The SAP® Project

PRESS

SAP PRESS is a joint initiative of SAP and Galileo Press. The know-how offered by SAP specialists combined with the expertise of the Galileo Press publishing house offers the reader expert books in the field. SAP PRESS features first-hand information and expert advice, and provides useful skills for professional decision-making.

SAP PRESS offers a variety of books on technical and business-related topics for the SAP user. For further information, please visit our website: *www.sap-press.com*.

Michael Doane
The SAP Green Book: A Business Guide for Effectively Managing the SAP Lifecycle
2012, 265 pp., paperback
ISBN 978-1-59229-407-7

Michael Doane
The SAP Blue Book: A Concise Business Guide to the World of SAP
2012, 190 pp., paperback
ISBN 978-1-59229-412-1

Venki Krishnamoorthy, Alexandra Carvalho
Discover SAP (3rd edition)
2014, app. 540 pp., paperback
ISBN 978-1-59229-987-4

Welz et al.
Rapid Deployment of SAP Solutions
2013, 401 pp., hardcover
ISBN 978-1-59229-910-2

SAP PRESS e-books

Print or e-book, Kindle or iPad, workplace or airplane: Choose where and how to read your SAP PRESS books! You can now get all our titles as e-books, too:

- By download and online access
- For all popular devices
- And, of course, DRM-free

Convinced? Then go to **www.sap-press.com** and get your e-book today.

Gerald Sullivan

The SAP® Project
More Than a Survival Guide

Bonn • Boston

Galileo Press is named after the Italian physicist, mathematician, and philosopher Galileo Galilei (1564–1642). He is known as one of the founders of modern science and an advocate of our contemporary, heliocentric worldview. His words *Eppur si muove* (And yet it moves) have become legendary. The Galileo Press logo depicts Jupiter orbited by the four Galilean moons, which were discovered by Galileo in 1610.

Editor Emily Nicholls
Acquisitions Editor Florian Zimniak
Copyeditor Laura Schreier
Cover Design Graham Geary
Photo Credit Shutterstock.com: 104572811/© Photoexpert; 34839997/© HomeStudio; 200780153/© Kisan
Layout Design Vera Brauner
Production Graham Geary
Typesetting SatzPro, Krefeld (Germany)
Printed and bound in the United States of America, on paper from sustainable sources

ISBN 978-1-59229-949-2

© 2014 by Galileo Press Inc., Boston (MA)
1st edition 2014

Library of Congress Cataloging-in-Publication Data
Sullivan, Gerald.
 Surviving in SAP projects / Gerald Sullivan. -- 1st Edition.
       pages cm
  ISBN 978-1-59229-949-2 (print) -- ISBN 1-59229-949-0 (print) -- ISBN 978-1-59229-950-8 (e-book) -- ISBN 978-1-59229-951-5
 (print and e-book) 1. SAP ERP. 2. Project management. I. Title.
  HD69.P75S85 2014
  658.4'04028553--dc23
                                                            2014016367

All rights reserved. Neither this publication nor any part of it may be copied or reproduced in any form or by any means or translated into another language, without the prior consent of Galileo Press, Rheinwerkallee 4, 53227 Bonn, Germany.

Galileo Press makes no warranties or representations with respect to the content hereof and specifically disclaims any implied warranties of merchantability or fitness for any particular purpose. Galileo Press assumes no responsibility for any errors that may appear in this publication.

"Galileo Press" and the Galileo Press logo are registered trademarks of Galileo Press GmbH, Bonn, Germany, SAP PRESS is an imprint of Galileo Press.

All of the screenshots and graphics reproduced in this book are subject to copyright © SAP AG, Dietmar-Hopp-Allee 16, 69190 Walldorf, Germany.

SAP, the SAP logo, ABAP, BAPI, Duet, mySAP.com, mySAP, SAP ArchiveLink, SAP EarlyWatch, SAP NetWeaver, SAP Business ByDesign, SAP BusinessObjects, SAP BusinessObjects Rapid Mart, SAP BusinessObjects Desktop Intelligence, SAP BusinessObjects Explorer, SAP Rapid Marts, SAP BusinessObjects Watchlist Security, SAP BusinessObjects Web Intelligence, SAP Crystal Reports, SAP GoingLive, SAP HANA, SAP MaxAttention, SAP MaxDB, SAP PartnerEdge, SAP R/2, SAP R/3, SAP R/3 Enterprise, SAP Strategic Enterprise Management (SAP SEM), SAP StreamWork, SAP Sybase Adaptive Server Enterprise (SAP Sybase ASE), SAP Sybase IQ, SAP xApps, SAPPHIRE NOW, and Xcelsius are registered or unregistered trademarks of SAP AG, Walldorf, Germany.

All other products mentioned in this book are registered or unregistered trademarks of their respective companies.

Contents at a Glance

1	Surviving in SAP Projects	17
2	How an SAP Implementation Changes Business	29
3	The ASAP Methodology	43
4	Types of SAP Projects	63
5	Start-Up Logistics	89
6	Systems Integrator Selection and Contracting	117
7	SAP's Role in the Project	141
8	Project Planning	163
9	Knowledge Management	183
10	Project Organization	199
11	Project Governance	219
12	Building the Right Project Team	241
13	Business Blueprinting	261
14	Realization	293
15	Configuration and Custom Objects Build	327
16	Systems Testing	355
17	Data, Reports, EDI, and Security and Internal Controls	379
18	Building System Environments	417
19	Change Management	439
20	Continuous User Training	463
21	Cutover Planning	485
22	Go-Live and Hypercare	503
23	Sustainment	527

Dear Reader,

In the age of smart telephones and the ubiquitous GPS, it's easy to hit the road empty-handed and trust you'll figure it out along the way.

But there are some journeys whose success or failure can most often be attributed to meticulous planning and calculated execution throughout. As a project lead, a systems integrator, or a C-level executive, you know that your SAP project is going to be one of them.

Whether you're upgrading, migrating, or simply adding widespread custom enhancements to existing applications, your project will drastically improve the way you do business—if you do it right. With Gerald Sullivan's *The SAP Project: More Than a Survival Guide* in hand, you can preview the road ahead, anticipate and bypass obstacles, and employ best practices in real time. You'll find that Jerry's decades of project experience and the invaluable wisdom he's amassed make the ASAP methodology manageable and the implementation process practical, from preparation to go-live and beyond into support.

We at SAP PRESS would be interested to hear your opinion of this book and whether it helped you arrive at your project destination. What did you think about *The SAP Project: More Than a Survival Guide*? How could it be improved? As your comments and suggestions are the most useful tools to help us make our books the best they can be, we encourage you to visit our website at *www.sap-press.com* and share your feedback.

Thank you for purchasing a book from SAP PRESS!

Emily Nicholls
Editor, SAP PRESS

Galileo Press
Boston, MA

emily.nicholls@galileo-press.com
www.sap-press.com

Contents

Acknowledgments 15

1 Surviving in SAP Projects 17

    1.1   Why Are SAP Implementations So Difficult? 17
    1.2   Levels of Preparation Required 20
    1.3   What this Book Will Do for You 22
    1.4   Factors Critical to Success 23
    1.5   How the Book Will Be Organized 26

2 How an SAP Implementation Changes Business 29

    2.1   Modifying Major Business Processes 31
           2.1.1   Process Standardization 32
           2.1.2   Process Simplification 33
           2.1.3   Process Automation 34
    2.2   Building New Skills in the Project Team 36
    2.3   Transforming SAP into a Company Asset 39

3 The ASAP Methodology 43

    3.1   ASAP Components 45
    3.2   Phase One: Project Preparation 50
    3.3   Phase Two: Business Blueprint 52
    3.4   Phase Three: Realization 54
    3.5   Phase Four: Final Preparation 56
    3.6   Phase Five: Go-Live and Support 58
    3.7   Quality Gates 60

4 Types of SAP Projects 63

    4.1   Full-Scale Implementation Projects 65
           4.1.1   Greenfield Deployment 66
           4.1.2   Carveout 68
           4.1.3   System Replacement 71
    4.2   Upgrade Projects 73
           4.2.1   Support Pack 73

		4.2.2	Enhancement Pack	75
		4.2.3	Version Upgrade	79
	4.3	Pre-Built Package Projects		82
		4.3.1	SAP Business One	82
		4.3.2	SAP Business One Starter Package	85
		4.3.3	Rapid Deployment Solutions	86

5 Start-Up Logistics ... 89

5.1	Project Preparation Timeline	90
5.2	Project Meeting Schedules	92
5.3	Headcount Forecasting and Ramp-Up Planning	96
5.4	Initial Planning for Integrator Selection	99
5.5	Project Procurement	108
5.6	Space Planning for Project Activities	112
5.7	Preliminary Project Budgeting	113

6 Systems Integrator Selection and Contracting ... 117

	6.1	Integrator Selection		118
		6.1.1	Initial Integrator Identification and Information Gathering	119
		6.1.2	Request for Proposal	121
		6.1.3	Reviewing RFP Responses	123
		6.1.4	First Cut Integrator Presentations	125
		6.1.5	Final Selection	126
	6.2	Integrator Contracting		127
		6.2.1	Types of Contracts	128
		6.2.2	Contract Structure and Contents	129
		6.2.3	Change Control	138
	6.3	Integrator Onboarding		139

7 SAP's Role in the Project ... 141

	7.1	Consultant Resources		142
	7.2	Custom Development		144
	7.3	Software Fixes		147
	7.4	Training		149
		7.4.1	Awareness Training	149
		7.4.2	Overview Sessions	150

Contents

		7.4.3	End-User System Training	151
		7.4.4	Change Management Training	152
	7.5	Technical Services		154
	7.6	Value Management		158

8 Project Planning 163

8.1	Defining the Project Schedule		164
	8.1.1	Project Complexity Factors	164
	8.1.2	Determining Overall Project Complexity	170
	8.1.3	Choosing a Deployment Approach	172
	8.1.4	Building the Implementation Wave Framework	173
8.2	Setting Top-Level Requirements		175
8.3	Achieving Cost Savings		178

9 Knowledge Management 183

9.1	Documentation		184
9.2	Knowledge Management Strategy		187
	9.2.1	SAP Solution Manager	188
	9.2.2	Collaboration Applications	192
	9.2.3	Specialized Document Applications	196

10 Project Organization 199

10.1	High-Level Project Organization		200
	10.1.1	Functionally Organized Project Organizations	200
	10.1.2	IT-Led Project Organization	203
	10.1.3	Matrix-Led Project Organizations	204
10.2	Program Management		206
10.3	Functional Workstream Leads		210
10.4	Horizontal Workstreams		214

11 Project Governance 219

11.1	Project Charter		220
	11.1.1	Project Description	221
	11.1.2	Project Plan Summary	222
	11.1.3	Roles and Responsibilities	224
11.2	Oversight and Guidance		229

11.3		Risk Management	231
11.4		Team Rewards and Recognition	237

12 Building the Right Project Team — 241

12.1		Team Recruitment and Selection	243
12.2		Onboarding the Project Team	249
	12.2.1	Team Logistics	250
	12.2.2	Bringing on the Project Team	254
12.3		Delivering Project Results	255
12.4		Roll-Off and Reintegration	257

13 Business Blueprinting — 261

13.1		Blueprinting Sessions	262
	13.1.1	Kick-Off and Session One	265
	13.1.2	Sessions Two and Three	271
13.2		Design Documentation	277
	13.2.1	Process Definition Documents	277
	13.2.2	Change Management Initiation	279
	13.2.3	Process Flows and Process Steps	280
	13.2.4	Business Controls Identification	282
	13.2.5	Managing the Documentation Process	284
13.3		Localization	288
13.4		Closing the Business Blueprinting Phase	291

14 Realization — 293

14.1		Transition to Realization	295
	14.1.1	Realization Project Plan	295
	14.1.2	Realization Kick-Off	298
	14.1.3	Realization Handbook	301
14.2		Organizing for Realization	304
	14.2.1	Workstream Management	304
	14.2.2	Regional and Site Responsibilities	306
14.3		Project Management	310
	14.3.1	Status Reporting and Performance Metrics	311
	14.3.2	Deliverables Tracking and Milestone Recognition	315
	14.3.3	Risk Management	317
	14.3.4	Resourcing	321

15 Configuration and Custom Objects Build 327

- 15.1 Configuration and Custom Development 329
  - 15.1.1 Configuration 330
  - 15.1.2 Custom Object Development 337
  - 15.1.3 String Testing 341
- 15.2 Security Design 341
  - 15.2.1 SAP Roles 343
  - 15.2.2 Data Level Security 346
  - 15.2.3 Company Policy Assessment 347

16 Systems Testing 355

- 16.1 Structure of Systems Testing 356
- 16.2 Systems Testing Processes 361
  - 16.2.1 Test Planning 361
  - 16.2.2 Script Execution 362
  - 16.2.3 Test Metrics 363
  - 16.2.4 Defect Processing 365
  - 16.2.5 Mega-Scenarios 370
  - 16.2.6 Regression Testing 372
- 16.3 Using Testing Systems 372
- 16.4 Systems Test Entrance and Exit Criteria 374

17 Data, Reports, EDI, and Security and Internal Controls 379

- 17.1 Data 380
  - 17.1.1 Data Types 381
  - 17.1.2 Data Cleansing and Conversion 383
  - 17.1.3 Data Governance 389
- 17.2 Reports 391
  - 17.2.1 Corporate-Level Reports 395
  - 17.2.2 Key Performance Indicators 397
- 17.3 Electronic Data Interchange 400
  - 17.3.1 EDI Structure 401
  - 17.3.2 EDI Project Deliverables 404
- 17.4 Security and Internal Controls 407
  - 17.4.1 Internal Controls Analysis 409
  - 17.4.2 Role Mapping and End-User Training 412

18 Building System Environments 417

- 18.1 The SAP Landscape 419
- 18.2 Environment and Client Structure 422
- 18.3 Infrastructure Build and Test 431
- 18.4 Performance and Failover Testing 434

19 Change Management 439

- 19.1 Business Transformation 440
- 19.2 Change Impacts 442
- 19.3 Stakeholder Management 452
- 19.4 Organizational Design 456
- 19.5 Project Communication 459

20 Continuous User Training 463

- 20.1 Course Development 465
  - 20.1.1 Delivery Methods 466
  - 20.1.2 Content Types 468
  - 20.1.3 Course Organization 470
  - 20.1.4 Development Tools 473
- 20.2 Trainer Preparation 474
- 20.3 Training Delivery Logistics 476
  - 20.3.1 Translation of Training Materials 477
  - 20.3.2 Course Scheduling 478
  - 20.3.3 Logistics Tools 481
- 20.4 Post-Go-Live Processes 482

21 Cutover Planning 485

- 21.1 Cutover Processes 488
  - 21.1.1 Business Preparation 489
  - 21.1.2 Data Load and Verification 492
  - 21.1.3 User Training 494
  - 21.1.4 Cutover Communication 496
- 21.2 Go-Live Authorization 497

22 Go-Live and Hypercare 503

22.1 Final Go-Live Processes 503
    22.1.1 Continuing Cutover Activities 503
    22.1.2 Granting System Access 504
    22.1.3 Business Ramp-Up Execution 504
22.2 Hypercare 506
    22.2.1 Hypercare Operations 506
    22.2.2 Hypercare Exit 523

23 Sustainment 527

23.1 The SAP Center of Excellence 528
    23.1.1 COE Organization 529
    23.1.2 The COE and the Project Team 535
    23.1.3 Staffing the COE 537
23.2 Sustainment Governance 540
    23.2.1 Governance Structure 540
    23.2.2 Managing COE Workload 544
    23.2.3 Critical Success Factors for Sustainment Governance 546
23.3 Continuing Company Projects 546

The Author 549
Index 551

Acknowledgments

Writing this book has been in the back my mind for some time. My many years of leading successful SAP implementations and reading the flow of newspaper stories about failed implementations have led me to believe that though success does not come easily, it can be achieved. Teams can make it happen; *your* team can make it happen by following a few straightforward rules. In my experience, close adherence to them really can make the difference between success and failure.

So this book is really is a labor of love. It is based on my professional work and highlights practical examples intended to make the way clear. It is dedicated to the success of SAP implementation teams everywhere in hopes that they will find this guide and these tools of great use to them in their journey.

So many former colleagues have always been there during the most difficult times of implementations. They are all shining examples of how to do things right: Chris Andersen, Amy Dale, Mark Farabaugh, Tom Flanagan, Jeri Lane, John Leffler, Vern McCrory, Ole Mikkelsen, Sanjeev Motwani, Jim Niehoff, Bill Piotrowski, Gloria Samuels, Claudia Tiuo, Mike Zahigian, Bob Buhlmann, Cathy Johnson and Raymond Wissenburg.

My utmost thanks go to everyone at Galileo Press for their assistance in making this book a reality. My editor, Emily Nicholls, has been a saint. She provided invaluable guidance and tirelessly worked to make the book the best it could be. Florian Zimniak made the decision to expand the Galileo Press repertoire and add SAP implementation coverage to its collection.

Finally, more appreciation than I can express goes to my wonderful wife, Lesley, who read and reread chapters and gave encouragement throughout the writing process.

1 Surviving in SAP Projects

Welcome to the world of SAP projects! If you are like most SAP project team members, your boss—be it the company CEO or a line manager—has tapped you on the shoulder and let you know how important you are to the company. Because of your importance, you have now been selected to work on Project X, your company's SAP implementation project.

At first, you no doubt felt a flush of pride that others recognized your capabilities and appreciated them. After that point, some doubt may have crept into your positive outlook, as you started wondering "Just what is an SAP project?" and "How does it work?" Likely included in this train of thought was some concern about the reputation that SAP projects have for difficulty and demanding time commitments.

1.1 Why Are SAP Implementations So Difficult?

"Survival" means more than personal survival. It also means company survival. After all, SAP implementation projects have a reputation for being extremely difficult to deliver. Newspaper stories recount the struggles that companies have had with conducting accurate financial closes, processing sales orders, and accounting for inventory. SAP is an integrated software package that performs thousands of functions essential to company operations—meaning that the implementation must go exactly as planned, or your standard company processes may no longer work.

Over the past several years, the complexity of SAP solution sets has substantially increased. Numerous releases have now made available a number of supporting modules in addition to the core SAP enterprise resource planning (ERP) functionality. These modules include applications supporting procurement, demand planning, supply chain management, and budget planning. The need to share data across modules with the basic ERP platform means that all solution elements must work together seamlessly. This requirement considerably raises the performance bar for implementation project teams.

However, the benefits of having an SAP solution as the "single source of truth" are fundamental. Once installed, an SAP solution means that management can access reliable information regarding company or business unit performance without the data massaging and manipulation so common to companies that lack this integrated set of systems. It also means that your company can now perform business functions on a robust and highly reliable system.

Moreover, SAP is not unconcerned with the popular view that its implementations are demanding tests for many companies. In fact, it has worked to address many of these concerns, and has offered some answers to common project struggles. SAP Rapid Deployment Solutions provides systems configured for targeted installation, and SAP Business One offers small and medium-sized businesses a standardized setup. However, for many companies, most challenges associated with large-scale implementations still remain.

In many ways, SAP implementations' reputation for difficulty is based on fact. You can expect your project to consume significant portions of your time and that of your team members. You may work longer hours than you or your colleagues are accustomed to. Challenges and emergencies will no doubt arise and require immediate resolution by your team. Sometimes you may feel at a loss for answers and not know what step to take next. Despite all of this, the life of a project team is directed by its implementation schedule, so problems must be identified and resolved quickly. This demand usually means much more than an eight-hour day or a 40-hour workweek. At times, you can expect project needs to be all-consuming. This especially holds true in the case of global projects where time zone differences between Asia and North America make *late* evening teleconferences routine.

No doubt these projects can be challenging. After all, few other activities in a company involve virtually all functional organizations—from its supply chain to sales operations to financial management. Such projects are undertaken only rarely, and your company's previous experience with projects on this scale may be limited. Virtually hundreds of company employees from IT and functional organizations will be mobilized to assess and redesign business processes. They then translate these process requirements into software configurations. Your company's level of preparation to meet this challenge is crucial, as we'll soon see.

You can also expect to see a very high level of attention on your project. An SAP installation for a typical Fortune 500 greenfield deployment (that is, a company that has never used SAP in any of its operations) can take several years and will certainly consume large amounts of company human resources. Further, these projects involve tens or hundreds of millions of dollars in investment. Very often, project progress and expenditures are tracked at the board-of-director level. Questions regarding project performance at the board level can become very pointed, which can be quite uncomfortable for those who are giving the answers.

SAP implementation projects can also place a company at substantial risk. The danger of implementing incorrectly is very real. Many companies transition to this heightened risk profile without foreknowledge of their potential negative impact or plans to handle specific risks. ERP implementation failures are not things of the past. Several Fortune 500 companies as well public agencies have recently reported their failures and litigated over the massive costs involved. Any company undergoing an SAP implementation places itself in a heightened risk category.

But these struggles are not limited to SAP implementation projects, as evidenced by recent experience with the Affordable Care Act website. Building and deploying a portal-based service is an extremely complex undertaking, similar to a large-scale SAP implementation. As reported in the *New York Times*, the ACA website experienced serious issues from the outset. As after-action analysis began to reveal the causes, they turned out to be a quite familiar list: continuing scope changes, inadequately constructed specifications, insufficient testing, and lack of an overall systems integrator, among other common obstacles.

Large-scale SAP implementation projects can encounter serious problems or even fail for many of the same reasons, such as insufficient system testing, inadequate business preparation, large numbers of SAP system customizations that degrade system performance, and the failure to integrate company operations to align with SAP constraints. These issues generally come down to a single cause: the ability of project staff to manage the implementation. This is likely due to lack of project skills in the team or among executive sponsors. Ultimately, any implementation project centers on business transformation. The company's ability to align the SAP system to perform needed business processes—and to prepare end users to operate them—is the major focus.

1.2 Levels of Preparation Required

Clearly, the project must be done right. Assigned employees from diverse organizations must learn to operate as a well-oiled team. Company outsiders, in the form of systems integrators and independent contractors, must also learn to function as integral members of this team. They must learn to think as though they were company employees. Management structures and operating procedures must be built to guide the overall team. Only then do the risks become manageable.

Company executives assigned to oversee the project will likely have very limited exposure to system implementation methods. They will need guidance relative to project processes, risks likely to be encountered, potential impacts to company performance, and high-level methods of progress tracking. Even systems integrators and contractors who perform much of the SAP technical setup will experience continuous flows of new staff into their organizations. Integrator staff may be well-versed in their specific professional roles, but may well not understand the full project process. Everyone assigned to the project requires a "nuts-and-bolts" understanding of project mechanisms, choice points, and risk mitigation options.

McKinsey & Company reported on the results of transformation projects at the Association of International Product Marketing and Management; its report was called "70% of Transformation Programs Fail." Other comparable studies indicate a similar failure rate. Based on the evidence, only a few companies have figured out how to reach the necessary level of success, and most companies still have something important to learn. Remember also that an SAP implementation is a twofold transformation: first, the process changes associated with the system, and second, those business process improvements deployed concurrently with the system—but not necessarily part of the SAP system. We have a double challenge in front of us!

However, the study does not end with reporting these attention-getting results. It goes on to discuss two of the major criteria separating successful company transformations from those that fail. McKinsey calls these *golden rules*. They encapsulate the core traits that differentiate success from failure. The study divided the company response set into four groups based on success. Those demonstrating the highest success rates also manifested the highest adherence to the golden rules.

Figure 1.1 outlines these two golden rules. The first emphasizes the importance of formal structure and systematic processes. Those companies that plan and organize for success are better able to attain it. The second underscores the essential aspect of information sharing and progress reporting.

Golden Rule #1
Formal systems and structures must support overall program success and accountability.

Golden Rule #2
Transparent information and stringent process tracking are major characteristics of successful transformations.

Figure 1.1 McKinsey's Golden Rules

Neither of the two golden rules is a new or radical concept. However, each does serve to reinforce the importance of committing to success and managing for it. Our book shares this premise. It will give you the guidance and examples enabling you and your team to replicate the McKinsey golden rules.

In the military, it's very common to hold rigorous training sessions before any mission. These simulations focus on creating situations that are as close as possible to the reality to be encountered on the ground. The underlying idea is this: Anything of such vital importance must be done right, and the only way to ensure correctness is constant repetition of proper technique. In contrast, it's common that project teams in SAP systems implementations get very little training, other than systems training. For this reason, you will see throughout the book continued emphasis on team training and setting clear performance expectations.

Those selected to lead the project or participate as project team members are usually chosen on the basis of their business knowledge, and this is how it should be. Your company will select project team members who best understand business processes in areas such as procurement, sales transactions, inventory planning, and financial accounting. They bring those skills to the SAP project team.

However, they will still need project operational skills. These include both team-building and the ability to manage deliverables in an often-chaotic environment. But unless your company already operates in a highly cross-functional manner, many of those selected for the project will not have previously worked with their new teammates. Even those assigned the same team can have limited working experience with their new colleagues. They may wonder just what is expected of them and just exactly how an SAP project operates.

Most importantly, their understanding of project operations and the activities of an SAP implementation will not yet be developed. Task sequences, durations, and performance expectations may not be well understood. Your company can expect a period of several months before its new SAP implementation group becomes a team. As a result, team members may become lost because they fail to understand project context, whether it be grasping the importance of individual deliverables or seeing how multiple deliverables fit with one another. Clearly, they need a resource that supplies this context.

If your project is successful, by the end of the project those team members will have developed skill sets that make them invaluable to the company. They will likely count their experience as one of the most important of their career. It will subject them to multiple pressures, teach them new responses, bring out the best in them, and leave them ultimately transformed as individuals and employees.

1.3 What this Book Will Do for You

Anyone assigned to your project team wants answers. They intensely crave sufficient guidance to make them act and feel effective. Later, as the project progresses, they will need even more guidance. As with all human enterprise, open-ended items make people uncomfortable. Having real-world answers will greatly increase the probability of project success.

If you are one of these individuals—whether company project team member, executive sponsor, systems integrator, or independent contractor—then *The SAP Project: More than a Survival Guide* is meant for you. It is designed as your project companion. It will serve as your guidebook to the workings of an SAP project. The lessons contained here apply no matter what the size and scope of your project. Whether you are participating in a full footprint implementation, a version upgrade to an existing system, or installation of a specific module such as SAP Business Planning and Consolidation, this book will provide capable guidance. While it may not provide answers unique to your project, it *will* give you firm grounding in project sequencing, deliverables, and success criteria.

This book follows the golden rules. Its fundamental premise is dedicated to the idea the major difference between successful SAP projects and failed ones lies in efficient and effective project management. This statement does not translate into "project management" as most people typically think of it. In the minds of many, project management means schedule updates and meeting minutes. However, management of the project is a far broader concept than this. It goes to the very organization and operation of the project — how it is structured, reported, and managed. If this management task is handled well, then many problems will never arise and those that do will exert a far diminished impact and can be resolved through existing procedures. Further, this management role becomes the responsibility of anyone assigned to the project. Each project team member is responsible and accountable for making the project succeed. As the project steps its way through the stages of its lifecycle, it will encounter its own set of problems and challenges. Navigating them well depends on the management of the project. Building this new set of skills and expectations requires a framework.

SAP has done an excellent job in designing the overall project foundation. The Accelerated SAP (ASAP) methodology outlines the project sequence from initiation to final delivery. While SAP has provided the project lifecycle framework, the real work of the implementation project team comes from supplying the details. However excellent the framework is, the project team must generate the individual work products in each phase: project preparation, business blueprint, realization, final preparation, and go-live and support. They organize the project sequence.

Together, we will use this framework to make your project succeed. Our book will outline the steps to follow — and you, the key resource, will apply intelligence and skill to the nuances of your project.

1.4 Factors Critical to Success

For your project to succeed, it should deliver agreed-upon scope and functionality on time and within budget. That said, project success will depend on achieving several factors that will enable positive results.

Throughout *The SAP Project: More than a Survival Guide*, we will build on the lessons of the golden rules. Those two success factors will apply to the entire ASAP lifecycle. Let's take a moment to elaborate on a more discrete list of success factors — those project behaviors that lead to a clear project pathway and help participants attain project goals. They apply to all phases of the project and will be discussed in many of the following chapters:

1. **Each person assigned to the project owns its success and takes real action to make his or her area of responsibility successful. All team members unhesitatingly work together to solve problems.**

   SAP projects prove the underlying value of teamwork. In projects, the agent of action is always the team. Well-functioning teams require little instruction. They simply recognize the problem, identify others who need to participate in the solution, and move forward to put the answer in place. Lacking this embedded success factor, teams will flounder and the entire project can be placed in jeopardy. Because this factor is so essential, *The SAP Project: More than a Survival Guide* will return to it again and again, discussing how to enable project teams and how to foster solid teamwork in every phase.

2. **Clear role specifications for all teams and team members that unite all facets into a single, committed organization. Additionally, this factor includes an unbiased assessment of members' skills and capabilities to perform those roles.**

   High-performance teams require structure. They must know their leader and have respect for that person. Both leader and individual team member must have a clear understanding of their roles as well as their boundaries. Assignment of project team members should also be preceded by a thorough skills assessment. It should provide clear evidence that a team member possesses the required capabilities, or the prospective member should not be assigned to the project.

3. **An integrated project schedule (applicable to both the company and the systems integrator) clearly showing all key deliverables throughout the project lifecycle, and their timing.**

   Project schedules become invaluable tools for unifying a project. When done well, they make project deliverable sequencing and timing expectations transparent. They also make clear which deliverables are on time and which are behind schedule. This builds accountability for those who own deliverables. For best effect, schedules should be graphical in format and printed on a plotter. They can then be posted in every work location.

4. **A management reporting method based on clearly understood and representative metrics. Reporting should foster transparency, teamwork, and accountability. The entire team should always know where it stands.**

   The team should agree very early on progress metrics and the methods for metric generation. Progress reporting should flow up the organizational chain. The project team requires close to real-time reporting; executive sponsors require reporting with a longer time perspective. In either case, teams accountable for deliverables should provide their own reporting and explanations where needed. Progress metrics can be posted in project work locations as a means of fostering communication and discussion.

5. **Business ownership for all key project results, and metrics to demonstrate achieved progress.**

    SAP implementation projects are very often viewed as IT operations, with IT holding the responsibility for company delivery. Clearly, the company IT organization *is* essential to project success. However, real success requires that company functional organizations ("the business") must take ownership for all facets of the project. Ultimately, functional organizations constitute the primary user group for the SAP solution. When those organizations step aside from their role, the solution will no longer be perceived as *theirs*. Ongoing project decisions and directions will suffer as a result.

6. **Mechanisms to capture the potential impacts of project risks, and the status of mitigations used to address them.**

    Almost all projects collect and tabulate risks. Many of these are very low-level and will play little part in overall project success. Those level one risks that place delivery and timing into question are quite another matter. Level one risks require an in-depth analysis and complete mitigation plans. Further, project executive sponsors should receive regular briefings on the status and success of mitigation measures.

7. **Executive sponsors who feel ownership for the project and who are eager to provide assistance when needed.**

    Each and every project has executive sponsors. Frequently, these are high-level senior executives who may not understand the importance of the SAP implementation to their organizations. However, without their understanding and commitment to the project, key decisions may not get made or decisions may be made whose ramifications are poorly understood. Executive sponsors should have skin in the game, both in holding the project accountable for its progress and providing needed C-level support when required. They must become part of the project team.

8. **Company employees who are technically expert in whatever parts of the SAP solution set that are being implemented.**

Without SAP experts of its own, the implementing company becomes entirely dependent on systems integrator system expertise. While this is not a problem in and of itself, it does have two potential impacts. The first of these is how the SAP solution fits or enables business processes. Integrator staff likely will not understand the detailed ins and outs of company business processes. Having company experts in these areas to explain the issue in SAP functional terms proves invaluable. The second potential impact lies with sustainment of the solution post go-live. Company-based SAP experts can play an essential role in managing any sustainment organization.

1.5 How the Book Will Be Organized

Our first three chapters in this book lay the overall foundation for your implementation project. They discuss the transformational nature of SAP project, describe SAP's ASAP implementation methodology in some detail, and then outline the different types of SAP projects:

- Chapter 2: How an SAP Implementation Changes Business
- Chapter 3: The ASAP Methodology
- Chapter 4: Types of SAP Projects

After laying this foundation, *The SAP Project: More than a Survival Guide* will closely follow the ASAP framework shown in Figure 1.2:

- *Project preparation* examines essential core project start-up activities. These chapters provide guidance in the logistics and planning needed to get the project off the ground, from initial project planning to integrator selection:
    - Chapter 5: Start-Up Logistics
    - Chapter 6: Systems Integrator Selection and Contracting
    - Chapter 7: SAP's Role in the Project
    - Chapter 8: Project Planning
    - Chapter 9: Knowledge Management
    - Chapter 10: Project Organization
    - Chapter 11: Project Governance
    - Chapter 12: Building the Right Project Team

- *Business blueprint* covers the main process assessment and design activities necessary for a company to organize its SAP usage. The chapter describes good blueprinting practices and discusses how to conduct business design reviews.
    - Chapter 13: Business Blueprinting
- *Realization* addresses the bulk of processes. Each chapter outlines a primary focus area for major activities within realization. These range from configuration and testing to change management.
    - Chapter 14: Realization
    - Chapter 15: Configuration and Custom Objects Build
    - Chapter 16: Systems Testing
    - Chapter 17: Data, Reports, EDI, and Security and Internal Controls
    - Chapter 18: Building System Environments
    - Chapter 19: Change Management
    - Chapter 20: Continuous User Training
- *Final preparation* emphasizes those critical planning and back-office activities that bring a project to the threshold of a successful implementation.
    - Chapter 21: Cutover Planning
- *Go-live and support* focuses on those crucial few days prior to go-live and operation of the intensive post go-live resolution period known as hypercare. These chapters discuss best practices for a positive hypercare experience, including transition to sustainment, training required for support staff, and incident resolution methods.
    - Chapter 22: Go-Live and Hypercare
    - Chapter 23: Sustainment

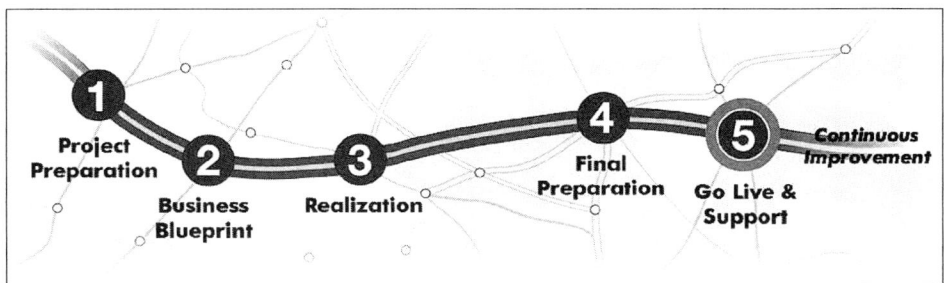

Figure 1.2 Accelerated SAP Implementation Methodology

In the interest of guiding you to salient tips and alerting you to common trouble spots, we have used the following icons:

- **Trail Marker:** These texts help you navigate the resource or explain terminology used in the book.

- **Pitfall Alert:** These notes make you aware of common obstacles that project teams face and that you can avoid through strategic planning.

- **Tip:** These suggestions underscore hints about project best practices.

In addition, we have offered many diagrams that help illustrate the SAP implementation process. The figures that appear on notebook paper are examples from hypothetical implementations.

Finally, for your assistance we have included several useful templates that you can apply for your own project activities. These templates contain descriptions of major project deliverables and cover such items as blueprinting, configuration, systems test, and cutover. For each area, the templates give a short description and then outline the inputs, major tasks, dependencies, and deliverables. They are all aligned with the SAP ASAP methodology, and can be accessed on the book's web page at *www.sap-press.com/3501*.

I have led several large-scale SAP implementations for major companies. Each of them has been successful in meeting its targets. *The SAP Project: More than a Survival Guide* builds on that experience and provides real-world, tested models for you to follow.

Now we are ready to move to the project fundamentals. Good luck!

We'll first focus on the business impact of an SAP implementation. Almost all implementing companies put an SAP system in place to enhance their business processes. However, we will see that the project affects far more than company business processes. It will strengthen the skills of the project team and make SAP a long-term company asset.

2   How an SAP Implementation Changes Business

Everyone knows that an SAP implementation project changes a company. Less well known are the ways those changes take place and their long-term impacts on the implementing company. Through the process of deploying the SAP system, these changes *will* take place—sometimes in unforeseen ways. And unless the implementing company makes careful plans for these changes, the effects may be less than optimal. They may even create negative or undesirable effects.

Most implementing companies understand, at some level, the business changes that these process modifications will introduce. While companies may experience difficulties in handling the impact of these changes, they are not unforeseen. Usually they are planned and intended to be accomplished during the SAP deployment. But implementing companies are likely to be less clear about the changes their project team members will experience and the potential effect on the company. Additionally, many implementing companies find themselves unprepared for the overall impact of the SAP system itself.

This chapter is dedicated to educating the implementing company's senior executives. It will outline how those changes occur in Section 2.1 and the methods by which an implementing company can manage them to its advantage.

Figure 2.1 outlines the three types of changes that will impact a company facing an SAP implementation project. These three types of changes can be quite profound and generate long-term alterations in company operations. Each change carries its own set of management challenges.

2 | How an SAP Implementation Changes Business

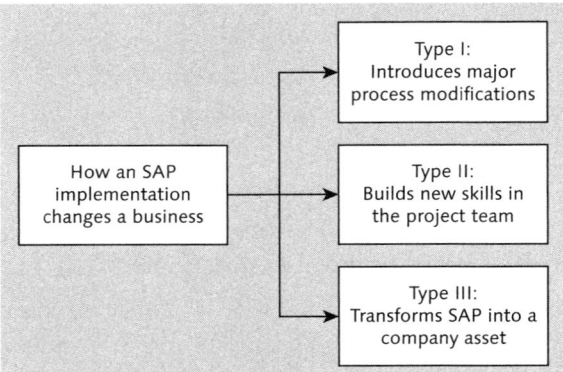

Figure 2.1 Changes Introduced as a Result of an SAP Implementation Project

This chapter will discuss each type of change and its impact on management:

- **Introducing major business process modifications**
  The project will modify company business processes in at least two ways. Generally, as part of the requirements-setting process in blueprinting, the implementing company will choose to adopt key business process changes. These will be known and clearly outlined during design discussions. Many of these will make significant changes to existing company operations. These are the changes that are most commonly identified as process transformations.

  A second type of business process modification results from the SAP system itself. Manual processes will now be automated, and process operations that were once limited to a regional purview will now have global implications. These often unintended results have far-reaching business consequences for the implementing company.

- **Building new skills in the project team**
  The project is a testing ground for company staff. Every SAP implementation project team, at every type of company, faces major challenges and extremely rigorous time constraints. While these do lead to fatigue—and, sometimes, burnout—they also create a huge opportunity for growth and development among the team members.

  Team members who complete the project will have been tested and will have expanded their limits as a result of participating in the SAP implementation project. From the most to the least skilled, each will have greatly enlarged his or her portfolio of accomplishments. Their values to the company will have doubled or tripled. It will be up to the implementing company to find roles for these individuals commensurate with their recent accomplishments.

▸ **Transforming SAP into a company asset**
Once the SAP system has deployed, it will change many of the company's fundamental operations. Redesigned business processes operating on the SAP system necessarily produce an integrated company—one where all functional organizations clearly depend on the performance of one another. We'll spell out some of those potential changes using examples in this chapter.

Additionally, as with any other major company asset, the system will require long-term care and maintenance. SAP is not a plug-and-play system. Rather, it requires a combination of user skills, system updates, governance, and continual bug fixes to keep it current. Many implementing companies don't fully grasp this, and they expect the heavy lifting is complete when the system has been implemented.

Let's begin by examining specific changes that implementations produce.

2.1 Modifying Major Business Processes

Many people believe that company-initiated business process modifications define the heart of an SAP transformation project. After all, they think, the list of activities that will change and the benefits that these changes will create is often the primary justification for an SAP implementation project.

In many ways, they're right. Unless the implementing company already has world-class business processes, the SAP systems project not only allows it to consider significant process changes—it encourages that kind of innovative thinking. The project can generate leverage for the company to rethink its ways of doing business. The SAP implementation methodology encourages this broad-based evaluation. As well, the SAP system can itself provide the foundation for these modifications.

Tip

Executives at the implementing company can provide valuable guidance to the project team by identifying needed business process improvement initiatives. The project team can use this input as a focus area. This ensures that executives and the project team are in alignment even in these early stages.

2 How an SAP Implementation Changes Business

Let's review three types of business process changes: standardization, simplification, and automation. Each has the advantage of using the system to reduce delays and improve process performance.

2.1.1 Process Standardization

Standardization of business processes can provide a powerful tool for an implementing company. Whenever business processes vary depending on geographical region or between functional organizations, standardization can bring consistency and positively affect the bottom line.

Figure 2.2 illustrates how significant standardization can be. It depicts the implementing company's order-to-cash processes with universally applied standardization across geographical regions. Prior to the SAP implementation project, these processes would have been performed in varying ways across regional operations. Ranging from customer identification, pricing, and shipping, the example shows where the benefits of standardization can be applied.

Focus area	Changes
Customers	Develop global customer system and numbers
Pricing	Adopt global pricing template for use in all markets
Sales orders	Standardize sales order types among all regions
Cash	Standardize global cash and collections processes
Rebates	Standardize global processes for trade promotions, rebates, and chargebacks
Exports	Standardize export processes and documents in all regions

Figure 2.2 OTC Standardization as a Process Transformation in an SAP Implementation Project

Prior to implementing a global SAP system, it is quite common for companies to operate in a very diverse fashion at the regional level. However, as the company supply chain begins to integrate globally, these regional variances will begin to cause problems in both efficiency and effectiveness.

For example, regions may utilize different numbering systems and formats for customer identification. In many cases, a single customer might have a different identifier in each region. For example, the same global company may have one customer number in North America and a slightly different name and totally unrelated customer number in Asia. The two customer instances will not reconcile. Simply collecting reliable sales information by customer means that the corporate headquarters will have to create and maintain translation tables to consolidate this data. If you multiply this situation several times by customer, vendor, or pricing, then the problem becomes a very substantial one.

Pitfall Alert

Regional differences, such as in the customer number example, can be resolved through the use of master data. The project team should understand the implications of these naming variances and work to address them during data cleansing. Executives can play a key role by making this a priority for the project team.

The situation with exports is very similar but often even more diffuse. Export documentation may vary not only by region, but at the country level as well! This creates a need for dedicated staff at the regional and country level whose main purpose is to assure that the disparate processes work as intended.

The SAP implementation project can create the single best opportunity for a company to break free from the mix of non-standard processes and to remedy the process differences. The impetus of the project and the investment involved can lead an implementing company to carefully assess its process imbalances. Including these process changes in blueprinting will move an implementing company toward unifying its operations and taking a step toward becoming *one global enterprise*.

2.1.2 Process Simplification

Process standardization isn't the only transformation tool available.

Even the very best companies contain examples of multi-person document reviews and approvals. These slow down the normal flow of operations, create unnecessary delays, and for many staff show company culture as behind the progress curve. An implementing company may also choose to examine overly complex processes for the purposes of eliminating non-value-added steps. For example, an implementing company could have large numbers of non-purchase-order invoices submitted for payment. Each of these is then handled as an exception item that must have managerial review and approval prior to payment, regardless of the amount involved. Handling these invoices through an approval process delays payment and uses company staff in a non-value-added manner.

The company could choose to simplify this process as part of the SAP implementation project. By conducting an analysis of the non-purchase-order invoices, their numbers and amounts can be determined. In most cases, the bulk of these invoices will have a small dollar value. The company can then shift to simplify the business process. This would include taking steps to reduce the number of non-purchase-order invoices and to require approval for those that represented larger dollar amounts.

By identifying those vendors that are approved to submit non-purchase-order invoices, the number of invoices can be dramatically reduced. By specifying a minimum dollar value that requires approval, the review process can also be curtailed. These process changes can then be configured into the SAP system and become standard practice across the company.

At one time or another, most companies have experienced large numbers of unpaid invoices in their accounts-payable backlog. Addressing these issues as examples of process deficiencies enables a solution to be developed. This solution results in better working relationships with suppliers and fewer staff members dedicated to these non-value-added activities.

So process simplification clearly applies in many situations. It will provide the most benefit in routine, large-volume transactions. When bottlenecks and delays occur, it's a sign that a process needs simplifying. The project team, whose members have considerable experience with the details of company processes, will be well equipped to generate solutions during the blueprint phase. Receiving encouragement from senior executives to conduct this type of work will serve to increase focus in these areas.

2.1.3 Process Automation

Automating processes is one of the most effective ways to create transformation. Automation uses the SAP system to build reliable and accurate processes. The development of custom objects that will be described in later chapters in this

Modifying Major Business Processes | **2.1**

book enables companies to replace manual steps with those that are entirely automated. An implementing company can make substantial changes to its operations by building workflows and forms.

> **Tip**
> Flag these automation opportunities for the project team. This will have two positive results. First, it helps them understand the important areas for transformation. Second, it builds a partnership between executives and the project team. Both will now work on the same page.

Figure 2.3 provides an illustration of the use of manual processing for company procurement processes. The steps from purchase order to invoice payment have all operated in a manual fashion. Purchase orders are created manually and sent to suppliers, who then send printed invoices to the company for products or services rendered. Once the company gets them, procurement staff and the holder of the purchase order physically review these invoices.

Manual purchase order » Printed invoice receipt » Physical invoice reviews » Physical invoice approval » Manual check payment

Figure 2.3 Manual Procurement Processes

If any item between the purchase order and the invoice does not reconcile, the process is put on hold and the supplier and company must exchange printed material to resolve the differences. Once they resolve any noted discrepancies in the paperwork, the printed invoice is forwarded for approval at the required level of management authorization. When this management approval is received, a check can then be manually issued and sent to the supplier in payment.

Take a closer look. The steps in this process are noticeably time-consuming. The parties spend much time checking for discrepancies and then searching out the reasons for them. Most inconsistencies are due to entry errors made by the sender or receiver rather than attempts at fraudulence. Each company involved, supplier and receiver, pays a penalty in employee time lost for these discrepancies. A great deal of this time lost can be restored through automation.

In the automated version of this process shown in Figure 2.4, all steps are accomplished in the SAP system and transition points from actor to actor are generated by workflow technology. Thus, the purchase order can be generated, approved, and distributed to the vendor by means of the SAP Supplier Relationship Management (SRM) application. Once the services are rendered by the supplier, the resulting invoice is either transmitted electronically or physically scanned by the implementing company.

Purchase order electronically issued → Invoice transmitted electronically and scanned → Invoice transmitted via workflow for review → Invoice approved in workflow → Invoice payment via electronic funds transfer

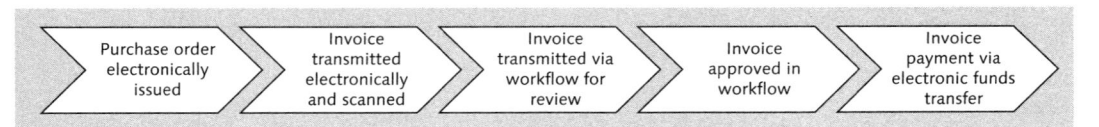

Figure 2.4 Automated Procurement Processes in an SAP Implementation Process

From that point forward, the invoice is an electronic document that can be immediately transferred using workflow to each reviewer or approver in the process. When final approval for invoice payment is received, the disbursement will be accomplished using electronic funds transfer (EFT) from the payer bank to the supplier bank. No manual check is required.

This and many similar automation processes are available through the SAP system using a combination of configuration, portal technology, and workflow. Chapter 6 will outline an approach where the implementing company's senior executives give direction to the project team regarding these types of process changes. The SAP client executive who is servicing the implementing company will be able to set up functionality demonstrations and thereby greatly facilitate use of the SAP system in support of process changes.

2.2 Building New Skills in the Project Team

An SAP implementation team is a special thing. In most cases, this is a group of people—many without any SAP system knowledge—who are expected to accomplish a minor miracle. Because this is comparable in scope and effort to the launch of a major software product, the individuals who accomplish a successful SAP implementation rise to rock star status within the company.

Many companies do not recognize the special human asset that they have created with the SAP implementation project. Unlike the product launch, many on the

SAP project team will have limited experience in the core subject matter. They may have never used SAP or understood how it works prior to the implementation project. They will generate this subject matter expertise through the lifecycle of the project.

Figure 2.5 shows this skill change along four different dimensions: achieving results, handling responsibility, working under pressure, and demonstrating leadership. When making the shift to the SAP implementation project team, circumstances will alter members' performance profile. By an almost magical process, they become a high-performance team. Similar to a fitness regimen, the added level of effort required can produce substantial gains for those participating. Some team members will make great changes, some will make marginal changes, and a few will change not at all or even not make the grade. For those who do make major changes, the implementing company will acquire human assets who have greatly exceeded their former capacity.

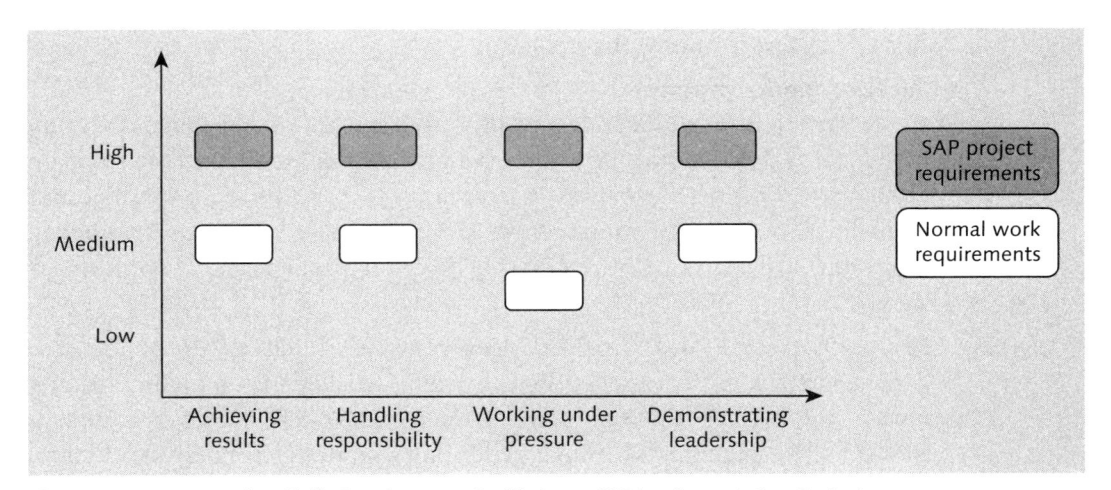

Figure 2.5 Team Member Skills Development Profile in an SAP Implementation Project

Compared to the effort involved in standard day-to-day tasks, the project team assignment brings continuous intensity and demand for rapid response to issues. This higher performance requirement creates new levels of capability. The four dimensions where these changes will take place are as follows:

- **Achieving results**

    An SAP implementation project is a series of ongoing demands for results. On a daily basis, the project team members are expected to produce according to the schedule and deliverables required. Every team member has an assignment and is expected to accomplish it. Achieving results is built into the DNA of an SAP project team and soon becomes a part of the DNA for every project team member.

The will to succeed and to resolve obstacles becomes a point of pride for virtually all team members. Each obstacle overcome becomes a matter of pride and reminds the team just how proficient it is. Teams create their own culture and this can manifest itself in many ways. However, at the core of an effective SAP project team is a shared drive to achieve results.

- **Handling responsibility**
Teams and team members fundamentally understand that they own their deliverables. The responsibility for success or failure lies with each individual. Over time, teams become adept at identifying their responsibilities and making sure they are accomplished. No one is looking over their shoulders and no one needs to. Nor does anyone spend time reminding team members of their deadlines. They already know them.

- **Working under pressure**
Implementing companies are especially familiar with the old adage that "time is money." Any delays to the project plan will undoubtedly cost the company and create unforeseen expenses. These, in turn, can necessitate a reallocation of financial budgets. Of course, these are not popular. Overruns may impact the company revenue stream by placing holds on product launches or hiring of new sales representatives.

Because everyone on the project team remains acutely aware of the costs attached to delays, they strive to do everything possible to stay on time. Almost always, this involves the team working longer hours and finding creative solutions to make deadlines. Working under this kind of pressure for two to three years leaves a lasting impression on team members' work habits. What was previously a difficult and stressful challenge now becomes a normal part of daily business.

- **Demonstrating leadership**
Everyone on an SAP project team becomes a leader at one time or another; more often than not, this occurs without the accompanying title. With so many things to be done and so little time to do them, team members quite commonly take on leadership roles when they see that initiative is required.

This is especially true during realization and final preparation when, compared to blueprinting, the number of deliverables per week can triple or quadruple. Team members recognize what tasks require leadership and then provide it. It is very common during systems testing to see team members take a leadership role on their own initiative for cross-workstream testing or managing defect resolution.

The message is clear: Companies that appoint an SAP implementation project team receive a secondary bonus. They greatly expand the capabilities of their staff assigned to the project team. The challenge is to provide job responsibilities and tasks after the project has been completed commensurate with these increased skill levels.

This requires planning on the part of project sponsors and constant assessment of each project team member. In this way, the implementing company is in position to take advantage of the high-performance team it has created.

2.3 Transforming SAP into a Company Asset

Michael Doane, author of *The SAP Blue Book* and *The SAP Green Book* (SAP PRESS, 2012), has urged implementing companies to see the SAP system as a long-term investment and treat it as such. Let's elaborate on this theme and connect it to the SAP implementation project.

Doane makes the case that a great many implementing companies focus almost exclusively on getting the SAP implementation project right and fail to recognize that, as a long-term asset, an SAP system will require considerable upkeep and maintenance during its likely 20-year period of use.

Doane's asset-based approach is important for two reasons.

1. It encourages companies to see the SAP implementation project as setting the stage for long-term system usage. Rather than completely emphasizing the success of the short-term implementation project, the company would also focus on how to make the system viable for company operations over time.
2. It provides a wake-up call to the company. Putting an SAP system in place is comparable to using company and system integrator resources to build a vehicle. Except this vehicle will exhibit properties of a mass-transit system, with

2 | How an SAP Implementation Changes Business

all its complexities. It will have large numbers of users located in different geographical locations. It will also require continual maintenance to stay in working order.

The argument goes something like this: Those elements that make for a successful project do not necessarily make for a successful long-term company asset. For reasons of cost, pride, and urgency, the implementation project centers on speed to deployment. This focus may cause the company to set aside those factors that would make for successful long-term use of the SAP system, including in-depth consideration of needed business processes or building user skills necessary to operate the system.

> **Pitfall Alert**
>
> If the implementing company already has an SAP sustainment organization, address how it will work together with the project team throughout the life cycle. Make sure that everyone is on board. If the implementing company does not have an SAP sustainment organization, begin the planning right now.

Figure 2.6 shows these two components: SAP system implementation and SAP system long-term usage. The implementation project has large numbers of resources devoted to it, is assigned a very substantial budget of company resources, and develops its own sense of importance. On the other hand, for most companies, preparing for continuous operations remains very much a back-burner activity; they wait until after the implementation has been completed to plan post-go-live operations.

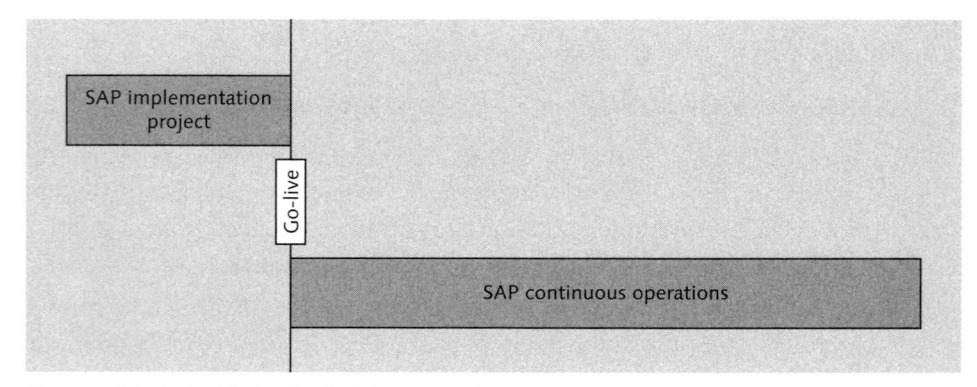

Figure 2.6 Relative Timing for SAP System Implementation versus SAP System Operation

Let's consider the relative timing of implementation and ongoing operations. An implementation may take three years, and long-term system operation may go on for at least five times that long. All of a sudden, it's apparent that the investment to put the system in place dwarfs the investment to keep it running.

Further, the *kinds* of investments to put the system in place differ markedly from those required to keep the system in place. As Table 2.1 indicates, the types of activities needed to deliver the system will likely vary considerably from those needed to maintain the system once it is live. By definition, the SAP project team is a delivery-focused organization. This means in practice that project leadership concerns itself solely with putting the system in place and relegates all other matters to second place. On the other hand, once go-live has occurred, the SAP sustainment organization pays utmost attention to how the system is operating and how to improve that experience.

System-Related Activities	System Delivery	System Operation and Maintenance
Essential activities	▶ In-depth understanding of business process changes ▶ Ability to create company commitment to delivering the system ▶ Proficiency in documenting system design decisions ▶ Capability to write test scripts and conduct thorough testing ▶ Ability to conduct data-conversion processes from legacy systems	▶ High degree of system user skills ▶ Committed super users and process owners active in system usage ▶ Effective system governance at all levels in the company that decides questions of system continuity ▶ Skilled SAP-focused IT business analysts who support the system ▶ Rapid and coordinated responses to system outages
Important activities	▶ Skills in developing targeted user-training materials ▶ Focus on timelines and deliverables	▶ Designing plans for system releases ▶ Monitoring system performance

Table 2.1 Activities Needed for System Delivery versus System Maintenance

The information presented in Table 2.1 makes an important distinction: The skills critical for system delivery will not be the same ones critical for system sustainment. Thus a company SAP governance team that has led a successful implementation will not necessarily be prepared for governing the now-live system for the years ahead. An implementing company making effective plans for system governance must make sure this transition point is well understood and needed skill sets are in place.

Our final chapter, Chapter 23, reviews the transition process to sustainment and how the governance process will operate in this new world. Sustainment will lack the drama and constant urgency of the implementation project. However, it will be equally important for the company to perform well. Building the home well is one thing; learning how to live in it is very much another.

But before arriving at sustainment, we have a good distance yet to travel and a great deal of material to cover. Our next chapter describes the Accelerated SAP methodology. It gives an overall roadmap for the project team to travel in its implementation journey. Let's head there now!

In this chapter, we'll learn the fundamentals of the Accelerated SAP methodology. It will guide us through the steps of the project from beginning to end and detail many of the corresponding actions. If you find the vocabulary proves different from what you're used to, stick with it. The effort is well worth it.

3 The ASAP Methodology

Many senior executives in implementing companies express profound reservations about bringing the SAP system into their enterprises. They believe that the time commitment required, the potential risks facing the company, and costs involved to implement the SAP system may outweigh the benefits. And truthfully, the list of failed or partially executed implementations might cause any reasonable person to have doubts.

SAP is well aware of these concerns, many of which have been voiced directly to its most senior executives. As a result, SAP has spent significant resources developing tools to improve the implementation experience. One of the most powerful of these tools is the Accelerated SAP methodology, known as ASAP.

At first glance, a methodology might appear to be of limited assistance to address the challenges of a full-scale implementation. However, once you understand the root causes of many of these challenges, the substantial value of ASAP reveals itself: ASAP acts as the glue that binds the project together.

When projects fail to achieve their objectives, it's usually due to a few key issues. Many of these were outlined in Chapter 1. Issues such as the inability to control project scope can result in confusion and conflicting expectations among key players. Lack of clarity about project timing, significant deliverables, and even how the project is managed can put a project off course. Insufficient attention to rigorous system testing can deliver a product that is unready to perform as the company requires.

Lack of management focus and structure are almost always at the heart of these challenges. None of them would be an issue if managers focused on effective core project operations. It is not a matter of competence! In most cases, these deficiencies stem from lack of knowledge. Key project leaders do not know how to manage scope, define a workable project schedule, or allocate the necessary time to system testing.

While ASAP is not the only thing you need to achieve project success, it goes a long way toward making that success possible. ASAP is not the total solution to these problems, but it does lay a foundation for their resolution. ASAP operates almost as a "program manager in a box." It lays out many of project delivery steps and guides the team toward their fulfillment.

First of all, ASAP is one of a group of similar methodologies called *software development lifecycles* (SDLC). These are used by information technology (IT) organizations to guide their own software development and implementation projects. Generally, each company has adopted one as a standard and uses it for any related activity. In this limited context, the chosen SDLC will usually prove very helpful.

Let's look at an example. Figure 3.1 shows a four-step SDLC that might be used for any medium-sized or large enterprise. Many of the commonly used SDLCs contain four to six phases in which they segment the project; our example uses four steps.

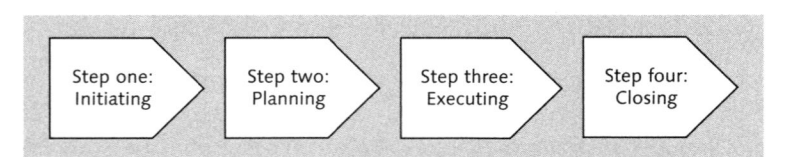

| Step one: Initiating | Step two: Planning | Step three: Executing | Step four: Closing |

Figure 3.1 Typical Software Development Lifecycle

So what's the problem? There are literally hundreds of different software development lifecycles, each with its own project steps and terminology. There is no one standard SDLC used by most companies, or even by most companies within an industry. Putting it mildly, the environment is unregulated. Each SDLC will call out different phase boundaries and define a singular project approach.

Viewed from the standpoint of a single company, this situation really doesn't represent a significant problem. Most company software implementations are relatively small in scale and utilize relatively few resources. Due to their small size, teams can easily adjust to lack of clarity about project definition. Potential confusion regarding a project roadmap can be resolved through discussion. Team members simply sit down together and work through any terminological distinctions.

However, the scale of an SAP system implementation greatly exceeds the size of virtually any other system implementation; in the end, an SAP implementation really does differ on a major scale. Implementing SAP will likely be the most complex systems undertaking in the company to date. It will involve greater costs, geographical reach, resource needs, and management challenges by a factor of 10. Thus, the scale of communication involved—even if it is limited to company staff—will cause any minor misunderstanding to soon mushroom out of control.

Add to this the large-scale involvement of a systems integrator team, other third-party participants, and SAP itself, and the number of participants can double or triple. In such an environment, miscommunications regarding scope definitions or project deliverables cannot be resolved by a simple meeting. Even holding such a meeting would require considerable logistics effort to schedule and prepare.

Imagine for a moment the situation of the poor systems integrator in the absence of ASAP. Each separate implementation would require a differing approach and terminology. Systems integrators would be forced to learn the conventions of whatever software development lifecycle that the implanting company had adopted. Every new employee assigned to the integrator project team would require training on how the implementing company conducted its projects. Obviously, this situation is untenable.

So now what?

3.1 ASAP Components

The solution is a common framework and set of operating expectations that help eliminate any points of confusion. As with any other SDLC, the ASAP method divides the project into manageable chunks or phases. Figure 3.2 identifies the five phases of ASAP. Together they range from project preparation at the very beginning of the program (phase one), to the business blueprint (phase two), to realization (phase three), to final preparation (phase four), and to go-live and support (phase five) at the conclusion of the program.

1. Project preparation
2. Business blueprint
3. Realization
4. Final preparation
5. Go-live and support

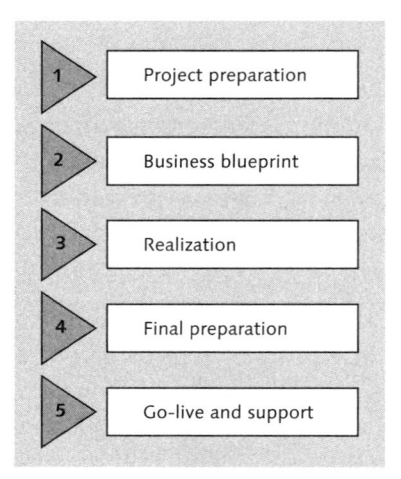

Figure 3.2 Five Phases of the ASAP Methodology

However, if the ASAP methodology were to offer only a set of phases, it would provide very limited assistance to the project team. After all, the phases provide only a set of buckets in which to classify project activities. What makes ASAP different — and truly valuable — are the features that accompany it. In addition to the project phase structure, ASAP also supplies core structuring elements:

- For each phase, ASAP identifies the *deliverable set* needed for the project team to accomplish. Not only are the core deliverables identified, they are also supported with templates. The project team can use these templates to outline the characteristics of its own deliverables. In some cases, ASAP even furnishes examples for documents that will be required, such as the project charter. Project teams are free to add additional deliverables as needed, but can work from a foundation set embedded in the methodology.

- As well, ASAP addresses many of the *project timing* challenges by supplying relative timing of key deliverables within each phase. While ASAP does not specify the length of a phase or a project, it does indicate the ordering of deliverables within a phase and, by extension, a project. An experienced program management office can use this information to generate a reasonably accurate phase or overall project schedule.

- ASAP does indeed provide the *common language* that ties all project team participants together. Acting almost as a Rosetta Stone, ASAP enables company project teams and systems integrators to understand one another virtually from day one.

But ASAP is not a panacea. It does not manage the project, construct deliverables, or build the design. Rather, it supplies the framework within which these actions can be accomplished. It is up to the project team to use the methodology effectively.

ASAP is not without its blind spots. It focuses almost exclusively on deliverables that directly affect the SAP system. Items such as program budgeting and financial reporting, systems integrator identification and contracting, and project team selection are barely mentioned at all. An implementing company must be aware of these coverage gaps and plan accordingly. The following chapters review many of these activities.

Additionally, some important systems integrators choose not to use ASAP, or they use a variant of it. Accenture has developed its own Accenture Delivery Methods for SAP. It uses a six-phase implementation process and has differing nomenclature. Otherwise it performs the same purpose as ASAP. Similarly, IBM has built the Ascendant Methodology, which is a variant of ASAP. It uses the basic nomenclature, but adds deliverables and the use of a common work breakdown structure for the project.

> **Tip**
>
> For those involved in the project management discipline, ASAP is aligned with the standards set by the Project Management Institute (PMI), which is the standard of reference in North America. It fits as well with the PRINCE2 framework most commonly used in the United Kingdom and British Commonwealth nations.

In addition to the five project phases discussed, the program will subdivide into several *workstreams* or *work breakdown structure* (WBS) elements. These are intended to clarify which part of the project team has responsibility for accomplishing the work product. Additionally, the workstreams organize the flow of deliverables across the entire project. Figure 3.3 outlines the workstreams currently in use.

3 | The ASAP Methodology

Project management	PM
Organization change management	OCM
Training	TRN
Business process management	BPM
Data management	DM
Technical solution management	TSM
Integration solution management	ISM
Value management	VM
Cutover management	COM
Application lifecycle management	ALM

Figure 3.3 Standard Workstreams in the ASAP Methodology

These workstream elements remain active and continue across the entire project lifecycle. Each will have deliverables designated for delivery within the subsequent phases until the project has reached its conclusion. For the most part the meaning for each workstream is self-explanatory, but we'll elaborate here:

- *Project management* focuses on planning, executing, and tracking the project. Activities associated with staffing, financial controlling, and facilities usage will fall in this area as well.

- *Organization change management* assures that the implementing company is prepared for the changes it will undergo. Activities here incorporate stakeholder management, project communications, and change readiness operations.

- *Training* comprises both the SAP-related training of the project team as well as the development of instructional materials for end users. Classroom instruction, scheduling of classes, and administration of course completions is included as well.

- *Business process management* (BPM) includes the identification of requirements and solution design. In addition, this element contains related activities such as user role frameworks and requirements for custom objects. BPM will align with functional workstreams such as record-to-report (finance) and order-to-cast (sales operations).

- *Data management* handles all data conversion steps. These range from data review and correction to data loading and verification.
- *Technical solution management* centers on project infrastructure operations. These will cover the installation and operation of all infrastructure, third-party tools, and SAP applications.
- *Integration solutions management* covers the full range of systems testing. Its major activities will encompass integration testing and user acceptance testing—as well as the related operations conducted, such as defect resolution.
- *Value management* centers on identifying the benefits the implementing company expects from the SAP system and ensuring that these benefits are actually achieved.
- *Cutover management* ensures that the project has completed all necessary items for go-live. Such activities involve business preparation, final loads of data and configuration, and user readiness.
- *Application lifecycle management* addresses the cradle-to-grave operations of those SAP applications included in the project, as well as any relevant legacy applications.

This workstream approach helps align the project. Once deliverables are allocated to a particular workstream, it has the major responsibility of ensuring their proper completion. With this assignment mechanism in place, project participants can clearly understand where task ownership lies and can turn their attention to meeting the deadlines.

> **Tip**
> Invest early in ASAP training for the project team. Building a common vocabulary and way of thinking about the project will prove to be a great investment for project success.

Irrespective of the workstream, deliverables are identified and assigned to a specific phase, as illustrated in Figure 3.4. In this way, all deliverables within a phase are tagged and can easily be tracked for completion status. Additionally, most deliverables will have one or more tasks associated with them. Generally, these are sequential steps within a hierarchy; the accomplishment of the first task under that deliverable will then lead to the second task.

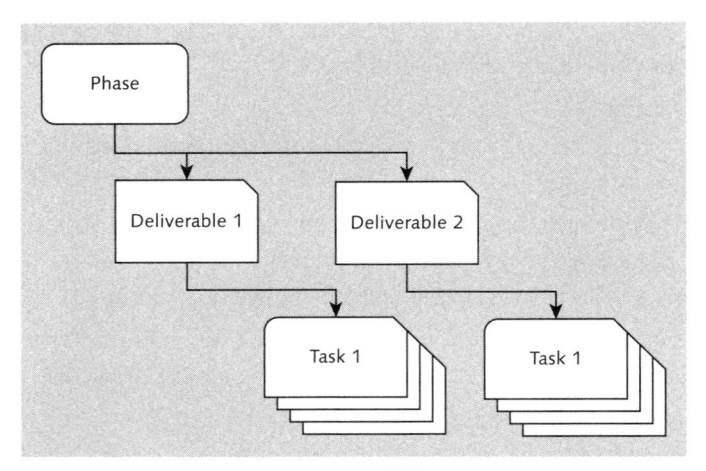

Figure 3.4 Deliverables Hierarchy in ASAP

If this deliverable identification and task assignment is done properly, the project team will clearly understand the workload in front of it. Workstream leaders can allocate these tasks to individual team members. This way, everyone knows what is to be done and who is responsible for doing it.

Obviously, both the deliverables and tasks will vary by project phase. Activities in blueprinting are far different than those in final preparation. So let's use the remainder of this chapter to review each of the phases in the ASAP roadmap and provide more detailed descriptions of the major deliverables. Subsequent chapters will supply greater detail regarding how the phase actually works.

3.2 Phase One: Project Preparation

Project preparation fully puts the project in motion and lays the foundation for all later phases. It focuses on making the shift from the "project as concept" to a living and breathing entity. This project will include staff, working locations, and an organizational structure. This transformation takes place through a series of incremental steps designed to construct the project.

Figure 3.5 identifies the many deliverables associated with the project preparation phase. As you can see, the deliverables are all about readiness. They are setting the project in motion and laying the groundwork for success in later phases such as blueprint and realization.

Phase One: Project Preparation | **3.2**

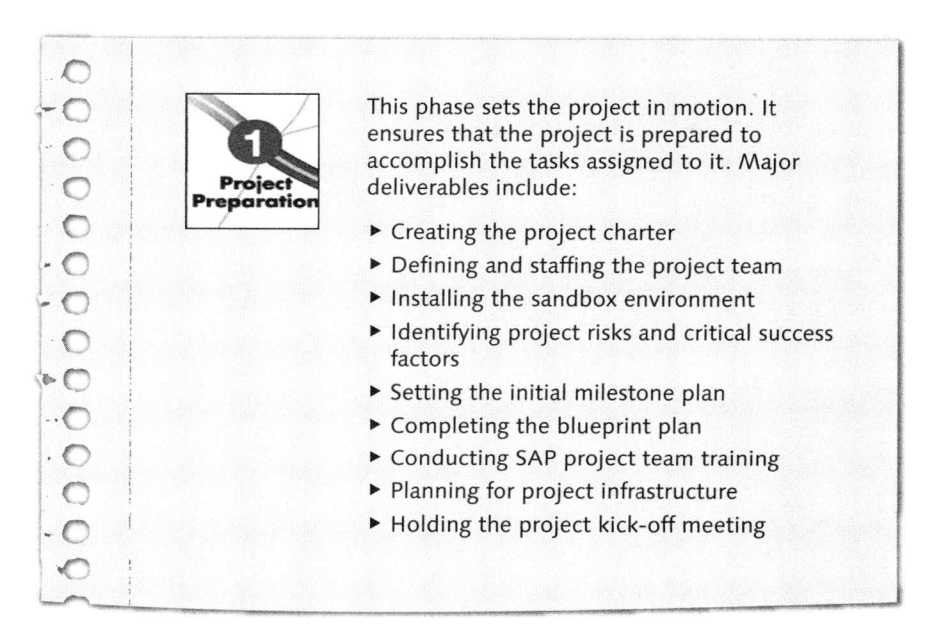

> This phase sets the project in motion. It ensures that the project is prepared to accomplish the tasks assigned to it. Major deliverables include:
>
> - Creating the project charter
> - Defining and staffing the project team
> - Installing the sandbox environment
> - Identifying project risks and critical success factors
> - Setting the initial milestone plan
> - Completing the blueprint plan
> - Conducting SAP project team training
> - Planning for project infrastructure
> - Holding the project kick-off meeting

Figure 3.5 Project Planning Phase Snapshot

The program management workstream has ownership of most of these deliverables. Of the nine deliverables outlined, six are owned by the project management workstream. Two others (installation of the sandbox environment and planning for project infrastructure) are owned by the technical solution management; the remaining item (conducting SAP training for the project team) is assigned to the training workstream.

However, other workstreams—such as data management and the functional workstreams such as procure-to-pay—have work to complete as well. The data team will be deeply involved in identifying data required for migration and the systems where they currently reside. Functional workstreams will be busy preparing for blueprinting activities, such as outlining the business process changes that will be essential components of the project.

Additionally, all remaining workstreams must review and agree to the project management deliverables described above. Those deliverables are intended to apply to the entire project. Every workstream must carefully assess any activities in which it participates and decide whether it can accomplish the timing and specification of the activities assigned to it. Once everyone agrees, the activities are booked as "scheduled" or "promised." They become core operating assumptions for project completion.

It is essential to get the project preparation phase right. We can't emphasize this enough. Any unfounded assumption here or task left undone will create difficulties in later phases. For that reason, this book spends a good deal of time on the elements of project preparation. As you can see in Table 3.1, seven chapters address elements of project preparation. These chapters detail the critical topics and should greatly assist with project team activities associated with this important phase.

Chapter	Title
Chapter 5	Start-up Logistics
Chapter 6	System Integrator Selection and Contracting
Chapter 8	Project Planning
Chapter 9	Knowledge Management
Chapter 10	Project Organization
Chapter 11	Project Governance
Chapter 12	Building the Right Project Team

Table 3.1 Project Preparation Phase Activities by Chapter

3.3 Phase Two: Business Blueprint

With the project foundation now in place, the team can turn to business blueprinting, or creating the solution design. Whereas the majority of deliverables in project preparation fell within the purview of project management, this orientation dramatically shifts during the blueprinting phase. Now the functional business workstreams play the lead role. These workstreams house the business process knowledge assigned to the project team and are most closely aligned with the functional business organizations in the implementing company.

Figure 3.6 identifies the major deliverables in the business blueprinting phase. These are noticeably different from the previous phase. Here the orientation has shifted to activities and documentation associated with the design workshops.

The functional business process teams have moved to the forefront. Five of the listed deliverables would fall in the business process management workstream (or, alternatively, the functional process workstreams). The remaining deliverables divide among the organizational change management team (setting change impacts), the technical solutions management team (installing the development environment), and the project management team (building the realization plan).

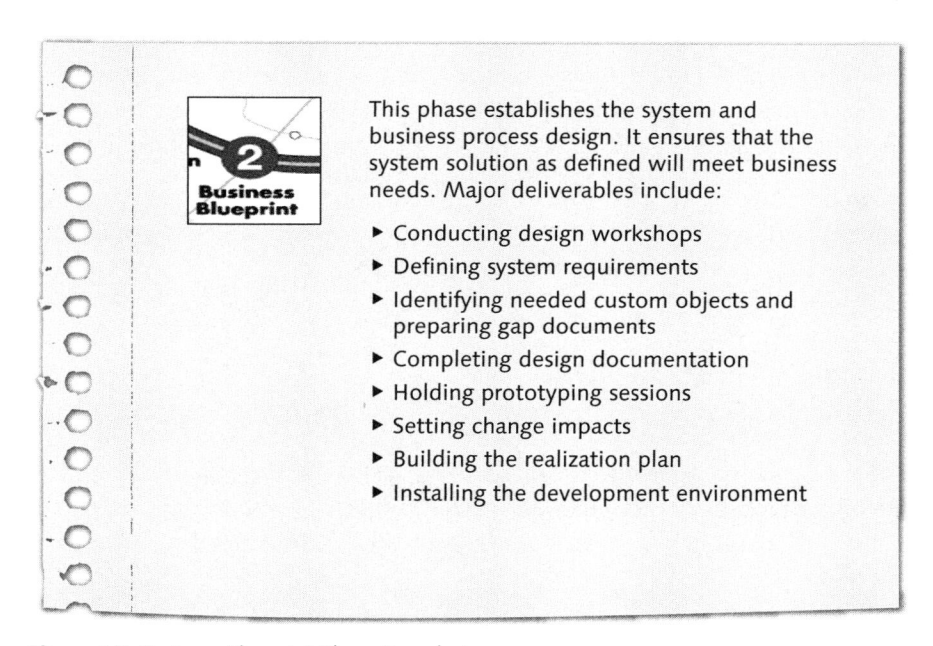

> **Business Blueprint**
>
> This phase establishes the system and business process design. It ensures that the system solution as defined will meet business needs. Major deliverables include:
>
> ▸ Conducting design workshops
> ▸ Defining system requirements
> ▸ Identifying needed custom objects and preparing gap documents
> ▸ Completing design documentation
> ▸ Holding prototyping sessions
> ▸ Setting change impacts
> ▸ Building the realization plan
> ▸ Installing the development environment

Figure 3.6 Business Blueprint Phase Snapshot

All other workstream teams will take an active role during business blueprint sessions. The training team will use this opportunity to discuss end-user training development processes and the need for locally based SAP team training needs. The integration solution management team will begin scoping for integration and user acceptance testing. The technical solution team will educate participants on the development process used to build custom objects. Finally, the organization change management team will initiate role-mapping discussions. There is no place for idle time on any of the teams.

A good part of the deliverables in business blueprinting consists of documentation. The teams will learn how to create, review, approve, and maintain the documents. Essentially, each of the functional workstreams has responsibility for its own documentation. Each team will come to understand the importance of preparing design documentation according to the instructions provided. Once reviewed and approved, the bulk of project deliverables will depend on the information contained in these design documents.

The degree of project support from company senior executives will depend on how well business blueprinting proceeds. If senior executives see excited and involved participants, they will view the project as a positive investment. If they see blueprints generating large-scale business process improvements, their interest levels will rise markedly. It will be up to the project team to assess the process improvement possibilities and incorporate them within the solution design.

Expanded coverage of business blueprinting will be located in Chapter 13. It outlines the processes and documentation required and provides concrete examples of completed blueprinting documentation.

3.4 Phase Three: Realization

The project team will have much to accomplish in the realization phase. In truth, realization is consists of two mini-phases. The first mini-phase is called "build," where configuration is completed and custom objects are built and tested. The second mini-phase is called "test," where the team verifies that the system performs to requirements.

> **Tip**
>
> The realization phase consumes the greatest amount of project time by far. In fact, realization frequently requires double the amount of time invested in blueprinting. It is here that project team fatigue is most likely to set in. Keep your finger on the pulse of team morale and hours worked.

Figure 3.7 lists the major deliverables included in realization. Those items completed during the build segment of realization are primarily accomplished by the systems integrator team. These include configuration, as well as custom object definition, development, and unit testing. Integration testing will, for the most part be performed by the project team. The systems integrator will also develop end-user training materials. The project staff from the implementing company will focus most of its efforts on review of materials prepared and preparation for user acceptance testing.

> This phase implements the system design through configuration and development. It ensures system performance through a staged series of rigorous testing. Major deliverables include:
>
> ▸ Building final configuration
> ▸ Defining custom object functional and technical specifications
> ▸ Designing, coding, and unit testing custom objects
> ▸ Assigning security authorizations
> ▸ Planning for and conducting system testing
> ▸ Developing user training materials
> ▸ Conducting data reviews and loads
> ▸ Installing the quality assurance and production environments

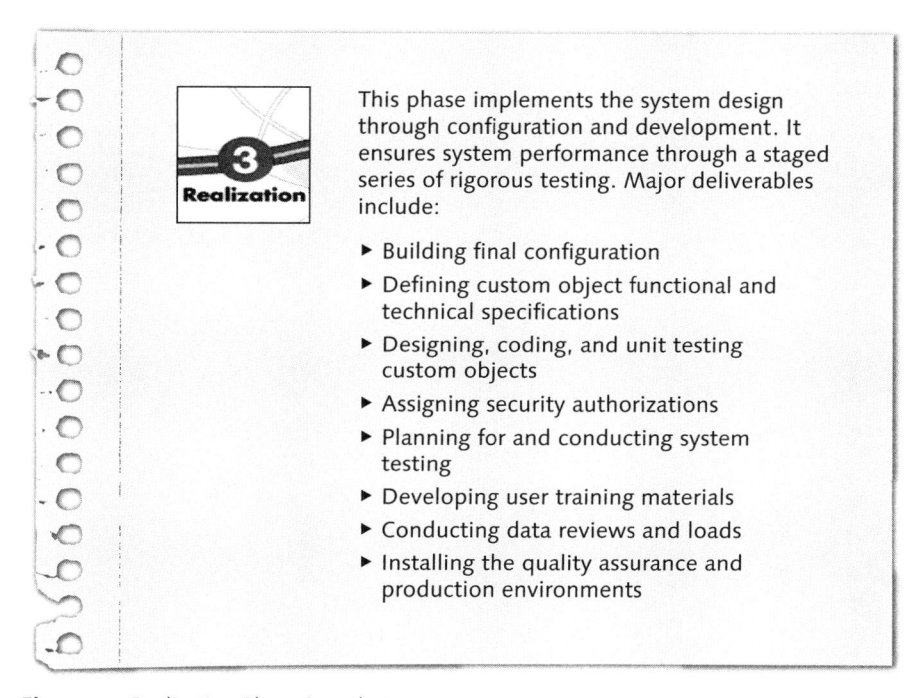

Figure 3.7 Realization Phase Snapshot

Not only does realization consist of numerous deliverables, but these deliverables are also largely technical. They center on the mechanics of making the SAP system work to meet business requirements. In this phase, the implementing company becomes very dependent on the skills and management abilities of its systems integrator partner. Even with the division of labor highly skewed toward the lead role performed by the systems integrator, the implementing company must still assure itself that adequate progress is being made. Monitoring time to completion of the individual tasks becomes a very critical job for the project management team. Additionally, even though the implementing company project team may not perform the actual work involved, it must carefully assess these work products and understand their content.

Governance activities will become prominent, especially in the later stages of realization. Implementing company senior executives will have concerns about project status and its ability to meet scheduled go-live dates. They will expect to receive regular updates that cover major risk areas and project performance schedule and costs. These updates will be very important in establishing and maintaining project credibility through this phase and following phases.

We'll offer expanded coverage of realization in Chapter 14 through Chapter 20, as shown in Table 3.2. These seven chapters encompass all major activities taking place during the phase. Coverage begins with an overall review of realization and moves into the two major components: configuration and custom object build, and system testing. The last four chapters of this sequence (17-20) address specific topics within the realization phase.

Chapter	Title
Chapter 14	Realization
Chapter 15	Configuration and Custom Objects Build
Chapter 16	System Testing
Chapter 17	Data, Reports, EDI, and Security and Internal Controls
Chapter 18	Building Systems Environments
Chapter 19	Change Management
Chapter 20	Continuous User Training

Table 3.2 Realization Phase Activities by Chapter

3.5 Phase Four: Final Preparation

Final preparation represents the short, very intensive period immediately prior to go-live. Here the project team focuses on making sure that all the different steps needed to move from a project environment to a production environment are in place. All the necessary go-live preparation steps must be accomplished in a very tight time frame.

Usually the implementing company will have shut down its production and shipping operations in support of the project. During this short window of time, all company data as well as configurations and custom objects to run the system must be moved into the production environment. In addition, it must be verified as accurate prior to releasing the SAP system to end users.

> **Tip**
>
> Final preparation will feel very rushed—and it is! Many activities have to be accomplished in a very tight time frame. Project sponsors should do everything possible to help the team understand this situation and respond to it.

Those same end users must receive required systems training in this short time frame. In this way, the instructional material will stay fresh in their minds and ready for use in a few weeks. Specially trained support personnel known as *super users* will be trained and prepared to provide end-user assistance on the new system.

For the first time, the cutover management workstream appears and plays the lead role during this phase. The project management workstream hands over the reins to cutover specialists. These individuals are specially trained to coordinate and handle the myriad of short-term tasks taking place during the shift from a legacy system to the new SAP production system.

Figure 3.8 identifies the major deliverables to be achieved during final preparation. These are, for the most part, very tactical deliverables that are intended to make the final push into an active production system.

One essential deliverable is the final go-live approval. Normally this is a very well-attended session with company senior executives. They will be eager to understand any remaining risks and their implications. Each senior executive is polled regarding her recommendation prior to the group's final decision. Assuming that decision is positive, the project team will have only a few days—three or four at best—to complete all remaining activities and get the system up and running for end-user operations. At that point, the SAP logins will be released and end users will have operational access to the system.

Expanded coverage of final preparation will be contained in Chapter 21. It outlines the steps to bring the project live and provides numerous examples of completed final preparation project materials.

3 | The ASAP Methodology

> This phase prepares for cutover and system go-live. It verifies business, end-user, and system readiness for final deployment. Major deliverables include:
>
> - Developing the cutover plan and conducting dry runs
> - Managing production data load and verification
> - Building the production environment
> - Assigning final end user role mapping
> - Issuing SAP UserIDs
> - Moving configuration and custom object transports to production
> - Conducting end-user training
> - Preparing super users for support role
> - Creating the hypercare plan
> - Receiving final go-live approval

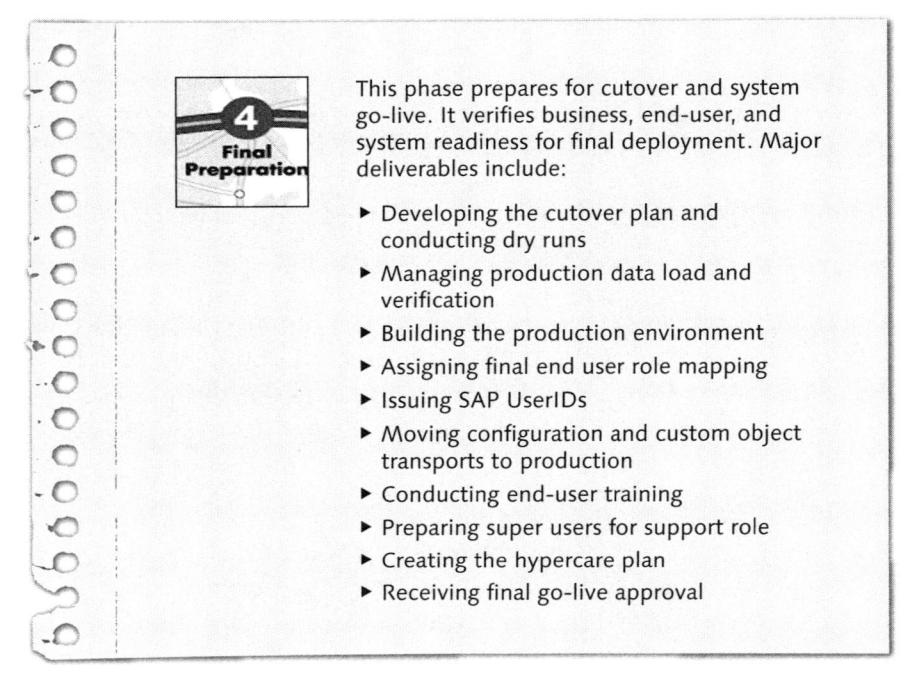

Figure 3.8 Final Preparation Phase Snapshot

3.6 Phase Five: Go-Live and Support

The system has now gone live and the intense period of final preparation is replaced by an even more intense period: hypercare. The reality is that very few go-lives result in smooth transitions to the new SAP system. Usually problems both small and large beset the project team almost from the beginning. End users may experience difficulties with access to all needed transactions, some portions of the system may not operate according to plan, and custom objects may not work as they did during testing. The discipline that has brought the team to this point will be greatly needed in go-live and support.

Figure 3.9 identifies the deliverables during go-live and support. Notice that each is centered on problem identification and resolution. The project status meetings have now shifted from tracking test script completions to monitoring incident closure status. As the help desk receives incidents and transfers them to resolvers,

Phase Five: Go-Live and Support | **3.6**

the entire project team now focuses on understanding the issues and bringing them to closure.

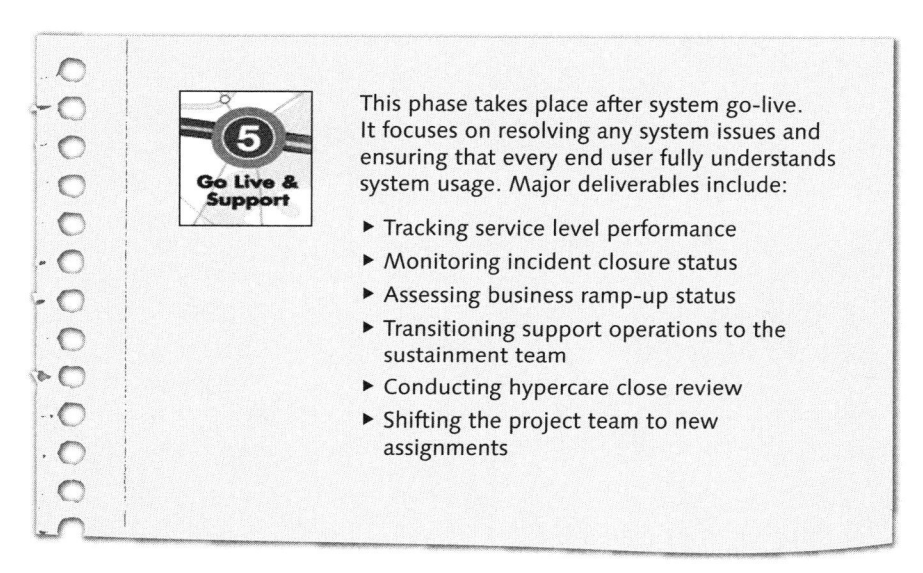

> **Go Live & Support (5)**
>
> This phase takes place after system go-live. It focuses on resolving any system issues and ensuring that every end user fully understands system usage. Major deliverables include:
>
> ▸ Tracking service level performance
> ▸ Monitoring incident closure status
> ▸ Assessing business ramp-up status
> ▸ Transitioning support operations to the sustainment team
> ▸ Conducting hypercare close review
> ▸ Shifting the project team to new assignments

Figure 3.9 Go-Live and Support Phase Snapshot

Hypercare will continue until some prearranged completion point is reached. This could be the attainment of some business performance metrics or achievement of incident volume targets. It could be both. At some point in the incident resolution process, the project team will begin to transition its responsibilities over to those who will maintain the system going forward. Approximately midway through the hypercare period, the sustainment group will assume ownership for incident resolution. In this way, the project team readies itself for new post-project roles and the sustainment team prepares itself for the problem-solving that is certainly ahead.

When the proposed hypercare completion point has been reached, project sponsors conduct their last program review. They assess hypercare performance, satisfy themselves that no major issues remain unresolved, and make a decision to bring hypercare to a close. This same decision brings the project to its close as well.

Expanded coverage of go-live and support will be found in the two chapters referenced in Table 3.3. They describe the operations of hypercare and outline the sustainment process.

Chapter	Title
Chapter 22	Go-Live and Hypercare
Chapter 23	Sustainment

Table 3.3 Go-Live and Support Phase Activities by Chapter

3.7 Quality Gates

Many projects have used quality gates with some success, so SAP has added this concept to the ASAP methodology.

Quality gates are end-of-phase reviews where the project must pass an examination before moving to the next phase. Such reviews provide project sponsors with targeted understanding of project performance. Because the reviews are formal in nature, materials are prepared in advance and then subjected to considerable scrutiny. The purpose is to establish where the project stands and whether it stands where it should.

These reviews have the advantage of capturing any significant issues early in the project, before they create delays or cost overruns. Figure 3.10 illustrates how this quality gate process would work. At the end of each phase, the project team would notify project sponsors on whether they were ready to proceed to the next phase. Project sponsors would schedule the phase gate review and make a decision based on the evidence the team submitted. An additional phase gate could be inserted at the completion of realization build so that project sponsors could assess the status of final configuration and custom object build.

All participants in these reviews fully expect a free give-and-take. The purpose is to give project sponsors the opportunity to ask questions of project team leadership and probe deeper when they need more clarity. Thus, when project sponsors make the decision to move to the next phase, they fully understand any risks and assume the responsibility as well.

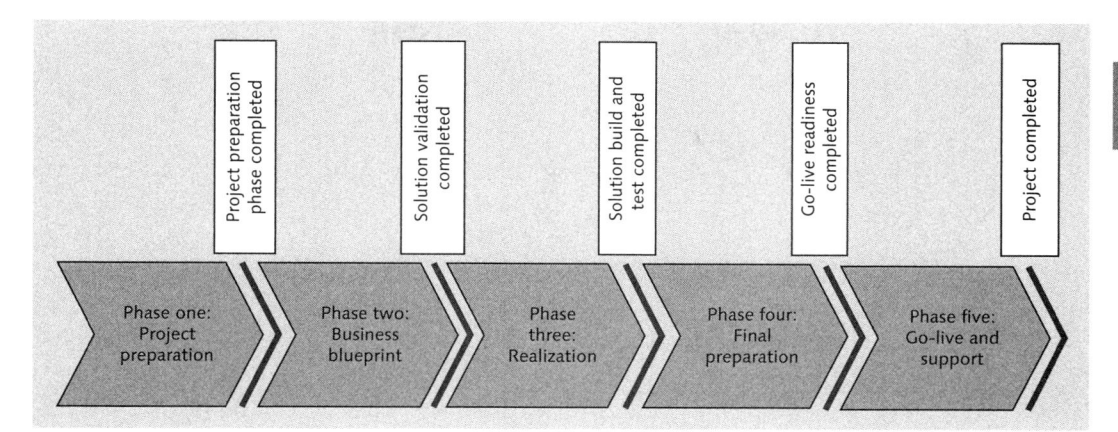

Figure 3.10 Project Quality Gates

Our next chapter describes the many types of SAP implementation projects. These run the gamut from highly complex, long-term efforts for which SAP is famous, to the deployment of SAP packaged solutions aimed at small and medium-sized businesses. Each type presents its own sets of challenges to the project team. The chapter will explain how to deliver each project type.

We are now headed into the nuts and bolts of SAP implementation. Because SAP projects come in many shapes and sizes, there really is no "typical" project. This chapter reviews the major project types and describes how one differs from another.

4 Types of SAP Projects

Despite the popular perception, there is actually more than one type of SAP project. The idea of a "big bang" SAP implementation involving the whole company is only one of many possible options. However, the "big bang" implementation has become increasingly less frequent over time. Many large corporations have already built their SAP-installed base. Their "big bang" projects have already occurred and are well in the past. These SAP clients now focus on improvements to and enlargements of their existing systems.

Yet large-scale SAP implementations do continue to take place. However, their emphasis has now shifted away from the original model. Rather than initial company-wide SAP deployments, they now represent the systems integration in support of IPO, merger, and acquisition efforts. In these cases, one company acquires another or makes a divestiture. The SAP implementation project integrates the two new entities.

The number of SAP projects also continues to remain at a very high level. Some of these projects will still fall into the large-scale implementation category. However, more and more projects represent extremely targeted deployments of specific SAP functionality. These projects may require a smaller number of resources and operate on a limited time frame. Nevertheless, each one will require a project team and program management capable of moving through the steps from initial preparation to go-live.

This chapter will introduce the primary types of SAP projects and discuss the defining characteristics of each. Figure 4.1 illustrates the three major categories of SAP projects. Each category identifies a distinctive implementation effort and provides a useful frame of reference to examine its challenges.

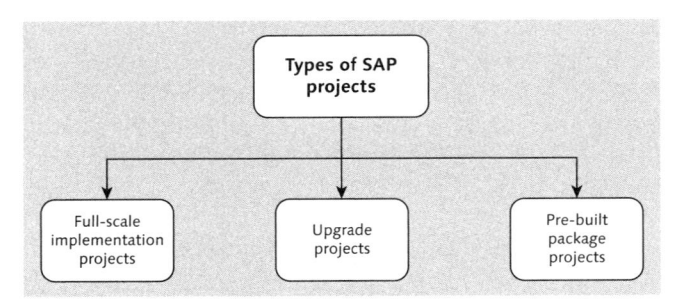

Figure 4.1 Primary Types of SAP Implementation Projects

- **Full-scale implementation projects**
  Any project that introduces the SAP system into a company operating environment can be termed a *full-scale implementation*. In these cases, the company is adopting major components of the SAP system and will be faced with across-the-board efforts to harmonize business processes. These implementation projects also entail data migration, system configuration, and custom objects, as well as significant system testing. When one first thinks of an SAP project, the full-scale implementation usually comes to mind.

> **Trail Marker**
>
> In this chapter and throughout the book, the large-scale implementation project will be used as the project base case. The most complex implementation project type can reveal relative differences and similarities among the remaining types.

- **Upgrade projects**
  For every company that already has an SAP system installed, the time will come when it is faced with making an upgrade from one version to the next. Such projects run the gamut in terms of complexity and amount of resources involved. However, they all introduce some degree of risk and must be managed very carefully.

- **Pre-built package projects**
  SAP has made a number of pre-built system options available. These pre-built solutions are intended to reduce the complexity of deployment and often even the time to deployment. Again, they each entail some level of risk and require project resources and capable project management to be successful.

Let's examine each project type more closely.

4.1 Full-Scale Implementation Projects

Relative to the other project types shown in Figure 4.1, the full-scale implementation project owns "top gun" billing. It consumes more time and resources, has greater complexity, and, in the event of failure, triggers the greatest consequences to the implementing company.

These are very often multi-year engagements and represent the attempt to place large portions of the company on the SAP platform. They also involve considerable financial investment by the implementing company—sometimes tens to hundreds of millions of dollars. These funds cover the fees for a systems integrator staff, necessary purchases of software licenses, and server hardware. A full-scale SAP implementation project is guaranteed *not* to be an inexpensive undertaking.

Additionally, in the case of a full-scale implementation, one does not implement just SAP. The idea of a single SAP software set does not fit with current reality. Instead, every full-scale implementation will deploy a host of SAP software, all intended to support the master enterprise core component, SAP Enterprise Resource Planning (ERP). Figure 4.2 illustrates the many application elements of a typical SAP installation. This complexity will affect the timing and difficulty of the implementation.

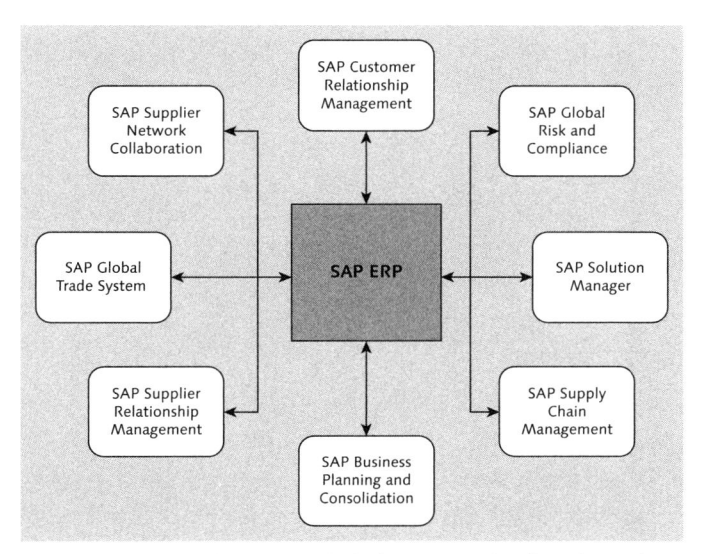

Figure 4.2 SAP Applications Included in a Typical Full-Scale Implementation

Full-scale SAP implementation projects are conducted for a number of different reasons. To help clarify, Figure 4.3 describes three of the most common approaches to full-scale implementation: the greenfield deployment, the carveout, and the system replacement.

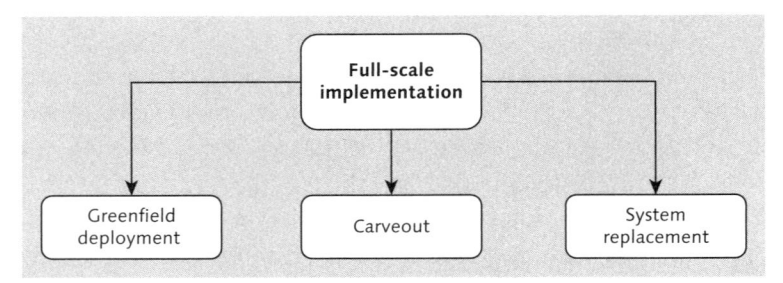

Figure 4.3 Primary Types of Full-Scale SAP Implementation Projects

Let's zoom in one step further.

4.1.1 Greenfield Deployment

A greenfield deployment takes place when the implementing company has no prior history of use with an ERP system. The name "greenfield" indicates that the SAP implementation is taking place in a company that lacks not only SAP experience, but also ERP experience. Thus, the challenge for the implementing company will involve not only learning how to operate the SAP system, but also familiarizing itself with the concept of an enterprise resource planning system.

These are not small tasks. Operating any ERP system requires discipline and a cross-functional approach to doing business. Shifting from using primarily manual or spreadsheet activities to conducting these tasks on a highly integrated system often comes as a shock. Due to its very structured approach to business processes, operating the SAP system requires a higher degree of company discipline. Usually it takes some time for these system-based processes to become second nature. For these reasons, greenfield implementations prove to be among the most complex and difficult-to-manage SAP implementation projects.

The absence of any ERP experience on the project team makes for still more difficulty. Most successful ERP project teams are already familiar with business processes performed in a systems framework. For the greenfield implementation, there will likely be very few members of the implementing company project team with this experience set. Even such fundamental project mechanisms as documentation and testing will be brand-new experiences.

> **Tip**
>
> Survey your project team and identify all members with prior SAP experience. It will help to go one step deeper to discover the details of this experience. For example, has a project team member been part of a previous SAP implementation or has a team member operated in a sustainment role? The more you know about this experience, the easier it will be to use specialized knowledge and skills.

These obstacles can be overcome, but it will take considerable effort. A systems integrator must be carefully selected—someone who understands the situation and comes prepared to help the project team build its SAP competency. The integrator staff should be selected to focus as much on instruction and support as it is on system configuration.

Table 4.1 provides four risk assessment factors for the greenfield deployment. These same risk assessment factors will be applied to all remaining project types reviewed in this chapter. As the table indicates, these types of projects reflect a high risk profile across the board. Their scope will generally encompass the entire company and its associated business processes. From the standpoint of the SAP implementation project, this means that the business processes for the complete company will undergo transformation and shift from manual actions to system-based transactions. This creates the need for a significant management effort.

Risk Assessment Factor	Greenfield Deployment Risk
Scope and business process complexity	Very high
Geography and languages	Medium to very high
Size of user base	Medium to very high
Degree of system integration	High to very high

Table 4.1 Risk Assessment for an SAP Greenfield Deployment

Depending upon the size and geographical scope of the implementing company, both geography and user base size entail medium to very high risk. If the implementing company has a large employee population and expects many of its employees to be SAP users, this will expand the risk profile. So, too, does the number of countries involved and languages to be used on the system. Finally, the degree of systems integration required can also have a significant effect on project risk. Building, testing, and maintaining the interfaces to several company legacy systems also increases the project risk profile.

This demonstrates the high risk inherent in a greenfield deployment of any large-scale system. Companies that decide on a greenfield implementation place themselves in a high-risk category.

> **Trail Marker**
>
> This constitutes one major reason why the reputation for SAP implementations is so problematic. It is based in large part on greenfield implementations. The companies least prepared by experience to conduct an implementation are faced with the most difficult and high-risk implementations of all.

However, fewer and fewer greenfield implementations are performed each year. Most of the full-scale implementation work falls in the remaining two categories: carveouts and system replacements.

4.1.2 Carveout

Carveout projects are almost always the results of some merger, acquisition, or divestiture action in the implementing company. In the case of an acquisition, the acquired company (or segment of the acquired company) almost always adopts the ERP system used by the acquiring company. In the case of a divestiture, the remaining entity must adopt an ERP system within a specified period of time. During this interim period, the divested entity continues to utilize the ERP system of its former company. After the interim period is concluded, the divested entity must have its own ERP system in place or face the prospect of substantial penalty payments.

As Figure 4.4 illustrates, the carveout scenario most closely resembles the greenfield SAP implementation. The divested entity retains interim usage of the ERP system used by the divesting company. Otherwise, however, much of the greenfield scenario applies. The divested entity must select an ERP system and implement it within an aggressive timeline. In most cases, the expertise and knowledge-base for the old ERP system continues on with the remaining entity.

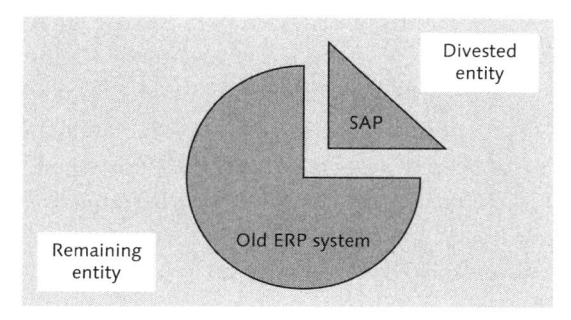

Figure 4.4 Carveout Scenario for Full-Scale SAP Implementation Project

The divested entity must learn to operate its new system and adapt its business processes accordingly. Additionally, it is faced with one complicating factor not confronted by the greenfield implementing company: The divested entity must identify its operating data on the old ERP system and learn the mechanisms of migrating it to its own SAP system. Effectively cleansing data and shifting it to a new system often proves a stumbling block for many implementing teams. In this case, however, the divested entity may lack even a basic familiarity with "its" data. After all, the former company or remaining entity likely performed all previous data maintenance.

In the acquisition scenario, the acquired company generally has the advantage of support from the acquiring company. That staff will well understand the setup of its SAP system and can assist the acquired company to align its business processes to be consistent with baseline system configuration requirements. If a systems integrator is used, that will make the process easier still. Yet at the end of the day, the acquired company is faced with an SAP implementation that it did not choose. Whether the shift goes from one SAP system to another or from a different ERP system to SAP, the difficulties encountered may have more to do with the circumstances underlying the acquisition. If the acquisition process was turbulent, one can expect the SAP implementation to experience some amount of discord.

> **Tip**
>
> Do everything you can to provide support for the acquired company project team. Let them know their importance, encourage them, and provide incentives for them. After all, they will have the best knowledge of business processes in the acquired company.

Table 4.2 assesses the risks associated with the carveout SAP deployment. Due to the external impetus for both divestures and acquisitions, scope identification and business process transformation can be problematic. The acquired company may undergo major business process alterations in adapting to those that are consistent with the new company. The divested company may be faced with actually designing many of its business processes for the first time. The degree to which either company type—acquisition or divestiture—knew of its future and could plan accordingly will have a great influence on the probable success of the SAP implementation project.

Risk Assessment Factor	Carveout Risk
Scope and business process complexity	High to very high
Geography and languages	Medium to very high
Size of user base	Medium to very high
Degree of system integration	High to very high

Table 4.2 Risk Assessment for an SAP Carveout Deployment

Risks associated with size of user base and geography involved could vary considerably. The greater the variability within the company—such as business operations in several diverse countries, multiple languages spoken, and large numbers of likely users—the greater the risk.

For each type of company, the issue of systems integration will present a challenge. For the divested entity, many of the systems used on an everyday basis may disappear at the end of the support agreement. This may require acquiring systems that perform many of the same functions. This will definitely complicate the SAP implementation.

A similar situation occurs with the acquired company. Many of its legacy systems may simply be declared redundant and taken off-line. It's likely that the acquiring company will choose to continue with its own systems and integrate the acquired company on those systems. In this scenario, the acquired company not only faces the simultaneous hurdle of learning to use SAP in rapid fashion, but also learning to use a host of supporting systems. Clearly the degree of difficulty in both instances could prove quite formidable.

4.1.3 System Replacement

Companies decide to replace their ERP systems for many reasons. One of the most common has to do with the desire to adopt a more modern, state-of-the-art system as opposed to its current system. Many companies still run portions of their operations on 30-year-old ERP systems. These legacy systems may no longer fit company business processes, and certainly their infrastructure would not align with modern distributed processing models. Additionally, Oracle Corporation's purchase of the older-version PeopleSoft and JD Edwards ERP applications led many companies to have concerns about their long-term viability. Many chose to abandon those systems and move to adopt SAP systems.

Figure 4.5 illustrates the shift from a legacy ERP system to an up-to-date and functional SAP solution. The implementation project needed to accomplish the shift will have all the trademarks of a full-scale SAP deployment. The project team will be faced with migrating data from the previous system and training its end users to make the transition to the new SAP system. It will also likely transform many of the company business processes and create the SAP system configuration designed to accomplish those redesigned processes.

Figure 4.5 System Replacement Scenario for a Full-Scale SAP Implementation Project

The company will most likely have few (if any!) resources familiar with the SAP system. For that reason, a good deal of the project preparation phase will center on developing SAP skills and knowledge among the project team. The entire infrastructure package from the current system will need replacement and the IT support staff will be faced with learning the nuances of SAP Basis operations.

On the positive side, the entire company will welcome the new SAP system. Everyone involved will quickly see how SAP can improve company business processes and create automation efficiencies in many areas. Excitement over a new SAP system and its prospects is a powerful motivator. The project team will face a daunting task but have enthusiasm for the eventual result.

Table 4.3 reviews the risk assessment profile for the system replacement SAP deployment. Due to a strong desire to improve existing processes on the legacy system, the blueprinting phase will elicit many views as to the direction needed for the company. These discussions can be very heated. The project team will sort out those views and create a proposal about how to best use the SAP system.

Risk Assessment Factor	System Replacement Risk
Scope and business process complexity	Very high
Geography and languages	Medium to very high
Size of user base	Medium to very high
Degree of system integration	High to very high

Table 4.3 Risk Assessment of an SAP System Replacement Deployment

Many legacy systems have been built for regional or country-based support. Consequently, many regions have their own systems with little or no integration at the enterprise level. Most reconciliation in these circumstances is performed by reporting where the numbers are collected regionally and then realigning them to reflect corporate realities.

This approach will not work with the SAP system. In the case of a global company, it will have to align its operations during the SAP project. All using entities will collect and report the same information. Obviously, for any regionally segmented company, adopting common standards will challenge its operating model.

A similar situation occurs relative to the degree of system integration involved. Where these legacy systems have been used, the implementing company may also have a number of end-of-life support systems. These may face replacement or, at the very least, version upgrades as a result of the SAP implementation project. The company must review each support system and adopt a strategy for its retention or replacement. It must then figure out how to integrate the remaining systems as needed with the SAP system.

Clearly each one of these full-scale implementations faces significant challenges. The most difficult of the varieties, the greenfield implementation project, has greatly reduced in number over the years. However, the carveout project and the system replacement project have continued to flourish in this ever-changing business climate. Project teams taking on those types of implementations will find many lessons for success in the later chapters of this book.

4.2 Upgrade Projects

An upgrade project builds on the fact that the implementing company has already deployed its SAP system. Even though the system is in place, SAP will continue to make improvements in the functionality of its applications and to correct errors that may have been reported by client organizations. Many implementing companies that have experienced the rigors of an SAP deployment are understandably reluctant to make any additional system changes. Yet any SAP client should carefully weigh the benefits to be gained from upgrades against the risks involved before making the decision to move forward or postpone.

Compared to full-scale implementation projects, an upgrade project team would appear to have an easier time of it. After all, the hard part has been done. The SAP system is in place and operating.

In reality, each of the three types of upgrade projects—discussed in this section and shown in Figure 4.6—has its own specific challenges. We'll examine support packs, enhancement packs, and version upgrades in more detail.

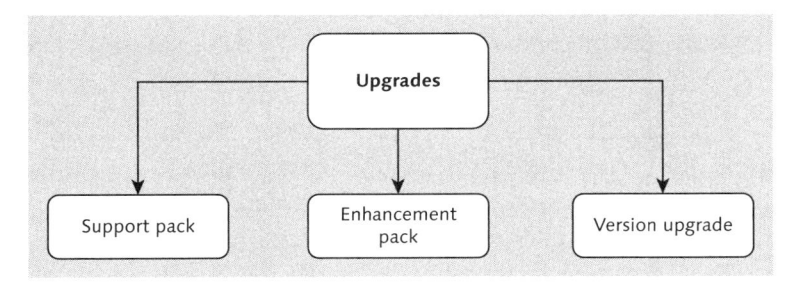

Figure 4.6 Primary Types of Upgrade SAP Implementation Projects

4.2.1 Support Pack

Generally the SAP support pack installation represents the least impactful of the upgrade paths. When an SAP customer discovers some issue with its system, these are reported via the Online Support System (OSS) Notes process. Fixes or recommended actions to mitigate the problem are then posted to the system. All customers who encounter the same issue can then refer to the OSS Note for guidance.

> **Trail Marker**
>
> Chapter 7 provides more information regarding the role and purpose of the SAP Online Support System.

Support packs are released on an interval schedule and generally include all software fixes or enhancements issued since the most recent release. On the face of it, one might conclude that the most rational action would be to install each support pack as it became available. However, circumstances often arise that make this apparently intuitive approach less desirable.

There are risks on either side of the spectrum. Companies opting to implement a support pack at time of release must consider how that decision could affect the stability of their systems. In fact, without careful vetting, implementing the support pack could create even more problems than those currently identified. Support pack documentation does not call out all potential problems. It leaves the client company to assess the support pack before deciding whether to adopt it. Often regression testing (that is, testing for the impact of system changes to the existing system) is the only mechanism available to determine how the support pack will affect current system performance. This testing can prove time-consuming and resource-intensive. Some companies choose to make the investment and others do not.

Companies opting to postpone support pack implementation face risks as well. Without adopting the most recent support pack, the company may also place its system in jeopardy. Instead of introducing unknown problems, the decision to postpone ensures that issues identified by SAP and addressed via a support pack will not be resolved in the system. After even a relatively short period of time, this company will face the task of reviewing all documentation associated with each of several previous support packs and understanding their potential system impact. All this must take place before moving forward with the support pack installation.

Alternatively, the company may choose to defer all support pack activity. In this situation, it may not be possible to perform upgrades. Those support pack fixes needed as foundations for the upgrade must be present in the system. This situation places the system in real jeopardy and puts the entire system at risk. Without a very expensive and protracted system review, the company may be forced to abandon its system altogether.

Table 4.4 discusses the risk factors associated with the support pack installation. The most significant risks are connected to the back-office operations of the implementing company. Systems administrators and business analysts who have responsibility for the SAP system must conduct thorough reviews of the support pack. Their reviews should identify any potential negative implications for the client system contained in the support pack. Additionally, this same group must work to ensure that the necessary regression testing takes place.

Risk Assessment Factor	Support Pack Risk
Scope and business process complexity	Medium to high
Geography and languages	Medium
Size of user base	Medium to high
Degree of system integration	Low to high

Table 4.4 Risk Assessment of an SAP Support Pack Deployment

The degree of system integration will likely be the critical success factor in the support pack installation. Direct interfaces to other company systems (a common indicator of business process complexity) can all be affected by the support pack. Technical staff must carefully test for support pack impact on these interfaces. Otherwise, once the support pack is installed, the interfaces may break and require extensive remediation action.

4.2.2 Enhancement Pack

Chapter 1 emphasized the complexity of the SAP system. Over the years, SAP has moved from storing base functionality a single platform (what is now known as the SAP ERP) to storing it in a multi-platform structure. Much of this has been due to marketplace considerations. Customers have requested additional functionality and SAP has responded by developing or purchasing additional applications.

For many companies, this has created difficulties with system upgrades. Instead of merely facing the task of upgrading ECC, they are now faced with that task in addition to upgrading several other support applications. To address this issue, SAP has developed the SAP Business Suite concept. Available as an option since 2009, SAP Business Suite links together the most recent version of SAP ERP and the following applications: Product Lifecycle Management (PLM), Customer Relationship Management (CRM), Supply Chain Management (SCM), and Supplier Relationship Management (SRM). The suite also includes the current SAP NetWeaver release.

SAP Business Suite requires SAP ERP 6.0 as a condition of use. Companies operating earlier versions will have the choice to upgrade to the newer version or continue to use their current system but without SAP Business Suite functionality.

One of the primary advantages of SAP Business Suite is the enhancement pack (EHP). Created in response to customer requests to streamline the upgrade process and make it more predictable, EHPs greatly simplify upgrade operations. They also bring a measurable ease to upgrade projects.

EHPs work in somewhat similar fashion to support packs but have additional benefits. In contrast to the support pack, EHPs are not error correction mechanisms. Rather, they deploy added functionality to the existing customer system. Table 4.5 outlines some of the main characteristics of enhancement packs relative to support packs.

Characteristic	Support Pack	Enhancement Pack
Cumulative	Not cumulative. Previous support packs must be installed.	Cumulative. Each enhancement pack contains all previous releases.
Total installation	Entire support pack must be installed in customer system.	Selective deployment. Only customer-required functionality activated.
Degree of effort	Modest degree of effort to implement but does require testing and system downtime.	Greater degree of effort to implement than a support pack but less than an upgrade.

Table 4.5 Comparison of Support Packs and Enhancement Packs

Note that the effort to implement an enhancement pack may be greater than that to implement a support pack, but it does provide the implementing company with control over its systems environment. Being able to decide which functionality best fits its business model and implement *only* that portion proves to be a great advantage. In that way, the system will contain only those elements useful to it and not all those solutions added across the board in a support pack installation. Those more discrete elements in an enhancement pack focusing on business processes are known as *business functions*. Only the specific business functions selected by the customer will be implemented. The remaining alternative business functions will not be activated.

In comparison to the standard SAP application upgrade path, installing an enhancement pack takes about half the time. Many of the requirements of the normal upgrade process have been eliminated. Data conversion or migration of custom objects will not be necessary. Further, the SAP Solution Browser (also known as the Enhancement Package Information Center) allows customers to identify functionality improvements available in an EHP prior to installation.

SAP has made considerable effort to document and automate the enhancement process. The Enhancement Package Information Center contains detailed documentation regarding each business function included in the package. In this way, company SAP support staff can look up this information and supply it to business users for their input. Additionally, the sandbox system can be used for a more hands-on evaluation of the business function.

Even with their reduced scale, enhancement packs nevertheless require an implementation project team using the Accelerated SAP methodology. Once the selected business functions have been installed in the sandbox environment, business blueprinting can initiate. This will include a review of existing requirements and the effects that the enhancement pack will have on them. It will also likely include the identification of any new requirements. These will be described in new requirements documentation.

If all stakeholders agree to deploy the enhancement pack, the technical team can then install it in the development system and begin the promote-to-production process. Having this agreement is essential! Once business functions are installed in the production system, they cannot be removed.

When a determination has been made regarding which business functions to select, the technical aspect of the installation then begins. The company downloads the enhancement pack. SAP has made available a tool solely to implement enhancement packs. The Enhancement Package Installer (EPHI) automates the selection of business functions and deploys them to the development environment. This will begin the build and test period.

Both regression testing and user acceptance testing will take place during the realization phase. When all required configuration and testing is complete, the production system is taken off-line until the chosen business function can be loaded into that environment. Once this step is complete, user access can be re-established for the system.

During this period, there will be some amount of system downtime. Relative to an upgrade procedure, this period has been greatly reduced. It will still require careful planning and coordination with the affected business functions. Companies operating on a round-the-clock schedule may need considerable advanced notification prior to actually taking the system off-line.

EHP installation should entail careful monitoring of incident reports. The project team can request the help desk to forward incidents in specific categories and then handle them according to their severity. Once the project team has confirmed that incident levels remain unaffected, it can report its status to business stakeholders and have the project concluded.

Table 4.6 indicates the lower risk levels associated with the enhancement pack. The option to allow selective installation of business functions considerably reduces the risk level relative to support packs (which are also still required). The unintended activation of conflicting functionality that may occur with a support pack installation is greatly minimized.

Risk Assessment Factor	Enhancement Pack Risk
Scope and business process complexity	Low to high
Geography and languages	Medium
Size of user base	Medium to high
Degree of system integration	Low to medium

Table 4.6 Risk Assessment of an SAP Enhancement Pack Deployment

The major risk has to do with the possible addition of unrequired or unplanned business functions. Obviously, this risk increases depending upon the complexity of the company business processes. You can substantially decrease this risk level by carefully vetting business functions.

4.2.3 Version Upgrade

Although many SAP applications have version numbers associated with them (and therefore require upgrades), the term is most often associated with upgrading SAP ERP. As newer versions are released, older versions are removed from contract maintenance. Companies utilizing those older versions are faced with the prospect of making the change to the newer version or remaining on the out-of-date version. Thus, companies operating on SAP ERP 4.6 must decide whether to shift to SAP ERP 6.0 or suffer the consequences.

Those companies choosing to remain on the older version can be shifted into a customer-specific maintenance category. In practice, this means an end to periodic support pack releases aimed at fixing problems with the current version. It may also impose a requirement for payment to SAP to repair any new, unexpected problems that occur.

Companies continuing on the older version also make sacrifices on the benefits side of the equation. By definition, they may forego access to new technology only found on the latest version. Access to the SAP HANA in-memory database and technologies such as Unicode will not be available on the older version.

Companies that move to the latest version will participate in an upgrade project. Of the three types of upgrade projects, the version change is the most ambitious. For that reason, it will also require far greater company resources to complete.

Many of the reasons for upgrade complexity are not readily apparent. After all, it's just the change of one software version to another, right? In fact, many of the complexities lie beneath the surface and must be brought to the light of day. Many of these have to do with the structure and operation of the existing system. A few of the complexities merit discussion:

- **Degree of customization in the existing system**
  As will be discussed extensively during the chapters on blueprinting and realization, most large SAP systems are heavily customized. This means that the implementing company has modified system functionality in some way to fit

its business needs. This is commonplace and only becomes a concern during the upgrade process. The upgrade project team will be faced with tracking down each customization made to the current system and assessing its impact on the newer version. This always proves to be a time-consuming and laborious task.

- **Amount of system downtime required for the upgrade**
  Placing the newer version in operation will require system downtime. The company must decide the amount of downtime it can live with and how to live with it. It may well require manual operations for a period of time. Downtime can be reduced, but this generally requires additional company and support resources. These cost money.

- **Project timing and cost**
  Major multi-national companies with an extensive SAP footprint take up to two years to make a complete upgrade. This entails a sizeable company project team and likely the services of a systems integrator as well. The cost will always be larger than initially expected. During the upgrade period, business conditions can change rapidly. Projects that began in favorable business conditions can find midway through that the marketplace has shifted. It is not uncommon to find upgrade projects placed on hold to await better business conditions.

- **New functionality requirements**
  Very often, the company will include some degree of additional functionality within the upgrade project. This decision ensures that the upgrade project team conducts blueprinting to outline that functionality and decide how to provide it. All this must be documented, built, tested, and trained.

- **Changes in the SAP system environment**
  The upgrade may require changes in hardware and infrastructure support operations. The new version may not operate on the same hardware or the company may require faster, more consolidated operations. These changes will introduce both complexity and incremental cost to the upgrade project.

The upgrade project is conducted under the ASAP methodology described in Chapter 3. However, many of the activities differ from those in the full-scale implementation project. With the exception of meeting the requirement for new functionality, the upgrade project will largely be a back-office operation. Basically the project team will spend most of its time during project preparation in analysis mode. The team will examine all facets of current system operations:

- System usage patterns such as number of transactions performed in geographical regions, by business functions, and by user types
- Number and types of current system modifications including their frequency of use
- Current SAP system landscape profile to include data centers and hardware profiles compared to those required by the newer version
- The identification of new transaction codes and those that will be made obsolete

This information becomes the foundation for the upgrade project plan. The analysis will define where effort must be placed. Essentially, the team must verify that all items brought to the newer version reconcile and that no needed functionality is lost.

Other than the need for user acceptance testing for specific changes, end users will likely feel minimal effect from the upgrade project. Training will be limited to any new functionality that the company decided to implement.

Table 4.7 provides the risk assessment for the version upgrade. It reflects many of the issues already raised. Again, both business process complexity and degree of system integration drive the potential risks. The possibility for error in the system upgrade will depend on the complexity of the business processes and how many customizations are in use. The more non-SAP systems that interface to SAP, the greater the possibility that one or more of these connections could be broken during the upgrade process.

Risk Assessment Factor	Version Upgrade Risk
Scope and business process complexity	High to very high
Geography and languages	Medium to high
Size of user base	Medium to high
Degree of system integration	High to very high

Table 4.7 Risk Assessment of an SAP Version Upgrade Deployment

Let's turn our attention to the final type of SAP project.

4.3 Pre-Built Package Projects

SAP has addressed two sets of challenges with these pre-built packages. The first challenge has to do with making it easier for small and medium-sized businesses to access the SAP platform. Many of these businesses lack the resources and technology base to participate in a full-scale deployment project. Instead, they require some assistance from SAP to make the deployment process easier to accomplish.

The second challenge concentrates more on delivering specific business-requested functionality. Operating in similar fashion as the enhancement pack, SAP has developed targeted solutions that provide business performance in a fraction of the time needed for a standard implementation project.

Figure 4.7 outlines the three major pre-built solutions. Each is constructed to solve a specific business problem and greatly ease the implementation process. SAP Business One and the SAP Business One starter package focus on the needs of small and medium businesses. These packages make the SAP system available to these companies by reducing the complexity of the implementation project and by making the system easier to maintain. SAP Rapid Deployment Solutions are basically out-of-the-box solutions targeted to solve specific business problems for existing SAP customers. They offer ease of implementation and rapid availability.

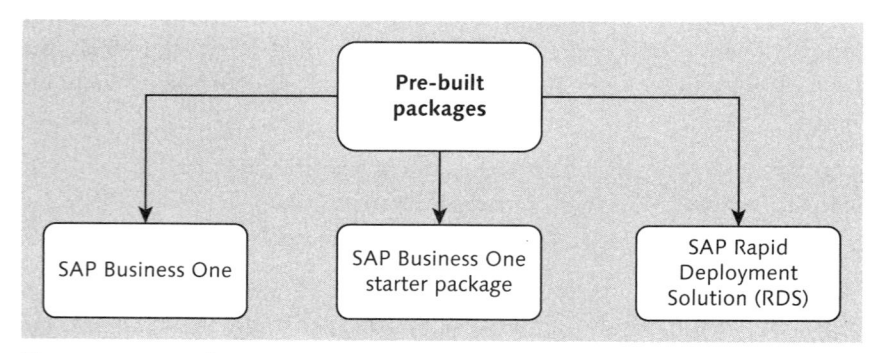

Figure 4.7 Types of SAP Pre-Built Package Projects

As before, let's dig deeper.

4.3.1 SAP Business One

SAP Business One delivers a packaged solution especially to fit the needs of small and medium-sized businesses. It approach can best be understood by comparing it with a full-scale implementation project. In the full-scale implementation, the client company reviews the range of application offerings available from SAP, identifies which best fit its needs, and moves forward with the SAP project. This will usually involve several SAP applications and cover a broad range of business functionality. Decisions about how the company will align its processes to each application take a major portion of time. Other time-consuming activities follow from decisions made during blueprinting. All these lead to extended projects and the investment of a significant amount of company resources.

SAP Business One changes the implementation model. It reduces the scale by restricting the scope. SAP Business One offers the key functionality needed to operate a business, and it limits the amount of modifications that can be made to the system. This allows an implementing company to utilize a relatively small project team and to complete the entire implementation process in one to two months. However, this reduced implementation model only applies if the implementing company remains generally within the scope of the standard SAP Business One model.

SAP Business One substantially reduces the implementation time by shifting the blueprint phase. It moves from an endeavor focusing on how to fit the SAP system to company business processes, and shifts a much more limited role. Under SAP Business One, blueprinting focuses almost exclusively on how company business processes will be aligned with the SAP system requirements.

This represents a very different model. Reducing business process variety creates all kinds of downstream project impacts. Not only is blueprinting greatly shortened, but realization becomes abbreviated as well. Custom objects and special configuration need not be built. And as a result, the time spent on integration and user acceptance testing contracts to a fraction of their normal levels.

The SAP Business One solution set in Figure 4.8 represents an extensive range of SAP functionality. In addition to the basic ERP solution that handles most internal business transactions, it includes the SAP sales support tool (SAP CRM), the SAP procurement tool (SAP SRM), and an SAP reporting solution (usually SAP Crystal Reports). This means that most company functions—including accounting, controlling, purchasing, inventory, and distribution—can be handled in the system.

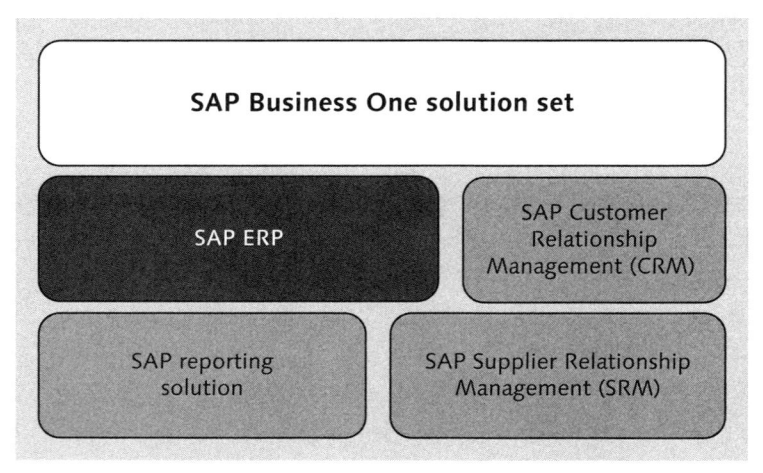

Figure 4.8 SAP Functionality Elements Contained in SAP Business One

With the reduction in project scope, demands for company project team resources are correspondingly decreased as well. Extensive business process documentation and specially developed user training packages, both major resource consumers in a typical full-scale implementation, no longer require major time commitments under SAP Business One.

> **Tip**
>
> Find time to conduct a thorough review of all SAP Business One supporting documentation provided by SAP or your systems integrator. Address any questions to the systems integrator and get clear answers before moving forward. Time saved at this point on clarification can ensure that the project hits its deadlines.

Table 4.8 demonstrates the much-reduced implementation risk assessment profile associated with SAP Business One. The working model limits configuration and custom objects. This makes the implementation process a much more vanilla effort than the full-scale implementation. With low levels of business process complexity and required system integration, the level of risk associated with the SAP Business One implementation will certainly be acceptable to most companies.

Risk Assessment Factor	SAP Business One Risk
Scope and business process complexity	Low
Geography and languages	Low
Size of user base	Low to medium
Degree of system integration	Low

Table 4.8 Risk Assessment of an SAP Business One Deployment

4.3.2 SAP Business One Starter Package

The SAP Business One starter package is aligned with the needs of small business. It offers most of the same functionality as the standard edition of SAP Business One. Some functionality, such as material requirements planning (MRP) and cost accounting, are not supplied. The primary difference between the two packages has to do with limitations on the number of system users. Whereas SAP Business One allows for unlimited users, the SAP Business One starter package is limited to a total of five end users. This limitation can work for a small business, but since the company will grow over time, this may prove a hindrance. Companies using the SAP Business One starter package can easily migrate to the standard SAP Business One package. Only a few adjustments are required.

The starter package is intended to be plug-and-play. Implementation time with the assistance of an integration partner will take no more than a couple of weeks. Additionally, SAP furnishes a set of support documentation to structure the implementation process:

- **Starter package scope documentation**
  This material outlines the business process functionality delivered in the starter package. It helps the implementing company understand exactly what is contained in the starter package.
- **Package implementation plan**
  These documents give an overview of the tasks that will be completed during the implementation. This will essentially provide project management guidance for the starter package implementation activities.
- **Predefined implementation work packages**
  These work packages structure the tasks that must be accomplished during the

implementation. Tasks are identified and divided between the integration partner and the implementing company.

▶ **End-user documentation**
Aimed at educating end users to the new system, this material includes work instructions and demonstrations for completing business process transactions.

Table 4.9 illustrates the low risk associated with the SAP Business One starter package. The restriction on available customization and limitation to five users means that the implementing company will face almost no implementation risk.

Risk Assessment Factor	SAP Business One Starter Pack Risk
Scope and business process complexity	Low
Geography and languages	Low
Size of user base	Very low
Degree of system integration	Low

Table 4.9 Risk Assessment of an SAP Business One Starter Pack Deployment

4.3.3 Rapid Deployment Solutions

SAP Rapid Deployment Solutions aim to reduce the complexity of SAP implementations. They follow the template model discussed with SAP Business One. The implementing company chooses to augment its SAP system with targeted functionality; these pre-packaged solutions address the specific business problem. Additionally, they are much faster to deploy than a standard SAP upgrade. SAP marketing documents claim that a rapid-deployment solution implementation will take at least 40 percent less time and effort than a project of similar scope. SAP has released a number of rapid-deployment solutions and continues to add to that number.

Rapid-deployment solution projects are intended to be accomplished in rapid fashion. For that reason, SAP has adopted a variant to the ASAP model to guide them. Once again, since they are pre-packaged solutions, the blueprint timing is substantially reduced and realization time can be halved. Most effort is spent preparing the rapid-deployment solution for implementation and assisting end users with any new operations.

Figure 4.9 illustrates the rapid deployment model. Here, the "start" phase has replaced blueprinting, and "deploy" has supplanted realization and final preparation. The rapid-deployment model emphasizes speed; its objective is for implementing companies to have the solution in hand as quickly as possible.

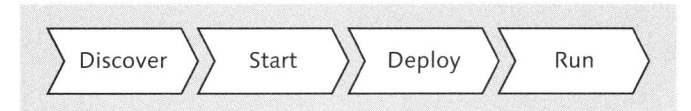

> Discover > Start > Deploy > Run >

Figure 4.9 Rapid-Deployment Solutions Implementation Methodology

The risk factors associated with SAP Rapid Deployment Solutions are relatively low. As long as the implementing company stays within the parameters of the solution it has selected, the risk factors are favorable. To the degree that the implementing company customizes the solution, that choice will introduce complexity and the risk factors increase. If the degree of customization rises above a certain level, the project will shift from a rapid-deployment solution to a standard implementation program. At that point, costs and resource requirements will also increase.

Risk Assessment Factor	SAP Rapid Deployment Solutions Risk
Scope and business process complexity	Low
Geography and languages	Low to medium
Size of user base	Low to medium
Degree of system integration	Low

Table 4.10 Risk Assessment of an SAP Rapid Deployment Solutions Deployment

SAP has made strides in minimizing the cost and effort associated with an implementation project. However, the pre-packaged solutions have thus far targeted very specific situations. They focus on smaller companies with more standardized business processes or on targeted solutions for the existing customer base.

Companies with global operations will continue to face the challenges of full-scale or upgrade projects for the foreseeable future. This will mean projects with extended duration, significant costs, and the need for substantial systems integrator support.

Now we are ready to enter the project preparation phase. We'll begin the discussion by outlining the project start-up logistics and planning. Getting it right always takes considerable attention but will pay dividends in the months ahead. Let's get started!

Start-up logistics truly initiates the project planning phase. During this time, teams will form, the systems integrator will be selected, and the program management office will begin its operations. These activities set the stage for the remainder of the project.

5 Start-Up Logistics

Once you've selected SAP as the system of use and you've worked out those contracting details, it's time to turn attention to the early stages of project planning. Start-up logistics brings the program from a gleam in the eye of executive management to a fully functioning project delivery team.

This chapter examines the steps involved in moving the project from zero to 60 miles per hour. Later chapters in this project preparation section will shift the discussion from initial planning to project governance. This chapter will cover the following areas of project preparation:

▶ **Project preparation timeline**
Critical deliverables will be required during this phase of the project. Many of them are not explicitly called out in the ASAP methodology due to their close connection with your company's business requirements. This section will review the key project preparation deliverables and provide a timeline for their accomplishment.

▶ **Project meeting schedules**
The meeting schedule to be followed by the project for the remainder of its lifespan is also established during project preparation. We'll outline the main meetings and their recommended frequency.

▶ **Headcount forecasting and ramp-up planning**
The project team fully comes together at the beginning of blueprinting. Final preparation also calls for the logistical effort of building the team so that it is ready on time. This section describes the initial steps for forecasting the numbers needed and planning for their onboarding to the project team.

- **Initial planning for integrator selection**
  This topic will consume a large part of the project cadre's attention during project preparation. Initial activities include defining the request for proposal and internal review processes involved.

- **Project procurement**
  Some items—primarily third-party software and servers to house SAP and other necessary applications—must be purchased by the project. In order for them to arrive on time, they should be procured during project preparation. This section supplies details concerning the procurement of these items.

- **Space planning for project activities**
  The project team will require adequate workspace. The cadre team must forecast the types of space needed and its timing. While later activities in project preparation will finalize those initial forecasts, this section covers the initial planning involved.

- **Preliminary project budgeting**
  Your company will require expedited estimates of the financial outlays for the SAP implementation project. Due to the size of the investment involved, an SAP project can substantially impact the company bottom line. This section reviews methods for constructing the initial financial projection.

Let's begin by discussing the preparation timeline that will govern delivery of key items.

5.1 Project Preparation Timeline

Recall from Chapter 3 that the Accelerated SAP (ASAP) methodology focuses almost exclusively on system-related deliverables. ASAP doesn't address many other important company-focused activities that must be accomplished during the project preparation phase, so let's examine how to schedule these items. We'll later explore the primary activities that your company will conduct during project preparation.

During this time, your company will be gearing up to put its SAP implementation project in place. Many of these start-up activities are tied to existing company processes and will reflect this orientation. As Figure 5.1 shows, this project preparation period is very compressed and contains a large number of simultaneous deliverables.

This period will give the program management office (PMO) time to gain experience with managing deliverables. These activities will have minimal systems integrator effort involved; the tracking and management will be completely in the hands of your company project management staff.

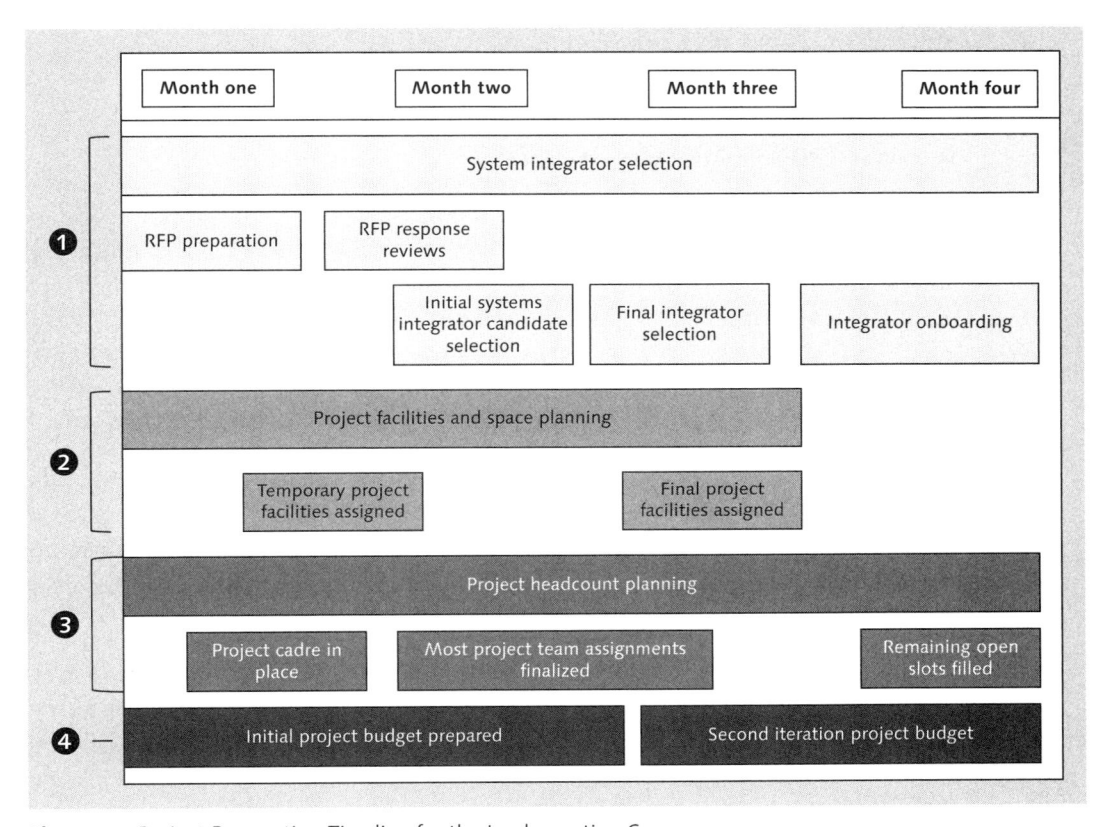

Figure 5.1 Project Preparation Timeline for the Implementing Company

The timeline shows four major deliverable sets due during project preparation. They begin with systems integrator selection ❶, which will consume a major portion of the project team effort. They also include finalization of a work space ❷ and headcount planning ❸ for the project team. It additionally involves several iterations of the project financial plan ❹. These are all clearly important tasks to get right.

We can assume that systems integrator selection and project headcount planning will take place over the entirety of the project preparation phase. Several sub-activities will occur during that period and are shown in the timeline. Project facilities and space planning should conclude at least a month before the end of the phase. Additionally, at least two iterations of the project budget should be complete by the start of blueprinting.

5.2 Project Meeting Schedules

The framework of standing meetings should be set during the project preparation phase. These meetings are intended to serve as the primary communications device within the project team. They will ensure the two-way sharing of information between project leadership and those assigned to specific work teams. In this way, project leadership can stay abreast of progress and status updates, and those assigned to work teams can receive the most up-to-date information regarding major project activities.

Table 5.1 lists the standard meeting set that will be established at this point of the project and continued throughout the remainder of its lifecycle. As the project advances into the later stages of blueprinting and through all stages of realization, the PMO may decide to modify the timing and duration for some of these meetings. However, the core meeting structure will remain in place.

The key to project success lies in a continuous and reliable information flow among core participants. While there will certainly be a need for regular informal communication, the meetings listed in Table 5.1 provide the details regarding where the project stands. Having access to a regular forum enables sponsors, the PMO, and team leads to develop a shared view of project progress. As the project moves into the turbulent world of blueprinting, realization, and final preparation, this will prove a very valuable entity.

Standing Meeting Title	Frequency and Duration	Purpose	Attendees and Meeting Lead
Project operating review meeting (managed by the PMO)	Twice weekly for one hour; duration can be adjusted according to material to be covered	▶ Program and workstream updates ▶ Issue identification and management ▶ Cross workstream topics ▶ Lessons learned and best practices ▶ Schedule review	Project leadership to include systems integrator leadership: project sponsors, PMO, and workstream leads
Project leadership meeting (managed by project sponsors)	Every two weeks for one hour; duration can be adjusted according to material to be covered	▶ Review of enterprise-level issues ▶ Reporting on benefits realization ▶ Review of high-impact risks ▶ Evaluation of program resource status ▶ Strategic decision assessment	Project sponsors, PMO, and systems integrator executives
Program management review (managed by the PMO)	Weekly for one hour	▶ Updates on project planning ▶ Project budget status ▶ Changes to the project schedule ▶ Project issue resolution	PMO from the implementing company and systems integrator representative
Project governance meeting (managed by project sponsors)	Every two weeks for one hour	▶ Overall project status ▶ Major risks and issues ▶ Change management topics	Project sponsors and leaders of participating functional organizations
Senior executive meeting (managed by project sponsors)	As required	▶ Major project milestones ▶ Overall budget and resource status ▶ High-level project issues	Project sponsors and members of the company executive team

Table 5.1 Key Meetings for the SAP Project Team

It is also important that the number of meetings and their frequency does not exert a negative impact on project team performance. They should be scattered across the week rather than taking place in one or two concentrated days (no one likes a day full of meetings!). Otherwise, the team may come to see the meetings as a burden rather than as an opportunity for team interaction.

Table 5.2 outlines a monthly standing meeting calendar. The most important factor in setting meeting dates is the availability of the major participants. Planners should carefully assess the calendars of each participant to identify any standing meetings, especially ones that cannot easily be changed.

Another factor that will require attention is the travel schedule of systems integrator staff. At a minimum, project leaders from the systems integrator company will take part in the program management review, the project operating reviews, and the project leadership meeting. In many cases, systems integrator staff will work at the company site, alongside the project team, from mid-day Monday to mid-day Friday.

> **Tip**
>
> Participants generally travel to their homes on Friday afternoons and arrive back on site about noon on Monday. To maximize participation and morale, don't schedule any meetings requiring their participation on Monday morning or Friday afternoon.

	Monday	Tuesday	Wednesday	Thursday	Friday
Week One	Program management review	Project operating review	Project leadership meeting	Project operating review	
Week Two	Program management review	Project operating review	Project governance meeting	Project operating review	
Week Three	Program management review	Project operating review	Project leadership meeting	Project operating review	
Week Four	Program management review	Project operating review	Project governance meeting	Project operating review	

Table 5.2 Calendarized Project Meeting Schedule

The project phase will determine the focus areas for these meetings. The focus of an SAP implementation project team is incredibly time-constrained. As a rule, *meeting content will target those items of interest during the most relevant phase.* Topics that may generate considerable interest and debate during project planning will likely elicit minimal discussion during realization. By that point, the former topic will have proven to be "old news."

Figure 5.2 outlines some of the topics that will garner the attention of the project team. As you can see, these often correlate to the project phase. Subjects such as staffing and systems integrator selection will occupy a sizeable portion of the project team's attention during the project planning phase. By the time that realization enters the picture, most of those issues will have receded into the background. The only exception will be project staffing levels, which will no doubt remain an item of intense discussion throughout the project lifecycle.

Project planning	Blueprint	Realization	Final preparation	Go-live and support
▶ Staffing	▶ System design	▶ Configuration	▶ Production build	▶ SAP UserID distribution
▶ Team on-boarding	▶ Localization	▶ Custom object	▶ User training	▶ Incident resolution
▶ System integration selection	▶ Design documentation	▶ System test	▶ Super user preparation	▶ Business ramp-up
▶ Facilities review	▶ Change impacts	▶ Training build	▶ Business planning	▶ Sustainment
▶ Financial planning	▶ Business controls	▶ Controls	▶ Role mapping	
		▶ Reporting		
		▶ Security build		
		▶ Data migration		

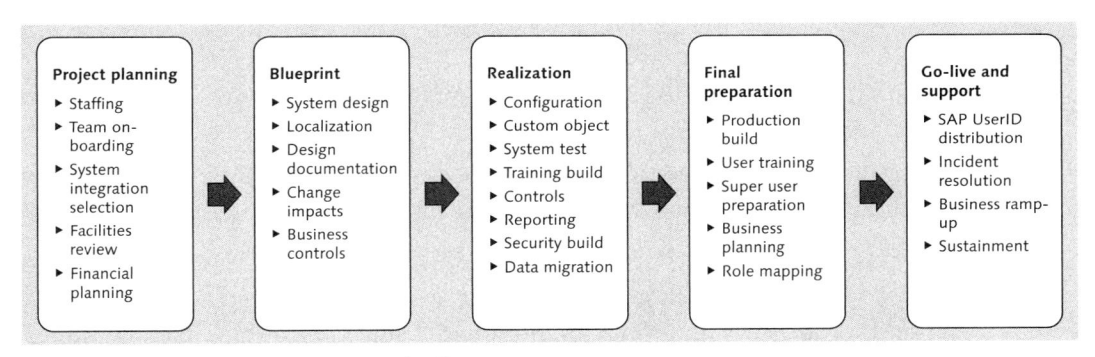

Figure 5.2 Primary Project Focus Areas by Phase

By the time the project team reaches the realization phase, the focus will have shifted to more SAP system-related technical issues. At this point, completing the configurations and custom objects needed to accomplish blueprinting will be foremost in the team's thoughts. In similar fashion, those subjects will have faded from view when the project team reaches final preparation. At that point, the team will be in a sprint to meet its go-live deadline and will focus only on those subjects necessary to accomplish that task.

The one constant across the entire timeline will be the project operating review meetings. Regardless of the project phase or issues encountered, these review meetings are always needed to identify problem areas and resolution strategies. The subjects may change, but problems of some kind will remain a constant. The project review meetings will serve as a primary operating framework for the project.

5.3 Headcount Forecasting and Ramp-Up Planning

Project team assignments should be finalized before the completion of project preparation. In order to finalize the specific team assignments, the PMO will forecast numbers and types of required staffing during this start-up period. So how does headcount forecasting work?

> **Trail Marker**
>
> Chapter 10 on project organization and Chapter 12 on building the right project team will provide details on the later stages of this process.

Forecasting headcount requirements has both a financial and a human resources component:

- On the financial side, it enables the company to compare reasonably accurate headcount costs against the number of staff forecasted for the project team.
- On the human resources side, it begins the process of transferring staff from functional organizations to the project team.

Not everyone will be needed at once. Although the project team's final numbers should be clear by this time, only a small group will be needed in the beginning. In start-up, the project team is built around a small cadre organization. Its purpose is to conduct the early portions of project preparation. As the project moves farther along in readiness for blueprinting, this small team will grow rapidly.

Figure 5.3 illustrates the headcount ramp-up process generally seen for an SAP implementation process. In the beginning portion of final preparation, the small cadre team just discussed will be the only staff directly assigned to the project. As this team completes its planning activities, additional members of the project team will be needed. These additional staff members will play a lead role in preparing for systems integrator selection and integrator presentations.

By the time project preparation reaches its final stages, almost the entire team will be in place. Some assignments, however, will still remain in flux at this point. The go-forward, complete version of the project team will likely not be fully assembled until the initiation of blueprinting and kick-off meetings designed to begin that stage of activity.

The forecasting of headcount requirements should reflect this phasing. Assuming a three-month project planning phase, the staffing numbers requested for the early stages should be approximately 15 percent of the total numbers expected overall. For month two, the staffing numbers should be approximately 40 percent of the expected total. For month three, staffing should have reached the 85 percent to 90 percent range.

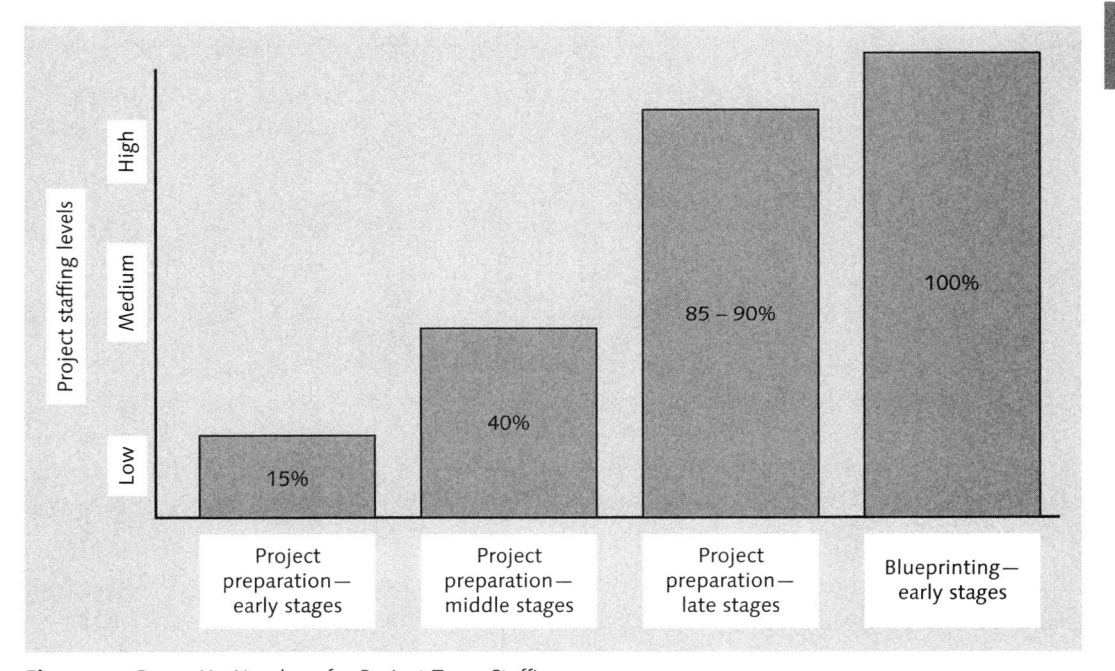

Figure 5.3 Ramp-Up Numbers for Project Team Staffing

Clearly, the actual numbers requested for the project team will be a function of program size. A full-scale implementation will require a much larger project team than an upgrade or application installation. The numbers portrayed in Figure 5.4 represent staffing needed for a full-scale implementation. Projects smaller in size and duration can adjust these numbers to fit the scope of their installations.

This table does not include senior leadership roles for the project team. These special roles will be discussed further in Chapter 11. Additionally, the most senior positions place director and associate director into a single classification. Some companies have eliminated associate directors altogether by consolidating the position into a single director classification; in a similar fashion, senior manager

Area	Level	Director or Associate	Senior Manager or Manager	Exempt Professional	Total
Supply chain	Operations	2	4	4	10
	Quality	1	1	2	4
	Procurement	1	3	3	7
	Logistics	1	2	3	6
	Subtotal	5	10	12	27
Finance	Accounting	1	3	4	8
	Planning	0	1	2	3
	Treasury and tax	1	1	2	4
	Controls	0	1	2	3
	IT	5	5	6	15
	Subtotal	7	11	16	34
Sales and marketing	Sales operations	2	2	4	8
	Customer finance	1	2	4	7
	Subtotal	3	4	8	15
Total		15	25	36	76

Figure 5.4 Forecasted Headcount Requirements for a Full-Scale SAP Implementation Project

and manager have been grouped together. It will be up to your company to determine the levels required for particular roles on the project team.

Additionally, the IT headcount requirements are contained within the finance organization. It is very common for the IT organization to report to the chief financial officer; Figure 5.4 has followed that practice by including IT within the finance organization. The contribution needed from IT will be substantial, and our estimate may even fall on the conservative side.

In any case, this forecast for headcount numbers can provide a starting point for filling out the SAP implementation project team. Depending on scope and assessment of need, add or reduce numbers to reflect the scale of the project. Having these estimates in place permits functional organizations to begin planning for how they will handle their contributions. It also enables them to begin planning for team member selection. Finally, the estimates allow the finance organization to plan for the cost factors associated with project team headcount requirements.

Once project sponsors review and approve the headcount projection, the next step can be taken. This centers on cadre positions needed in the early stages of project planning. At a minimum, these positions generally include functional workstream leads; technical leads such as data conversion and systems testing, and much of the PMO. This early assignment process would give the cadre time to plan for onboarding the remainder of the project team and for blueprint planning.

Thus, the initial group would consist of between 10 to 15 individuals. They would have ownership for setting up a great deal of the project. As additional staff members join the project team, this cadre group can brief new arrivals on decisions made to date and ensure their alignment with planned project activities.

5.4 Initial Planning for Integrator Selection

Selection of the project systems integrator stands out as one of the most important deliverables during project preparation and is well worth emphasizing here. The integrator selected will take on many of the technical SAP-related tasks to be performed during the project lifecycle. Thus, the selection of a systems integrator is a critical decision; the project depends on the skill and reliability of the company chosen.

Our following chapter, Chapter 6, will discuss the dynamics of integrator selection in some detail. For now, we'll cover the preliminary steps that set the process fully in motion. During these early stages, those team members already in place and those slotted to join the team will focus on defining the fundamentals of the project. These building blocks not only provide guidance to the remainder of the team as it merges with the project, but especially provide the necessary background information that permits the systems integrator candidates to prepare their proposals.

In many cases, the required answers will not be readily available. Those cadre members from the project team will be faced with digging out the necessary information and deciding on the best method of presenting it to systems integrator candidates unfamiliar with your company. However, this assignment will prove to be an excellent learning experience for the cadre team. It not only accustoms them to finding the needed data, but it also gives them a first occasion to work together as a team. This initial deliverable—the systems integrator request for proposal (RFP)—helps them understand the strengths and weaknesses of each team member.

Figure 5.5 indicates the major topic areas for what will become your company RFP. The major headings provide a framework for the information needed. The team can assign small work groups from the cadre organization to collect and format the necessary information.

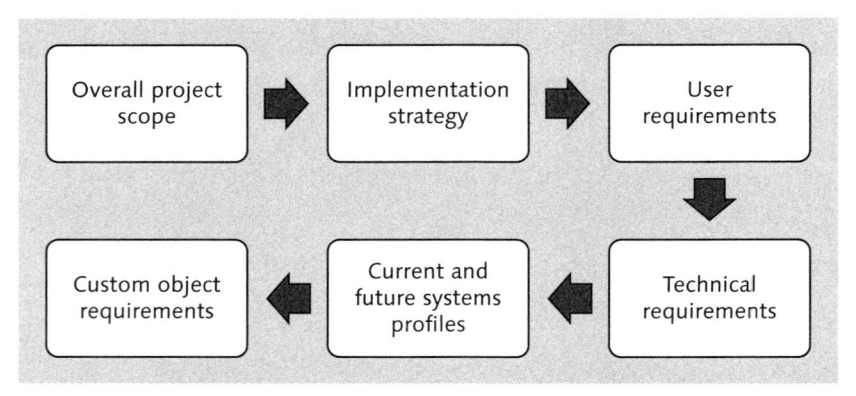

Figure 5.5 Major Topics for the Implementing Company Request for Proposal

Your company RFP provides information necessary for a third-party services provider, possibly unfamiliar with the company itself, to understand the scope and purposes of the project. The headings shown in Figure 5.5 are commonly used in RFPs to organize this information. Let's examine them further.

Overall Project Scope

The project scope is outlined in two separate sections. The first section discusses the business scope of the project and the second section reviews the functional processes to be included in the SAP implementation project.

- **Business scope**

    This subsection gives detail about implementing company's business operations. The section begins by describing the company business focus and other relevant data such as annual revenue and major product. It also includes major company locations and operations performed at those operations (e.g., Amsterdam, the Netherlands—Regional Headquarters and Distribution). Normally the listing will include only those geographies or entities that will participate in the SAP implementation. For a global program, all major geographies and entities should be provided. This listing will enable candidate systems integrators to assess potential locations for their teams.

- **Functional processes**
  This subsection outlines those functional business processes that will be included in the scope of the SAP implementation project. Most commonly, these functional processes will align with the workstreams defined for the project. Thus, the hypothetical project used as an example throughout this book has five functional processes in its scope:
  - Order-to-cash: Develops global standard business processes to receive customer orders, determine product availability, forecast demand, manage export operations, and conduct invoicing and collections.
  - Plan-to-stock: Develops global standard processes to plan production, manage materials, ensure product quality, and deliver products.
  - Procure-to-pay: Develops global standard processes to design company sourcing strategy, handle supplier selection and contracting, manage chosen suppliers, create requisitions, and pay vendors.
  - Record-to-report: Develops global standard business processes for company financial management, planning and budgeting, asset management, tax and statutory reporting, period-end processing, and general company accounting practices.
  - Human capital management: Develops global standard business processes for workforce planning and reporting, recruitment and hiring, staff development, benefits and compensation, and staff services.

In addition, certain types of mechanisms that overlay these processes may be included. Master data management, a mechanism that crosses all these processes, could be specifically listed to emphasize its importance to your company.

Implementation Strategy

This section of the RFP details the approach that your company has adopted for its SAP deployment. The section generally includes a prospective project timeline and any phase structure for the project. Very often the implementing company will request feedback on this implementation framework during the RFP process. Supplying this information early can begin a dialogue on timing estimates and the definition of phases. Candidate systems integrators will have long experience with similar implementations and will be very open to sharing their assessment of the proposed approach during the RFP process. The team can provide a schematic of the current project plan for systems integrators to review, as shown in Figure 5.6.

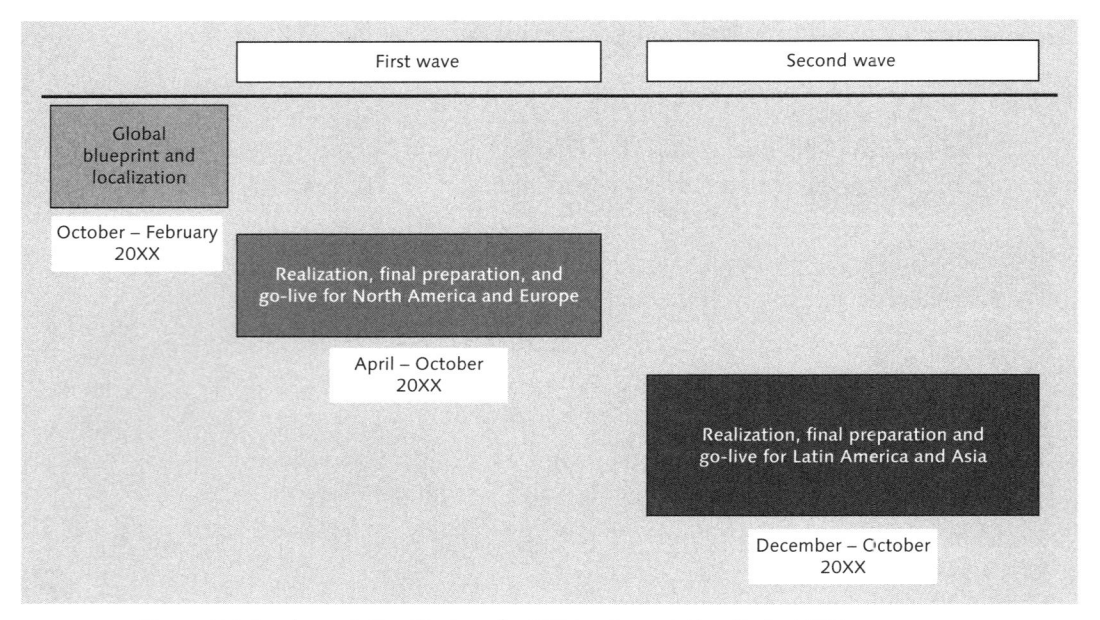

	First wave	Second wave
Global blueprint and localization October – February 20XX	**Realization, final preparation, and go-live for North America and Europe** April – October 20XX	**Realization, final preparation and go-live for Latin America and Asia** December – October 20XX

Figure 5.6 Implementation Strategy for SAP Implementation Project RFP

The implementation strategy section outlines a proposed approach for a global SAP implementation. It consists of complete blueprinting at the beginning of the project and two subsequent deployment waves thereafter. The first wave combines company operations in North America and Europe; the second wave combines operations in Latin America and Asia.

Candidate systems integrators will certainly raise questions regarding this deployment strategy. They might ask whether your company can complete blueprinting activities for all regions in a single attempt instead of over two waves. Perhaps they might recommend alternative approaches that entail a lower degree of risk.

Additionally, candidate systems integrators might raise questions about the two-wave approach and the grouping of regions in each wave. They could well request additional information regarding the business volume in each region and its level of process maturity. Here again, they might provide suggestions regarding different approaches.

This dialogue can assist your company to reevaluate or redevelop its thoughts around a proposed approach. In some cases, it might even lead to changes in timing and implementation strategy. Further, it can give your company some initial insight into the capabilities of integrator candidates.

Additional contextual information can be provided in the implementation strategy section as well. This includes known project constraints, overall project objectives, and completion requirements. Let's look at a few examples of this contextual information:

- The company will undergo a major business expansion in the next three-year period. The ERP system implementation must be complete by that time and capable of supporting those operations.
- A new regional headquarters for Europe is planned for the next two years. The ERP system must be in place for that region and ready to support the new headquarters.
- The project aims to develop and foster globally integrated and standardized operations for the listed business processes. The systems integrator will be expected to assist in defining best practices for those processes and support the company transition to this operating model.
- The company requires a reporting solution that provides an enterprise-wide view of critical data and the ability to use that data to support functional processes.
- The company currently operates multiple charts of accounts—in fact, a different chart of accounts for each regional entity. The ERP project should develop a global chart of accounts that accommodates the statutory reporting requirements for each region.

User Requirements

At this point in the project, user requirements will likely be known only at the high level discussed in Chapter 2. However, even at this relatively broad level, the requirements furnished to systems integrators will prove very useful. Having a listing of the process standardizations, optimizations, and automations envisioned by your company will help systems integrators understand the intended use of the SAP system. At this point, the systems integrator is working to establish how it will support the implementation and which integrator resources will be needed. User requirements certainly assist in this determination.

The procurement process automation example from Chapter 2 shows an integrated supply management mechanism with the SAP system at its core. It depicts the use of workflows and electronic documents from purchase order issuance to invoice remittance via electronic funds transfer. This process outline demonstrates to the systems integrator RFP response team that your company has high expectations for the SAP system and will apply it throughout its business processes.

Technical Requirements

This portion of the RFP is written by your company's IT organization. This behind-the-scenes material gives important direction about costs and operating parameters. It is very common for SAP systems integrators to manage the hardware in the system during the implementation project. Even if your company intends to manage the systems infrastructure after the project is complete, the systems integrator will nevertheless provide some part of this service during the project lifecycle.

Integrator technical staff will have experience with building the system components and maintaining them in a project environment. They can work effectively with their counterparts in other areas of the integrator project team to load data effectively. They will also have experience with the transport of custom objects and configuration according to standard procedure. Unless your company has considerable background in building and maintaining an SAP system, it's more prudent to assign these tasks to the systems integrator.

This technical requirements section will generally be very detailed. These responses will play a substantial role in determining the systems integrator to be selected. Although they may appear to be very back-office focused, they will outline requirements in a number of operating areas:

- **System architecture**
  The RFP will request information on the sizing of servers to be used and their locations. The RFP will probably also request recommendations on the number of servers to run in parallel and machine capacity. This section will solicit suggestions regarding operating system to be used, data storage approach, and failover strategy. Make sure to discuss the question of performance management and any system latency.

- **Network operations**
  This segment will describe current wide-area network configuration and Internet presence for your company. The RFP will request recommendations from systems integrator candidates regarding network infrastructure architectures for the SAP system. These recommendations should address any latency and bandwidth requirements as well.

- **Storage and backup**
  In this component, your company will describe its current file and database services as well as back-up and recovery mechanisms. The RFP will solicit recommendations on back-up and restoration operations for SAP system data objects and system components. Moreover, it will seek suggestions on disaster recovery, failover, and business continuity from the candidate systems integrators.

- **Server platforms**
  This element will outline the current server platforms used for business support in your company. The description will primarily focus on operating systems such as Linux, AIX, Citrix, and Windows. The RFP will ask for proposals on platforms and operating systems to be used for the SAP system.

- **Portal, Web, and middleware**
  In this area, your company will identify the portal, Web, and middleware solutions it currently uses. It will request candidate systems integrators to outline Web and application technologies to be used, as well as integration mechanisms.

Current and Future Systems Profiles

One of the final sections of the RFP will supply an overview of your company's current systems profile. Generally this will take the form of a schematic that shows the major systems currently in use by your company and their relationships. Thus, if the systems share data in some way, this should be reflected in the schematic. This information can be used by candidate systems integrators to identify likely SAP integration points.

Figure 5.7 shows the high-level systems profile for a typical implementing company. The schematic reflects only the major systems in use and only those related to the scope of enterprise resource planning. For this reason, it does not contain any research and development systems, as they are not normally used in conjunction with an ERP system.

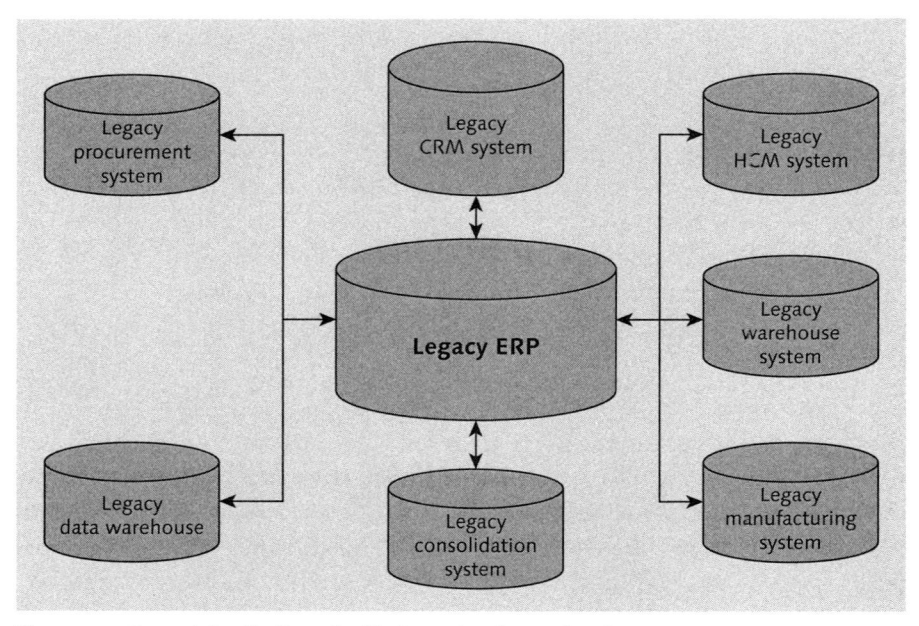

Figure 5.7 Current Applications Profile for an Implementing Company

The diagram shows a number of interrelated core legacy systems. Some, such as the customer relationship management (CRM) system, support sales and marketing activities. Others, such as the manufacturing execution system and the warehouse management system, support production activities. All identified systems now participate in two-way data sharing with the legacy ERP system.

The future systems profile shown in Figure 5.8 illustrates a much-changed topography. In this example, the SAP system has replaced virtually every legacy application. The sole remaining legacy systems are the manufacturing execution system—which automates many production floor activities—and the CRM application used primarily for sales and lead tracking.

SAP applications have taken over all remaining legacy systems. SAP will handle procurement, financial planning and consolidation, warehouse management, human resources, and enterprise resource planning functions. This decision places the SAP system at the very core of your company application portfolio.

Once deployed, SAP becomes essential to performing most company operations. For the remaining legacy systems, the candidate systems integrators will plan to build data-sharing integrations that enable the entire apparatus to operate as a single entity. These interfaces become a primary deliverable for the SAP implementation project.

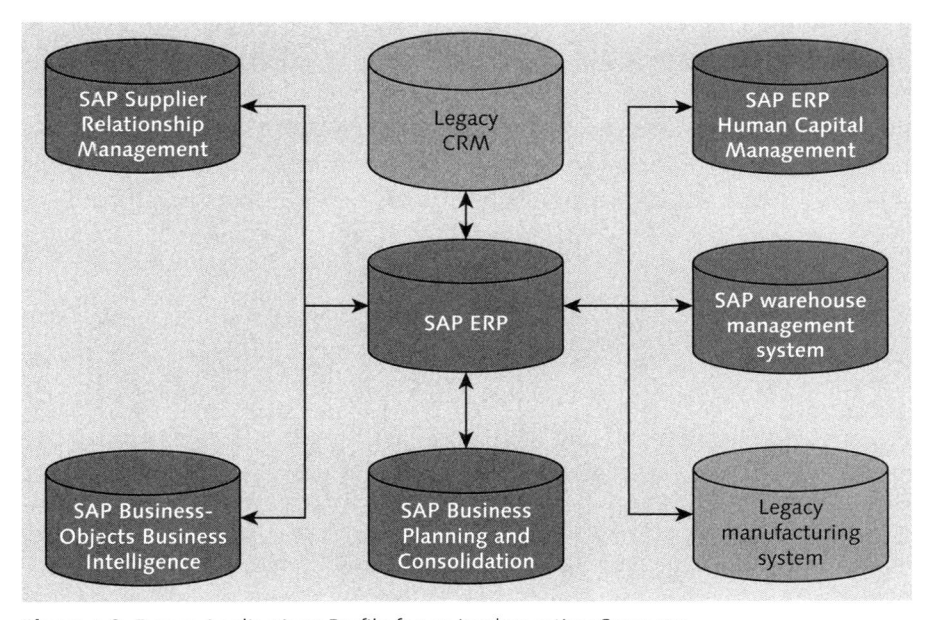

Figure 5.8 Future Applications Profile for an Implementing Company

Custom Object Requirements

The final portion of the RFP addresses the known requirements for custom objects (WRICEFPs). Although this list can be expected to grow as the project moves into the blueprinting phase, these elements will represent a major work requirement for the systems integrator. It is essential, therefore, that the listing—even if partial—be provided at this time. It's also important to enumerate areas where the SAP system will interface with legacy systems or where automation will be needed for workflows and reports.

Most important on the list will be any needed system enhancements. These are often the most complex custom objects to build, and the candidate systems integrator must understand as fully as possible the rationale for these enhancements.

The literature on SAP system implementations is filled with examples of requested enhancements whose complexity to develop spelled the demise of the project schedule. Your company can expect any candidate systems integrator to question the need for and probable design of these enhancements in some detail.

Once all this material has been prepared, reviewed by your company procurement organization, and approved by senior executives, it is ready to distribute. The remainder of the systems integrator selection process is outlined in the following chapter. It goes into the selection methods for determining which systems integrators to involve in the proposal process. It also details the mechanisms for reviewing proposals and selecting the final choice, contracting with the chosen integrator, and onboarding systems integrator staff prior to the initiation of blueprinting.

5.5 Project Procurement

Although early phases of the SAP implementation project are not usually capital-intensive, some purchases will be required at this stage. If the implementation company hasn't already purchased licenses for SAP system components, then licenses to support the number of planned users will have to be purchased.

Two other sets of items may require procurement as well. Each area can consist of high-ticket items requiring substantial due diligence and careful negotiation in the purchasing process:

1. **Third-party software that will support the SAP implementation project**
   In most cases, these software components are essential to the operation of the SAP system, to the design specified by your company, or to the activities of the project team. First on the list is the database to be used for the SAP system. Most implementing companies have long-standing relationships with database vendors such as IBM, Microsoft, or Oracle and so will make independent recommendations about which application to choose. Assuming their preferred organization's database is sufficiently robust to operate with the SAP system, many companies adopt this recommendation. Others, however, make an altogether different decision. Once the final choice has been made, the procurement process should begin.

   After database decision and procurement, a few other software choices remain. These can be categorized as software in support of the SAP system and software in support of the SAP implementation project in particular. The SAP system does many things, but it does not do all things. Thus, third-party software is needed when your company requires functions that are outside the SAP system purview.

Figure 5.9 illustrates two types of support systems: those needed by the business to accomplish augmented functions (left) and those needed by the project team to support the implementation project (right). They are analytically separated because their purpose is very different. In both cases, the need for these ancillary systems can go overlooked early in the project and can cause unforeseen budget impacts if the need becomes apparent well after the budget has been finalized.

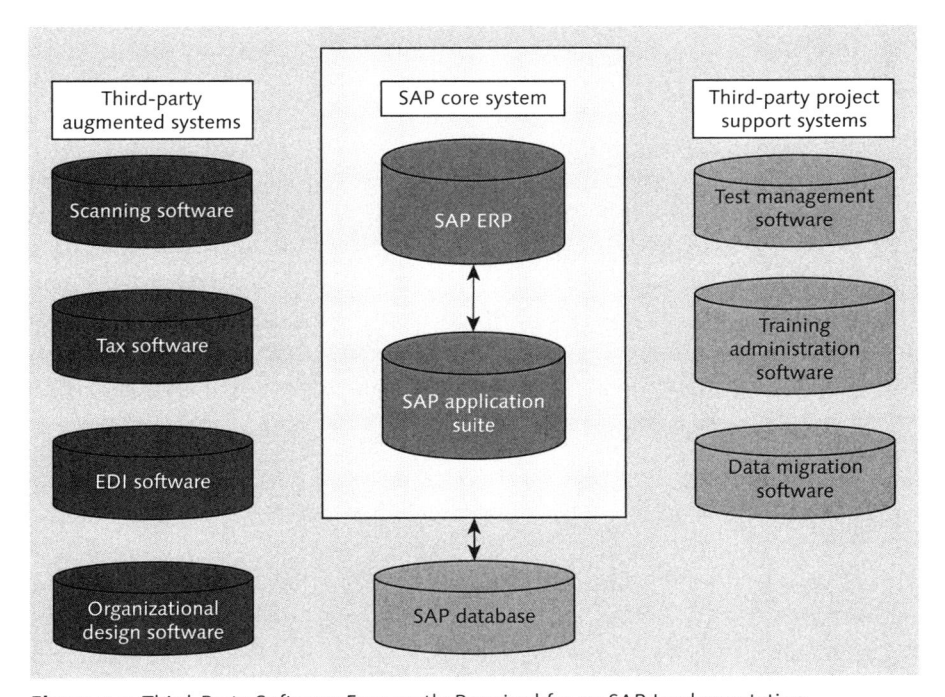

Figure 5.9 Third-Party Software Frequently Required for an SAP Implementation

For example, the full operation of an SAP system will frequently depend on the use of third-party software or "tools." Document-scanning would be a good illustration of this concept. Chapter 2 outlined an automated procurement process built on workflows that utilizes invoice-scanning as a main process component. Vendor invoices would be received as electronic documents and then scanned for distribution to reviewers and approvers. In most cases, this software will be acquired from third-party software vendors.

The SAP implementation project team will often require third-party software for its activities as well. For example, in a full-scale implementation, the volume of systems testing will overwhelm manual tracking systems' capacity to report on test completions and defect resolution. Many implementing companies choose to adopt systems that enable tracking and reporting of systems test status. These are not required by the SAP system and are not associated with SAP. They are used in order to facilitate activities associated with the implementation project.

2. **Infrastructure required for the operation of the SAP system and for related third-party software**
The described applications and the SAP system itself will require infrastructure. Often the servers that will house these applications must be purchased and separately installed. This will require specification and planning for the data center in which they will operate.

Any applications and servers required to support the SAP system will entail user or operator training, storage setup, and ongoing maintenance. These will have to be factored into the procurement process to ensure that all incremental costs are known and accurately forecasted. Purchase and installation of each should be handled according to standard practices in your company. Even though the purchases and deployment are made within the framework of the SAP implementation project, there should be no relaxation of company standard practices.

For each application to be purchased, your company IT staff will prepare a specification document to describe its operation. This specification ensures that the third-party system will operate effectively with the SAP system as well as any other company systems with which it will be expected to interface. Additionally, the specification will identify functionality of the third-party system and its working parameters.

From the perspective of working parameters, the specification will outline the following items:

- Licensing requirements
- Network operating needs
- Storage

- Operating system
- System architecture
- Database server

Let's look at a design schematic for a scanning tool like the one discussed for Figure 5.9. Figure 5.10 shows a relatively complex landscape of servers and external interfaces required to operate the system. It also outlines the SAP workstreams that will be using the tool.

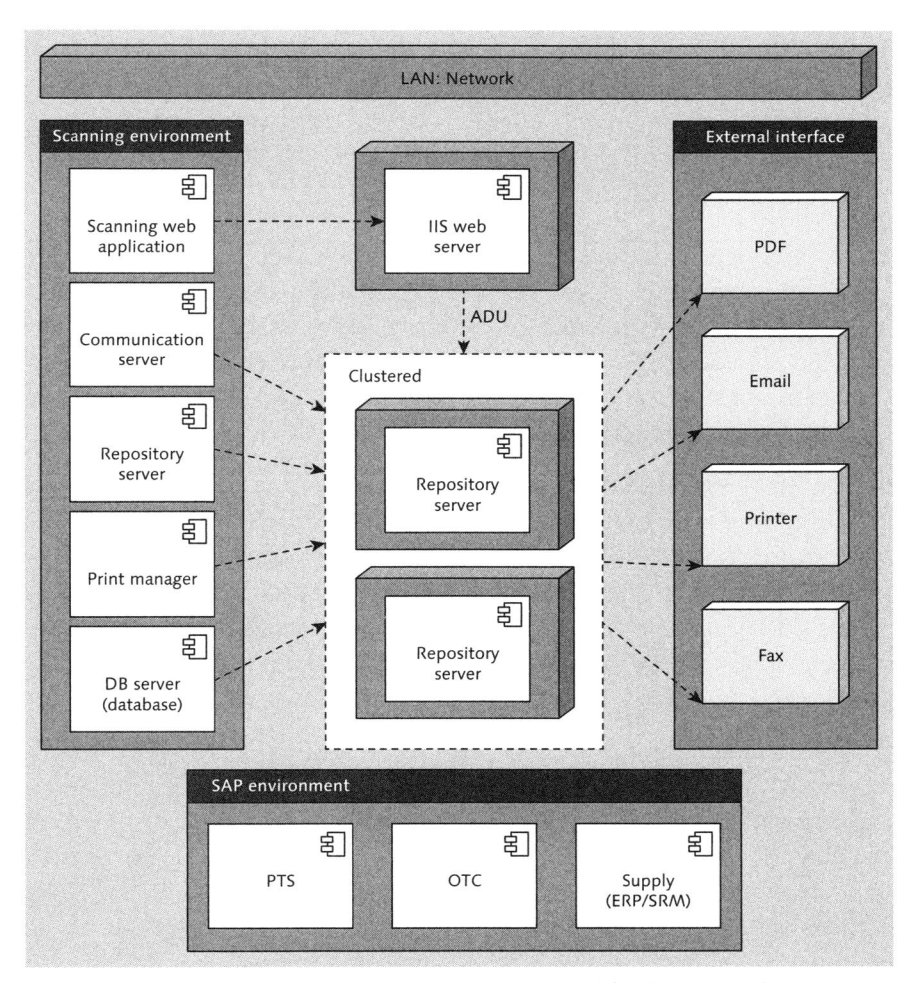

Figure 5.10 Design Schematic for Third-Party Tool Required for the SAP Implementation Project

5 | Start-Up Logistics

> **Tip**
> The acquisition and installation of these third-party systems, as well as the entire infrastructure package necessary for the project, will represent a substantial work effort. It must be scheduled and tracked very carefully. The project will depend on these items meeting their delivery times and "ready-for-use" points.

A substantial work effort will go into the acquisition and installation of these third-party systems and the entire infrastructure package necessary for the project. It must be scheduled and tracked very carefully. The project will depend on these items meeting their delivery times and "ready-for-use" points.

5.6 Space Planning for Project Activities

Even at this early stage in the project lifecycle, the cadre project team will require collocated working space to accomplish many of the activities described in this chapter. Assuming a cadre team of approximately 20 members, most implementing companies should easily be able to find space capable of housing this small team. It will require workstations for each individual, telephone connections, and one or two conference rooms for group meetings.

Chapter 12 describes these facilities logistics processes in some detail. Though the bulk of housing needs will become clear in the middle of project preparation, you should begin preliminary project planning now. It includes an estimate of the space required to house the project team and to conduct project activities, such as blueprinting and systems testing. The likely lead time to identify and acquire facilities capable of housing the project team means that this item must be high on the cadre checklist.

The checklist would enumerate the "facilities drivers," as they are known at this time. Table 5.3 lists a number of these drivers and their current requirements. Though the project cadre must understand that their space requirements may not prove feasible—for example, not everyone on the team will need or receive an individual office—the team will receive no more than what it requests. These requests should receive careful attention.

Facility Driver	Current Estimate
Total project headcount	▶ 100 full-time company staff ▶ 80 systems integrator staff
Number of workstreams	▶ 5 functional workstreams ▶ 8 technical workstreams
Number of working locations	▶ Project will operate out of company headquarters ▶ Subsequent deployments will require dedicated project workspace for two to three months
Collocation requirements	▶ Entire project team should be located in a single facility. This includes both company staff assigned to the project and systems integrator staff ▶ At a minimum, workstreams must be collocated

Table 5.3 Initial Facility Planning for the SAP Project Team

5.7 Preliminary Project Budgeting

Initial spending estimates are developed during the start-up portion of the project preparation phase as well. We've already discussed the capital projections for the SAP system, third-party applications, tools, and project-related infrastructure needs. These would come first on the list. Due to the potentially large amounts of money involved, these big-ticket requests receive careful vetting.

Overall project budgeting activities should take the next priority. Establishing the budget categories, whether expense or capital, is relatively straightforward. Table 5.4 shows the top-level budget categories for a standard SAP implementation project. Most budget categories show up both as expense and capital items. Each company has adopted its own rules for these charges and some examples of these are covered in Chapter 11. However, once the rules are established, most of the remaining effort will focus on expenditure tracking, accounting, and forecasting of project financial performance.

Budget Area	Budget Category	Description
Expense	Company headcount costs	Costs charged to reflect compensation for those assigned to the project team and any backfill charges incurred
	Company travel and expense	Costs to support travel and related expenses for company staff authorized to travel in support of the SAP implementation project
	Systems integrator service charges	Payments made to the systems integrator company for the resources assigned to and working on the SAP implementation project
	Systems integrator travel and expense	Costs to support travel and related expenses for integrator staff authorized to travel in support of the SAP implementation project
	Third-party contractors	Costs charged to reflect compensation for those assigned to the project team
	SAP service charges	Costs charged to reflect compensation for those assigned to the project team
	Office supplies	Office supplies and office equipment used by the project team in support of the SAP implementation
	Facilities allocation	Any costs allocated by the implementing company to cover facilities utilized by the SAP project team
	Software licenses	Payments made to software vendors for the use of their systems by the implementing company
Capital	Company headcount costs	Costs charged to reflect compensation for those assigned to the project team and any backfill charges incurred
	Systems integrator service charges	Payments made to the systems integrator company for the resources assigned to and working on the SAP implementation project
	Third-party contractors	Costs charged to reflect compensation for those assigned to the project team

Table 5.4 Standard Budget Categories for an SAP Implementation Project

Budget Area	Budget Category	Description
	SAP licenses	Payments made to SAP for user licenses to employ the SAP system
	Software licenses	Payments made to software vendors for the use of their systems by the implementing company

Table 5.4 Standard Budget Categories for an SAP Implementation Project (Cont.)

> **Trail Marker**
>
> Some of the budget categories show up under both expense and capital. The cost of systems integrator service is a good example of this situation. Accounting rules cause some integrator activities to fall in the expense category and others to fall in the capital category. Chapter 11 will cover the rationale for determining which category to use.

For global projects that have regional components, this approach will likely require each region to construct its own project budget. Regional budgets will be reviewed and approved by assigned project controllers and consolidated into the overall SAP implementation budget. Using this mechanism enables controllers to ensure that all regional elements are aligned with the general budget. Figure 5.11 provides an example of a budget for a European region.

Category	Primary Location	Other Locations	Total
Company headcount costs	$3.5M for 25 full-time employees	$1.5M for 7 full-time employees	$5M
Facilities allocation	$0.6M		$0.6M
Expatriate expenses	$0.5M for housing and tax support		$0.5M
Company travel and expense	$1.5M for travel and localization	$0.5M for travel and localization	$2M
Third-party contractors	$2.5M for regionally based skills		$2.5M
Other staff and super users	$1M	$4M	$5M
Total	**$9.6M**	**$6M**	**$15.6M**

Figure 5.11 European Budget for a Global SAP Implementation Project

As the figure illustrates, the budgetary amounts requested from regional organizations may prove quite sizable. It will be necessary for project controllers to assess each line item and confirm that it falls within the standards used in the project. Obviously some regions may have unique business needs; these will have to be accommodated in the amounts allocated.

> **Tip**
>
> In general, your company can expect to allocate its total project spend as 40 percent in the expense category and 60 percent in the capital category.

Financial controllers assigned to the project will doubtless pay very close attention to the proper assignment of these charges. They also will be a top-of-the-list subject of any corporate audit and external auditor reviews.

Overall, systems integrator charges will represent by far the largest single line-item for the project. It is not uncommon to find over 50 percent of the total project expenditures devoted to capital and expense charges for integrator headcount as well as supporting travel payments. For this reason, the company procurement organization and accounting staff should be closely involved in the integrator contracting process. Both groups will ensure that formats for defining allowable charges are well-reviewed and agreed to prior to signing the final contract.

Now on to systems integrator selection. Chapter 6 covers the major facets of finding the systems integrator right for your project. Clearly, finding the best integrator is hard work. It requires a great deal of due diligence, but the reward is worth the effort.

A number of the following chapters address other topics specific to the project preparation phase. It is important that the project team pays attention to laying this foundation very carefully. Many of the decisions made in this phase will have significant ramifications for later phases of the project. Team formation, project governance, integrator selection, and project planning outline how the project will operate and receive resources. If incorrect, they will be difficult to undo and may limit the ability of the project team to achieve its objectives.

Your company must carefully weigh and review its systems integrator selection decision. Let's walk through it.

6 Systems Integrator Selection and Contracting

Selection of a systems integrator is probably your company's most important project-based decision. An effective systems integrator adds definite value and ensures that the project meets its targets. A *very* effective systems integrator can even ensure project success. However, a less-effective systems integrator will at best require continuous management attention, and at worst create problems with deliverables and an on-time go-live. As you can see, there are lots of potential problems here.

Our chapter assumes that your company has already decided to adopt the SAP system. So the chapter will focus instead on the steps of selecting, contracting, and onboarding the systems integrator. This overall process requires considerable effort from the company project team and provides the first set of coordinated project team tasks.

The systems integrator team works hand in hand with the company project team (generally at the company project site) and offers needed SAP technical expertise. The integrator staff can be counted on to possess significant application knowledge and skill; most integrator team members will have worked through numerous SAP implementation projects. Their experience of "been there, done that" will prove of immense assistance to your company project team. Additionally, the overall integrator project lead is most often a highly experienced leader with several SAP implementations under his or her belt. This person will know well the risks and difficulties your project will face.

The marketplace has many systems integrator companies to choose from. They range from very large-scale global organizations—such as Accenture, Capgemini, Deloitte, and IBM—with thousands of SAP consultants, to small shops with 10 to 20 SAP consultants.

> **Tip**
>
> For sizable SAP projects, we recommend that you consider at least one of the global integrators. These global integrators have resources available to support regional activities no matter what the location. For smaller implementations, a local integrator may work well.

In any case, the selection must include a careful review of integrator capabilities, anticipated cost, and whether it can fully commit to the company project.

Identifying the right project integrator goes through three distinct phases, as shown in Figure 6.1.

- The first of these phases is integrator selection. Here, you identify and review multiple candidate firms and make a final selection.
- The second phase initiates after contractor selection and requires you to focus on defining details of the project contract.
- The final phase centers on you bringing integrator personnel on site to begin project activities.

Step one	Step two	Step three
Integrator selection	Integrator contracting	Integrator onboarding

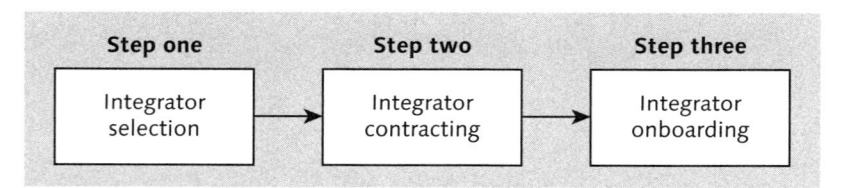

Figure 6.1 Systems Integrator Selection Phases

Each phase presents a different set of challenges and needed skills. For larger projects, the entire sequence of activities may take from three to six months to complete.

6.1 Integrator Selection

Your company should identify the systems integrator that best fits its project needs. Not all integrators are created equally. The integrator playing field is very diverse, and successful selection requires a major time investment.

> **Pitfall Alert**
>
> An integrator with exceptional skills in one industry may not prove the best fit for another industry. For example, great skill levels in the oil and gas industry do not translate into the very different skills required to implement SAP in the consumer packaged goods industry. Likewise, not all integrators can support a global implementation. Many are centered on North America or Europe and would experience difficulties supporting project activities in Latin America or Asia.
>
> Only a careful review of integrator capabilities will reveal the full picture. If a company has a longstanding relationship with a systems integrator, then that integrator should certainly be considered for inclusion.

When deciding which integrator will work best for your company, numerous additional factors come into play. Many of these factors may be unique to your company or project. Others are more general in nature and apply to almost all companies. However, the process to select that systems integrator does follow a consistent path. The following sections outline a method for finding that "best-fit" systems integrator for your project.

6.1.1 Initial Integrator Identification and Information Gathering

Full commitment to due diligence during the selection process will pay you great dividends. Remember, your task is to find the right integrator. Most likely, many more integrators will receive consideration than will make the final grouping. Your initial list of candidate integrators may be quite long—as many as 20 prospective integrators. The selection process continuously winnows down this group, operating as a funnel that evaluates and removes potential integrators from the list. Each step should bring your team closer to discovering the *right* integrator for your project.

Expect this process to be time-consuming and fraught with difficulty, but keep in mind that finding the right systems integrator will both save company money and reduce project uncertainty in the long run. Begin by making use of previous connections with other companies in your industry that have recently performed an SAP implementation. Gathering references from those connections will provide a helpful building block.

This initial integrator report card data is best collected with a pre-arranged conference call involving personnel from the reference company who had major roles and responsibilities during their own SAP implementation project. You may want to consider using a standard checklist for these calls. In this way, all important information is collected and available for review. Checklists also enable the comparison of one integrator to another. This checklist targets the most relevant information to gain about the integrator. At a minimum, you should obtain the following information:

- Basic information about the reference company, including its name, industry segment, annual revenues, and locations, as well as names and positions of reference call participants.
- Scope of the reference company's SAP project, including the project's planned and actual timelines, names of SAP component systems implemented, the business case for the project, and approximate project budget (if the interviewing company will make this information available).
- Reasons for selecting the integrator (and for not selecting other integrators) and, on a related note, the size of its project team. Reasons impacting selection can include estimated cost, skill set of the proposed integrator project team, references from other integrator clients, relationships with integrator senior executives, or fit with project scope and parameters.
- Relevant experiences with the integrator, both positive and negative. Questions can focus on project governance, team composition and performance of the integrator project team, financial relations over the life of the project, degree of company fit with the integrator, and ability of the integrator to cover the full scope of the project, as well as an overall recommendation regarding using the integrator for future engagements. This last group of qualifications should reflect as much in-depth information as can be obtained. Your selection team should make it a point to follow up with any questions where additional detail is required.

Your program management office (PMO) will designate a small but broadly skilled group to make all due diligence calls. You'll get the best results by having all functional business organizations represented, as well as company IT resources. This across-the-board participation ensures a good degree of standardization regarding information collected and reported.

This small team will synthesize its findings and make them available to project leadership. Once this team has completed its report, the project team can review and rank results. Project management will assess these results for final determination. Only those integrators that make the cut will receive the request for proposal (RFP). Due diligence in data collection will discover integrators with positive experiences in your company's industry and the ability to support your implementation. At this point—after the initial review—your total number of integrators under consideration should be in the neighborhood of five to six candidate firms.

> **Pitfall Alert**
>
> You may decide to include a larger number of potential integrators. Take care here, because this decision will impose significant time demands on the project team. Moving forward, those integrators still under consideration will now participate in a rigorous and time-consuming vetting process. Limiting integrator candidates to a select few permits your project team to focus on those most likely to be selected.

6.1.2 Request for Proposal

Most companies issue an RFP to its selected group of candidate integrators. We recommend that your company do so as well. The RFP supports the review of prospective integrators on a level playing field. Specifying common formats and requesting similar information from integrators is a big help in making integrator comparisons.

> **Tip**
>
> Because of the RFP's importance, company procurement staff should be heavily involved in the preparation and review of the RFP. They will have extensive knowledge of best formats and necessary content to make it an effective document. They will also have experience in the review and evaluation of RFP responses. Normally, these high-dollar-value decisions will benefit greatly from their experience.

Preparing a comprehensive RFP document has many advantages. It provides an effective unifying method for your project team to distill its objectives and proposed approach into a single document. Many implicit assumptions about the project, such as timing and approach, can be discussed among the team and resolved at this time. The results of your discussions, the agreed-upon baseline information, will then be included within your RFP document. Another important advantage of the RFP is how it will serve as your project's primary communication device with the candidate systems integrator group. The RFP should lay out the essential parameters of the project, such as number of localities involved, systems to be included, timeline expectations, and general project scope. This will be important information for your integrator candidate pool.

One important purpose of the RFP is to educate responders. At least some integrator candidates will have limited experience with your company, so the RFP will be their best source of information. Candidate integrators should receive as much company-relevant data as needed to create an informed response. Thus, an effective RFP should describe the project in some detail. This will include at a minimum:

- **Project objectives and prospective impact to the company**
  Give integrators insight about why your company is proceeding with its SAP implementation; the business case used to justify your company's investment should be outlined in the document. This section should also describe any business imperatives that create important deadlines or make special change management requirements.

- **Company business processes, including company locations and third-party business partners**
  You should cover any major business process changes expected as a result of the project in this section. Also make it a point to identify any major business processes that will *not* be involved in the implementation.

- **Project organization**
  Include any project governance mechanisms, workstream structure, and project management staffing in terms of teams, numbers, and locations.

- **Anticipated project timelines and major cost parameters**
  Attach a copy of the most recent project timeline along with any relevant contextual information that might explain your rationale. If you have chosen to supply anticipated project cost information to integrator candidates, include this as well.

- **System implementation scope**
  Here you should identify all SAP and related third-party systems to be implemented, legacy systems to be replaced, and existing company systems that will interface with the SAP solutions. If available, this section would also include a listing of known custom objects that will be required. These include work-

flows, reports, interfaces, data conversions, system enhancements, forms, and portal operations. These custom objects are normally built by the systems integrator and this information will serve as an essential financial planning tool.

Here is the most important step: Make sure that you make available draft copies of the proposed RFP for review and approval by project stakeholders prior to creating the final version. Stakeholders should specify any requested changes so that the RFP team can track them. Confirming stakeholder approval of changed wording will prove crucial as well. Once you have reached a final version, the procurement organization will distribute copies to all participating integrator candidates. For their own reasons, some integrators will choose not to participate. They may or may not inform your company of their decision.

The RFP will include an RSVP date by which all participating system integrators should submit their responses. Prior to this date, you should hold a question-and-answer session with participating systems integrators as well. This session serves as a public forum where integrators can raise questions or concerns and receive answers from project staff. Team leads and project management should attend the session. You should solicit integrator questions in advance. Make the complete list of questions available to all participants, integrator and company alike. At the actual session, only submitted questions should be answered. This way your project team will have the opportunity to prepare answers in advance. Some questions will be technically focused, and the last thing your company needs is for the project team have to speak off-the-cuff. At the company's discretion, clarification questions and follow-ups can be answered at this time.

6.1.3 Reviewing RFP Responses

Once the RSVP date has passed and all responses have been received, your team will now turn to evaluating those packages. During the RFP response period, your project team should have developed its scoring mechanisms for the received RFP packages. The most common scoring mechanisms identify categories and assign a weight to each category. Clearly the challenge lies in finding the right categories and their relative weights for a specific implementation.

Table 6.1 shows a sample set of categories and weightings. Notice that the categories reflect major focus areas in the RFP and their weightings represent the emphasis placed on each category.

Category	Description	Weight
Project timelines	Degree of proposal fit with proposed schedule submitted by your company. Satisfactory rationale provided for any deviations if outlined in the submitted proposal.	15%
Staffing model	Numbers and skill profiles of identified staff in the proposal. Extent of fit with the project workload.	20%
Cost estimate	Reasonable cost basis for the proposal and support provided for the cost estimate.	20%
Systems approach	Methodology to be used for delivering the SAP system, any custom objects required, and integration with legacy systems.	10%
Management team	Relevant experience and skills shown by those individuals the integrator has nominated to operate in project leadership roles.	20%
Industry experience	Documented experience with SAP applications particular to your industry. Indications in the proposal that the integrator understands the specific challenges of your implementation.	15%

Table 6.1 RFP Categories and Scoring Weightings

As with RFP preparation, project management should form a small team to review each RFP submission in detail and assign scoring values to each category. The experience of assigned procurement staff will prove invaluable here. They, along with business and IT representatives, should play major roles in ensuring reliable scoring.

Once scoring is complete, you can rank prospective integrator submissions and outline the rationale for scoring decisions. The project team can then brief its leadership and assigned business stakeholders on the integrator rankings and scoring.

> **Tip**
>
> Take some time to prepare these briefings. To the extent possible, they should be open and free-flowing discussions that encourage significant participation from all attendees. Your objective here is to develop a common viewpoint on the strengths and weaknesses of each integrator so that everyone is on the same page. Subsequent steps in the selection process will benefit from building this shared understanding.

6.1.4 First Cut Integrator Presentations

Assuming that leadership briefings created a consensus on the relative ranking of each integrator, you can schedule on-site presentations. These sessions will serve as the first opportunity for the project team to meet and assess integrator candidates and many of their staff who could be assigned to the project.

> **Tip**
>
> We recommend allocating a day for each prospective integrator. These sessions are scripted and organized by the project team. Normally, morning sessions focus on the integrator's general approach to the project, including timeline and methodology. Afternoon sessions focus more on specialized requirements of particular workstreams, infrastructure, and project management.

Again, preparing assessment checklists for use during the presentations will greatly assist in standardizing comparisons among integrator candidates. These should be more comprehensive and subject-matter-specific than those used to review RFP submissions. Each checklist should target concerns for each workstream. For example, subjects could include previous specialized experience with implementing SAP Advanced Planning and Optimization (APO) for sales and inventory planning, or export processing for order-to-cash using the SAP Global Trade System (GTS). Ensuring that the selected integrator has significant background supporting key areas for your project is crucial. Of course, having the opportunity to assess integrator staff who would potentially be assigned to these areas represents a plus as well.

Your company can request that integrator candidates provide demonstrations of SAP software functionality. This approach has two definite advantages:

1. First, it educates the project team. Integrators can give in-depth presentations of specific SAP applications. This provides for the project team to view any unfamiliar functionality even if it uses mocked-up data.
2. Second, it gives the project team one more chance to assess integrator skills in system setup and offering explanations. These kind of real-world situations closely parallel project operations during realization and are excellent points of reference to evaluate integrator competence.

Additionally, ask each workstream to develop a listing of target questions. In order to make the session more productive, these should be assigned to specific team members and asked at each integrator session. The ability to compare answers will provide important benchmark information during your integrator assessment process.

Your project team leadership should meet at the conclusion of each integrator presentation. This way it can receive immediate feedback about integrator performance. Informal scoring generated at this time can be collected and used to baseline each integrator.

Make it a point to post and discuss integrator scores, both by workstream and overall performance. At the conclusion of the presentations, your team should meet to review its findings. If one systems integrator has scored substantially better than all others, this makes the selection decision much easier. If two or more are grouped quite closely, then additional review steps will be needed. You can schedule conference calls or on-site meetings with these integrators to help make your decision.

6.1.5 Final Selection

Figure 6.2 shows an example of the overall results from integrator scoring. Those tabulations point to a decision to select systems integrator Company B over its competitors. Company B has outperformed other integrators in the competition by a wide margin. It represents the best fit. Unless compelling alternative information were available to support another integrator, your project team should go with this selection.

Of course, prior to finalizing Company B as the integrator selection, a few review steps still remain. Major stakeholders—including the head of procurement and the CFO—should receive in-depth briefings on the selection process to date and the rationale for choosing integrator Company B. Additionally, stakeholders from other affected functional organizations must be brought on board with both the process steps and integrator selection. Until you reach an agreement among stakeholders, you cannot proceed with the next steps. Once agreement is reached, though, your team can inform the selected integrator and move forward with establishing a contract.

Integrator	Scoring Highlights	Score (out of 100)
Company A	Proposed management team assigned to the project has limited experience in our industry. Many proposed workstream leads show the same lack of industry experience.	66
Company B	Overall best performer. Positive performance in all categories. Second-lowest cost among all integrators.	91
Company C	Estimated cost 50% higher than the lowest bidder even though staffing numbers are slightly less than all other submissions.	73
Company D	Lack of global staffing support needed to complete a multi-continent roll-out. Use of subcontracted personnel adds risk to the project.	49
Company E	Submitted project plan shows completion date three months later than requested. All other integrators accept the proposed timeline with minor revisions.	78

Figure 6.2 Integrator Scoring Matrix

6.2 Integrator Contracting

Integrator expenses will represent the largest line item in the project budget—in fact, very likely by a factor of three or four. Understanding the exact responsibilities and performance expectations for the selected integrator will take place during the contracting process.

> **Pitfall Alert**
> It is of utmost importance that sufficient time is allocated and project resources fully assigned to complete a rigorous and enforceable integrator contract.

At minimum, your contracting team should include project leadership, senior-level procurement resources, and stakeholder participation where available. The contracting team will achieve best results by taking the initiative. Having the company's position ready to put on the table when negotiations begin ensures that you're able to take a leadership position during the subsequent weeks of discussion.

Several small to medium-sized consulting firms specialize in assisting companies with integrator contracting. Because systems integrator selection is both a high-cost item and an activity that companies undertake in very rare instances, using external specialists to support contract completion may make sense for an implementing company. If your company chooses to adopt this option, the assigned consulting staff should be made an integral part of the company contracting team.

6.2.1 Types of Contracts

The terms and conditions of the contract will play a major role in the success of the project, but so will the type of contract signed. Two primary contract types are used in establishing a legal relationship with an integrator:

1. The first type, a *fixed-price* contract, provides for a highly limited set of cost adjustments. Such contracts are used when the implementation scope is clear-cut and where both the company and its integrator have a firm understanding of costs to be incurred. The contract sets fees to be paid to the integrator for work performed and generally only modifies those amounts if broad economic changes lead to price adjustments. Noticeably, the fixed-price contract imposes most of the risk on the integrator by ensuring that cost overruns are its responsibility to assume.

2. The second type of contract, *time-and-material*, is more basic. It pays the integrator for labor and materials used on the project. Integrator manpower resources are reimbursed at an hourly rate for time worked. Integrator expenses, such as travel and materials utilized, are reimbursed at cost. Time and material contracts place most of the cost risk on the project company. These contracts are only used when implementation scope is not set and neither participant has a defined picture of potential project costs.

Within the framework of either type of contract, you can apply various approaches to cost risk-sharing. The most common type is an incentive payment for exceeding predetermined performance levels. These are often schedule-based, where the integrator is paid an incentive for achieving on-time or early delivery of a particular milestone. These incentives can also be applied for on-time or early delivery of the entire implementation. While incentives are used more frequently in fixed-price contracts, they can be utilized in time-and-material contracts, since pre-provided deliverable dates can be agreed on here, too.

Another incentive type, the holdback, is used only in the fixed-price contract. Holdbacks are applied to monthly or quarterly achievement targets. If the integrator fails to make delivery for an agreed-upon milestone, a percentage of the payment due is placed on hold. If the milestone is satisfactorily met within a specified period of time, the amount placed on hold is paid to the integrator. If the milestone is not met within the contracted time period, the integrator forgoes the holdback amount and it is not paid.

> **Pitfall Alert**
>
> Holdbacks require considerable attention to detail. To work effectively, all milestones must have specific completion criteria and a common understanding of those criteria among company and integrator project leadership. Unless those are in place, use of holdbacks can generate misunderstanding and distrust. However, with a skilled project management team, holdbacks can serve as an excellent financial device to keep a project on track.

In the end, incentives can be both positive and negative in terms of project cost. However, incentives will most likely play a positive role in managing project performance. If incentives are to be used, company financial staff should closely monitor their cost impact and adjust the project forecast to account for incentive payments made or holdback receipts.

6.2.2 Contract Structure and Contents

Most systems integrators prefer to use *statements of work* (SOW) to outline their contractual performance agreements. Provided the involved companies have a *master services agreement* (MSA) in place formalizing their general working relationship, the SOW will be an excellent vehicle. Elements contained in the SOW represent the real contract subject matter for the SAP implementation. They will also represent the focal point of contract negotiations. Standard SOW sections include project scope, approach, timing, staffing, fees and expenses, and major assumptions. Let's walk through each.

Fundamental Program Scope

From the integrator's standpoint, fully understanding the client's project scope definition is the most important information target. Knowing the project scope in as much detail as possible has significant implications for project timing, staffing requirements—both in numbers and specialties—as well as fees requested. Larger integrators build their fee quotes using very sophisticated spreadsheets. Once project parameters are inserted to the spreadsheet, they can derive accurate costs. For this reason, the chosen integrator is likely to spend considerable time making sure that project scope is well understood. Indeed, you may find that the integrator will also work to identify those areas that do not fall within the project scope.

> **Pitfall Alert**
>
> The integrator's negotiation team will be experts in working through project scope parameters with the client company. Remember, though, that few, if any, members of the integrator negotiation team will work as assigned members of the project team. Much of the historical continuity for decisions made will not be easily available. For this reason, it is very important that the client negotiation team document all major decisions, including scope decisions, in detail. Otherwise, substantial differences of opinion about contractual points may cause disagreements among the parties and possibly affect long-term working relationships.

The first steps will involve delineating processes in scope and those outside of scope. Using the project workstream structure, the integrator will seek to understand those process elements that will be part of the project and those that fall outside of scope. The company RFP will provide the initial guide for process discussion. However, during the contracting phase, the integrator will drill down into the RFP material to ensure that it provides a complete picture. The integrator will also spend time verifying what processes will remain out of scope. The focus here is to assure clear boundaries around the work and to preclude any assumptions that particular scope items were included under another process.

For human capital management (HCM) processes, the delineation of items in and out of scope might look similar to Table 6.2. Notice that the list of items out of scope is quite robust, taking considerable potential work off the table. Items such as master data management and reporting represent placeholders for custom objects that will be identified later in the contracting process.

HCM Processes in Scope	HCM Processes Out of Scope
Workforce planning and reporting	E-Recruitment
Staffing	Enterprise learning (LMS)
Staff services	Workforce deployment
Employee self-services	Travel management
Compensation	Time management
Succession planning	Payroll
Payroll interfaces	Environmental health and safety
Contingent workforce management	
Performance assessment	
Performance management	
Master data management	
Reporting	

Table 6.2 Human Capital Management Process Definition

Once scope is agreed for all company workstreams, the discussion will then center on identifying SAP modules that will be part of the implementation or placed under evaluation for potential later inclusion. These lists will generally identify the version to be used when the application has a version assigned to it.

Table 6.3 shows a listing of SAP modules that will comprise a hypothetical implementation. Having the agreed listing of modules and processes included greatly enables the flow of contracting discussions. At this point, both parties understand the framework of work to be completed.

SAP Modules in Scope	Functional Area Supported
Human Capital Management (HCM)	Human resources
Sales and Distribution (SD)	Sales operations
Materials Management (MM)	Procurement

Table 6.3 SAP Modules in Scope for a Hypothetical Implementation

SAP Modules in Scope	Functional Area Supported
Production Planning (PP)	Supply chain
Quality Management (QM)	
Advanced Planning and Optimizer (APO)	
Financial Accounting (FI)	Finance
Financial Controlling (CO)	
Asset Management (AM)	
Profitability Analysis (PA)	
Business Planning and Consolidation (BPC)	
Project Systems	
Supplier Relationship Management (SRM)	Procurement
Contract Lifecycle Management (CLM)	
Business Intelligence (BI)	All

Table 6.3 SAP Modules in Scope for a Hypothetical Implementation (Cont.)

Much of the remaining scope definition work falls in the category of custom development scope. Here, the negotiating parties will come to a common understanding of custom objects to be created or supported during the project. These custom objects—known by the acronym WRICEFP—represent software development required by the client for SAP to work as the company needs. The integrator, which will perform the software development, will identify each requested item and assign a work complexity to it (e.g., high, medium, and low). The estimating spreadsheet will contain embedded cost parameters for each object type and complexity of development so that an aggregate cost estimate can be assigned to the work.

The integrator SOW will list all known custom objects agreed to by both parties. Those specified in the SOW will be priced and an overall cost for development work will be assigned. Both parties will recognize that the list is incomplete. They will also understand that the need for other custom objects, especially workflows, interfaces, enhancements, and reports, will arise during blueprinting. In this case—where estimates are recognized as incomplete—the parties agree on a reasonable placeholder number and insert it in the SOW for that area. The placeholder assumes that more or less development work may be required in that area (usually more—much more!) and the correct number can be addressed at a later stage in the project.

Other Scope Areas

Other scope areas included in the SOW consist of organizational and geographic scope, training scope, change management, testing, and compliance. These sections cover the division of responsibilities, such as which party develops user training materials versus which party delivers and manages the training. They also provide an outline of the deliverables in an area such as testing. This scope definition identifies the types of tests to be performed during the project and how they might support project quality assurance objectives. The compliance section will identify those areas where the Sarbanes-Oxley Act of 2002 or other regulatory activities apply and the project documentation that will be prepared to satisfy those requirements.

Project Approach and Timing

In the case of large-scale SAP projects, there will usually be some type of specific phasing used. Your project will be subdivided into multiple rollouts, each with its own timing and deliverables. It is extremely important that both your company and selected systems integrator fully agree on the sequencing of phases and their relationship to one another. The SOW should detail the phases and any staffing or locational issues associated with each phase. This section of the statement of work should also address any specialized testing, post-go-live readiness, or knowledge transfer steps that will be needed.

In almost all cases, the integrator will utilize the ASAP methodology. The SOW will describe each stage and identify major milestones to be accomplished during that stage. Your company can also make the case to add milestones specific to its project. These milestones should be relevant and acceptable to the integrator. The SOW will also specify dates for each phase and its ASAP stages. For example, if the project is divided into three phases, the SOW should list those high-level dates as well as the dates for any stages within those phases, as shown in Table 6.4.

Phase	Step	Date
Phase one: project preparation		July 2015
Phase two: initial blueprint and realization	Blueprint	August 2015
	Realization	December 2015
	Final preparation	March 2016
	Initial go-live	May 2016
Phase three: final blueprint and realization	Blueprint and realization	July 2016
	Final preparation	January 2017
	Global go-live	April 2017

Table 6.4 Example of Multiple Phases and Their Dates

Organization and Staffing

The organization section generally covers the way the project is structured. Staffing also addresses the roles performed by either your company or the integrator. Even when one of the parties has primary responsibility for a specific deliverable set, the other party has individuals assigned to monitor or guide those deliverables. For that reason, this portion of the statement of work identifies responsibilities assigned to each role. In this way, all parties attain clarity regarding their scope and boundaries.

Table 6.5 and Table 6.6 list a subset of full-time roles typical for an implementation on the client and integrator sides, respectively.

Client Project Roles	Role Description
Business transformation office	▸ Responsible for program delivery and business acceptance ▸ Accountable for necessary financial and human resources ▸ Clarify program priorities and sponsor change management initiatives ▸ Sign off on contracted project deliverables ▸ Manage all program vendor relationships

Table 6.5 Role Descriptions for Client Staff

Client Project Roles	Role Description
Senior advisory team	▶ Own the process and business solution ▶ Champion the program and remove any barriers to success ▶ Act as a final decision point for process design
Process owners	▶ Generate business process requirements ▶ Guide process design activities in functional areas ▶ Own the final design and project deliverable materials
Process team member	▶ Contribute process and business expertise to the program ▶ Ensure business understanding and acceptance of the solution ▶ Develop and execute testing protocols
Super user	▶ Act as an advocate for the SAP solution in area of responsibility ▶ Participate in system testing ▶ Deliver end-user training
Technical leads	▶ Take responsibility for technical design and solution ▶ Own technical standards in area of responsibility ▶ Resolve functional and technical issues

Table 6.5 Role Descriptions for Client Staff (Cont.)

Integrator Project Roles	Role Description
Engagement lead	▶ Manage contract performance and delivery ▶ Assure quality status of all deliverables ▶ Work closely with client executives and handle risk
Project manager	▶ Deliver specified system on time and on budget ▶ Maintain project schedule and track its performance ▶ Generate work plans and ensure assignment of resources
Process team lead	▶ Ensure adequacy of system design to meet business needs ▶ Manage required configuration and test activities ▶ Provide technical guidance to the process team

Table 6.6 Role Descriptions for Integrator Staff

Integrator Project Roles	Role Description
System configurator	▶ Deliver assigned configuration tasks during realization ▶ Conduct unit and integration tests for configuration items ▶ Document all design and testing activities
Technical lead	▶ Manage technical team staff and deliverables ▶ Provide technical guidance to the project ▶ Ensure delivery of assigned technical milestones
Change management lead	▶ Develop and manage the project change management plan ▶ Deliver all change management milestones ▶ Coordinate all internal and external communication
Test lead	▶ Develop plans for unit, integration, and user tests ▶ Ensure test script and test execution delivery ▶ Manage resolution of any test defects

Table 6.6 Role Descriptions for Integrator Staff (Cont.)

> **Pitfall Alert**
>
> The integrator will also designate staff with key roles during the project. That listing includes partners assigned to the project, the program manager, and workstream team leads. These designated individuals should be carefully vetted and approved by your company. These individuals will provide the primary sources of technical and management guidance to integrator staff during the span of the project. In cases where the individuals nominated do not meet company requirements, your PMO should communicate this fact and ask the integrator to designate substitute resources.

Additionally, the organization and staffing section will specify integrator executive sponsors assigned to the project. These more senior individuals will serve as the primary point of contact in the event of difficulties or significant questions that cannot be resolved by the integrator project team. At a minimum, the list will contain the integrator executive handling the industry practice and a quality assurance lead from the integrator's SAP leadership.

Project Management

This section outlines how your integrator will manage its portion of the project. It details the duties of the integrator project manager with respect to how planning and documentation of deliverables will take place. It also specifies how deliverables will be tracked and reported to client management.

It is greatly to the client's advantage to review and provide input on this section. In many ways, it forms the foundation of the relationship between the client and integrator teams.

Fees and Expenses

Integrator fees represent a central focus of the negotiation process. You can expect to spend considerable effort on ensuring that integrator services are provided at a reasonable cost. In practice, the negotiation will vary between attention to overall integrator fees and the constituent items that make up these fees. Your company can expect that a very large percentage of the integrator cost quote will center on two items: staffing costs and company-paid integrator expenses.

The integrator will furnish the implementing company with a rate card outlining hourly charges for each consultant type assigned to the project. The rate cards will detail hourly rates for landed on-site consultants as well as off-site consultants. Even though the eventual contract will be a fixed-price arrangement, these rate card standards can serve as useful mechanisms for establishing a reasonable cost basis. By figuring overall length-of-the-program costs for each consultant type, the implementing company can closely estimate the basis for integrator pricing. Focusing negotiation on the ratio of on-site consultants versus off-site consultants will be an important cost control item as well.

Once your company and integrator agree on an overall price, this can be adopted as a not-to-exceed fee. In this case, the integrator agrees to abide for a fixed fee during the length of the contract. Even if its costs exceeded its fees, the integrator would continue to work until project completion at the agreed rate. Integrator payment levels would be adjusted only if your company changed the parameters of the project in some way due to its business circumstances.

Expenses usually cover travel and expenses associated with consultants working on client sites, such as lodging and meals. These can be handled in two ways.

1. By far the easiest to administer is the *expenses as a percentage of fees* model. In this case, the implementing company and the integrator agree on an additional percentage of the contract fee that will be allocated to expenses. Most often this figure falls somewhere between 15 percent and 20 percent of the overall agreed fees. Consultants assigned to the project will report their expenses internally and reports will be furnished to the implementing company to assure compliance with the expense policy.
2. A second method for handling consultant expenses is much less restrictive *open-ended model*. Basically, each consultant charges expenses consistent with the expense policy and no cap is applied. This method places more of the tracking burden on the implementing company and also removes the incentive for the integrator to live within an assigned budget.

Assumptions

This section allows both parties to stipulate any key items that require attention and management. Assumptions may include such items as project location, normal working hours, user training, access to integrator company management, billing practices, responsibility for delivery, and limitations on scope modifications. Change control procedures are used to resolve any challenges while adhering to agreed-upon assumptions.

Signature

Once the SOW is accepted by both parties, it is signed by implementing company and systems integrator senior executives. Once signed, the SOW becomes a legally binding document. The project is now a step closer to beginning implementation activities.

6.2.3 Change Control

Once both parties approve the SOW, modifications to the agreement will be handled through a change control procedure. This process permits either party to identify recommended changes and introduce them through a formal decision-making mechanism. The change control procedure ensures that all submitted changes are dispositioned and, if approved, work is completed.

Items that could initiate change control actions include additions to functionality or modifications to the agreed scope. For example, a decision by the client company to implement the SAP Warehouse Management System (WMS) would enlarge the project scope as defined in Figure 6.3. Or on a smaller scale, additions to the approved custom object list would be handled through change control mechanisms. It's important to the success of the project that all parties take a reasonable approach concerning the type and volume of change requests. Maintaining solid working relationships between both parties makes the change process an effective tool.

The process begins with submission of a change request. It should specify the rationale for the change and include estimates for the following:

- Charges specific to making the change
- Benefits to the company paying for the change
- Time frame for implementing the proposed change
- Business case for approving the change
- Resources required to implement the proposed change (especially resources with limited availability)
- Significant potential risks if the change is or is not approved

The change process will operate through a *change control board* (CCB). This body will contain representatives from both your company and the systems integrator. It meets on a regular basis from blueprinting through the end of the project to review submitted change requests.

The CCB has several decision options: It can approve, reject, or defer. Those change requests that are approved are transferred into change orders. The CCB will also monitor work progress through to completion. Final sign-off will take place as work is finished.

6.3 Integrator Onboarding

With the signing of the SOW, the clock has now started on the project. Integrator resources will now become available for assignment to the project. Their onboarding should be accomplished in a measured way. Leadership resources will be the first to arrive. In this way, integrator leadership can assume planning responsibility for each wave of consultants. As the two teams—your company project team and your systems integrator—sit down together to plan initial activities, you should make deciding the arrival order of each wave the first order of business.

Implementing company and integrator project managers should identify any early work products required. From that listing, they can then target specific resources needed to handle that work and schedule them accordingly. Special attention should be paid to having adequate work space available and management resources assigned to review work products.

Your PMO should develop onboarding packages for new integrator staff. These packages should include information on the history and rationale for the project, descriptions of project leadership, any helpful location maps, and information on handling project travel and expense submittal.

We've spent considerable time discussing the systems integrator. All this time you may have been wondering, *"Just what does SAP do during an implementation project?"* You may be surprised to know that SAP takes a very active role. Our next chapter gives you that answer.

SAP plays several key roles in the implementation project, ranging from software licensing to several types of technical support.

7 SAP's Role in the Project

An SAP implementation project will have three major players: the implementing company, the designated systems integrator, and SAP itself. Though some implementing companies may choose to involve additional third-party providers (e.g., data migration services) on their project team, the three key players shown in Figure 7.1 represent by far the main drivers of your implementation project. Each of the three entities has a significant but varied role to play during the project.

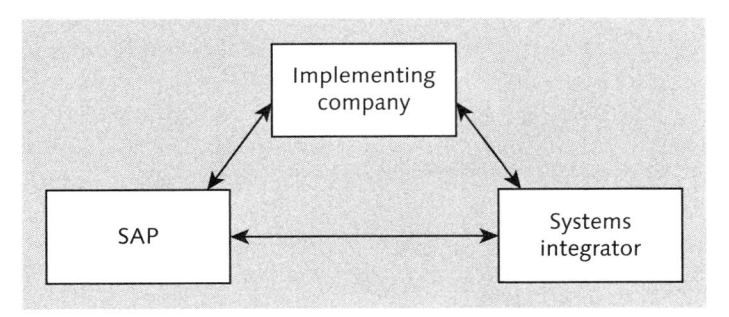

Figure 7.1 Primary Players in an SAP Implementation Project

Of these three key partners, the implementing company and its systems integrator are involved daily in the project. Together they work the deliverables and meet the milestone schedule. In contrast, while directly involved in the project, SAP does *not* have this daily working relationship with the deliverables.

Many project participants are surprised to learn that SAP is not a systems integrator. In fact, SAP rarely if ever takes on the integrator role for large-scale projects. It leaves this task to the professional systems integrators. SAP does, however, ensure the competence of systems integrators through close working relationships with certified SAP Partners and recognition of those with superior performance.

Table 7.1 outlines the roles that the implementing company, the systems integrator, and SAP itself all play during an implementation.

Organization	Primary Role
Implementing company	This is the overall owner of the delivered system, and the one that pays for all services. It is the decision-maker regarding solution design, business process changes, and adequacy of project deliverables. The implementing company will supply approximately half of the dedicated project team and the working locations for all team participants.
Systems integrator	The systems integrator ensures that the system is delivered to specification and operates to technical requirements. It provides resources to guide configuration and custom object development, and acts as an on-site SAP technical resource for the project team. The systems integrator will provide the remaining half of the full-time project team. Integrator staff will normally operate at implementing company locations.
SAP	SAP provides the application software that will constitute the company SAP system. It can assign specialized consultant resources to the project team as needed, and makes technical and development services available on a contract basis.

Table 7.1 Roles for the Implementing Company, Systems Integrator, and SAP

This book has already covered one significant SAP contribution: the intellectual property contained in the ASAP methodology. As we mentioned earlier, SAP focuses almost entirely on application software and leaves systems integrator activities in the hands of its partners. Instead, SAP will handle activities such as user licenses, technical issues with system performance, training of the project team, and technical support services. Additionally, for many projects SAP assigns a senior executive as a project sponsor and makes that person the primary point of contact for questions from your company.

7.1 Consultant Resources

The provisioning of specialized consultant resources is an area where SAP plays a more involved role. In the case of recently released or highly complex applications, SAP makes technical consultants available to augment the systems integrator project team. Otherwise, this essential expertise might not be available on the systems integrator project team. As you might expect, the numbers of consultants assigned will be fairly small—usually less than 10 even in a large-scale SAP implementation project.

Your company would contract directly with SAP for these resources. Contracting will define the types of consultants required, the duration of their assignment, and the rates of compensation provided. These contracts reflect the defined scope of SAP consultant resources on the project. As a rule, these consultants are treated as full members of the project team and given direction by the systems integrator workstream leads. While the consultants remain SAP employees, they are essentially subrogated to work under the management of the systems integrator.

> **Tip**
> For human resources purposes, an SAP point of contact will liaison with the group. This point of contact is usually appointed from the SAP technical services organization.

These SAP technical consultants perform a series of very valuable project roles. Their high level of subject matter expertise and knowledge of supported applications make them essential participants in all project phases. As part of blueprinting, they will conduct in-depth prototype sessions for your project team. This helps those less familiar with the application to see how the application can be utilized within company business processes.

During realization, the SAP consultant resources prove of great assistance in areas where in-depth application expertise is at a premium, such as configuration and test script preparation. Helping the project team to design rigorous test scripts that verify application performance will prove of great importance. Finally, during hypercare, the SAP consultants are often able to target root causes of reported incidents based on this same expert skill set.

The SAP consulting contract stipulates the number of working hours each consultant is assigned to the project. Obviously these amounts can be negotiated upward or downward as project circumstances permit. The hours are stipulated on an annual basis; hourly requirements can be adjusted as well.

7.2 Custom Development

Virtually every implementing company receives a warning at the beginning of its project about the dangers of modifying SAP. Sometimes these warnings are clear-cut and easily understood. Other times, the message gets blurred and understanding is lost. After all, the whole process of constructing workflows, reports, interfaces, conversions, enhancements, forms, and portals (WRICEFPs) or custom objects consists of *some* modification. It is important to be clear regarding the degrees of distinction.

To some extent, nomenclature is to blame. Custom objects *are* modifications — but not all modifications will create problems. For the purposes of this discussion we can subdivide modifications into two types: enhancements and modifications. Figure 7.2 illustrates the distinction between an enhancement and a modification. Enhancements are those forms of customization (of which there are many) that the SAP system will support. Modifications, on the other hand, represent those forms of customization that SAP does not support and will likely cause future problems for any company that chooses to implement them.

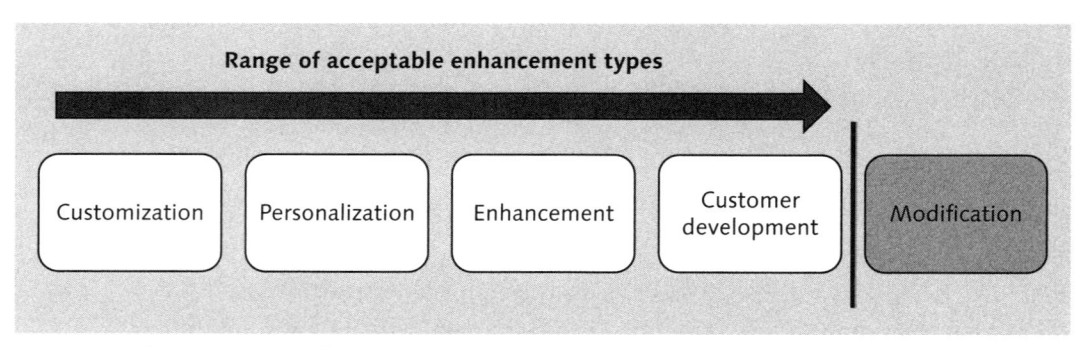

Figure 7.2 Forms of SAP Enhancement

Enhancements range from customization to customer developments. At the very end of the array is the SAP modification. Let's focus for a moment on the implications of each on the overall system:

- **Customization**
  Customization is simply another term for configuration. It permits the implementing company to adapt the SAP system to its own specific business uses. Customizations include such items as building a set of company codes, profit

centers, or sales organizations. These unique identifiers for how you will do business are built by the systems integrator. Customizations are a common feature of the implementation process and have no long-term negative system impact.

- **Personalization**
  This type of enhancement is similar to customization. However, in the case of personalization the focus is on end users or groups of end users. Personalizations simplify or accelerate business transactions by making navigation more user-specific or by building screens that assist end users. Personalizations are also a common feature of the implementation process and have no long-term negative system impact.

- **Enhancement**
  When an implementing company requires some type of derivative functionality to a standard SAP operation, this will generally be known as an *enhancement*. SAP recognizes that not all implementing companies opt to use the system in the same way. For example, your company may choose to utilize a natural rebates process in order-to-cash, which would involve the use of user exits in free goods, sales order processing, and customer billing.

  To support this type of option, SAP has designed *user exits* and *customer exits* that reinforce customer-requested add-ons. Enhancements allow your company to add code that meets specific requirements. They are tracked through a system feature called an SAP Software Change Registration (SSCR). If the SSCR has been completed and approved, SAP guarantees that it will support the enhancement in future releases.

- **Customer development**
  Larger-scale enhancements may involve creation of programs, data dictionary objects, or function modules. These substantial adjustments to SAP functionality must be carefully planned, developed, and tested. If performed correctly and documented in an SSCR, SAP will support the development during future releases. We'll spend more time on this option shortly.

- **Modification**
  Any changes to the SAP system conducted outside the standard processes described above are known as *modifications*. The system recognizes them as adjustments to normal functionality and has them identified in the customer namespace. However, modifications have no ongoing credentialed status. This means that while the modification may work in your current system, any

future change to that system, such as an upgrade, may disturb or disable that modification.

This last condition occasions some warnings about modifications. Whether developed by internal IT resources or third-party organizations, their effects can prove to be disastrous. Conducting an upgrade with non-approved modifications creates an untenable situation. The upgrade may simply not be possible without deleting the modification. This also highlights the significant advantages in contracting with SAP-certified systems integrators, which would never make such unauthorized system changes.

If conducted in these "under-the-radar" conditions, the modification's creators and installers may not provide quality documentation to sufficiently explain the changes actually made or the reasons for them. Additionally, the SSRC registration information may not have been delivered.

When the time comes to upgrade your system to a later version, the previously invisible costs of the modification now become clear. To remedy the situation, your company may find itself conducting exhaustive reviews of all systems. Even then, fully identifying the impact of the modifications will prove challenging. Further, the cost to rebuild those modifications according to correct procedures may be prohibitive.

This long analysis of the different enhancement types allows us to understand where SAP adds value in the process. When your company's choice lies between creating sub-optimal modifications or building robust, long-lasting solutions, SAP has an answer. The customer development enhancement option is intended to furnish your company with an effective alternative to highly undesirable modifications.

> **Trail Marker**
>
> This terminology can become rather twisted. We have made a distinction between modifications and SAP-produced system enhancements in support of complex company business processes. Generically, these enhancements are *custom developments*. However, to distinguish them from other types of enhancements and modifications, we have adopted the term *customer development*.

SAP customer development operations builds requested customer solutions that are outside the scope of existing SAP applications. The SAP customer development team constructs software that meets your company's requirements and, best of all, integrates seamlessly with core SAP functionality. SAP also supports these solutions through upgrades and enhancements.

When coupled with an SAP implementation, your company will usually handle customer development work as a "project within a project." Your company agrees to a contract with SAP for the construction of the solution. After both parties have signed the contract, the resulting project is managed through a variant of the previously discussed ASAP methodology. Known as *assemble-to-order*, it outlines the steps required to bring your development to reality.

Your company could potentially accrue cost savings from using the SAP custom development team. In some cases, SAP incorporates the customer development as part of its standard application package. SAP makes this decision when additional customers have need for similar functionality. In those situations, SAP will adjust the pricing for your customer development in the form of cost sharing and make the enhancement available to other customers.

7.3 Software Fixes

During the course of any SAP implementation project, issues will arise regarding potential software errors in the system. As with any large-scale system such as SAP, users continuously report software errors. When you discover errors during the implementation project, technical resources assigned to your team must identify the error, find a fix for it, and apply it to the project system.

SAP has developed a mechanism to track and resolve software errors called the Online Service System, or OSS Notes. This service system supplies project teams and sustainment groups with the latest status on identified software errors. Because it is Web-based, it requires minimal direct participation from SAP technical resources.

The OSS Notes system does require careful use, however. As Figure 7.3 indicates, the project team must first verify that the issue is associated with SAP code. Your team will have to initially rule out any possible code errors introduced during your project by the systems integrator or other third parties. Otherwise, the issue may prove to result from non-SAP code and an OSS Note won't resolve the issue.

Such non-SAP code changes include custom developments delivered during the project; OSS Notes focus on SAP base code only.

Once your project team has eliminated non-SAP code as a potential source of the problem, the technical resources can review the OSS Notes database. This review requires access to an SAP UserID. Because your company now has an SAP system installed or is in the process of implementing an SAP system, it will have received an SAP UserID. This ID verifies that the user is associated with the particular company installation.

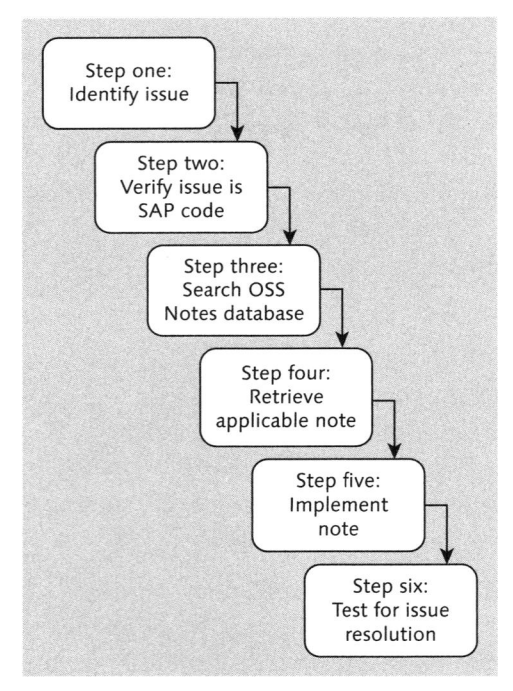

```
Step one:
Identify issue
    ↓
Step two:
Verify issue is SAP code
    ↓
Step three:
Search OSS Notes database
    ↓
Step four:
Retrieve applicable note
    ↓
Step five:
Implement note
    ↓
Step six:
Test for issue resolution
```

Figure 7.3 Software Fix Process Using OSS Notes

With the SAP UserID, your project team can execute step three. This means logging on to the OSS Notes database and searching for symptom descriptions similar to those you are experiencing. For several reasons, this process is not particularly straightforward. The search will likely identify several possible solutions to the problem. However, only the right solution will remedy the problem, so you must find the specific OSS Note. OSS Notes apply only to specific application versions. If your company's version is more recent than that used for the OSS Note, then that solution will not work.

Additionally, each OSS Note contains an implementation status. The note description specifies which notes can be implemented and which cannot. This latter status indicates that while the problem is known, no code fix is currently available to repair it. When this occurs, the note may identify certain steps that will provide workarounds for the problem.

A status indicating a note can be implemented means that a code fix to solve the problem is available. Your project team can then download the fix and apply it to the system. Any fix requires testing to verify that it does indeed resolve the problem, so your team should test the solution in the development and quality assurance environments before posting it to the production environment. Clearly, this is one of those cases applicable to change control. Assuming all testing verifies that the fix does indeed repair the problem, the fix will receive a change order assignment and then be transported to the production environment through normal processes.

OSS Notes works extremely well as a mechanism for resolving SAP software issues. During the SAP implementation project, the systems integrator will handle most needed repairs. After the project is complete and the system is live, your company sustainment organization will conduct issue resolution.

7.4 Training

SAP has a well-developed education and training organization. It offers educational support to implementing companies in a number of areas. These offerings break down into the three core areas shown in Figure 7.4.

7.4.1 Awareness Training

Awareness training, or project team preparation training, has the most immediate value to your company. These courses build an early SAP baseline competency among those assigned to the project team. Many members of your team may have limited experience with the SAP system and will need assistance in quickly getting up to speed. Awareness training addresses this need.

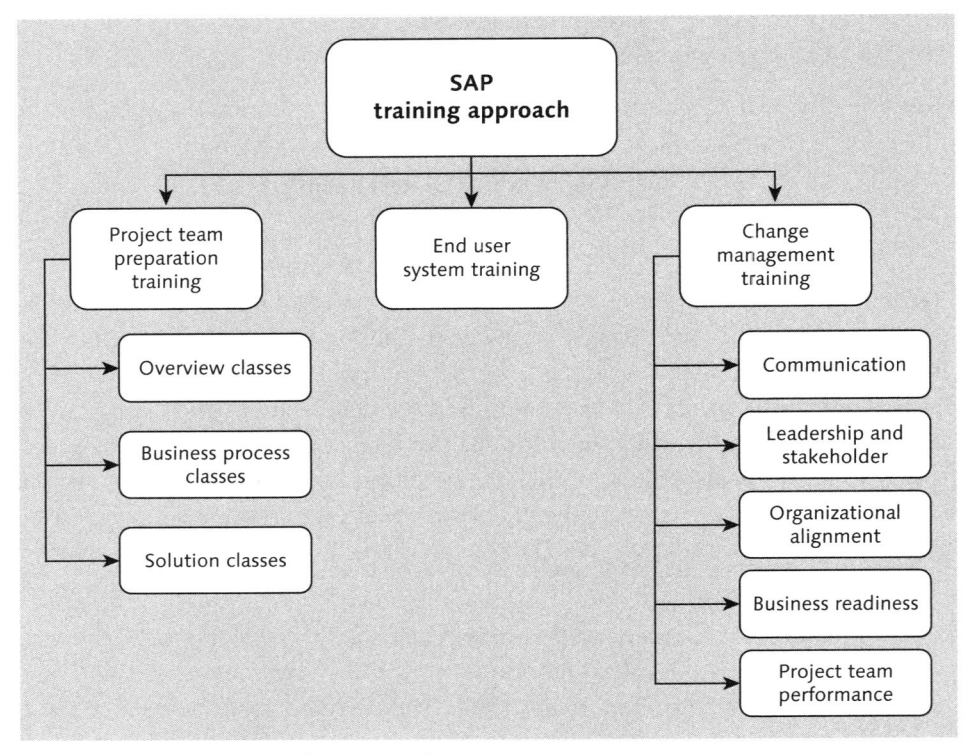

Figure 7.4 SAP Education and Training Solutions

Project team preparation training divides into three categories: overview classes, business process classes, and solution classes. For a project team in the process of forming during project preparation, the entire team or project leadership will likely participate in an SAP overview. This class reviews the entire range of business process transactions supported by SAP. The course demonstrates how transactions can vary through company business processes, from sales order receipt to delivery of finished product.

7.4.2 Overview Sessions

SAP offers these overview courses in a variety of settings. They include public courses where attendees travel to the course location, as well as classes conducted at your company location, the course instructor travels to the site while attendees remain at the workplace. For obvious reasons, you are likely to prefer that sessions be held at your company in this early stage of the project. This familiar setting gives your team time to become acquainted and encourages sharing of perspectives as the instruction progresses. These overview sessions are pre-packaged and will apply to a range of implementing companies, including your own.

> **Pitfall Alert**
>
> Make sure that your project team is well-trained in SAP. Each team member should become familiar with the purpose and operation of relevant SAP transaction sets. Project preparation offers the best time to complete team awareness training. Plan for extensive training up front and ensure that your team attends any needed sessions.

Once your team has completed any designated overview courses, it can then move on to business process courses. These courses provide more in-depth coverage. For example, where the overview course touches on materials procurement, individual business process courses address more specific subjects, such as direct materials procurement and indirect procurement. These courses build an even deeper knowledge and greater SAP system competency.

Solution classes are the final step in project team training. In solution courses, instruction focuses either on detailed transactions or more technical subjects such as configuration of master data or setting up SAP infrastructure. These classes are intended to build mastery skills among your team.

As classes progress from awareness to mastery level, the number of project team participants per class likely decreases. Whereas the overview sessions will enroll a sizeable portion of the project team, mastery sessions will require only one or two attendees. Many companies believe that attending a public session may make the most sense for small groups. Public sessions bring together participants from diverse SAP clients across global locations. Attendees then have the advantage of seeing and hearing how different companies operate SAP. This information can be of great assistance in building a broader context among your project team.

7.4.3 End-User System Training

End-user training assumes greater and greater importance as your project moves into realization and final preparation. The project team will have received its needed training and is now in the midst of delivering the final system. Project success will depend on carefully managed training of end users. Every one of your end users must become proficient in the skills required for system operation.

End-user training differs substantially from project team training. The objective of project team training was to learn the vanilla SAP system (that is, basic SAP with no customer-specific augmentation) and how it functioned. However, your end users will not operate a vanilla system. The configurations and custom objects now built into your system make it unique to the specific needs of your company. To the extent that your system contains extensive custom objects and widespread configuration, the end-user training should reflect these changes.

As a result, the training courses cannot be pre-packaged like the initial team training was. Instead, the training will require specific design and development that reflects your individual system. Both SAP and the major systems integrators build end-user courses designed to teach skills related to your system. The choice of which entity to use—that is, SAP or the contracted systems integrator—will be addressed during your contracting process.

SAP has a well-developed methodology for constructing end-user training materials. Analysis of training requirements is conducted during blueprinting. Its purpose is to identify those processes that are most impacted by system configurations and custom objects. Using the pre-packaged training materials previously discussed, it would then prove possible to assess the likely curriculum design.

Those courses developed would be supported by classroom instructional materials, simulations, quick reference guides, and hands-on exercises to solidify learning. Chapter 20 provides a general discussion on the development and instruction of end-user training materials and should be used as a reference here.

7.4.4 Change Management Training

In keeping with the concept of an SAP system implementation as a business transformation experience, SAP assigns considerable importance to change management. Citing evidence showing that human performance factors are key to achieving successful implementation results, change management is the tool best adapted to address these factors. When end users are able to execute system technology and effectively operate within the context of transformed business processes, the prospects of success are considerably improved.

Return to Figure 7.4, in which change management preparation is subdivided into five separate elements. Again, most large systems integrators will also provide change management services; which organization takes the lead role will be a function of contracting.

Many of the SAP change management services are delivered through a classroom environment or facilitated sessions. This approach shifts the key organizational attendees out of their normal roles and onto those most important to change management.

SAP change management resources work with the organization to develop robust communication plans aligned to the needs of target groups. This same approach works to align leaders and stakeholders on the requirements for successful change. This will involve helping leaders understand the changes, addressing their impacts on company operations, and seeking ways to support the changes at all levels of the company.

The business transformation will also likely involve changes in the organizational structure. This may include reporting relationships, the creation of new organizations, or changes in global responsibilities. SAP change management resources work closely with the implementing company's human resource organization to address how these organizational changes can best be carried out as the project progresses.

Business readiness and project team effectiveness are closely related. At the line level, change management may come down to policies, procedures, work instructions, and quick reference guides for end users. The project team will be the primary delivery agency for these tools and must be fully prepared to perform this change management role. SAP change management resources will assist in supporting these activities as well.

A successful change management program will require careful planning and attention to those business processes experiencing the most substantial transformations. Chapter 19 on change management provides greater detail on this important process, irrespective of whether it is carried out by SAP or the contracted systems integrator.

7.5 Technical Services

Even with a systems integrator in place, the implementing company may well still need support from SAP Active Global Support (AGS). At first glance, an implementing company might wonder why it would need such services. After all, it has contracted with a systems integrator to assist with the implementation. It has also engaged with SAP through software licensing fees. Implementing company executives may believe that this combination will cover any eventuality.

While all this may be true, it really does not cover *every* eventuality. Whereas your systems integrator may do an excellent job in assisting with system setup and operation, that organization may lack the in-depth competence and experience required to resolve complex SAP systems issues. As a general rule, SAP licensing fees cover the use of systems software and changes to it. Ongoing support for the system is left to the implementing company. Some companies are extremely well-prepared for that role and others are not.

It's somewhat like buying a car. When the consumer buys a car, the manufacturer agrees to supply a defect-free vehicle. But that purchasing contract makes no claim about the ability of the buyer to maintain the car properly or even to drive it in accordance with state laws. Once the title changes hands, all that is up to the new owner. While the manufacturer might wish the buyer well, continuing responsibility for the vehicle is left up to new owner.

Things *can* go wrong with an SAP system. In most cases, when things do go wrong, it stems from a company's lack of familiarity with system nuances. Some SAP system components may create tricky issues. These issues can further manifest themselves in such symptoms as portal processing difficulties, inflated infrastructure transaction volumes, and interface performance shortfalls. These will make a huge difference in user satisfaction with the system. Resources available from SAP AGS can help implementing companies to address these kinds of complex problems.

SAP makes available a range of technically based services to assist implementing companies with infrastructure and application challenges. Many of those services fall under a heading referred to as *safeguarding*. SAP targets these service offerings to the special needs of implementation projects and operates them on a time-and-material contract basis. Your company indicates the range of services required and, working closely with SAP AGS, comes to an agreement regarding the number of hours to be contracted.

Once the contract is executed, a *total quality manager* (TQM) is assigned and becomes the operational point of contact for the engagement. This individual both manages the contract activities with the implementing company and works as a conduit between the implementing company and SAP AGS.

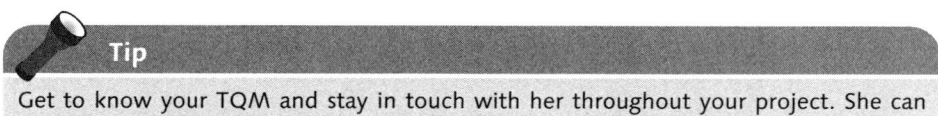

> **Tip**
>
> Get to know your TQM and stay in touch with her throughout your project. She can greatly assist you in identifying SAP-related issues and tracking them through to resolution. SAP is a huge, geographically dispersed company. You cannot do it alone, but your TQM will immediately know whom to contact and how to phrase the problem. Make use of her!

Figure 7.5 shows the range of services provided under safeguarding.

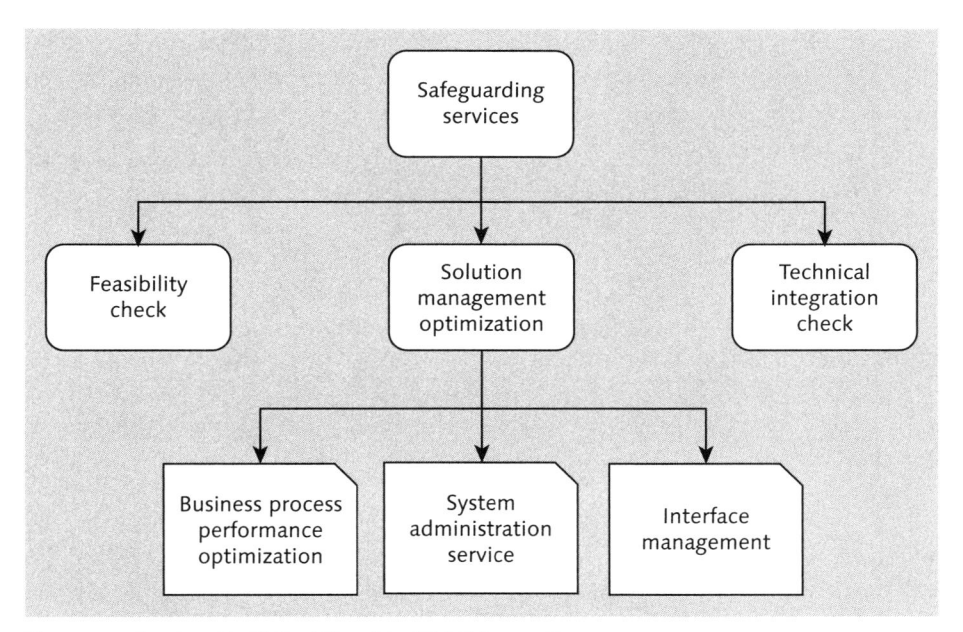

Figure 7.5 Services Portfolio Offered by SAP Safeguarding

Let's take a look at each.

7 | SAP's Role in the Project

▶ **Feasibility check**

This three-to-five-day data-gathering step is conducted during the later stages of business blueprinting. The information collected becomes the foundation for any subsequent safeguarding activities. Focused on applications and technology, the feasibility check assesses exactly where your company project stands relative to any potential systems issues.

The feasibility check begins by using documentation generated from blueprinting. It will identify the integration levels inherent in the design, the number and scope of custom development objects, and expected volumes associated with system usage. Just a word of caution, though: The feasibility check is very SAP-centric. It emphasizes the collection of information relevant to how SAP works in your environment. It will not focus on such items as integrator performance or the adequacy of configuration. SAP AGS is very clear about setting boundaries related to your systems integrator. The safeguarding team will not offer assessments of integrator performance or make suggestions about how the integrator might perform differently. Everything is focused on gathering data to find how the system is designed and its effects on SAP functionality.

Thus, on the application side, the intent is to describe how your company will use the SAP system and for what purposes. The check intends to identify any risks in how you intend to use the SAP system. Figure 7.6 gives a very high-level view of a feasibility check output.

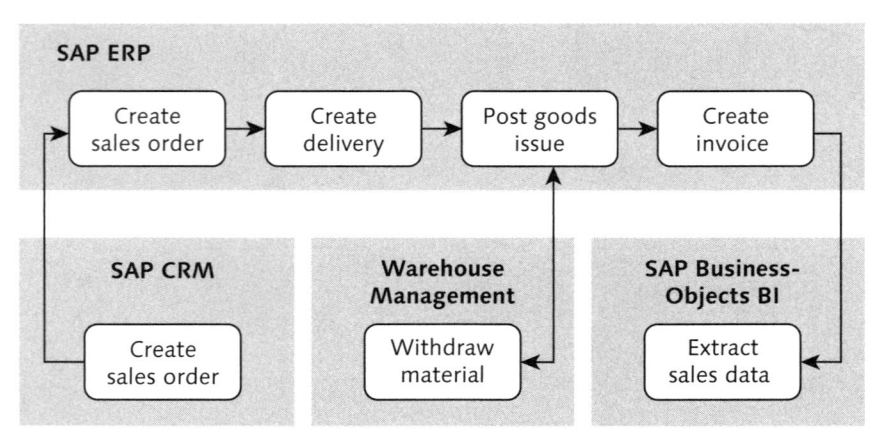

Figure 7.6 Simple Feasibility Check

A similar assessment takes place on the technology side. This involves painting a portrait of the solution landscape with all SAP and non-SAP components, including the operating system and database. The feasibility check team will examine the number and types of interfaces and their expected record volumes.

Once the feasibility check is complete, your company will have a better understanding of how its system is expected to perform. You will also have a good understanding of any risks affecting the stability and reliability of the SAP solution.

- **Technical integration check**
  The safeguarding team performs this four-day technical integration check (TIC) at the conclusion of the realization phase. By this point in your project, all configuration and custom objects should have been tested, and all infrastructure should be in place and working (with the exception of the production environment). Using the baseline information collected during the feasibility check, the TIC team can now evaluate how the as-built system performs in real time.

  The TIC team will utilize performance benchmarks to examine such areas as central processing unit usage to identify where bottlenecks may occur; to assess database performance in executing custom object transactions; and to estimate the impact of database volume consumption over time. The TIC team will issue a final report documenting the issues it has identified, in order of importance to future operations.

- **Solution management optimization**
  This suite of services has numerous components. Each addresses a specific target area and can be accomplished in the latter portion of realization. The service provides an assessment of any challenges the implementing company is likely to face.

  - **Business Process Performance Optimization**
    The safeguarding team will perform end-to-end analyses of selected essential company core business processes. This will include a trace analysis of the individual steps for each selected process, an analysis of the performance of any custom objects in those processes, and a review of any non-optimized structured query language (SQL) statements. This latter has the potential to greatly slow processing times and, when repaired, can greatly accelerate the timing.

- **System Administration Service**
  In this service, the safeguarding team works closely with the implementing company or systems integrator basis team. The objective involves critical back-office procedures that may impact overall SAP system performance. It will include such areas as core interface (CIF) monitoring processes, data consistency check, live cache administration, system performance, and back-up and recovery operations.

- **Interface Management**
  This services centers on the performance of interfaces to legacy systems that were constructed during realization. Using specifically designed datasets that mimic likely volumes in the production environment, the safeguarding team verifies that the interfaces will perform at expected levels. If issues arise, the team will examine the code created to find potential remedies for the problems.

- **MaxAttention**
  SAP AGS also makes available a service called "MaxAttention." The service is not specifically intended for SAP implementation projects but is certainly available and useful for an implementation. It places full-time quality management resources at the company site. They act as integral members of the project team: Using information gained from real-time understanding of project issues, they coordinate the overall SAP response to all service problems.

> **Trail Marker**
>
> Many companies feel that having SAP AGS resources on site greatly assists with communication on service needs. Ranging from problem reporting and follow-up to assisting with OSS Note reviews to monitoring service levels, a MaxAttention team can facilitate resolution for many of the technical needs of the project team—especially in that critical time of go-live and hypercare.

7.6 Value Management

You may remember from Chapter 3 that value management was one of the workstreams identified in the ASAP methodology. It addresses how to get the most value from your company's SAP investment.

Unfortunately, many companies fail to realize the potential business benefit of their SAP investment. After listening to implementing company senior executives voice concerns about the value they were receiving from their system investments, SAP responded by creating a value management practice. Its purpose is twofold: to demonstrate the value of implementing the SAP system, and to assist implementing companies in maximizing their own return. Over the years, this practice has matured greatly and it now offers a number of very valuable services.

At the foundation of the SAP value management program is the performance benchmarking database. Established in conjunction with the Americas' SAP Users' Group (ASUG), this database contains performance information submitted by thousands of companies. It also has data on over 30 end-to-end business processes and hundreds of key performance indicators.

> **Tip**
>
> Take advantage of the SAP process benchmarking services. The database contains considerable information relevant to your company. It allows you to see where your company stands relative to similar companies. Further, it can give perspective to your blueprinting activities by indicating the range of improvement that you can expect from specific process changes.

Reports from the benchmarking database permit your company to select a peer group for comparison. Based on such measures as unplanned system downtime, support staff per 100 active users, number of critical interfaces, and IT spend per employee, your company can rate its position relative to similar companies. For each measure, your company will see the peer group average and the score of the top 25th percentile. Nor is the data limited to systems-related measures. You can use this same comparison process for one or more business processes such as procurement, supply chain planning, and order-to-cash.

Your company can use this information on its own or with the assistance of the SAP value management team to track where you stand relative to peer organizations. Using this benchmarking data helps set executive expectations regarding the types of improvements that can be accomplished with the SAP system. Your company can then incorporate these value improvements in the project metrics and assess progress as the system is implemented and placed in operation.

Figure 7.7 illustrates the output framework that your company might use to define business process benefits. The benefit categories coincide with the five major project workstreams used in this book. Once specified, value targets give the workstreams a metric to assess their progress in benefit realization. The categories are color-coded to indicate the source of benefit: revenue, efficiency, or cost-reduction. The framework also supplies a conservative benefit estimate and the most likely result.

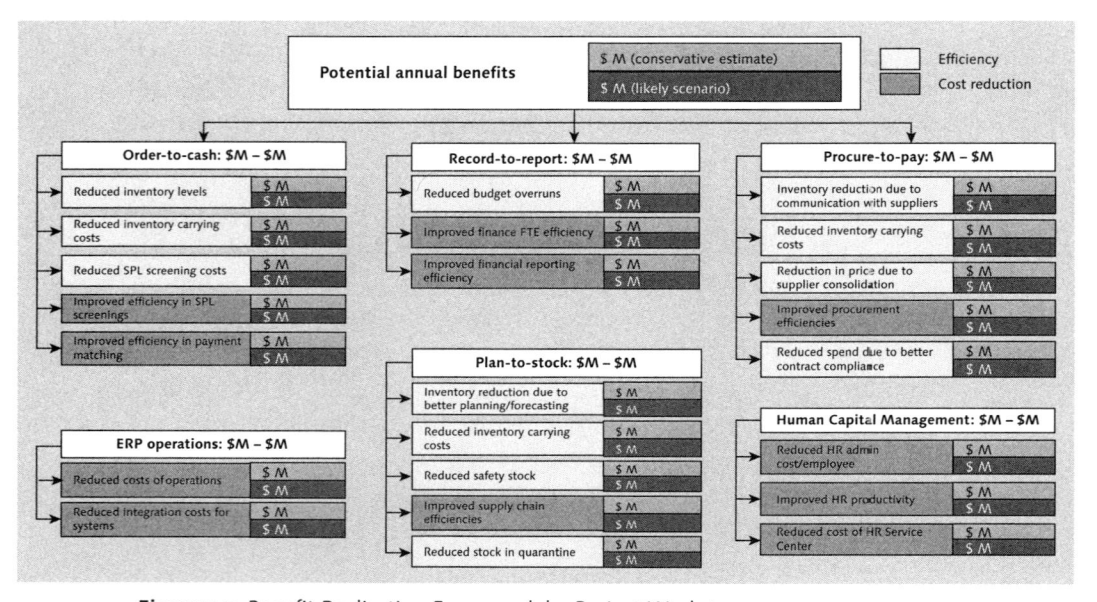

Figure 7.7 Benefit Realization Framework by Project Workstream

SAP also offers a value academy, which provides hands-on assistance to those companies that need to identify the full range of potential business benefits from the SAP system. Offered in a number of formats such as by industry or line of business, the academy consists of a three-day workshop. Topics range from business case development to benchmarking to value-based governance. To date, several hundred companies have participated in these sessions. They have gained perspective on identifying benefits and effectively presenting information to company boards of directors.

SAP will play a key role in the project. Its participation may not be as visible as that of the systems integrator or the implementing company, but the contributions are equally valuable.

Now that you have selected the systems integrator and aligned SAP with projected operations, we will move even deeper into project preparation. Our next subject, project planning, looks at the complexities of building a reliable schedule for your project.

This chapter outlines several aspects of project planning. These include defining the parameters of the project schedule, setting top-level requirements, and adopting cost savings targets for the project.

8 Project Planning

This chapter covers guidelines for planning an SAP implementation project. Rather than discussing planning methodology for several project types, our chapter focuses on a single type: the global SAP implementation. Planning techniques used for global implementation timelines and deliverables are the most ambitious and can easily be adjusted to fit the needs of smaller-scale projects. Our discussion builds on the ASAP implementation framework outlined in Chapter 3.

Following up from Chapter 2, where we reviewed SAP business transformation, this chapter also examines two additional planning elements: top-level requirements and achieving cost savings. They must be defined at this early stage of the SAP implementation project because they constitute the major process changes that will be incorporated into the SAP blueprint.

- **Setting top-level requirements**
  The project begins with a very general set of requirements. As the project team commences its work, project sponsors will engage in constant dialogue regarding requirements or functions they would like the system to perform. As the project moves forward, they will provide additional input and review the functional workstreams' initial formulations. Setting these early boundaries on blueprinting expectations saves workstreams from exploring unneeded options or spending valuable time on unnecessary pursuits.

- **Achieving cost savings**
  A great many SAP implementation projects contain cost savings targets set by the company. These targets may include savings associated with both improved process efficiency and improved information technology generated by

the new system. The inventory of these cost targets would be maintained by the program management office, which will periodically assess whether the project is achieving those goals.

Before arriving at top-level requirements and cost savings, we'll first discuss the overall project schedule. It will give us a framework to cover requirements and cost savings.

8.1 Defining the Project Schedule

The duration of the project depends on its scope. This in turn will depend on a number of factors. Almost universally, anyone hearing the word "scope" immediately begins to think in terms of the business processes involved in the project.

While this certainly represents one part of the scope equation, it is only but a part. Other scope parameters may play a far larger role than business processes in determining project duration. Let's look at the total set of scope parameters, which include project complexity factors, overall complexity, implementation in waves, and the wave framework.

8.1.1 Project Complexity Factors

Project complexity provides an effective way of looking at scope. In this section, we will examine several contributors to project complexity. At its conclusion, we will use these components to generate an overall project complexity score.

Business Processes in the SAP Implementation

As a rule, the more business processes included in the SAP implementation project, the more complex it will be.

> **Trail Marker**
>
> We'll review several aspects of project complexity. Each one can individually exert substantial impact on the project schedule. Together, however, they definitely exert an effect. We will focus on determining this combined impact.

But the complexity of the individual business processes themselves also becomes a variable. For example, one project may include every company business process in a functional process area. Another project, on the other hand, may include only a single company business process and one functional area. The complexity and likely duration of the first project would exceed that of the second project. However, the one-process project could present a very similar level of complexity. It could redesign processes extensively and from the ground up. Assessing complexity demands close examination.

Another factor that will come into play under this same umbrella is the amount of business process change that the project introduces. Clearly, an SAP implementation project that retains most existing business processes will prove a far easier and more rapid task than its opposite. That undertaking is mostly technical, while an SAP implementation project that includes major business process changes will thoroughly stress test all facets of the project team.

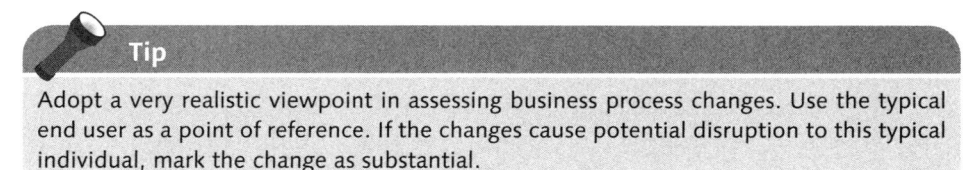

> **Tip**
>
> Adopt a very realistic viewpoint in assessing business process changes. Use the typical end user as a point of reference. If the changes cause potential disruption to this typical individual, mark the change as substantial.

Figure 8.1 illustrates this project complexity concept. From left to right, the project increases in the scale of business process complexity. A very complex project involves a substantial number of business processes, with planned changes in many of them. This complexity increases the length and depth of blueprinting, as well as systems testing and related activities. Both resources and time required for the project will be substantially less in the relatively simple projects.

Relatively simple	Somewhat complex	Very complex
Small number of business processes involved. Little business process change.	Moderate number of business processes involved. Some changes in those business processes.	Many business processes involved. Considerable change in business processes.

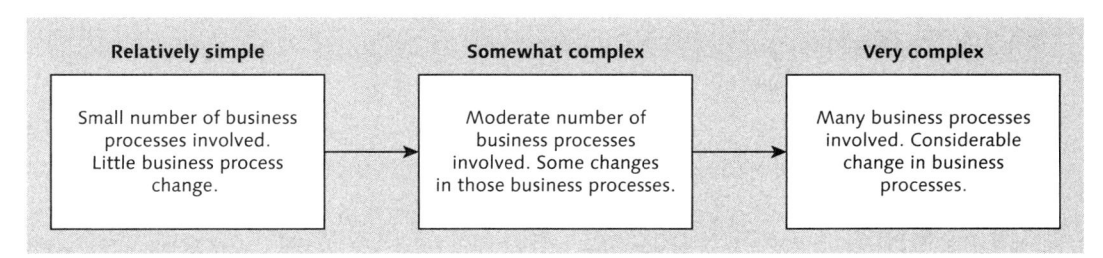

Figure 8.1 Dimensions of Business Process Complexity

Company Locations Participating in the Project

This same continuum applies to company locations. If a company has sales operations and manufacturing sites in only a single region, this greatly eases the challenges for system testing and end-user preparation. At the other end of the spectrum, companies with sales operations and manufacturing sites in multiple regions will find the SAP implementation to be a much more complex undertaking.

Considerable complexity will accumulate in a global operations framework, which has to account for statutory and regulatory requirements for several countries and regions. Additionally, differences in business processes between regions will require harmonization during the SAP implementation project. Finally, the multiple languages used within regions and built into the system will have to be factored into end-user preparation planning as well.

Figure 8.2 demonstrates the effects of geographical complexity on the SAP implementation project. Companies operating within the boundaries of a single continent and with only a few manufacturing facilities will find their way to a final go-live much faster than companies operating on a global basis. As geography expands, so too does scope and project team workload. Global projects, as a rule, take much longer to reach their final go-live than those limited to one or two continents.

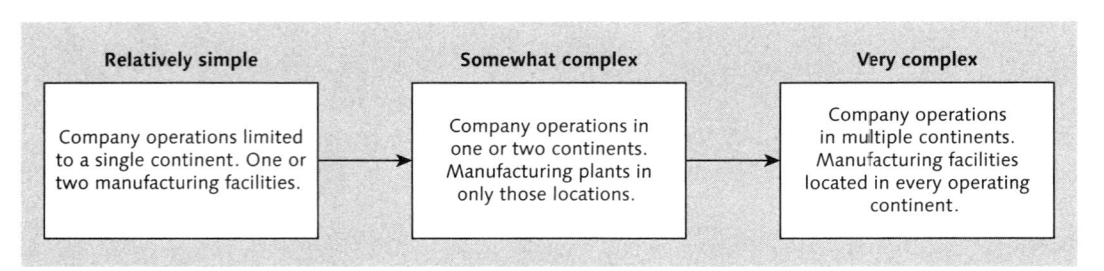

Relatively simple	Somewhat complex	Very complex
Company operations limited to a single continent. One or two manufacturing facilities.	Company operations in one or two continents. Manufacturing plants in only those locations.	Company operations in multiple continents. Manufacturing facilities located in every operating continent.

Figure 8.2 Dimensions of Company Geographical Scope

Number and Type of Legacy Systems Being Replaced by the SAP System

For purposes of our book, the term *legacy system* will be used to describe previously installed company systems that predate the SAP implementation project.

Although not all company legacy systems will be impacted by the SAP implementation project, some will no doubt be affected. In these situations, your company has a decision to make: It can continue to use the legacy system, or it can replace the legacy system with available SAP functionality.

> **Tip**
>
> The effects of legacy systems will be more visible to the IT members of the project team than business process members. Your IT colleagues will be familiar with the operational nuances and complexities of legacy systems. Make it a point to invite their input on this portion of the assessment.

Figure 8.3 indicates how the increase in legacy system replacement can affect the SAP implementation project. Where legacy systems are candidates for replacement, the number of such systems and their complexity definitely affects the SAP implementation project. Replacement of one or two secondary systems will have a modest effect on the project. In contrast, replacement of five or six core legacy systems simultaneously with the SAP system has a far larger effect.

Relatively simple	Somewhat complex	Very complex
One or two legacy systems are being replaced by the new SAP system.	A small number of core legacy systems are being replaced by the new SAP system.	Several very complex, core legacy systems are being replaced by the new SAP system.

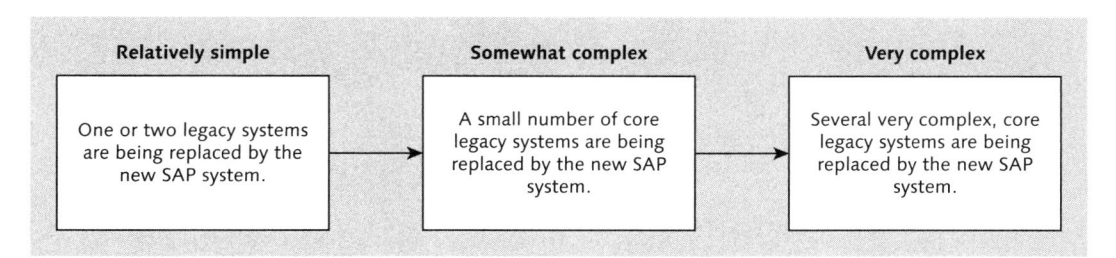

Figure 8.3 Dimensions of Company Legacy System Replacement Scope

When you decide to replace legacy systems, their data must be migrated to the SAP system during the project. The data migration process for core systems will be time-consuming and likely difficult. Additionally, previous legacy system users will have to transfer to the new SAP system and face the challenges of becoming familiar with a new system that is complex in its own right.

A corollary issue for the project team will be those legacy systems retained by the company but required to share functionality. For example, a legacy product lifecycle management (PLM) application in use by your company requires a mechanism to share bills of material and related data with the SAP system. This data sharing process is normally accomplished by using a "system interface" linking the two systems. Even a modest number of these complicated interfaces can extend the duration of an SAP implementation project.

Number of Expected Company SAP Users and Previous SAP Experience

Any implementing company with a broad base of experienced SAP users will find it far easier to conduct an SAP implementation project than a company that lacks previous SAP experience. Familiarity with the SAP system makes it easier to find effective project team resources. It also reduces the need for extensive user preparation and training to use the system.

Figure 8.4 illustrates the dimensions of prior company usage experience with the SAP system. In cases where previous company usage and understanding of the SAP system is high, the project becomes correspondingly easier. Users will intuitively understand operations of the new SAP system. Where a company does not have this previous user familiarity with the SAP system, all user understanding will have to be developed from scratch—including basic SAP competency within the company's project team.

Relatively simple	Somewhat complex	Very complex
Almost all company users are familiar with the SAP system.	Many company core users are familiar with the SAP system. Other users have no SAP experience.	Very few company users have experience with the SAP system.

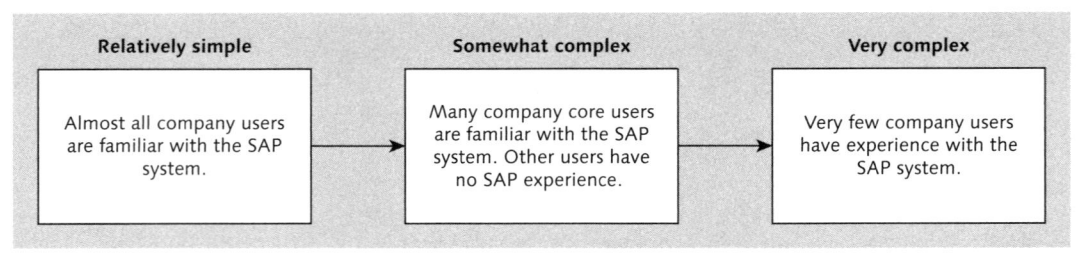

Figure 8.4 Dimensions of Company Prior SAP System Experience Scope

Number and Type of SAP Applications Included in the Implementation

The basic SAP functionality is contained in SAP ERP. It includes functionality for materials management, sales and distribution, and finance and controlling, among others. In addition to these core functions, SAP also makes available a number of more targeted applications.

These additional applications run the gamut from the SAP BusinessObjects Business Intelligence reporting tool to more specialized tools, such as the SAP Global

Trade Services (GTS) and the SAP Advanced Planning and Optimization (APO) modules. SAP GTS, for example, greatly enables international trade activities. It assures regulatory compliance and enhances electronic communication with customs authorities. Its installation requires considerable setup and testing with both third parties and participating governmental customs agencies.

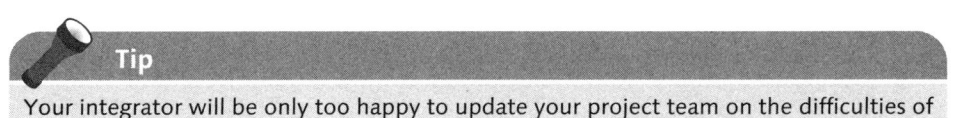

> **Tip**
> Your integrator will be only too happy to update your project team on the difficulties of specific SAP applications. It is one of the best sources for this type of information.

Figure 8.5 describes the continuum between implementing only the core SAP ERP functionality and that involved with implementing SAP ERP as well as several SAP applications. While there is no doubt that these applications are quite powerful and provide necessary functionality to your company, they are also often very complex to implement. As in the case with SAP GTS, they require a significant time investment from the project team, including the systems integrator and possible third-party organizations. You should carefully weigh the overall project plan timing when making the decision to implement several such applications concurrently.

Relatively simple	Somewhat complex	Very complex
The company SAP implementation includes only core modules from SAP ERP.	The company SAP implementation includes SAP ERP modules and a few SAP applications.	The company SAP implementation includes a large number of SAP applications in addition to SAP ERP.

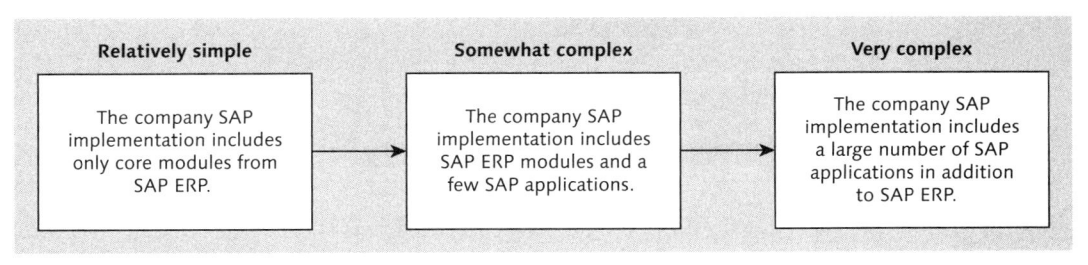

Figure 8.5 Dimensions of Included SAP Applications

Number of WRICEFPs Included in the SAP Implementation

Recall the role of system interfaces in the SAP solution set. During the early stages of the project, your team will identify the custom objects you need for core business processes. An initial listing of needed custom objects should be in place prior to the start of blueprinting. The list should be nearly finalized by the completion of blueprinting and localization.

Some custom objects, such as workflows, enhancements, and interfaces, entail extensive development work. Later on, they will also require extensive testing to confirm that they operate to specification. Relatively large numbers of difficult-to-develop custom objects will extend your project schedule.

Figure 8.6 indicates the range of custom object complexity for an SAP implementation project. In a relatively simple case, the implementing company has decided to build only a small number of custom objects. In a very complex case, the implementing company has chosen to include a large number of custom objects in its SAP system solution. Again, this may represent a purposeful business decision. However, it definitely impacts the project schedule. Developing and testing a large number of these objects—especially workflows, enhancements, and interfaces—greatly enlarges project difficulty and the level of effort required to deliver it.

Relatively simple	Somewhat complex	Very complex
The company SAP implementation includes few, if any, custom objects.	The company SAP implementation includes some custom objects, but only a few are complex.	The company SAP implementation includes a large number of complex custom objects.

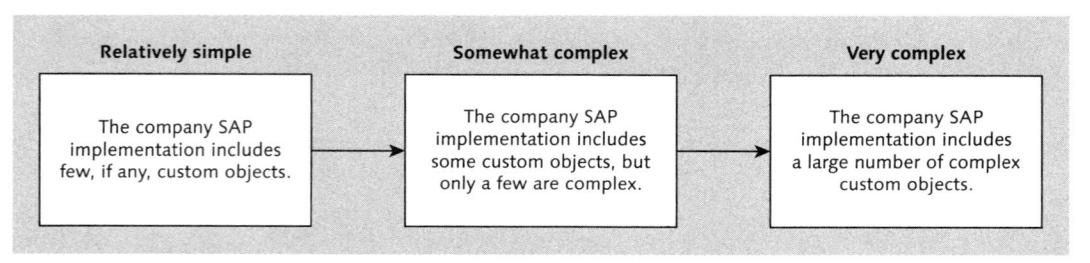

Figure 8.6 Dimensions of Included Custom Objects

8.1.2 Determining Overall Project Complexity

Systems integrator companies use algorithms to calculate project complexity. They then estimate the effects of that complexity on the overall project timeline. They make these calculations as a prudent business practice. Because it identifies their exposure to any factors that may produce project delays, they adjust project delivery schedules to reflect the complexity confronting the implementation. For an implementing company, it makes good sense to make similar calculations. Creating a risk-based project schedule outlines realistic timelines and specifies any up-front financial impacts to on-time project delivery.

Lower-complexity projects would, all other things being equal, have reduced delivery timing. On the other hand, projects with more complexity will require a much longer timeline. Each factor receives its own independent rating. For example, relatively simple project factors receive a two; somewhat complex factors receive a four; and very complex factors receive a six. This equation enables program management to assess where its project stands in comparison to these important dimensions.

Figure 8.7 reports the results of a sample project complexity assessment. As you can see, this particular SAP implementation project reflects a substantial degree of variability on its complexity ratings. The project demonstrates a low-complexity situation with legacy systems, but substantial complexity in its geographical locations, lack of user familiarity with the SAP system, and the large number of custom objects involved.

Complexity Factors	Relatively Simple	Somewhat Complex	Very Complex	Total
Business processes		4		4
Geographical locations			6	6
Legacy systems	2			2
User familiarity with the SAP system			6	6
Number of SAP applications involved		4		4
Number of custom objects involved			6	6
Total	2	8	18	28

Figure 8.7 Rating of Project Complexity Factors

A score of 28 places the project at the high end in terms of project complexity, which has a range from 12 to 36. The results indicate that this particular project should place great stress on site preparation, end-user training, and both integration and user acceptance testing. Project sponsors can use this information to apprise senior executives—who are likely less familiar with the demands of an SAP implementation—of the risks facing the project and their potential effects on the schedule.

8.1.3 Choosing a Deployment Approach

Each SAP implementation project must wrestle with the question of whether to deploy everything at once (the "big bang") or to deploy in waves.

Clearly, either approach has its advantages and drawbacks. The big bang approach potentially shaves time off the project schedule by delivering the entire SAP system at a single point in time. Thus, all users are able to use the system simultaneously. Additionally, the implementing company will be able to accrue system benefits earlier.

But big bang deployments entail substantial risks as well. They operate on the presumption that all parts of the SAP system are ready for implementation at a single point in time. If this presumption does not, in fact, hold true, the results can be quite profound. User problems with system operation can pour into the project team from all over the globe during hypercare. Not having lived through the rigors of post go-live support, the project team will probably be unprepared for this 24-hour, unceasing onslaught.

To be clear up front, this book is biased towards multi-wave implementations for global projects. The primary advantage of a multi-wave implementation is this: They do not put all the eggs of an implementing company in a single basket. Let's look at some of the pertinent advantages of a multi-wave implementation:

- Most importantly, multi-wave global implementations space out the risk and allow it to be handled in manageable chunks. In this way, the project team has the opportunity to learn as it goes. Mistakes made in one wave become the lessons learned for any following waves.

- Resources are also conserved in a multi-wave implementation. Instead of having all global resources working on the project simultaneously, only resources involved with the current wave participate in the implementation. As one wave completes and the project team moves on to the next wave, resources specific to that next wave are then ramped up as resources from the previous wave are rolled off.

- User preparation is far more targeted in a multi-wave implementation. Activities quite specific to a particular region, such as user training, super user recruitment, and role mapping, can receive the focus they require. Each region receives dedicated attention from the project team. As a result, user preparation is enhanced and the go-live flows more smoothly.

- Technical activities, such as custom object development, data migration, and systems testing, can be addressed within the framework of individual waves. The big bang increases risk by causing all these activities to be handled simultaneously.

Assuming that an SAP implementing company wants to proceed with a multi-wave deployment, it must then decide how many waves to plan for and which entities to assign to each wave.

8.1.4 Building the Implementation Wave Framework

For the most part, wave planning decisions revolve around company business operations. For example, if some regional business operations supply resources or products to other parts of the company, those must be implemented prior to that of the receiving regional operation.

> **Trail Marker**
> Waves come in all sizes and shapes. They can include regional groupings, as we have discussed here. They can also include functions such as supply chain or finance, companies within a multi-company organization, and geographies within a single region. The planning approaches we discuss next apply to all.

Additionally, if possible, any single region that represents a very high risk to the company should be scheduled among the final set of implementation waves. In this way, an implementing company can build the capability of its project team through earlier waves and then apply those skills to the more high-risk region. Figure 8.8 illustrates this concept. It shows four company geographical regions participating in the SAP implementation. Two of those regions have a "high" risk profile, one has a "medium" risk profile, and one has a "very high" risk profile.

Based on this projection, the project team would recommend—and likely have accepted—a three-wave solution. Due to supply chain considerations, the North American region would participate in the first implementation wave. Europe would have to precede Asia, but it lacks the overall business volume to justify its own wave, so it would combine with the medium-risk Latin America to make up the second implementation wave. Finally, the Asia region, with all its company supply chains in place, would participate in the third and final implementation wave.

Company Regions	North America	Europe	Latin America	Asia
Risk profile	High	Very high	Medium	Very high
Rationale	Major portion of company plant sites and revenues in this region. Supplies other regions. Complex 3PL and customer relationships.	Relatively low business volume. Entire OTC business process will be replaced by SAP system. Supplies Asia region.	Previous regional SAP usage. Considerable statutory and legal operating requirements.	No previous regional SAP usage. Existing ERP systems all country-based. Major growth area for company sales.
Recommended wave	One	Two	Two	Three

Figure 8.8 Potential Wave Structure for an SAP Implementation Project

Once an implementing company has decided to adopt the multi-wave implementation strategy and to ratify the three implementation waves, the next steps of project scheduling then begin. The ASAP methodology provides substantial assistance by supplying the framework for the elements to be scheduled. Blueprinting and localization will be conducted only once, but realization, final preparation, and go-live and support will be conducted three times—once for each implementation wave.

Figure 8.9 shows this three-wave approach. Once the full scope of configuration and testing is known, program management can identify the timing for realization, final preparation, and go-live and support activities.

> **Tip**
>
> As a rule of thumb, the combined realization and final preparation phases will take twice as long as the blueprinting and localization phases. Also, realization and final preparation for the first wave will take longer than those phases in later waves. The first wave will accomplish considerable configuration, custom object development, and master data conversion that will all be used by subsequent waves.

With the scheduling decisions in place, let's now turn, as promised, to top-level requirements and cost savings estimates.

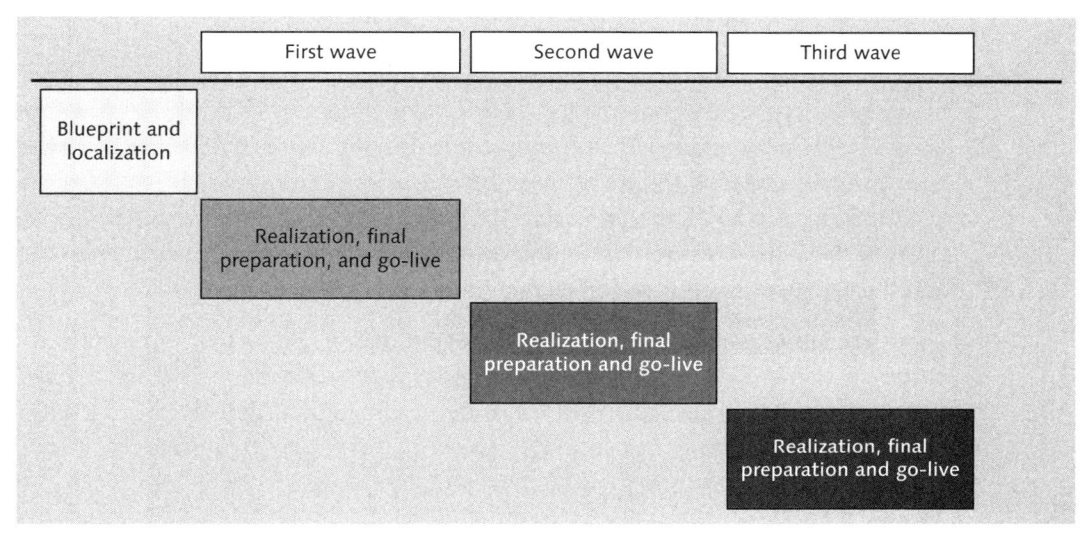

Figure 8.9 Three-Wave Implemention Project Schedule

8.2 Setting Top-Level Requirements

Recall from Chapter 2 the many ways in which an SAP implementation transforms company operations. In most cases, these business transformations are the company's primary reason for doing the implementation in the first place. Having a firm grasp on transformational requirements is the first step to achieving them.

The SAP implementation project also provides an opportune time for making needed business process changes. The SAP system dictates some process changes needed for its effective operation. Now is the time for company senior executives to give direction to the project team. As a means of giving direction to the project team, these changes will be defined as *top-level requirements*.

Later blueprinting activities will define the particulars of the SAP system design. Top-level requirements, on the other hand, enable senior executives to set the future course for the project. This can be done in two ways. In the first way, senior executives outline a set of transformation requirements. In the second and most common approach, functional business process leads work together to recommend top-level requirements. The two groups—functional leads and senior executives—hold a series of design meetings to review and agree on the requirement set.

This second approach has the advantage of using the more in-depth expertise of business process leads and leaving senior executives in a more familiar decision-making role. Rather than expressing desired outcomes in a very cut-and-dried fashion, these top-level requirements identify the process performance solutions that the new SAP system would enable.

These executive requirements sessions are best conducted as part of formal definition sessions. Participants include project sponsors, leadership from the systems integrator team, workstream leads, the program management office (PMO), and a trained facilitator. This last role assures that top-level requirements are collected and reviewed in a very systematic and deliberate manner.

Thus, a top-level requirement might be to simplify or reduce cycle time in certain processes. During this specification process, it will prove extremely helpful to have the participation of the project's systems integrator. Integrator staff can provide perspective on the SAP system's ability to support these top-level requirements. The performance gains envisioned in these top-level requirements can also result from business process changes made outside of the SAP system.

Table 8.1 lists the partial output from an early top-level requirements gathering session. Given the probable level of SAP system knowledge in the implementing company, these are expressed at a fairly general level. They capture points where senior executives want to have major business process improvements. Once enhanced, they would be in operation by the completion of the SAP project. The requirements do not yet capture the detailed design information that would assist in configuring the SAP system.

That step would come later, in the intensive blueprinting sessions. These top-level requirements are intended as guidance for that blueprinting activity and would be deployed to the project team for its use. As the table indicates, many of these requirements create shared responsibilities among business process workstreams. Where responsibilities are shared, those workstreams are listed in column two. The workstream with overall ownership for making the top-level requirement a reality is shown in column three.

Top-Level Requirement	Assigned Workstreams	Blueprint Ownership
1. Reduce time to complete contracting for new suppliers from 10 days to five days.	Procure-to-pay Plan-to-stock	Procure-to-pay
2. Improve the financial accuracy of sales and inventory forecasting process.	Plan-to-stock Record-to-report	Plan-to-stock
3. Decrease the number of shipments with incorrect customs documentation that are placed on process holds.	Order-to-cash Plan-to-stock	Order-to-cash
4. Enhance the accuracy and cycle time of indirect procurement supplier invoice payments.	Procure-to-pay	Procure-to-pay
5. Upgrade company financial consolidation and close times.	Record-to-report	Record-to-report
6. Improve the cycle time of accounts receivable from major customers in Asia and Latin America.	Order-to-cash Record-to-report	Order-to-cash
7. Upgrade the new hire provisioning process to ensure that all new hires are fully provisioned by first day on the job.	Human capital management	Human capital management

Table 8.1 Top-Level Requirements for an SAP Implementation Project

These top-level requirements are not intended to be all-encompassing. Rather, they represent those requirements that are connected to essential management business objectives. Nor do they preclude teams from identifying other, unrelated requirements, such as the need for a statutorily required invoice for Ecuador. The latter type of more specific requirement would not be included in the deployment process described in Table 8.1.

After blueprinting is complete, project sponsors conduct design reviews to examine exactly how these top-level requirements will be achieved. Time would be set aside to discuss each requirement in detail. The workstream that has ownership of the requirement would lead this discussion. Blueprinting results would not receive approval from project sponsors until each requirement is satisfactorily addressed.

> **Tip**
>
> The PMO can maintain an ongoing scorecard for these top-level requirements. The scorecard can be plotted on posters and distributed to each workstream. In this way, workstream staff gets a very real sense of the progress they are making.

Interim reviews would be conducted as the SAP implementation project progresses. During these interim reviews, process workstream leads report they steps they have taken to achieve the requirement at that point, and the results of those steps. In this way, these top-level requirements remain in full view during the SAP implementation project lifecycle.

8.3 Achieving Cost Savings

Closely aligned with top-level requirements are cost savings targets assigned to the project. Business transformations associated with an SAP implementation project can be stated either in terms of process improvements or cost savings achieved from those transformed processes. Often they are stated in terms of both. Top-level requirements, however, need not include cost savings. They may simply represent process improvements necessary to company operations.

Chapter 7 discussed value realization services as part of the range of assistance that SAP provides to companies. Cost savings initiatives within implementing companies can build on these value realization services, or they can use their own internal calculation methods.

These cost savings can be expressed in terms of hard or soft savings. *Hard cost savings* specify actual cost reductions, such as decreases in headcount or material costs as a result of the cost savings initiatives. They could also include process changes that improve company revenues.

These hard costs savings would be booked in the company annual financial planning process and expected to materialize as a result. Given its temporary nature, the savings generally would not be booked in the project budget. Rather, they would be booked in the functional organization that exercises leadership over the specific workstream involved. For example, if cost savings were realized in the procure-to-pay workstream, the company procurement organization would budget and take ownership for those results. This provides a very useful point of accountability.

Soft cost savings often fall more into the category of cost avoidance. Their status is more ambiguous. Generally, they cannot be booked as part of company financial plans or as part of any proposed project savings. They may include decreases in future working capital or reduced cash flow. Many companies take the view that soft cost savings must turn into hard dollar returns within a specified period (e.g., three years) or they will not be considered successfully proven.

Some cost savings attributable to SAP implementation projects can include headcount reductions closely connected to process improvements. Table 8.2 outlines several cost reductions—primarily from full-time employee (FTE) count decreases—associated with a hypothetical SAP implementation project. Many of these cost reductions stem from process automations associated with SAP operations. Clearly, others could be identified and added to the company list as a result of those top-level design activities.

Workstream Involved	Subprocess	Cost Savings Improvement	Benefit
Record-to-report	Cash management	▸ Daily electronic bank reconciliations ▸ Automation of manual clearing tasks	Reduced FTE required for cash management
	General ledger close	▸ Single chart of accounts with common rules and definitions ▸ Reduction in use of individual sales companies	Reduced FTE required for closes and reduced time to close
	Inter-company postings	▸ Automation of inter-company postings reduces manual coordination and inputs	Reduced FTE required for inter-company postings

Table 8.2 Potential Cost Savings for an SAP Implementation Project

Workstream Involved	Subprocess	Cost Savings Improvement	Benefit
	Financial reporting	▶ Single system for all sales reporting ▶ Global cost of goods reported in one system ▶ Supports U.S. GAAP reporting ▶ Global inventory visibility	Reduced FTE required for financial reporting
Order-to-cash	Pricing	▶ Manage contract expirations ▶ Online rebate payments	Reduced FTE to handle credit notes and improved accuracy for rebate payments
	Exports management	▶ Automated screening of customer and vendor shipments for sanctioned party lists (SPL)	Reduced FTE to process SPL screenings
	Shipments	▶ Automated generation of customs documents and shipment request forms	Reduced FTE to process late shipments
	Accounts receivable	▶ Automated invoice matching	Reduced FTE for invoice processing
Procure-to-pay	Spend control	▶ Regional spend visibility established to review suppliers and specifications	Reduced material spend
	Procurement efficiency	▶ Linkage of all procurement processes through workflows (sourcing, contracting, order, and payments) to reduce errors	Reduced FTE for procurement processing

Table 8.2 Potential Cost Savings for an SAP Implementation Project (Cont.)

Workstream Involved	Subprocess	Cost Savings Improvement	Benefit
	Direct material procurement	▸ Improved efficiency and control over material purchases from approved suppliers by automating purchase order approval process	Reduction in unauthorized procurement spend and FTE to monitor it
Plan-to-stock	Product disposition	▸ Adoption of global product expiration dates that can be changed with one system transaction	Reduced quality assurance FTE to monitor product expirations
	Warehouse and inventory management	▸ Automated calculation of expiration dates for procured materials	Reduced quality assurance FTE to monitor procured materials expirations

Table 8.2 Potential Cost Savings for an SAP Implementation Project (Cont.)

Within the planning framework described in this chapter, the core team can move forward with building the project organization, detailing the governance structure, and staffing the full project team. The following chapters will describe these processes. First, our next chapter will give you a good view of the knowledge management tools available to the project team. We will also show you how they can be used to best effect.

Your project team will create a whole host of documents during the SAP implementation project. These range from specifications to user training materials. All must be effectively stored and versioned using a knowledge management approach.

9 Knowledge Management

It may seem a bit strange to see knowledge management in a book focusing on SAP implementations. After all, *knowledge management* usually refers to how an enterprise handles its information assets. The term is most often used to describe a highly conceptual approach to understanding and utilizing these company information assets. However, the more mundane approach to knowledge management simply means the collection and re-harvesting of information created in the company. Often, this entails document creation, versioning, and maintenance.

Although it may seem counterintuitive, an SAP implementation project is usually as much about documentation as it is about systems. From project preparation to final preparation, each phase contains major documentation deliverables. They are not systems fixtures, but rather documents describing some aspect of the project. Nor do these documents merely represent bureaucratic requirements. They are core aspects of the project and many will live long after the project is complete and the project team is released to new roles.

For example, the project preparation phase entails building the project charter, budget, and headcount plan. These are core documents for the project and will surely undergo revision as circumstances change at multiple points in the lifecycle. Team members will need access to each deliverable and must have assurance that they are using the most recent version.

It will pay significant dividends for your project team to have defined a methodology for ensuring document continuity throughout the project lifecycle. This may involve developing manual processes for small projects or using document-focused systems for large-scale projects.

9 | Knowledge Management

> **Tip**
>
> Your project knowledge management strategy is one of those deliverables *not* covered by the ASAP methodology. Do set aside the time to think through how your team intends to handle all the documentation. It will be time well spent.

Figure 9.1 displays only a few of the document deliverables common to an SAP implementation. Many of them are discussed in later chapters. In this chapter, we'll focus on the preparation, storage, and maintenance of each document type. Your project team will face the challenge of keeping documents current and retrieving those documents needed throughout the SAP implementation lifecycle.

Project preparation	Blueprint	Realization	Final preparation
▸ Project charter ▸ Request for proposal ▸ Project budget ▸ Head count plan ▸ Governance plan ▸ Project risks and issues	▸ Process definition documents ▸ WRICEFP gaps ▸ Data definitions ▸ Change impacts ▸ Training plan ▸ Business controls plan ▸ Final scope definition	▸ Test scenarios and scripts ▸ Functional and technical specifications ▸ Configuration rationales ▸ Standing operating procedures ▸ Work instructions ▸ Training courses	▸ Cutover approval ▸ Hypercare plan

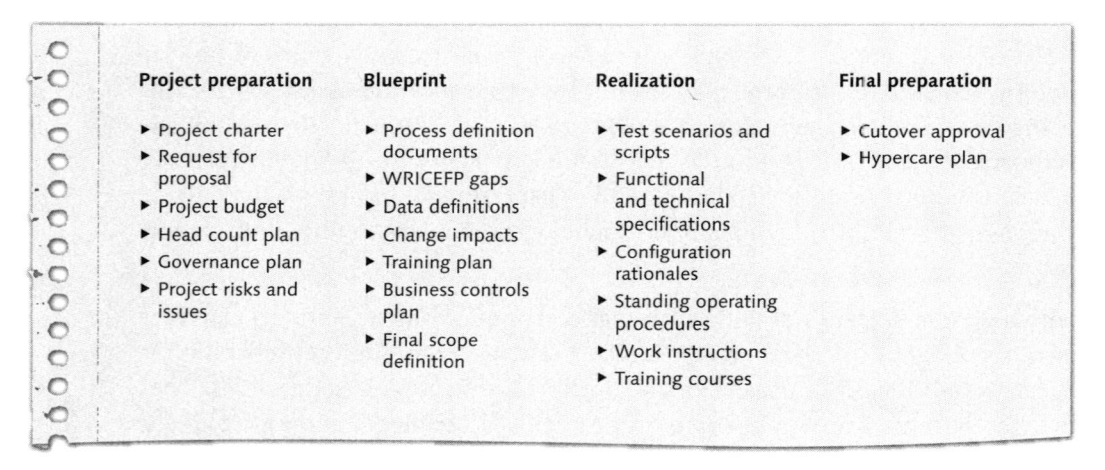

Figure 9.1 Core Document Deliverables During an SAP Implementation Project

9.1 Documentation

The primary knowledge management roles for the project team will be the orderly creation and systematic maintenance of these documents. By the end of the project, your team will have generated thousands and thousands of documents. The team must have an efficient process in place to manage all these documents, and the knowledge management approach will help put a working classification in place to address all this output.

We can classify project documents into three types:

- *Type one* documents have a limited lifespan outside the project lifespan. They are specific to back-office project operations, and have the least need for a retention strategy. They include the following:
    - Workstream meeting notes
    - Calendars
    - PMO status reports
    - Presentations
    - Working documents
- *Type two* documents contain project-centric details, and also have a lifespan only for the length of the project. However, given certain circumstances, such as audit requirements, they may be retained well after project completion. Type two documents either encompass plans describing how the project will perform an operation, such as the business controls implementation, or include documents intended to exercise control over project operations. Type two documents will require wide access among the project team. They can include the following:
    - Risks and issues
    - Deliverables
    - Budgets
    - Project schedules
    - Milestones
    - Governance documents
- *Type three* documents are intended to long outlive the project and remain in place for the lifespan of the SAP system. For example, the configuration rationale—a realization deliverable itself—describes the process used and the underlying foundation for the project team's configuration decisions. These documents can be accessed for the full span of the project as well as during the sustainment period. They will no doubt be updated and receive more recent versions during this time. The technical support team will use them to understand how the system was configured long after the project team has departed.

Type three documents require continuity from the project team to present-day operations, so care must be taken to make them easily available. Additionally, these documents are living artifacts that will be updated and versioned as the system is modified to meet new requirements. They can include the following:

- Requirements
- Specifications
- Test results
- Configuration rationales
- Standing operating procedures

When creating or modifying documentation, all team members should be aware of how long the document will be used. Many type one documents may not even need to be retained during the entire project lifecycle. The project documentation policy should identify which documents require retention and which could be disposed of at an earlier time.

Type two documents have a more clearly defined lifespan. They are needed until the project is complete. Some type two documents, such as governance reports or project schedules, may need to remain active well after the project has been completed.

Type three documents are a different class altogether. They *must* be retained and made available for use until they are superseded or otherwise not needed. These documents serve a number of uses. For example, sustainment operators will commonly review project technical documents. Or, during onboarding, new company employees will need the end-user training materials that the project team created during realization. For cases like these, type three documents require an especially well-defined strategy for retention and versioning.

> **Tip**
> Type three documents definitely require your project team's attention. Many of these, such as functional specifications and configuration rationales, will be completed by your systems integrator. Do ensure that applicable workstreams review and verify the documents before sign-off. These documents will have a long shelf-life!

9.2 Knowledge Management Strategy

Smaller implementation projects likely do not need a formal knowledge management strategy. These projects often use manual processes and can be handled without instating a formal mechanism. Larger projects, however, will most often use a systems-based approach to their knowledge management operations. This demands a clearly articulated strategy stipulating which documents are to be managed and which systems will be used to enable that process.

At least three different categories of systems are typically used for knowledge management during an SAP system implementation. Each one takes on a defined role based on its operating parameters and can encompass the management of all three document types, lasting throughout the system lifespan. Figure 9.2 illustrates three types of systems most often used for project documentation.

SAP Solution Manager	▸ Design documentation ▸ Functional specifications ▸ Technical specifications ▸ Configuration rationales ▸ Data definitions ▸ WRICEFP gap documents
Enterprise Document Management System	▸ Standing operating procedures ▸ Work instructions ▸ Document templates ▸ Approval histories
Enterprise Learning Management System	▸ User training instruction ▸ Attendance records ▸ Training translations ▸ Instructor certifications ▸ Role mapping assignments

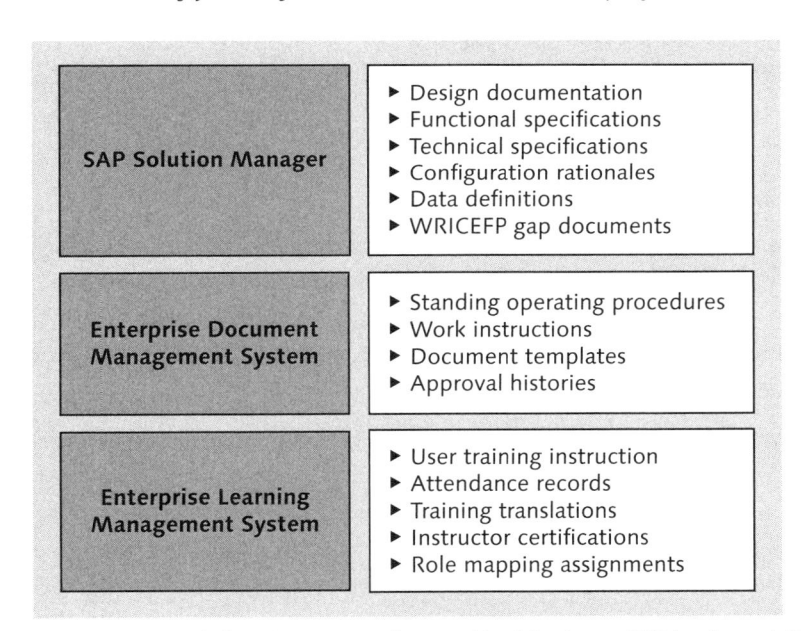

Figure 9.2 Knowledge Management Systems Used During an SAP Implementation Project

The first system type, SAP Solution Manager, can work as a document repository for items related to SAP system design and operation. This system houses and maintains correct versions for these types of documents. This section will provide additional information about how SAP Solution Manager is used for these purposes.

Enterprise collaboration tools, or enterprise document management tools, represent the second category of system used for project knowledge management. As a rule, these systems have broader applications than those of the SAP implementation project. They are used for enterprise knowledge management but can be applied to project purposes as well. For that reason, they may house all three document types. Their most common usage for type three documents is to house the company's standing operating procedures and work instructions.

Finally, for those specialized applications having to do with user training and related functions, learning management systems (LMS) can be utilized to house that information. Most often an LMS will house type two and type three documents that will be reused after the project is complete. They include all course materials prepared for user training and records of employee attendance. If the training material has been translated for use in alternate languages, this information can be stored on the LMS and used for new hire training in those regions.

9.2.1 SAP Solution Manager

Both SAP Solution Manager and any enterprise collaboration systems used by the implementing company require setup and configuration decisions in order to meet the needs of the project. SAP Solution Manager in particular requires special attention. It will house those project documents needed to define the system and to support it moving forward.

SAP Solution Manager is basically an administrative system that operates as a central platform for the entire SAP system landscape. It treats the other components of the SAP system as "satellite systems." Through use of SAP Solution Manager as a knowledge management tool, the project team can create all major design documents and house them in a single repository.

Figure 9.3 shows the relationship between SAP Solution Manager and the remaining SAP system components. Companies most commonly implemented SAP ERP as their SAP implementation projects—SAP ERP does most of the heavy lifting with regard to finance, supply chain, procurement, and sales processing. However, as the SAP system has evolved, components such as SAP Supplier

Relationship Management (SRM) have been added to the mix. These components offer more specialized functions but nevertheless operate in tandem with SAP ERP.

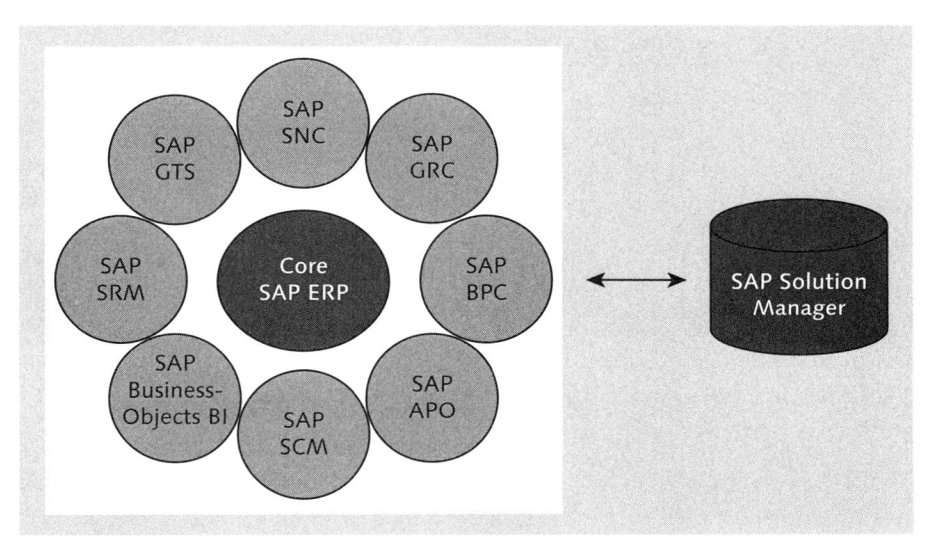

Figure 9.3 Relationship between SAP System Components and SAP Solution Manager

Leaving aside for the moment the numerous three-letter acronyms involved in an SAP system landscape, Figure 9.3 illustrates the relationship between SAP ERP, additional application components that might represent part of a company SAP implementation, and SAP Solution Manager. SAP Solution Manager works with all components as part of a single point of access to an integrated SAP system. In previous iterations, each SAP application operated as an independent entity with no simple way to integrate the components. Now SAP Solution Manager provides a single point of access, and it can house design and realization documents for the entire landscape.

> **Tip**
>
> SAP Solution Manager is a great tool. Your systems integrator will likely install and configure the tool for your team's use. Delegate an individual from your project's IT team to become intimately familiar with its workings. That way, your company will have the skill set in place when your integrator team rolls off.

The fact that SAP Solution Manager is an SAP system has several advantages for both the implementation period and following into sustainment. SAP Solution Manager benefits from the common SAP login and security setup. Thus, the permission structure that applies to SAP system user roles can be adopted and incorporated within Solution Manager as well.

SAP Solution Manager provides a single point of access for all end-to-end business processes. So it doesn't matter whether a business process resides in SAP ERP, SAP Supplier Relationship Management, or the Supplier Portal (to use procurement as an example); the entirety of the process can be documented in SAP Solution Manager.

The primary drawback of SAP Solution Manager concerns its scope. It is primarily limited to the set of SAP applications used in an enterprise. Companies that intend to combine legacy systems with the SAP system in their portfolio will find SAP Solution Manager covers only the SAP portion of that portfolio in the integrated fashion that we have described.

Figure 9.4 shows a fragment of the business process hierarchy, and an example for a company order-to-cash implementation. Focusing on the order-to-cash process, it breaks the customer management scenario into discrete components. The diagram identifies three business processes: manage customers, manage pricing, and trade promotion planning. For one of those business processes, manage customer, the figure shows three steps that will be completed during the process. Creating the customer master, maintaining the customer hierarchy, and handling customer credit applications represent three of several steps in this single business process.

The complete company business hierarchy—as well as the design and specification documents that will describe how the system will operate for each scenario—can be stored in SAP Solution Manager. Figure 9.5 depicts this same information as it would appear in SAP Solution Manager. Each folder defined for that step will contain the relevant information for that business process.

This document hierarchy matches the business process hierarchy. The project team is able to place its completed design materials in SAP Solution Manager for later retrieval. Similar to a document management system, SAP Solution Manager allows for updates and versioning of the completed documents.

9.2 Knowledge Management Strategy

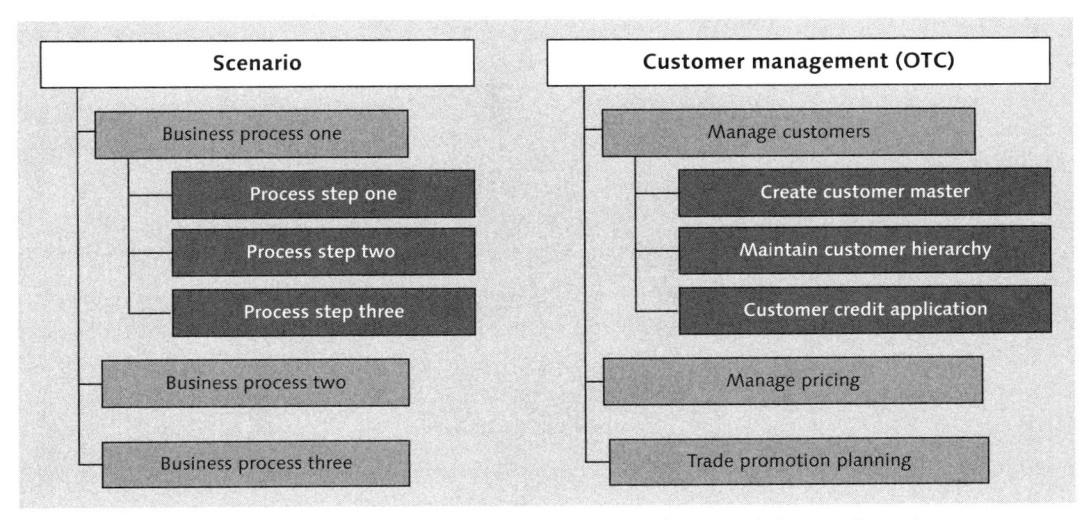

Figure 9.4 Sample Business Process Hierarchy with a Company Order-to-Cash Process Example

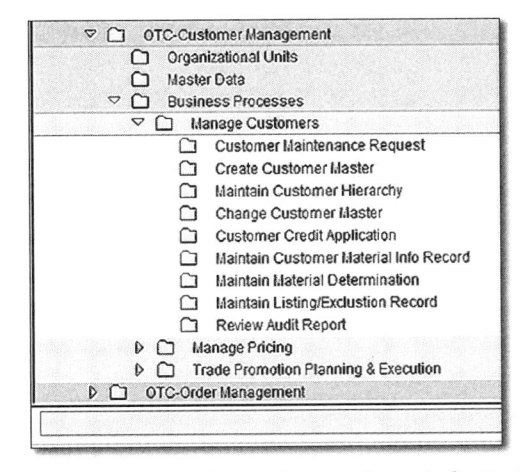

Figure 9.5 SAP Solution Manager Example for Business Process Data

Effective naming conventions are the key to using Solution Manager effectively. These naming conventions reflect the hierarchical process structure and provide a mutually exclusive designation for each document. In this way, each document is assigned its own unique identifier. Figure 9.6 shows the naming conventions for each design document type. The example uses OTC as the team identifier, but could have just as easily used any of the other four teams in the set of hypothetical project workstreams.

Document Type	Project Deliverable	Solution Manager Identifier
Blueprint	Process definition document (PDD)	OTC_PDD_4.4.1_Create Customer Order
Custom objects	Gap definition (describes the need for the custom object)	OTC_GAP_4.4.1_Material Description
Data specification	Data definition document (DDD)	OTC_DDD_4.2.1_Customer Master
Functional specification	Functional specification	OTC_FS_4.1.2_ENH_0225_ Ship to locations
Technical specification	Technical specification	OTC_TS_4.1.2_ENH_0225_ Ship to locations
Configuration	Configuration rationale	OTC_CRS_4.1.1_005_ Maintain Sales Group

Figure 9.6 Naming Conventions Used for Major Design and Configuration Documents

The actual documents referenced in the table are created in blueprinting and the early stages of realization. Once in place, they can be maintained in a correct version for the remainder of the project. Recall as well that the sustainment team can reference them during the lifespan of the SAP system.

9.2.2 Collaboration Applications

Other project documents may reside in enterprise document management systems or enterprise collaboration systems. Similar to SAP Solution Manager, the purpose of these systems is to house documents where they may be available for reference or reuse. Unlike SAP Solution Manager, these systems are most often multi-purpose. They are used by the implementing company to handle a multitude of tasks, of which the SAP project is a single usage.

Table 9.1 indicates only a few of the many uses of these collaboration applications. The table focuses primarily on project-based uses and does not discuss general, enterprise-wide services. The collaboration application permits the enterprise to house almost all remaining project documents (excluding the type three documents housed in SAP Solution Manager) in a single location. This provides a great benefit to the project team. Using a single system with a standard user interface simplifies the entire document management process and reduces errors.

Collaboration Environment	Functions Enabled
Controlled documents	▶ Makes available a Web-based system to manage controlled documents such as policies, standing operating procedures, and work instructions ▶ Permits standardized templates, hierarchies, and naming conventions ▶ Delivers workflows that can be used for approvals and "read and understand" with e-signature functionality
Content management	▶ Provides central access, management, and storage on a common platform for project type one and type two documents ▶ Allows for a consistent mechanism for navigation and finding needed documents ▶ Enables workflows for processes such as document review and issue and risk tracking
Enterprise portal	▶ Supplies a global, interactive online portal for up-to-date information on project activities ▶ Permits project teams to establish project-specific sites for internal project information as well as sites for more general company access

Table 9.1 Project Uses for an Enterprise Collaboration Application

Table 9.1 depicts three primary uses for the enterprise collaboration application. The first centers on controlled documents that may be required to conduct company business. Especially prevalent in life sciences and other highly regulated companies, controlled documents detail business processes involved in the manufacturing, test, and distribution of their products. In these cases, governmental agencies require that process operations be documented. Additionally, they require that employees who perform those operations receive training and can verify compliance with the documents.

Having an application available to house these type three documents and to provide electronic signature evidence of employee understanding of controlled documents is a valuable resource. The SAP implementation projects in these regulated companies will usually prepare numerous controlled documents as part of the project deliverables. Prior to go-live, employees will receive specific training that incorporates the use of these controlled documents. The controlled document repository offers an electronic record to assure regulators and auditors that the required project training and documentation is in place.

The second project use for the enterprise collaboration application comes in the area of content management. The type one and type two documents described in Figure 9.1 will most often reside in the content management space. Unlike the controlled document repository, which is constructed specifically to house and manage procedural documents, the content management area is more free-form. It must be configured specifically to fit the purpose of the using group. In this case, it must be structured to fit the needs of type one and type two documents.

Figure 9.7 illustrates the structuring involved for these project documents. The project team develops the folder structure and then gives it to the systems administrator for the collaboration application, where it would be configured and made ready for use.

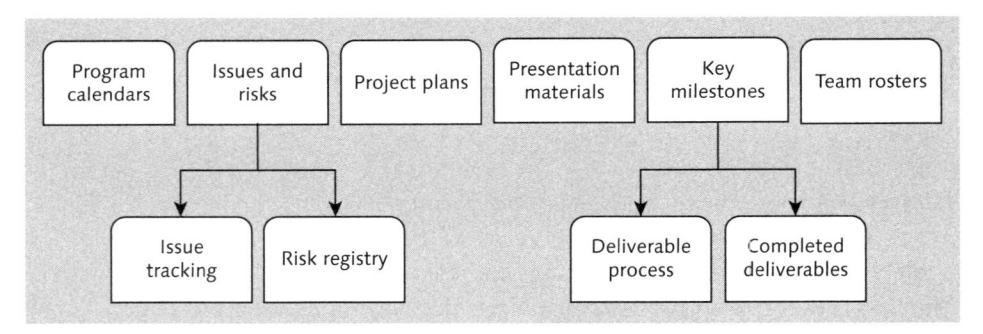

Figure 9.7 Content Management Folder Structure

This folder structure generally operates at several levels of indentation. In the Figure 9.7 example, only the issues and risks folder and the key milestones folder reflect this subdivision. In reality, each of the folders would likely have many subfolders beneath it. Once the folder structure was in place and ready for use, the PMO would develop standards and rule sets to ensure common usage across the project teams.

The top-level folders should encompass the full range of materials to be housed. Thus, the listing should thoroughly outline where any project document should be able to find a home.

Figure 9.8 illustrates the extension of the folder structure. Most projects will have multiple calendars; this example shows five types of calendars to be used in the project. From this perspective, any user can locate the needed folder and information without having to sort through multiple calendars. Administrators can easily maintain this structure and ensure that the most recent versions are available to interested users. Having the approach defined and in place early in the project minimizes confusion and ensures easy access to information.

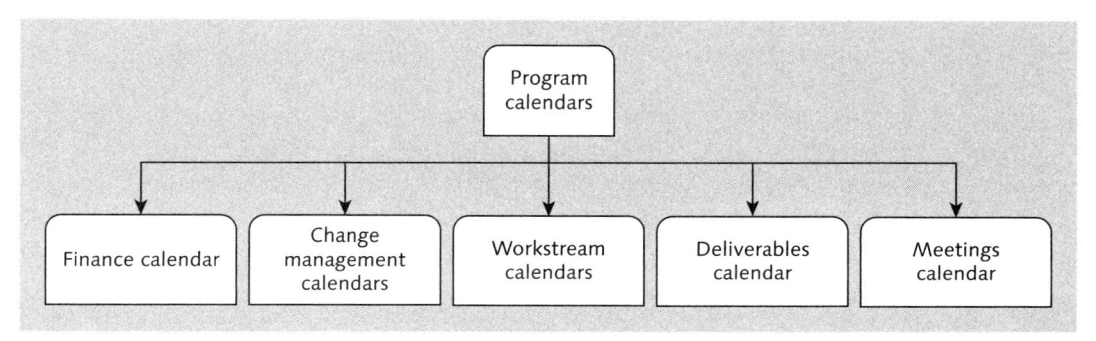

Figure 9.8 Calendar Document Structure for an SAP Implementation Project

A more formal submission and approval process is required for project deliverables. Many of the deliverables will fall under the scope of the systems integrator contract and have financial implications to the project. In these cases the following mechanism would be used:

1. **Document preparation for submission**
   When the deliverable is completed and ready for submission, the responsible team member notifies the team leader that the document is ready for review. In this case, completion means that the document meets project standards and correctly uses applicable project templates. The team lead then reviews the documentation to ensure that it is correct and complete.

2. **Document submission**
   The team lead then submits the documentation to the appropriate location within the document repository. This could be a team folder within the deliverable folder structure.

3. **Document sign-off**
   The team lead responsible for the deliverable would notify the designated reviewer that the document was available for review. This reviewer would verify

that the document was complete and was appropriate to the purpose intended. The reviewer would also validate that the deliverable met project standards and requirements. Any hard-copy documents containing reviews or sign-offs would be submitted to the PMO, which would scan the copy and post it to the correct folder as approved.

> **Tip**
>
> As a rule, your project financial controller will take charge of deliverable verification. Your controller will probably be very detail-oriented—a trait that will serve the project well. Often this verification consists of continuous discussion with your systems integrator on the details of "complete." Best to have detail-oriented team members handle the negotiations.

The final use of the enterprise collaboration application revolves around construction and use of portals. The project team may decide to create two types of portals.

The first type would be primarily internal in focus and furnish the project team with information and updates relevant to project activities. This use would be limited to the project team and those immediately involved with the project.

The second portal type would generally be a segment on the company portal devoted to the SAP implementation project. Employees who wish to access the latest project information could use this portal or link within the overall company intranet site. This site could be used for special project announcements, achievement of major milestones, or to request involvement such as recruitment of super users.

9.2.3 Specialized Document Applications

In addition to SAP Solution Manager and enterprise collaboration applications, other systems may be used to house project documents. Figure 9.2 made reference to the use of enterprise learning management systems (LMS) as a repository for project-related training materials. In addition to the actual training coursework, these could include training attendance records, any training materials that were translated and likely to be reused in regional instruction, and instructor certifications issued by the company.

Regulators and auditors often focus on verifying that training has been prepared and performed. Having the material housed in a single system location and maintained by your company training organization ensures that the materials are kept up-to-date and complete.

A similar situation prevails with systems test documents. These will be key to validating that the project team conducted all required testing, especially user acceptance testing. The project can use enterprise test systems to track test script completions and records of defect closure. Any auditor or regulator requests to provide test verification can be addressed with materials housed on the test system. A more complete description of test systems will be found in Chapter 16.

With knowledge management in place, the following chapters conclude discussion of project preparation with descriptions of project organization, project governance, and building the right project team. At that point, the project will be ready for full-scale operation and the initiation of blueprinting.

Project organization establishes the framework for building the company SAP system. It sets the foundation for project activity and, ultimately, project success.

10 Project Organization

Your project organization supplies the framework for virtually every project activity. Once established, the project organization will operate very much in the background. It affects every action but its very presence makes it taken for granted — not seen and not heard. However, your project sponsors must make a very conscious decision regarding how the project will be organized. Once this is done successfully, then the organization can recede into the background.

The decisions about how to organize the SAP project must take account of several requirements. The most important requirements are as follows:

- Provide an organizational home for all company employees assigned to the project, systems integrator staff participating in the project, and external contractors hired to deliver the system.
- Manage the hundreds of work products required during the project lifetime and ensure they are accomplished on time and on budget.
- Develop, flesh out, and deliver all company business transformations needed as part of the project scope.
- Prepare end users for the new system and ensure that it works according to plan at go-live.

Each of these components should be in place by the midpoint of project preparation. To determine this organization, your necessary decisions range from structuring the high-level organization to establishing mechanisms capable of controlling project work products.

This chapter reviews several methods of organizing the SAP project and provides assessments of situations where each method works best. Our discussion centers on four separate components: the high-level project organization, program management and its components, the functional workstream leadership, and horizontal or technical workstreams.

Let's begin by examining high-level project organization, which sets the stage for all our subsequent discussions in this chapter.

10.1 High-Level Project Organization

At the highest—or senior executive—level, the project organization must reflect the implementing company's management culture. To do so, the project must understand and adapt itself to that management culture. Some companies, motivated by a desire to follow existing management culture, decide to house the project within one of their functional organizations. In other cases, this will mean constructing a special matrix organization for the project as a means of accommodating all functional organizations. Each approach has its advantages and challenges, and differs in terms of the benefits to be gained. We'll consider two functional approaches: the business-led model and the information technology (IT)-led model. We'll also examine the matrix-led project organization. We'll take a look at these approaches next.

> **Trail Marker**
>
> Functional models vary considerably from industry to industry. This chapter assumes that the implementing company is a manufacturing entity and is divided into three top-level groupings: global supply chain, global finance, and global sales. The discussion will not include any company marketing or research and development organizations, since these functions generally do not fall within the scope of an SAP ERP solution.

10.1.1 Functionally Organized Project Organizations

Most large organizations operate according to a functional model, in which tasks are assigned to a functional organization and staff members, in turn, are allocated to achieve those tasks.

Companies frequently adopt a functional approach to implementing an SAP system. In these cases, the functional organization that is the primary system user will often serve as the home for the project. For example, companies with significant manufacturing and distribution operations routinely select their supply chain organization as the project organizational location. Financial services companies, on the other hand, often choose to house the project within the global finance organization.

Figure 10.1 illustrates this functional arrangement. For our example, the global supply chain organization owns the leadership role and hosts the project organization. That relationship is designated with a solid line running to the project organization. The dotted lines between global finance/global sales organizations to the project organization indicate that they perform a secondary role.

As an operational matter, all three organizations would participate in the project and furnish any necessary resources. However, because project leadership would come from the global supply chain organization, much of the day-to-day decision-making would come from executives in that organization as well.

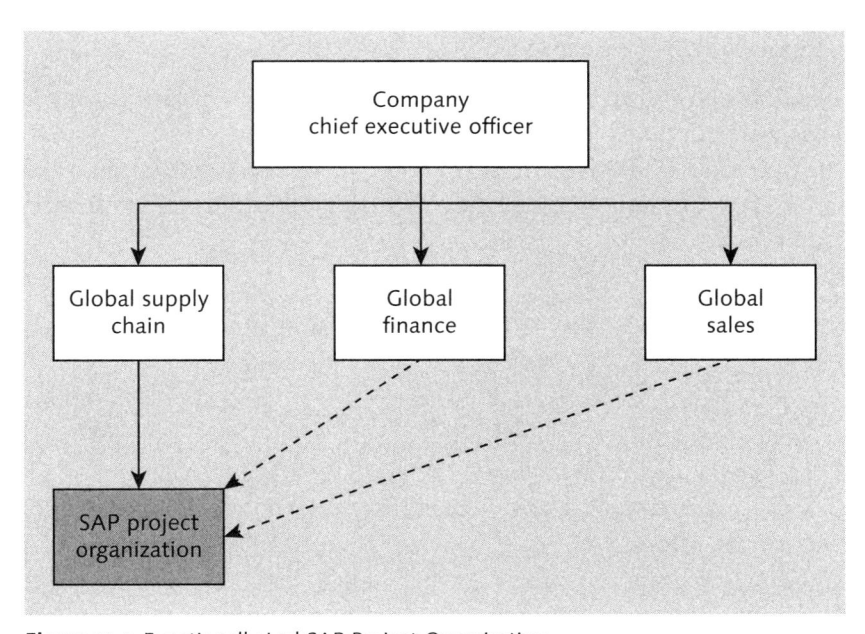

Figure 10.1 Functionally Led SAP Project Organization

There are several clear advantages to the functionally led project organization:

- **Places the responsibility for project success in the hands of the organization most impacted by the system**
  The lead organization will feel ownership for the project that another, less system-

dependent organization might not. Housed in this location, the project has direct access to critical resources, solutions, and support as are needed.

▶ **Gives the project legitimacy and stature**
Having the lead functional organization in a company solidly behind the project creates momentum for it. This makes many of its tasks all the easier. Rather than having to seek recognition, the project acquires it through its organizational location.

▶ **Gains access to key process expertise**
Many of the key process transformations will be attached to the host functional organization. Correspondingly, the existing process skill base in the company will also be located in this organization and remain available to the project team.

Of course, not even these essential advantages can always compensate for some potentially significant disadvantages:

▶ **Limits the amount of project buy-in from other functional organizations in the company**
Rather than jumping on board with the project, those organizations may participate with lukewarm involvement and leave the major effort to the primary functional organization.

> **Pitfall Alert**
> Unfortunately, it's possible that this lukewarm participation includes the company IT organization, and any reduction in this crucial area could greatly impact project performance. IT resources and expertise will have great value during the implementation.

▶ **Minimizes the project stature and access to process expertise from other functional organizations**
Appointing one organization, such as global supply chain, as the lead group can diminish the stature and process access among those organizations not selected as the primary host.

If an implementing company chooses to adopt a functionally led management approach for its SAP project organization, it will have to do so with care. To ensure project success, the primary host organization must reach out to the remaining company functional organizations. Including them in initial planning meetings and ensuring their participation in project governance are essential first steps to mitigate any reservations in those other functional organizations.

Let's consider an alternative functional approach.

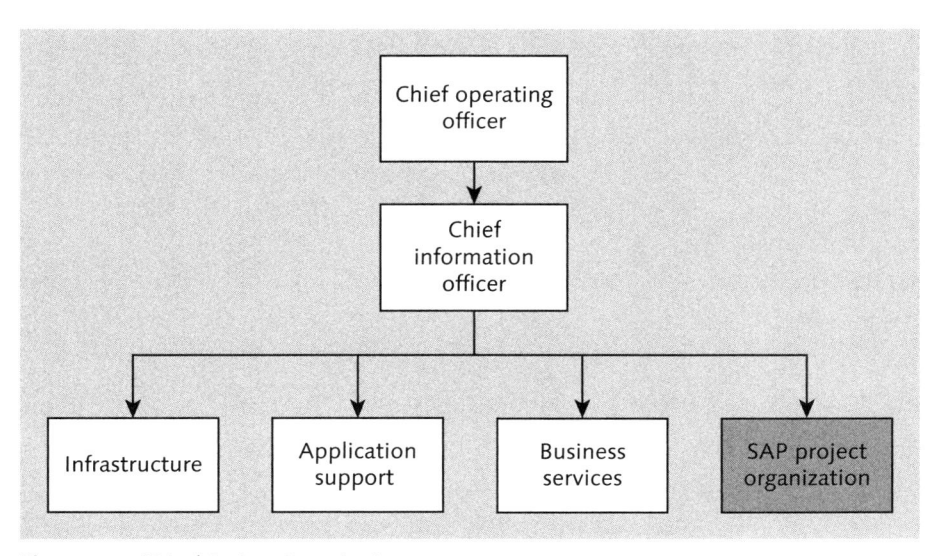

10.1.2 IT-Led Project Organization

In this approach, the project organization would be housed within the company IT organization. Many companies have adopted this tactic and some have had success with it.

Figure 10.2 illustrates how the project organization would be appended to the sub-organizational structure within IT. The project would report to the chief information officer (CIO); that individual would take on primary management control.

There is one very clear advantage to this arrangement; it matches essential skill needs and experience base. After all, SAP is a system, and it makes sense to place the project organization within the company systems function. IT organizations also have considerable experience with implementing systems. This means that systems resources and company systems expertise can be easily accessed by the project organization; it will be an integral part of information technology.

Figure 10.2 IT-Led Project Organization

However, the disadvantages to an IT-led project are numerous and must be addressed with determination at the very beginning of the project, while they can still be overcome:

- **The company IT group will generally lack the stature of other major functional organizations.**
  IT is often assigned to the chief financial officer (CFO) and becomes part of that reporting network. Alternatively, the IT organization is one of the many service reports assigned to the company chief operating officer (COO).

  As a result, the IT group may find it difficult to exercise leverage with other functional organizations. Those business units may not see the IT organization as an equal and could simply choose to discount direction received from the project team due to its placement with IT.

- **The SAP system definitely is a business tool.**
  Functional organizations must take ownership of the system and ensure that their processes operate effectively. Housing the project organization in IT tends to create a "leave it to IT" attitude, which could work against the very system adoption activities that must take place for the system to be successful.

- **Acquiring committed business expertise may prove difficult.**
  While some project deliverables depend heavily on IT skills, other equally critical deliverables depend on skills coming from company business units. Almost the entirety of blueprinting focuses on business processes, as do many downstream activities in realization and final preparation.

For this organizational arrangement to prove successful, it requires that the CIO connect extremely well with the leaders of major functional organizations. They will have to see him as an ally in reaching their objectives and as having their interests at heart. These are rare skills for a technology leader, but in those instances where those skills have been in place, this has proven to be an effective organizational strategy.

10.1.3 Matrix-Led Project Organizations

Matrix-led project organizations place the ownership outside of company functional business units. Instead, they use special organizational formats to house the project.

The most popular matrix option is the use of a company business transformation officer (BTO) in a leadership role, as shown in Figure 10.3. This individual usually reports to the company CEO and holds the company charter for leading business transformation efforts.

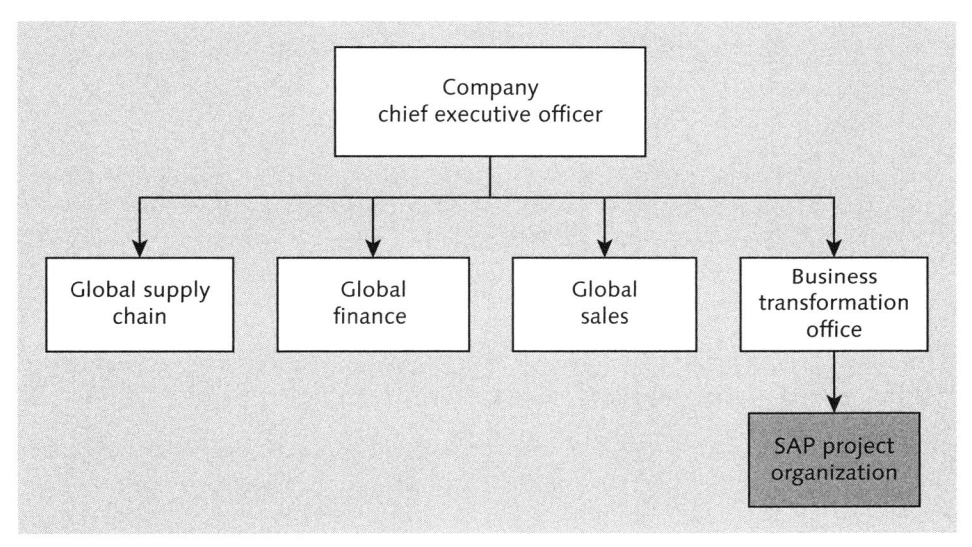

Figure 10.3 BTO-Led Project Organization

Placing the project organization under the guidance of the company BTO has several advantages:

- The BTO who reports to the CEO will have equal status as other functional business unit heads. Reporting to the CEO means that the BTO can exercise leverage on behalf of the project and its objectives.
- Functional business units will see the BTO as "one of them." This arrangement shields the project from the potential divisiveness of reporting to a single functional organization. The executive will likely not be seen as biased, and this mitigates prospective jealousies from those functional organizations not chosen as the lead business unit.
- The BTO will have an intimate familiarity with business transformation and with those critical business changes needed to make the project a success. She will understand how to make change happen and will bring that skill set to the project.

The matrix-led project organization is not without its challenges. Prior to adopting this format, the implementing company should check a few things:

- The BTO possesses a real skill set and track record in leading transformative change. In most companies, BTO positions have modest, if any, staff assigned to them, so it is expected that sheer competence and force of personality will primarily make this individual a success in creating change. However, some companies assign these roles to executives with limited experience and may find that their selection is not capable of performing the tasks needed to lead the project.
- Since the BTO is unlikely to have deep systems or SAP skills, some reinforcement may be needed. Either the company IT organization can supply a support resource, or it can hire a skilled contractor to provide needed SAP expertise.

Provided that the required qualifiers are met, this hybrid approach serves most companies well. Further, SAP project experience will build a deep-seated expertise that the BTO can apply to future transformational assignments.

Once your company has made its choices about the high-level project organization, management can turn its attention to subsidiary project organization decisions. We'll consider program management as the first of these.

10.2 Program Management

Program management takes operational responsibility for leading the project through its lifecycle, from project preparation to go-live and support. An effective program management office (PMO) can be the glue that holds the project together.

The overriding purpose of project management is to systematically administer all major project activities. This includes the anticipation of negative events before they happen and day-to-day planning of project operations.

Large-scale projects that have a high number of participants, involve global locations, and require the investment of financial resources are often known as *programs*. An SAP implementation is one such program; the SAP implementation requires a seasoned program manager who combines SAP technical knowledge with an ability to manage all the interrelated parts of an implementation. While the company senior executive heading the project has a role primarily focused on company business units, the program manager identifies the necessary deliverables, schedules their completion, and ensures that those schedules are met.

As Figure 10.4 shows, the implementation PMO combines a number of functions.

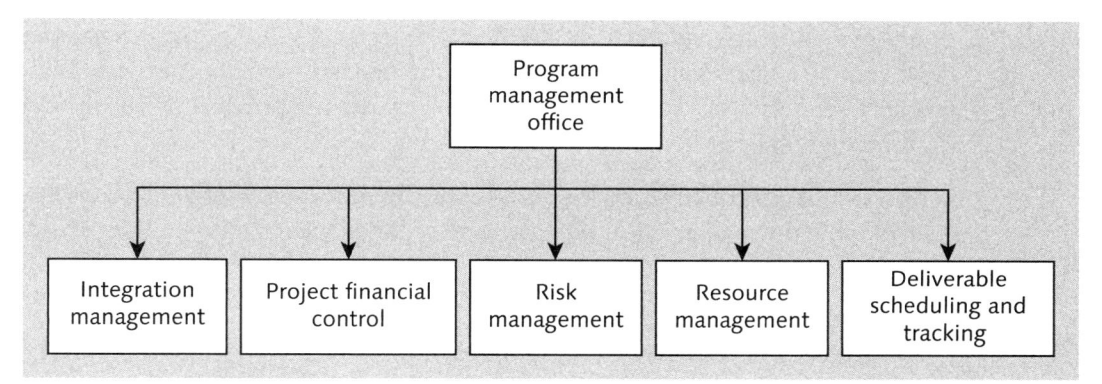

Figure 10.4 SAP Implementation PMO Functions

Depending on the size of the project, the five components of the SAP implementation PMO can all be performed by a single person or by multiple individuals per function. In a very large project (total costs greater than $100 million), workload size and complexity will require at least a small staff assigned to the PMO.

The numerical size of staff required will also greatly depend on the role assigned to the PMO. Some projects adopt a "weak" PMO approach, in which the PMO acts as a scorekeeper and coordinator among workstreams participating in the project. The weak PMO operates with workstream leads to acquire status information and then reports this information to stakeholders. Where the scheduling is concerned, the PMO identifies deliverables and due dates for work assignments.

The "strong" PMO approach, on the other hand, puts the program manager in charge of daily project operations. The program manager and any assigned staff define the project schedule, clear any obstacles impacting deliverable completion, and push to ensure that all activities are accomplished on time. The program manager represents the project and its objectives.

Let's compare these two. The weak program manager approach diffuses responsibilities among the project team. No one person would own the accomplishment of essential work products. In this case, the program manager could track and report on status, but would likely be unable to influence its execution. The weak program manager style is not well suited to the urgency and time demands of an SAP implementation project.

The strong program manager approach is much better suited to SAP implementation project. It places the locus of decision-making in a single point and enables rapid response to critical issues. It also provides needed direction for project participants who lack background and experience with the demands of an SAP implementation project.

Let's return to Figure 10.4 and the components to the SAP implementation PMO. Each of the following tasks is fundamental to on-time delivery and on-budget execution:

- **Integration management**
  The project will consist of software, hardware, and process elements that range across several workstreams. The timing of activities and their resourcing must be closely managed. The integration management team identifies cross-workstream activities and ensures a unified and coordinated approach to their performance.

  Whoever performs the integration management role should possess substantial technical and implementation project experience. They will be familiar with the challenges that face workstreams and every discrete element involved. This track record will enable them to intervene successfully at these major coordination points.

- **Project financial control**
  The SAP implementation project represents a significant company expenditure, with both capital and expense components. On top of that, numerous vendors will invoice the project, and regional offices in the company will submit charges to cover any employee backfill costs incurred.

  PMO staff controlling the project's finances should have sufficient background to work closely with the company's accounting organization. In addition to doing standard financial reporting, this position will include participating in budget planning cycles and financial forecasting.

  Project sponsors will be very sensitive to budget overruns of any kind. As part of its normal operating protocol, the PMO should conduct monthly and quarterly reviews of financial performance. The objective is to address major deviations from the financial plan and to examine root causes for those deviations during these reviews.

- **Risk management**
  SAP implementation projects are fraught with risk. The statistics on troubled or failed projects provide true reflections on how well the project identified and handled the risks it encountered. Clearly reporting and tracking significant risks is a significant part of the equation. Most important, however, is the skill and perseverance the PMO demonstrates in resolving those risks.

  To address potential risks, many projects maintain a risk registry where any project team member can designate a risk. This produces a large number of identified risks, some very significant and many others of far lesser importance. The PMO must ensure that these risks are triaged and those of a critical nature are flagged for special attention. Having a "top-10" risk list that the project continuously tracks and updates will prove essential during the project lifecycle.

> **Trail Marker**
> We'll expand our coverage of risk management in greater detail in our next chapter (Chapter 11).

- **Resource management**
  The project begins with a resourcing plan that estimates the number and types of resources needed during the project lifecycle. Even the very best estimates require constant monitoring and occasional corrective actions. PMO staff will evaluate staffing needs and report both shortfalls and overages to project sponsors.

  A project can't meet its schedule without having the right resources in place at the right time. Project sponsors will often find that they spend a good portion of their time making—and following up on—resource requests directed to company business units.

- **Deliverable scheduling and tracking**
  Many people believe that scheduling and tracking deliverables is the sole function of a program management office, but this is inaccurate. However, scheduling and tracking deliverables does represent a very critical activity. The project schedule serves as its map. The schedule shows where the project is

expected to be on its journey. Those who create the schedule do so with an experience set that helps them reliably estimate duration times of project activities.

The timelines built into the project schedule are based on these estimates. The PMO will track a project to determine whether it is meeting its deadlines. Progress reporting can be accomplished several ways. The most effective mechanism is the general project operating review meeting (As we discussed in Chapter 5), managed by the PMO, where activities' progress updates can be discussed in full.

With the program management team in place, we can turn to the roles of functional workstream leads.

10.3 Functional Workstream Leads

With top-level project organization in place, addressing workstream arrangements is the next step. Our discussion focuses on the organization of functional business processes within the project structure. Functional business processes are generally introduced to the project via workstreams. These are self-contained organizations led by a company expert in the specific process. SAP projects are well known for their liberal use of acronyms, and this tendency becomes very clear in the naming of these workstreams. Almost all are referenced by a three-letter acronym. For example, "procurement and accounts payable" are commonly linked together in a single workstream known as procure-to-pay. From the time the project gets fully underway, the procure-to-pay workstream will be known as "PTP."

> **Tip**
>
> Someone who does not interact with the project on a regular basis can feel overwhelmed by the use of multiple acronyms used in a single sentence, sometimes known as "alphabet soup." To combat this communication problem, many projects create acronym glossaries to reduce confusion among those outside the project.

Table 10.1 provides several common three-letter acronyms for process workstreams. Many of these differ only in the scope included. For example, procure-to-pay (PTP) and contract-to-pay (CTP) differ only in the addition of supplier contracting in the scope of CTP, while PTP limits its scope by excluding the contracting process. Human capital management (HCM) and recruit-to-retire (RTR) have exactly the same scope. HCM is often chosen as a workstream designator due to the popularity of record-to-report (RTR) as workstream designator for finance processes.

Team Name	Acronym	Description
Contract-to-pay	CTP	Full procurement process, from supplier contracting to payment for services
Human capital management*	HCM	Full human resources process, from hiring to discharge
Order-to-cash*	OTC	Full order fulfilment process, from order processing to funds receipt for invoice
Plan-to-report	PTR	Full financial process, from financial planning to reporting of earnings
Plan-to-schedule	PTS	Production planning to master scheduling
Plan-to-stock*	PTS	Production planning to completion of warehouse stocking
Procure-to-pay*	PTP	Procurement process, from materials purchasing to vendor payment
Produce-to-demand	PTD	Production of product to factory shipment
Record-to-report*	RTR	Financial processes, from recording of financial transactions to reporting company results
Recruit-to-retire	RTR	Full human resources process, from hiring to discharge

Table 10.1 Common Acronyms for Business Process Workstreams

This book has adopted five workstreams as a device to illustrate a model SAP implementation project. These selected workstreams (HCM, OTC, PTP, PTS, and RTR) are all marked with an asterisk in Table 10.1. These workstreams represent the standard process components of a typical full-scale project and are shown in Figure 10.5. They will be used throughout the book to portray workstream scope, blueprint definition, configuration, and system testing. Through this recurring usage, we hope that readers will become familiar with the real-world specifics of many process workstream activities.

10 Project Organization

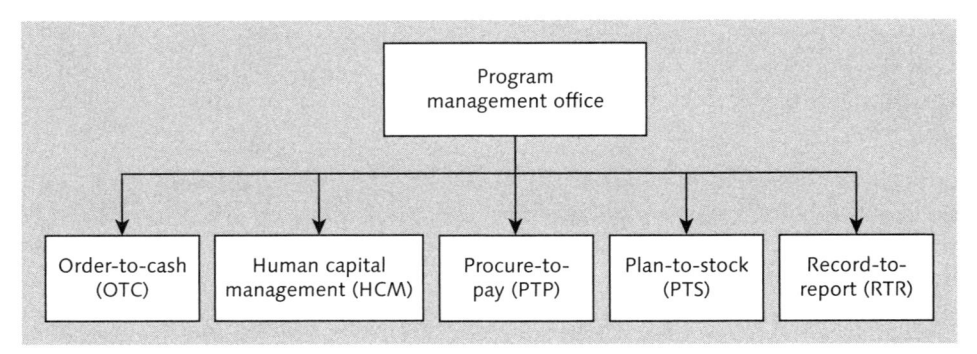

```
                    Program
               management office
     ┌──────────┬───────┼────────┬──────────┐
     ▼          ▼       ▼        ▼          ▼
Order-to-cash  Human capital  Procure-to-  Plan-to-stock  Record-to-
   (OTC)       management (HCM)  pay (PTP)    (PTS)       report (RTR)
```

Figure 10.5 Workstream Components of a Model SAP Implementation Project

> **Tip**
>
> Although all the acronyms may seem very strange at first, the oddity will soon wear off. Encourage everyone to adopt this strange language. It does make for clarity of communication once everyone becomes familiar with the usage.

Functional workstream leads are key players in the SAP implementation project. For many companies, these workstream leads are also the global process owner for their areas of expertise. In this way, they not only make decisions about how their processes will be operated in the company, but also have considerable say in how the SAP system performs those processes.

Additionally, functional workstream leads are sometimes known as "vertical" leads—which indicates that they have responsibility for all project decision-making and activities relevant to their function. For a typical SAP implementation project, both the company and the systems integrator will assign designated staff to support the process owner. These individuals will complete all deliverables in their respective areas of responsibility. These deliverables include outputs in blueprint, realization, final preparation, and go-live.

Figure 10.6 provides an example of workstream organization for record-to-report (RTR). The RTR functional process lead is supported by both systems integrator and IT technical analysts. On the systems integrator side, these analysts will have extensive background in the SAP setup for the FI/CO modules and SAP Business Planning and Consolidation (BPC). On the IT side, this set of business analysts will be well-versed on company systems requirements for RTR enablement.

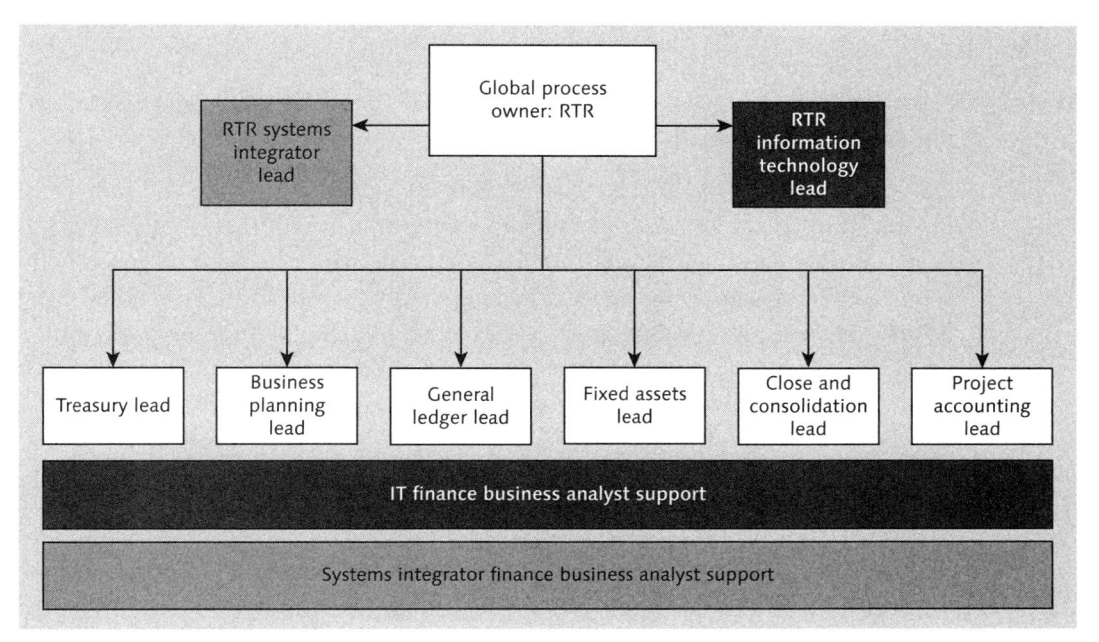

Figure 10.6 Typical RTR Workstream Organization for an SAP Implementation Project

Each lead for a discrete process area will have been assigned from the company global finance organization. Normally, these leads have expert-level knowledge in the business process under their control, whether this be treasury or fixed assets.

Additionally, the overall RTR functional process lead at the top of the figure will have assistance from an overall systems integrator lead assigned to the workstream, as well as an IT lead on the left and right, respectively. Each has ownership of the workstream deliverable set partitioned to that area. This "three-in-a-box" leadership pattern applies to all other functional workstreams. It assures coordination, but also places the global process owner in overall control.

Other workstreams will be organized in quite similar fashion as RTR, though they may differ as to the type and number of leads involved. Some workstreams may also have more than one process owner assigned. Often, accounts receivable will have a process owner designated for order-to-cash, and pricing may have a process owner assigned to order-to-cash as well. In procure-to-pay, there may be a process owner assigned to accounts payable. And plan-to-stock may have an additional process owner who handles production forecasting and scheduling.

In general, no matter how many process owners are assigned to a workstream, one individual will act as the overall workstream lead. This person has domain expertise. He or she will assign work and will sign off on all deliverables the workstream completes.

One of the primary ways that project updates make their way to the functional organizations is for workstream leads to stay in touch with their home organizations. Workstream leads brief their functional senior executives on design requirements, resource needs, and challenges during realization. Functional executives will have long-standing, trust-based relationships with the workstream leads. If possible, project management should encourage these dialogues and set aside time for status briefings between workstream leads and functional executives. Maintaining this communications link is essential for project well-being; the benefits will prove substantial.

10.4 Horizontal Workstreams

Our discussion recently characterized functional workstreams as vertical organizations. Their deep focus on function-specific scope enables them to take charge of the business solution approach that will be needed for the SAP system. For example, procure-to-pay handles all procurement and accounts payable activities that are within the scope of the project. For activities that include procurement activities in addition to those from another workstream, both process owners would work together to define a solution.

This functional scope provides a powerful way to organize business-related activities within the project: Any functional deliverable is automatically allocated to the correct process team. The team contains the necessary functional expertise and will take charge of the solution.

However, not all project deliverables are functional in nature. Many very important deliverables have a functional component but have a more technical character. For example, activities such as data conversion and security receive significant input from functional teams, but the bulk of the work is performed by technical teams. These are known as *horizontal teams*.

Shown in Figure 10.7, these technical teams span across all functional process groupings. Usually they are staffed by a combination of company IT and systems integrator resources. Their expertise lies not in the functional process area but in system support. They have deep understanding of how the system works and how best to perform in their particular support area.

So how does it work? Process teams make decisions about how their submissions will be structured — while referring to rules supplied by the horizontal team. Once the process material is complete, the horizontal team takes the activity from that point on. The functional process teams continue in a monitoring role. They assess horizontal team output to ensure that it meets their specifications.

This methodology is common to all horizontal teams. Each horizontal team serves as an integration agent within its coverage area. Rather than having each functional workstream independently handle its data conversion, the data conversion team puts processes in place to assure uniform data submissions. The team then performs the back-office data transformations to make the converted data "SAP-ready."

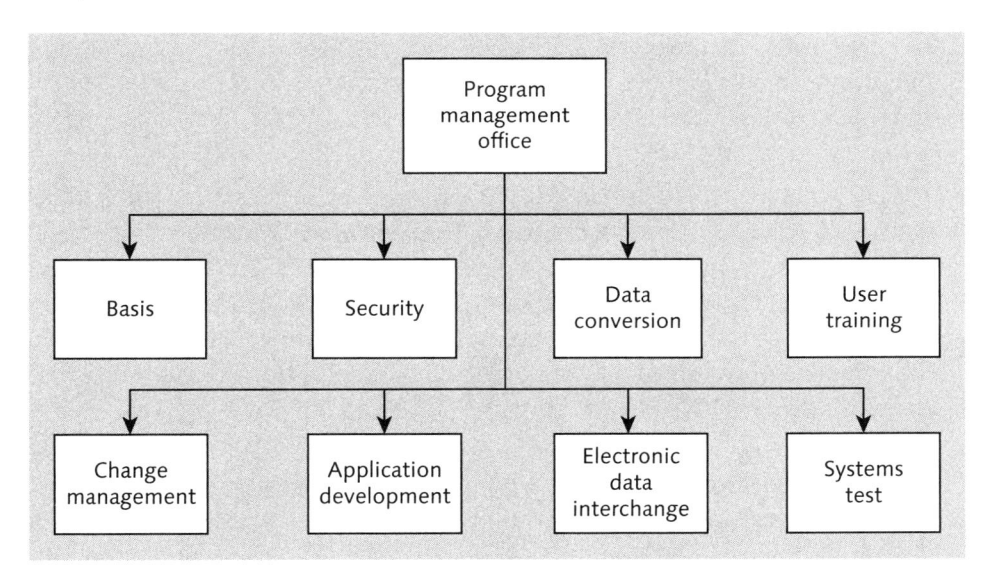

Figure 10.7 Horizontal Workstreams in a Typical SAP Implementation Project

Typically these horizontal teams are collocated with the project PMO. In this way, the PMO can get immediate access to status information, and the horizontal teams can receive any needed support.

> **Pitfall Alert**
>
> Your PMO should make time to familiarize vertical and horizontal teams with their division of responsibility. Clarity here can defuse any potential ownership conflicts that could show up later in the project.

The upcoming chapters will discuss each horizontal team in more detail, but for now let's get an overview of the associated tasks:

- The Basis team is responsible for purchasing, installing, operating, and maintaining the hardware necessary to run the company's SAP system. Its purview will also include loading all SAP applications to include the core SAP ERP and any additional applications, such as SAP Supplier Relationship Management (SRM) or SAP Advanced Planning and Optimization (APO).

- The security team constructs the system security design controlling the scope of user access and works closely with process owners to ensure that all necessary user role assignments are complete. It participates in any segregation of duties assessments and will oversee verification of security roles during testing phases. It will also ensure that the provisioning of SAP UserIDs remains consistent with this design during go-live activities.

- The data conversion team handles the migration of master and transactional data from legacy systems to the newly implemented SAP system. The team works closely with functional teams to ensure that they cleanse and prepare data properly. From that point forward, the transformation and loading of this data is conducted under the supervision of the data conversion team. Remember—the functional process teams continue to monitor the accuracy of conversions throughout.

- The user training team develops training packages intended to prepare users for the system prior to go-live. The team works with process experts to gather information on individual processes and then transfers that information into course modules for instruction. The process teams remain involved in the ongoing review of this material. Once it is ready for delivery, the training team prepares instructors and handles the logistics associated with training.

- The change management team prepares the company and system users for new processes used in the SAP system. The change management team works with functional process teams to identify major change points. Through briefings, communications, and process education, the change management team ensures that users understand what will be different after SAP has gone live and how to operate in this new environment.

- The applications development team completes the technical design work needed for all approved custom objects. Functional process teams prepare the specifications to guide this work. From that point forward, the applications development team creates the technical specifications, delivers the custom objects, and conducts unit testing to ensure their proper functioning.
- The electronic data interchange (EDI) team ensures that electronic transactions with banks, customers, vendors, and distributors are built and tested. The functional teams—especially OTC, PTS, and PTP—directly participate in the identification of business partner organizations and ensure their involvement. Once this commitment has occurred, the EDI team works closely with partner EDI teams in the transacting organizations to assure that all needed specifications are complete and that all transactions are fully tested.

Figure 10.8 illustrates the matrix nature of the relationship between vertical functional process teams and the horizontal technical teams. Each is dependent on the other for the success of its deliverables.

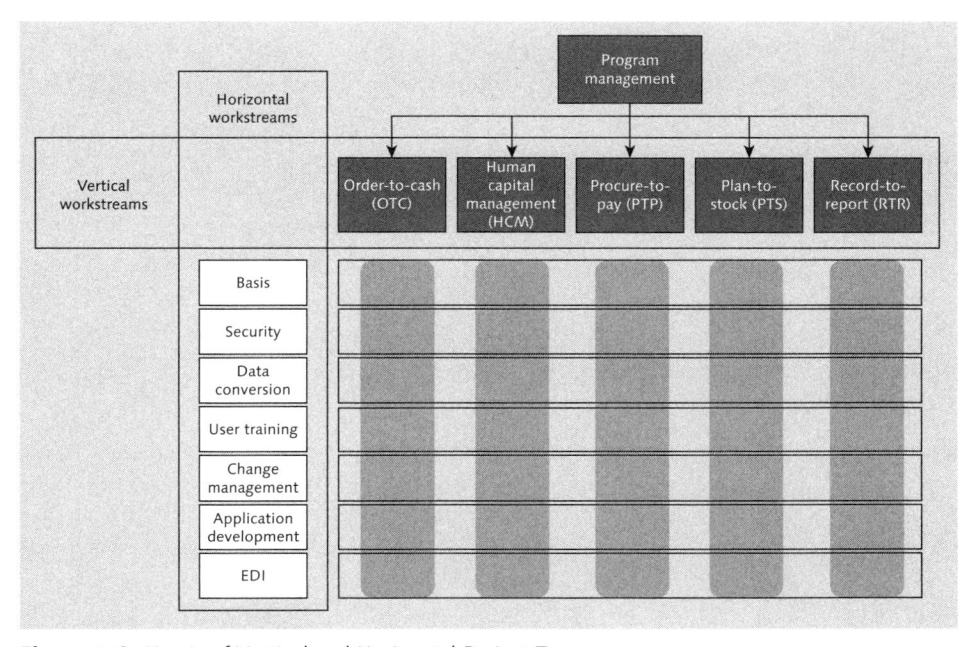

Figure 10.8 Matrix of Vertical and Horizontal Project Teams

The overall project team represents a combination of talents and skills, all of which are needed to successfully deliver the project. Working together in this way may be a new experience for many. However, without this positive combination, the project could not create the results that everyone is counting on.

With project organization in place, we now turn to how the organization will be used to govern its operations. Our next chapter gives you substantial detail on governance methods you can consider.

Like a captain guiding a ship from the bridge, governance provides overall direction to the project. While the captain sets the course and tracks its progress, the rest of the crew puts that guidance in place.

11　Project Governance

In project governance, company sponsors define the objectives for the SAP implementation program and evaluate its attainment of those targets. Additionally, it provides the primary connection to company executive leadership and ensures that project results are consistent with corporate goals.

Project governance is not just a single entity; rather, it has several components. Performed well, and in synchronized fashion, these pieces make a major contribution to project success. We've already alluded to one governance component: oversight and guidance. The remaining components in the governance portfolio act to support and extend this focus area:

- **Project charter**
  While project sponsors need not personally construct the project charter, they must take full ownership for its contents. The *project charter* defines the overall framework for what the SAP implementation will accomplish and how the project will operate throughout its lifecycle. These core descriptions let all participants know what is expected from the project and, in turn, what is expected from them.

  Some in your project team may take the position that the project charter is just one more incidental box to be checked prior to beginning the real work of blueprinting and realization. However, this view ignores the guidance that the charter can provide to the newly formed project team. This public and easily available document imparts needed project context, so any team members who lack previous implementation experience can gain guidance from and place value on the project charter. It will be the single best source of information about where the project is headed and what it intends to accomplish.

- **Oversight and guidance**
  When the charter is complete, project sponsors can now begin to focus on the details of oversight. These include monitoring the status of major project deliverables, checking their performance relative to the schedule, and reviewing financial results for forecasts and budgets. Project sponsors will establish critical review points at which the overall health of the project can be assessed.

  Oversight and guidance will also ensure project alignment with corporate targets.

- **Risk management**
  The program management office (PMO) will maintain a risk registry of all known risk factors that could potentially affect project success. Project management will closely track any risks deemed of major importance. Project sponsors, in turn, will monitor changes in the profiles of these risks, so they can include modifications in their likelihood, potential impact, and mitigation strategies.

- **Team rewards and recognition**
  The duration and intensity of SAP implementations places considerable burden on the project team. Many companies choose to reward teams at various points in the project lifecycle. These rewards can take many forms. It is the responsibility of project governance to decide whether rewards are warranted and, if so, the type and amounts of rewards to be offered.

Let's explore each of these facets of effective project governance in more detail, beginning with the project charter.

11.1 Project Charter

The project charter is a comprehensive document divided into a number of constituent sections. As a general rule, it contains at least four multi-part sections, as outlined in Table 11.1.

Section	Description
Project description	Contains overall information about the specific project. Identifies project goals, the approach to be used, the project organization, and its scope.
Project plan	Outlines the major milestones for the project and their dates. Identifies all major project deliverables.
Roles and responsibilities	Specifies all major roles that will be part of the project, including project sponsors, team leads, project management, and team members.
Project management approach	Describes the project planning methodology as well as scope, issue, and cost management.

Table 11.1 Outline of the Project Charter

The project charter is often prepared with significant input from the systems integrator. In this way, the document outlines how the two groups intend to work together. Having this agreement—in the form of a document signed by company project sponsors and systems integrator executives—makes it something similar to a contract that binds both groups. It lays out operational expectations that will guide both teams throughout the project lifecycle, and for that reason is often signed by executives from both organizations.

Let's take a closer look at each piece of the project charter.

11.1.1 Project Description

This section covers the major nuts and bolts of the project, and it identifies the major project goals or intended results. The SAP implementation program should have three to five major objectives that are phrased like talking points, such as "build for a global organization" or "standardize all major processes." These should quickly become the mantra for all those assigned to the project. These few sentences specify the core purpose of the project.

The project approach will depend on the ASAP methodology and its primary phases. What is especially important in this segment is the listing of major deliverables by each phase, which will align the project team's understanding of what is due, and when.

> **Tip**
> This milestone list should cover the top 10-15 primary deliverables in each phase, and should not attempt to provide an all-inclusive listing.

The project organization segment identifies all functional process workstreams and their primary areas of coverage. The segment also identifies any horizontal technical workstreams, as well as the project management organization that will be used during the project.

The scope section addresses a number of elements. These have to do with major business processes to be included in the project, the entire listing of SAP and third-party applications that will be involved, all implementing company organizations and locations involved in the project, and technical infrastructure to be addressed. The scope section will also describe all custom objects known to be required at this stage in the project.

11.1.2 Project Plan Summary

The summary outlines key portions of the project plan. Because blueprinting is the first phase in which the entire project team is involved, it devotes considerable space to laying out the approach to that phase. The section contains both a description and timing for blueprinting events. This will alert the functional teams to the chronology of blueprinting and encourage them to plan for these activities. It will also discuss exactly how blueprinting works.

The project plan's summary section also introduces the concept of *localization*, which identifies any global blueprint decisions against statutory or legal requirements for a specific marketplace. Localization can be seen as an adjunct to blueprinting, where local requirements may, in a very limited fashion, modify the global blueprint decisions.

The project plan's summary section contains an explicit description of all blueprinting deliverables. Again, this listing performs both educational and notification purposes. It lets workstreams begin their planning by focusing on the first deliverables that the project requires. This not only supports program objectives, but begins building a delivery-based culture within the project team.

Figure 11.1 shows the project blueprint deliverables. Note that the figure provides a numerical designation to each deliverable, identifies each deliverable by name, and supplies the date on which it is expected to be complete. Each deliverable also includes a short descriptive statement regarding its purpose and content. Finally, the figure specifies the delivery mechanism for each deliverable. Most often, it references the software application on which the deliverable will be supplied.

Ref	Deliverable and Date	Purpose and Content	Delivery Mechanism
1	Program charter (6/01/20XX)	Defines the ERP program.	MS Word document
2	Benefit opportunities (6/05/20XX)	List of benefit opportunities, descriptions, and matrix showing relative desirability.	MS Word or PowerPoint document
3	Benefits case (6/20/20XX)	Defines and quantifies the benefits to be derived from the SAP program.	MS PowerPoint document
4	Benefits action plan (7/01/20XX)	Lists actions to achieve defined benefits. Shows estimated timing and assigned owners.	MS Excel spreadsheet or MS Project plan
5	Defined and configured sandbox system and development environment (7/15/20XX)	Overviews SAP systems to support blueprint prototyping activities.	Physical system and supporting documentation in MS Word
6	List of common processes and data within scope (7/25/20XX)	Lists global, local, common, and unique processes.	SAP Solution Manager and attachments in MS Office formats
7	Workshop schedule (7/30/20XX)	Shows number, location, and attendance at workshop meetings.	MS Word or PowerPoint
8	Blueprint workshop materials (8/05/20XX)	Lists facilitation materials for workshops.	MS PowerPoint

Figure 11.1 Partial Blueprint Deliverable Listing in Hypothetical Project Charter

11.1.3 Roles and Responsibilities

The project charter also outlines all major roles and their responsibilities during the SAP implementation project. Making all these role descriptions available in a single, easily accessible document permits everyone on the project team to compare and contrast the various roles.

Let's explore the depth and scope of the roles and responsibilities for the business transformation officer (BTO) and the business process owners. Other roles, not listed, require this same level of articulation.

The BTO has the following tasks:

- Assume responsibility for delivery of the program and address any conflicts between completing company initiatives.
- Ensure that the delivered SAP solution matches business needs and requirements.
- Be accountable for the program budget and the program's ability to achieve that budget.
- Deliver program progress updates to company senior executives and solicit their input on program performance.
- Provide overall guidance to the project team and represent business interests. Clarify and resolve differences in business and program priorities.
- Ensure that necessary financial, human, and knowledge resources are available to accomplish the program's objectives.
- Set direction on program priorities and policies.
- Work to resolve issues in a rapid manner and remove impeding obstacles.
- Take the lead in supporting change management initiatives, including communications, process transformations, and organizational changes.
- Hold regular update meetings with the PMO to review project status and resolve major issues.
- Manage relationships and contracting with the systems integrator and other key vendors.
- Sign off on and approve key program deliverables.

- Serve as the program's global spokesperson with regional executives.
- Ensure that the program follows the project charter and revise it as the program evolves.

Business process owners (or functional workstream leads) have the following tasks:

- Exercise responsibility for the process content of the SAP solution.
- Lead process design activities for the SAP solution.
- Contribute process, functional, and business expertise throughout the project lifecycle.
- Lead the process team and oversee company staff assigned to functional workstreams.
- Develop process business requirements, and design process scenarios and business transformation scope.
- Develop and document the transformational business model to include changes to processes, people, and organizations.
- Take a lead role in identifying and resolving cross-functional process issues throughout the program lifecycle.
- Deliver blueprinting deliverables, including process definition documents, change impacts, and business controls.
- Manage functional process activities, such as system testing, data conversion, and user training development during realization.
- Create an extended team of subject matter experts (SMEs) to assist with regional implementation activities.
- Conduct ongoing communications with functional executives to update them on program progress and continuing business-related issues.

Project Management Approach

This project management approach section of the project's charter outlines a number of related components. They describe the fundamental workings of the program, including descriptions of processes for issue resolution and scope management, methods of financial control, and the meeting structure that the project will use for the remainder of its lifecycle.

Issue Management

Project governance focuses considerable attention on issue management. Any member of the project team can identify and submit an issue. In general, issues describe some facet of the project that is not working as planned. Issues cover a number of areas, including schedule construction and its attainment, performance of the project team and infrastructure, and project processes such as system testing.

Issue resolution generally follows the project chain of command outlined in Figure 11.2. When workstream members report issues, the first point of resolution will be that workstream's leader. Even if the issue crosses workstream boundaries, it will still be the responsibility of the reporting lead to manage the issue with other workstreams. If workstream leader cannot resolve the issue, it will be escalated to the PMO to address. If the PMO cannot resolve the issue, it will be forwarded to project governance.

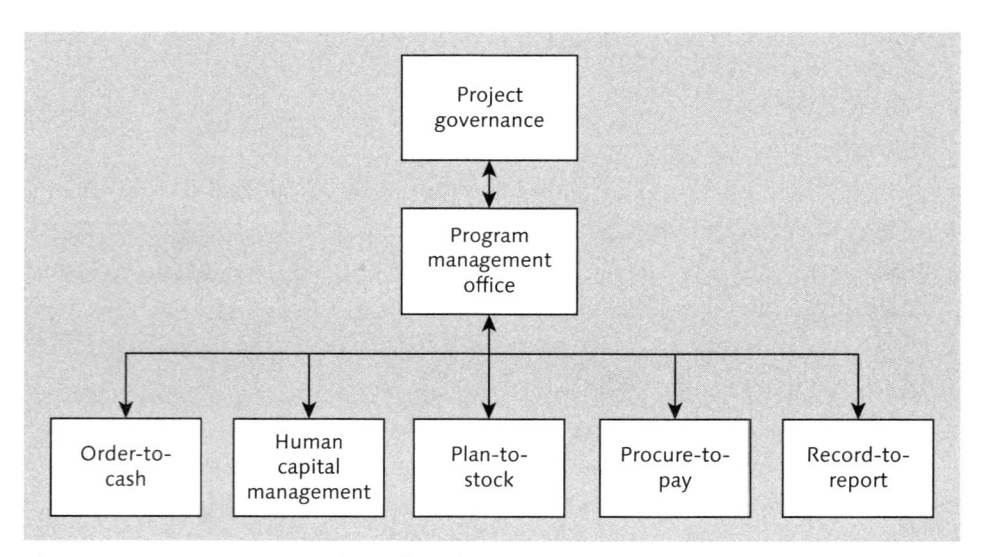

Figure 11.2 Issue Management Chain of Resolution

Once an issue reaches project governance, it can be handled by any of three entities. First, the issue will be assigned to the BTO. If the issue cannot be resolved at that level, it will be assigned to the project sponsors group. This will take place where the project lacks the authority or the mandate to resolve the issue. Project sponsors can most often mobilize the necessary resources and make a binding decision for resolution.

If that approach proves unsuccessful, the issue can be assigned to the company executive committee. This will be a very rare occurrence. Only a very few issues are likely to make their way even past the PMO. In most cases, they are resolved at that point. Generally, only issues with major policy implications for the company will rise to the level of the BTO or higher. Certainly those that make their way to the company executive committee will have broad impact for an implementing company.

Once an issue is resolved, the agreed-upon solution is outlined in the issue registry that is maintained by the PMO. At that point, the issue is tagged as "resolved" and removed from the active issue registry. It can then be placed in an "inactive" status.

The issue registry should receive very scrupulous maintenance. Corporate auditors who focus on the SAP implementation program may assess program operations adequacy; to do so, they often request access to the program issues registry. By reviewing input, documentation, and resolution of reported issues, auditors can very quickly assess the quality of PMO operations.

Cost Control

The SAP implementation program will have a very large budget to manage and report its performance against. To enable this reporting, some cost collection mechanisms will be needed. These include assigning charge numbers for those working on the project, and procedures for assigning capital versus expense reporting.

By far the largest component of the project budget will be headcount charges for company project staff and for systems integrator staff. These should be carefully collected and reported.

For those accustomed to working on capital projects involving physical objects, such as adding a new manufacturing facility, the rules of a software implementation project operate somewhat differently. There are two operating rules of thumb:

▶ All costs related to the design, configuration, and custom objects software development are considered to be direct *capital costs*.

- All planning and testing activities are considered to be expense costs. Activities involving development and delivery of end-user training are also considered to be *expense costs*. The project preparation phase and early aspects of blueprinting are most often handled as expense charges.

For companies tracking staff time charges, the team should receive capital and expense charge numbers for the purposes of reporting time allocations. These charge numbers should be distributed only to personnel who are formally assigned to the project. If possible, a dedicated department number should be created within the company cost centers. Use of a specific department number makes it far easier to collect and report accurate staff charges.

Some project staff may remain housed within their home departments and not transfer to the central project location. Usually these staff members continue to perform their normal duties while exercising a limited role on the SAP implementation project team. These staff members should receive charge numbers and be permitted to charge their time in accordance with the functional organizations' agreements.

In the case of global projects, regional operations will assign their staff to work for the project on a dedicated basis. Their time commitments vary considerably over the lifecycle of the project but will expand during blueprinting, localization, and user acceptance testing. Regional operations may receive charge numbers to report time spent on project activities.

In some situations, regional staff assigned to the project—as well as full-time core project staff—will have some of their costs covered by using a "backfill" mechanism. For full-time or part-time project assignment, functional organizations could temporarily replace or backfill their resources assigned to the project. In those cases, the project would pay for the backfill cost out of its budget.

If a cost center were dedicated to project headcount costs, it would collect costs for full-time assigned staff. That money, normally allocated to costs within their home department, could now be used to hire contract or temporary labor for the duration of the project. This simplified method reduces the recordkeeping associated with funds transfers between the project and home functional organizations.

For part-time regional staff assigned to the project in an SME role, the project could agree to a backfill funding amount that would enable regional organizations to hire temporary replacement workers as needed. Project sponsors should agree on the percentage of time spent on the project that would be eligible for backfill. Once a threshold was established, regional organizations could receive funds transfers from the project to cover these costs.

Clearly, the project charter has an essential role to play in project governance. It basically sets the foundation and outlines rules of the road for project operations. For it to serve its purpose fully, it must be carefully reviewed and kept up to date during the project lifecycle. Because the project charter must be a living document, making sure that it remains current is one of the major roles of the BTO who leads the project.

11.2 Oversight and Guidance

Over the span of the program, project governance ensures its accomplishments are consistent with the project charter. The bulk of this essential oversight role will fall to the BTO, who conducts periodic project reviews; of course, other project sponsors will assist in regular reviews by participating in them as needed.

The key oversight role will consist of phase reviews as the project moves forward in its lifecycle. *Phase reviews* provide solid evidence that the project is ready to deliver the functionality required by that phase. As formal phase reviews, the project team will present evidence of readiness and project governance will assess, question, and render its judgment of readiness.

Figure 11.3 indicates the scheduling of these phase reviews. The blueprinting completion, localization, and build completion phase reviews would be conducted once. The remaining three reviews would be conducted for as many go-lives as required to complete the project. Thus, if the project were constructed around three implementation waves, there would be three user acceptance test completion reviews, three go-live readiness reviews, and three hypercare completion reviews. This would total 12 reviews during the project lifespan.

> **Trail Marker**
> Remember the connection to the ASAP quality reviews discussed in Chapter 3? These are those same reviews, now adopted for use by your project team.

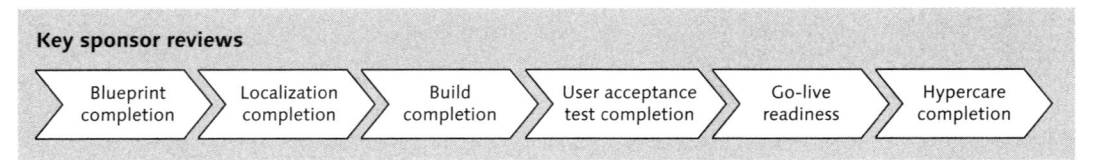

Figure 11.3 Major Project Governance Phase Reviews

Clearly, the focus of each phase review depends on its purpose and timing in the project. Each phase review would have a set of defined objectives:

- **Blueprint completion**
    This first phase review examines major design decisions made during blueprinting. Functional workstream leaders would present their design objectives before beginning blueprinting and demonstrate how these objectives materialized in terms of actual system design content. Project sponsors would have the opportunity to question all decisions in detail and understand the rationale behind them. This review would provide final approval to the blueprint for each workstream.

- **Localization completion**
    Normally, localization takes place in the months immediately following blueprinting. This review examines all significant localization issues and how they were handled. Again, project sponsors would have the opportunity to question all localization decisions. After this review, the system design would be complete.

- **Build completion**
    The build phase of realization translates blueprinting decisions into concrete system configuration and custom object build. During this period, the systems integrator applies needed configuration to the SAP system. Additionally, the systems integrator will develop and unit test all custom objects (WRICEFPs) required to operate the system according to company specifications.

    Your team can't initiate integration testing until the system build is complete. During this review, project sponsors would emphasize completion of all custom object development, the success of unit test results for those custom objects, and the accomplishment of all configuration required. When the review has concluded, the team will have authorization to move onto integration test.

- **User acceptance test completion**
  This review confirms the close-out of system testing. It assesses performance during the integration test and the second testing phase, which is the user acceptance test. At this point, the system should be verified as working to requirements and ready for the final steps to go-live. Project sponsors examine completion of all test scripts and resolution of all system defects discovered during testing. When this review is complete, the team will have authorization to move into go-live preparations.

- **Go-live readiness**
  This very important review evaluates the project's readiness for go-live, so naturally it is held in the period directly before go-live. Its focus includes transport of configuration, custom objects, and master data into the production system. It also focuses on completing required user training, super user preparations, final role mapping, and hypercare planning. If the review concludes successfully, the project team will receive permission to take the system live.

- **Hypercare completion**
  After go-live, the project team shifts into a very intensive problem resolution mode. The project team resolves all issues or incidents affecting the new system. The review assesses incident levels, resolution timing, and the ability of business functions to operate the system effectively. When the project sponsors decide that the system has reached stable operating parameters, hypercare will terminate. The team will now be free to move on to any following implementation waves.

These scheduled phase reviews are in no way intended to place limits on project sponsors. They can conduct project status updates or progress assessments at any time. This list constitutes a minimal set to recognize what is absolutely necessary for effective project governance in terms of an implementation project's charter. Your company can add other reviews to the schedule or perform ad hoc assessments as warranted.

11.3 Risk Management

Every SAP implementation project faces daily risks. Because the very act of placing so many company business processes under a single software system poses a risk unto itself, your company must decide whether the prospective benefits outweigh the risks. A project performs only as well as its mechanisms for working risks. In fact, it is not uncommon for a project to face hundreds of major risks during its lifecycle. Risk recognition and mitigation skills among key program staff will prove essential throughout its implementation phases.

Some risks, such as the ability of the project team to complete constructing its test scripts on time, are relatively small and easily handled. Others are very major in scale and require coordinated effort to overcome. Major risks can run the gamut—from the project's ability to generate its deliverables, to business control issues that may hurt the company's ability to report its earnings accurately. Project governance and the PMO operate as the major point for identifying, assessing, and resolving all major risks.

In this context, the term *risk* will be used to identify any prospective events that may jeopardize the project's ability to meet its objectives. Project risks may be phrased as either positive or negative in nature. Thus, a risk may indicate that some positive event for the project, such as completing the user acceptance test on schedule, will not take place or be only partially complete. It may also indicate a negative event, such as if a major infrastructure component would not be delivered on time to meet project needs.

All risks should be viewed through the prism of their effects on project objectives. These objectives are writ large (and necessarily include causing no damage to the company business profile or existing supply chain). Often, the project charter will contain a listing of any top-level risks that have been defined at the onset of the project. These should be the first items on the project risk register.

> **Tip**
> Take an active role in risk identification. Talk to executives, project team members, and prospective end users to find out what *they* are worried about. Add these to your risk register. Effective risk mitigation begins with knowing the real risks. One test for your register should be: Was every major risk we encountered already identified on our risk register?

Often these initial top-level risks identify potential issues that have the attention of company senior executives. For this reason, they should be carefully managed throughout the duration of the project. Other top-level risks can be added to this listing as they are captured.

Figure 11.4 illustrates an effective risk classification system, which consists of six risk classifications:

- Executive risk
  - Verify that key executives are involved
  - Check that these stakeholders understand and are committed to support the project objectives
- Project risk
  - Assess that the project is properly planned, scope is well-defined and managed, and decision-making is timely and accurate
- Functional risk
  - Assess whether user requirements are well defined and aligned to business processes
  - Verify strong user commitment/involvement to manage expectations and gain acceptance to the delivered system
- Resource risk
  - Assess proper definition of resource requirements (skills and time) for project
  - Assess whether project team is effectively positioned to perform
- Organizational risk
  - Verify that communications strategies are in place to manage expectations and gain buy-in
  - Verify appropriate training and support for business user community
- Technical risk
  - Verify technology architecture is sound and stable
  - Verify integrity of the data in the new system
  - Verify appropriate security controls are in place

By classifying risks in this way, project governance personnel can not only assign a potential severity to the risk, but can also denote what agency in the company might take responsibility for its mitigation.

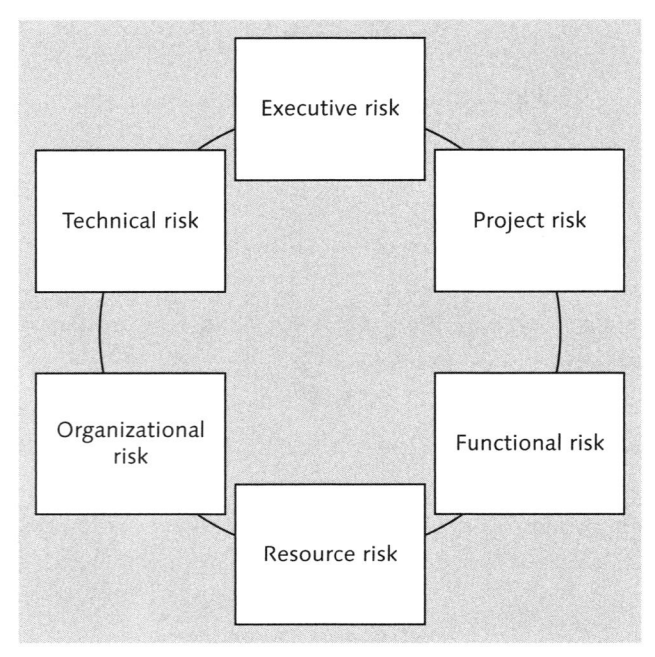

Figure 11.4 Project Risk Classification System

> **Tip**
> One way to generate an effective initial risk listing is by conducting a brainstorming session with project sponsors. It will help to provide a few examples in each category and then have attendees flag risks that could most impact the project. This encourages them to think about project risk, and it will also begin the process of teambuilding among the group.

Table 11.2 outlines a set of hypothetical—but realistic—top-level risks in each category. The listing also contains two realistic project risks as well as other pieces of essential information about the risks. In addition to the risk description, these include its impact on the project, its likelihood of occurring, and mitigating actions that can be taken.

11.3 Risk Management

Number	Description	Project Impact	Probability	Mitigation
Executive risk				
1	Project sponsors do not fully engage with or support the project.	Critical business support will be missing. Team leads will not receive needed guidance.	Low	Use change management team to engage stakeholders. Generate regular communications.
2	Regional leaders will not support changes in business processes needed to make the project a success.	Changes will take place at the corporate level but encounter difficulty at the regional level.	Medium	Engage with regional leaders on needed changes. Solicit their concerns.
Organizational risk				
3	Preparation for go-live will not be thorough. This may substantially raise incident levels during hypercare.	Hypercare will be protracted and will cause the schedule for later implementations to slip.	Medium	Establish rigorous review formats as conditions for go-live approval.
4	Changes in the Asia organization are still underway. Focus on the project may be difficult to obtain.	The critical Asia market may not have the time to fully participate in the project.	Medium	Reach out to Asia regional director. Confirm the importance of the project to company success.
Technical risk				
5	Implementation of recently introduced SAP functionality may cause delays.	New functionality will not perform as expected. Testing and hypercare will be extended.	High	Identify recently released SAP applications and place them on a special "watch list" to verify their performance.
6	Needed SAP infrastructure may not be delivered on time.	Without needed infrastructure in place, the project cannot begin development activities.	High	Periodically review infrastructure delivery schedules with systems integrator to validate adherence to delivery schedule.

Table 11.2 Initial Program Top-Level Risk Registry

11 | Project Governance

Number	Description	Project Impact	Probability	Mitigation
Resource risk				
7	Project workstreams do not have adequate staffing levels	Workstream resource coverage issues will cause delays in blueprint and in later phases.	Medium	Identify key staffing issues and supplement workstreams as needed.
8	SMEs in Latin America do not fully cover needed business processes	Blueprint and localization for Latin America may not complete on time or have adequate coverage.	Medium	Reach out to Latin America regional director for additional resources as needed.
Project risk				
9	Project schedule and timing may be too aggressive	Working to an unrealistic schedule will cause team burnout, errors, and incomplete work.	High	Closely review schedule and its rationale with PMO.
10	Project scope is not as yet well-defined.	Inadequate project scope definition will cause confusion and wasted effort among workstreams.	Medium	Schedule working session with team leads and the PMO to generate final project scope.
Functional risk				
11	Great deal of variation in the experience levels of workstream leads assigned from functional groups.	Workstream leads have considerable responsibility for project deliverables. Those without necessary experience will not represent their functions well.	Medium	Review experience levels of workstream leads and provide supplemental resources where needed.
12	Business process differences between regions will not be resolved prior to go-live.	Operating the SAP system as a single entity depends on common business processes. Without these, the system will not perform as expected.	Medium	Identify key business processes where differences now exist. Conduct periodic reviews to ensure commonality.

Table 11.2 Initial Program Top-Level Risk Registry (Cont.)

Risks such as these require constant vigilance from project governance. Monitoring the mitigation methods' effectiveness should be part of that oversight as well; merely indicating that a mitigation effort should be attempted does not ensure that the effort was made or that it had the desired impact. Project sponsors should take ownership of top-level risks that fall in their area of functional scope. Receiving updates on actions taken and success attained will keep these risks at the forefront of sponsor attention.

11.4 Team Rewards and Recognition

At the beginning of the SAP implementation project, sponsors should make preliminary decisions concerning the recognition and rewarding of team members. Though awards are generally given at the end of the project or at various phases in the implementation cycle, we recommend that project governance leadership map out an approach to this often-contentious subject early on. Doing this is very positive; it ensures that a framework has been put in place and that necessary funds are available to pay for these rewards.

Basically, an implementing company adopts its own method for constructing team rewards for successful projects. Projects that do not complete or are flawed in some major way are not eligible for recognition awards. Companies that do make awards available, however, are faced with answering the following questions:

1. **Who will be rewarded?**
   The easy answer to this question is "everyone on the project team." However, not everyone will play the same role—some will be more critical to project success than others. Additionally, some members of the project team will participate only on a part-time basis, so their efforts on the project will not be as consistent as full-time members. Likewise, in the case a global project with multiple regional implementation waves, project team members from those regions may participate only in that wave and no others. Project governance must decide which individuals to reward and by how much.

2. **When will rewards be made?**
   In the case of a project with a single go-live, project governance could decide to distribute recognition awards after the conclusion of hypercare. For a project involving multiple implementation waves, the decision is not so clear-cut.

Multi-wave SAP implementation projects take place over years at a time. Some type of award for each wave may prove a reasonable course of action.

3. **What form will the rewards take?**
Some companies choose to make monetary awards only. Other companies award money along with stock option grants.

> **Tip**
> Money is always welcome. The reception given to stock option grants depends on how their strike prices compare with the company stock value and the timing at which the options might vest.

4. **How much will be awarded?**
Clearly, the amount to be awarded depends on the importance of the project to company operations and to the financial condition of the company. If the SAP implementation project is central to long-term company strategy, then the awards should be as generous as they are practicable. Where the project is less central, the amounts to be awarded would be somewhat less.

Table 11.3 provides an example of how project rewards might be structured for a multiple-wave global SAP implementation. The awards are divided into three levels:

- Level one is targeted to project leadership. This group includes functional and technical workstream leads as well as staff from the PMO.
- Remaining full-time project staff would be designated as level two. This grouping would include full-time global SMEs who were regular participants in a project workstream.
- Project team members who participated in a single implementation wave, such as regional SMEs, would be placed in the level three grouping.

Those in the level one group would receive a full share of the amount offered by the company. Team members in the level two group would receive some fractional share. The rule here is that leadership is absolutely essential to the outcome of the project and should receive a significantly greater reward. Due to the more limited role, level three would receive an award of much smaller value.

Award Level	Recipients	Timing
Level one: Full share	Project leadership, including the PMO and workstream leads	At completion of major implementation waves
Level two: Partial share	All other full-time project team members	At completion of major implementation waves
Level three: Partial share by wave	Regional SMEs and other regional staff	At completion of regional implementation waves

Table 11.3 Structure for Project Recognition Awards

Assuming a three-wave SAP implementation project, levels one and two participants would receive awards following each wave—provided it was successful. Level three recipients would collect their awards after completion of the wave in which they participated. For level one and level two participants, the amounts awarded at each wave could be pro-rated depending on the duration and complexity of the wave. Thus, instead of receiving one-third of an award at each wave, recipients could obtain their bonuses at 40 percent for wave one, 20 percent for wave two, and 40 percent for wave three.

> **Pitfall Alert**
>
> SAP implementation project team rewards are always difficult to administer. As we've shown, there are so many different combinations of service—and so many candidates for recognition—that it makes equitable solutions hard to find. However, they can be found. Just remember that there will be future projects on the horizon and they will require excellent teams as well. The message sent by *not* rewarding your team will have lasting effects. Recruiting for your next project may, as a result, encounter a very lukewarm reception.

While it is absolutely essential to recognize difficult work and long hours, administering these recognition awards is not without its challenges. Team members often feel that they should be classified in one group rather than another. Others who were not included in the awards often feel unjustly excluded. It will be up to project governance to develop clear-cut rules and rationales for these decisions. These rules should be transparent and made available to those who have questions. Even then, there may still be a bit of controversy—but it will be manageable.

We have now accounted for all aspects of project governance: Your project charter will now be in place, along with oversight mechanisms and a risk management process. The stage is now set to build your project team. Our next chapter outlines methods for selecting and on-boarding team members.

We're now ready to build our project team. In this chapter, we discuss team member selection, onboarding, and the final return to home organizations in the company.

12 Building the Right Project Team

Chapter 10 outlined the SAP project organization. It reviewed arrangements for the functional alignment of the project and described the overall structure of workstreams. Chapter 11, in turn, described the project's governance structure and how oversight and risk management take place. This chapter takes matters one step further. It focuses on how best to staff those roles throughout the entire project lifecycle. Our coverage includes finding and retaining the very best resources available to complete the project.

Finding resources for an SAP implementation project goes outside "business as usual" activity, if only because of the sheer size of the project and its required personnel. Large numbers of qualified individuals will be needed immediately. Though many candidates will come from the existing company employee base, finding the right people for an implementation project team will constitute an arduous assignment. Those employees selected will be required to work for long hours for the entire duration of the project—usually somewhere between two to four years—under challenging conditions, and they will frequently travel away from home.

So, recruiting an effective project team is essential for a successful project. To the extent that team members are qualified and motivated, the project stands a good chance of realizing its objectives. To the extent that team members are *not* qualified or motivated, the project is in jeopardy.

Figure 12.1 shows project teambuilding to be a long-term process, taking place across the project lifecycle. It consists of finding the right team, bringing team members on to the project, helping the team deliver results, and then reintegrating the team within their home organizations.

12 Building the Right Project Team

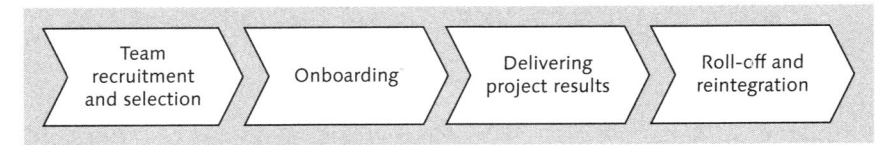

Figure 12.1 Four-Step Project Teambuilding Process

This process model divides teambuilding into four discrete phases. The lesson here is that teambuilding does not stop once the team is selected. It continues for the duration of the project. Depending on where the project stands in its delivery cycle, teambuilding will remain a focus even as activities change.

- **Team recruitment and selection**
  This represents the initial and most intensive phase of project team building. During this period, candidates for all project roles must be identified, interviewed, and vetted before selections are made. Given the size of the project, this may involve reviewing as many as 500 candidates to fill 100 roles.

- **Onboarding**
  Once the project leadership has made its final selections, the onboarding process begins. Each project team member will receive a briefing regarding duties and expectations. Locations and working space both for teams and individuals must be allocated. Work processes must be initiated.

- **Delivery of project results**
  With the team on board, the project moves into the major delivery phases: blueprint, realization, and final preparation. During this period, teams undergo significant stresses. They will likely experience burnout from working on tight deadlines, as well as fatigue from the years-long project schedule. Project leadership will need to constantly monitor all individuals and their ability to withstand the rigors of an SAP implementation.

- **Roll-off and reintegration**
  When the last project go-live has taken place, team members who have contributed to its success will be ready to roll off. They will relinquish their project roles and return to their functional organization. Your project leadership will have planned for this transition period and ensured that each team member has a challenging and rewarding role to fill.

This chapter uses the four-phase teambuilding model as its organizing principle. We'll discuss each phase in detail and offer guidance about how to make the project time a positive experience for all team members.

12.1 Team Recruitment and Selection

Building a solid SAP implementation team can be a daunting task, and it sometime feels like accelerating from zero to 60 in the blink of an eye. The project now has an agreed-upon start date but can't move forward until the project team has been built and is ready to perform.

Often, recruitment and selection takes place over the course of a month. During this period, the project organizational structure must be decided, candidates identified to fill necessary roles, and selections made to bring on the best choices from among the candidate group.

Almost every SAP implementation project operates by the staffing mantra "bring on only our best and brightest." In some cases, these results really are achieved: The project really is staffed with the very best performers from the company organization. In other cases, this goal is not achieved. The project team consists of middle-of-the-road performers and the results confirm this condition. To take aim at success, this chapter is oriented toward finding the best candidates available. We hope that your company can adopt this orientation as well. Where circumstances make this option impossible for your company, it can perhaps compensate in other ways to obtain a high-quality team.

Our first step entails focusing on project leadership roles. These include the program manager, functional workstream leads, and horizontal workstream leads. Because these personnel will carry a large part of the burden for achieving project results, take considerable care with their selection.

Let's walk through the process of making these major selections, as outlined in Figure 12.2.

Position description → Candidate grouping → First cut candidate interviews → Candidate vetting → Final selection

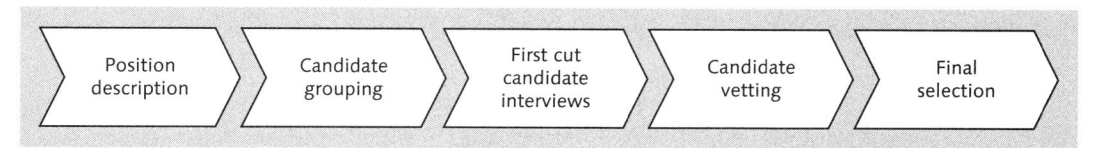

Figure 12.2 Project Leadership Selection Process

For each leadership position, prepare a job description to guide candidate selection. This involves a listing of key knowledge, skills, and attitudes required for the position. In addition, it would also include those leadership attributes needed to perform the role successfully.

These job descriptions should be prepared in close working partnership with the company's human resources organization. Having a skilled HR practitioner directly assigned to the project during this period will greatly assist. HR practitioners prepare job descriptions and conduct candidate evaluations as a matter of course. Their deep experience in these areas will make the process move along much more smoothly.

Figure 12.3 provides a sample job description for the procure-to-pay lead. It outlines the major requirements of the position and helps candidates determine whether they are prepared to take on the role. It also provides guidance to project leadership in the later steps of the selection process. Prior to posting the job descriptions, your project leadership should assess the managerial level needed for each position (e.g., director, associate director, senior manager, or manager-level positions). This information would be included with the job description as a guide to those who might wish to apply.

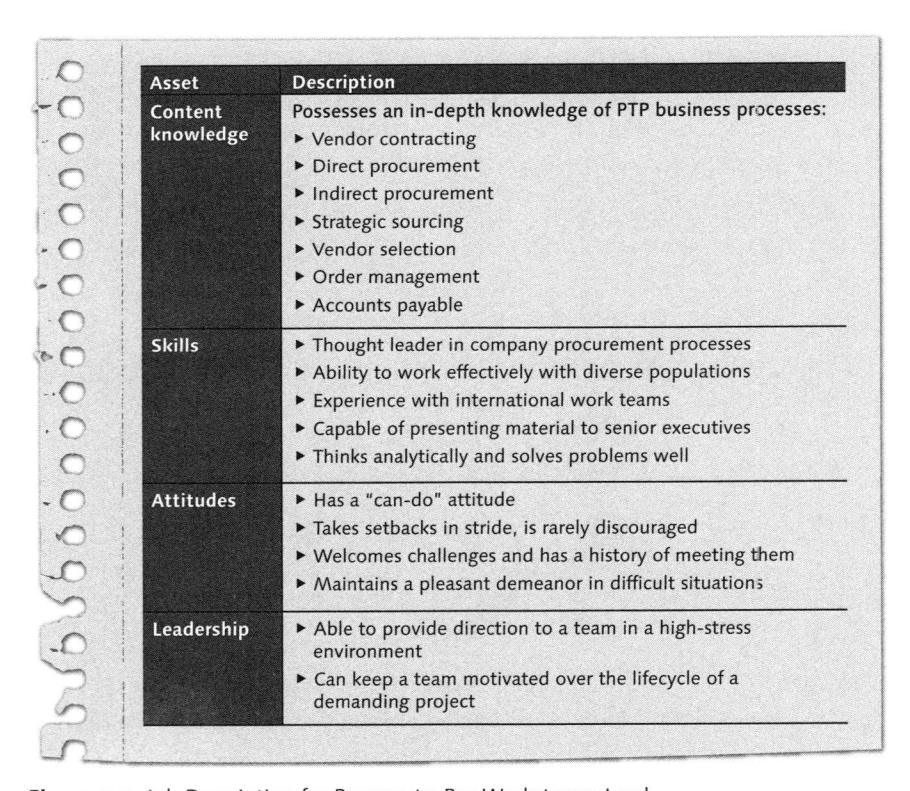

Asset	Description
Content knowledge	Possesses an in-depth knowledge of PTP business processes: ▸ Vendor contracting ▸ Direct procurement ▸ Indirect procurement ▸ Strategic sourcing ▸ Vendor selection ▸ Order management ▸ Accounts payable
Skills	▸ Thought leader in company procurement processes ▸ Ability to work effectively with diverse populations ▸ Experience with international work teams ▸ Capable of presenting material to senior executives ▸ Thinks analytically and solves problems well
Attitudes	▸ Has a "can-do" attitude ▸ Takes setbacks in stride, is rarely discouraged ▸ Welcomes challenges and has a history of meeting them ▸ Maintains a pleasant demeanor in difficult situations
Leadership	▸ Able to provide direction to a team in a high-stress environment ▸ Can keep a team motivated over the lifecycle of a demanding project

Figure 12.3 Job Description for Procure-to-Pay Workstream Lead

Pitfall Alert

Pay a great deal of attention to these job descriptions, but try not to forget the human element. Many of your project "stars" will be as expected. Others, however, will surprise everyone. Some people relish taking on a challenge and flourish in its attainment. They may not be impressive in interviews but have an internal guidance system that just gets things done. Seek these people out.

It's likely that a number of candidates will make their interests known. However, because these are project positions with a limited term, the standard formal rules for position applications may not apply. Your company may have leeway to invite individuals to apply or to seek nominations from company functional executives.

As Figure 12.4 indicates, a company can cast a wide net in finding its senior workstream leads. Considerable weight should be placed on recommendations from company senior functional executives. These individuals will have long-term experience with many of the prospective candidates and will have dealt with them under a variety of circumstances.

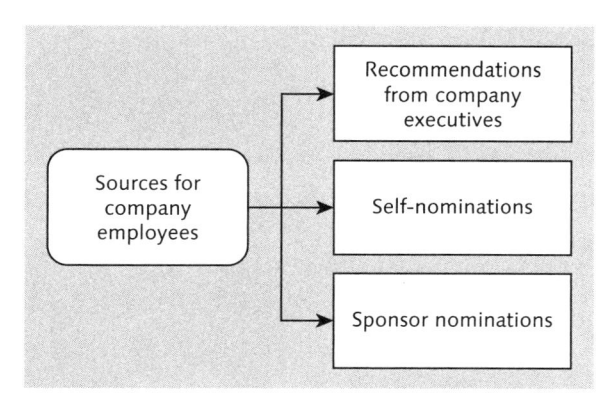

Figure 12.4 Sources for Company Project Leadership

Additionally, many of the horizontal workstream leads will no doubt come from the company IT organization. The company CIO will be well placed to provide input on self-nominated candidates and to suggest additional candidates who might be good fits. Many in the IT organization can be expected to have previous project experience. While they may not have participated in an SAP implementation project, any previous project experience serves as a good indicator of their ability to flourish in the SAP project world.

Once project sponsors complete this initial review, they will be in a good position to make decisions regarding staffing. The simplest way to begin is with an inventory of staffing needs and applicants. By tracking the availability of program manager and workstream leads, project sponsors can immediately grasp the numbers needed and progress in filling positions.

The full inventory should register each position required along with potential candidates. It should also include positions where a likely fit is available and where no good fits have yet been found.

Table 12.5 provides a compilation of the recruitment status. It breaks down the three primary position categories and displays the current status in the search for candidates. Additionally, comments describe the likely prognosis in finding suitable candidates for the positions.

Leadership Role	Number Required	Number of Candidates	Comments
Program manager	1	3	No strong program manager candidates available. Those applying have limited experience managing large-scale project.
Functional process leads	7	22	Solid candidates for every workstream. Preferred candidates for OTC and PTP will require special recruitment effort.
Horizontal technical leads	8	16	Small number of candidates but a strong field. Only EDI and data conversion leads needed additional attention.
Total	16	41	

Figure 12.5 Tracking Summary for Project Leadership Roles Selection

Figure 12.5 shows that staffing for functional process leads is proceeding well. There are two qualified candidates for every position available. The horizontal technical lead situation indicates a small number of candidates but qualified individuals available for all but two roles: EDI and data conversion. The program manager position stands out as the greatest challenge. Company internal resources do not have the necessary background to direct a project of this magnitude.

Based on this evidence, the program manager search requires immediate attention and close scrutiny, as will the search for the two horizontal workstream leads. Likely project sponsors should turn to the CIO to seek evaluation information regarding potential candidates. The CIO's recommendation or rejection of potential candidates will make the choice of actions much clearer. If the CIO suggests that the in-house candidates can perform the tasks, then sponsors will likely move forward with those individuals. If the CIO does not have confidence that in-house candidates will suffice, then the project sponsors must adopt a different course of action.

> **Tip**
>
> Your company CIO will be the best source of information about project IT staffing. The CIO understands the technical skills each staff member possesses. Trust the recommendations and solicit the CIO's suggestions regarding contract staffing for these positions.

Figure 12.6 outlines the three primary staffing sources for project roles. Clearly, in-house candidates offer the preferred alternative for a few reasons: They are immediately available, they have long-standing experience in the company, and they do not impose an additional cost burden on the project.

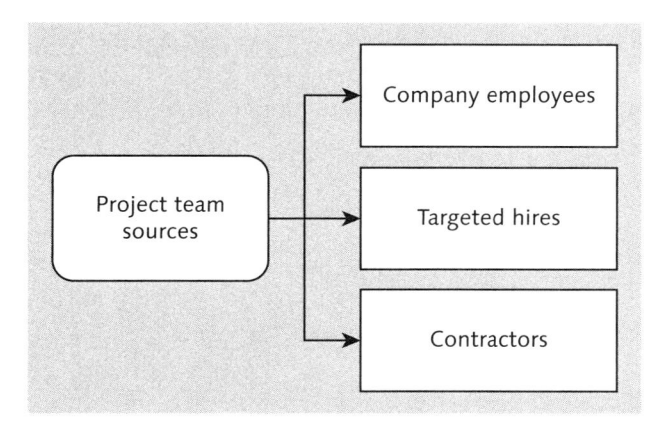

Figure 12.6 Sources for Project Team Staffing

However, remember that finding qualified company employees may not always be possible. In these circumstances, other courses of action must be followed. Two alternatives are available, each with its own set of advantages and disadvantages.

The first option, recruiting for a new hire, may appear to be the best choice. It would provide the project with a full-time and skilled company employee. Yet finding full-time employees is often a time-consuming process. Even under the best of circumstances, it will usually take three to six months from the time that the hiring requisition is approved until the new employee is brought on board. By that time, the project would likely be well along its delivery cycle.

Additionally, the project roles under discussion are temporary in nature. When the project is complete, many of these roles will disappear and all project participants will return to their host functional organization. Any full-time employees hired to participate in the project would be at potential risk. They would lack a home organization and might be subject to lay-off when the project came to a close. For this reason, job-seekers may choose to avoid signing on for project roles, no matter how appealing.

The second option, turning to a contractor, is the remaining course of action. This option often represents a more rapid turnaround approach. Many SAP-qualified project managers and technical resources normally operate as contractors who transition from one project to another as the current finishes and the next one begins. As a result, these resources are readily available in the marketplace.

Generally, contract hires are sourced through specialized recruiting companies. These recruiters work directly with the hiring company to establish discrete position requirements and then furnish a list of suggested candidates for the company to review. Company sponsors and project staff will conduct interviews with those who meet their requirements.

Unlike full-time hiring, these interviews are usually handled through teleconferences with the candidate, a representative from the contract recruiting firm, and members of the company's SAP implementation team. Running from 30 minutes to an hour in length, these interviews are open-ended and all company project team members can pose questions regarding skills, strengths and weaknesses, and relevant experience.

It is quite common for contractor hiring to be concluded within the span of a few days. Contractor recruiting firms work to make the process as painless and rapid as possible. Once the company has agreed on a specific contractor, only two potential obstacles stand in the way of bringing that individual on board the company project team.

The first obstacle is financial. The individuals under consideration are often very seasoned project experts. With their extensive project background, they can come up to speed on their role and be prepared for productive work very quickly. However, they will expect an hourly rate that may cause sticker shock in the hiring company. Their bottom-line rate will usually exceed that paid to standard contractors. If the project budget did not anticipate contract hiring, funds to pay for these contractors may prove difficult to come by.

The second obstacle is more procedural in nature. It's likely that many of these contract recruiting firms will not have a prior working relationship with the implementing company. In this case, making the initial hire will entail adding the recruiting firm to the company-approved vendor list and establishing a contractual understanding. Depending on the efficiency of your company procurement organization, this can turn into a more drawn-out process than expected. Having a single buyer who handles procurement activities for the project can greatly mitigate the time required.

Assuming that the financial and procedural obstacles have been overcome, the team will be staffed and ready for operation. The next step will center on the onboarding process for the team: moving team members from functional mode to project mode.

12.2 Onboarding the Project Team

Onboarding consists of two highly interrelated components. The first component centers on logistics arrangements for the team. This includes setting up work spaces, preparing communications devices, and allocating conference rooms for the teams. When the logistics process has concluded, the project team will move into whatever housing has been provided for it. The second component focuses on the actual onboarding of project staff. At that point, the team will have shifted into project mode and the SAP implementation will be fully underway.

This section covers each component. It also reviews team logistical options and their impact on team performance, and examines methods for bringing the team into its new home to begin project work.

249

12.2.1 Team Logistics

Once members of the team have been identified, final work can take place in setting up the project work space. Several options are available; each one can have a significant effect, either positive or negative, on team accomplishments.

Figure 12.7 indicates only some of the possible alternatives for team facilities setup. Basically any arrangement that fosters team interaction and communication is preferable to siloed, silent setups. Communication among and between teams is universally beneficial to project progress.

	Most preferable team options		Least preferable team options	
Location	All teams located in a single building	Intact teams located in multiple buildings at the same site	Teams located at the same site; no common team work areas	Teams scattered across several geographical locations
Conference rooms	At least one dedicated conference room per team		Some project-dedicated conference rooms; other conference rooms available to schedule	
Telephones	Individual team member phone connections; conference phones allocated per each team		Assigned team conference phones located at work sites	

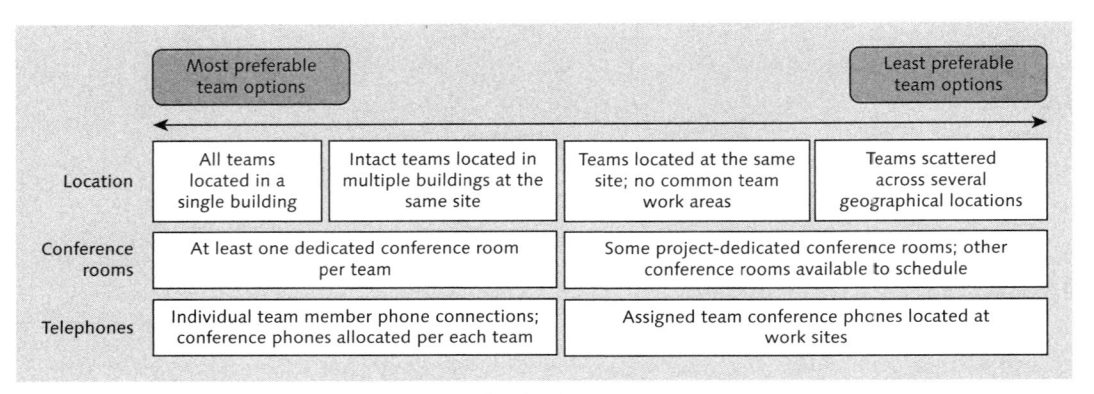

Figure 12.7 Team Logistics Options for the Project Team

Let's examine each alternative in this figure more closely.

Team Location

The most important of these facilities choices is the physical location of the project team. For this reason, project sponsors should make it a point to include a facilities coordinator in their team location discussions. The four options available are depicted in Figure 12.7. Options one and two can generally include a "bull pen" common work area and at least one office for workstream leads. Clearly many more options are possible, but these represent typical arrangements with close approximations to other alternatives.

> **Tip**
>
> We have a very strong bias in favor of team collocation and want to make that clear. Other options *can* work, but are not so well positioned for success. If you have the opportunity to create collocated workspace, seriously consider it.

1. **All teams collocated in a single building**

   This option is by far most preferable for supporting efficient project working conditions. It minimizes any barriers to communication by permitting real-time interaction. Project team members in different workstreams can become acquainted with one another and understand each other's perspectives.

   Ownership of major business processes is often shared among several functional teams. Housing the teams in a single physical location enables the informal day-to-day communication necessary for effective coordination. Team members are able to simply walk across the hall tesolve issues as they arise, instead of being hindered by time zones.

   This same situation holds for interaction with project management and horizontal technical teams. Thus, the data conversion lead will have easy access to all functional workstream leads. The status of data cleansing or difficulties in data verification can be immediately gathered by a short trip to the workstream lead office.

   The challenges with this option relate to facility availability and cost. Some companies will have sufficient vacant building space to house the team easily. Other companies will be more limited and may have to consider leasing space to house their project team. Where cost is a limiting factor, the implementing company may have to examine other options.

2. **Intact teams located in multiple buildings at the same site**

   If space and cost constraints prevent the implementing company from housing the project team in a single building, this represents the next-best choice. In this situation, some teams would likely operate from one building and other teams would operate from others. However, every team would be housed in its own adjacent work area.

   Having significant physical separation between teams — but having all teams in the same site location — is less preferable than option one, but good program management and a commitment to communicate among workstream leads can circumvent these limitations. Response times may be slower, but good results will still be achieved.

3. **Teams located at the same site with no common work areas**
   In this alternative, team members would essentially retain their current office location but have a full-time assignment to a functional or technical workstream. It is more of a "business as usual" approach to the project. It does, however, assume that all team members are stationed in a single geographic site. While the option also has the advantage of creating almost no incremental facilities requirements, it does little to support the unique needs of an SAP implementation project. For this reason, the option is clearly less desirable than the two alternatives previously discussed.

   Maintaining the necessary team identity under these distributed circumstances will prove very difficult. Without critical mass, even basic actions such as assigning tasks and assuring follow-up will place considerable demands on workstream leads. Without the ebb and flow of continuous team interaction, team unity may well never develop. Without physical points of contact, even maintaining the project schedule and achieving project discipline will prove challenging.

4. **Teams and members located across several geographical sites**
   This alternative distributes the team even more broadly than the previous option. It places team members in many locations. Basically, this option imposes no facilities requirements on the implementing company.

   Effective team functioning requires a shared sense of project ownership. It is built on common purposes and commitment to their achievement. Only by bringing the team together at a single location—and on a regular basis—will it be possible to build this shared commitment.

   While option four *could* prove successful, it would take considerable skill among program management and workstream leads to make it work. Otherwise, the likelihood of attaining project objectives under this alternative is very low.

Conference Rooms

Meetings are the lifeblood of an SAP implementation project; workstreams will hold meetings at all times of the day and night. Many times these meetings will involve the entire workstream team, but more often than not they will include only a selected subset of the workstream. Holding these sessions in the assigned common area invites confusion and disorder. Attendee discussions will constantly disrupt those not involved in the meetings and made it difficult for meeting participants to focus on the topic at hand. Dedicated project conference rooms are the solution to this problem.

These rooms need not be large. A conference room holding 10 to12 occupants with a conference table and seating should suffice. For teams distributed across a site, each will need its own dedicated space. For teams that are located in a common area, two rooms can be allocated to three teams. They can arrange their own scheduling mechanisms.

For the third and fourth location options, some number of dedicated conference rooms is a must. In these options, assigned conference rooms will be the primary source of team continuity. Dedicated rooms enable team members to gather for meetings and to post project-specific materials such as schedules on the walls.

If space or financial constraints make common project areas an impossibility, project sponsors must find some way to allocate dedicated conference rooms. Teams will form their own working styles, including the frequency and timing of their meetings. During realization and final preparation, many meetings will take place via conference calls scheduled at the local time of the implementing region. Project teams implementing in Asia will especially need access to a conference room to meet these needs.

Dedicated project conference rooms should be entirely removed from the company online scheduling tool so that there's no question about the availability of the room for non-project users. Further, each room should have a sign posted at the door indicating that it has been assigned to the sole use of the SAP implementation project.

Conference Calls

If meetings are the lifeblood of the SAP implementation project, then conference calls are the circulatory system. Global implementations in particular depend on conference calls with teams in other regions to apprise them of project progress, to address team-specific issues, and to answer questions from regional team members.

By far the most effective way to conduct these sessions is with team members gathered together in their locations. Having team members scattered across a site on their individual telephones means they lose the opportunity to see and respond to reactions of others in the same room.

Conference calling technology allows teams to dial into a single conference number. That way, those conducting the meeting know who is in attendance. It also permits access to network operators who can immediately respond to technical issues with the call.

> **Tip**
> Conference call services such as those run by major carriers are a must. Each team lead and PMO member should receive a specifically assigned calling card number. These numbers can be used for calls hosted by specific teams, and call-in numbers can be distributed in the meeting scheduling notices.

Sound station technology permits those gathered in a single conference room to clearly hear what others are saying from remote locations. It also enables people in remote locations to clearly hear what is being said in the team conference room. Throughout the project, this will represent the primary mechanism of communication.

Facilities operations can provide or order sound stations for every project-dedicated conference room. Using these tools, the team can establish regularly scheduled meetings regardless of the time of day.

12.2.2 Bringing on the Project Team

Once facilities have been arranged, the project team begins its movement to new locations. Two sets of packing boxes are delivered to each team member. One set of boxes contains materials needed during the project and will move to the team location. The second set of boxes stores personal materials not needed during the project and will be moved to a designated storage location.

On moving day, boxes needed during the project are delivered to selected team locations. On this same day, team members report to their new work spaces. Assuming that all has gone well with preparatory facilities logistics, teams will now begin to focus on planning for blueprinting and realization.

At approximately the same time, systems integrator project resources begin to join their workstreams. Company project staff and systems integrator resources usually work in the same area. In this way, each has ready access to the other. Systems integrator staff will likely seek out information about the company's business processes, while company workstream resources will seek out information about the SAP system.

Normally, blueprinting begins with a kick-off meeting involving the entire global team. However, prior to the kick-off, each workstream must decide which types of business process changes are needed to support the SAP system. Additionally, each team may decide to include other significant business process changes that will be introduced simultaneously with the SAP system implementation.

Workstream leads hold briefing meetings to discuss how the SAP system supports their functional area. These sessions can include technical presentations from the systems integrator and in-depth examinations of how company business processes will operate in specific functional areas. The idea here is to build a common understanding among all those assigned to the workstream.

This will also be a great opportunity for team members to get to know one another. At this point, teams will face minimal pressure to generate deliverables. Team leads can set aside time for in-depth discussions and team get-togethers. These might include sessions with functional senior executives to gather their views on needed process changes, or team dinners at local restaurants. These activities contribute to team cohesiveness, which will be very much needed at the beginning of blueprinting—and certainly in later stages of the project.

12.3 Delivering Project Results

As the project team moves into its regular rhythm, many of the team preparatory activities recede in importance. The constant pressure to meet deadlines and deliver to schedule now overshadows virtually every other concern. However, two team concerns will continue in the forefront throughout the remainder of the project.

The first has to do with team member performance. SAP implementation projects oftentimes continue for two to three years. During this time, constant pressure to deliver can result in fatigue and eventual burnout. As a result, some team members' performance may drop below acceptable levels.

Throughout the project lifetime, program management keeps its finger on the pulse of team member performance. This monitoring entails identifying and assisting team members whose performance does not meet expectations. Program management and project sponsors also conduct monthly reviews of all team members whose performance is in question. For each individual so identified, a mentor is assigned. Mentors provide support to team members who need assistance and feedback to program management on team member improvement.

When needed improvement does not take place, program management will take remedial action. These actions may take several potential paths. At the most conservative level, the team member's assignments may be reduced to more manageable levels for the individual in question. However, in some cases, it may prove necessary to remove the individual from the project team and to search for a replacement.

These are always difficult situations and must be carefully managed. The feelings and future career of the affected individual are at stake here, but there's a lot at stake for the workstream, too. Every step should be taken to help the individual clearly understand the nature of the performance issue. Additionally, every step should be taken to assist the project team with the transition. Care should be taken to reinforce the existing positive working relationships among the team.

> **Tip**
>
> Finding suitable candidates to replace the departing team member should be done with all possible speed. At this point in the project, the schedule could be adversely impacted by loss of key personnel without a replacement available. Once a solid candidate has been identified, the workstream lead personally manages the onboarding process. This will assure a smooth transition for the new team member and for the workstream.

The second and somewhat related concern is turnover among the project team. Because these projects build skills and generate leadership in virtually every project team member, the job market seeks potential employees who have SAP implementation experience. Expect recruiters to call existing team members throughout the project lifecycle. In some cases, these recruiters may put such compelling offers on the table that one or more valuable team members leave the company during the project.

Often, employees who leave the project make an effort to delay their start dates with their new employers. This gives the company time to find a solid replacement and to conduct extensive knowledge transfer, which minimizes much of the negative impact.

In cases where an employee leaves the project without warning, the team will have to work together to alleviate the shortfall. Coordinated efforts to identify a replacement and handle the increased workload can, under the guidance of a skilled workstream lead, create a bonding experience among the remainder of the team.

12.4 Roll-Off and Reintegration

By project's end, after the final go-live has been completed, the team will now be ready to disband. In some implementation projects, this process is known as "repatriation"; in others, it is known as "reintegration." Irrespective of the terms used to describe it, the process entails company staff moving from project roles and returning to full-time company functional roles.

At this same time, systems integrator staff will also be rolling off the project and shifting to new projects and different locations. This process is quite familiar to long-time systems integrator staff. Their role is transitory and they fully expect to leave the implementing company when the project is complete. The only challenge here centers around the timing of roll-offs given any remaining project demands.

Company staff assigned to the project will not experience the end of the project in the same way. They will not see it as "business as usual." For them, the end of the project represents a time of uncertainty. For several years the project has been their organizational home and has consumed virtually all their waking hours. Now all the demands and urgencies have suddenly stopped. The immediate future is no longer so clear.

> **Pitfall Alert**
>
> It is absolutely essential that your company handle this transition well. The folklore of many companies is filled with stories of successful project team members of who had no job at the end of the implementation, or project team members who were laid off en masse six months after the implementation completed. These situations destroy trust and leave scars that make it difficult to recruit teams for the next project.

Employees have long memories and they will remember circumstances like these. When the next project arises, the memories will resurface. Recruitment will no doubt suffer as those asked to participate in the next project reflect on what happened to their colleagues and then decline the invitation to join.

Your company can very easily resolve this kind of negative situation. By handling the employee reintegration well, only positive memories will arise when responding to future project staffing.

Reintegration takes careful planning. It should be led by the company human resources organization and, at a minimum, begun midway through the realization phase. Human Resources should maintain records on each full-time employee project team member. The records would include details on project roles performed and any evaluation materials provided by the workstream lead or project sponsors. This information would be used to match reintegrating team members with available positions.

Every implementing company will encounter three primary challenges to successful team member reintegration. If the company meets them successfully, it will have laid a solid foundation for future projects. If the company does not meet them successfully, that foundation will instead be shaky.

1. **Sufficient positions are not available for reintegrating team members.**
   If a company assigns 50 employees to its full-time project contingent, this requires that at least 50 positions are available at comparable grade and skill levels by the end of the implementation. For best results, these positions targeted for reintegration should be identified and allocated during the planning process. As the project progresses, prospective assignments can be periodically reviewed and updated.

   Where implementing companies fail to complete timely reintegration planning, results rarely prove satisfactory. The most common difficulty centers on the number of positions available. During the project, an implementing company may have hired new employees or transferred existing employees into the positions formerly occupied by project team members. This leaves the reintegrating project team member without a clear path back to his or her original position.

Being assigned to clearly jury-rigged positions sends a harmful message to the project team members. It communicates to them that their contributions and sacrifices during the implementation cycle were not highly valued, and indicates that their future with the company is not secure.

2. **Anticipated promotions for reintegrating project team members were not received.**
Very often at the beginning of projects, prospective team members receive explicit or implicit promises of promotions when the implementation is complete. During reintegration, those expectations now become very acute. The project team member will feel that the promised change in grade is now due.

Whether this expectation is the result of an explicit promise or is based on a team member's unsupported belief, it must still be addressed in an equitable fashion. If the belief results from explicit promise, then discussion with the team member should promptly begin focusing on the timing of the promotion. If the belief results from more subjective factors, like hints or veiled language, management can now sit down with the team member and discuss career and promotion plans. The company must take pains to avoid situations in which individuals who have worked under trying circumstances feel that they have not received proper recognition. Explicit discussion at the beginning of and during the project will mitigate many of these situations.

3. **Reintegration positions offered to the project team are not sufficiently challenging.**
Very often, those employees who complete an SAP implementation are greatly changed from those who began it. They will be comfortable working at a very rapid pace and with handling significant responsibilities. They will have come to reach much more of their potential.

The positions offered during reintegration should reflect this changed circumstance. The former team members will welcome responsibilities and often will expect to be treated as such. Whether or not the positions offered contain a promotion, they should at the very least include an expansion of duties.

If this reintegration process is planned and handled well, the company will now come full circle. It will have its new SAP system and it will have a group of employees with greatly expanded capabilities—two very positive outcomes.

With the foundations built during project planning, we are now ready to address project operations. We begin with blueprinting activities that establish system design and then drive most of the remaining project deliverables.

Most time thus far has been spent focusing on start-up activities, but now blueprinting begins the heavy lifting for the project. Here, we'll build the business processes needed to operate the SAP system.

13 Business Blueprinting

Business blueprinting defines your company's business-related design deliverables. During this period, the team identifies current business processes used throughout the company or those specific to its locations; these are known as the "as-is" processes. However, concurrent with the SAP implementation, your company may also wish to introduce new processes or standardize processes across all locations; these are the "to-be" processes. Once these processes are clearly identified and understood, project teams then work to define any new business processes suitable for the SAP environment.

So why spend all this time on preliminary process definition? Our objective here is to know the full details of all new processes during blueprinting. The emergence of unanticipated, unknown, or unclear requirements in later stages of the project could lead to missed delivery dates and project cost overruns.

However, planning and logistics considerations still underlie blueprinting. Teams must identify both the mechanism for blueprinting and select participants for blueprinting sessions. In fact, they must decide the number of sessions, their locations, and cost projections before moving forward. For implementations that involve major changes to business processes, blueprinting sessions should be extensive. They should involve participation from all regions of company operations and span a number of sessions.

This chapter covers all parts of blueprinting. Discussion ranges from setting up and running the blueprinting design sessions to constructing the required design documentation. We will also spend some time examining integration points between project teams and conclude with an extensive discussion on the identification of any regional design differences.

13   Business Blueprinting

> **Trail Marker**
>
> In *The SAP Project: More Than a Survival Guide*, we will use the larger scale project as the base case. Other, more limited projects can scale this approach to their own needs.

13.1 Blueprinting Sessions

Many companies have not yet achieved the level of integration needed to see how business processes are used in various locations or operations. This condition especially holds true where legacy ERP systems are in use, which could include older versions of SAP or ERP systems that are no longer marketed. In fact, having multiple ERP systems in a company virtually ensures that common business processes haven't yet been adopted at all locations. To encourage a common perspective, blueprinting sessions should take place in a single location, but should include regional participants in all sessions.

Single-location blueprinting sessions have quite a few advantages. First, they indicate to all participants the amount of integration and process standardization required in the company. More importantly, they create team-building opportunities across the project. Many regional team participants will be strangers to the other participants or unfamiliar with culturally driven working patterns of other countries; some will have traveled from distant locations and will require time to acclimate to the host nation's working styles. So team building that takes place in the blueprinting sessions can go a long way to develop team cohesion.

Following a few other guidelines for single-location blueprinting sessions can produce a positive, productive experience for participants. The project should encourage a full transparency and "no-surprises" philosophy early in the lifecycle. Regional participants should expect to represent and liaise with their more numerous colleagues in home offices, so they should be explicitly encouraged to convey design decisions to regional management for its review and approval. Design decisions should be documented formally and provided to regional staff to supplement their understanding.

Planning for blueprinting meetings takes considerable effort and must be done in a rigorous way. On the logistics side, scores of company employees will travel to the blueprinting location. Many of these individuals will have limited experience with international travel. Participant information packets with customs and country entry requirements should be distributed to each participant. Additionally, your team should make sure to arrange lodgings, meals, transport from the arrival airport, and transport to and from the central blueprinting location. Project administrative resources should be posted at designated locations during blueprinting sessions to answer any questions and provide needed directions.

If your project is global, you'll need to keep language differences in mind. All participants should have the opportunity for understanding, regardless of their host-country language skills. One critical error that some companies make is to let regional team members sit in sessions where they do not understand the content discussed. Any potential language issues should be identified and solutions put in place. This might mean pairing fluent team members with coworkers who are less familiar with the project's common language; they can translate phrases as needed or even ask questions for these participants and translate the answers.

Figure 13.1 shows a template approach for blueprinting sessions. It uses three separate sessions to accomplish the design work. Each session should be at least three to four days in length.

Before detailing each of the three sessions, let's consider what preparation entails. Prior to session one, each team prepares its initial process maps. These will clearly designate which process steps will remain unchanged and which will be modified to achieve project objectives. Before disseminating them, team leads will review their maps with company senior management to ensure alignment and agreement. Once approved, these maps—accompanied by written explanations—should be distributed to all team members who will participate in the blueprinting sessions. Holding conference calls prior to the blueprinting sessions serves to clarify explanations and answer questions. This will help create a participatory atmosphere.

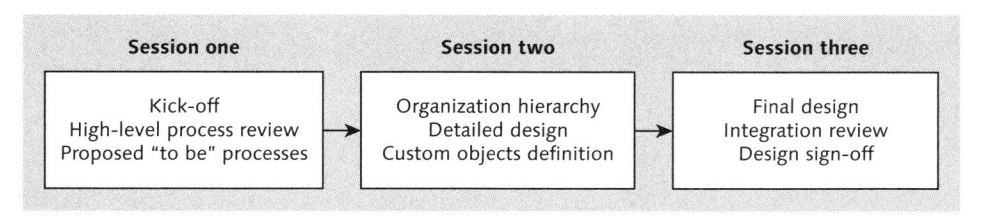

Session one	Session two	Session three
Kick-off High-level process review Proposed "to be" processes	Organization hierarchy Detailed design Custom objects definition	Final design Integration review Design sign-off

Figure 13.1 Blueprinting Sessions Organization

Let's preview each blueprinting session now. Session one introduces the project and its objectives during a kick-off and begins the actual design work. Teams conduct high-level process reviews to develop a common understanding among all participants. To do this, each team spends the necessary time outlining its scope. This will be time well spent; it achieves clarity about what is included for discussion and what is not. Full engagement of all attendees is needed here. During this review, team leads begin discussing proposed new processes or possible changes to existing processes. All problems with proposed changes should be surfaced as early as possible. In this way functional teams can work through any objections or difficulties in the interim between sessions.

Session two builds on the foundation established by session one. This second meeting focuses on detailed design. In the period between sessions, regional participants will have had the opportunity to discuss and bring forward any implications of proposed process changes. Participants should communicate any implications or issues in common sessions and resolve them prior to initiating the detailed design work.

Once agreement is reached, high-level processes can begin to be translated to a much more detailed level. During this session, integrator staff can play an important role in explaining how the SAP system will handle this process and in suggesting any improvements based on their work with other companies. By the session's end, most major design decisions should be in place.

Session three serves several purposes. It provides the opportunity to review and resolve any outstanding design details. It also specifically allocates time for integration meetings among teams where any cross-team issues can be discussed and decided. Finally, session three ends with each team conducting an extended presentation of its final design to company senior management. Project management should provide templates to teams ahead of time in order to align formats and presentation styles. In this way, management can more easily provide targeted input to the teams and give earned pats on the back as a result of effective team performance.

With the general objectives of each session in mind, let's examine each one.

13.1.1 Kick-Off and Session One

The kick-off sessions at the start of session one are critical to project success. For many participants, this will serve as their introduction to the project. Many of their questions, such as "Why was I selected?" and "What are we expected to accomplish?" should be answered by end of the session. Senior company leaders and project management take the lead in presenting groundwork for the project. Subjects discussed should at least include the following:

- **Purpose of the project and its importance to the company**
  This should include any business imperatives that make project timing critical.
- **Organization of the project (team composition and structure)**
  All major roles, and those occupying each role, should be identified. If time permits, key team members should be introduced to the group as well.
- **Methods of selecting project members and their roles**
  Many participants will have questions about why they were selected to participate in the process and what their roles will be. At a general level, the kick-off meeting should supply answers by discussing selection process specifics and rationale.
- **High-level schedule and its purpose**
  For many in the project team, the kick-off event serves as their introduction to ASAP terminology, so offering analogies to other developmental lifecycles can clarify the specific phases and their schedules. Timing of each phase should be discussed in detail. In fact, this is the first step in building commitment to achieving the schedule.
- **Introduction to the project systems integrator and its team leads**
  Systems integrator senior executives will usually make themselves available for kick-off sessions. These executives should have assigned roles during the kick-off session. Their presentations should include the function of the systems integrator and introduction of integrator team leads.
- **Project scope and applications involved (both SAP and any legacy systems)**
  Maintaining scope will prove a challenge during blueprinting and realization. Regions and functions will no doubt request changes and additions. Many of these will not be needed. Clarifying the project scope at this point will help

define and maintain scope boundaries. The aim at this time will be to develop standardized business processes to be used across the company where possible.

Once you have demonstrated the general picture, make sure to allot time for individual team breakout sessions. The agenda now shifts to initial knowledge-sharing. These first workstream sessions also give an initial opportunity for team members to ask questions pertinent to their individual team. Early in the breakout session, make time for all members to introduce themselves and share information about their background and experience. This offers a great first step in making the workstream an effective team.

Session one of the actual blueprinting begins in earnest immediately after kick-off has completed. An immediate transition from the kick-off meeting is necessary to maintain momentum. Teams are directed to gather in their designated spaces to begin work on their assigned tasks. At this point, major responsibility for blueprinting success passes over to company and integrator functional team leads. They direct the sessions and serve as process knowledge reference points. The integrator leads can play an especially important role in describing how the SAP system will operate with the designs under consideration.

> **Tip**
>
> Do everything possible to involve the systems integrator team members in system design discussions. They will be very happy to participate! They will have detailed knowledge regarding exactly how the SAP system will process transactions or how it will handle specific business process setups.

First, plan to have a thorough discussion of team scope, especially in reference to other teams in the project. Setting the boundaries for which activities to include and which to exclude serves as an excellent structuring device for initial team discussions. You can expect almost all team members to have questions about why some areas fall on their workstream's plate, but especially why other areas are excluded from the workstream's purview. This leads to a real sharing of ideas.

Figure 13.2 gives a high-level view of the scope of the five project teams: plan-to-stock, procure-to-pay, human capital management, order-to-cash, and record-to-report.

13.1 Blueprinting Sessions

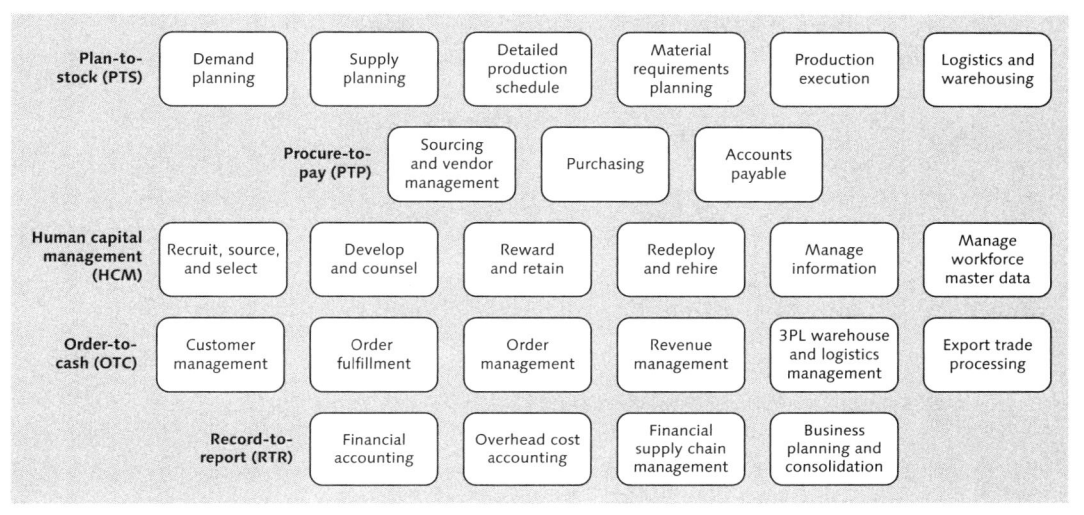

Plan-to-stock (PTS)	Demand planning	Supply planning	Detailed production schedule	Material requirements planning	Production execution	Logistics and warehousing
Procure-to-pay (PTP)		Sourcing and vendor management	Purchasing	Accounts payable		
Human capital management (HCM)	Recruit, source, and select	Develop and counsel	Reward and retain	Redeploy and rehire	Manage information	Manage workforce master data
Order-to-cash (OTC)	Customer management	Order fulfillment	Order management	Revenue management	3PL warehouse and logistics management	Export trade processing
Record-to-report (RTR)		Financial accounting	Overhead cost accounting	Financial supply chain management	Business planning and consolidation	

Figure 13.2 Project Scope Definition by Team

> **Tip**
>
> Expect to continue revisiting scope definition throughout the project. Scope discussions are never a one-time topic. As the teams gain knowledge of the overall design implications, they will no doubt revisit questions about the correctness of previous scope decisions. Identifying scope issues and resolving them early in blueprinting is to everyone's advantage.

Once this first-pass scope conversation has concluded, teams can now address detailed design areas. As part of blueprinting preparation, each functional team will have prepared an end-to-end overview of its process "to-be" vision. Reviewing this vision provides an early opportunity to align the team on business process changes. Team presentations should be very extensive and focus particularly on areas designated for change. Make sure to provide adequate time for a free-flowing discussion. An open dialogue concerning all business implications is very important. Time spent in give-and-take discussions will offer a learning experience for all participants. Discussions will certainly bring up business processes specific to locations or regions that do not fit with the overall "to-be" vision. The project team should document any unresolved questions as items to be resolved before the next design workshop.

Each of your design workshops should have a defined set of deliverables. Project management will specifically monitor progress to ensure completeness and adherence to standard documentation processes. Most deliverables addressed during the remainder of team blueprinting sessions will focus on completing items begun in session one. Each deliverable outlines the design decisions in greater and greater detail. Team deliverables from the initial design workshop include the following:

1. **A completed business process hierarchy (BPH)**
   The BPH defines team scope to at least one more level in order to clarify team scope and to ensure complete coverage for team blueprinting products.

2. **Agreed organizational hierarchy**
   The organizational hierarchy serves as a foundational document for SAP system setup and configuration. It translates company operations into master data elements so that all transactions fall into the proper container. Examples of organizational hierarchy components include company codes, plant codes, warehouses, and cost centers.

3. **The initial requirements listing**
   The final first session deliverable is the first-cut set of business requirements for the system. In order to assure adequate testing during the realization phase, your teams must define individual requirements for all system-related activities. Systems integrator staff will have extensive experience with each deliverable and can serve as a ready source of information.

Each deliverable outlines design decisions in greater detail. The BPH defines team scope to at least one more level. This further clarifies team scope and ensures complete coverage for team blueprinting products. Additionally, the organizational hierarchy serves as a foundational document guiding SAP system setup and configuration. It translates company operations into master data elements so that all transactions fall into the proper container. The final first session deliverable is the initial set of business requirements for the system.

The BPH details the scope for each team and enables team leads to identify key areas for integration review (where teams assume shared responsibility for deliverables). Let's return to Figure 13.2; note that the BPH provides an additional level of detail. In this example, another level is provided and uses order-to cash (OTC) as a reference point in Figure 13.3.

High-Level Business Process	Low-Level Business Process	Major Change
Customer management	Manage customers	
	Manage pricing	
	Trade promotion planning and execution	
Order management	Quotation processing	X
	Contract/chargeback processing	X
	Sales order processing	X
	Special sales order processing	
	Credit management	
Order fulfillment	Demand management	
	Backorder processing	
	Perform availability check	
	Outbound delivery processing	X
	Transportation and logistics cost	
Revenue management	Rebate agreement processing	
	Billing/invoice processing	X
	Intercompany billing	
	Manage cash application	X
	Manage collections	
	Manage disputes and deductions	
Foreign trade processing (export)	Embargo checking	
	Export control	X
	Export license management	
	Customs processing	X

Figure 13.3 Expanded BPH for Order-to-Cash Workstream

Most often, OTC has more complexity than other workstreams and has functional responsibility spread across a number of company organizations. Consequently, any expansion of these processes offers additional points for team discussion and resolution. To encourage that discussion — and to help team members and executive reviewers focus their energies on the areas where the most change is taking place — your team leaders can highlight the specific areas where process changes will be most substantial. The areas of major change are marked in the right column for our OTC example in Figure 13.3. Workstreams should discuss these change areas in great detail. In this way, implications for all facets of the business process become clearer and can generate continuing interaction among teams.

In contrast, the organizational hierarchy has a much different purpose. It lays out the master data elements (more on master data later) which the systems integrator will build into the system. Organizational hierarchy elements include standard reference points such as company codes, plant codes, profit centers, and warehouse storage locations. Many potential organizational hierarchy entries have a very specialized purpose in the SAP system. Completion of the organizational hierarchy will entail a cooperative effort between the functional team that understands company business processes and the systems integrator that understands common uses for these master data fields.

Throughout business blueprinting, all system requirements should be identified and documented. Requirements represent the primary connection point between business process needs and system build. Integrator staff configuring the system will utilize system requirements as the primary guidance for assuring configuration accuracy. System requirements should be very specific and stated in a way that is testable. Thus, "the system shall produce sales orders with unique and incremental numbering sequences" would represent a testable requirement. The more general version, "the system shall produce numbered sales orders" leaves too much open-ended. The more specific, the better.

During business blueprinting, team members will have many questions regarding how the SAP system performs a specific operation. Integrator staff can assist in demonstrating standard SAP functionality for any area in question. These demonstrations make clear where standard functionality will suffice and where special configuration will be required. (Remember, we are now deciding how to elaborate on the vanilla SAP system.) Additionally, the integrator team can build simple prototypes showing how company processes and data would operate in the system. Not only does this practice provide needed detail to the team, but it can also build the team's essential confidence in the SAP system's ability to meet company business needs.

Upon completion of session one, the team should carefully review its decisions and documentation. Deliverables such as the BPH, the organizational hierarchy, requirements listing, and overviews of "to-be" visions should be packaged and delivered to all team members. Members from other regions should be charged with briefing their executives on proposed business process changes and their implications for regional operations. Team members conducting the briefings can capture feedback received and bring it to following blueprinting sessions for discussion.

> **Tip**
>
> Team dinners during blueprinting sessions, especially in the first session, serve as an excellent team-building device. They permit team members to converse in a more relaxed atmosphere and for individuals to build relationships. These dinners can be held at the blueprinting location and can be relatively informal.

13.1.2 Sessions Two and Three

At the completion of session one, the remaining two blueprinting sessions target an increasing level of detail. Both sessions two and three review feedback from regional team members and ensure resolution to any open items. Additionally, these sessions flesh out more detailed requirements. They will also continue to examine any operational implications of new business processes.

Organizational impacts and revised role definitions initiate the change management process. *Change management* refers to the personnel and organizational supports needed to operate the new SAP system. It includes company-wide communication, user training, and system implementation preparation for users.

This first step, accomplished in blueprinting session two, identifies organizational impacts the new system will produce. Session two also examines any role additions, changes, or deletions required to operate the system. Attending to this "human" side of the implementation represents a critical factor for project success. As the teams uncover more details, operational responsibilities for processes may shift from one business organization to another or new roles may be needed to handle the new process. While some changes may be minor, several will probably be significant enough to have substantial organizational impact. Possible changes could include the following:

- Shifting a portion of inventory reconciliation to a third-party logistics provider
- Using SAP Advanced Planning and Optimization (APO) for supply and inventory planning with associated new processes

- Shifting process accountability to regional organizations instead of a central organization
- Hiring and training additional staff to accomplish newly designed functions
- Identifying significant change points, such as performing consolidation with the SAP Business Planning and Consolidation tool

These and similar changes should be monitored by each workstream. Once thoroughly vetted and approved by company executives, they can be passed along to the change management team for its action.

Understanding and working through points of integration between teams will be one of the most important outcomes of blueprinting. Many processes will require the input of two or more teams. Such processes usually involve complex operations and require complete understanding of which team owns which part. Any missing delineation of responsibility will show up in testing and potentially impact the schedule, so it's better to ensure all coverage is allocated, even if it may mean overdoing integration sessions. Integration required during design will reappear during testing to verify that it works as planned. Any misses must be worked through at that late point.

Table 13.1 shows common integration points among teams. Individual projects can expect to define additional points unique to their business models.

Teams	Integration Focus
RTR and OTC	Accounts receivable, pricing
RTR and PTP	Accounts payable
PTS and PTP	Direct material, contracting
OTC and PTS	Supply planning, sales projections

Table 13.1 Common Integration Points between Teams

Integration meetings between teams should be formally scheduled during session three. Because the sessions involve two or more teams, it requires up-front planning to alleviate any possible confusion. Each integration meeting needs a specific agenda and objective that has been reviewed with participants in advance. Whenever possible, meetings should be facilitated by team leads. Meeting results, including agreements reached and items deferred, should be documented and approved by team leads and affected company management.

Once blueprinting work is complete, the final portion of session three focuses on team presentations of proposed designs. All blueprinting team members participate in this final presentation. Additionally, company senior executives will attend to provide guidance and design approval. Team presentations should be very thorough and center on major accomplishments. Each team should have approximately one hour to complete its presentation.

Standardizing the presentation format ensures that all presentations will cover similar material. Include the following items in team final presentations:

- **Team scope**
  Scope identification sets the stage for the presentation. It reminds all participants of what will follow in the discussion.
- **Business process hierarchy**
  The BPH should be outlined during the presentation. This serves to ground subsequent presentation information.
- **Key design decisions**
  This will be the heart of the team presentation. It outlines all major design decisions. One of the best ways to accomplish this is to use the BPH as a classification mechanism. Each section should define the existing process and the design changes that will improve or change it. At this time, plenty of time should be left for questions. Having clarity among all participants is essential at the conclusion of blueprinting.
- **Change impacts**
  The teams should identify all major change impacts and their importance. Significant change impacts may include such items as staffing changes produced by new processes, knowledge and performance requirements needed by the process, or effects the process will have on individual company locations.
- **Known integration points with other teams**
  Having teams point out their integration points is a great step in having them own the integration work. During later stages of the project, it will be essential to revisit integration work to ensure that it is complete. Any team identifying an integration point with another team should have a corresponding recognition from its partner team. For example, accounts payable as a procurement

integration point should also show up in record-to-report as an integration point.

- **Key performance indicators (KPIs)**
  Performance indicators are called for wherever improvement is planned or major changes will be instituted. Supplying recommended baseline measurements for success shows whether the design is working as planned. KPIs could include improvements in process cycle times or cost reductions in processes.

- **Open issues and concerns**
  Teams should identify any open issues still requiring a design decision. Additionally, teams can point out concerns, such as challenges in adopting new processes, needed level of preparation for regions of the company, or complexities likely to cause future problems.

Custom Objects Definition

Additionally, the second and third sessions will include definitions for all needed custom objects. Basically, these objects are tools that are not part of the out-of-the-box SAP system, but are required to help the system meet company needs.

Custom objects require careful scrutiny. Not only do these WRICEFPs—remember the workflow, reports, interfaces, conversion program developments, enhancements, forms, and portals?—usually entail special additional funding, but they can substantially degrade system performance if not carefully reviewed. Company management—especially in the IT function—should keep a careful eye on custom objects requests. Table 13.2 describes the composition and functions of these items.

Item	Description
Workflow	Automated steps created in the system to execute processes. These supersede existing manual processes. Instances could include automation of process steps to change employee status such as location, position, bank information, or salary.
Report	SAP system data that is compiled and formatted for decision-making purposes falls under the reports area. These can range from simple lists to highly complex computational results. Examples could include daily sales reporting and profitability analysis.

Table 13.2 Custom Object Types and Uses

Item	Description
Interface	When connection between an existing company system and the SAP system is needed for data-sharing, an interface will be required. The interface must assure that each system—both sending and receiving—handles the data transfer accurately.
Conversion	Any data elements from existing systems needed for the new SAP system will require conversion. This entails preparation of data and an eventual move to the production system. Conversion of master data, such as vendor master or customer master, would fall in this category.
Enhancement	Used when a company decides that additional SAP functionality is needed. Enhancements can be relatively straightforward or extremely complex. Examples could range from altering screen views of certain transactions to changes in sales order processing.
Form	For handling system-outlined templates that capture and replicate structures that the business commonly uses. They enable you to post needed information to the individual form location. Companies commonly build forms for invoicing or customs documentation.
Portal	Construction of Internet access for customers, suppliers, or employees to use the system. For example, a supplier portal would enable vendors to provide information regarding purchase order completion in real time.

Table 13.2 Custom Object Types and Uses (Cont.)

Establishing a review board to evaluate and approve all custom objects requests serves as a useful mechanism to keep the number of custom objects at a minimum. A review board ensures cost control and assures limited impact to system performance. This review board should include both senior business representatives and company senior IT staff. Often company IT staff will have ready knowledge of the custom objects' potential impacts and can provide that information to business decision-makers.

Workstream leads will own preparation of custom objects documentation for their areas. Their ownership ensures that personnel with significant business knowledge manage and define use for custom objects. At the review board, team leads identify the need for these objects in a presentation. They can, of course, ask technical members from their workstream to assist with the presentation. The review board will require a complete picture of need and impact produced by the custom object.

All approved WRICEFP items will almost certainly be constructed by the implementation integrator partner. Most often, an integrator contract specifies a base number of possible approved WRICEFPs to be built by the integrator, with an incremental cost assigned for any custom objects exceeding that projection. Consequently, teams should exercise care during blueprinting to ensure that all custom objects have significant business needs. As the project moves through to realization, the team may discover additional requirements for custom objects. At that point, the budgetary threshold may have been reached and unbudgeted costs assigned to the project. Knowing the number of custom object types during blueprinting has its advantages!

The custom objects review board will utilize a simple request form. It includes a description of the requested custom object, rationale for its need, and an estimate of the man hours required to complete it. Project functional teams prepare the request forms and submit them to the board for consideration. Once the board receives a sufficient number of requests, it schedules a formal review session. During this session, each project team will have the opportunity to present its case for any requested custom object. Teams can also call upon assigned integrator staff to provide any technical input regarding the object.

Once the board decides to approve a custom object, it then forwards it to the integrator for inclusion in the custom object queue. All approved custom objects are assigned to the integrator development team for completion; all work should be finished during the early stages of realization. The PMO will monitor them for completion status.

Project management must ensure that all possible custom objects are identified and reviewed during blueprinting. Carrying over WRICEFP requests into succeeding phases will negatively impact project timelines and budget for several reasons. First, integrator developmental resources are assigned to the project for a limited time and then scheduled for roll-off. Keeping them on board past agreed-upon dates becomes the financial responsibility of your company. Second, identifying new custom objects after system testing has begun will mean additional, unplanned testing or retesting. Any new testing requirement is likely to extend the timeline for integration or user acceptance testing. The bar for approving custom objects *must* become very high after completion of blueprinting.

13.2 Design Documentation

The baseline deliverable of business blueprinting is fully documented design. This mechanism makes all the teams' design decisions fully tangible. Further, your integrator will use documentation to guide SAP system configuration as well as create the foundation for post-go-live user support.

13.2.1 Process Definition Documents

Because of its importance as a lasting project legacy, we will spend some time on design documentation. The fundamental document is called the *process definition document* (PDD). The PDD digests all output from blueprint sessions and operates in a one-to-one relationship with process designs. Each named process will have a corresponding PDD assigned.

Approved PDDs become controlled documents. Each PDD receives the affixed signatures of your company approval authorities. Additionally, since these are living documents, each PDD will contain a version history listing all changes and the reasons for them. Once signed and approved, the PDDs are transferred to the project document repository. Any changes from that point forward require approval. They will also update the current document version.

The PDD begins with an overview of the specific process covered. The overview outlines in text format how the process is intended to work, as shown for a stock transfer order in Figure 13.4.

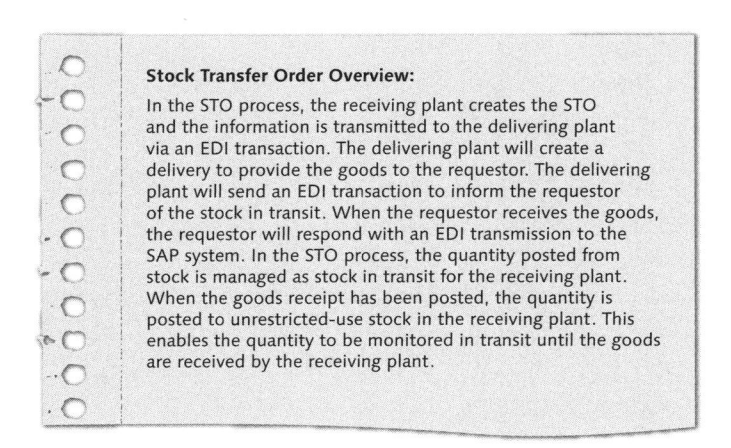

Stock Transfer Order Overview:

In the STO process, the receiving plant creates the STO and the information is transmitted to the delivering plant via an EDI transaction. The delivering plant will create a delivery to provide the goods to the requestor. The delivering plant will send an EDI transaction to inform the requestor of the stock in transit. When the requestor receives the goods, the requestor will respond with an EDI transmission to the SAP system. In the STO process, the quantity posted from stock is managed as stock in transit for the receiving plant. When the goods receipt has been posted, the quantity is posted to unrestricted-use stock in the receiving plant. This enables the quantity to be monitored in transit until the goods are received by the receiving plant.

Figure 13.4 Stock Transfer Order Overview

Notice that this PDD contains a considerable level of detail. The overview puts the entire process in perspective and outlines process mechanisms. A reader familiar with the process described will understand how it is intended to work and the transactions involved.

Following the process overview, there will be a description of key process inputs and outputs. Table 13.3 shows sales order inputs and outputs (if any).

Inputs	Description	Outputs
Order type	Type of sales order: Standard order	Sales order document
Sales area	Sales organization/distribution channel/division (legal entity that is performing the sale)	Order confirmation for customers having this requirement
Sold-to party	Customer number (sold-to party)	
Ship-to party	Ship-to address number	
Quotation number	Quotation number to use as reference in creating the new sales order	
Purchase order	Customer purchase order number if applicable	
Purchase order date	Date of customer's purchase order document	
Plant	Plant code where product will be shipped from	
Material number	Finished-good product number (SKU)	
Quantity	Quantity ordered	
Price	Sales price, either system-derived or manually entered	

Table 13.3 Key Process Inputs and Outputs

Notice the one-to-one correspondence between inputs and their descriptions. This isn't the case with outputs, though; they may be fewer in number (as in this example) or greater. Again, the description should proceed towards a greater amount of detail. Inputs and outputs should be exhaustively described. Any input or output used within the process should be referenced.

Next, the document identifies any process integration considerations. For the example in Table 13.3, these integration considerations include those with supply chain management during product availability check, with finance during credit check, and with EDI processing in order receipt and order acknowledgement. By defining specific integration points linked to processes, each team can fully understand its integration responsibilities and the overall project management team can determine the entire integration scope for the project.

13.2.2 Change Management Initiation

Earlier in this chapter, we discussed change management activities. One of those activities included key changes and change impacts. The PDD will document all process change impacts. For every process, the team must thoroughly and completely identify all changes affecting the company. Thus, depending on the amount of change introduced by the specific process, a single PDD may house several key changes and change impacts.

As an example, let's work through a change impact for introduction of SAP Business Planning and Consolidation (BPC) as a new financial tool.

- **Change number one**
  All regions of the company will move from the existing consolidation tool to the SAP BPC system.
- **Overall change impact for the process (rated high, medium, or low)**
  High impact; the change introduces new systems and greatly changes the existing process. Skills enhancement and user training will be required.
- **Local differences**
  Some process adjustments to support local tax differences will be made.
- **Activities affected**
  Monthly, quarterly, and year-end close will be accomplished through these new processes.
- **Organization (rated high, medium, or low)**
  Medium impact: Some currently centralized close activities will shift to regional finance organizations.
- **Role and skills (rated high, medium, or low)**
  High impact: New roles and additional skills will be required to complete close and consolidation activities.

- **Communications and reports (rated high, medium, or low)**
  Medium impact: Forms and reports currently used as part of the consolidation process will be replaced. New reports have been identified through the custom object definition process.
- **Policies and procedures (rated high, medium, or low)**
  Medium impact: Existing procedures will require updates to fit the new system and all process modifications.
- **Human resource management (rated high, medium, or low)**
  Low impact: Some modest amount of hiring activity will be required to support regional close processes.
- **Culture and behaviors (rated high, medium, or low)**
  Medium impact: Changes in the working relationships of the company corporate office relative to regional operations will change. More of the process will be performed regionally.
- **Locations (rated high, medium, or low)**
  Medium impact: Regional locations will assume more responsibility than under the current process model.
- **Systems (rated high, medium, or low)**
  High impact: The existing consolidation system will be replaced. BPC system learning must be addressed.
- **Suppliers and customers (rated high, medium, or low)**
  No impact: Consolidation activities do not affect customers or suppliers.

Each change impact requires this full description. Using this listing, the change management team constructs a change impact matrix outlining all impacts by workstream and by degree of impact. This becomes the primary working document for the change management team throughout the project. That team works to ensure that all change impacts have been addressed by go-live.

13.2.3 Process Flows and Process Steps

Next, the PDD details process flows and process steps. The example in Figure 13.5 for order management shows the general structure of the process flow. In addition to standard process flow features, note the use of swim lanes identifying process inputs or outputs as well as the organization performing the specific action. Additionally, where possible, each action is further identified by the system performing the transaction. If a system other than SAP performed the transaction, it would be noted. Further, process steps identify the applicable PDD describing the step.

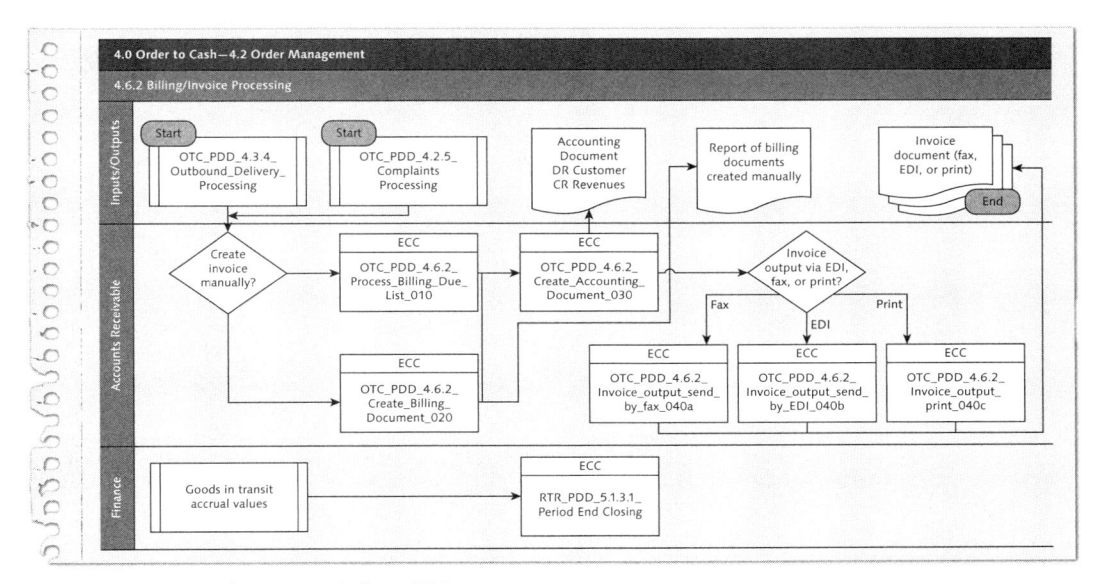

Figure 13.5 Process Flow Example for a PDD

Each step in the process is then described in detail. This description outlines many specific attributes of that individual step. It lists all requirements associated with the step, any design requirements for that step, the SAP transaction code or custom object identifier (if applicable), the role performing the step, any internal controls requirements (more about internal controls later in this chapter), and any financial impact of the step. Consider the example in Figure 13.6, which shows a completed process step for sales order generation.

The more specific information contained in the process step description will prove essential during the realization phase. Your systems integrator will utilize the aggregated listing of design requirements to assure a full capture of configuration needs. Additionally, the process step requirements serve to tag testing needs during realization. These requirements will be gathered by the testing team to assure a complete range of testing.

13 | Business Blueprinting

Process step	OTC_PPD_4.2.3_Sales_Order_Create_020
Process step requirement	System must be able to create a standard order.
Process step design to meet requirement	Configuration required: Order type and associated item category, schedule lines, etc.
	When customer places an order via purchase order, fax, email, or any other form of communication for manual order entry, the customer service representative should be able to enter the order type along with sales area information. After entering the required information, the system should allow the representative to enter sold-to party, ship-to party, and material number with quantity required by the customer.
SAP transaction or WRICEFP number, if applicable	VA01
SAP position	Customer service representative and manager
Specify applicable internal controls and/or segregation of duties (SOD)	The system should prevent the user who is processing sales orders from being able to maintain customer master data, maintain credit management, maintain revenue pricing conditions, process A/R entries, and/or release/approve sales orders.
Financial impact	☐ High ☐ Medium ☒ Low/None Creating/changing a sales order triggers credit management.

Figure 13.6 PDD Example

This section of the PDD concludes with a listing of all system interfaces needed for the process to function as required. They include listing of output requirements and any custom object approved by the review board for this process.

13.2.4 Business Controls Identification

The final element in the process definition document identifies any required business controls or segregation of duties (SOD). Mandated by statutory financial regulations, these controls assure that financial reporting is complete, accurate, and in compliance with regulations. From a PDD standpoint, the intent is to assure that only authorized individuals have access to sensitive transactions and that this authorization is limited to the minimum users needed. We will cover business controls in more detail in Chapter 17.

Figure 13.7 outlines the PDD entries for business controls. The first block identifies the three aspects of risk in the process. Items rated highly in any one area will usually require a business control. Controls can be completed through system automation.

The second section in the form provides detail regarding the control to be built. "ICS" refers to the internal control standard, and "CAVR" designates the control objective met via the business control. Since automated controls can be achieved using configuration in some cases and custom objects in others, the remainder of this section outlines the method adopted.

The final section in Figure 13.7 specifies any SOD risks. A common concern, for example, is when the same individual is responsible for both issuing purchase orders and distributing checks in payment. In some small offices, this may be common practice and will have to be mitigated. This section also requires identification of sensitive-area access, because access to employee salary information or current company sales information represents a sensitive area and access should be controlled.

Completion tracking can be accomplished through the SAP Solution Manager approach, described in depth shortly. As with other documentation items, the exact status must be visible and issues made available to project management.

Financial impact	☐ High ☐ Medium ☒ Low/None					
Operational impact	☐ High ☐ Medium ☒ Low/None					
Compliance impact	☐ High ☐ Medium ☒ Low/None					
Business controls requirement	ICS Ref #	Control requirement/ standard	CAVR	Standard (S) or custom (C)?	Detailed configuration spec	Config. control (C) or report (R)?
Segregation of duties risk area?	☐ High ☐ Medium ☒ Low/None					
Comments						
Sensitive access risk area?	☐ High ☐ Medium ☒ Low/None					
Comments						

Figure 13.7 Process Controls PDD

13.2.5 Managing the Documentation Process

Large projects will create over a hundred PDDs, all of which must be completed before the start of the realization phase. Managing PDD completion initiates the formal status reporting phase of the implementation project. The program management office (PMO) will develop status collection mechanisms and deploy these to workstreams for their reporting.

Each project should adopt naming conventions for its documentation. The blueprinting stage is often the first time these conventions are used, and the naming protocols must be clear to all team members. The document set must have a clear hierarchy and a mechanism to identify the different document types.

Figure 13.8 shows an example of a workable naming convention for PDDs. In this case, each project workstream will receive a classification number for all its documentation. For example, OTC uses the number "3" to identify any documentation assigned to that workstream. The 3.2 identifies a primary process within order-to-cash. If further subprocesses were required, they would be indicated by an additional digit, such as 3.2.5. This procedure maintains mutual exclusivity for all related documents.

Team	Document	Number	Process Name
OTC	PDD	3.2	Sales order processing

Figure 13.8 Documentation Naming Convention

Fortunately, SAP Solution Manager makes available an excellent documentation tracking tool. SAP Solution Manager contains document management capabilities enabling initial assignment, changing of document status, and status reporting. The systems integrator team will configure SAP Solution Manager to fit project documentation requirements. By using this tool project-wide, all project participants will have a common view of documentation progress and challenge areas.

SAP Solution Manager enables configuration that makes status tracking possible. Teams can assign their status items and assess movement of documentation through that process. Additionally, documents can be checked in and out, comparable to a document management system.

> **Pitfall Alert**
>
> Take care to ensure that documents do not remain in the "checked out" status for long periods because it could negatively affect the accuracy of SAP Solution Manager document completion reporting. Additionally, some team members may leave PDDs active on their desktops without changing the version, resulting in incorrect versions where the desktop version has not been uploaded. In these cases, SAP Solution Manager would not reference the most current version.

Many SAP projects also use company document management systems, such as Microsoft SharePoint, as an adjunct to SAP Solution Manager. These document management systems have more easily utilized check-in and check-out functionality. In cases where such systems are used, final approved versions are posted to SAP Solution Manager while the document management system controls work in progress.

Tracking could involve several ordinal classifications, as shown in Table 13.4.

Status	Description
Not started	Initial entry created in SAP Solution Manager.
Assigned	Individual completion responsibility assigned in SAP Solution Manager.
Baseline draft complete	PDD first draft completed and ready for review.
Baseline draft review complete	Baseline draft has been reviewed and comments received from team members.
Final draft complete	All open items in the PDD have been closed. Workstream sign-off is complete.
Blueprint complete	All required sign-offs for the PDD have been received. The document is complete.

Table 13.4 Documentation Status Classification Example

The PMO has the responsibility for tracking completion status and providing update reports to the entire team. Workstream leaders, however, own completion of all PDDs assigned to their workstreams. Business blueprinting completes only when the required documentation is approved and posted as final approval (*blueprint complete*). Accountability for accuracy and completeness rests with the workstream leads. They present their status and they own the accomplishment of their deliverables.

Please note this critical division of labor. Almost all deliverables created during business blueprint are owned by the functional workstreams. This ownership situation will change considerably, however, during the realization phase.

Blueprinting documentation requirements truly initiates the schedule-driven deliverable cycle. The PMO will ensure reporting transparency and accountability for achieving assigned project deliverables. For many team members assigned to the project, this serves as a first taste of the deliverable completion discipline required to meet deadlines. PDD completion errors will impact the fulfillment of the project schedule, and increase the likelihood of financial impacts caused by delivery slips.

At this time in the project lifecycle, the project operating review meetings discussed in Chapter 5 begin in earnest. Prior to this point, the meetings will have centered on information sharing. Now they center on deliverable status. The overriding purpose of these update meetings is to present current project progress and uncover or communicate any completion problems. Each workstream lead presents team documentation accomplishments. Additionally, they share any problems or issues they encountered in documentation completion. Participants will discuss recommended courses of action to resolve issues during review sessions.

If possible, hold these meetings in a single location and expect all team members in leadership positions to attend. Global project team members located in different regions should attend via telecommunication.

> **Tip**
>
> If you must use teleconferencing, adopt strict rules for speaking. Any speaking member in the host location should be immediately in front of an input device. Any member in the same location who has a comment should also speak only into an input device. In this way, all participants in the call will be able to hear and contribute.

The example in Figure 13.9 shows a relatively straightforward approach to documentation completion tracking. You can expect considerable variation in workstream completion status. When workstreams fall well behind expectations, the

PMO should give immediate attention to the problem and identify the causes. Reasons can include insufficient resources, the complexity of the assignment, or a need for improved leadership skills in the team lead.

PDD Status	OTC Team	PTP Team	PTS Team	RTR Team	Total
Not started	6	16	8	2	32
Assigned	22	5	7	5	39
Baseline drafted	10	6	15	6	37
Baseline review complete	6	4	10	20	40
Final draft complete	5	1	3	3	12
Blueprint complete	2	0	4	4	10
Total	51	32	47	40	170

Figure 13.9 Sample Blueprint Documentation Tracking Sheet

Viewed from this perspective, some workstreams are clearly in better positions that others. RTR has half of its PDDs in *baseline review complete* status and almost all have been started. PTP, on the other hand, has yet to begin work on half of its PDDs. OTC also faces some challenges as well; over half of its PDDs fall in the *not started* and *assigned* categories. The PMO and project sponsors will focus on issues facing those teams and help resolve them. The PMO may assign OTC and PTP to the project watch list as a mechanism to ensure heightened attention to their completion status. The watch list involves meeting with team leadership to gather information regarding problems encountered and solutions currently applied. Each team should remain on the watch list until the completion status has been resolved.

This same tracking model can also work for custom object definition status, especially since custom object documentation follows a similar sequence as the PDD.

13.3 Localization

Some readers may already be familiar with localization, but for others it might occasion a look of wonderment. *Localization* identifies specific regional or locational business process needs that must be incorporated within the SAP system. In many cases, local business operations will have requirements unique to their own legal or regulatory environment. These must be identified and configured in the SAP system.

Localization begins during formal blueprinting sessions with the building of a commonality matrix. This matrix identifies, by process, where differences in transaction take place within the company. More detailed localization steps normally take place in special sessions after general blueprinting has ended.

Figure 13.10 gives a sample commonality matrix. It divides the company into four regions (North America, Europe, Latin America, and Asia) according to a single business process. Regions where transactions are performed differently are marked with an X in the matrix and totaled on the right. It makes sense also to capture underlying reasons for process differences during blueprinting discussions.

Subprocesses	North America	Europe	Latin America	Asia	Total
Billing due list	Standard	Standard	X	X	2
Create billing document	X	Standard	X	X	3
Create accounting document	Standard	Standard	Standard	Standard	0
Invoice output	X	X	X	X	4
Goods in transit accruals	Standard	Standard	Standard	X	1
Period end closing	Standard	X	Standard	Standard	1

Figure 13.10 Billing and Invoice Processing Matrix

This commonality matrix example shows considerable variation in the mechanisms used across the company for billing and invoice processing. In all subprocesses but one (accounting document creation), some variation exists in a least a single region. During blueprinting, teams should work to uncover the reasons for regional process differences and to discover whether the standard design can apply there.

In many ways, localization represents a change management effort. Regions may report some localization requirements that simply represent current ways of doing business and which can be standardized. The power of inertia in keeping known processes in place is very strong and must be addressed by workstream leads and project management. This will mean extensive discussions with regional team members to elicit concrete reasons for maintaining process differences across the company.

Normally, regional localization sessions are held after completion of general blueprinting. The project team schedules and conducts a localization session for each region. To be effective, your sessions should be held at a regional location with the core project team traveling there. Localization sessions will gather additional information about known special regional requirements and uncover more requirements from regional staff in attendance. For sessions to be most effective, you should encourage significant numbers of regional staff to attend. That provides a more diverse viewpoint, and it also permits the core team to present the overall blueprint to the regional audience. In this way, the team encourages feedback and discussion at the regional level.

At the very beginning of each localization session, make sure that your project team presents and explains the meeting ground rules. Your team can expect each region to identify more localization requests than will receive actual approval, so it's essential to build understanding about the purpose of localization and the need to standardize company processes. Nevertheless, it will require a fair amount of diplomatic skills to build this shared understanding among regional participants. The attempt is certainly worth the effort.

> **Tip**
> Regional teams should not feel that the project team is dictating all the outcomes. Rather, in the best of cases, regional teams should come to an understanding of their real requirements. More discussion and questions should always be encouraged.

During blueprinting, your project team should have already agreed on languages to be used in the system and for screens required in local languages. The team should clarify the system language decisions and those for translation of user documentation during localization. In many cases, user guide translations exceed the number of system languages. For example, the system languages for the company referenced in Figure 13.9, with four regions, would probably be limited to English, Mandarin Chinese, Thai, Spanish, and Portuguese, depending on its business locations. User documentation translation languages could also include languages such as French, German, Russian, and Polish depending on the coverage that primary system languages provided. This should be a subject of discussion during localization sessions.

Many companies drive localization decisions from the standpoint of legal and regulatory issues. Customs documents, invoices, and required governmental reporting will certainly fall within this grouping. However, be careful to ensure that these requested localization requests are indeed required. In many cases, local sources have embedded and categorized certain requirements as statutory without researching whether they are in fact required by regulation or law. Where there is any doubt as to the validity of a proposed statutory requirement, the team should request the region to supply a translated copy of the purported requirement.

Regional localization requests and their resolutions will fall into one of several categories. The first category centers on a country's statutory requirement for extended financial reporting. Here the solution depends on using an SAP country version that adapts the system to provide required governmental reporting. County versions with broad-scale, country-specific requirements are indicated. The *notas fiscal* financial reporting method in Brazil gives a good example for this type of localization requirement.

The second localization category involves requested local solutions addressed through SAP setup or configuration. For instance, it is quite common for plant warehouse storage locations to differ across sites and by facility characteristics. SAP makes storage location master data configurable by location. This enables each warehouse to be configured according to size or number of storage bins. A similar example comes from the requirement for country-specific or regional pricing procedures. Again, SAP makes available configurable pricing procedures by region or country as needed.

The real team decision-making begins where neither a country version nor available configuration option solves the problem. Any remaining localization requests should receive careful consideration. In some cases the team may deny localization requests, and in others the requests will be accepted as business needs. In those cases, the solution often requires some type of custom object.

For example, many Latin American governments require copies of the original invoice. This, in turn, requires use of multi-copy impact printers to operate on the SAP system. In addition to purchase and setup of impact printers, the team will have to design special forms to transact the necessary information. These types of localization decisions add to the custom object development work performed by the systems integrator.

Once your team has determined the full range of localization decisions, you will know the total of all custom object work. Some requirements may show up later during realization — though, of course, this is not ideal — but your team should have identified and dispositioned the bulk of requests during localization sessions. Your team should ensure that each region understands and accepts those localization decisions. If the regional team ever believes that a decision was incorrect or incomplete, make it a point to revisit and thoroughly discuss the difference of opinion before bringing localization to a conclusion.

Additional requirement and custom object requests can be tracked through the use of SAP Solution Manager as described earlier in this chapter. Your team can adopt supplemental classifications to reflect the localization document process for PDDs and custom object requests. These will be closed out in the same fashion.

13.4 Closing the Business Blueprinting Phase

After your team has completed localization sessions and all blueprinting documentation has received final approval, the project is ready to exit business blueprinting. Project workstreams will conduct presentations to senior executive as the final step in the phase exit process. (Remember the phase gates from ASAP?) The team invites its project sponsors to a half- or full-day session where it reviews blueprinting accomplishments. At a minimum, presentations will focus on the following areas:

- All major business changes adopted by a workstream, along with the tangible benefits to be achieved by the changes
- Status of the blueprinting documentation process, especially process definition documents and custom object approvals

- Reports of approved localization changes and their system solutions
- Identification of any remaining open issues and their impacts
- Specification of risks facing the workstream and proposed mitigation plans

At this point, senior company executives give their approval to move forward or register any reservations concerning the blueprinting work. Assuming they make a decision to move forward, the business blueprinting phase now concludes and the project moves to realization. Here, an entirely different set of challenges awaits.

Our next chapter does in fact address the challenges of realization. It will clarify the many deliverables and continuing resource requirements that the phase brings on. It will also emphasize how the project shifts from the functionally oriented approach in blueprinting to a greater reliance on the technical teams.

With business blueprinting complete, the project has now moved into the realization phase. Here, the project team will find itself presented with significant tasks across the board, including making the shift to realization and beginning work on all those deliverables.

14 Realization

Not only is realization generally the longest of the ASAP phases, but it is the most complex. In many implementations, realization comprises up to 80 percent of total project time. Not only does this phase represent the bulk of project duration, but it also has by far the largest number of deliverables to manage. Many of these deliverables have overlapping due dates and require virtually the same resources to complete. The project team and its management will have to juggle numerous conflicting priorities and incompatible resource allocations. Effectively meeting the demands of realization will test everyone on the team.

Let's take a look at the kinds of challenges that are coming down the pike during this multipart stage:

- System configuration and its documentation
- Specification, development, and testing of custom objects (WRICEFPs)
- Infrastructure and application installation
- Data cleansing, extracting, and conversions
- Testing of system components
- Security role design, build, and testing
- Reports build and user verification
- User training design and documentation
- Change management and communications activities
- System performance testing

- Business controls and necessary regulatory documentation
- Initial site readiness preparation
- Electronic data interchange (EDI) design activity with partners and customers

This inventory of high-level realization deliverables underscores the diverse demands placed on the project. Indeed, the sheer volume of simultaneous deliverables can lead any team to struggle in meeting its schedule. Additionally, as this list makes clear, many of the realization deliverables are system-based, meaning that they require use and understanding of the SAP system. Business processes, as they utilize SAP, will be the central focus of realization.

Because it's so important to the overall success of the project, realization requires considerable attention. This chapter serves as an introduction to realization and focuses most of its coverage on project management activities. Later chapters will address individual realization activities such as build, test, custom object development, and related topics in more detail.

Before we move more deeply into this chapter, let's spend a moment previewing what we'll cover in the next few pages. We've already discussed some of the differences between blueprinting and realization. This chapter underscores those differences by describing the shift from one phase to the next. It outlines some methods, such as the realization kick-off and the realization project plan, which can help your team make the transition.

Realization also brings on changes in project organization. The role of technical or horizontal workstreams becomes much more pronounced. These workstreams now take the lead in managing many fundamental activities during realization, such as test and data conversion. The role of regional organizations expands as well, since these regional organizations have many of their own deliverables to manage.

This chapter also describes the workings of project management. Subjects will include deliverable tracking and project operating review management, as well as assessing project resourcing needs and handling risks during realization.

Let's get started with the realization transition process.

14.1 Transition to Realization

Your team members will likely have strong reactions to the new world of realization, especially if they have just been involved in the blueprinting process. Experience in blueprinting, with its single focus on design, doesn't really serve as a useful model for this next phase. In fact, you can expect that it will take some time for teams to learn the purpose of realization and to adapt to the multiple sets of deliverables required. Additionally, you will find many of your team members to be unfamiliar with the systems-based terminology used in realization.

Project management can anticipate these reactions by team members and therefore plan to address the variances between phases. Successful projects take care to prepare their team up front, so take advantage of two tools that are available to assist with this transition: the realization project plan and the realization kick-off. If used well, these tools can greatly ease the entrance into the new phase.

14.1.1 Realization Project Plan

The realization project plan helps ease the transition. It comes in two views. The first view serves as an orientation mechanism. It gives a very high-level portrait of realization, focusing only on the names and timing of primary top-level deliverables. It provides a common point of reference for new terms and timing and so enables transition to this next phase. The second view supplies substantially more operational detail. It shows the more numerous B-level realization deliverables and will be the reference point for project team status reporting. This second view definitely brings home the fact that realization is very different from blueprinting.

> **Tip**
>
> Team communication becomes even more important during realization. Plan to take advantage of upcoming suggestions to make sure everyone on your team is on the same page before even starting realization. Once the deliverables come due, you won't be able to find the time for building a common understanding. Use the opportunity now.

As a first order of business, your program management office (PMO) should make available an easily understood graphical view of realization similar to Figure 14.1. This plan grounds the team and helps illustrate how realization will work. Figure 14.1 depicts a project going live in October. It begins at the close-out of blueprinting with localization in January, and then shows eight sets of high-level realization deliverables and their timing. This first view can serve as a baseline for discussions about how realization works.

Such a plan helps illuminate the scope and duration of realization. The left column presents major realization deliverable categories, while the monthly columns show their timing. The schedule calls out deliverables in critical areas such as user training, custom object development, configuration, and testing. Your team receives just enough detail to set clear expectations regarding the deliverable schedule, but without additional confusing detail. This presentation reinforces how realization continuously demands deliverables from the project team.

Project management prepares numerous copies of this high-level plan and distributes them to every team member. Additionally, the PMO will post larger, plotter-generated copies in project work areas where they can serve as easily available reference points for workstream discussions. As changes are made to the plan, the PMO can distribute revised copies and post them in work locations.

The PMO can introduce the high-level realization plan in one of the project status meetings very close to the end of blueprinting. During this meeting, team leads can ask questions or pose issues in a public setting. Using this presentation method, all meeting attendees hear the same answers and the same message. Adopting this type of graphical and easily understood internal communications creates and maintains a common orientation among the team, and you should use it liberally throughout the project lifecycle.

Later, given the large number of deliverables in play during realization, project plans will reflect a much higher degree of granularity. These more granular, or "low-level," plans will supply operational guidance through the remainder of realization to final preparation.

Providing this visibility accomplishes two major objectives:

1. It enables a clear view of requirements and their timing for all project team members. Maintaining team alignment during this time is critical. Otherwise, teams may inadvertently slip deliverables by placing their focus on other targets. Used as a tracking mechanism, the project plan can keep all parts of the team aligned on the big picture.

2. It encourages effective executive governance. The plan points out where your team is making progress and where it is experiencing difficulties. With this information in hand, executives can concentrate on those few deliverables where oversight can pay dividends.

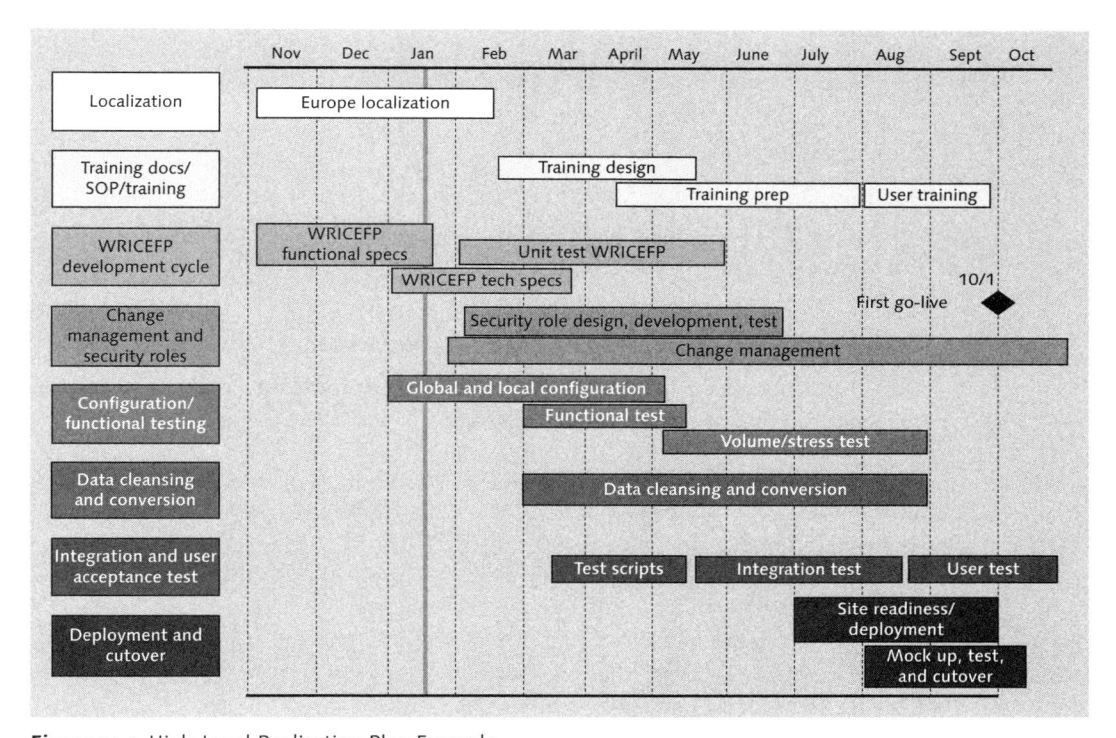

Figure 14.1 High-Level Realization Plan Example

> **Trail Marker**
>
> We cannot overemphasize the need for building a plan with the right level of granularity. It is a matter finding a middle ground between the forest and the trees. Too general a focus, on the one hand, will lead the team to miss important details. Too much detail, on the other hand, creates difficulty in seeing all the right deliverables. In the same way, using a graphical business plan for team status activities minimizes confusion and generates clarity.

Build the plan of record in Microsoft Project so that project management can track the overall status. However, if that plan is used for project status reporting, most teams will become lost in the details—so aim for somewhere in the middle. Use color-coding or shading to separate deliverable types and, where possible, combines them into separate areas on the schedule.

The detailed realization project plan portrays multiple layers of information on a single page:

- First, it shows realization deliverables from an "earliest to latest" perspective, with the earliest deliverables placed at the top of the page and latest deliverables at the bottom.
- Secondly, it groups deliverables according to the infrastructure environment in which they will be built. This helps the team to understand how the infrastructure transitions during the realization phase.
- Third, the plan color codes or shades the activities of different workstreams. This allows for ready referencing of specific workstream deliverables.
- Finally, it includes an icon (for example, a star) to indicate project go-live date and keep the overall target at top of mind.

Placing all this information on a single readable copy helps all program participants remain aligned. Questions concerning timing or sequencing can be resolved through reference to easily available editions. As these plans will change over time, it is imperative that the PMO distribute updates wherever they are posted.

14.1.2 Realization Kick-Off

Unless the team has numerous SAP implementations under its belt, the special demands of realization make an introductory kick-off session an absolute requirement. Similar to previously held blueprinting sessions, the realization kick-off meeting should involve the entire project team. Rather than multiple sessions over several days, the realization kick-off is usually a day-long meeting. Workstreams should leave the meeting with a clear idea of the demands of realization and how to meet them.

Project management will assume responsibility for the realization kick-off logistics. This includes taking care of a number of items:

- **Locating and booking a facility in which to hold the sessions**
  The facility will need a large room capable of seating the entire project team. It

will also require break-out space for each deliverable session since these will be delivered concurrently.

- **Identifying and preparing presenters who will deliver the sessions**
  This will mean preparing topic outlines for each presenting team and reviewing materials prior to the kick-off meeting.

- **Conducting dress rehearsals for the sessions**
  Make sure to provide feedback to each presenting group.

- **Deciding on the attendee list and ensuring that each identified person is invited to the session**
  Among a large team, participants should receive name tags to improve communication.

- **Preparing and distributing all hand-out materials**
  Participants should also receive a realization handbook. It can be used as a reference guide during the remainder of the project.

- **Introducing the kick-off presenters and ensuring the smooth flow of activities during the laboratory sessions**
  As you will shortly see, the lab sessions involve numerous changes in location. The PMO should assign guides to assure ease of movement from one meeting spot to the next.

- **Arranging for breaks, meals, and related participant events**
  All meals and breaks from breakfast to a team dinner should be scheduled and held on time.

> **Trail Marker**
>
> By designing a realization learning lab, the PMO can effectively convey all necessary information. Learning labs turn what could be a dull experience into a small group activity.

Prior to the kick-off, the PMO divides attendees into eight to 10 small groups and assigns rotations through the individual sessions. An example break-out structure is shown in Figure 14.2; each learning lab is parsed into a 30-minute time slot. Each subject session is devoted to a specific deliverable set and provides information that the project team will need.

The high-level realization project plan sets the session framework and ensures comprehensive coverage for each listed deliverable. Each workstream will prepare and present the laboratory materials on its own area of responsibility. Sessions should be to the point and designed to engage the project team. Rather than by-the-book presentations, each deliverable team should work to make its session an enjoyable experience. Weaving in humor, team participation activities, and learning games all help achieve this objective. Offering how-tos should be the focus of each presenting group. Every attendee should leave the kick-off with a clear understanding of the workings of realization.

Subject	9:30-10:00	10:10-10:40	10:50-11:20	12:40-1:10	1:20-1:50	2:00-2:30	2:40-3:10	3:20-3:50
	Round 1	Round 2	Round 3	Round 4	Round 5	Round 6	Round 7	Round 8
Localization	Team 1	Team 8	Team 7	Team 6	Team 5	Team 4	Team 3	Team 2
User training development	Team 2	Team 1	Team 8	Team 7	Team 6	Team 5	Team 4	Team 3
Configuration and functional testing	Team 3	Team 2	Team 1	Team 8	Team 7	Team 6	Team 5	Team 4
Integration and user acceptance testing	Team 4	Team 3	Team 2	Team 1	Team 8	Team 7	Team 6	Team 5
Data conversion/master data/data cleansing	Team 5	Team 4	Team 3	Team 2	Team 1	Team 8	Team 7	Team 6
Change management/job role design and security	Team 6	Team 5	Team 4	Team 3	Team 2	Team 1	Team 8	Team 7
Cutover and deployment	Team 7	Team 6	Team 5	Team 4	Team 3	Team 2	Team 1	Team 8
WRICEFP development and unit testing	Team 8	Team 7	Team 6	Team 5	Team 4	Team 3	Team 2	Team 1

Figure 14.2 Realization Learning Lab Break-Out Sessions and Rotation by Round

Individual learning lab sessions emphasize work products created during realization. Where possible, presenters demonstrate these work products using actual examples. Session exercises offer hands-on examples for building these work products. Participants will understand not only the deliverable content, but also how to construct it in actual practice.

In addition to the lab sessions, the kick-off includes an overview of the realization project plan. Scheduled at the beginning of the meetings, this introduction begins with a discussion of the just-completed blueprinting phase and any outstanding items still remaining. Once that discussion completes, the topic shifts to an in-depth overview of the realization project plan. Presenters should encourage questions from participants and be sure to bring any lingering concerns to the open. At that point, project management can discuss them in detail.

The realization kick-off concludes with a wrap-up. Project leadership can take this opportunity to thank all those involved as well as to congratulate everyone on a successful day. Spirits should be high as participants leave the meeting.

14.1.3 Realization Handbook

The realization handbook offers another tool to clarify this phase. It contains essential background information about each deliverable set and should be distributed to each kick-off participant.

The handbook contains two primary sources of information: copies of realization project plans and descriptors for each realization deliverable. Figure 14.3 through Figure 14.7 show the template used and material provided for a localization example. This same format is followed for all other realization deliverables.

Localization Purpose

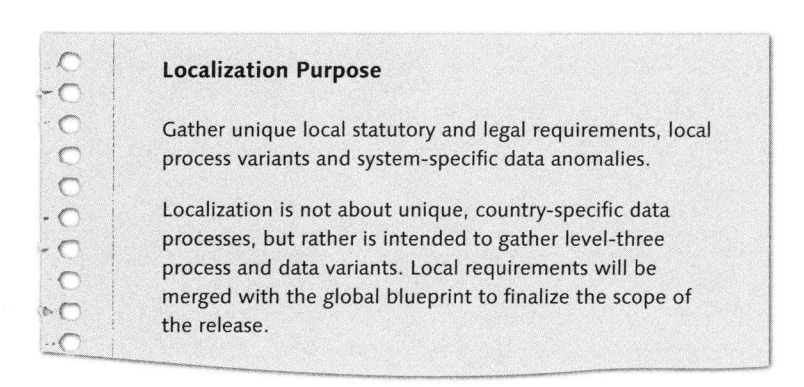

Gather unique local statutory and legal requirements, local process variants and system-specific data anomalies.

Localization is not about unique, country-specific data processes, but rather is intended to gather level-three process and data variants. Local requirements will be merged with the global blueprint to finalize the scope of the release.

Figure 14.3 Localization Purpose

14 | Realization

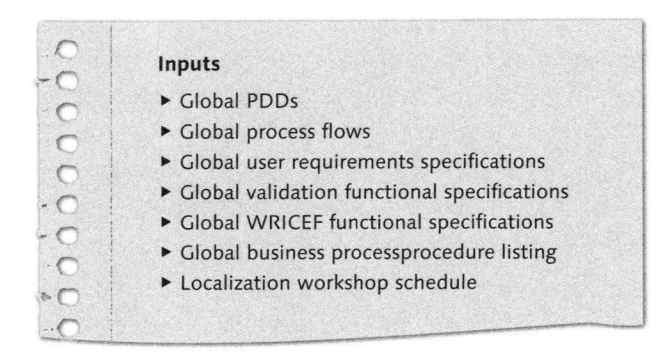

Inputs

- Global PDDs
- Global process flows
- Global user requirements specifications
- Global validation functional specifications
- Global WRICEF functional specifications
- Global business processprocedure listing
- Localization workshop schedule

Figure 14.4 Localization Inputs

Localization Tasks

Task	Tool	Who?	End Date
Localization workshops and interviews	MS SharePoint	Global process owners	2/10/20XX
Integration to countries	MS SharePoint	Integration manager	2/10/20XX
Complete localization requirement documents (by business process team)	MS SharePoint	Global process owners	2/10/20XX
Update global blueprint documents (PDD/PFL) with EU requirements	MS SharePoint	Global process owners	2/10/20XX
Solve design issues and alternatives with local businesses	MS SharePoint	Global process owners	3/15/20XX
Localization approval (prior to global BPO approval)	MS SharePoint	PMO	2/24/20XX

Figure 14.5 Localization Tasks

Localization Key Dependencies

Global blueprint documents must be updated with localization requirements by 2/10/20XX.

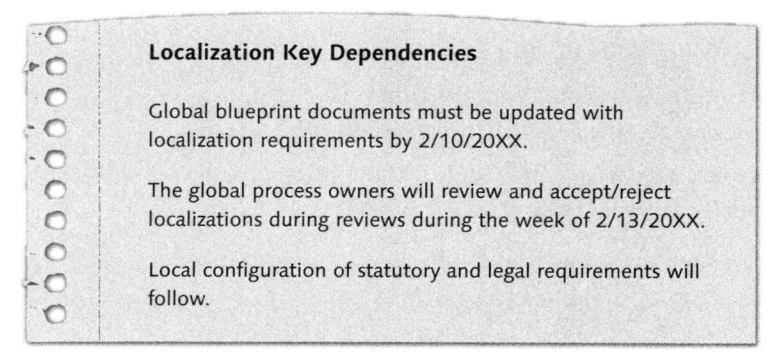

The global process owners will review and accept/reject localizations during reviews during the week of 2/13/20XX.

Local configuration of statutory and legal requirements will follow.

Figure 14.6 Localization Key Dependencies

Localization Deliverables and Outcome

Deliverables:
- Change impact analysis
- Localization requirements document
- Local PDDs
- Local process flows

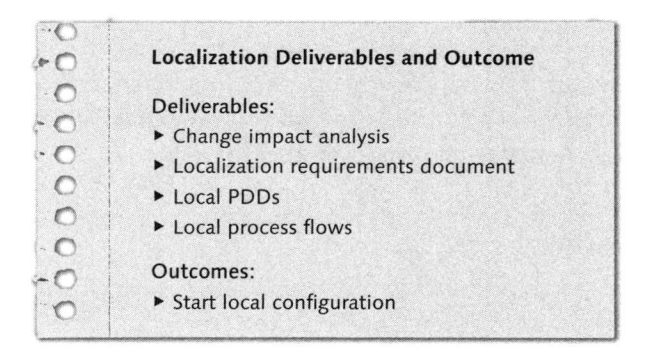

Outcomes:
- Start local configuration

Figure 14.7 Localization Deliverables and Outcome

Each section outlines critical data for the specific deliverable. This includes the following:

- An overall description of the deliverable, including any specialized information that will be required by the project team.
- Inputs that will be needed to complete the deliverable. These are often documentation items that were compiled during blueprinting. The remaining items are documentation sections compiled during early stages of realization.
- The task listing identifies items used as elements of the deliverable. Task listings are represented in chronological due-date order. The section also specifies any tools used to deliver or record the task. It also describes the project organization responsible for the task.

14 | Realization

- The key dependencies segment shows the name and timing of any major milestone that depends upon the item to be finished.
- Any documentation that will be required when work is finished. In this way, the project team knows exactly what "done" looks like.
- Outcomes represent next-step items that can be initiated once the deliverable in question is ready for final review.

Once the project team has received all realization transition materials, the real work of the phase can begin. The team is now prepared for the challenges it will face.

14.2 Organizing for Realization

The next step is to ensure that your team is properly organized to accomplish its realization objectives. While blueprinting focused everyone on the same deliverables, realization divides up assignments and responsibilities.

14.2.1 Workstream Management

Blueprinting was driven by the functional workstreams. Each workstream worked to complete an SAP system design that met business needs and operational processes. During this time, horizontal or technical workstreams conducted intensive planning activities and provided support for the design effort. Once that design is developed and confirmed as complete, the roles of functional and horizontal workstreams change markedly.

> **Pitfall Alert**
>
> Emphasize, emphasize, and re-emphasize the realization workstream role shift. Otherwise, functional workstreams will continue to manage their technical deliverables (such as test and data conversion) while the horizontal teams fail to take overall ownership of their deliverables. Your expectations about the management role of the horizontal team must be very clear.

Functional workstreams continue to own the design and provide company business process expertise. However, many of the new activities specific to realization are both technical and centralized in nature. Testing, user training, security, data conversion, and configuration have technical components and apply across the entire project. This makes it essential for the horizontal workstream leads to manage their processes by establishing a common framework.

Table 14.1 shows that each vertical or functional workstream has a role to play in all realization activities. Additionally, each horizontal workstream has a role to play in its area of responsibility. For example, the horizontal workstream for system testing ensures that system tests are properly planned, performed, and recorded. The vertical workstream ensures that tests reflect required business processes, and it executes the tests in its area. For vertical workstreams, learning how to share leadership represents one of the challenges of project realization.

Workstream	Human capital management	Order-to-cash	Procure-to-pay	Plan-to-stock	Record-to-report
Change management	X	X	X	X	X
Configuration	X	X	X	X	X
Data conversion	X	X	X	X	X
EDI processing		X	X	X	
System testing	X	X	X	X	X
User training	X	X	X	X	X
WRICEFP development	X	X	X	X	X

Table 14.1 Relationship of Functional and Horizontal Worksteams

Trail Marker

The table emphasizes the shared roles of functional and horizontal workstreams. Each has a role to play in the completion of assigned deliverables. However, unlike blueprinting, the horizontal workstreams manage and take responsibility for the tasks under their purview. This ensures a standard approach across functional workstreams.

In some cases, such as configuration, data conversion, and custom object development, the work is very system-specific and requires technical skills. In these areas, the horizontal team and the integrator staff assigned to it will play the primary role in delivery. The functional workstreams often assume a support role during realization.

Project management manages the balance of work between the two sets of workstreams. It begins with very explicit clarification of roles and continues through to the day-to-day management of deliverable completion. It also includes smoothing over any rough edges in working relationships among the two types of workstreams. Differences of opinion can be expected, but if you address them quickly, they can certainly be worked through.

14.2.2 Regional and Site Responsibilities

In addition to the shifts taking place in workstream relationships, regions and sites involved in the project experience changes as well. In blueprinting, regions and sites had very cut-and-dried responsibilities. They supplied input to the business design and reviewed its impact on local operations. The regional and site project teams also assured that management understood and were involved in any new business process designs. This limited role left much of the project decision-making in the hands of the central team and vertical workstreams in particular.

During realization, regional teams' roles expand considerably. Regional leads now take a more active part in ensuring that relevant deliverables will be completed; in addition, regional leads help plan for deployment. These expansions shift greater demands to regional and site team members as well.

Recall from Chapter 10's discussion on project organization that each region has a regional lead assigned to manage its project deliverables. During blueprinting, this lead managed the overall coordination of regional resources assigned to the project. The regional lead also manages area subject matter experts (SMEs). This responsibility continues in realization, but acquires increased scope. Similar to the central project team, as seen in Figure 14.8, the regional team will now emphasize horizontal team organization. For that reason, the lead will now also manage horizontal staff, who will handle specific technical topics relevant to regional requirements. If the technical work reaches a sufficient level, a regional integration lead can be assigned. In most cases, the regional IT organization takes on the integration lead role.

Organizing for Realization | **14.2**

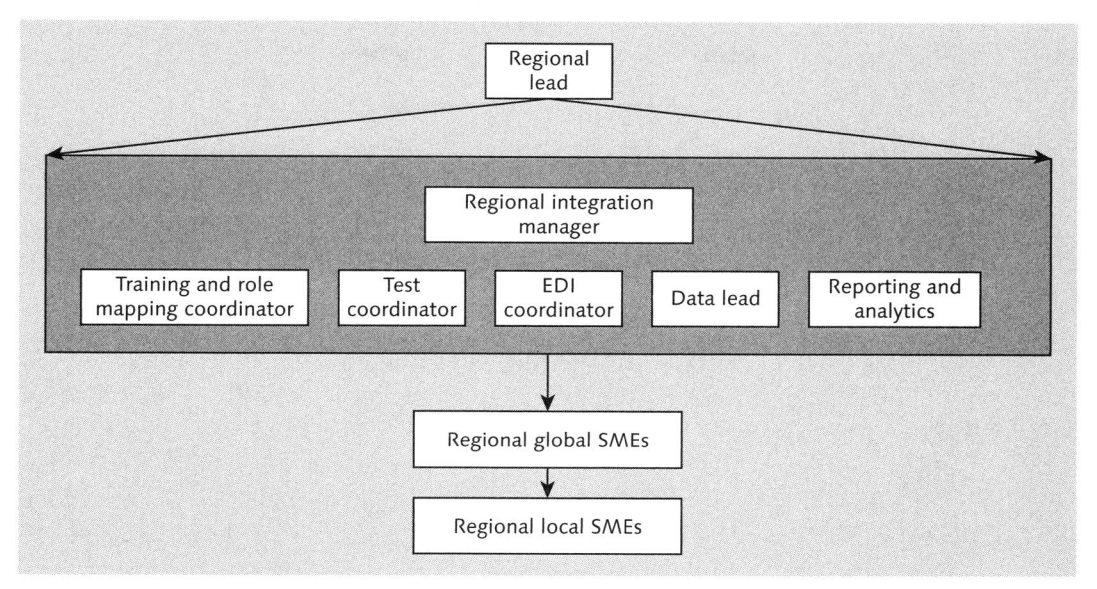

Figure 14.8 Regional Project Organization during Realization

These regional integration leads work directly with their counterparts in the central project team. During the region implementation wave, they are responsible for ensuring that deliverables in their scope are correctly fulfilled. Often, they manage regional SMEs to complete these activities. In this way, the regional horizontal organization will closely parallel the organiztion of the central project.

More specifically, the regional integration manager would perform the following roles during realization:

- Managing and assuring effective completion of all technical deliverables assigned to the regional team
- Reporting on the status of deliverables to the regional lead and to the central PMO
- Ensuring that adequate technical resources are assigned to the regional team and raising requests for additional resources where needed
- Working closely with key regional stakeholders to build alignment with project objectives and timelines

- Operating as the regional central point of contact on project system-related issues
- Ensuring that regional end users are ready to operate the SAP system when delivered
- Verifying system readiness prior to regional deployment

Together, the regional lead and the regional integration manager coordinate activities in support of the deployment. Often the regional lead focuses on business readiness actions, while the regional integration manager handles more systems preparedness issues.

The PMO ensures necessary coordination of responsibilities between the central and regional project teams. If any overlap exists, the PMO makes clear which group has ownership. In all cases, the central project team has some task ownership. However, in some cases, the regional project team owns the realization deliverables for its area. Table 14.2 indicates the division of labor between the two groups. In the table, X indicates primary ownership and O indicates secondary ownership.

Task	Central Team	Regional Team
Data verification	O	X
Integration testing	X	O
User acceptance testing	O	X
Third party/EDI	X	X
SOPs and work instructions	X	X
Role mapping	O	X
Super users preparation	O	X
Training materials design	X	O
Training delivery	O	X
Reports and controls	X	O

Table 14.2 Deliverable Responsibility Between Project Core and Regional Teams

In many cases, your project will have large sites involved in its SAP implementation. These sites are usually manufacturing plants or distribution facilities with several hundred staff. Each type of site will both accomplish site deliverables and provide project support. For large regional sites, local resources should directly participate in the project organization. Otherwise, the very detailed activities intended to be accomplished at those locations may not proceed as planned.

These site-related activities fall into three major groupings:

- Site preparation
  - Warehousing and storage location labeling
  - Production planner preparation
  - Facilities management readiness
  - Data cleansing and preparation
  - Identification of existing operating procedures
  - EDI processing assessment
  - Coordination with third-party logistical providers (if used)
- Site project support deliverables
  - Planning for user testing
  - Review of project training curriculum
  - Assessment of operating procedures
  - Participation in data conversion
  - Involvement in site-based regional cutover planning
- Site deliverables
  - Evaluation of interfaces to other site-based systems
  - Revising applicable site operating procedures
  - Mapping staff to security roles
  - Executing user acceptance testing
  - Review and approval of data conversion results
  - Planning for any needed organizational change
  - Communicating to staff regarding project objectives and timing

This list underscores how important it is for sites to fully participate in this project. Company sites will own many of the essential and complex project regional deliverables. Site deliverables require effective preparatory work. If the site definitely feels it has ownership of its deliverables, it will accomplish this work effectively. Having site resources assigned to manage its own deliverables builds local buy-in for your project.

If your project touches operations in multiple countries, you may require a country coordinator to ensure that affected country-based operations are prepared for implementation. Coordinator duties would include the following:

- Provide a country "voice" to regional lead
- Participate in change management activities and role mapping activities impacting the country
- Provide translation language support for user training materials, SOPs, and other controlled documents
- Identify end users for training, coordinate training logistics, and manage training schedules

Now that we've outlined changes in project organization, we will move to the changing role of project management. In realization, project management functions as a traffic light, a scorekeeper, and a facilitator, as we'll soon show.

14.3 Project Management

Once the team has been aligned for realization, the work products begin to flow. At this time, project management processes and structures put in place during blueprinting expand to encompass the broader demands of realization. Status reporting—which in blueprinting focused on only a few deliverables—now shifts to monitoring progress on a broader front. The reporting involves a far larger number of deliverables and an extended project organization.

In realization, project management becomes the hub of the project. It ensures that all deliverables are known, have an owner, and are making required progress. The functional workstreams still own business deliverables, and horizontal workstreams still own technical deliverables. However, project management operates in the midst of this matrix to assure that all is proceeding as planned. Where it is not proceeding as planned, project management points out the shortfall and assists with the resolution.

14.3.1 Status Reporting and Performance Metrics

Project operating review meetings, initiated during blueprinting, take on an even greater importance during realization. They show progress against the full range of deliverables now assigned. Any deliverable whose failure to meet the schedule could affect go-live is reported and assessed. As discussed in Chapter 5, these meetings are held on a regular basis—two or sometimes three times per week—and involve key project team members from both the central and regional organizations.

With a large number of project members on the conference calls, there is considerable potential for confusion. The PMO prepares documents for each session and distributes them via email at least an hour prior to the session. It standardizes the meeting format as much as possible and assigns ownership for status reporting to the workstream or location that owns a deliverable. Each meeting session is limited to an hour.

Effective meeting tempo and duration depend on the degree of session discipline established. Good meetings limit questions only to matters of understanding. Delving deeply into individual issues during the meeting, no matter how important, is to be avoided. The moderator controls off-topic comments or problem-solving. These discussions can rapidly begin to use technical terms or acronyms. As a result, project team members who are not familiar with the terms—or are experiencing language difficulties—can become confused or distracted.

In lieu of problem-solving, the PMO identifies issues during the meeting and assigns small task teams to work them. In later meetings, task team leaders can provide reports on progress and solutions identified. Due to the large number of deliverables reported during the status meetings, a single individual should provide the report for the entire deliverable area.

> **Tip**
>
> When possible, use numerical values in reports. Dependence on percentages requires a consistent denominator for ease of understanding. Where those denominators are in flux—as is very often the case with test scripts or data objects reporting—percentages may lead the team to assume incorrectly that all is well. In situations where your team is encountering major problems, numerical values with both numerator and denominator shown allow for a clear picture and point out where problems are occurring. Often, the true numerical status provides the initial step in problem resolution.

14 | Realization

Later chapters will cover individual performance metrics in greater detail. However, Table 14.3 shows the types of metrics used during realization. These metrics depict horizontal workstreams' status in completing their deliverables. Project status meetings report this performance to all participants. Having this information generally available enables the team to take ownership of issues and to resolve them. It also assures that everyone sees the same information.

Reporting Workstream	Performance Metric
System testing	▶ Test scripts written ▶ Test scripts approved ▶ Test scripts loaded ▶ Test executed ▶ Test rejected ▶ Defects identified ▶ Defects resolved
Electronic data interchange	▶ Company mapping developed ▶ Partner mapping developed ▶ Unit tests executed ▶ Integration tests executed ▶ User acceptance tests complete
User training	▶ Courses in progress ▶ Courses approved by workstream ▶ Courses scheduled ▶ Courses translated (where needed) ▶ Instructors assigned ▶ Facilities assigned ▶ Course attendance
Application development	▶ Functional specification prepared ▶ Technical specification prepared ▶ Developments complete ▶ Unit tests executed ▶ Objects accepted

Table 14.3 Sample Metrics Used During Realization

Reporting Workstream	Performance Metric
Configuration	▸ Configuration objects complete ▸ Configuration rationales complete
Change management	▸ User roles designed ▸ User roles mapped ▸ User role segregation of duties analysis ▸ User roles assigned in system ▸ Change workshops completed ▸ Communication issued
Data conversion	▸ Data objects cleansed ▸ Data objects loaded in development ▸ Data objects loaded in quality ▸ Data objects verified ▸ Data objects loaded in production

Table 14.3 Sample Metrics Used During Realization (Cont.)

Functional workstreams may well maintain their own metric views. The functional workstream owns many of the resources that execute or resolve what is measured, so workstream performance tracking plays an extremely valuable role. It assures that both management elements—the horizontal and functional workstream—are aligned.

Figure 14.9 provides a sample order-to-cash workstream. Notice that the items reported reflect metrics from a number of horizontal workstreams. Combined ownership greatly increases the probabilities of success.

Additionally, your project team may choose to color-code deliverable status. This may introduce a certain level of subjectivity into the reporting process. For example, the three colors (green, yellow, and red) don't have objective meanings assigned to them.

Description	Metric	Comment
Integration test cycle 3 scripts	277 total/253 completed	
Integration test defects	0 urgent; 11 total	3 routing for QA review, 3 assigned, 3 QA review reject, 2 deferred
WRICEFP development objects	0 outstanding	
Data loads	18 total/18 verified	
User acceptance test scripts	428 total/405 completed	To complete testing for UAT need to retest: 14 accounts receivable scripts and 3 for trade promotions 6 EDI
User acceptance test defects fix applied or less	20 critical defects; 61 total. 8 fix applied, 9 assigned, 2 QA failed, 1 defect.	4 accounts receivable, 3 warehouse inventory 5 SOP, 1 security, 2 exports
SOPs and work instructions	33 of 33 SOPs approved. 208 or 219 work instructions approved	11 work instructions in process
Training materials	41 of 41 approved	
Design, functional specifications, and technical specifications	385 of 385 signed	

Figure 14.9 Functional Workstream Realization Metrics

Pitfall Alert

The preference of many workstreams to show progress and not to hinder on-time schedule delivery may cause teams to prefer green and yellow while carefully avoiding red. Sometimes, even projects that are facing major difficulties, mark virtually no late or incomplete deliverables. This creates a false sense of security among the project team. A very rocky go-live and hypercare period may result from these *safe* choices. Far better to present things as they are and deal with the consequences. Manipulated reporting causes everyone to discount the information.

Providing clear definitions regarding the meaning of each color goes a long way in resolving ambiguity. As with the project schedule, these definitions can be posted in project work areas. The PMO can also continually reference their status during project status meetings. This ensures that color coding conforms to a standard.

For example, consider the following color code guidelines:

- The color green indicates that the activity is on schedule to meet milestones or deliverables.
- The color yellow indicates that issues have been raised that make the milestone or deliverable questionable, or that a milestone or deliverable date has been missed but approved plans to recover have been initiated and have no impact on long-term milestones or other teams' deliverables.
- The color red indicates that a deliverable or milestone has been missed and that either no recovery plans have been initiated or recovery plans are not possible without major program delay.

But the PMO does far more than manage project reporting statuses.

14.3.2 Deliverables Tracking and Milestone Recognition

In addition to verifying the deliverables' status with regard to the project schedule, project management verifies deliverables' status for systems integrator progress payments. Quite often, the integrator's statement of work (SOW) outlines the categories of deliverables and the timing associated with progress payments. Each deliverable is described in broad terms. Assuming that the identified deliverables meet their agreed-upon dates, the client company then owes some portion of integrator fees for that successful effort.

Using the SOW as a reference, the project manager verifies when the work is complete. It also includes approval to release funds for payment to the integrator. In point of fact, this deliverable verification mechanism serves as an excellent control device for integrator management.

Figure 14.10 shows a subset of realization deliverable packages. Each milestone identifies those deliverables due and provides specifics as to the completion criteria. It also stipulates an acceptance review period within which the deliverable must be accepted.

Milestone Package	Required Completion Date	Deliverables	Deliverable Description	Acceptance Review Period
Cycle one unit testing complete	3/15/20XX	1. Configuration and unit test results 2. Data conversion functional specification 3. Functional systems specifications	1. All configuration complete and problems logged 2. All specifications for data received and approved 3. All WRICEFP functional specifications received	Five days
Cycle two unit testing complete	5/15/20XX	1. WRICEFP technical specifications 2. Quality assurance environment 3. Integration test schedule	1. All WRICEFP technical specification complete 2. QA system built and delivered 3. Integration test schedule complete	Five days
Cycle one integration testing complete	7/15/20XX	1. Unit testing results 2. Configuration rationales 3. Production environment	1. Unit testing complete 2. Configuration rationales complete 3. Production environment delivered for use	Five days

Figure 14.10 Systems Integrator Deliverable Packages

Project management can use this opportunity to apply more detailed standards for deliverable acceptance than those contained in the statement of work. For example, as the number of integration test scripts planned for execution becomes clearer, these numbers can be used to replace those more open-ended values in the original SOW (such as 435 integration test scripts built and executed).

This approach applies to the full range of integrator deliverables. Similar to our earlier discussion on status tracking, take care to avoid percentages and terms such as "complete," which are always open to interpretation. Applying numerical values to technical specifications totals, configuration rationales, and WRICEFP functional specifications to be delivered makes both parties clearly understand what is "done." Accountability becomes even more fine-tuned.

These package milestones are tied to payment schedules. As each is submitted for review, project management assesses it according to completion criteria. It then either accepts and approves the milestone for payment, or rejects it. In the case of rejection, this rationale must be couched in terms referring to the integrator SOW. Here is another good reason being precise in deliverable criteria. Cut-and-dried criteria makes management acceptance far simpler. For example, indicating that only 376 integration test scripts were built and executed instead of the agreed-to 435 clarifies the situation considerably. This reduces the debate over whether the integrator met deliverable conditions.

14.3.3 Risk Management

Realization is fraught with risk. All the conditions just discussed—such as multiple deliverables management and activities carried out in distant regions or remote sites—make high risk levels extremely likely. The project as a whole contains significant risk, and each decision made in such an environment poses some degree of risk. Because the project contains this risk profile, the team must act to minimize risks by any means possible.

> **Pitfall Alert**
>
> The ability to manage risk is a key determinant of your project's success. Some projects pay little explicit attention to risk—at their peril. Risks—whether they're completely unforeseen, or seen and simply not addressed—are the rocky shoals upon which your project ship can crash. Pay attention to risk and then pay even more. The return is worth the investment.

Project management owns the overall identification and tracking of risk. A system capable of tracking project risks must be in place during realization. Chapter 8 introduced this topic, but this chapter offers more detail in terms of the structure of risk management. It outlines the types of risks posed during realization and risk management tools available to address them.

Risk analysis is divided into two tasks: identifying the risk, and then specifying tracking actions taken to mitigate the risk. Project management will establish a *risk register*. It captures any known risk and puts it through an initial filter. First, it can be categorized according to the type of risk it poses. Here are some commonly used realization risk categories:

- **Leadership**
  Without dedicated leadership commitment to the project, from senior executives to middle management, the project will fail. Success requires daily involvement and effort in all major functional areas. Anything less entails a significant risk. Particular focus is needed during realization in these areas:
  - Ongoing evidence of active management commitment to the project. This includes stepping in to assist the project team when it runs into problems.
  - Frequent, targeted formal and informal communications from management to the user community regarding the project. These can range from regular written updates to small group meetings.
  - Senior executives' energetic participation in project governance.
- **Project management**
  Unless project management has the skills and ability for effective coordination of core activities, it cannot run the project. Deliverables will be missed and confusion will develop within the project team. Risk items in this category include the following:
  - Adequate definition and management of project scope. The project will face constant pressure to include additional deliverables or to modify them in some way. Without effective scope management, the project may take on more work than it can handle in the time allotted. This will result in missed or incomplete deliverables.
  - Full understanding of global requirements. In global projects, it is difficult to gather a complete requirements list. Regions may have greatly differing business processes or have operated on site-specific systems. Uncovering these requirements takes a real focus by the project team. To be successful, project management must allocate the time and emphasize the need.
  - Development of project team organization and accountability. Lines of communication and responsibility must be clear to all project team members. Ownership for decisions must also be crystal clear.
  - Ability to coordinate activities with other projects. It's very likely that the company will have other projects underway that impact the SAP systems project. Project management must identify these impacts and coordinate with other project teams to understand their status.

- **Resources**

  The PMO must ensure that the project has the right number and skill mix of resources assigned. Lacking adequate resources, your project team will continually run on the ragged edge and constantly face looming schedule dates. Resource risks involve the following:

  - Sufficiency of staffing on the project team. Staffing levels among the core team (including integrator staffing), regions, and sites must be adequate to accomplish project deliverables. Where these levels are not sufficient, reporting mechanisms must be in place to address any need.

  - Continuity on the project team. Turnover on the project team can present challenges to the project. Important team members can leave the company or the systems integrator. Alternatively, team members can receive new assignments that remove them from the team. Processes must be in place to assist management in understanding impacts of proposed staffing changes. The effects of these changes must be managed.

  - Ability to attract the highest-caliber staff for the project team. The SAP systems project requires the best and brightest staff for functional and horizontal teams; if the company is unwilling to recruit at that skill level, the risks increase.

- **Technical**

  SAP is, after all, a very technical system. The project requires staff with an in-depth understanding of the processes and infrastructure that will be needed to operate the system. Without this skill set, many of these risks could come to fruition:

  - Shortfalls in technical and system performance. The project may encounter difficulties with infrastructure installation, application performance, or the skills levels among integrator staff. These can all disturb the system's smooth operation and have downstream effects on testing, cutover, and go-live.

  - Issues with custom development. The team may find that custom objects were inadequately specified, built incorrectly, or simply not built to the agreed-upon schedule. If these problems impact critical custom objects, they'll greatly affect the schedule.

  - Difficulties in linking to legacy systems. Most projects will either supply or receive data from existing company systems. These interfaces to legacy systems must work as planned. If not, either the legacy system or the SAP system will not work as planned.

▸ **Execution**
Knowing what to do and executing based on that knowledge represent two different project needs. Your project team will require skill in executing the correct actions. Otherwise, the following risks become a reality:

- Ability to pilot test new processes or procedures. Go-live will bring on new processes or procedures for portions of the company. Pilot testing ensures that users have verified the performance of these new processes and their ability to complete the tasks prior to go-live.
- Effective delivery of end-user training. Users must receive training, especially where the SAP system will be unfamiliar to them. This also means there must be an entire logistics operation to train these users.
- Thorough planning for post-implementation support. Hypercare (the support period immediately after go-live) and the transition to a full-time sustainment organization requires careful planning. Support personnel must be trained on the new system and capable of resolving incidents from end users.
- Preparation of super users. After go-live, it's critical to place user support on-site to provide first-level problem solving. Users will encounter problems, and their satisfaction with the new system depends on easy access to resolving their questions. On-site, first-level support is provided by super users. They, in turn, must be prepared and trained for their roles.

The risk register collects identified potential issues and places them into one of these five categories. Project management, in conjunction with functional workstream leads, then assigns each risk a probability of occurrence and an impact rating. Because of their importance, risks with high probability and high impact are highlighted for special attention. The PMO tracks them in a special register. Each critical risk receives additional attention regarding its impact and the mitigation actions that the project team should take.

Figure 14.11 provides an example of this special register. It shows two risks the project team has identified: one risk that impacts acceptance testing and another that impacts data load into the production system. Both issues have high probability and would have high impact if they were to come to pass. For that reason, they would be highlighted in red in the system.

Each risk entry lists a cause. Where there are multiple causes, the registry lists all primary contributors. The mitigation actions outline the steps that the team will take to eliminate or minimize the risk. Finally, the registry assigns an owner for the mitigation actions. In some cases, the PMO assigns multiple owners.

Date Mitigation Required	Key Deliverables Affected	Probability	Impact	Cause	Mitigation Actions	Owner
7/18/20XX	Readiness for user acceptance test	High	High	▶ Testers have not yet received systems training. Unable to complete tests	▶ Special classes established for testers. ▶ Instructors assigned from project team	Training team
9/01/20XX	Start of cutover data load	High	High	▶ Production system not performing at needed speed. Data loads cannot take place in allotted time	▶ Complete performance testing on production system. Resolve performance issues.	Basis team

Figure 14.11 Special Risk Register

Project management ensures that every high-probability and high-impact risk receives a review during the project operating review meetings. This review assesses progress for all mitigation actions. The workstream that has been assigned ownership for the risk reports actions taken since the last meeting. This review will continue for as long as the risk remains in the high-probability and high-impact category.

Seeing the risk mitigation status allows the team to focus on those real-time critical issues that are likely to affect project performance. Creating accountability for achieving results makes the risk register an important tool.

14.3.4 Resourcing

Once the project moves into the realization phase, it should review its resourcing plans based on any new information. When faced with the specifics of competing resource requirements during realization, new resourcing needs often appear.

This resource review includes staffing for the core team as well as regional staffing requirements.

Addressing Additional Resource Needs

It's very possible that the project will need additional regional SMEs. A typical project would assign SMEs a percentage-based time allocation for project activities ranging from 50 percent for regional SMEs and 25 percent for local SMEs. However, before beginning realization, the PMO can conduct a review of actual usage to date. If multiple regions are involved in the project, usage may differ substantially from region to region. It is important to understand the underlying causes for any substantial differences. Differences could be due to issues with consistent labor reporting or because the actual SME manpower usage varies from region to region.

> **Pitfall Alert**
>
> Some project teams feel uncomfortable raising the question of additional resources, since they understand that the initial response will not be positive. However, the team must have the willpower to make its case despite any fears that it may feel. Otherwise, the work does not get done or gets done only partially. Take a deep breath, experience the discomfort, and then move forward anyway.

However, at this point in the project your PMO must determine whether the current resourcing plans address the SMEs' requirements for the phases ahead. Resourcing plans formed in the early days of the project may prove insufficient in the face of newly discovered demands. For example, the project team may have underestimated critical needs for SMEs, such as testing, user training, and hypercare in the original resourcing plans. Any requests for additional resources should be addressed with company senior executives as soon as they are known.

Figure 14.12 shows a situation in which labor projections met needs early in the project, but additional SME staffing allocations became necessary in the later stages of realization. Note that these differences represent major changes and could cause difficulties with the functional organizations supplying these resources. Changes will impact project funding as well.

After reviewing this with project sponsors, the PMO should communicate these changes directly to regional leads. Specific information about SME assignment changes will be very important. Whether the shifts involve requirements for new SMEs or additional work delegated to existing SMEs, the regional lead will be faced with managing the changes.

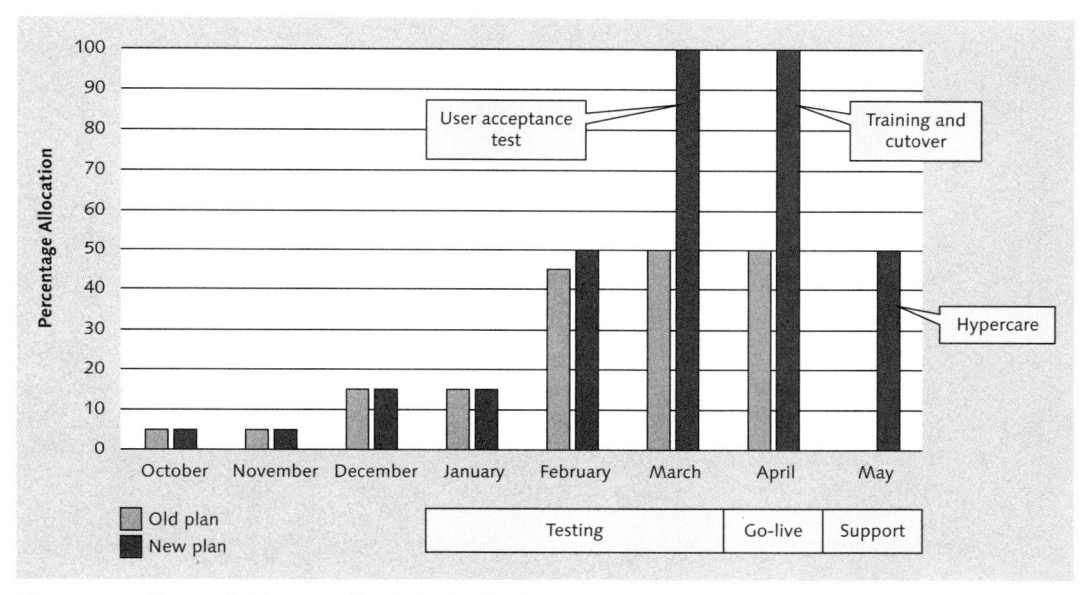

Figure 14.12 Changes in Resource Needs During Realization

Your meetings with senior executives to discuss changing resource requirements require detailed explanations. Making the rationale very clear and compelling greatly improves the chances of success. For this reason, any prepared materials should focus especially on how and why requirements have changed. Whether the reasons are inadequate resourcing planning, a decision to enlarge project scope, or the project team's inability to perform at anticipated levels, these facts must be made crystal clear. Otherwise the request is likely to be met with a lukewarm reception, and requested resources may not be received. In this case, the project team will have reduced its credibility with senior executives and still face the same resourcing challenges.

> **Tip**
>
> If the project is global in nature and deploys through multiple implementation waves, this will also be the time to address how the project can use SMEs from wave to wave. In a three-wave project, SMEs from regions already implemented can become a ready source of reliable and experienced staff for future waves. Thus, for the wave two implementation, SMEs from wave one assist the project team. In the same way, SMEs from wave one and from wave two can assist wave three implementation. Again, this approach should be approved by company senior executives and by regional management supplying the resources.
>
> Some projects have successfully used SMEs to augment the project team staff. Functional workstreams faced with the multiple demands of realization can use global SMEs to assist in multiple areas, such as documentation and training material review. Having the SMEs working with the core project team at this time can greatly expand their understanding of SAP and project operations in general.

Once approved, these additional assignments should be carefully explained to all regional SMEs affected to ensure their buy-in and commitment. These explanations should be clearly outlined. For example, the project team would craft an introductory communication, to be followed later with more detail. This high-level message might appear as follows:

- Wave one SMEs will assist with the implementations of wave two and wave three. This will require their 100 percent participation, from user acceptance testing through hypercare in both waves.
- Wave two SMEs will assist with the implementation of wave three. This will require their 100 percent participation, from user acceptance testing through hypercare in wave three.
- SMEs will operate as super users and problem resolution resources during hypercare for any assigned implementation wave.
- Some SMEs will work at the central command center to assist the core project team during hypercare. Staff assigned to these roles will be separately notified.

In this way, the central message provides overall guidance. Follow-up slides can offer additional details concerning names, assignment location, and role. Providing the utmost clarity on these types of assignments is essential to reduce any uncertainties.

Using Contractors to Augment the Project Team

Where core team resourcing shortfalls are the issue, one solution is to bring on technically experienced contractors.

Using contractors has concrete advantages. Their experience in SAP implementations allows them to come up to speed quickly on project teams, and they can provide a ready source for technical solutions. Also, since your company has hired them, contractors can provide alternative points of view to the systems integrator's recommendations on project issues.

However, some disadvantages also come into play. Identifying the right contractor to meet specialized project needs is a time-consuming process that could take several weeks. But cost is the main disadvantage to using contractors. Top-flight contractors may charge $200 per hour and above, and these pose an extra, unplanned cost. Incremental funds to cover contractor costs will not appear in the project budget. Authorization to move forward with contracting requires separate justification by project management and approval by senior company executives. Even the addition of three to four contractors at this rate may cause overruns in the project budget. Project management can expect intense scrutiny on the rationale and need for these resources. Still, if the project can afford the expenditure, then it is an option certainly worth considering.

Evaluating Integrator Staffing

The beginning of project realization is as an excellent time to address integrator staffing. If the contract operates on a fixed-price basis, overall staffing numbers remain the responsibility of the integrator. However, the status of individual integrator staff members—especially when they fill significant roles on the project—is certainly open for discussion. Your company has a contractual right to request replacement for any integrator staff member not performing at necessary levels. Where your company has performance concerns, these should be raised with systems integrator management as early as possible, but certainly by the start of realization.

Project management and workstream leads should pay careful attention to the quality of integrator staff performance. Potential issues could include lack of technical skills, inadequate work habits, and difficulties with communication. As noted, these concerns should be relayed to the systems integrator project lead.

This will allow time for the issues to be discussed with affected staff and resolved, if possible. If the integrator has taken remediation steps and you are still not satisfied with the results, your company should request replacement staff be assigned to the project. In this way, the overall integrator team can be improved to meet your company requirements.

The staff replacement or "rolling off" process should be accomplished quickly. The integrator project lead should identify candidate replacements in short order. Project management would receive replacement résumés for review. The PMO and applicable workstream leads can schedule interview calls with potential replacement candidates. Only make the change after your review group members all agree they've found a satisfactory replacement.

In cases where senior members of the integrator project staff are in question, a different process should be followed. Your company sponsors should reach out to their executive counterparts at the systems integrator firm. Those discussions can point out which issues are impeding progress, and your company sponsors should request that integrator executives start the replacement process. Again, a small group consisting of your senior project management and sponsors would interview replacement candidates and decide on their suitability.

Remember all that design work done during blueprinting? It means that our team must do a lot of work during realization. Our next chapter outlines the build process and will focus extensively on configuration and custom object development. Here we go!

Realization comes in two parts. In the first part, your project team configures the system and builds those custom objects identified during blueprinting. This chapter shows how the build takes place.

15 Configuration and Custom Objects Build

While realization project management activities are taking place, so too are technical activities supporting system build. The two parts of realization, build and system test, combine to ensure that required functionality is in place and works as planned. This chapter covers core events in the build phase: system configuration, custom object development, security design, and evaluation of company procedures. Next, Chapter 16 will address the fundamental aspects of testing.

Let's take a look at a typical timeline for the build part, as shown in Figure 15.1.

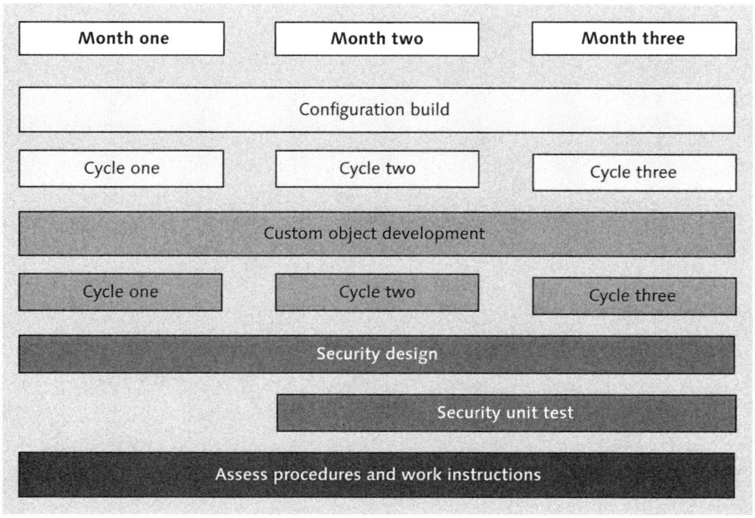

Month one	Month two	Month three
	Configuration build	
Cycle one	Cycle two	Cycle three
	Custom object development	
Cycle one	Cycle two	Cycle three
	Security design	
	Security unit test	
	Assess procedures and work instructions	

Figure 15.1 Three-Month Realization Build Timeline

It shows the four activities described, each consuming an approximately three-month window. In order to manage the work efficiently, configuration build and custom object development break their activities into three deliverable cycles. All work is assigned to one of the three cycles and completed within that time frame, which makes it easier to monitor and manage that work progress.

Configuration build and custom object development work together as highly integrated activities. Custom objects must function with the configuration in place, and configuration must support custom object operation. They are both essential to basic system operation. On the other hand, security design and evaluation of company procedures proceed independent of configuration and custom object development. They take place within the build time frame but do not depend on completion of the technical work. Our chapter will address all four as elements of the build process.

- **Configuration**
  This building block organizes elements of the system to perform company business processes according to defined requirements. SAP is a very configurable system, meaning that it can perform business processes in many different fashions. During configuration, technical resources specify the combination of system settings that will enable the system to operate as needed.

- **Custom object development**
  During blueprinting, the project team identified additional SAP functionality required to operate company business processes. Once built, these custom objects—recall the acronym WRICEFP from Chapter 14—will provide the needed services. Each custom object requires specification, development, and testing. All activities take place during realization build.

- **Security design**
  SAP security controls the access and transactions permitted for end users. These controls are established in the system and channel users to only those system activities required for their job functions. Each company has its own set of security requirements. These are built and tested during the build phase of realization.

- **Company policy assessment**
  All industries face some degree of regulatory oversight. Business process performance must conform to the requirements of this oversight. At the end-user level, companies assure this conformance using policies and work instructions.

They provide employee guidance on how processes will be performed. During an SAP implementation, existing policies must be reviewed to make sure they correspond to new business processes. Additionally, where existing policies do not conform to these business processes, policies must be revised or created. The initial review and assessment of policies take place during the build phase. Construction of any new policies occurs later in realization.

For any participants new to an SAP implementation project, the build portion of realization brings about a dramatic shift in focus. Operational business process discussions are now superseded by coding and configuration. Most of the build process is very technical in nature; it goes to the core of the SAP system. It concerns itself with translating design elements defined during blueprint into system functionality.

The building blocks put in place during this period lay the foundation for all testing and deployment activities which will occur later. For this reason, all project team members should understand the elements of realization build, even if only at a conceptual level.

15.1 Configuration and Custom Development

We've already indicated that configuration and custom object development can be considered interdependent activities. Each one greatly depends on the other for its operating mechanisms. Let's take a look at how each of these realization build activities takes place.

Figure 15.2 outlines the high-level steps in configuration and custom object development. Each has its respective build activity performed by the project team and each receives an individual test to assess performance. Once the team has verified each part as operating according to its specification, those elements designed to work together are confirmed through string testing. After the team has confirmed their operational performance, these elements are considered to be "built" and realization moves on to integration testing and other higher-level tests.

The following sections cover each of these build processes in some detail. We will examine the processes involved, rather than focusing on the setup steps for configuration or the coding steps for custom object development.

15 | Configuration and Custom Objects Build

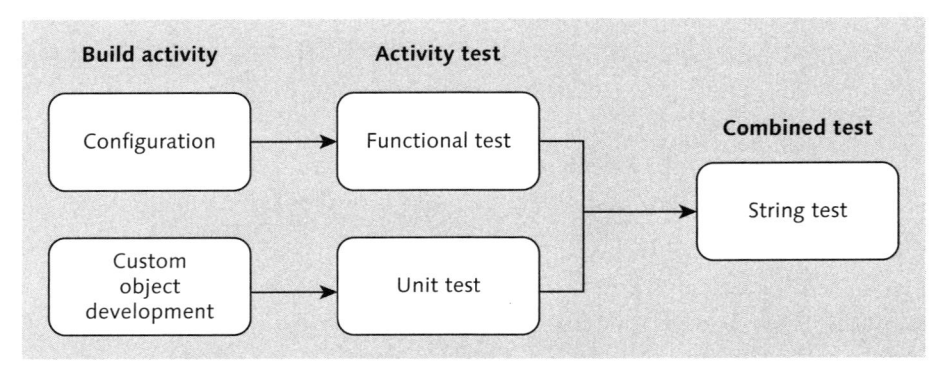

Figure 15.2 Build and Test Processes for Configuration and Custom Objects

15.1.1 Configuration

Configuration deliverables take the form of actual changes made to the system and documents describing those changes. Configuration takes the essential "blank slate" or vanilla SAP system and organizes it to perform the company-specific business processes defined in blueprinting. It is analogous to placing plumbing, electrical connections, heating, air conditioning, and lighting in a new house to make it livable for its occupants. With configuration, the complete system structure to support your business processes comes much closer to reality. Almost all of your company-requested functionality will be delivered through configuration.

The pyramid shown in Figure 15.3 outlines the three levels of configuration. Level one constructs the operating framework. Configuration elements such as company code or sales organizations are inputted at this level. They remain unchanged throughout the system lifecycle unless the company undergoes major changes in ownership or organization. Level one configuration provides the baseline for all subsequent configuration inputs.

Level two of the configuration pyramid enters the company master data. These data provide standard information used in most transactions. Thus, company master data relieves end users from entering standard, repeatable information such as customer address (customer master) or vendor payment terms (vendor master) for each transaction. These data are accessed by the system to populate transactions as they take place.

Configuration and Custom Development | **15.1**

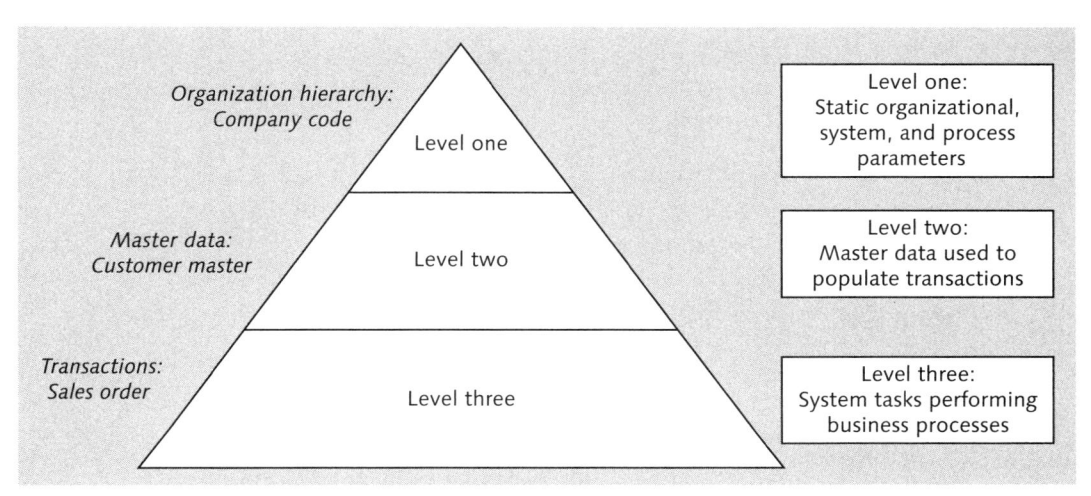

Figure 15.3 Configuration Levels Used in System Build

Lastly, level three places company business transactions in play. These online tasks implement company processes through the SAP system. From sales orders to purchase orders, transactions represent the system as end users will operate it.

Figure 15.4 shows the relationship between configuration activities and the end-user view of the system. As an end user completes a transaction, the SAP system runs programs and applies configuration tables in the background. All this activity remains invisible to the end user. The end user only sees that the requested transaction is complete and the associated document representing that transaction has posted.

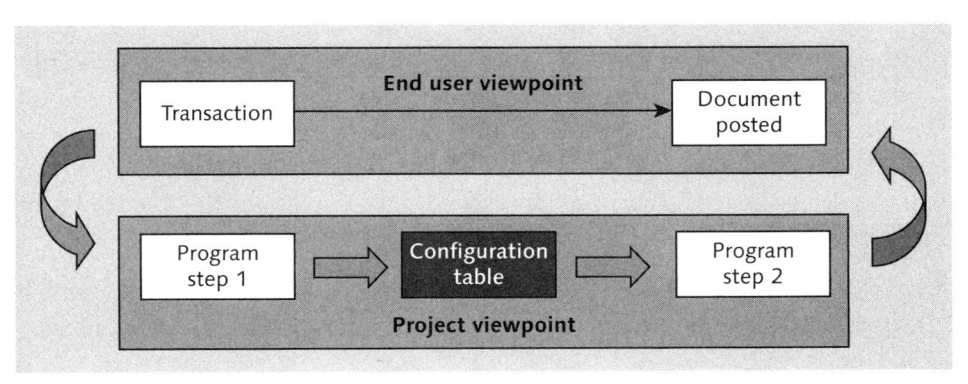

Figure 15.4 Configuration Results from an End-User Perspective

331

The workings of configuration are a background operation, and the activity of configuration itself will be in the background for a good portion of the project team. Your systems integrator project team performs almost all configuration actions. Integrator staff with business process knowledge—generally those assigned to functional workstreams—identify configuration requirements called out within process design documents. They then identify the configuration steps needed to post these to the system.

> **Trail Marker**
>
> Assign your IT team to review a sample of completed configurations. They can conduct this review alongside the integrator configuration analyst. Your reviewer can assess the quality of configuration build and learn more about system setup at the same time.

These integrator configuration analysts remain quite busy during the build part and are responsible for the following tasks:

- Handling day-to-day configuration activities within the project workstreams
- Documenting configuration decisions through requirements specification documents
- Initiating configuration transports once complete and approved
- Supporting functional testing of configuration

Let's use Figure 15.4 as a reference to make this process clearer. Let's assume, for instance, that the end user wishes to create a sales order and post it. As an SAP transaction code, this would translate to VA01 (create sales order). This transaction immediately reaches out to a table (TVKO) containing a list of sales organizations. An associated embedded program identifies and inputs needed sales order header data. It also associates the correct sales organization (master data) and utilizes the taxes and prices contained in other master data files. Finally, all collected information would be conveyed to the posted sales order. Thanks to proper configuration, all of this business process execution takes place behind the scenes for the end user.

The act of configuration takes place using table structures. These tables contain relevant data selections, such as company codes or product pricing structures.

Configuration analysts specify which tables are referenced and the detailed items to be used for a particular transaction, as shown in Figure 15.5.

SAP makes available a tool to support configuration. The SAP Implementation Guide (IMG) permits configuration to take place within the confines of the system. The IMG is accessed through the SAP Solution Manager tool. Here, the responsible analyst links company-specific configuration entries to selected SAP physical tables. When entry is complete, SAP Solution Manager posts the entries to the applicable SAP system via transport. In this way, a major portion of the blueprint design is built.

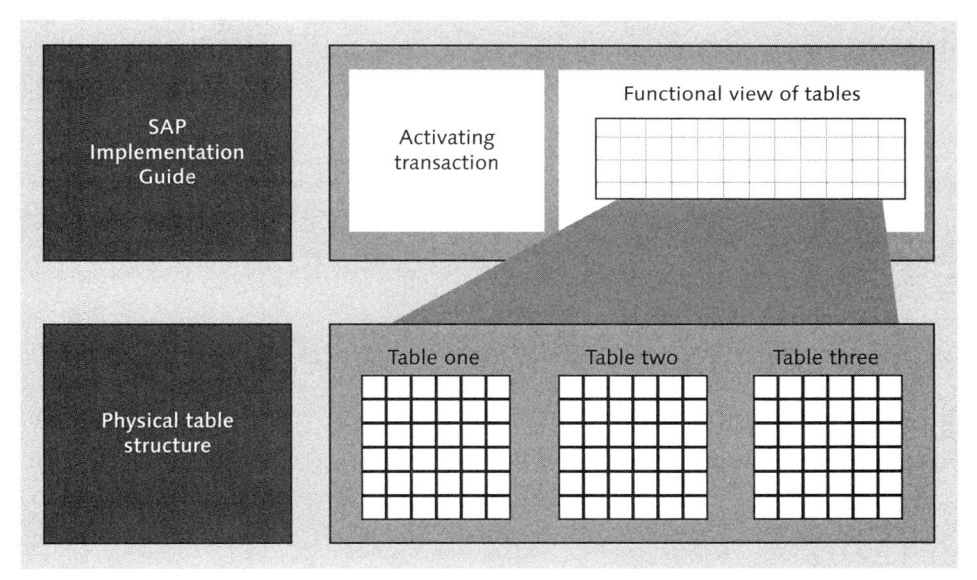

Figure 15.5 System Configuration Using the SAP Implementation Guide

SAP Solution Manager is also used to house configuration documentation. These configuration rationale specifications (CRS) record configuration steps performed by the project team as well as the rationales to support individual configuration decisions. Each configuration rationale specification links to the overall process definition document (PDD) that provides requirements for that business process element. Figure 15.6 shows this one-to-many, parent-child relationship.

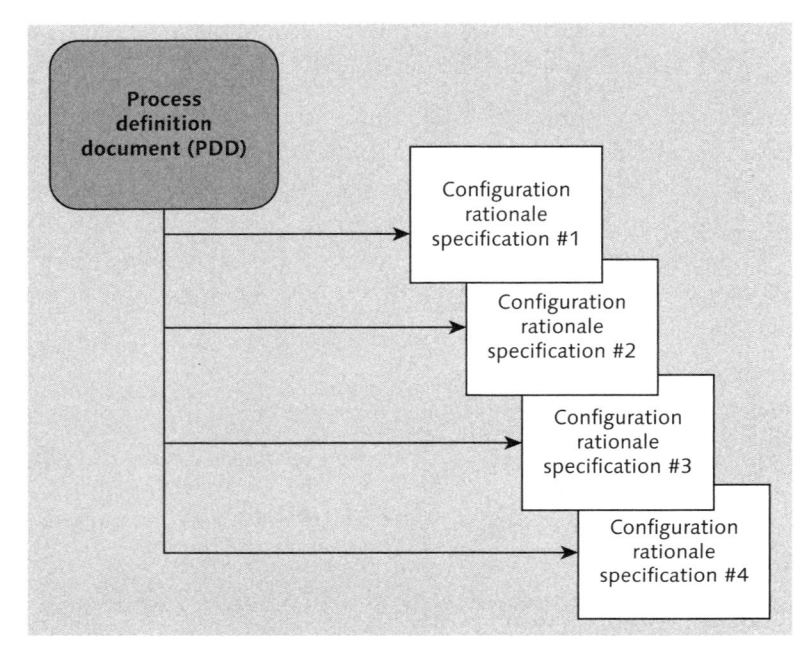

Figure 15.6 Relationship of the PDD and CRS

Your integrator project team will have constructed a CRS template in SAP Solution Manager. Configuration analysts use this template to enter requested information describing their actions. As reference points, the analyst identifies the workstream where the business process resides, any needed sub-process information, step traceability in the IMG menu, the SAP transaction code involved, and any related PDDs. The CRS template will contain a section identifying all configuration steps used.

When complete, the analyst will send CRS to company functional workstream leads for their review and approval. Due to its technical nature, this review is generally assigned to IT staff assigned to the workstream.

CRS documents prove invaluable for company sustainment operations once the system is implemented. By that time, the integrator project team and its configuration analysts will have rolled off the project and be unavailable to answer questions. The CRS documents serve as the primary record for sustainment staff to understand the reasoning and specific decisions underlying configuration actions. Configuration rationale specifications will guide subsequent system support activities.

> **Pitfall Alert**
>
> Pay very close attention to the quality of the CRS. In the rush of activity, the need for this quality check may get lost, and you'll be left with CRS documents that lack the necessary detail or are incomplete. More than one company has found itself trying to figure out how or why the system was configured. Remember, once the integrator team leaves, your company is on its own. Your sustainment team will be left to reconstruct the rationale for configuration decisions. Help them out now!

As CRS approvals are received, the configuration analyst prepares the configuration for transport. This process places the configuration in an operational SAP system where it can be accessed for project team and eventual end-user transactions. The analyst prepares documentation describing the transport item and forwards it to the infrastructure or Basis team where the transport will be carried out. At that point, the configuration will be available in the system.

Configuration work is most often delivered in cycles. This arrangement permits work to be subdivided and structured by need and complexity. Consider this standard cycle approach and its contents:

- **Cycle one**
    Organization hierarchy and major master data components, such as customer master, vendor, master, material master, product master, and charts of accounts
- **Cycle two**
    Remaining master data elements such as purchasing information records (PIR), storage locations, credit master, and sales pricing
- **Cycle three**
    Simple transactions (with limited system dependencies) such as fixed-assets transactions
- **Cycle four**
    Complex transactions (with significant system dependencies such as create sales order or create stock transport order)

As was the case during blueprinting and as has been discussed in the broader view of realization, configuration activities have assigned completion targets. The program management office (PMO) monitors and reports their status. Tracking can be arranged to fit these four cycles and includes completion of configuration actions, submission of configuration rationale specifications for review, approval of review, and accomplishment of transport. As the build process moves into testing phases, functional test results should be monitored and reported as well.

Functional testing verifies that configuration works as intended. By verifying that the configuration supporting a transaction is correct, it confirms that the SAP system configuration operates according to the process design. This will be the first of many test sequences that the project will perform. It prepares the team for those later tests, although these take place on a smaller and more manageable scale.

As with all subsequent tests, functional testing requires testers, data, and recording of results. In this case, testers will come from the group of project team members who did not build the individual configuration. Normally, these testers will come from the company project workstreams. This separation prevents a conflict of interest and ensures that the review of test results occurs separately from the configuration analysis. These analysts, however, are able to provide needed support for testing.

Functional test execution focuses on all possible entries for any key field in a single transaction. It uses a very limited set of test data, specifically prepared for functional testing. These data represent a small number of cases but are otherwise quite similar to actual company data. Simplified informal test scripts, which outline the testing to be performed, are used to guide the testing. As with configuration itself, functional testing is managed by individual workstreams. They schedule the work and manage resource assignments.

> **Trail Marker**
>
> We will refer to formal and informal testing. The distinction between the two refers primarily to recordkeeping requirements.
>
> For formal testing, such as the integration test and user acceptance test, the team maintains test scripts and test results for the life of the project and beyond. They remain available for auditor review in the case of any questions regarding the degree of system testing or its results.
>
> Informal testing indicates that the recordkeeping requirements are less stringent. Often informal test documentation is maintained by the project team but has a very limited lifespan.

Once all cycles of configuration and functional testing have finished, the project team will be ready to take its next steps.

15.1.2 Custom Object Development

While configuration has progressed on one track, custom object development will have proceeded along a parallel track. During the early stages of build, the application development group will increase its size from a small number of programmers to a far larger number—likely triple or quadruple the original group. These programmers, who are project integrator staff, build and test all custom objects (or WRICEFPs) identified and approved during blueprinting.

The development team constructs custom objects using SAP's propriety programming language. The SAP R/3 system itself is constructed from this language. Called by the acronym ABAP, which stands for Advanced Business Application Programming, it is also used to add custom functionality.

Ownership of custom object development flows between the application development group and business process workstreams. Managing these hand-offs will be essential to their on-time delivery. Figure 15.7 shows how each team owns and completes the process steps. Steps owned by the functional workstream are shown in ovals and those owned by the application development team are shown in rectangles. The sequence begins with the list of approved WRICEFPs and a description contained in their respective gap documents.

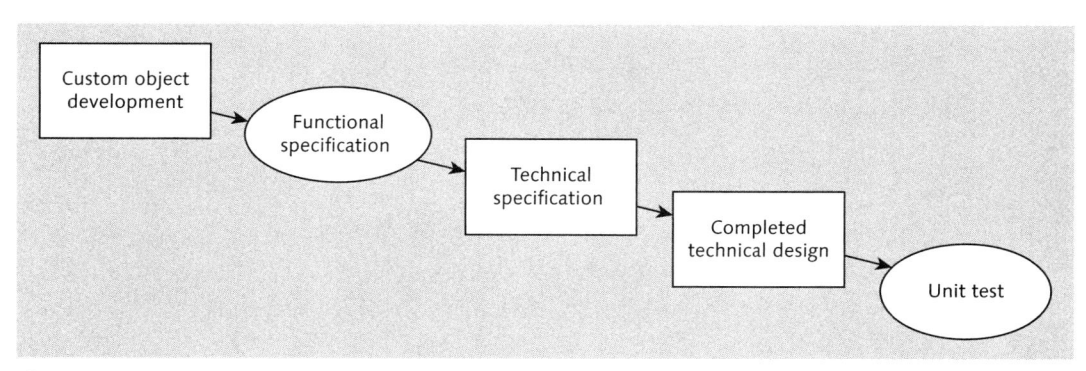

Figure 15.7 Custom Object Development Process

> **Trail Marker**
>
> Throughout the book we will use the term *on-time delivery*. It refers to the production of a project activity to schedule. A deliverable is either on-time or late (*late delivery*).

The applicable business process workstream prepares the functional specification. It explains how the custom object will be used, in as much detail as possible. This document provides guidance to the developer. It describes the business process where the WRICEFP will be used and identifies any process-specific requirements for the custom object. Additionally, it lists all design documentation containing a requirement or description of the object. Finally, it calls out any business controls or training impacts for the item.

Using this information, the application development team lead assigns the programmer best suited to complete the technical work for the custom object. This individual writes the technical specification and delivers the working custom object. The technical specification expands on the information provided in the functional specification. It documents both the SAP transactions involved and the internal SAP ABAP programs that execute the transaction. It also verifies the SAP menu path involved in the transaction.

The developer calls out any options or parameters that will be used in the custom object. The technical specification identifies any existing tables or structures that will be required, as well as any necessary modifications to existing tables or structures. Finally, the technical specification points out any new domains or data elements needed to operationalize the custom object.

The application development team lead and any system architect resources assigned to the project review the technical specification. Once the technical specification receives approval, the actual custom object construction can begin.

When the object is complete, developers then perform unit testing on the delivered WRICEFP design. The unit test assesses the operation of the individual custom object relative to its technical specification. Once the object passes the unit test, it is then delivered for additional testing.

While configuration tasks will generally hit their targets, custom development timing is more difficult to predict and requires careful management. Development tasks often progress by fits and starts. Sometimes days will pass without apparent progress. These delays can substantially impact the project schedule. Unless project management understands the process steps and hand-offs at the individual item level, deadlines could be missed.

> **Pitfall Alert**
>
> Your PMO and project sponsors should pay special attention to completion of custom development work. If the development team encounters difficulties and runs late, meet with the integrator lead immediately to identify the causes. Make sure that the integrator lead understands your concern and has an action plan to resolve the situation. Work the situation methodically, custom development object by custom development object. Make sure the integrator lead is accountable for improvement. Otherwise, schedule slips are just over the horizon.

String testing can't begin until the custom objects have passed the unit test hurdle. This situation can further jeopardize the beginning of the integration test. If custom objects have trouble passing the unit test, that will hold up the string test. As a result, the entire project test schedule—and eventually the go-live date—soon become a moving target. As we discussed earlier, any slips in your project will have both financial and business process consequences for the company. All top-level milestones in realization carry substantial downstream impacts to the remainder of the project schedule.

Figure 15.8 illustrates a sample tracking mechanism used for custom development. It shows our five functional workstreams and the number of WRICEFPs assigned to each. The entire project has 200 custom objects assigned to it; 47 are currently in functional specification, 88 are in technical specification, and 75 are in unit testing. The figure shows progress in a waterfall style. Once an object passes through a stage of development, it is no longer counted under that step. Thus, the 47 objects in functional specification are accounted to one of three statuses: assigned, completed, and approved. When all functional specification work is complete, the total and subtotals revert to zero.

The figure also indicates the number of custom objects assigned to each workstream. Note that OTC has twice the number of WRICEFPs as any other workstream and four times as many as two of its fellow workstreams. The volume and complexity of these objects makes OTC a prime candidate for close monitoring. Your project will likely encounter the same workload distribution, where OTC will own the bulk of the workload.

Workstream	OTC	HCM	PTS	PTP	RTR	Total
Functional Specification	25	5	10	0	7	47
Assigned	10	0	4	0	3	17
Complete	5	0	4	0	3	12
Approved	10	5	2	0	1	18
Technical Specification	35	6	4	25	18	88
Assigned	25	0	0	3	0	28
Complete	5	0	0	12	9	26
Approved	5	6	4	10	9	34
Unit Test	30	9	6	15	15	75
In Progress	20	3	3	6	5	37
Passed	10	6	3	9	10	38
Total	80	20	20	40	40	200

Figure 15.8 Custom Object Tracking Mechanism

Notice that over half of the objects with in-progress functional specification work belong to OTC. Significantly, only 10 of its WRICEFPs have passed unit test or completed the custom development process. On the other hand, PTP has a total of 40 objects to develop. All of them have a completed functional specification and 10 have passed the unit test.

Each functional team lead should have a full handle on the objects assigned for delivery. However, development process sequencing assigns a great deal of responsibility to the application development lead. That person assigns tasks to developers and manages work progress. Functional team leads and the development lead must work closely together to assess areas of difficulty and plan how to resolve them.

Depending on where the project stands relative to its schedule, the data presented in Figure 15.8 may only indicate a concern, and not yet an emergency. If the application development deadline is fast approaching, though, this completion picture would be cause for alarm. Appending an expected completion number to each of the table cells could provide a baseline for comparison.

15.1.3 String Testing

When configuration has passed its functional test and custom objects have passed their unit test, then string testing is ready to begin. During this segment, all custom objects will be tested in conjunction with the configuration that supports them. As with functional test, the team prepares special company-relevant test data and transports it to the development system. String testing will be the first time that configuration and custom objects coexist in the same environment. The testing assures that both elements perform as required and are ready for integration test.

Either the test management team or individual workstreams can administer string testing. Having the test management group oversee script generation and test completion gives it a good practice opportunity prior to the integration test. In either case, however, the PMO must take care to ensure that all required deliverables are in place and meet quality requirements.

Project management prepares reports showing test progress and defect resolution status. It tracks completions on a daily basis and identifies any potential trouble spots. Once all string testing scripts have passed, the project will move on to the greater complexities of the integration test. These later stages of testing will be covered fully in Chapter 16.

15.2 Security Design

SAP security ensures that only authorized users are able to have system access and complete transactions on the system. For that reason, correct security setup is essential to maintaining system integrity.

15 | Configuration and Custom Objects Build

> **Trail Marker**
>
> This section will describe the structure of SAP security. Chapter 17 will address project-related security deliverables in greater detail.

Similar to other large-scale systems, SAP uses role-based security to assure transaction integrity. It is a very conservative approach. Users receive access only for that set of transactions necessary to perform their specifically assigned tasks. However, unlike other systems, the number of users and the breadth of transactions make security a major component of your SAP implementation project.

Let's walk through this process, which is illustrated in Figure 15.9.

1. Step one initiates first-level SAP access security. The end user attempts to log on to the system using the assigned SAP UserID and password. The user will be able to access the system only if the SAP UserID and password match.

2. Step two executes a selected transaction. The end user attempts to perform an SAP transaction such as Transaction ME21N (create purchase order).

3. Step three calls the SAP program responsible for that transaction code. ABAP programs built in the system will execute the transaction code providing the user his authorization.

4. Step four calls security routines by providing the required authorizations to execute that transaction code. These security routines are called each time an end user requests to run a transaction.

5. Step five matches the required authorizations to those contained in the user profile. Each user profile will contain a list of all transaction codes available to that end user. If the transaction contains a number of elements, SAP will verify access for each element.

6. Step six grants or denies access based on the comparison to the user profile. If the end user was denied access and needs it to perform that transaction, the profile can be modified to include it. Only then would access be granted.

User profiles discussed in this scenario utilize job roles as their organizing principle. Roles performed in your company business processes specify the transactions that each end user can access. SAP security design proceeds by grouping authorized transaction codes in accordance with role requirements.

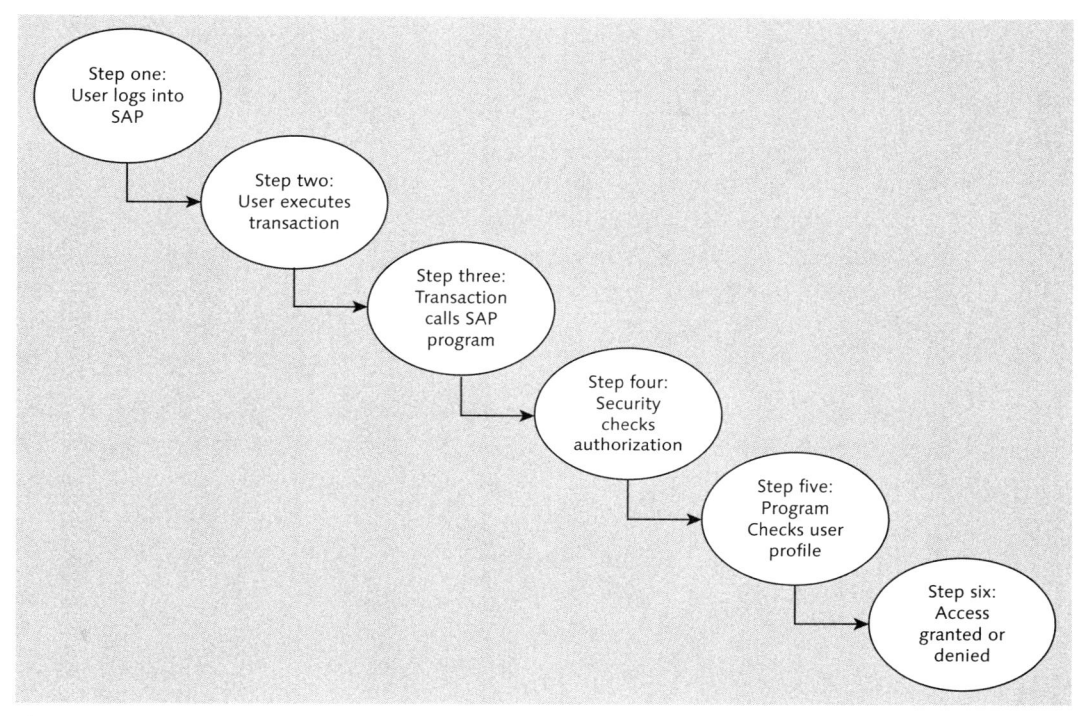

Figure 15.9 SAP Security Access Process

> **Tip**
>
> Security build is an integrator responsibility. Often it will hover in the background without the necessary attention. Schedule a design review with the security lead and the integrator project manager during this build process. Make sure that you understand the security design and agree with the approach. At go-live, a complex security design can create a host of problems.

15.2.1 SAP Roles

In terms of the SAP system, a job role is a group of related transaction codes that allow end users to perform their duties. The SAP transaction codes making up a job are determined by the actions needed to complete a specific task.

For example, accounts payable administrator is a common function in almost all companies. However, each company likely assigns some different duties to that function. If your company assigns common duties to all accounts payable administrators, a single job role would be created within SAP. This would enable all accounts payable administrator to have access to the accounts payable transactions needed to perform their jobs.

However, the real world is usually not so simple. It is far more common to see job functions and transaction access differ by region, organization level, or even by individual—often, people who perform essentially the same operation but have some minor differences. These permutations exist in every organization and make it imperative that the security team understand which work is assigned to each role. Only in that way will SAP security function as your company requires.

In the example in Figure 15.10, there are two accounts payable administrators: User A and User B. One of the users, User A, requires access to a transaction not needed by User B (Transaction FB04, document changes). If User B were given access to the unneeded transaction code, potential compliance problems could result. Additionally, it might well set a pattern of enabling unneeded access across the entire company.

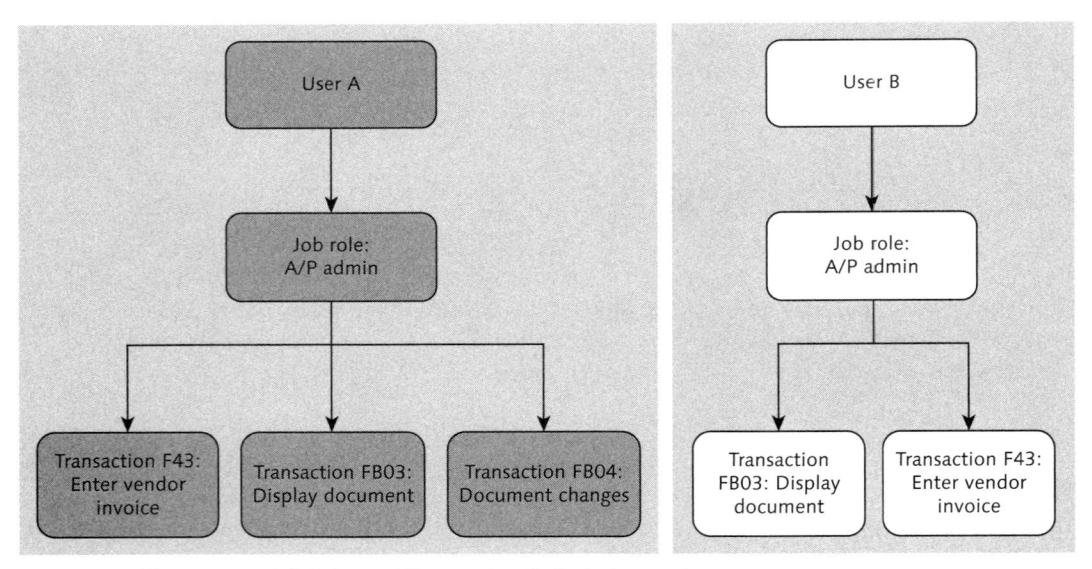

Figure 15.10 Job Roles and Transaction Code Assignments

On the other hand, setting up separate roles for each user may move one step closer to having unique roles for each end user. This would create significant difficulties in managing user access and for limiting users to required transactions only. This dilemma lies at the heart of building an effective SAP security design.

For that reason, the first step in addressing security design is to create usable employee job roles in the SAP system. Companies that have developed and put in place well-defined job roles for their employees will find that they have done much of the preliminary work. In comparison, organizations operating without this job role structure will be faced with the need to create it or construct an acceptable substitute.

An effective role structure aligns as closely as possible with specific business processes. This alignment enables the SAP system to operate in concert with normal business activities. Figure 15.11 shows how company business processes, SAP transaction codes, and roles work together. In this example, the business process includes production planning and scheduling in the supply chain function. The business process further divides into business sub-processes, one of which is to analyze the supply network. Your project team would identify transaction codes associated with this sub-process. Finally, the project team would specify a set of base SAP roles involved in performing the network analyst function. Naming and grouping of these roles would follow from roles already in place or roles constructed especially for SAP system use.

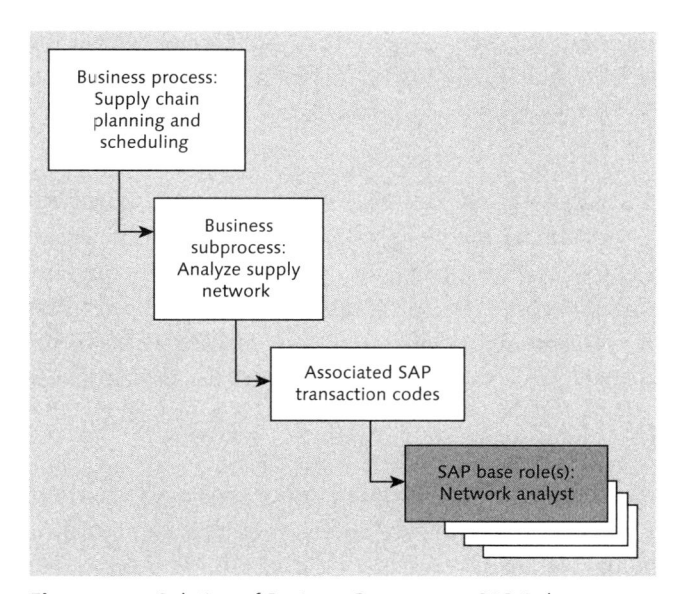

Figure 15.11 Relation of Business Processes to SAP Roles

Base SAP roles form the building block of security design. They group like sets of tasks—ones that that end users are most likely to perform in executing the activities of a network analyst.

15.2.2 Data Level Security

In addition to controlling system access through role-based security, SAP uses another access restriction as well. Data level security puts limits on which data a user can access. These limits prevent end users from accessing unauthorized information from other departments or business units in the company.

Let's reference the accounts payable example, in which both accounts payable administrators could access all payables transactions from across the company. This situation also permits administrators to view information not required by their particular role assignment. Data level security limits access based on the types of data a user can view. Thus, if User A were assigned to support North American operations and User B were assigned to support European operations, each could be limited to their rightful role by restricting their activities to their geographical company code.

The organizational hierarchy that your project team constructed in blueprint contains a number of entries that can be applied as data level elements. Each one can limit user access by restricting transaction to tagged numerical values within the organization hierarchy. The following entries are often used for data level security, but several other hierarchy tags can be used as well:

- **Company code**
  This is the legal entity for which a financial statement and an income statement are produced. It will be the central recipient of financial transactions completed under its auspices. Generally, a company will use several company codes that roll up to the overall company entity. Each one can be used to set data level permissions. In this case, those operating in the framework of one company code would normally not have access to data from other company codes.

- **Plant code**
  A location either where the company produces and stores materials or where goods and services are provided. The plant subdivides an enterprise according to product, procurement, maintenance, and material planning aspects. For

example, if a company has five plants identified in its organization hierarchy, each can be used to provide data level security. Those assigned to one plant would not normally have access to the data from another plant.

- **Purchasing organization**
  An organizational unit that procures materials and services. It also negotiates conditions of purchase with vendors. A purchasing organization can be aligned with a company or plant for restriction of data access. Again, buyers within one purchasing organization would receive access only to their home purchasing organization and no others.

- **Sales organization**
  An organization responsible for the sale of products and services. It will be the legal selling unit and responsible for product liability and customer claims. Sales organizations can be aligned with company codes for the purpose of access limitation.

Data level security is most often constructed using derived roles. These roles essentially associate base SAP roles with organizational hierarchy elements such as company code, plant, or cost center. Derived roles limit base role transaction access only to the organizational hierarchy entity.

15.2.3 Company Policy Assessment

For companies that operate under substantial regulatory requirements, an SAP implementation means writing or updating their policies and procedures. If your company is one of these, you can expect to spend considerable time writing or revising your policies. Especially prevalent in life sciences, banking, and utilities industries, these policies and procedures are intended to guide the actions of company employees in performing their work. They also demonstrate to regulators that the company has adopted business processes consistent with regulatory requirements.

For companies with large numbers of policies and procedures in place, revising content to reflect SAP system operations represents a substantial undertaking. In life sciences companies, an entire validation organization will be in place to review the documents and monitor compliance with their provisions.

Functional business organizations own their policies and procedures and are responsible for drafting them. The heaviest workload will fall in the company's IT and supply chain organizations, with sales operations following closely behind. Finance will also have some workload here relative to Sarbanes-Oxley requirements.

Policies and procedures come in two levels. The first level, standing operating procedure (SOP), documents the overall process. It outlines how a company policy will be implemented. The SOP provides high-level information about how the process will be performed, who will complete the tasks involved, where it will be performed, and what materials or tools will be required.

The SOP standardizes the way a process is performed. If it is well-constructed, employees can complete many tasks simply by following the guidance in the SOP. In many cases, no further instruction is required.

System-related SOPs will include high-level business scenario information and process flows containing key steps in the operational sequence. They clearly identify the steps to perform an activity but often will not explain how to execute them.

The second level, work instructions, applies in cases where users require additional information to perform their tasks. This requirement usually kicks in for more complex tasks. In these cases, work instructions are provided to staff in addition to SOPs. A work instruction provides the detailed, step-by-step guidance needed complete the task. In the case of tasks using SAP transactions, work instructions will likely include screen shots and system guidance on how to complete the activity as the transaction progresses through its steps. It is this system-to-process connection that creates the need for SOP or work instruction rewrites during your implementation.

Thus, a company having hundreds of system-related SOPs and work instructions will find itself with a substantial workload to complete within the project duration. Much of this workload will fall on those who understand process details and the SAP system operations used to achieve it. Normally, this means using the labor of the already well-burdened project team.

If the workload burden appears beyond the capacity of the project team, some assistance may be available. Many technical writing companies furnish resources to help. They place small teams on company sites to perform the document construction and to administer the review processes. These resources will be skilled technical writers familiar with the documentation process in general. However, they will not be familiar with the specifics of your company's processes. They will still require some level of company process experts to guide their efforts.

Additionally, if the company has regional plants and country sites, it will likely have global documents and regional documents. Each group must be managed and revised. The project team must also ensure that regional documents remain consistent with global documents. Any deviation here would invite regulatory scrutiny.

Figure 15.12 outlines the workflow for this documentation mini-project. If the number of affected documents is large, project management should appoint a single individual to direct all document construction and revision activity.

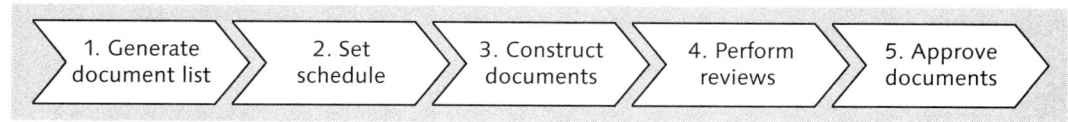

1. Generate document list → 2. Set schedule → 3. Construct documents → 4. Perform reviews → 5. Approve documents

Figure 15.12 Workflow for SOPs and Work Instructions

Let's walk through these steps.

1. **Generate lists of all potentially affected documents.**
   These lists will be assessed to identify which documents are unaffected and can remain in place as-is. They will also be reviewed to establish which documents require revision, which ones can be obsoleted, and where new documents are needed. The team can create relation diagrams of PDDs and existing documents to determine where any needed documentation is required.
2. **Use the number and types of documents identified in the previous step to build a work schedule.**
   Not only should a documentation preparation schedule synchronize with the overall project schedule, but it should reflect the number of resources assigned to the work. If these numbers are insufficient, the PMO should immediately address the situation with project sponsors. At this point as well, the assessment of regional and site documents can begin.
3. **Initiate the document construction process.**
   Generally, this step consumes the bulk of the schedule. During this stage, the team would write all new documents and revise existing documents as needed. If the project contains several implementation waves, the global documents as well as any regional documents for the first implementation will be written

during that wave. The team would write regional documents for later waves at the time of each implementation.

4. **Conduct reviews of documents written during step three.**
Draft copies of SOPs and work instructions are used as references in integration and user acceptance testing. Not only do the documents assist in guiding testing activities, but the documents themselves can be assessed during the testing process. Testers verify that the documents conform to system operations. For this reason, all required documents must be ready for the applicable round of the integration test.

5. **Get final approval for the completed documents.**
At this point, designated reviewers affix their signatures as an indicator of approval. Documents are then posted to whatever repository the company may use.

Completion of these steps involves a number of roles, so let's take a look at the most important of these. As the proposed document moves through steps three through five — prepare, review, and approve — these roles will provide the major effort:

- **Process lead**
  The functional process lead is responsible for all global, regional, and site documents in the workstream. This individual ensures that documents have been inventoried and resources assigned to construct them.

- **Document owner**
  Document owners are the individuals who are most affected by and knowledgeable about required document content. They perform final review and approval of the completed document.

- **Author**
  Authors create or revise documents using subject matter experts and existing procedures. They prepare the content using company formats and standard templates, manage document reviews, and collect feedback for document revisions.

- **Reviewer**
  Reviewers provide expert guidance concerning the document in progress. They verify that the content is correct and suggest needed revisions, and they review each iteration as requested. When the document is complete, they give their authorization.

▶ **Approver**
Approvers are individuals designated by the company to provide final document authorization. Usually this will consist of the process lead, the document owner, and representatives from the company's quality assurance organization.

These policy documents will undergo an iterative construction and review cycle. To assure that documents are ready on time, project management will schedule required completion dates for each review cycle. This will alert authors and reviewers to the necessary deadlines. Each review cycle brings the documents closer to achieving finished product status.

Figure 15.13 illustrates this preparation, review, and approval process.

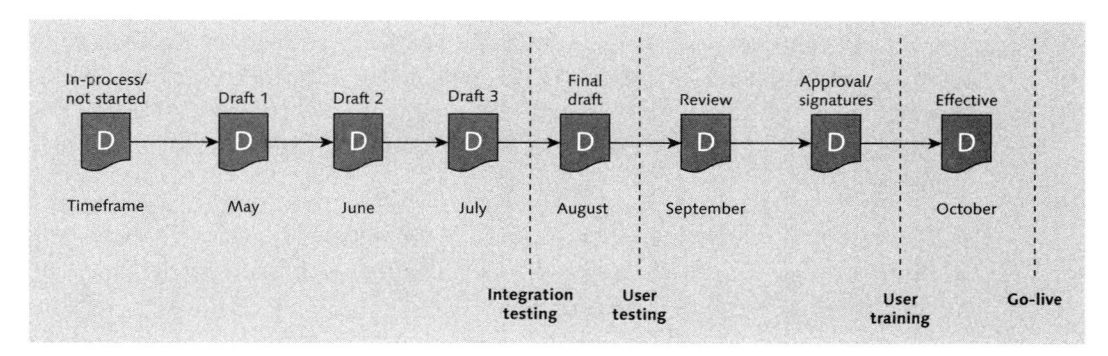

Figure 15.13 Document Preparation, Review, and Approval Process

> 🧭 **Trail Marker**
>
> Your company's controlled documents organization (if you have one) must place these project SOPs on a fast track. This should include the assignment of dedicated resources to handle the review and any format conversions. Otherwise, the volume of documents the team delivers can prove overwhelming to processes designed to handle one or two documents a week.

Documents that have completed the third draft cycle will be used to support integration testing. Testers will use them as process points of reference. Questions about process methodology will be referred to these draft documents, so the answers should be found there. Additionally, after completion of the integration test, testers can provide feedback to the documentation team. The documentation team can then incorporate this feedback into later revisions.

Testers will use final drafts of the SOPs and work instructions in much the same way during user acceptance testing. These testers will provide a different and more demanding audience. Integration testers, coming directly from the project team, will have greater familiarity with system design and transaction steps. User acceptance testers come directly from the business. They may have had some limited connection to the earlier stages of the project, but will lack overall system familiarity. As a result, they will depend far more heavily on the SOPs and work instructions to guide them in business process execution. Difficulties with document content, especially in lack of detail, will become more pronounced during user acceptance testing operations.

During cutover—prior to go-live—the approved SOPs and work instructions are used to supplement end-user training. For regulated companies, end users must furnish evidence that they "read and understand" document content. From this point forward, end users will be responsible for accomplishing business processes within the framework of these documents.

As the system is released to users at go-live, these documents are released as well. New or revised business processes will have the documentation support that end users need to perform their tasks.

Although much of this documentation preparation process is handled manually, some tools are available to assist. These come in two types: some to maintain document integrity during the review and approval sequences, and others to securely house documents once they are approved and declared effective for use.

Several PDF applications allow for data entry and editing. These applications enable secure processing of changes, additions, or deletions. Once saved and versioned by a user, any subsequent alterations require the creation of a later document version. This feature means that authors and reviewers can pass versions back and forth with confidence during the review process. The author maintains control of the master version while managing edits from several possible reviewers.

Other tools assisting the documentation process are repositories that use Web-based functionality for company control. These document management solutions allow any authorized user to gain access to the most recent or effective version of SOPs or work instructions.

Generally, these tools come with some overhead. Staff resources are required to administer document intake and control. Formats and content must be verified. All approvals must be confirmed prior to posting for general access. However, adoption of a repository can prove especially helpful for companies in regulated industries. The back-end control of content ensures that only documents that meet specific release criteria are posted. This, in turn, ensures that the content meets regulatory guidelines

Now that the system is built, we have to turn to the second part of realization — we have to test everything to make sure that it all works as planned. We'll go there now.

With build complete, many discrete elements of the system have now been verified to work independently. The project now moves into the systems test phase, in which we see how well the system works as an integrated entity.

16 Systems Testing

During the test phase of realization, your project team assesses the adequacy of the build in a more direct way. It evaluates how well the recently constructed system components work together to execute company business processes. These must operate correctly and produce accurate results. A well-planned testing program assures these outcomes.

Not all projects pay the necessary attention to systems testing. Many unsuccessful projects shorten test cycles to accommodate an aggressive schedule. Or, overwhelmed with the magnitude of defects, projects push forward with insufficient testing. This is a dangerous course of action. Inadequate testing ultimately ensures that the system will not work as planned. More testing—instead of less—is the prudent course. Delivering an error-prone system is not a positive experience.

Earlier discussion of the Affordable Care Act's website implementation shows the dramatic impact of shortened or incomplete testing. Remember that testing was deferred too late in the project lifecycle, and that the system had so many defects that it proved extremely difficult to identify the root causes of major problems. Issues must be identified and corrected prior to go-live and the beginning of full user involvement. At that late point, when users transact on the go-live system, it's far more difficult to resolve errors. Extreme pressure from unhappy user communities simply adds to the workload of an already stressed project team.

Testing serves as the essential quality check on build activities; it becomes the company's ally in protecting itself against the effects of a poorly built system. If your build was completed incorrectly, the testing phase will expose those errors. Even in testing, however, a large number of errors will exert a major impact on

16 | Systems Testing

your project schedule; all defects must be identified and resolved before advancing past the test phase gate. A high error level adds to team workloads and makes meeting the schedule even more problematic.

> **Trail Marker**
>
> Do note that it's quite normal to find some degree of error in system build. As was discussed in Chapter 16, most of this build work will have been performed by the systems integrator. Encountering a large number of errors indicates that a portion of the system build or specification was executed incorrectly. This could be due to integrator process problems, misunderstanding the assignment, poor documentation, or skills deficiency. In any case, your PMO should find root causes for the errors and ensure that all of those defects are corrected. Root cause analysis represents a time-consuming activity that project management will not have factored into the schedule.

In the optimal case, build was done correctly. In that scenario, the number of defects will be manageable and the project will meet its timelines.

16.1 Structure of Systems Testing

Figure 16.1 shows systems testing divided into two parts: integration testing and user acceptance testing. Each has its own agenda and purpose. In a moderately sized project, each test type will take two to three months to complete.

The integration test verifies that the system works as a single entity. Testing validates that end-to-end business required functionality is in place. This includes verification of all logic paths, data boundaries, and custom object performance. Integration testing is most often performed by integrator staff with the assistance of the core project team. The integration test must complete before user acceptance testing can begin.

User acceptance testing validates that the system performs as intended in its actual business environment. The testing ensures that each element of the system meets requirements specification targets. As its name implies, user acceptance testing is executed by business users who will operate the system once it's implemented. All testing and defect resolution must be completed before final system build and production data load activities can go forward.

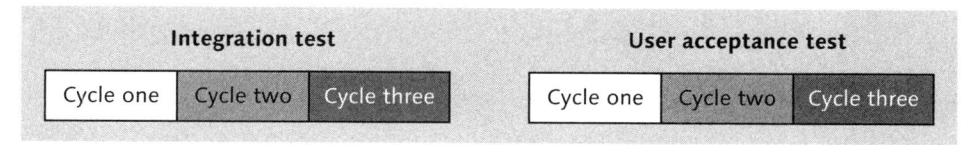

Figure 16.1 Systems Testing Structure

Integration test and user acceptance test are quite similar; in fact, they often execute the same test scenarios in each. The logistics of the user acceptance test, however, bring far more challenges. Users must receive their required training on the new system prior to conducting tests. All this must be scheduled or arrangements made for project team members to train testers personally.

Additionally, your team must take special care to ensure that testers are well utilized. Testing sometimes comes to a halt due to defects and the time it takes to resolve them—which is always unpredictable. Test management must ensure that testers are released to do their normal work tasks when these problems do occur; if they're forced to wait, they'll become impatient. Test management must also ensure that they'll be called back immediately when testing is able to proceed.

Each testing part—that is, integration testing or user acceptance testing—divides into cycles. These are partitions that enable some testing to proceed and restrict other testing from taking place. In our example, each part contains three cycles. Cycle one, for example, tests only the configured system. Custom objects are added in cycles two and three. Cycle two would add certain custom objects to the test process such as workflows, enhancements, interfaces, and forms. Finally, cycle three would add and then test any remaining custom objects such as reports, portals, and data conversions.

> **Tip**
> Adopting the test cycle approach ensures that the configured system operates as planned prior to adding the newly developed custom objects. Once the configured system is verified, the team will know that any defects in cycles two and three have most likely been caused by the added custom objects.

Usually, earlier cycles are complete before you move to the next cycle in the sequence. In cases where a later sequence's test activities don't require completion of earlier items, there may be some cycle overlap. These circumstances, however, must be carefully examined ahead of time. The team must ensure that no possible interference exists. The test management team will carefully manage test scope.

Individual testing items are arranged according to scenarios. These scenarios are defined based on the business requirements outlined in the process definition documents (PDDs) from blueprinting. Scenarios subdivide the process into discrete sections. They form the molecules for testing and may involve some of the following activities:

- Creating a customer master record
- Completing an inventory transaction
- Setting a customer credit limit
- Adding a new vendor to the vendor master

Test scripts form the operational items within a scenario. Where scenarios are the molecules, scripts are the atoms. Knowledgeable members of the functional workstream prepare the scripts and ensure that their scripts translate business process requirements into SAP executable transaction code steps. In this way, workstreams can assess whether system configuration and any custom objects operate according to the business process.

Often, several test scripts will demonstrate a *business scenario*. The scripts divide into granular process steps. Each step completed executes a script. When the body of scripts is performed without defects, the scenario is deemed to operate effectively within the system, and the scenario passes.

Each script stipulates an expected result for the test. This expected result establishes the basis for concluding whether the test has been passed, so it is very discrete in nature. Expected results specify what exactly should take place when the test is executed. For example, the script would specify actions such as "Execute the material transfer report with Transaction PF41 using material X12." The expected result should detail the exact values required to pass the test. If these values are not obtained, the test would then be failed and a defect recorded.

At a more general level, discrete scenarios can be combined to form an *end-to-end scenario*. This would represent an overall business process within a process team. However, end-to-end scenarios may also include processes that involve legacy or third-party systems, as well. The number of scenarios combined to produce an end-to-end scenario is limited by the scope of the business process involved.

Generally, the end-to-end scenario will comprise more than one PDD. For example, end-to-end scenarios from order-to-cash might include the following:

- Receiving an electronic data interchange (EDI) sales order
- Invoicing the customer
- Receiving a customer payment
- Applying the payment to the invoices

The broadest level of scenario structure is the *mega-scenario*. These involve major company business processes and will generally cross workstreams—in fact, they sometimes involve all workstreams. Mega-scenarios provide the ultimate check of the business process as implemented in the SAP system. Examples of mega-scenarios would include the following:

- Planning of production orders
- Purchasing of material requirements for production
- Receiving goods
- Receiving vendor invoices
- Executing a production order
- Creating a sales order

Mega-scenarios noticeably increase the level of complexity for test planning and execution. First of all, they involve multiple workstreams. In the case of end-to-end scenarios, each workstream operates independently. With mega-scenarios, major degrees of cross-workstream coordination are required. This means that test management and workstream test coordinators must carefully monitor progress to assure that workstreams perform their testing activities in the correct sequencing. Second, mega-scenario execution requires overall planning to assure smooth execution. Because the testing will flow from workstream to workstream, test management must oversee the transitions.

Figure 16.2 shows the testing scenario hierarchy. As the project moves from business scenarios to mega-scenarios, the testing process becomes more complex.

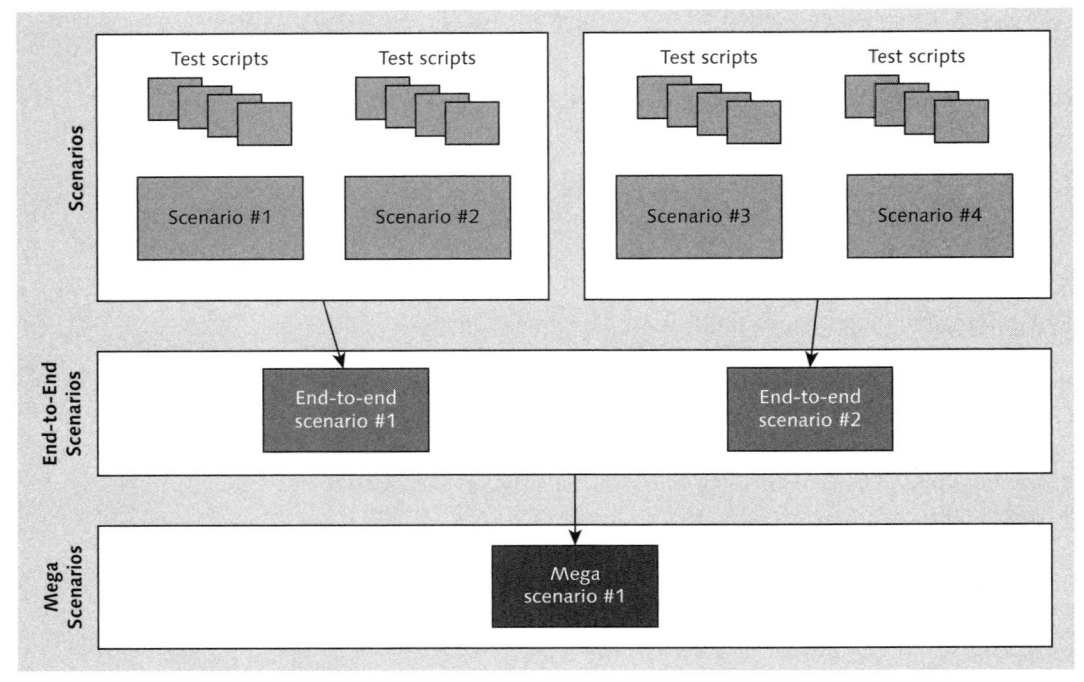

Figure 16.2 Testing Scenario Hierarchy

The project test management team remains closely connected with workstreams during the planning and execution portions of testing. This valuable team includes knowledgeable members who have participated in a number of previous system tests. They will know the pitfalls and how to plan for them. Additionally, they are experts in the testing process and can provide directions to workstreams regarding the following:

- Constructing test documentation
- Training testers and assigning a location for testing activities
- Applying any system tools used in testing
- Producing reports on test progress
- Recording and processing of defects

Each functional workstream designs its testing approach. Using guidelines furnished by the testing team, functional workstreams will identify requirements that need to be tested. Team members then convert these requirements into executable test scripts.

16.2 Systems Testing Processes

We can divide the system testing process into three separate elements, as shown in Figure 16.3. Each one ensures that testing moves from identifying the items to be tested and working through until all defects are closed. These elements will be discussed in the following sections.

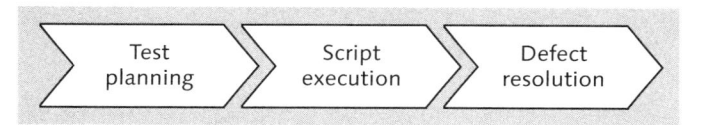

Figure 16.3 Testing Process Steps

16.2.1 Test Planning

Several steps are necessary to ensure balanced and thorough test planning. Many of these involve scope setting and scenario planning. Other portions of test planning focus on building the proper foundation.

1. **Define testing scope.**
   Identify all systems functionality that must be tested. Identify goals and strategies for the testing process. Construct test objectives for each workstream based on these goals. Assign test scope for all cycles using this foundation.
2. **Create scenario listings and sequencing.**
   Establish high-level scenarios for each workstream and the ordering of those scenarios.
3. **Evaluate requirements coverage.**
   Assure that all systems requirements have been identified. Verify that these requirements fit within one or more of the test scenarios.
4. **Build test scripts.**
   Using the test scenarios, establish the testing steps that will be needed for each. Generate test scripts for each of the steps.

5. **Assess requirements linkage.**
   Confirm that all requirements link to one or more test script. Establish that scripts, as written, will provide clear indication that the system would meet the requirement.

Your test management team will assign special roles to be used during testing, as shown in Table 16.1. These roles will call out designated activities required during systems test. These roles are formally assigned and range from script author to defect resolver. Holders of these roles will be trained to perform them. Only they are authorized to perform the activities described in the table.

Role	Description
Test script author	Constructs tests for a workstream based on its scenarios and testing strategy.
Test approver	Approves test scripts submitted by the test script author and approves adequacy of defect resolutions for those scripts.
Tester	Executes the tests using scripts developed by the workstream and under guidance from the test management team.
Post-execution reviewer	Verifies that test execution and documentation were completed correctly after passage.
Workstream test coordinator and defect manager	Assures that workstream scripts are assigned to testers and monitors test completion. Handles defects assigned to a workstream. Assigns defects to resolvers and tracks resolution progress.
Defect resolver	Identifies causes for test defects and makes fixes to correct the errors.

Table 16.1 Systems Testing Roles

Once test planning has completed, we can move to the actual test execution activities.

16.2.2 Script Execution

Once test scripts have been approved, they are now ready for execution. Management of script execution involves reviewing the setup steps and then ensuring that testers are prepared to perform their assigned scripts.

> **Tip**
>
> Tester training is mandatory. It should include information about the test schedule, including the cycle structure. All testers should receive hands-on instruction regarding test script execution, defect identification, and retest requirements in the event of defects.

- **Create test sets and schedules.**
  Using the testing goals as a guide, scripts are combined into test sets. These sets are then assigned to testers for the conduct of testing. Each workstream, as well as the test management team, constructs schedules for the completion of these sets.
- **Execute tests.**
  Testers are assigned test sets according to the schedule. They then execute the tests and either pass or reject the test result.
- **Assess test outcomes.**
  Completed tests are forwarded for post-execution review. Here, the reviewer assesses documentation provided by the tester according to project test procedures. The reviewer also assesses the results for accuracy. Tests that do not fulfill the review requirements are returned to the tester for retest.

Once the testers have completed the required scripts, the PMO will begin to collect and distribute progress reports.

16.2.3 Test Metrics

Project progress depends on timely and accurate test metrics reporting. At this point, they become the project manager's best friend. From project management to workstream leads, everyone involved in the testing process must know where they stand at all times. Test metrics supply the answer to this question. They reveal exactly where the project stands.

Figure 16.4 shows a sample report that tells exactly where the project stands. First of all, the report displays test status by workstream. Each workstream has all its assigned scripts tabulated in the columns. It also shows test performance by type. The scripts divide into four groupings: process scripts (tests of business processes), EDI customer, EDI third-party logistics providers, and EDI banks.

Notably, only the order-to-cash team has test scripts underway in all four test groupings.

Integration Testing: Process Scripts	OTC	PTS	PTP	HCM	RTR	TOTAL
Total # of test scripts	384	30	232	27	526	1199
# of test scripts executed	372	26	230	27	518	1173
# of test scripts complete	371	26	230	27	518	1172
% executed	96.9%	86.7%	99.1%	100.0%	98.5%	97.8 %
% complete	96.6%	86.7%	99.1%	100.0%	98.5%	97.7 %
EDI Testing: Customers						
# of test scripts	16					16
# of test scripts executed	15					15
# of test scripts complete	15					15
EDI Testing: Third-Party Logistics Providers						
# of test scripts	127	23				150
# of test scripts executed	127	23				150
# of test scripts complete	127	23				150
EDI Testing: Banks						
# of test scripts	11		10		1	22
# of test scripts executed	1		10		1	12
# of test scripts complete	1		10		1	12
% executed	92.9%					92.9%
% complete	92.9%					92.9%

Figure 16.4 Sample Test Metrics Report

The matrix of workstream and type of test permits test management to identify any bottlenecks or problem areas in the testing process. In the process area, OTC and PTS show significant numbers of tests remaining. In the EDI areas, bank testing reveals the largest number of tests still to be executed. This situation may result from poor test performance or stem from difficulty communicating with banks to complete the tests on time. In any case, test management will focus its attention on these areas of potential concern by identifying and researching the source of the problems.

The test management team produces these performance reports on a daily basis. Having real-time status visibility enables project management to detect trends where they occur and to assign additional resources where they are needed. Without regularly available reporting, the project can lose valuable time by assuming that all is well when it is not.

Of course, these test reports can also reflect whether testing is on schedule. Each workstream has its daily schedule, and the report shows whether teams are on time. Those teams that diverge markedly from their schedules should be closely observed. Those teams that do extremely well can be used as guides for other workstreams. Teams that consistently lag far behind schedule should be monitored and potentially assigned added resources.

16.2.4 Defect Processing

Some scripts will not pass the test and subsequently become defects. Each workstream will establish the causes for failure and assure that a remedy is in place. Defect resolution is the final step in the testing process, and includes the following steps:

- **Design a defect handling process.**
  Prior to testing, the test management team defines how defects are to be handled. The process includes criteria for defects, requirements to be a defect resolver, and methods to be used to verify that the defect has indeed been resolved.

- **Assess and assign defects.**
  All defects identified during the testing process will be reported. They will then be assigned to resolvers based on the category of severity and urgency. Defects remain open for action until they are established as resolved.

- **Resolve defects.**
  The assigned defect resolver is responsible for finding the solution to the issue. Once a solution has been found and implemented, the resolver conducts preliminary testing to verify that the solution remedies the problem.
- **Retest.**
  Defects reported as resolved are returned to the original tester. This individual applies the previously used script to test the solution. Provided that the solution works, the script is now marked as passed. If the solution does not work, it is returned to the resolver for additional investigation and resolution.

Any test script where the actual result falls short of the expected result constitutes a defect. Testers will be trained to record defects and report them to test coordinators. For ease of tracking, each defect should be linked to the test script where it was produced. Testers will provide detailed descriptions of the problem. Required supplemental materials would include:

- The SAP UserID of the tester
- References to data that were used in the testing process
- Expected results that should have been achieved
- Copies of any screen shots for the test step where the defect occurred

Test coordinators compile defects identified and submit them to the test management team for review. The test management staff verifies that the defect is valid—that is, not a result of tester error.

The test management team is responsible for coordinating defect resolution. This includes establishing defect severity levels and defect resolution urgency. In many cases, defects will not only prevent a script from completing, but also place a hold on any downstream testing that embeds that step in the affected business process.

For this reason, defects must be actively managed and closed at the earliest possible opportunity. The first step means having all project team members understand how defects will be classified. As stated above, this is a two-step process that weighs the importance of a defect by its severity and urgency.

Severity concerns the impact that the defect would have on business process operations. Although the defect may produce minimal problem on systems functioning during testing, it could have substantial negative effects once the system is fully live and production data are in use. Table 16.2 shows how the three severity categories operate.

Severity Rating	Description
Critical	▶ Problem encountered during testing can create a shutdown in business operations or negatively affects an entire company function ▶ Defect violates a legal or regulatory requirement
Major	▶ Problem affects a large number of users or a large number of SAP transactions ▶ Defect slows business processes ▶ Business deems resolution important
Minor	▶ Problem affects a small number of users or a small number of SAP transactions ▶ Business deems resolution of low importance

Table 16.2 Defect Severity Ratings

Urgency reflects priority assigned to defect resolution. This is especially true for testing activities. High-urgency items recognize the effect on testing. Thus, some low-severity defects may substantially affect testing and are assigned a high urgency. Table 16.3 outlines the three urgency rating categories.

Urgency Rating	Description
High	Testing cannot move forward. Some needed functionality is not operating (e.g., invoices not processing in SAP or forms such as customs documents not populating correctly)
Medium	Problem affects testing but downstream activities can still continue
Low	Creates no testing impact. Needed changes are cosmetic in nature

Table 16.3 Defect Urgency Ratings

The actual priority assigned to individual defects will reflect a combined scoring of the two ratings. Project management, test management, and workstream leads will work together to review the defect list and assign correct resolution priorities.

Once testing is underway, defect review meetings can begin. Held daily during cycles of integration and user acceptance testing, these meetings track open defects. The meeting participants include test management, test coordinators, integrator management, and workstream leads. They assign defects to resolvers and establish target dates for resolution based on severity and urgency.

To facilitate these discussions, each defect is assigned to a category reflecting its primary cause. These categories generally point to the horizontal workstream responsible for handling the defect. Table 16.4 lists example categories and their descriptions.

Defect Category	Description
Configuration setup	The SAP systems configuration does not perform as expected. Testing shows results inconsistent with functional requirements.
Custom object performance	Custom object (WRICEFP) does not perform in accordance with technical specifications or functional requirements.
Data issue	Test data appears to be invalid. Testing produces incorrect results due to incorrect or incomplete data.
Legacy applications	Defect occurs as a result of interaction with an existing legacy system. The incorrect test result stems from an error in legacy system processing.
New requirement	The defect indicates the need for a new or changed requirement. Build work proceeded correctly but the system does not work as planned due to incorrect requirements.
Tester error	The defect arose due to incorrect testing processes. This could be due to test training, misunderstanding of the test script, or incorrect test execution.
Security error	User roles assigned to the test case were incorrect. Either the role was incorrectly designated or did not have the necessary authorizations to perform the test.

Table 16.4 Defect Categories

> **Tip**
>
> Whether you use this set of defect categories or some other, do *use* categories. They will clarify the underlying cause of the defects you are seeing. If you are seeing large numbers of defects attributable to tester error, it means that testers have likely missed some key point in their training. Get all testers together and review their instructions. Focus on the areas where errors are prevalent and make sure that everyone understands the information before closing the meeting.

Each day, the group meets to review newly opened defects and to receive progress updates from resolvers on assigned defects. Test management will report on the aging of defects relative to the date they were opened and status of defects relative to their target closed date. Where discovery of defects identifies the need for changes in system design, actions in support of design improvements will be tracked as well. Considerable emphasis will be placed on the closure of defects according to their target dates.

In tracking defect progress, the test management team can prepare documentation showing the steps from defect origination to closure. Either through automated processes or manual methods, the test team will follow the defect through to closure. Figure 16.5 outlines the defect resolution steps that the team will follow.

| New defect | Assigned | In process | Ready for review | Transport | Test | Complete |

Figure 16.5 Defect Resolution Steps

Let's walk through this process, from the discovery of a defect through completion. Based on severity and urgency ratings, defects will be assigned to technical staff for resolution. For the most part, defect resolvers will be members of the systems integrator project team. Resolvers will work to identify root causes for each defect. Once the root cause is known, resolution can begin. In the case of SAP system issues, this generally consists of a configuration change; in the case of custom objects defects, it usually requires a code fix.

Once the defect resolution is known and the technical fix generated, changes must be made to the testing system. The fix must be introduced to the system as a replacement for the former, error-producing configuration or code. This will be accomplished through a system transport. In order to have traceability to the problem and its resolution, the transport description should include the defect number that generated it.

When the resolution has been transported to the testing system, it will be available for retest. In every case, the tester who identified the original defect will conduct the retest to verify that the defect has indeed been resolved. If the retest is successful, the defect can be reported as closed.

The test management team will keep a record of all open and closed defects, including the transport numbers that resolved them. This provides full traceability to the defect closure process, giving any auditor access to records that indicate that the defect was opened, resolved, transported, and retested.

16.2.5 Mega-Scenarios

Earlier sections in this chapter touched on the need for—and some of the challenges of—mega-scenario testing. Now we'll discuss some of the operation details. Verifying system performance through this large-scale, multi-workstream testing is the final opportunity to exercise the system prior to go-live. Although mega-scenarios are executed both during user acceptance testing and integration testing, user acceptance testing provides the best chance to discover hidden process issues.

Integration testing is performed by company IT staff or by systems integrator personnel who may not be familiar with business process nuances. But if the mega-scenarios are not tested by fully knowledgeable process experts, issues may go undiscovered. This may lead to later system difficulties. User acceptance testing, where experienced business users are directly involved, provides the most rigorous test setting.

Because mega-scenario testing involves multiple workstreams simultaneously executing test steps and making hand-offs to other workstreams, it generates special logistics challenges for the project team. Mega-scenario testing must be organized to a very detailed level and constantly monitored for any obstacles encountered. Each mega-scenario requires an owner—generally, the lead from the workstream that is most impacted by the process under test.

> **Tip**
>
> Additionally, take care to ensure that your scripts link together in an effective way. Transfer of testing responsibility from one workstream to another must be specifically called out. This can best be accomplished if the mega-scenario test takes place in a single location so that teams can discuss any problems encountered with other teams in the testing location.

Figure 16.6 shows an intercompany shipment transaction, which illustrates how complex these mega-scenarios can be. The closer they come to replicating real-world processes, the more difficult the testing management. Testing the "handling intercompany shipments" mega-scenario involves processes from four of the five workstreams: order-to-cash, procure-to-pay, plan-to-stock, and record-to-report. In this case, it will also include demand from a regional market to ensure that imports and exports are contained within the scope.

The mega-scenario owner and test managers must ensure that each step is completed in the proper sequence. Unless this is handled carefully, test results will not be accurate. Potentially incorrect conclusions might then be drawn from the test.

Plan-to-stock	1. Forecast demand 2. Plan MRP 3. Create bill of materials 4. Manufacture produce 5. Ship finished goods to warehouse
Procure-to-pay	1. Create purchase order 2. Generate imports documents
Order-to-cash	1. Stock transfer order 2. Export product 3. Ship to market 4. Receive finished good
Record-to-report	1. Set transfer pricing 2. Financial reconciliation

Figure 16.6 Process Components for Intercompany Shipment Mega-Scenario

16.2.6 Regression Testing

Regression testing introduces a slight variant to the verification process. Unlike most testing performed during realization, regression testing aims to ensure that introduction of the SAP system does no damage to existing systems. For global implementation projects consisting of several waves of deployment, regression testing comes into play as the project moves from wave one to wave two or wave two to wave three.

> **Pitfall Alert**
>
> Please pay close attention to regression testing during any subsequent deployment waves in your project. Any changes to configuration and new custom objects developed during wave two should be tested to ensure they have no impact on data or functionality now in the wave one production system. Unless your project team performs regression test with care, your wave two go-live could encounter problems during hypercare. Transactions may not work correctly. Unraveling the issues with the system after it's live will introduce complications and user frustrations.

In this scenario, regression testing would be performed during waves two and three. Each would focus on verifying that no element of the system built for the new wave produced a negative impact on the wave currently in use.

Regression testing is most often conducted by technical staff, either from company IT or from the systems integrator. Although this testing may be performed as a back-office activity, it is essential for verifying that a newly introduced code or configuration does no harm.

16.3 Using Testing Systems

Using automated testing systems can greatly ease test execution during a project. Several companies market these systems, and it would be wise to review several before initiating your project. Essentially, the systems serve as a platform where many major test activities are performed. Scripts are loaded in the system, where they are available for test and retest.

Automated testing systems have several additional advantages that may make them—in combination with SAP Solution Manager and Microsoft SharePoint—the third leg in your project system. Let's examine a few:

- Because all testing takes place in the test system, the system can accurately track testing performance, even for regional locations. Built-in reporting capability makes providing test status much simpler than with manual processes.
- Many companies have stringent regulatory requirements. These can come from external auditing organizations or governmental regulatory agencies. Automated testing systems enable auditors to receive real-time visibility on tests they would like to examine.
- Many regulators also require that the company show an explicit connection between system requirements and the tests used to assess them. These requirement traceability matrices are included as standard functionality in the test systems. Having a test system in place is a real advantage where multiple tests may test a single requirement or where multiple requirements are verified by a single test.
- These systems are Web-based, which means that data entry and collection processes are greatly simplified. Each level of the project organization—whether it be the core team, regional teams, or site operations—can slice the output data for its own needs. Each group can receive reports that provide visibility to specific problem areas and guidelines for its actions.
- Defect tracking can be managed in the system as well. This permits the test management team and test coordinators to know which defects have been resolved and which fixes have been transported.

However, these advantages do come with a cost. Test systems must be configured for use as the company requires. Preparation and the actual configuration take time and resources. Additionally, your company must prepare project team members to use the system. Extensive training will be required to enable testing, defect management, and tracing of requirements. Security setup unique to the system must be performed as well. Staff familiar with testing systems must be hired and brought on board prior to beginning the project.

So these will not be simple tasks. Each implementing company must make the decision regarding use of a test system. However, in the case of large-scale, global projects, the benefits will usually greatly outweigh the costs.

16.4 Systems Test Entrance and Exit Criteria

Reporting the status of activities required for entering and exiting cycles is an excellent way to ensure the integrity of test processes. Developing and tracking measures that provide empirical evidence of readiness prevents the team from premature beginnings or endings of test cycles. This applies for both integration and user acceptance test.

Normally test entrance or exit reviews are conducted as formal meetings. They should be scheduled so that company executive sponsors can attend, discuss test progress, and decide whether to move forward. In these meetings, the team provides data and recommendations. The sponsors alone make the decision to shift to the next phase.

Figure 16.7 provides an example of test entrance criteria. Project and test management work together to identify criteria representing those items that *must* be complete prior to the initiation of a cycle. These criteria should not only be essential to risk-based entrance to test—they should also each be measurable. In this way, all members of the project team can independently assess progress.

In this example, the team has selected 11 items for its entrance criteria. Many of these represent preparation that must be complete for testing to initiate. These include movements (or transports) of configuration and custom objects into the test environment. Of course, testing cannot move forward without the system elements built to company specifications.

Items three through eight represent test preparation activities. Test management systems and testers must be readied for testing to proceed. Thus, decisions on defect management, server access, test scripts loads, resourcing requirements, and testing schedules all represent necessary conditions for starting the test.

> **Pitfall Alert**
>
> Some may argue that many of these items can be completed once testing is underway and therefore are not true entrance criteria. However, allowing necessary preparatory work to be addressed *after* the start of testing adds risk to the project. It assumes that the activities will finish early in the test cycle and will not create any delays to testing. The project can simply eliminate this risk by requiring items to be closed prior to beginning test. Often that requirement will cause the work to be done in a timely manner.

No.	Task	Status	Comments
1	Configuration transports complete	Green	Configuration transports complete
2	Custom objects transports complete	Green	WRICEFP transports complete for cycle two
3	Defect change control and transport process reviewed and approved	Green	Defect change control process approved
4	All resources/roles (testers, reviewers, approvers, etc.) identified	Green	All testers identified for test system and SAP
5	Access confirmed to all required servers, applications, and tools for each resource	Green	All required access granted
6	Training complete for all resources	Green	All testers trained on test system and SAP
7	Test scripts loaded into testing system and approved	Green	All scripts loaded
8	Detailed test schedule complete	Green	Schedules in place
9	Security build complete	Green	Security build for test roles only
10	Test data created and verified	Green	
11	System integration and connectivity (including peripherals, such as printers) verified	Yellow	Some required impact printers still to be configured

Figure 16.7 Integration Test Entrance Criteria

The final three entries, nine through 11, focus on security roles to be used in testing, availability of requisite test data, and connection among elements of the SAP system and its peripherals. Each of these represents a function that horizontal teams must provide in support of testing. The importance of data for proper testing cannot be overestimated. Additionally, peripherals such as specially configured printers are necessary to demonstrate that the functionality is in place to print invoices and regionally specific customs documents.

Notice that all entrance criteria except item 11 are tagged as "green." As the comments demonstrate, items one through 10 are all complete. The work needed has been accomplished. Item 11 is tagged as yellow because it is not complete. It will be up to executive sponsors to decide whether testing should move forward without having the impact printers configured and ready.

This example shows the value of entrance criteria and the transparency they produce. Unless the subject of peripheral readiness was called out and made a subject for discussion, the project might move along. If printer performance caused delays to testing, senior management might feel that full disclosure was not provided. *It's always better to make everyone aware of potential problems early.*

At the conclusion of each test cycle, the same type of discussion can be held regarding exit criteria. Generally, these reviews are more straightforward; they focus almost entirely on test performance. The example shown in Figure 16.8 contains only four exit criteria. They clearly emphasize passage of test scripts, effective defect management, performance of custom objects in testing, and the ability to work with third-party and legacy systems.

Activity	Status	Due Date
One: All cycle two test scripts completed	Green: 471 of 471 test scripts tested	28 Jun 20XX
Two: Resolution of all outstanding Urgent and Very High priority defects	Yellow: 17 Urgent defects, 12 Very High defects. One very high, defects still outstanding. It will not impact cycle three testing.	28 Jun 20XX
Three: All cycle two custom objects integration tested	Green: 51 of 51 custom objects delivered. All passed test	28 Jun 20XX
Four: All cycle three test plans and legacy and third-party integration test plans in place	Green: All tests executed and passed	28 Jun 20XX

Figure 16.8 Integration Test Exit Criteria

As with the entrance criteria, performance in exit criteria should be discussed with company executive sponsors as the primary decision makers. The question to be answered is whether the testing cycle has proceeded sufficiently well to move to the next cycle. Based on the information provided, testing activities have proceeded to plan. However, one risk still appears with an open defect. Senior management will expect a full explanation of the defect involved and the reason why it is still open.

In the interest of time management, you can schedule reviews concurrently. Thus, the exit review for cycle two can be combined with the entrance review for cycle three. In the case where project sponsors decide to remain in a test cycle rather than exiting it, the following entrance review will be held at a later date.

You'll now see that realization encompasses far more than just build and test. An entire set of additional activities proceed simultaneously through realization. Our next chapter addresses four of them: data conversion, reports building, EDI, and security and internal controls. Here we go!

> *SAP implementation projects can fail for a number of reasons. Most news stories list incomplete blueprint design and insufficient testing at the top of the list. Less well known, but certainly equally potent contributors to failure, are these four horsemen of the project apocalypse.*

17   Data, Reports, EDI, and Security and Internal Controls

The biblical book of Revelations identifies four horsemen as foretellers of coming calamity. Each horse has a different color and represents a different disaster: pestilence, war, famine, or death. Though certainly not as dire as these calamities, significant problems with data, reports, electronic data interchange (EDI), and security and internal controls can each produce potentially fatal consequences for the SAP implementation project.

Unfortunately, very often our four horsemen fall below the project radar. Their issues may not be visible until it is too late to address them. At that point, the only available options might be postponing your go-live or deploying a flawed system. Unless these four horsemen are carefully managed and closely monitored, project sponsors may be left with these very undesirable choices.

> **Tip**
>
> Desolation is not preordained; it need not occur. We take the position throughout this book that good information goes a long way toward solving any problem. We believe that the information offered here will enable you and your team to understand the potential pitfalls and then take action to avoid them. Good luck!

This chapter provides the background for understanding how the four horsemen can impact a project. This background will include a discussion of the underlying importance of each one and a description of where project leadership can make major missteps without being aware of the consequences.

17 Data, Reports, EDI, and Security and Internal Controls

17.1 Data

Earlier chapters identified configuration as supplying the superstructure for your company's SAP system. By creating the framework for transactions, configuration enables the operating structure for your company's SAP system. Data, however, takes things one step further. Data is the very lifeblood of the system. Company data—your customers, vendors, financial records, and organization—reflect the reality of your company.

Data in an SAP implementation project generally means the incorporation of company information from an existing legacy system. *Data conversion* transfers that data from one or more legacy systems to your new SAP system. The project team conducts this process over several iterations during realization. If all goes well at go-live, this reviewed and verified company data is transferred to the SAP production system. Once embedded in this way, the transferred data now confirms the SAP system as a core part of company operations.

If all does *not* go well, SAP transactions may search for erroneous data and then utilize it in company business processes. Vendors and customers may have incorrect addresses; inventory records may reflect inaccurate balances; financial accounts may have incomplete transactions. Mistakes with data can have enormous consequences for your company. An effective project can prevent these harmful situations; avoiding data issues such as these depends on management attention at the highest levels of the company.

Data conversion is a time-consuming and complex operation. While this fact contributes to the potential for difficulties, it is not sufficient unto itself to create problems. Project teams will successfully handle many other time-consuming and complex operations throughout the project lifecycle.

What makes data different and more challenging is its task ownership. Data conversion is technical in nature; it demands system understanding and knowledge of data structures. Most technical tasks during the project are handled by the systems integrator. For example, configuration, custom object development, and system build are all performed by the systems integrator. With data, the bulk of conversion activities are accomplished by company staff. Integrators, operating from the guiding principle that a company owns its data and is therefore responsible for it, focus on the more technical aspects of data load to the system.

This principle becomes clear in Table 17.1. It shows that almost all data work, with the exception of data load activities, is performed by the company project team.

Company Data Responsibilities	Systems Integrator Data Responsibilities
▸ Data identification and review ▸ Cleansing ▸ Extracting and verifying ▸ Preparing data load files ▸ Data mapping ▸ Preparing manual files ▸ Defining test data ▸ Preparing data functional conversion specifications	▸ Preparing data loads ▸ Managing load files ▸ Operating conversion tools ▸ Building data transformation rules ▸ Preparing conversion technical specifications

Table 17.1 Data Responsibility Allocation between Company and Systems Integrator

Data conversion represents one of the few areas where the company team is expected to assume a technical role. Project team members must understand the structure and usage of company data. They must also respond to the very tight time frames involved in data conversion. System testing and cutover activities depend on data being loaded on time. If the team is unprepared to handle this level of responsibility or lacks the necessary skills, the data conversion effort may not go well. The results can be disastrous.

> **Pitfall Alert**
>
> Early in the project, clarify data conversion roles with your systems integrator. Each integrator works differently and the contract may not cover this topic in detail. Meet personally with the integrator leads to discuss their expectations about which organization performs exactly which tasks. The time will be well spent. Remember our watchword—no surprises.

17.1.1 Data Types

Before proceeding with the data conversion process, it is important to point out the framework of data types: master and transactional data. Each type presents its own set of challenges to the project team.

Master data supplies a template information source for specific transaction entries. That means, for instance, that the bill-to and ship-to for an individual sales order will be referenced and auto-populated from the customer master. Using master data in a transaction ensures that the information is correct. End users are saved the trouble of adding this standard information during a transaction because the SAP system performs that task for them.

Master data is often used by more than one functional organization and stored in many different systems across the company. This represents one source of complexity. And although it would be ideal for the master data to remain unchanged over time, this is not the case. Master data changes constantly. Customers and vendors change or add locations, and these must be referenced and updated. Pricing conditions and storage locations will also change. This creates another source of complexity with master data—making sure that it is accurate and up to date.

Examples of master data include the following:

- Customer master
- Vendor master
- Material master
- Pricing information
- Human resources master data
- Bills of material
- Work breakdown structures
- Work centers
- Profit and cost centers

Clearly, this is essential information and must be correct at all times. Errors in the conversion of master data from legacy systems will directly result in errors in SAP transactions. For this reason, the data conversion team will spend a great deal of time making sure that master data is correct.

The second type of data, transactional data, is related to a single business event. It utilizes master data in completing the event, but it also creates a unique data entity. Thus, when an end user creates a purchase requisition, the SAP system generates an electronic document as a record. The SAP system assigns a document number to the transaction and adds that record to others collected in the system. Examples of transactional data include the following:

- Warehouse inventory
- Sales transactions
- Asset records
- General ledger transactions
- Invoices
- Shipments
- Requests for payment

17.1.2 Data Cleansing and Conversion

During blueprinting, your project's data conversion team created data definition documents. These deliverables described the data elements that are required from source systems for migration to the SAP system. Data definition documents establish the foundation for conversion activities that will be completed during realization.

Figure 17.1 outlines a prototypical data conversion schedule for a six-month realization process. Months one through three describe activities to be delivered during the build phase discussed in Chapter 15. Months four through six outline activities to be delivered during the testing phase discussed in Chapter 16.

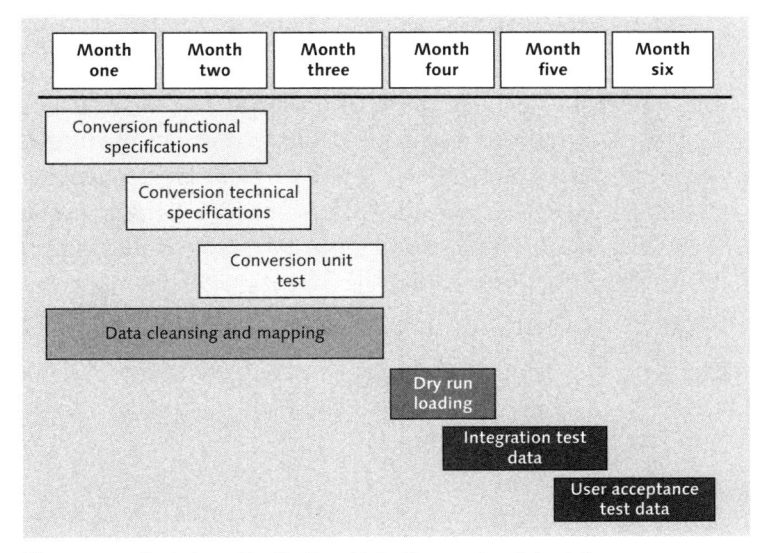

Figure 17.1 Prototype Realization Data Conversion Schedule

Conversion functional specifications, conversion technical specifications, and conversion unit testing follow similar patterns to the custom object development process discussed in Chapter 15. Through this process, the data team identifies data objects from the legacy system that are required to populate the company SAP system. The company data resources simultaneously focus on data cleansing and data mapping.

These last two activities are essential conditions for successful data migration. Data cleansing investigates and resolves any issues with current legacy system data. It makes sure that the data is "clean" and free of errors or duplicates. Once again—any data migrated to the SAP system must be accurate and reliable; effective cleansing ensures that data migrated to the SAP system can be used without reservation. Typical cleansing issues include resolving any duplicate records, incomplete records, or records with errors in the legacy system. Prior to go-live, the data team must know that all these issues have been resolved.

> **Pitfall Alert**
>
> Make the time for data cleansing. Most legacy system data contains errors and duplicates. Finding them depends on your team's subject matter experts (SMEs). Only those who know the data well can find the often-hidden errors. One good method is to address cleansing in workstream sessions. The functional lead facilitates the session and includes integrator experts who understand SAP data requirements. SMEs, working as a team, can identify and resolve many of the issues in these sessions.

Data mapping, on the other hand, defines the relationship between fields and records in the legacy system and in the SAP system. Figure 17.2 shows the overall migration process where data are sourced from three different legacy systems, mapped to the SAP system, and then converted. In the best-case scenario, fields required in SAP will match those in the legacy system. Mapping would simply identify the two fields with instructions to place the legacy information in the comparable SAP field.

This best-case scenario, however, is only rarely encountered. More often, fields and records differ in some way. This is where the complexity of data conversion comes into play.

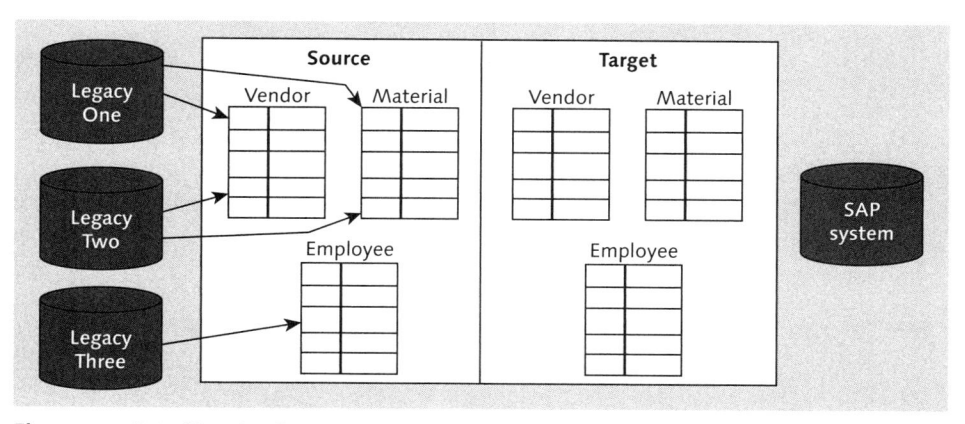

Figure 17.2 Data Mapping Process

Let's consider a few situations related to these fields that fall outside the best-case scenario.

- Fields may not match. This situation can include a range of issues.
  - The legacy field may host alphanumerical information while the SAP field requires only numeric information.
  - SAP may need information of a particular field length (e.g., 15 characters) while the legacy system uses a different field length or even a mix of them.
- The purpose of fields in the legacy system may vary from those in the SAP system. Thus, even though the fields appear to be comparable, they are not.
- SAP's required fields may not be present in the legacy system.
- SAP's required field information may be needed from additional systems outside the framework of the target legacy system.
- Record amounts in the two systems may differ. For instance, customer information in the legacy system may span across multiple records, while in SAP it is found on a single record.

Both data cleansing and mapping must be performed by those who are expert in specific company data items. Only personnel with the knowledge base to analyze legacy files should be involved. Experts in the current customer master should lead the customer master effort, experts in the current vendor master should lead the vendor master effort, and experts in current company pricing structure should lead the pricing structure effort.

Often, the foremost experts on a company's data will be the functional workstream leads. They will know its ins and outs—why it operates as it does. The challenge will come with making these leads available to participate in the data effort. With so much on their plate, workstream leads may find it difficult to allocate the necessary time. However, unless others with as much skill can be found, the leads still provide the best resources to oversee this data conversion task. Project executive sponsors must brief the workstream leads on the importance of data and emphasize the need for their participation.

These experts will know which legacy data is useful and which can be deleted. More importantly, they will know which data requires enhancement and which requires modification.

This will be an ongoing effort. Cleansing and improving source data quality will continue until the days just before go-live. Each iteration should bring the data closer to perfect—and by go-live, the data should be 100 percent correct.

This iterative improvement model is accomplished through a series of data loads. During these loads, the data team produces reports indicating which files, records, and fields have errors. The team uses this information to correct errors. The data team will do correcting work in between loads, so the next load should show reduced error rates. The team can also improve its timing on the load sequence. During cutover, data load into the production environment must take place in a very limited time period. It is important for the data team to have confidence that it can achieve excellent results in the time allotted.

> **Tip**
>
> Data loading is a pedal-to-the-metal exercise where the data team works virtually nonstop to transfer converted data into the SAP system. At the end of this grueling process, the team will have data available for integration test or user acceptance test.

These loads also supply the data used for integration test and user acceptance test. Data in the early cycles of integration test are limited to smaller sections of the total amount. However, by the time later integration test cycles begin, almost all data should be available. For user acceptance testing, full data availability is a requirement.

To meet this requirement, the team will schedule several extracts from source systems and subsequent loads into the SAP system. Each extract should reflect higher data quality and each load into SAP should demonstrate progress in achieving desired times. Table 17.2 shows the alignment of extracts and loads, beginning with the end of the build step and continuing through the entirety of test in the realization phase.

Realization Month	Extract	Load
Month three (approximately two weeks between extract and load)	First extract of master and transaction data	Initial load for cycle one integration test; 10-20 % of data
Month four	Second extract of master and transaction data	Second load for cycle two and three integration test; 15-20 % of data
Month five (cleansed data extracted for previous load used in user acceptance testing)	No additional extract	Third load for user acceptance testing; 30 % of data
Month five	Extract of master data for cutover simulation	Load master data for cutover simulation
Month six	Extract of transaction data for cutover simulation	Load transaction data for cutover simulation

Table 17.2 Data Load and Extract Schedule through Realization

Now that we have the conversion process under our belts, let's discuss the tools that can be used in data conversion.

Conversion Tools

Application support is available to assist in the data conversion process. Choosing which application type to use depends greatly on the volume of data you need to migrate. Where the volume is large, an automated system will enable handling of the extract, transformation, and load (ETL) steps. These automated systems not only conduct transformation, but also supply reports on such items as record duplicates and field errors. Additionally, they provide record counts for all records processed in a file. These system reports prove invaluable in correcting mistakes in large-volume files.

Figure 17.3 shows how this automated conversion process would work. The source system provides the files, records, and fields to be migrated. Depending on the scope of the SAP implementation, there may be only a single source system or there may be multiple systems. Additionally, the conversion may involve large numbers of files from some systems and relatively few from other systems. In our example, three source systems supply data for conversion to the SAP system.

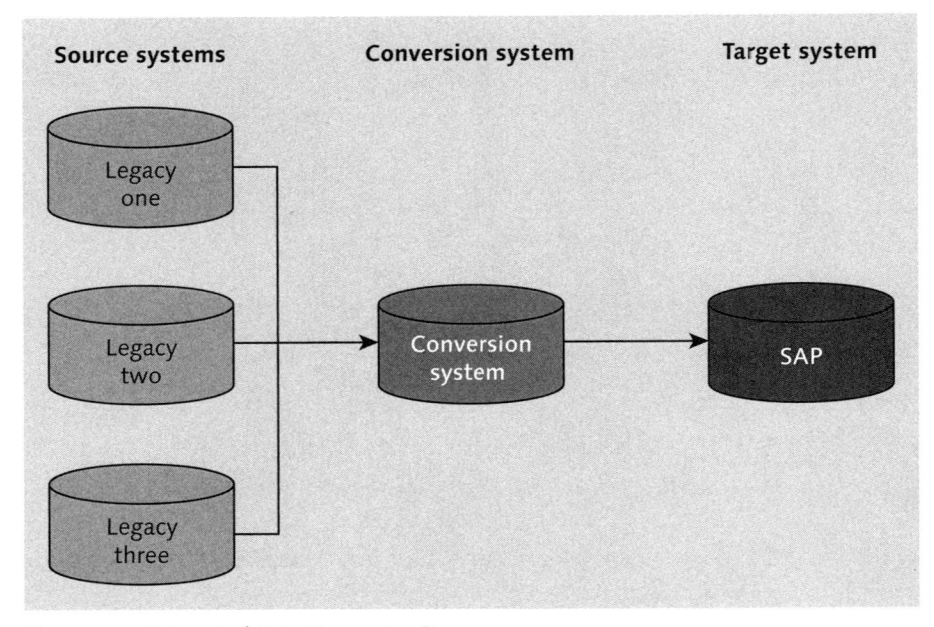

Figure 17.3 Automated Data Conversion Process

The conversion system (identified in the second block) represents an application designed to handle large volumes of data transfer. Sometimes these applications are owned and operated by companies specializing in data conversion services. In other cases, they are applications marketed by large software companies for multiple uses. However, they all perform the same basic function. They use algorithms to transfer the data to a target system according to the project data team's mapping tables. The team may also supply data using manual enrichment files. These files provide data supplementing or expanding the source system information.

The target system—in this case, SAP—receives the information according to the mapping tables. These tables will align the data to SAP's file, record, and field formats. Once installed in the production system at go-live, this data will be used as primary information for SAP end users.

The data team is responsible for ensuring that connections between source, conversion, and target systems all result in valid and reliable data. Any errors identified are generally handled as defects. Cleansing errors will be addressed by company data experts, and conversion errors will be resolved by the systems integrator data team. As defects are reported, they are managed in similar fashion to those encountered in testing (see Chapter 16). The data team defines a resolution and verifies it through the input of the company data experts.

In many projects, the volumes of data won't be big enough to require automated conversion tools. In these situations, a manual process can be used and a different tool applied. The team prepares source data on spreadsheets and cleanses it manually. These completed spreadsheet files are called *manual load-ready files*. Once ready for load, an SAP tool called the *Legacy System Migration Workbench* (LSMW) can be used for migration purposes. LSMW imports the source data using the manual load-ready spreadsheets, converts it using mapping files, and finally posts it to the SAP database.

Once done, the information migrated through this more manual process will prove as accurate and reliable as data from automated conversions. The end result—that is, the right company data in the SAP system—is the fundamental target of both.

17.1.3 Data Governance

Some companies have invested considerable resources in data governance, while others have not yet addressed how they will govern their data in a systematic way. Companies falling in this second grouping may find that an SAP implementation project serves as an especially good time to initiate data governance—especially with master data.

17 | Data, Reports, EDI, and Security and Internal Controls

> **Tip**
>
> Do take advantage of your SAP implementation to address master data governance. Whether it means putting a governance process in place for the first time or improving the processes already in use, good data governance can only improve your company's business processes.

SAP is a highly integrated system that depends on master data to work effectively. If a company will use SAP in multiple regions and functions for the first time, data governance becomes essential. In this multi-region, multi-functional model, lack of aligned data definitions can lead regions to have different interpretations and uses for the same data. Changes made to master data in one location can impact processes in other locations that remain unaware of the change. After all, remember that many changes to master data also impact transaction data such as external partner communications, cash flow values, and inventory levels. These alterations could be highly damaging to business operations unless carefully planned.

Data governance ensures consistency by managing data creation and changes. Essentially, it defines a governance model for each data object that balances central and local needs. Appointed data stewards can oversee data object management processes. These can operate both centrally and locally. Each data object would have specific definitions regarding the amount of local control available.

Master data objects with central control would still have some degree of local control. Table 17.3 indicates where central control would be shared with local control and where central and local control only would operate.

Data Object	Central Governance	Shared Control	Local Governance
Customer master	X	X	
Vendor master	X	X	
Material master	X	X	
Bills of material	X		
General ledger accounts	X		

Table 17.3 Governance Control by Master Data Object

Data Object	Central Governance	Shared Control	Local Governance
Profit centers	X		
Sales pricing conditions			X
Equipment			X
Assets			X

Table 17.3 Governance Control by Master Data Object (Cont.)

Data owners participating in implementation project conversions could apply their lessons learned to the new SAP data governance process. This would represent a definite win for the company in the days forward. Data management will improve overall company data quality and make roles and responsibilities clear to all.

17.2 Reports

If data is the lifeblood of a company's SAP system, then reports are its eyes. At the executive level especially, the perceived value of SAP comes from the availability of up-to-the-minute views of company performance. These views may include overall sales levels, fill rates in plants, or revenue-versus-plan projections. Many executives have limited visibility to the SAP transaction process. Only rarely would an executive actually execute a transaction. But most will attach great importance to reports based on this data and will use them extensively.

However, most reports—as an executive would define them—do not appear out of the box with SAP. Rather, they must be constructed in the same painstaking way as other WRICEFP custom objects, such as forms or workflows. Reports are one more in the series of technical deliverables commonly not provided by the project systems integrator. Similar to data conversion, most of the report-building effort will come from the company project team.

The application development team will build a small number of SAP system reports and the Basis team will manage servers on which SAP reporting tools operate. Beyond this set of services, the systems integrator will offer limited assistance unless specifically contracted to do so.

Unlike data conversion, it's difficult to make an urgent case for reporting. Data conversion is absolutely necessary for project progress. It must be delivered on schedule or the project cannot test, conduct cutover, or go live. Reporting, however, has none of these concrete drivers for urgency. It can remain an abstract requirement in the minds of many. Thus, those on the project team who work to mobilize resources and fight for the needed time commitments will often find themselves facing an uphill battle in the struggle to complete reporting deliverables.

> **Pitfall Alert**
>
> This situation described above can happen to your project team as well. Take a leadership role by making the case for the importance of reporting. Just remember, your senior executives will judge system performance by a small number of parameters. One of these will be: "Can I get my reports and are they accurate?"

Executives, on the other hand, generally expect business-level reports to be available immediately after go-live. Project sponsors and project managers, especially, must understand what SAP reporting can provide, what it cannot provide, and how to accomplish required deliverables. This group should take every opportunity to educate company senior executives.

Some of the challenge likely derives from the range of SAP reporting solutions available. They run the gamut, from literally hundreds of pre-built reports available in SAP as standard functionality, to large-scale reports that are built to order. Table 17.4 shows the scope of reporting functionality available within the SAP system. The first two examples describe reports built within SAP ERP. These either come pre-built as just outlined, or built by the application development team as part of custom object work.

SAP Business Planning and Consolidation (BPC) contains its own report set. This will mostly be used by the record-to-report team and distributed to management as part of the close and business planning process.

The final piece of reporting functionality is where the company will build most of its executive-level reports. It consists of a data warehouse as well as reporting tools that utilize this warehouse.

SAP Tool	Functionality Provided	User Base
Standard SAP ERP reports	Abundant options to personalize, represented by transaction codes added to appropriate security roles.	All users involved in transaction processing and master data management
ABAP reports (custom ERP reports)	Can deliver high-complexity solutions. The costliest ERP reporting option built by the application development team and attached to a transaction code in production.	All process teams, but usually restricted to: ▸ Statutory/legal reports ▸ Real-time reporting not met by standard reports or report writer
SAP Business Planning and Consolidation	Solution specific to SAP Business Planning and Consolidation	▸ RTR to generate reports ▸ Supply chain and general management as consumers
SAP BW/SAP BusinessObjects Business Intelligence	SAP BW provides the data warehouse for selected SAP information. SAP BusinessObjects Business Intelligence provides the Web-based ad-hoc reporting tool and SAP BusinessObjects Dashboards for use with BW or other data warehouse solutions.	Available to all users, but generally used for management reporting, metrics and trending/analysis

Table 17.4 SAP Reporting Tools

Most of this design work will center on SAP Business Warehouse (BW) and the SAP BusinessObjects suite. Virtually all management reports will be generated through these two sets of tools. All requests for specially built reports will go through the gap definition process in blueprint. Once approved, the work also undergoes functional specification, technical specification, development, and unit testing. The major difference in this process concerns those doing the development and unit test work. The resources assigned are normally employed by the company or are directly contracted by it.

This places the burden of managing the process on your company. These resources must have technical skills in SAP BusinessObjects and be capable of engaging and guiding business resources and meeting deadlines for the project.

Figure 17.4 shows the three levels of a reporting pyramid. For the most part, operational- and analytical-level reports will derive from standard SAP ERP reports and custom-built ABAP reports. Those custom-built reports will be constructed by the systems integrator's developers. Those reports usually require little in the way of special formatting or presentation styles.

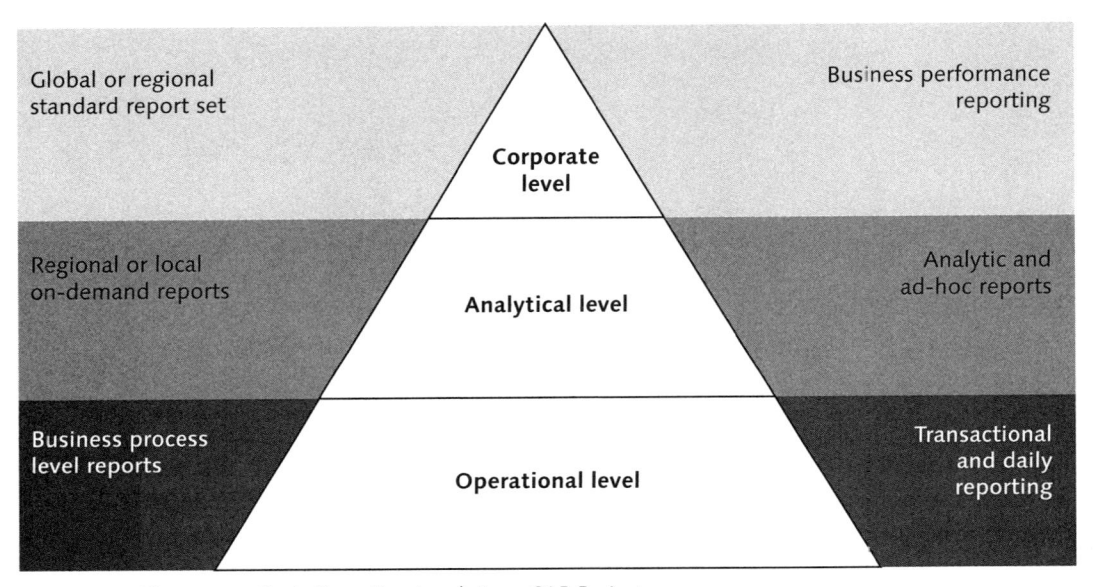

Figure 17.4 Basic Reporting Levels in an SAP Project

Notice that we have three reporting levels. The bottom level, operational reporting, pays attention to business process dimensions, such as daily shipments. These reports give functional managers performance detail on the transactions taking place in their areas. The middle level, analytical reporting, contains reports designed for special needs. These reports are created by expert business users and are also designed for middle management. The top level, corporate reporting, supplies performance information for your company's senior executives. They include such reports as company profitability or daily net sales by region. These reports are highly complex in nature and require the ongoing participation of the project reporting team to construct. For that reason, we'll describe the most difficult case—corporate reporting. All other levels follow the same general path, but with significantly fewer resources and expertise required.

17.2.1 Corporate-Level Reports

Corporate-level reports are those intended to support executives' and senior managers' decision making. These reports are often very complex. They require elaborate formatting, will utilize multiple data sources, and can be put to several different uses. The project reporting team will spend the bulk of its time in this area. The team will face many challenges, including all of the following:

- **Finding a really knowledgeable business resource**
  Most functional teams place reports far down the list of their priorities. When asked to define their requirements, the pressure of other events can lead to minimal time invested in the answer. Unless the reporting team is very persistent, it's easy to incorrectly assume that all requirements have been identified. The reporting team's success in locating all requirements depends on its ability to enlist a knowledgeable functional resource as its guide.

- **Identifying the "real" requirements**
  Executives who use the reports likely have only the most general idea of their requirements. They are users at the end of a long chain of people who work to make the report useful. At best, the reporting team can expect a busy executive to look at a report prototype and identify faults or features still needed. It will be up to the reporting team to work with all levels in the functional business organizations to identify detailed requirements.

- **Locating all the data sources**
  Data to supply the report may come from a variety of sources. Some of it may be SAP data, some may be data from other SAP applications such as SAP BPC, and some of it may come from other systems altogether. The report team must identify source data for its reports and develop a solution that enables the data to be integrated in a single report.

- **Testing the report as used**
  Despite the fact that functional experts in the organization prepare and massage reports for executives, they often are unaware of how executives use them. Only company executives—who are the real users—know the importance placed on each piece of information and how the report flows together for them. The report team must find a way to conduct its testing with all parts of the report's users.

As you can see from Figure 17.5, reporting complexity extends to the application structure. Accessing and making SAP data for reports requires extensive preparation. First, SAP BW must be installed. Specific to SAP, SAP BW serves as a central data repository that integrates data from various parts of the overall SAP system. Similar to other data warehouses, it stores current and historical data. Based on defined requirements, the reporting team will determine which data are needed to be stored in the business warehouse.

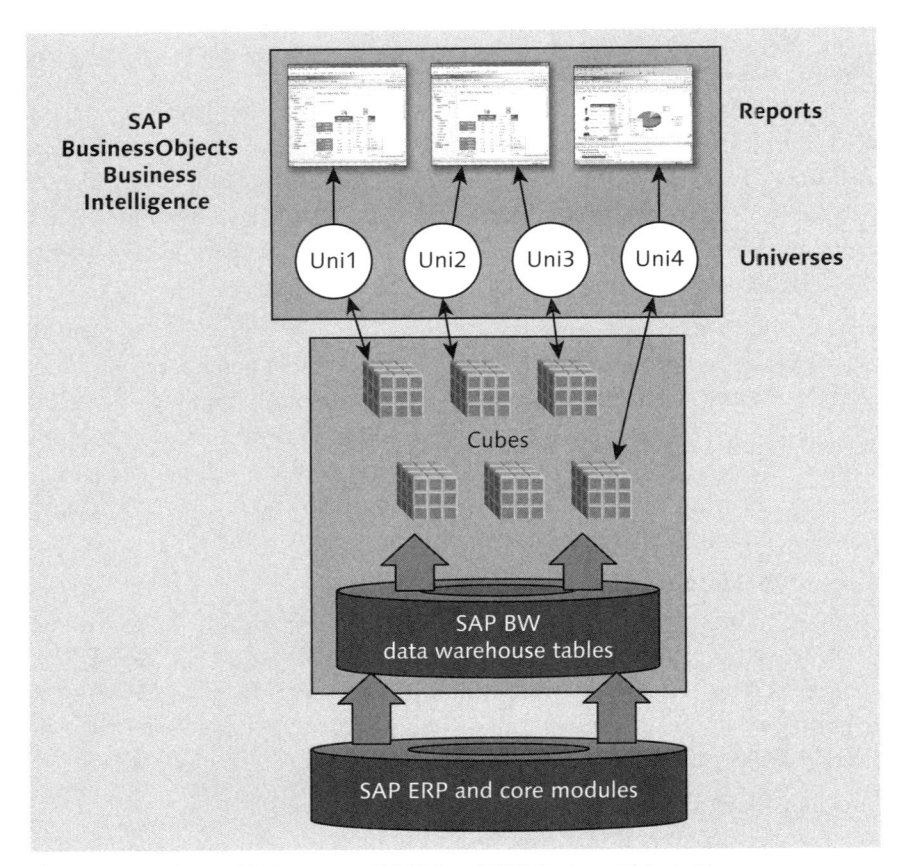

Figure 17.5 Relationship between SAP BW and SAP BusinessObjects BI

Data is constructed in InfoCubes containing SAP data. The specific design of these cubes will again be defined by the reporting team. InfoCube structure depends on the purpose of the data and the frequency of *refreshes* needed. Most cubes will require a daily refresh while others may require refreshing every four hours. This refresh rate is determined by the amount of change taking place in the data over that period of time.

> **Tip**
>
> "Refresh" refers to the timing required to rebuild data in the InfoCube. If the InfoCube operates with a daily refresh, any new transactional data to be included in the report will not appear until the refresh is completed.

End users do not normally access the data warehouse. Rather, accessing and reporting this data is the function of the SAP BusinessObjects application. It provides the information management, query, reporting and analysis tools available to end users. The reporting team will build *universes* to facilitate report building.

Universes are built on a selection of tables or InfoCubes. The reporting team decides which data sources are required and makes them available via universes. For ease of use, the universes are often grouped into classes. In this way, end users can easily locate and utilize needed data.

In addition, the reporting team can organize the data within a universe by using classes and subclasses. Classes would constitute such items as customer, vendor, or material. For the class of "customer," subclasses could be sold-to customer or ship-to customer.

SAP BusinessObjects contains tools that enable report design and online running of the reports. InfoView operates through a Web browser and allows users to run, view, and schedule reports online. SAP BusinessObjects Web Intelligence (WebI) permits users to design and analyze reports via the Web.

All this information makes a single point: Designing and making available corporate reporting requires considerable skill and readily available resources. The implementing company must commit fully to the effort for it to be successful. Clear benefits will accrue from a strategic approach to corporate reporting. In this way, your company can fully realize the value it expects from the purchase and deployment of the SAP system.

17.2.2 Key Performance Indicators

Key performance indicators (KPIs) represent a special case of reporting. The tools used to build the datasets are much the same, but they are applied for the purpose of tracking overall company performance in some critical areas. Generally, these

17 | Data, Reports, EDI, and Security and Internal Controls

KPIs quantitatively demonstrate company progress in achieving important corporate goals.

The SAP implementation project can include identifying and building dashboards for key performance indicators as part of its reporting scope. SAP BusinessObjects Dashboards supports dashboard construction within the framework of SAP BusinessObjects. The underlying design effort will remain much the same. However, a central part of the work will involve working directly with company senior executives. It takes careful investigation to understand specific company goals, to agree across organizations as to how the KPIs will be measured, and to construct the universes in business intelligence with SAP data.

Figure 17.6 shows the interrelationship of company earnings, taxes, and investment levels, with a subset of measures. These measures are quantitative in nature and can be reported through a dashboard that the project team has constructed.

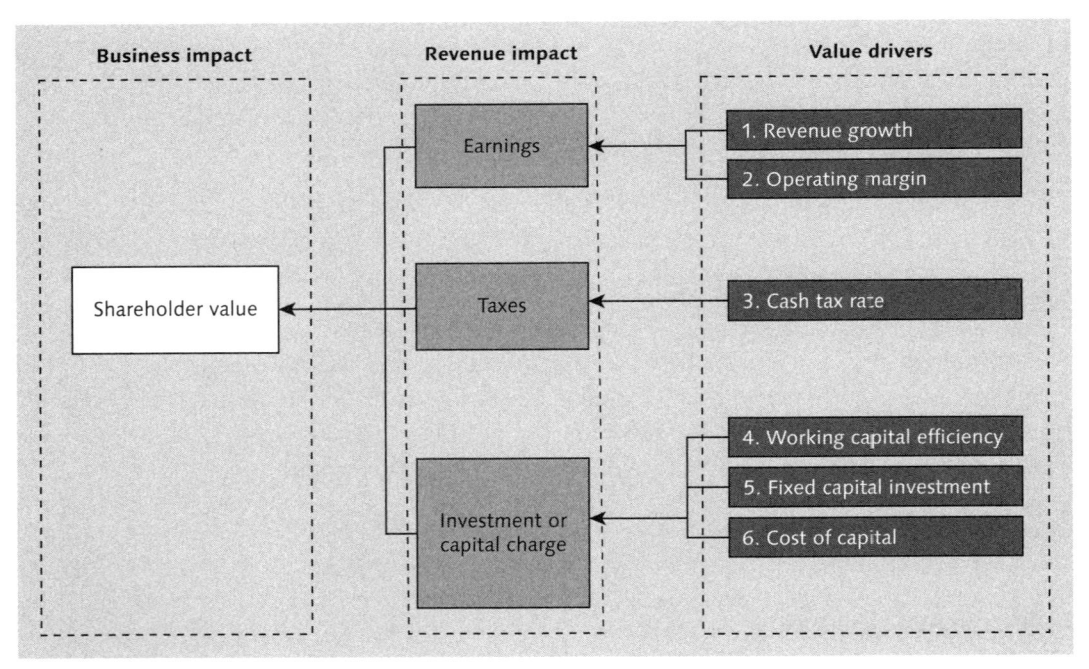

Figure 17.6 Company Goals and High-Level Tracking Measures

Well-constructed dashboards help ensure that your global workforce is working toward established company goals. The dashboard provides up-to-date indications of how well the company is doing, and this information can be made available to all levels of management.

> **Pitfall Alert**
>
> Building an effective dashboard *takes a lot of work*! Understand this going in and plan for it. Executives will be hard to schedule and will oftentimes have their attention elsewhere. Don't get discouraged. This requires patience and commitment to getting the job done. But it can be done.

Constructing the right company dashboard is the first order of business. Guidance as to what measures to use must come from company senior executives. It will be challenging to gather all affected executives in a room and to gain their perspectives. As a fallback position, members of the reporting team may have to schedule working sessions with small groups of executives to work through the dashboard content.

Coming to agreement on the correct mix of measures for each company goal represents the first challenge. However, the second challenge—reaching consensus on the exact parameters for each measure—will prove more difficult yet. Commonly used metrics such as days sales outstanding (DSO) or inventory days on hand (DOH) can have a specific meaning for each company and even for functional organizations within your company.

For example, for DSO, should 30, 45, or 60 days be the metric used? Often customer contracts stipulate terms for payment. If the DSO measurement were set at 30 days and major customers operated under 60-day payment terms, the measure would likely not reflect the expected payment status.

DOH reflects a similar situation. In this case, the measurement decision is about which inventory to count. Which inventory should be included in the measure? Should it include restricted stock and distributor inventory, or should it be limited to inventory that is stored in company warehouses and available to ship?

Once company executives agree on which measures to use and on the nuances of each measure, the reporting team can begin work on the universes needed to populate the dashboard. The reporting team can schedule progress reviews with executives. These can demonstrate the framework of the dashboard and specific measures to be represented.

17 | Data, Reports, EDI, and Security and Internal Controls

Figure 17.7 illustrates a final dashboard product. It contains financial graphics showing company performance over time in both revenues and expenses. Having this type of dashboard as a product of the SAP implementation only adds to its overall value. Executives seek this type of balanced scorecard information, and the implementation project can supply it.

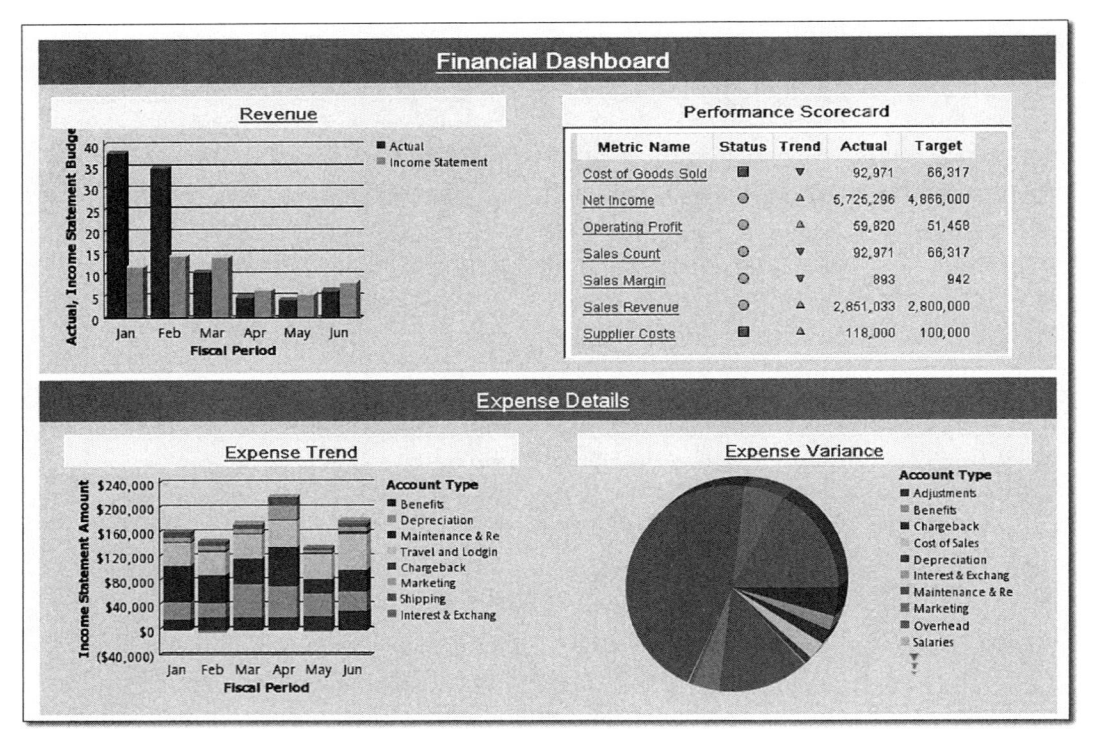

Figure 17.7 Company Financial Dashboard Example

Now that you understand the dynamics of the reporting challenge, let's transition to a more mysterious topic: EDI.

17.3 Electronic Data Interchange

To continue the analogy, if data serves as the lifeblood of the SAP system and reporting as its eyes, then EDI is its nervous system. EDI operates as a messaging system by which your company can communicate with its business partners. SAP is designed to enable and support this messaging process. If your company already has EDI in place or decides to implement it from the bottom up, it will likely form a core effort of the company's SAP implementation project.

Virtually all major companies use EDI; in fact, many executives are surprised at the extent to which trading partner communications within their own company use this mechanism. EDI replaces paper-based partner transactions with automated computer-based transactions, and so offers the advantage of reducing errors associated with paper transactions. By using real-time computer messaging, EDI also dramatically improves transaction speed compared to the use of paper documents.

17.3.1 EDI Structure

At heart, EDI is a standard that lays out a common computer interface between transacting parties. Each transaction has a numeric identifier, such as 810 for an invoice and 820 for a payment order. EDI transactions operate on a two-way basis. Those originating from the selling company to its trading partners are termed *outbound messages*; similarly, those from the trading partner back to the originating company are known as *inbound messages*. Clearly, inbound for one company will be outbound for the associated trading partner.

EDI operations include a full range of partner communications. These consist of standard business-to-business (B2B) transactions such as customer invoices, customer and supplier purchase orders, payment orders from customers, and payments from banks. Transaction sets offer financial, supply chain, and transportation functions that will operate in virtually any industry. In most cases, the information contained in an EDI document will match information found in a comparable paper document. An EDI 810 invoice will contain customer identification information, payment terms, and price, similar to a paper invoice.

Although the format of each transaction set has been established by specifications, trading partners still have considerable leeway in deciding which particular information to communicate and what formats to use. Similar to the mapping process used in data conversion, EDI uses implementation guidelines to specify what information will be transmitted and how it will be used by the trading partners.

Obviously, this can become a time-consuming process if the number of customer, supplier, and bank trading partners is quite large. Negotiating field usage with every possible partner—and in cases where each has somewhat differing requirements—is one of the challenges of installing EDI. Many companies take the position that they will negotiate individual implementation guidelines only with very large-scale trading partners. Smaller-scale trading partners are left to use the standard implementation guideline of the larger partner. Due to contractual requirements to utilize EDI, these smaller-scale trading partners must accommodate the larger partner's standard as a cost of doing business.

Many companies may have previously implemented EDI in a piecemeal fashion. Thus, even if all regions use EDI, each region may have structured its messaging operations in differing ways. If the implementing company has not yet adopted a global approach to EDI, the SAP implementation may serve as a useful catalyst for it to do so.

> **Pitfall Alert**
>
> Expect to find considerable diversity in your company EDI processes. In some regions, especially your home region, many customers will have individual implementation guides. In practice, this means that each customer must be addressed and handled individually. Just shrug your shoulders and get it done. Otherwise, sales orders will not post properly at go-live. You don't want questions sent your way as to why you allowed this to happen.

If EDI is included under these circumstances, the project team will have to pay considerable attention to underlying business processes. These will include any agreements with trading partners that may affect messaging structure, since the SAP design may not support them. They will also include standardization of EDI-related business processes from region to region, which can take considerable effort to achieve.

Two primary EDI standards guide how this process is implemented. The United States standard, ANSI X12, is commonly used in North America, while the United Nations standard, EDIFACT, is more common in Europe, Latin America, and Asia. These standards dictate how information will be structured and will include character sets, formats, and data acceptable to transmit. Implementation guides will stipulate which standard will apply in communications between trading partners.

Figure 17.8 shows how building a company EDI system requires extensive setup. Looking at the diagram from an inbound company perspective (reading from right to left), the EDI system will handle transactions received from customers, distributors, vendors, and financial institutions. From an outbound perspective (reading from left to right), the EDI system would distribute your company's messages to customers, distributors, vendors, and financial institutions. This would represent a robust use of EDI and would require implementation guides capable of structuring all transactions.

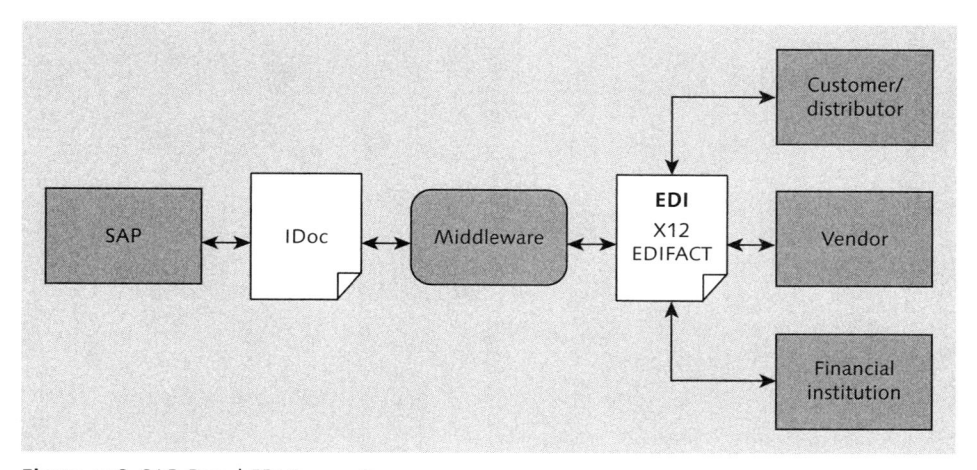

Figure 17.8 SAP-Based EDI Transactions

Let's walk through the diagram. Middleware provides the mapping software that accepts the inbound message (generally sent in AS2 or FTP formats) and prepares it to be accepted by the SAP system. Among other things, the middleware solution verifies the sending trading partner is authorized and meets applicable EDI standards. Most importantly, it utilizes the implementation guide to map the data to be received by the company SAP system.

The final step is the actual transfer mechanism to SAP. Called an *intermediate document*, or IDoc, these objects carry the data from the middleware system directly into SAP. The middleware system triggers the IDoc, and the information is then posted into SAP, where the final processing occurs.

In some cases, companies choose to use middlemen or value-added networks (VANs) to handle connections with trading partners. This has the advantage of placing responsibility for final trading partner mapping in the hands of the VAN.

It will receive outbound messages and translate them to the formats used by trading partners. It will also receive outbound messages from trading partners and translate them for use by the implementing company. Figure 17.9 shows the outbound EDI process using files sent to a VAN and further translated to company customers.

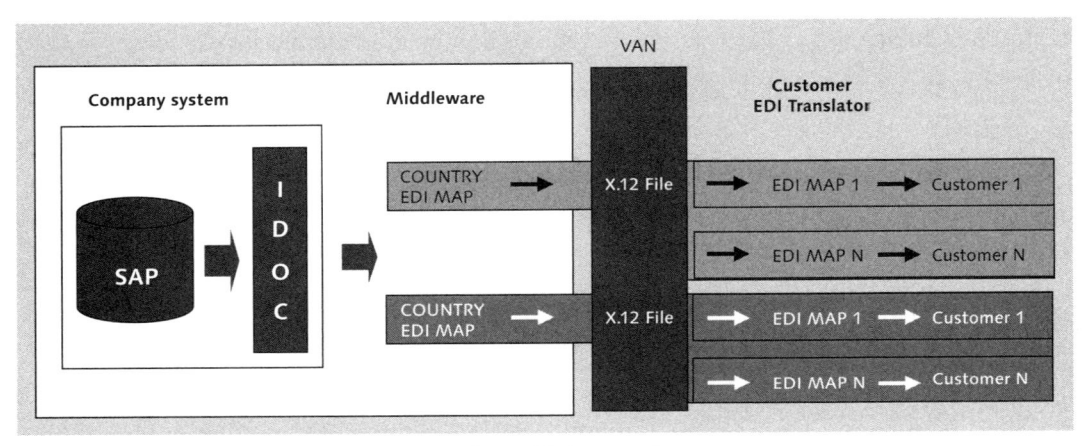

Figure 17.9 EDI Process using a Value-Added Network

17.3.2 EDI Project Deliverables

No matter what the final arrangement, if EDI is placed within the scope of the SAP implementation project, it will require considerable effort to deliver this functionality on schedule. There are many steps to be completed, and they depend on external organizations—such as trading partners and VANs—to meet the timeline. The amount of effort you will need depends greatly on the number of trading partners involved, the quantity of different EDI transactions included, and the extent of custom mapping required for individual trading partners.

Custom mapping requirements are normally the biggest resource drain on the EDI team. Custom mapping requires that the EDI team make contact with each applicable trading partner. Any additional requested features will mean some negotiation with those partners. The EDI team must understand what is driving the requirement and identify its impact on project resources. This will always be a trade-off: It's clearly easier to use standard transaction sets, but this might not work for trading partners' business needs.

A number of process steps are involved in putting the EDI solution in place. Most of these steps will entail working directly with external trading partners. Additionally, each trading partner must perform development and testing work on its end. This work verifies that the company trading partner can send reliable inbound messages to the implementing company and receive consistent outbound messages from your company. This introduces a level of complexity to the EDI project. Few other workstreams depend so heavily on external third-party performance for their success.

Figure 17.10 outlines the three-step EDI solution-building process. All three steps depend on close coordination with the comparable trading partner's EDI team. This close dependence should become clear as we discuss each step.

1. Identify trading partner information → 2. Complete internal development activities → 3. Test EDI performance

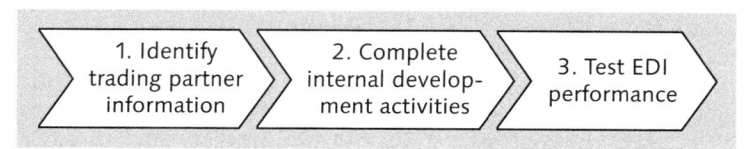

Figure 17.10 EDI Solution-Building Process

Step one focuses on collecting trading partner information and supplying company EDI requirements to these same trading partners. During blueprinting, the project EDI team begins the work of identifying each trading partner that will participate in the EDI solution. This identification must include a listing of each EDI transaction to be used with that partner and also identify both inbound and outbound messages in scope. If some trading partners utilize VANs for EDI processing, those VANs and their EDI methodology should be identified as well. Additionally, for each EDI transaction type used by a trading partner, the team will collect the following:

- Agreed-upon EDI implementation guides for each EDI transaction type
- Identification of EDI standards (X12, EDIFACT, or other standards) used by the trading partner
- Sample data that will be used in each transaction type

Step two involves working with the middleware team and the project application development team. The middleware team conducts analysis on sample data to assure that it works with the middleware application. Also, the middleware team creates all new maps or modifies existing ones and builds communication links with the trading partners. The team also performs unit testing on the results to ensure that they are internally consistent. The application development team will set up special configuration in SAP to support EDI transactions. These include items such as partner profiles and output conditions.

Step three ensures that the designed system works as intended. Unit testing comes first in the progression, and verifies three things:

- That each EDI transaction has been exercised separately to ensure that its format is correct and complete for all applicable business scenarios
- That all EDI data is correct to specification
- That all systems—both in the implementing company and its trading partner—process the files according to the implementation guides

Integration testing takes on a much more ambitious scope. It begins the verification of business process operations. During this testing phase, files are sent to and received by your company and its trading partners. Generally, integration will be structured in cycles to represent sales order, shipping, product delivery, and post goods issue. For example, the test cycles might work as follows:

- Cycle one (clean cycle): Test all EDI transactions per trading partner.
- Cycle two (exception cycle): Test all EDI transactions per trading partner with such exceptions as short-shipments, over-shipments, split orders, and wrong quantity.
- Cycle three (special business scenarios cycle): Test returns, annual physical count, and subcontracted purchase orders.
- Cycle four (combination test): Test all combinations of circumstances from previous cycles.

User acceptance testing for EDI is the final hurdle. Until this point, the testing has centered on EDI transactions as independent activities. In user acceptance testing, EDI processes will be incorporated within overall company business scenarios as part of end-to-end testing. Selected trading partners will be asked to participate in the testing to ensure that processing truly extends from end to end. Successfully demonstrating that the process works as designed will prove that the system operates correctly.

> **Tip**
>
> The PMO should pay close attention to this testing. It goes by fits and starts because it depends greatly on the performance of your trading partners. Understand where issues arise and be ready to assist the EDI team where they may need your help.

This last confirmation is especially important. At go-live for the SAP system, EDI transactions will carry orders from major customers, financial transactions with banks, purchase orders to vendors, and shipping information to distributors. If the EDI system cannot process these transactions as planned, the company will be faced with falling back to manual processes. The damage to your company's reputation among major trading partners would be very difficult to undo.

17.4 Security and Internal Controls

Earlier chapters (Chapter 13 and Chapter 15) discussed identifying needed business controls during blueprinting and security design during the build portion of realization. As the implementation project moves further along to the later stages of realization, these items become intertwined—and the complexities of each become more apparent. To continue with the analogy used throughout this chapter, security and internal controls apply the brakes to the system. The project team must decide when to apply the brake and how much pressure to apply.

The realization deliverables for security and internal controls depends on an intricate dance with four different teams. Table 17.5 identifies the four horizontal workstreams involved and their primary deliverable sets. The security team has the initial set of deliverables with the security design. Recall from the previous chapter that the security team defines the set of user roles needed to operate the system through access controls.

Team	Task	Primary Activity
Security team	Security design	Build roles to facilitate company operations and maintain transaction security.
Change management team	Security role mapping	Deliver role mapping assigning users to security roles and data access.

Table 17.5 Workstream Deliverables for Security and Internal Controls

Team	Task	Primary Activity
Internal controls team	Install internal controls	Develop and implement internal controls to remediate risk and segregation of duties.
Training team	Deliver training based on role assignments	Assure user training designed and delivered according to role assignments.

Table 17.5 Workstream Deliverables for Security and Internal Controls (Cont.)

Figure 17.11 shows the steps and timeline for security design throughout realization. The first three components of the timeline are central here. Either your company will have assigned jobs to employees on the basis of clear roles, or role sets will have been created during security design. Using the principle of providing transaction access only where required, the security team and functional team leads assign transactions to roles. At approximately the same time, any restrictions in the operations of these roles are identified and constructed.

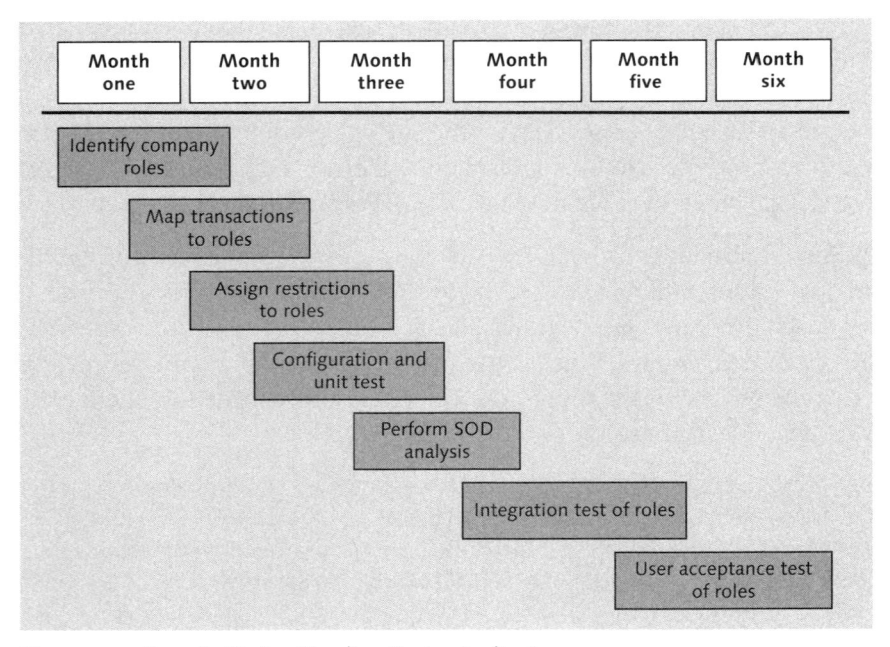

Figure 17.11 Security Design Timeline During Realization

Let's discuss the first item in the timeline.

17.4.1 Internal Controls Analysis

The internal controls team will have already delivered the controls requirements outlined in the *process controls definitions* (PCDs). This effort will now include segregation of duties (SOD) analysis. The internal controls team begins its analysis with the security design discussed above and assesses the combination of roles and associated transactions for potential conflicts. SOD analysis targets fraud prevention. With large-scale systems such as SAP, fraud prevention identifies roles that enable a single person to initiate or approve related transactions. It would also include recording and reporting related transactions, especially those affecting company assets. Any potential SOD violation would be reported to the security team for remediation action.

The internal controls team assesses all identified SOD violations using a risk analysis tool. Each violation would be placed in one of four categories, as described in Table 17.6.

Category	Description
Critical	There are enough functions available to an individual user to complete a process without the use of collusion, resulting in an increased likelihood of financial misrepresentation and/or fraudulent activity which may result in high personal gain.
	Let's look at examples of what a single individual can do to process independent transactions without review:
	▸ Ex. 1: Create vendor, process purchase order, and receive goods
	▸ Ex. 2: Process accounts payable payment and perform bank reconciliation
	Critical risks are unacceptable and cannot be mitigated with the use of a compensating control.
High	High risks are similar to critical risks but lack the ability to perform all components of the process/transaction.
	▸ Ex. 1: Process purchase order and receive goods
	▸ Ex. 2: Open/close general ledger posting periods and post journal entries
	High risks are still deemed unacceptable, however. If violations are identified, they must be removed or mitigated by the use of compensating controls.

Table 17.6 SOD Risk Categories

Category	Description
Medium	Activities may exist in the same process but are far enough removed that the likelihood of financial misstatement and/or fraud is minimal. ▶ Ex. 1: Release credit holds on sales orders and apply cash ▶ Ex. 2: Process inventory adjustments and post journal entries Medium risks are undesirable but should be reviewed for excessive access and removed or mitigated by the use of compensating controls.
Low	There exists a large separation in the business process for the functions being performed and there are multiple areas where collusion would be necessary to perpetrate fraud. The resulting fraud is not easily achieved and there exists no potential for personal gain. ▶ Ex. 1: Maintain fixed assets and received goods ▶ Ex. 2: Approve purchase order and process inventory adjustments Low risks may compromise the effectiveness and efficiency of the business, which may affect performance and return on investment.

Table 17.6 SOD Risk Categories (Cont.)

Clearly, any risk falling in the critical and high categories must be remediated. The controls team would focus especially on areas with a history of issues, activities with high material impact, and those that are operationally or administratively important to the company.

Wherever a single individual has the opportunity to create fraud undetected, this role must be changed. Where two or three individuals have the same opportunity to operate in collusion but likely remain undetected, this must be remediated as well. One option available to the security team will be to redesign the specific role, which could include limiting the transaction codes assigned to that role or creating a new role with only some of the former transaction codes allocated to this new role.

The example demonstrates some of the challenges that the security team will face. Subdividing roles and allocating transactions in a very fine-grained way greatly increases the number of roles available. This can make the roles so granular that the potential for SOD violations during role mapping is actually increased.

Other alternatives to address the problem are available, however, in the form of preventive or detective controls. Preventive controls work to block the error or fraud activity from taking place on the system. On the other hand, detective controls are primarily after-the-fact activities. They identify any errors or fraud that may have already occurred. Obviously, preventive controls are generally preferred over detective controls.

Either type of control can be automated or manual. Automated controls operate without human intervention. Some automated controls can be achieved via system configuration while others can be based on workflow requirements. Automatic three-way invoicing is an example of an automated control.

Manual controls require some form of human intervention. A system may enable the control, but human action is needed for the control to be exercised. In the case of review of service invoices prior to payment, the owner of the service order must create a query to access the information, perform a review, and approve or reject the invoice for payment. It's clear that automated controls improve efficiency, but they may require complex system coding to create. In many cases, manual controls may prove to be the only option available.

The project team can establish audit trails for sensitive transactions. These audit trails will use the system to track changes to a record, file, or document. They will indicate the initiator of the transaction by SAP UserID, provide timing information about the transaction, and indicate what exactly was changed during the transaction. This would mostly fall in the automated controls category. However, even with automated flagging, a supervisory or other authorized individual would still make the decision as to whether a controls violation took place.

The project team can also require the use of exception reports. In this case, the system would send reports indicating a system exception to supervisors or managers. These reports may require clearance from an authorized manager—so they sometimes may sit, awaiting action, for long periods. To prevent this, they would have to be monitored for aging.

Periodic audits represent more of a manual control activity. Whether performed by the company internal audit function or other assigned individuals, these audits would especially focus on sensitive transactions and any discrepancies noted during the examination. System transaction logs, as well as other manually produced reports, serve as a primary tool in this type of analysis. Table 17.7 provides a more complete listing of the manual and automated control types.

Manual Control Types	Automated Control Types
▸ Policies and procedures ▸ Reconciliation ▸ Authorization controls ▸ SOD ▸ Key performance indicators ▸ Management review ▸ Exception report review ▸ Detailed (data comparison)	▸ Edit and validation checks ▸ Tolerance limits, alerts, warnings, error ▸ Default values ▸ Key calculations ▸ Key reports, monitoring, review

Table 17.7 Business Controls Examples

Assuming that the role design is complete and all identified SOD observations have been remediated, attention now turns to the change management team.

17.4.2 Role Mapping and End-User Training

In most projects, role mapping comes under the responsibility of this group. Role mapping consists of assigning security roles and their associated transactions to individual company users.

As a final step, the change management team will conduct role mapping sessions where SMEs review the array of possible roles. At this session, SMEs decide which roles will be apportioned to individual end users.

Depending on the number of end users and the number of sites involved, this can create a very complex process. Figure 17.12 depicts the relationship between SAP transaction codes required by end users on the right and the various role configurations that might be assigned. For the most part, end users will receive a combination of single and composite roles, as shown on the left.

> **Tip**
>
> Role mapping will continue to experience changes even into final preparation. Expect regional operations to fine-tune their assignments in an attempt to get them right. Build this understanding into your project schedule.

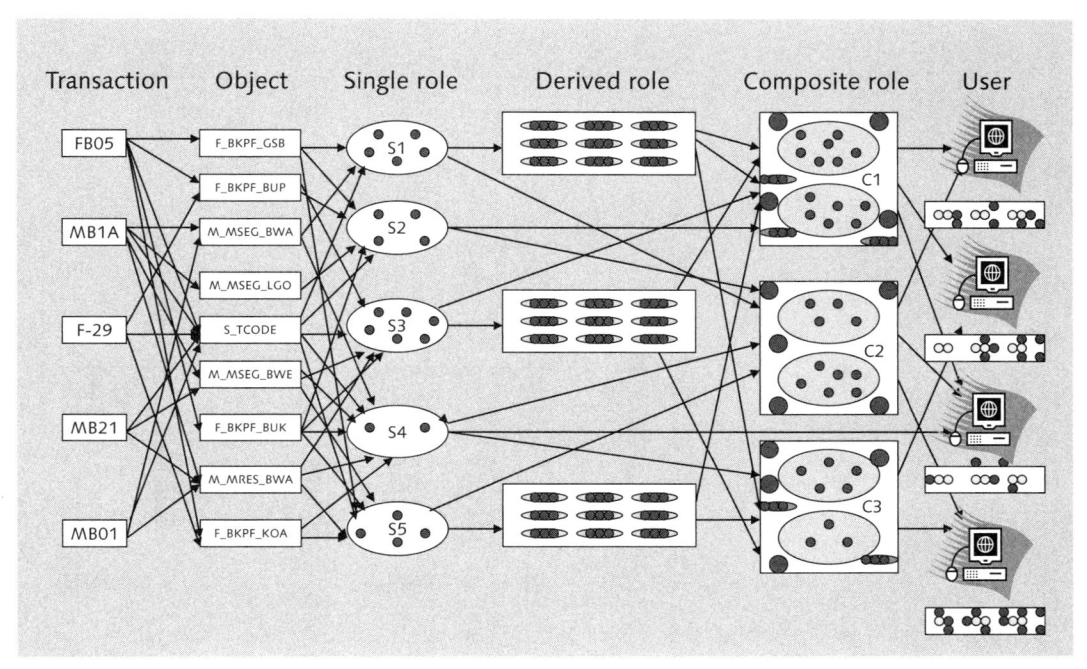

Figure 17.12 Relation of Transactions to Role Allocations

Role mapping often requires several iterations before it can be deemed complete. The objective is twofold: to provide each user with only the access required to perform assigned tasks, but to also ensure that all required access is granted. During role-mapping sessions, the specifics of user tasks are discussed in detail. The job of Person A may be quite similar to the job of Person B, with the exception of a few tasks. The team must decide whether to assign the same roles to both or to make differing role assignments for each person.

Figure 17.13 illustrates the results of role mapping for a buyer in company code 1000 as divided into four tiers. Those aspects of tier three and tier four produce combinations of single roles and composite roles required to perform buyer tasks within that company. When a company has hundreds of roles similar to this, making the right decisions regarding role mapping can become a daunting task.

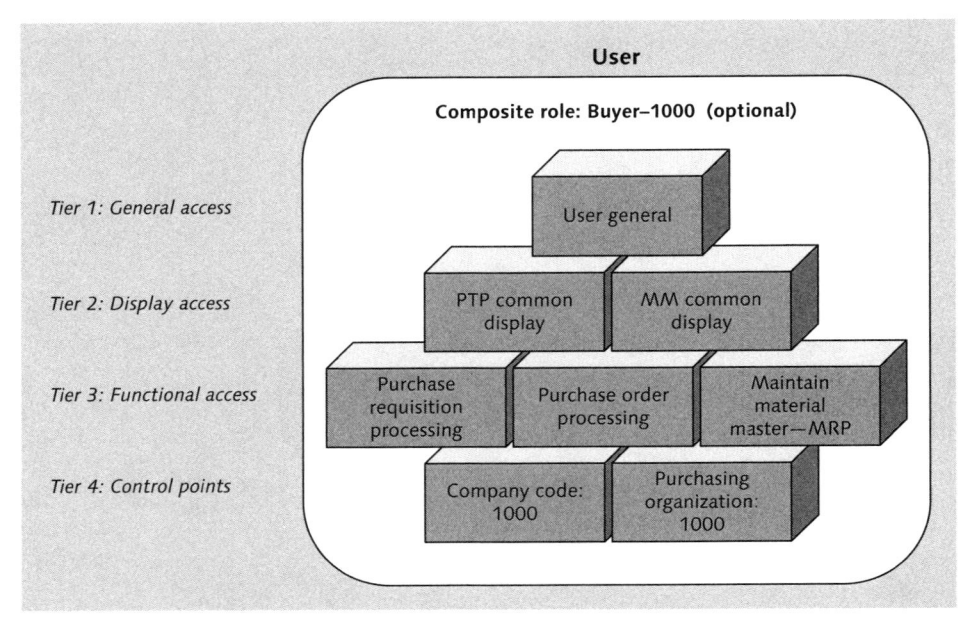

17 | Data, Reports, EDI, and Security and Internal Controls

Figure 17.13 Role Mapping for a Buyer in Procurement

Let's walk through the various tiers shown in the figure:

- **Tier 1: General access**

    General access is provisioned via one single role, made up of tasks common to all users such as printing, inbox, SU53, etc.

- **Tier 2: Display access**

    Display access is provisioned via a set of roles, defined by functional area, that allow display and reporting access intended to complement the functional roles of the users.

- **Tier 3: Functional access**

    Functional access is provisioned via multiple single-task–based roles. This groups together activities that are the lowest common denominator of tasks and permission components to suit the needs of the end users. These groupings usually are SOD-free and part of a sub-process such as invoice processing or material master maintenance.

- **Tier 4: Control points**

    Roles that provide additional control point access or granularity needed by the first three tiers, such as company code, plant, etc.

Once role assignments have been made, the internal controls team must perform another SOD review. Role mapping will produce users with multiple roles allocated to them. These combinations may result in users with SOD issues. Each user with these role conflicts must be analyzed, and a mitigation strategy decided upon, prior to go-live. In some cases, the SOD conflict may be left in place. Reporting can then be used to track any possible fraud or error-producing situations.

At the end of the day, end users will participate in training based on their role assignments. Class scheduling uses role mapping as the mechanism to build class rosters. Figure 17.14 shows the relationship between role design, role mapping, and course curriculum. If these are not closely linked, end users might be assigned to training, which is for the most part not needed, or they could be assigned to numerous courses to cover the several components of their role.

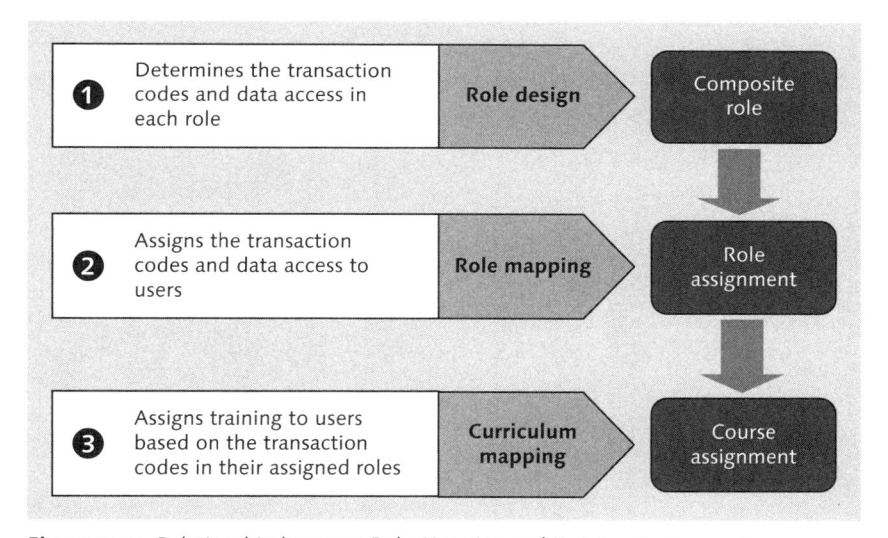

Figure 17.14 Relationship between Role Mapping and Training Assignments

The training team will be responsible for designing a curriculum that is consistent with the role design and to schedule classes consistent with user role mapping.

This should be enough information to ward off the effects of the four horsemen. Let's turn now to the hardware and application software needed for your SAP implementation.

System build activities are taking place during project preparation, yet they don't really get into full swing until realization. There, the main components of the SAP system environment are assembled and tested.

18 Building System Environments

The entire systems build and maintenance process is usually well hidden behind the scenes—that is, until things go wrong.

Even many project team members remain unaware of the critical role that these systems build activities play in implementation success. After all, those responsible for systems build and operation (the Basis team) are often housed in different locations than the rest of the project team and may be unknown to many team members. Additionally, for many projects, both sponsors and team members find the systems nomenclature so confusing that they shrug their shoulders and cease to pay attention to any of it.

But this decision, even if it is an unconscious one, places project team members at a real disadvantage. Being on a first-name basis with the system nomenclature brings an important source of clarity. A great deal of discussion in project status meetings is taken up with system code words and various build plans. Without some basic knowledge of the underlying meaning, all understanding will be lost.

Further, familiarity with this nomenclature helps project team members to understand how the system is structured and how the various pieces fit together. As will soon become evident, systems build is a complex and carefully orchestrated process. It ensures that all parts of the system are ready when needed, and that they are prepared to perform their functions.

The chapter focuses on bringing clarity to the systems build process. It begins with a (hopefully painless) discussion of SAP system nomenclature and the reasons behind its usage. It illustrates the components of an SAP system landscape and outlines the hierarchy of elements in that landscape. By chapter's end, much of the mystery surrounding systems build and operation should have disappeared.

Chapter 5 introduced the initial procurement activities needed to set hardware and software acquisition in motion. As we saw in that chapter, the number of servers needed to operate an SAP system depends on variables such as the number of SAP applications included, the geographical scope of the project, the number of end users to be supported, and response times required for the system. For a large-scale global implementation, the number of servers will likely be very large.

Servers represent the essential hardware element. Your SAP landscape will likely contain large numbers of servers under the Basis team. For the project team, the most important topic concerns how the SAP system is built to address business process operations. Our chapter includes the following topics:

- **Structure of the SAP landscape**
  We'll identify the major features of an SAP landscape. This includes parts ranging from applications to environments. We'll also touch on system identifiers and break the codes used to designate each.

- **Operating an environment and client arrangement**
  Here we'll cover the more detailed parts of the landscape: environments and clients. This will give you very useful information to understand how environments and clients are arranged to support project activities.

- **Conducting infrastructure build and test**
  Your project will utilize numerous servers to construct the SAP environment. This section describes the necessary delivery schedule to ensure that all hardware elements arrive on time. It also outlines the preliminary verification steps needed to ensure that the hardware functions as required.

- **Handling system performance and failover testing**
  We'll review performance testing that ensures your system can support required user volumes, and we will outline failover testing as well. This test confirms that your system can switch over to and operate on backup servers in the case of serious outage.

Let's get started on our journey through the SAP system landscape.

18.1   The SAP Landscape

Table 18.1 outlines the key terms that project team members will soon encounter in discussing how the overall SAP system will be organized.

Key Systems Term	Definition
Landscape	A landscape is a set of environments of a given application that are logically linked with one another. The logical connection allows objects to be created or changed in one instance (typically DEV), promoted and tested in another instance (typically QAS), and, after verification and approval, promoted to the production (PRD) instance.
Application	Applications are usually specific products used to accomplish a business purpose (e.g., SAP ERP, SAP BusinessObjects BI, or SAP Supplier Relationship Management).
Environment	An environment is a collection of applications (such as SAP ERP, SAP SRM, or SAP BusinessObjects BI) that perform a distinct function. Examples of environments would be development, quality assurance, and production.
Client	A client is a container within an SAP environment element built for a specific purpose. It is a self-contained unit with separate master records, data, tables, and transactions.
Instance	An installation of an application. A company may have multiple installations of an application or multiple instances. In the case that the company operates only one installation of an application, this is called a *single instance*.
System identifier (SID)	A system identifier (SID) is a unique three-character identifier for an SAP instance (e.g., QE1).

Table 18.1 Basic Nomenclature and Definitions for SAP Systems Organization

At first, many of the terms, such as landscape, environment, and application, may appear interchangeable. However, they exist in a hierarchical relationship and each element plays a specific role in that relationship.

Let's map this out. In Figure 18.1, landscape is the broadest level. It encompasses the entire SAP system organization.

Immediately below it comes the application level. Applications are the software that provides business functionality such as sales ordering or production planning. Most SAP system implementations consist of several applications. In the example provided, the landscape consists of three applications: SAP ERP, SAP Supplier Relationship Management (SRM), and SAP Supply Chain Management (SCM). The typical SAP system implementation includes many more applications, but to facilitate ease of understanding, only three are depicted here.

> **Trail Marker**
>
> Until recently, the key functionality in an SAP system was delivered by the SAP Enterprise Core Component (ECC). It contained the operating modules such as Sales and Distribution (SD) and Financial Accounting and Controlling (FI-CO). Now SAP has dropped the term ECC in favor of SAP ERP. This makes considerable sense and we have adopted this usage throughout the book.

Each application has at least one environment. Most often, it will have multiple environments. Each environment plays a distinct role in assuring that the application is properly built and ready for operation. Figure 18.1 shows three environments for each of the applications implemented within the landscape: Here, development (DEV), quality assurance (QAS), and production (PRD) work together to optimize the build process. More will be said about these environments shortly.

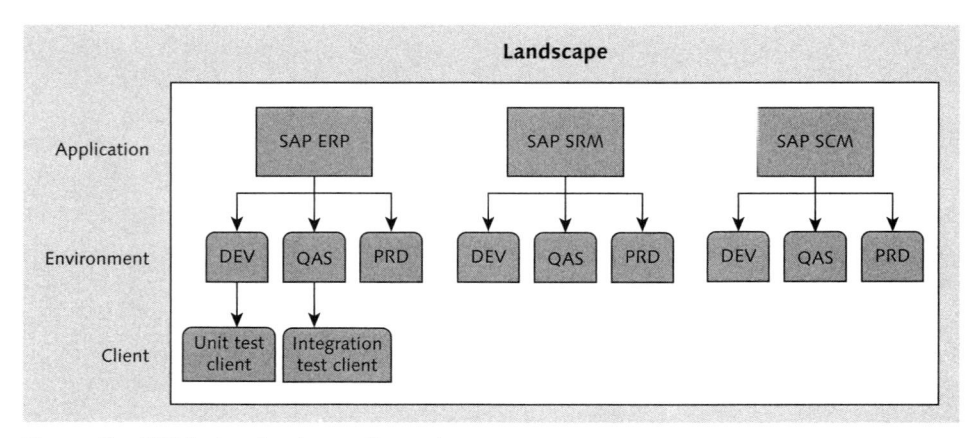

Figure 18.1 SAP System Landscape Elements

SAP ERP contains two clients. These are self-contained units dedicated to a specific purpose and restricted from other usages. In this example, the development environment in SAP ERP has a client assigned for unit testing. All unit testing to verify that custom objects are performing properly is carried out in this client. In similar fashion, the quality assurance environment in SAP ERP has a client assigned for integration testing. All integration testing activities are conducted in this client.

Table 18.1 makes reference to two additional terms: instance and system identifier. According to the definition, an instance denotes an application installation. When an implementing company decides to have its SAP installations support specific geographies or business functions, there may be multiple instances of the same application. Thus, in this scenario, SAP ERP or SAP SCM can have multiple instances.

Adopting a multiple instance strategy can result in different sets of master data and reporting that cannot easily be reconciled. Most recently, implementing companies have elected to consolidate their multiple instances into single instances. This option supports standardized business processes across the entire company and is known as a *single instance strategy*.

Systems identifiers (SIDs) apply mutually exclusive three-character reference designations for each of the environments and their instances. The example provided in Figure 18.1 would require a SID for each of the three application environments. In the case of multiple instances of the same application, each environment would operate under its own SID. This convention assures that each environment has its own unique reference name.

Table 18.2 illustrates the use of systems identifiers for an SAP application landscape. Note the naming conventions where all development environments have a first character of "D," all quality assurance environments a first character of "Q," and all production environments a first character of "P." The second character identifies the application referenced with "E" used for ERP, and so on. In some cases, the application reference point is a straightforward correspondence between the application name and the one-letter designation. However, as can be seen from SAP Global Trade System and SAP Solution Manager, this does not apply in all cases. The numerical designation "1" indicates that this is the first instance of the application.

Let's look at an example. In the case where an implementing company had installed two instances of SAP ERP, the second instance of the production environment would have the identifier of PE2. This naming convention would continue for all remaining environments in the second instance.

> **Tip**
> The shift in usage between system identifiers and environment abbreviations is one of those sources of confusion in project team operations. In most cases, the environment abbreviation will be used.

Application and Environment	Development	Quality Assurance	Production
SAP ERP	DE1	QE1	PE1
SAP BusinessObjects BI	DB1	QB1	PB1
SAP Supplier Relationship Management (SRM)	DR1	QR1	PR1
SAP Supply Chain Management (SCM)	DC1	QC1	PC1
SAP Global Trade System (GTS)	DW1	QW1	PW1
SAP Global Risk and Compliance (GRC)	DG1	QG1	PG1
SAP Solution Manager	***	QM1	PM1
SAP NetWeaver Developer Studio	DZ1	***	***

Table 18.2 System Identifiers for an SAP Landscape

Now that we've outlined the elements of the SAP landscape, let's move on to visit the details of system environments and clients.

18.2 Environment and Client Structure

For the sake of simplicity, Figure 18.1 displayed three environments per application. In some cases, an SAP implementation will follow this three-environment path. However, many times an application will require more than three environments. This is especially true with the core SAP ERP application.

> **Tip**
>
> Arrange a time to educate your entire project team on the SAP landscape and environment structure. Maybe not all the pieces and parts will stick, but the sessions will serve to introduce the concepts. Later, your PMO can create posters showing the landscape and environment. Having a ready reference on a nearby wall does wonders to improve recall.

Figure 18.2 illustrates the more realistic and complex scenario. In this example there are six environments, with three of them new to our discussion. The SBX environment denotes a sandbox that the project team will use, especially in the early stages of the project, for prototyping and demonstration. Note that it operates unconnected to the remainder of the environment set. A second quality assurance environment (QA2) and a training environment (TRN) have been added.

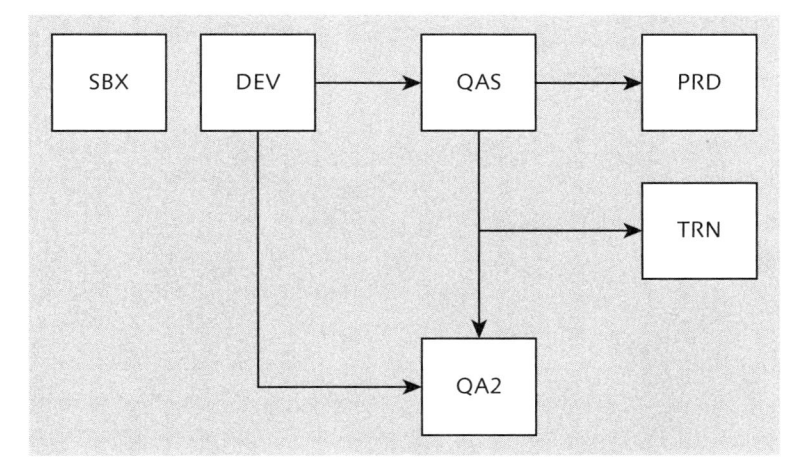

Figure 18.2 Realistic Environment Setup for SAP ERP Application

Table 18.3 gives the details and purposes for each of the six environments shown in Figure 18.2. The degree of interconnectedness among the environments depends on the function they perform. The sandbox operates as a standalone system. Because of the prototyping and demonstration function it performs, it will not have the same degree of control applied to it as with the remaining environments. Nor will changes in other environments necessarily make their way to the SBX environment.

Environment	Function
Sandbox (SBX)	This is used by the project team or sustainment team after go-live. Teams will use the environment to demonstrate or learn about product features. It also serves prototyping uses for new applications, upgrades, or for fixes to the operating system, application, or database.
Development (DEV)	This environment hosts project team activities such as initial data loads, custom object development, and configuration to meet blueprinting requirements. It will be the source system with version history for all configuration and custom development activities.
Quality assurance (QAS)	This is the environment used for integration and user acceptance testing. It receives via transport any data, configuration, and custom objects needed to support that testing. It is used primarily by testing team members and end users assigned to user acceptance testing. After the system is live, the quality assurance environment receives periodic updates from the production system to keep the two in synchronization.
Quality assurance (QA2)	In the case of a multi-wave deployment, a second quality assurance environment is often built. This second QA system incorporates configuration changes and custom object additions specific to subsequent waves.
Training (TRN)	This environment hosts activities supporting end-user training activities for the company. The training environment houses configuration, tables, and data required to demonstrate system operations.
Production (PRD)	This is the go-live system for end users. It houses all configuration, data, and custom objects required for end-user operation. Prior to go-live, these elements are moved through a transport process from the development and through the quality assurance system until arriving in the production system. After go-live, any updates to the environment go through this transport process as well.

Table 18.3 Common SAP Environments

Every environment, other than the SBX, is connected to the others in some way. The DEV environment serves as the foundation for all remaining environments. It contains the base SAP installation software and all configuration, data, and custom objects that create the eventual production environment.

Once verified through unit testing, these elements, such as data and configuration, are passed on to the QAS environment. At the conclusion of all integration and user acceptance testing, the PRD environment becomes active and receives configuration, data, and custom objects transported from QAS or QA2. The TRN environment will be constructed from the quality assurance environment. This ensures use of the most recent data loads and verified configuration.

Although environment identifiers are standardized, the same cannot be said for client identifiers. The identifier system for clients is usually defined by the systems integrator, as is the number of clients to be used. Clients are identified by a three-number sequence, of which the first number identifies the environment in which the client is housed.

As shown in Figure 18.3, the hypothetical project development environment contains six clients. With the exception of the SAP reference client, all other clients receive a "2XX" identifier. Each of these clients plays a unique role.

Client 000 is the SAP reference client. It contains the base SAP application software prior to any configuration or other addition to the system—a vanilla SAP scenario. This 000 client lays the foundation for the original versions of client 200 and client 210. Whereas client 210 will be used to build the master units of configurations and custom objects, client 200 will serve as the unit test bed. It provides a test location for all configurations and custom objects built in client 210. The arrow moving from client 210 to client 200 illustrates this relationship.

Once client 210 is complete, it is used as the foundation for clients 230, 240, and 235. Client 230 will be used for the sequence of initial data loads, while client 235 performs verification tests on the loaded data. Client 240 will—for many purposes—supersede the sandbox environment, as the actual configuration and custom objects required for company business processes will now be in place in this client.

As Figure 18.4 shows, the QAS environment has a much less complex client structure. It contains only two clients. Again, the base SAP reference client has been loaded to QAS. All QAS clients, with the exception of the SAP reference client, receive a "5XX" designator. In addition to the SAP reference client, QAS is built by receiving and incorporating transports from the development unit test client (DEV 200). It will have the most recent, verified configurations and custom objects. With these transports in place, QAS is then used for the integration test and user acceptance test.

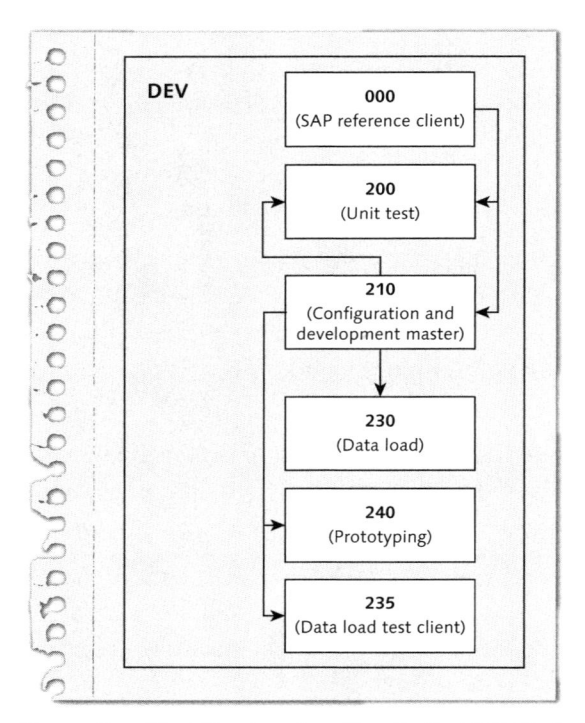

Figure 18.3 Client Structure for a Hypothetical DEV Environment

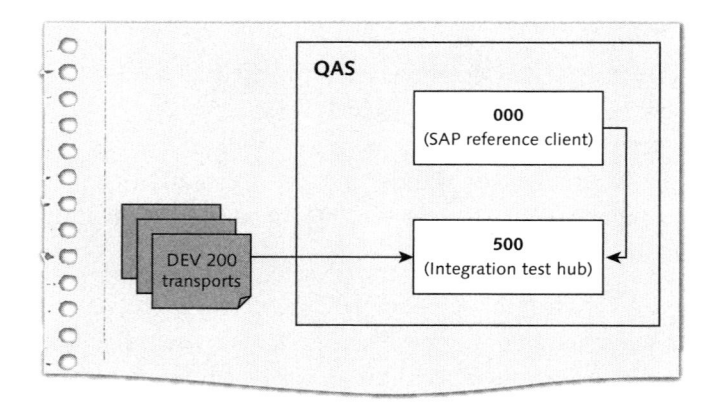

Figure 18.4 Client Structure for a Hypothetical QAS Environment

If a second quality assurance environment is required, it will generally have a more complex client structure. Figure 18.5 illustrates how this might work. Unlike the QAS environment, QA2 will not require an SAP reference client. However, it will receive transports from the client 200 of the development environment. These transports will be posted to the integration test hub similar to QAS. The remaining three clients are used to create an operational boundary between your company's now-live production system.

Remember that part of your company is now live on SAP while other parts of the company continue to operate on legacy systems and participate in their wave of the deployment. The two QA2 data clients will now operate the data conversion processes for the subsequent waves. Client 530 supports data load and verification, while client 540 hosts the data that will be migrated to the production system when remaining waves go live. Client 510 functions as the user acceptance test hub in support of testing in the remaining deployment waves.

The QA2 system is only used in multi-wave implementations. Once all parts of the company have deployed to the SAP system, the QA2 system is no longer needed. Those system resources can then be repurposed and applied to other needs.

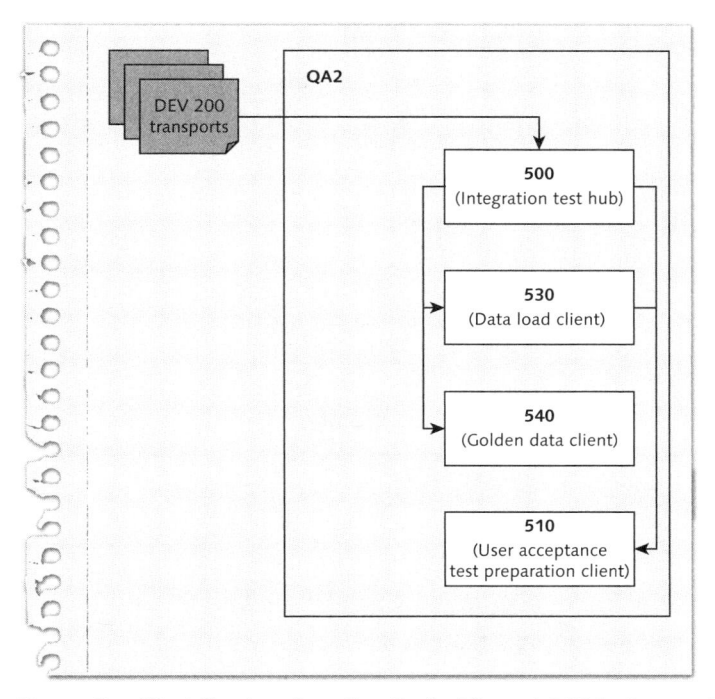

Figure 18.5 Client Structure for a Hypothetical Second QAS Environment

18 | Building System Environments

The TRN environment is applied to end-user course instruction. Given the large volume of courses administered and end users trained, the training environment may require a number of clients. Figure 18.6 depicts the training environment as being built from the QAS system. Since the QAS environment contains the most current configuration, data, and custom objects, it offers the most reasonable version of how the production system will eventually appear.

Once the client 500 is built, it is used to prepare client 510. The training team will then use client 510 to perform class preparation. The remaining clients (520, 530, 540, and 550) will be copies of client 510 and are assigned to support specific classes. Any data needed during the training classes is also loaded to the clients. This environment will be actively used during the latter parts of the realization phase and during final preparation when user training is conducted.

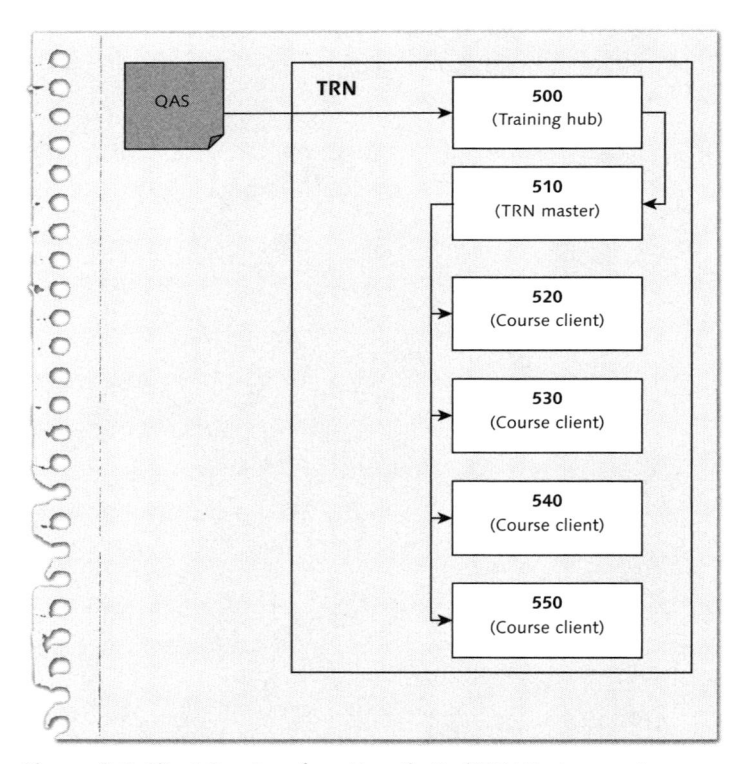

Figure 18.6 Client Structure for a Hypothetical TRN Environment

The final and arguably most important environment is production. When end users log on to the SAP system to conduct company business, they will work in the production environment.

There will be only a single PRD environment. In a multi-wave implementation, when some portions are live on the SAP system, they transact in the production environment. As other portions of the company go live in their own deployment waves, they will be added to this same production system.

The production environment houses company data and is the location for its business process performance. In many ways, the careful orchestration of environments is designed to protect the integrity of the production environment. During final preparation, movement or "transport" of configuration, data, and custom objects is carefully controlled. That process is tightly regulated in order to ensure that only verified and validated transports make it into the production environment. That way, the production environment houses only the configuration, custom objects, and data approved for use.

Once the system is "live" and the production system can be accessed by end users, great effort is made to quarantine later waves' data, configuration, and custom objects from the PRD environment. That second quality assurance environment (QA2) is an example of creating an environment to maintain this boundary.

The PRD environment holds a minimum number of clients. In our example, there is the standard SAP reference client used in basic environment builds, along with two others. The first client contains the production hub in which almost all company business process operations are conducted. For companies implementing portal-based applications, such as SAP SRM Supplier Self-Service (SUS), a separate production client is built to house them.

The promote-to-production process utilizes previously loaded configuration, custom objects, and data transported from the development environment to the quality assurance environment. These materials are transported into the newly built production environment immediately prior to go-live and system release. The project team uses the final hours before release of the production environment to verify that all data, configuration, and custom objects have been correctly assigned. Only when this final verification is accomplished is the production environment released for use and SAP UserIDs distributed.

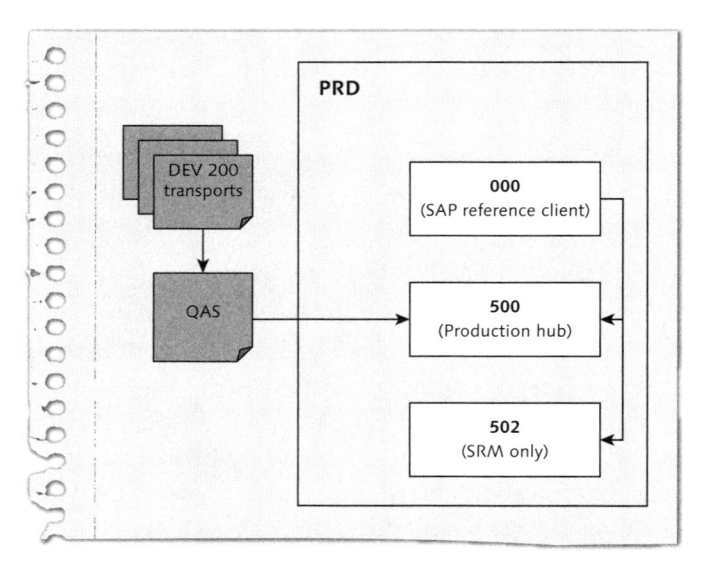

Figure 18.7 Client Structure for a Hypothetical PRD Environment

After go-live, and with the production environment now in place, the administration of the system becomes much more rigorous. This enhanced rigor begins with hypercare. Any modifications to any part of the production system are subject to change control. Many companies adopt formal change control systems to document completion of all required steps. Change control processes introduce overwhelming, thoroughgoing concern with ensuring that only correctly documented and tested changes ever reach the PRD environment.

> **Pitfall Alert**
>
> Anticipate the culture shock that introducing change control will produce. Understand also that the shock applies across all parts of your team, from your company team to systems integrators as well. Training all participants on the workings of the process will help greatly. Even more likely to gain everyone's attention are examples of unauthorized transports that made their way into the production environment and the damage they caused.

Figure 18.8 illustrates the components of this change control process. Generally, each change control work item must reference an incident number. The incident or problem becomes the rationale for the work to be performed; all subsequent activity ties to its resolution. When the solution to an incident is found, the team first assesses it in the development environment and determines its capability to resolve the problem. The project team or the sustainment team—depending on whether final deployment has taken place—then conducts the integration test to ensure that the solution performs as expected. If this step is successfully completed, the team will forward the proposed solution to an experienced end user for user acceptance testing. Once all required testing and documentation is in place, the solution is then verified as satisfactory and transported to PRD for widespread use.

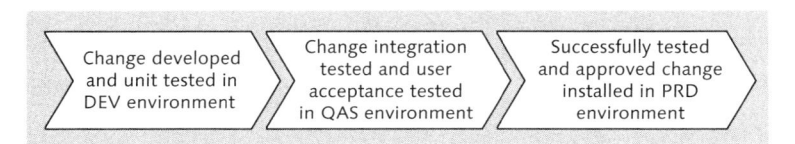

```
Change developed      Change integration       Successfully tested
and unit tested in    tested and user          and approved change
DEV environment       acceptance tested        installed in PRD
                      in QAS environment       environment
```

Figure 18.8 Change Control Process for Production SAP System

For many project teams, this shift to change control comes as a definite shock. Prior to go-live, the controls placed on transports and system changes are much less rigorous. They demand much less in the way of documentation and traceability than that required after the production environment is in place. When suddenly faced with the procedural differences during hypercare, the pace of problem resolution often slows quite substantially and affects team efficiency. Each transport request must generally be approved by a team lead and handled by a change owner assigned to the team. All changes targeted to move into the PRD environment must be reviewed and approved by a change control board prior to the transport taking place.

Nevertheless, change control processes are important to protect system integrity. They may seem like overhead to many on the project team, but rigorous change control processes will provide one of the foundations for effective sustainment.

18.3 Infrastructure Build and Test

Whether the infrastructure to operate the SAP system is operated by the implementing company, the systems integrator, or another third party, it requires careful planning for on-time delivery and subsequent effective performance. Figure 18.9 depicts a high-level to-do list showing major infrastructure deliverables by the phase in which they occur.

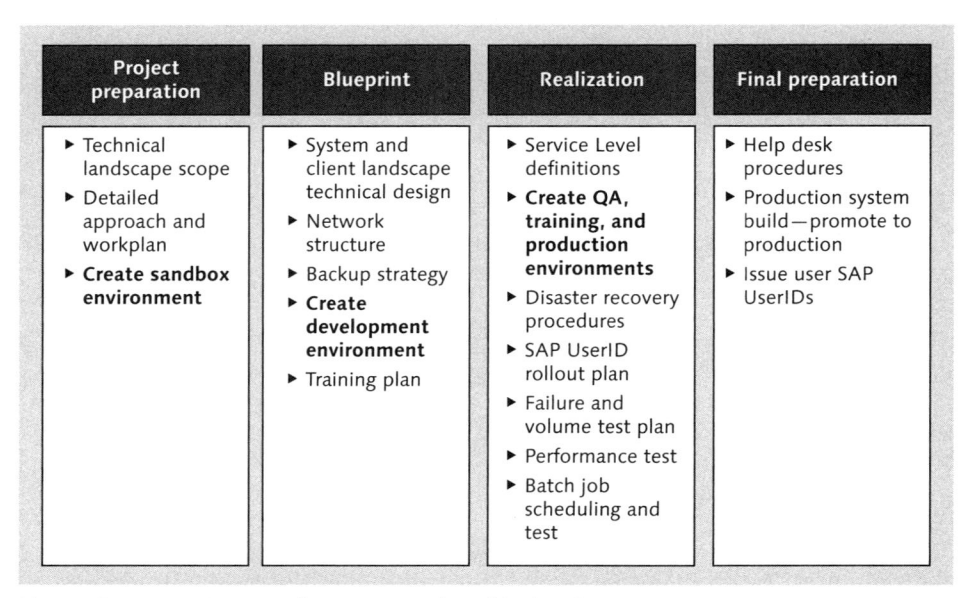

Project preparation	Blueprint	Realization	Final preparation
▸ Technical landscape scope ▸ Detailed approach and workplan ▸ **Create sandbox environment**	▸ System and client landscape technical design ▸ Network structure ▸ Backup strategy ▸ **Create development environment** ▸ Training plan	▸ Service Level definitions ▸ **Create QA, training, and production environments** ▸ Disaster recovery procedures ▸ SAP UserID rollout plan ▸ Failure and volume test plan ▸ Performance test ▸ Batch job scheduling and test	▸ Help desk procedures ▸ Production system build—promote to production ▸ Issue user SAP UserIDs

Figure 18.9 Major Project Infrastructure Deliverables by Phase

The environment creation deliverables have been emphasized to indicate how early in the project these infrastructure activities take place. For example, the sandbox environment will have been procured and likely received even before the project systems integrator was brought on board. Although it may appear that the servers and other infrastructure required to create an environment are simply "plug and play," that is not the case. Far more is involved than merely installing the needed hardware in a data center and beginning operations.

> **Tip**
>
> Remember to keep a very close eye on the server delivery schedule. If your sandbox environment is not in place during project preparation, it cannot support early prototyping activities in blueprinting. If your development environment has not arrived during blueprinting, it cannot support vital configuration and custom object development activities during the early stages of realization. If your quality assurance environment has not landed prior to test initiation, it cannot support integration test and user acceptance test. The list goes on.

Further, your company will likely use more than one data center. Each center can have its own set of operating procedures, training levels, and operator proficiencies. The project team must ensure that common standards are set for data centers and that each data center adheres to these standards.

Many implementing companies require an *installation qualification* (IQ) document to support the build process. The IQ documents the requirements for each infrastructure component and any items that are required in order to make it functional. Generally, the IQ is executed for each server designated to operate in the SAP landscape. The IQ is intended to verify that each server meets the requirements of the technical design specification. It is performed in much the same way as system testing during realization, and it uses test cases as the primary tool. This process assures that the components comprising an environment are built correctly and will work as planned.

These IQ components can include the following:

- Hardware installation script
- Operating system installation script
- Tools installation script
- Application software installation scripts
- Infrastructure environmental requirements qualification
- Infrastructure power supply qualification

For verification purposes, it is important to fully document all tests executed as part of the installation qualification. Most often, a data center technician performs the tests and is identified as the *test executor*. This technician works under the direction of the service manager who has responsibility for the entire IQ process. Test execution assignments are noted on an assignment log prepared and maintained by the service manager.

Test cases, which are combinations of test scripts, are conducted by the test executor. Records of the expected results to be achieved and actual results obtained are recorded and incorporated as part of the test record. To be consistent with good testing protocol, the test executor will make screen shots of the actual results wherever possible. Where any discrepancies are observed between expected and actual results, the test script and the test case are marked as failed.

When all cases have been passed, the service manager prepares an installation qualification report. It verifies the results achieved during IQ testing and identifies the specific components as ready for use.

Completing this installation qualification process for all servers used in the SAP system provides two advantages for the implementing company. First of all, it mandates a thorough review and assessment of the components prior to their use. This review establishes a baseline that shows that all needed installations were in place before the project team performed any operations. Second, the documentation generated during the IQ process can prove quite helpful in case of later issues with any component. The test results may establish the source of any problems, and for this reason are often the first points of reference in the event of a component failure.

18.4 Performance and Failover Testing

Two further safety checks are conducted during the final preparation phase. Performing these checks requires that the production environment has been built and is ready to operate. The first safety check, *performance testing*, verifies that the system will be able to handle the loads required of it. The second, *failover testing*, ensures that the system can continue to operate in the event of a catastrophic event affecting the main data center operations.

Table 18.4 supplies the definition for the terms associated with performance and failover testing. Of the two, performance testing is the most essential activity for the project team. It aims to demonstrate that system users will receive the necessary response times for their transactions and that the system is capable of handling projected transaction volumes. This testing utilizes sophisticated system tools that must be specially scripted in order to supply easily interpretable results.

Key Infrastructure Term	Definition
Failover testing	This includes processes and procedures required to shift operations from the primary data center to a secondary or backup data center.
Business continuity	Business continuity is the process of ensuring that a company can survive unforeseen events that cause interruptions to normal business processes. These generally consist of plans that the company will adopt in the case of a business interruption.

Table 18.4 Failover and Performance Testing Definitions

Key Infrastructure Term	Definition
Disaster recovery	Disaster recovery measures the ability of company systems to recover within an acceptable period of time after a major incident or disaster, and they ensure that end users are able to access critical business systems. It also ensures that mission-critical data are fully restored, operational, and accessible. The disaster recovery system would operate as a back-up.
Performance testing	Performance tests are designed to verify that the system will meet specified performance parameters, such as system response time, the volume of users supported, and ability of the system to service differing locations.

Table 18.4 Failover and Performance Testing Definitions (Cont.)

Effective performance testing requires considerable business input. It is not a matter of simply executing several tests and reporting the results. The implementing company must make several decisions, including the following:

- **Which business processes are important to test**
  Companies usually settle on 10-15 business processes. These processes represent a mix of high-volume transactions or transactions critical to company revenue generation. For example, demand planning and forecasting, creating a procurement shopping cart, and generating sales documents are standard candidates for performance testing.

- **What business performance requirements will be associated with the process**
  In order for the test results to be meaningful, they should have requirements associated with their performance. Thus, in the case of sales order creation, your company may want to use its existing sales order volume as a reference point. The details could be outlined as follows:
  - Average of 40 users online simultaneously
  - Average of 400 sales documents created per day
  - Average of 20 line items per sales order
  - Average response time of 10 seconds per sales order

- **Which test volumes to set**
  The performance test for sales order creation may then be set to track the

amount of time it takes to generate 20 sales orders with 20 line items per sales order.

- **How test results will be interpreted**
  For these transaction sets, the test results will generally specify components of the overall time consumed. Reported in milliseconds, the test results will indicate average response time, average central processing unit (CPU) time, average database execution time, and average wait time. For example, if the test results indicated sales order creation in less than a second, this portion of the performance test would rate a pass.

However, not all performance test executions produce such positive or clear-cut results. In some cases, the test cases cannot be completed due to system issues. In others, the system is not able to meet the business requirement. Where system performance has not met the business requirement, this often produces complicated situations. Your company must review the requirement to assure its validity.

Due to the close proximity of final preparation and go-live, solutions to such issues require rapid identification and action. Often the project team can make rapid system adjustments and successfully re-execute that segment of the performance test. In other situations, the team will not find an immediately available solution. In those cases—depending on the business impact—project sponsors may decide to continue with go-live and repair the issues after the production environment is in place. Alternatively, sponsors may decide that the business functionality involved is so critical to the company that the go-live date should be postponed until the performance issues have been resolved.

> **Tip**
>
> If your implementation includes the use of any portal technology, emphasize the need for extensive performance testing prior to go-live. These applications will encounter far higher volumes and require rapid response times. Make sure that your system can handle the load for supplier self-service in PTP or manager self-service in HCM before you go live. The comparable level of testing for overall system recovery is known as failover testing. Generally included as part of a company business continuity process, failover testing simulates some critical event and then establishes that company operations can be move to an alternate disaster recovery data center site and become operational within a required interval of time.

How this test is performed will depend on your company's adopted backup strategy. Each type has service and cost implications, and the decision to use one approach over another will reflect a trade-off on this mix.

The three primary types of back-up or disaster recovery solutions are as follows:

- **Cold back-up**
  In this approach, SAP system servers are set aside and designated for a back-up role. They are not operational until some event causes their use. The basic production system is installed and configured on the back-up system. Otherwise they are not updated in the interim between creation and first use.

  In this case, your company can expect that it will take between three to five days for this cold back-up system to begin performing business transactions. In the interim, your company would conduct its business processes manually and post those transactions to SAP when the back-up system became available.

- **Warm back-up**
  This more assertive approach has all the features of the cold back-up and some additional ones. The back-up servers to run the SAP system are set aside and the production environment has been installed. The difference lies with the update process. Whereas servers are not operational in the cold back-up, servers in the warm back-up are powered up periodically for the system to refresh itself. Thus, any changes or updates made during the preceding period would be located on the warm back-up system. After refresh, they are again powered down.

  This particular method supports a shorter interval between the critical event and the availability of the back-up system. The size of the interval depends on the number of changes made to the production environment since its last refresh to the back-up system. It should take no longer than 36 hours for the warm back-up system to become operational.

  Clearly, there will be additional charges to cover the costs of this periodic refresh process. Your company must decide whether its business processes are critical enough to offset the additional cost.

- **Hot back-up**
  This even more aggressive approach contains all the features of the warm back-up. In the hot back-up scenario, the system is periodically refreshed with all transactions and system updates that have occurred since the last refresh. The hot back-up differs in that the servers are never powered down. They remain

fully operational and available, similar to the primary production system. Similar to the warm back-up process, the interval between refreshes will affect system availability in the case of a catastrophic event.

Because the back-up system remains operational on a 24-hours-a-day, seven-days-a-week basis, it can take on the functions of the primary system more rapidly—likely a day. The cost increment to provide this quick turnaround is substantial. Essentially, the backup system will approximate a full production system and will require similar maintenance.

Even more failover options are available at considerably greater expense. Some implementing companies choose to adopt a "high-availability" approach in which the entire production system is replicated in the back-up system and operated concurrently. In this case, the disaster recovery design would immediately shift company operations to the back-up system and continue operations seamlessly. Needless to say, this represents a much more expensive option.

Because so many of your company's critical business processes will be housed on the SAP system, some disaster recovery testing is strongly advised. Any disaster recovery testing performed as part of the implementation project would work within the parameters of the back-up option you have chosen. Thus, if your company had chosen a warm back-up process, testing should verify that the replacement system was refreshed and operational within a 36-hour window. This should bring closure to the readiness of the system for go-live.

With the hardware and software in place, we will turn out attention to the more "people-oriented" aspects of the project. Our next chapter discusses the activities of change management. Here, we'll learn how the project team prepares users for the effects of business transformation.

Recall our initial change management discussion from Chapter 13. During blueprinting, the workstreams identified change impacts as a guide to the change management team. Now let's go deeper, and see what happens to the change impacts and how the change management team builds its business transformation activities.

19   Change Management

While system delivery activities are taking place during realization, so too are comparable activities that prepare functional business organizations to receive and operate the new system. Change management prepares your company for the business process changes that come with the system. A close associate of change management, continuous user training builds instructions that are geared to the specifics of SAP functionality and educates users. This chapter covers change management; the next chapter (Chapter 20) addresses continuous user training.

Figure 19.1 illustrates primary change management activities as the project moves through the realization phase and prepares for go-live. We can divide change management into four operational segments:

- The *change impacts* component focuses on identifying and preparing for the major business process alterations that the project will introduce.

- *Stakeholder management* concentrates on gathering information on the support for the project throughout your company. The change management team identifies major influencers throughout your company and keeps a close watch on how much they understand and support the project. The purpose here is twofold: to see where the project stands in the eyes of these influencers, and to furnish them with necessary information on project accomplishments and issues.

- *Organizational design* targets any significant company organization changes introduced by the project. Added or reduced staffing levels, changes in skill set requirements, and shifts in employee roles all fall under organizational design. Clearly, organizational design and change impacts are closely related. Not all change impacts have organizational design effects, but some will. The project change management team, combined with your company's human resources function, has a dual responsibility for completing work in this area.

▶ *Project communication* refers to any company-wide (or more) targeted messaging regarding the project. The change management team operates as the external communications hub for the project. Throughout its lifetime, change management will prepare and distribute all announcements about the project. Due to the almost constant flow of communications from the change management team, this operational segment does not show up in the Figure 19.1 timeline. However, later portions of this chapter do provide additional information regarding this topic.

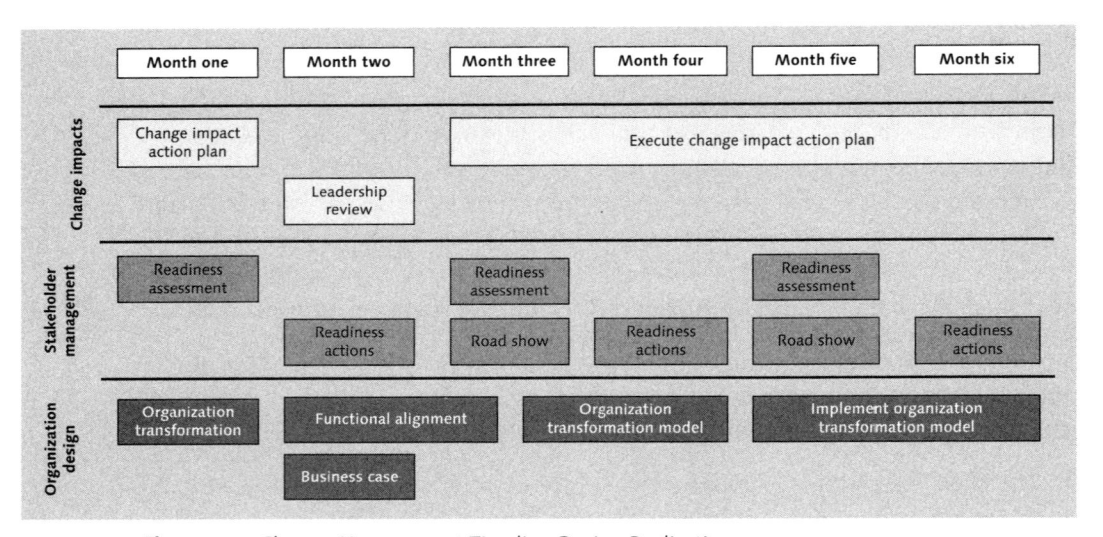

Figure 19.1 Change Management Timeline During Realization

19.1 Business Transformation

SAP implementation projects are often described as *business transformations*. When a company adopts SAP, it automatically accepts some degree of change; screen setups, transaction entries, and terminology will all significantly shift. However, business transformation entails something with far greater company impact than user interface changes. It refers to essential *intended* modifications to business processes, which often cross major functional boundaries.

When an SAP implementation includes transformational process modifications, the project's change management workstream takes on a very important role. Figure 19.2 shows the three-step transition from organizational alignment to full-scale organizational transformation. The difference between each stage lies in the degree of change encountered.

Degree of organization design programs and changes

Organization alignment	Organization redesign	Organization transformation
▸ Roles and responsibilities are more likely to be "tweaked" than redefined	▸ New roles and responsibilities may emerge as better alternatives to realignment	▸ Unit level design driven by top down framework
▸ Role changes need to be tightly coordinated with systems security and training departments	▸ Skill requirements may include those previously not considered, creating new training challenges	▸ Proposed changes in roles and responsibilities may be significant and require high degree of senior management "socialization"
▸ Transition planning should include participation of business unit management and leadership	▸ Implementation and transition planning should be aligned with other corporate initiatives or affected business units	▸ Large scale organization change may require multi-pronged phased implementation approach
▸ Implementation needs to be aligned with other tech and process projects		▸ Senior level leadership critical to success

Figure 19.2 Intensity of Organization Change Associated with a Project

For example, organizational alignment entails modest changes to company business processes. Existing roles and responsibilities remain very much the same. Role changes are limited to security setup and enough training to execute transactions. Depending on the scope of changes and number of users affected, projects involving changes in organizational alignment require significant attention to this dimension and require the participation of senior management.

Organizational redesign goes a step further. New roles and responsibilities created by the project have effects beyond system security and user training. Those areas will certainly be involved, but business process changes will expand roles performance in some way. New roles may be created or new skills may be required for existing roles.

Putting organizational redesign changes in place necessitates in-depth planning. Your HR organization and affected functional business units must decide how this initiative will be communicated to end users. Gaining end-user acceptance and support will be key to making a smooth transition.

The final step, organizational transformation, involves making large-scale changes in business processes. Due to its potential impact on the company, this change effort requires careful definition and communication. Company senior executives must not only lead but "own" the change effort.

Very often, a company will adopt major business process changes concurrently with an SAP implementation. Recall from Chapter 13 that blueprinting leads to a top-to-bottom re-examination of business processes and can build consensus around making substantial changes. While these changes may make considerable sense in terms of improving efficiency, they still require far broader explanation and justification. Support for change comes slowly. It takes constant effort to build backing for change among the user community.

> **Tip**
>
> Encourage your change management team to take an active role in the project. They should have a standing role in project operations and reviews.
>
> That said, however, the change management team must adopt a very fact-based reporting style. Some change management teams find fact-based communication very difficult to achieve. The team speaks in generalities, few listeners get the point being made, and eventually the team simply ceases to pay attention when change management is discussed.
>
> So be firm in your expectations—generalities often mean fuzzy thinking. Too much is at stake in your project to allow for anything but actionable information.

In the case of an SAP implementation project, the change management team takes ownership for most of the organization transformation deliverables. Rather than assuming a primarily systems-focused role similar to other workstreams, the team takes on a primarily business-focused role. The team works directly with company human resources and functional business units to increase the likelihood for successful change.

19.2 Change Impacts

Let's examine the first component of change management. Chapter 13 introduced the concept of "change impacts" as a blueprinting deliverable. During the design period, your project team identified changes that the SAP system would introduce. In addition to a full description of each change, portions of the change impact deliverable included such information as organizations affected, roles affected, and locations involved.

The change management team must first ensure that the project team has uncovered the full range of change impacts. Some teams may not have captured all downstream effects for the changes they proposed. The change management team now works closely with each team to ensure that all impacts are captured and their effects are described in sufficient detail.

Once functional process leads and the change management team members are satisfied that every significant impact has been identified, action planning can begin. This five-step process begins with an initial analysis and moves through a checkup on change impact mitigation steps. Figure 19.3 outlines this process.

Steps one and two further develop change impact material collected in the process definition documents (PDDs). These steps are both completed during blueprinting and they will build analytical frameworks to guide action. Classifications and categories, once established, can greatly assist with action planning. Using spreadsheets or even small-scale databases will help teams identify where change affects a functional organization most, or where specific business processes will undergo substantial alteration during the SAP project. Steps three, four, and five are completed during realization and focus primarily on making the change a reality. These steps are accomplished in change impacts briefings described shortly.

| Step one: Classify and analyze change impacts | Step two: Group change impacts into major categories | Step three: Create action plans addressing the change impacts | Step four: Implement the action plans | Step five: Monitor progress and report status |

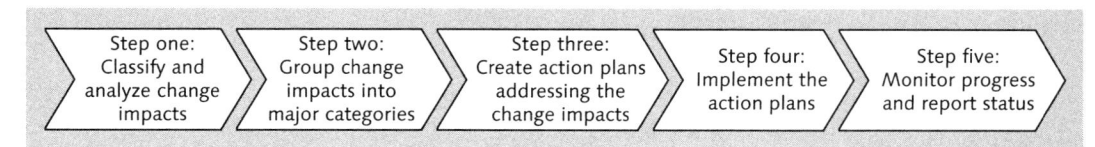

Figure 19.3 Change Impacts Action Planning Process

Grouping changes into high-, medium-, and low-impact categories usually represents the first classification cut. Simply knowing the overall volume of impacts creates useful information. For example, say a project has identified 200 change impacts. Of those, 100 have high impact, 50 have medium impact, and 50 have low impact. Outlining these numbers will clearly demonstrate the challenges facing the project team.

19 | Change Management

> **Tip**
>
> Find time to review these results prior to scheduling a session with senior executives. Ensure that the message is clear before communicating it more broadly. If *you* can't discern the underlying message, then anyone less familiar with the project will not be able to do so either. Always remember that senior executives grant you a limited time to make a point. If your first message is not clear, they may disregard all further messages.

You can also reveal important information when you further subdivide change impacts by functional workstream. Generally, the impacts will not distribute equally across teams. One or two functional workstreams will bear the brunt of major process changes. Uneven distributions will impact team resourcing needs and the degree of support required from supporting horizontal workstreams.

Figure 19.4 illustrates this point. Of the 200 total change impacts identified for a hypothetical project, 80 (or 40 percent) of them fall in the order-to-cash workstream. The next highest rates of change impacts fall in procure-to-pay and record-to-report, with 20 percent each. Human capital management and plan-to-stock each have 10 percent of the total impacts.

	OTC	HCM	PTS	PTP	RTR	Total
High	50	5	10	15	20	100
Medium	20	5	5	10	5	50
Low	10	10	5	15	15	50
Total	80	20	20	40	40	200

Figure 19.4 Distribution of Change Impacts by Workstream and Degree of Change

Even more telling still is the distribution of change impacts that have high impact. Remember that high-impact levels mean that the process change is significant and requires new skills, policies, training, and coaching follow-up to implement. Thus, a large number of change impacts in a workstream places some teams in a difficult position. If not implemented properly, high-impact changes can cause business process disruption.

Over 50 percent of the total high-impact changes belong to OTC. RTR comes next, with 20 percent of the total high-impact changes. Without knowing details about the substance of these changes, OTC must be closely monitored and assisted with additional resources if the need arises.

This workload disparity is a common feature of SAP projects. Some workstreams will bear heavier loads than others. It is also quite common to find OTC as the overall leader in high-impact changes. After all, OTC traverses many company business processes. Recall from previous chapters that OTC often lacks a fully established organizational home; rather, its processes span supply chain, sales, and finance. From a project standpoint, this may create difficulty in gaining traction for addressing change impacts.

Senior Management Change Impact Briefings

Once the total change impacts have been grouped and analyzed, the project team reaches out to senior management to ensure they understand the ramifications of these findings.

This will involve a series of meetings. The first meeting emphasizes senior management issue recognition; it should present the overall change impact situation and furnish details regarding significant items. These meetings will set the tone for change management success throughout the project and must be handled well by the project team. Later sessions will target how the change management team plans to address the impacts that have been identified.

First Meeting
Where possible, graphics and impact descriptions should deliver the message when your team first meets with executives. Showing the overall change impact patterns helps senior managers understand the broad-scale situation. Figure 19.5 illustrates a first-level graphic targeted to senior executives. Using each functional workstream as a point of reference, the figure shows its change impact condition by means of a color code and provides a corresponding legend. Additionally, the graphic uses data collected from the PDDs to provide detail about individual aspects of the workstream change situation. This same approach can be used to demonstrate the level of change experienced in regions and in functional organizations.

19 | Change Management

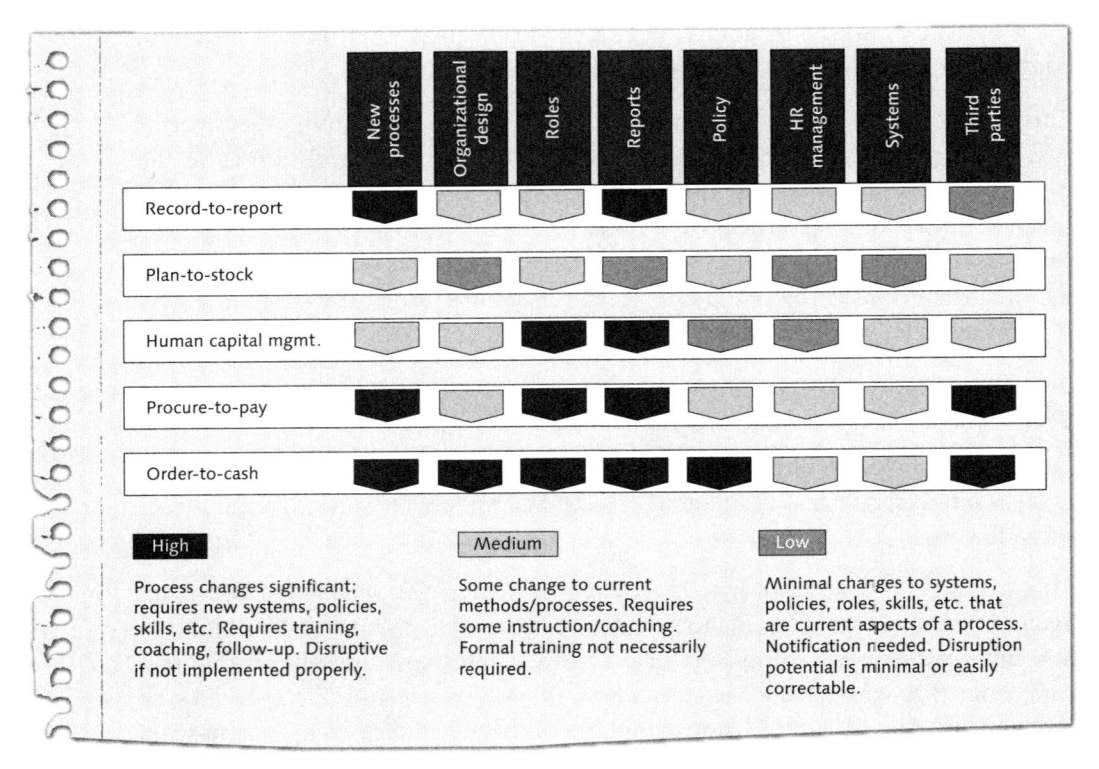

	New processes	Organizational design	Roles	Reports	Policy	HR management	Systems	Third parties
Record-to-report	High	Low	Low	High	Low	Low	Low	High
Plan-to-stock	Low	Medium	Low	Low	Low	Low	Medium	Low
Human capital mgmt.	Low	Low	High	High	Medium	Low	Low	Low
Procure-to-pay	High	Low	High	High	Low	Low	Low	High
Order-to-cash	High	High	High	High	Low	Medium	Low	High

High — Process changes significant; requires new systems, policies, skills, etc. Requires training, coaching, follow-up. Disruptive if not implemented properly.

Medium — Some change to current methods/processes. Requires some instruction/coaching. Formal training not necessarily required.

Low — Minimal changes to systems, policies, roles, skills, etc. that are current aspects of a process. Notification needed. Disruption potential is minimal or easily correctable.

Figure 19.5 Overall Change Impact Situation by Workstream

The single page graphic illustrates the change management challenges facing the overall project as well as each workstream. Your senior executives can easily visualize the task facing the company and the anticipated workload for each workstream. Again, the workstreams demonstrate considerable variability in change effort required. Here, order-to-cash faces an across-the-board change situation. Other workstreams, such as plan-to-stock, face a much more limited change situation.

At this initial session, it will prove useful to conduct additional discussion regarding change impacts. Drilling down into major subprocesses within workstreams helps to clarify the situation. Each workstream could potentially have only one or two subprocesses that will undergo change. Alternatively, each workstream could face substantial change in most of its subprocesses. Sharing this information helps senior executives assess the scope involved. However, your change management team should resist going much beyond this level of detail, or the overall message could become lost. This would not prove helpful.

> **Tip**
>
> Consider using your workstream leads to present the change situation for their areas. They will understand the situation in detail and can best present it to senior executives. Keep in mind that senior executives know the leads and have great confidence in their abilities. Take advantage of their skills.

Figure 19.6 illustrates a drilldown into one workstream's subprocesses. It shows the same format heat map as Figure 19.5 except it covers major OTC subprocesses. This example clearly shows that more than a single OTC subprocess will exhibit major change. Four of the five have some degree of significant change, and three have substantial change activities in many impact categories.

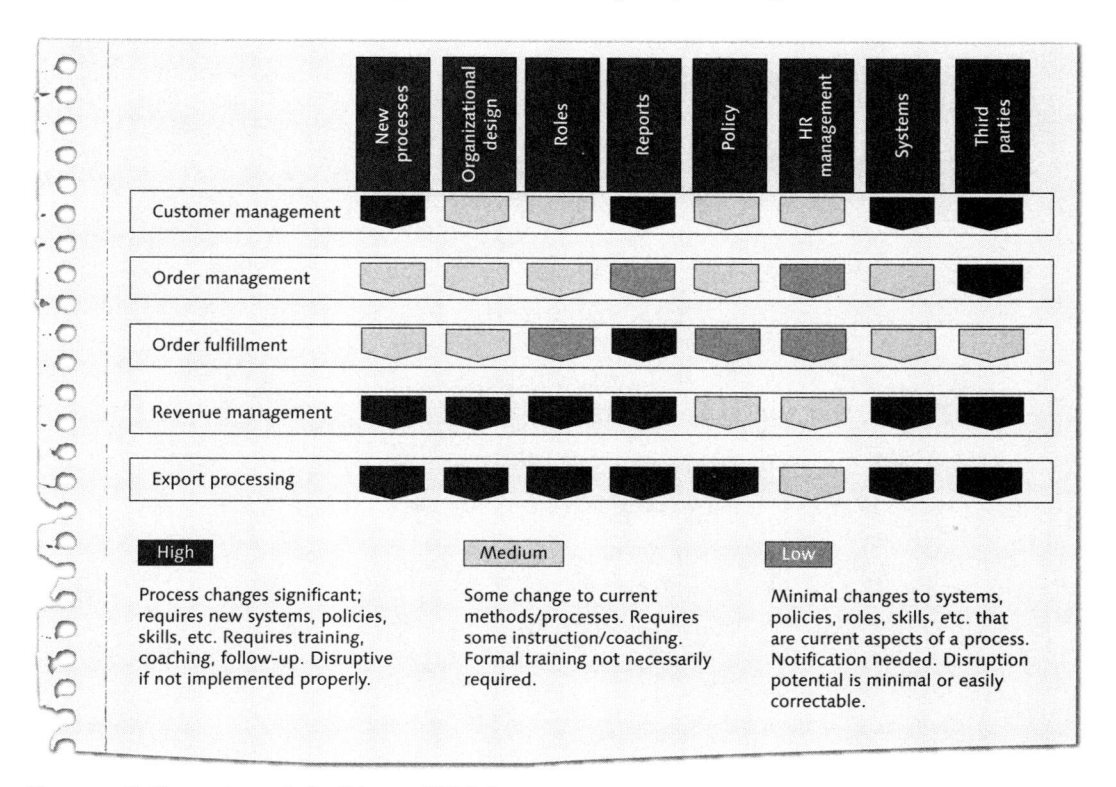

	New processes	Organizational design	Roles	Reports	Policy	HR management	Systems	Third parties
Customer management	High	Low	Low	High	Low	Low	High	High
Order management	Low	Low	Low	Medium	Low	Medium	Low	High
Order fulfillment	Low	Low	Medium	High	High	High	Medium	Low
Revenue management	High	High	High	High	Low	Low	Low	Low
Export processing	High	High	High	High	High	Low	High	High

High: Process changes significant; requires new systems, policies, skills, etc. Requires training, coaching, follow-up. Disruptive if not implemented properly.

Medium: Some change to current methods/processes. Requires some instruction/coaching. Formal training not necessarily required.

Low: Minimal changes to systems, policies, roles, skills, etc. that are current aspects of a process. Notification needed. Disruption potential is minimal or easily correctable.

Figure 19.6 Change Impacts for Primary OTC Subprocesses

Having access to this information not only contributes to senior executive understanding, it also assists them in making resourcing decisions. Workstreams participating in large-scale changes need the resourcing assistance that senior executives can supply.

In order to solidify senior executive understanding, your change management team should cover two other aspects of project change impacts during this initial meeting. The first aspect includes a description of which company roles are primarily involved in the change impacts. This type of information will help executives see the company-wide extent of the change impacts you are discussing.

Table 19.1 shows an example of the primary company roles that will be changing as a result of the SAP implementation. This first meeting with senior executives is intended to introduce them to the project and ground them in the extent and depth of these changes in company business processes. The list in Table 19.1 should cause them to take note, because it involves many of the most important roles in a company. This list of specific roles involved, in combination with the earlier illustrations, does a good job of introducing the scope of the challenge ahead.

Workstream	Roles
OTC	▸ Accounts receivable administrator ▸ Exports administrator ▸ Pricing specialist ▸ Customer service administrator ▸ Transportation planner ▸ Trade promotion specialist
HCM	▸ Recruiter ▸ Training developer
PTS	▸ Supply planner ▸ Demand planner ▸ Production scheduler ▸ Maintenance technician

Table 19.1 Company Roles Changing During an SAP Implementation

Workstream	Roles
PTP	► Commodity buyer ► Indirect buyer ► Accounts payable administrator
RTR	► Treasury analyst ► Tax specialist ► Internal auditor

Table 19.1 Company Roles Changing During an SAP Implementation (Cont.)

The second aspect for the team to cover would be representative examples of significant business process changes. These illustrate the extent of change. This information provides more concrete, real-world context for the change impacts. By having one or two in-depth examples placed in front of them, senior executives can directly understand the changes facing their company.

Figure 19.7 illustrates this type of example. It goes through the steps of initiating a purchase order as they would be performed on the new SAP system. The illustration shows five high-level process steps and identifies which ones would be executed using SAP. In our case, SAP would be directly involved in every step. The figure also includes high-level benefits to be achieved at the global or corporate level and those achieved at a local or regional level.

> **Tip**
>
> Generally, these types of change impacts presentations bring out many questions. The change management team should ensure that members of the functional workstreams are present to answer more detailed requests.

Second Meeting

The second meeting with senior executives to discuss change impacts would address mitigation activities. The initial meeting essentially defined the problem; this second meeting discusses how to resolve it. Even more than the first encounter, this session should engage senior executives in active problem-solving. It will not be enough to present a series of potential solutions to the group. Rather, company executives must walk away as *believers* in the solutions proposed and as *owners* of those action plans adopted.

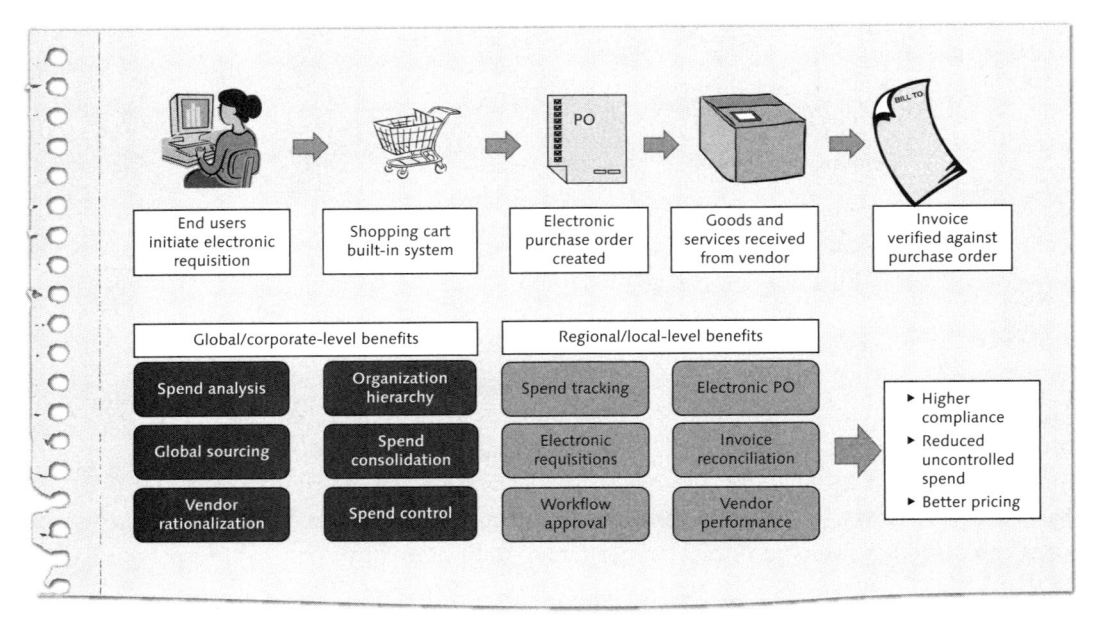

Figure 19.7 Change Impact Example for Senior Executives Presentation

Figure 19.8 shows how this meeting might proceed. For major changes, such as the adoption of an SAP-based central purchasing catalog, the change management team has prepared a framework for action planning. The third column outlines actions recommended to mitigate the impact of the change. They include communications, policies and procedures, organization and employee changes, and learning or training to be applied.

The change management team will have prepared a similar slide for each major change proposed. Your company executives will have the ability to discuss each change in full. Often these proposed changes lead to considerable discussion about the likely effects and how to mitigate them. These are positive responses. The change management facilitator should ensure that discussion comes to a close after a reasonable period of time. The facilitator should also ensure the each major change has an action plan identified and an executive owner for the change effort.

Change Impacts | 19.2

Impact	Organizational implications	Mitigating actions
All company purchases are requested in the SAP system using a central catalogue	Requisitions must have required information to be converted to purchase orders Material/vendor must be qualified by the company Requisitions are submitted by all employees via the system for direct and indirect material	**Communications** ▸ Develop a multi-channel communication campaign for employees around correct processes for requisition entry ▸ Develop "day in the life" scenarios to help high impact organizations understand the new purchasing function (materials resource planning [MRP] and maintenance, repair, and operations [MRO]) ▸ Develop key change guidance materials for buyers to assist them with driving purchasing compliance **Policies and procedures** ▸ Develop purchasing policy for buyers to convert requisitions to purchase order ▸ Identify and document end-to-end purchasing scenarios for direct, indirect, and new vendor purchasing events **Organization and employee changes** ▸ Centralize purchasing function and organization based on region/country ▸ Assign baseline requisitioning to the requestor of materials ▸ Develop strategic purchasing capabilities to take advantage of economies of scale **Learning or training required** ▸ Integrate policy and process training in end user training courses in purchasing ▸ Require Web-based learning for employees involved in the purchasing process ▸ Educate high-impact stakeholders such as MRP controllers and facilities management

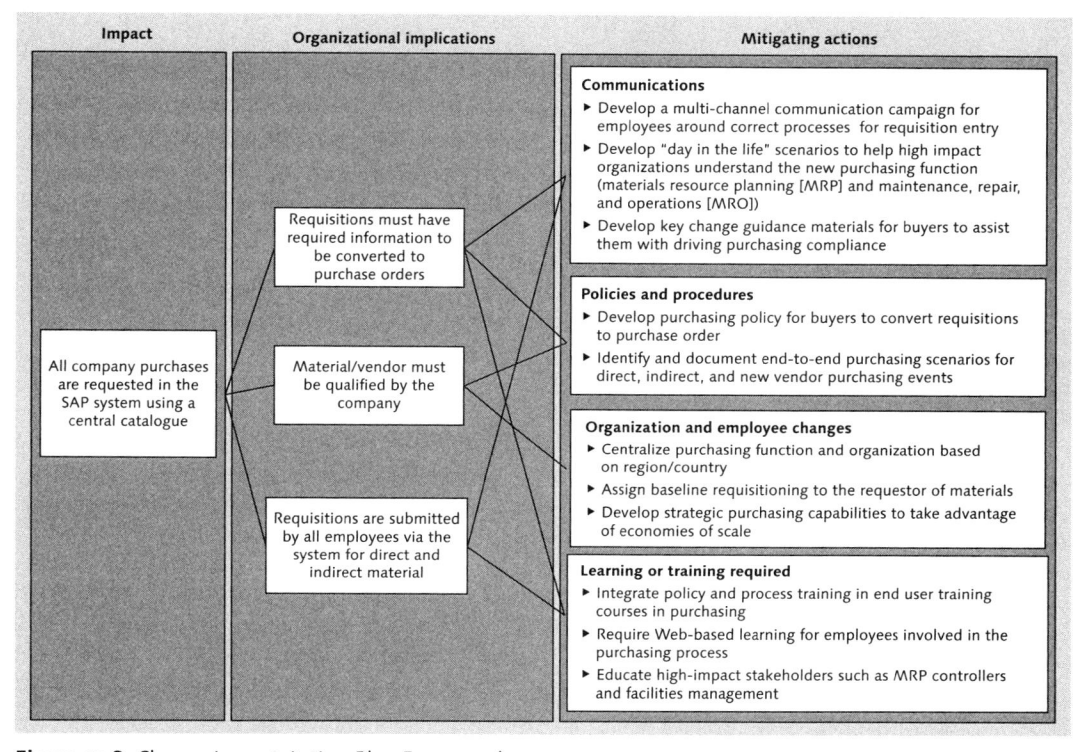

Figure 19.8 Change Impact Action Plan Framework

> **Tip**
>
> Again, consider asking the workstream leads to make the presentation for changes in their workstream scope. Having workstream leads visibly committed to these changes goes a long way toward convincing senior executives of their importance.

One key change mitigation tool not covered in this example is the "day in the life" exercise. Because it requires an enormous effort from the project team, it is only used for major changes that cross organizational boundaries. Essentially, a "day in the life" acts as a dress rehearsal; it brings together groups of users for the purpose of operating a process as it would be done after go-live. For example, participants in the manufacturing process—such as planners, buyers, material handlers, production personnel, quality inspectors, and others—could be brought together for the purpose of accomplishing each step in the process as part of an in-depth simulated environment.

The new process would be operated according to the standard guidelines. Each operator would in turn use the SAP system to execute transactions and pass the process to the next step in line. Production documentation, such as work instructions, would be used, and members of applicable project team workstreams would be in attendance to act as guides. Each attendee could observe other participants complete—in real time—all upstream and downstream operations.

The "day in the life" exercise is the best available tool to ensure that all participants in a new SAP process understand exactly how it works. Putting all participants in one room and showing them the full process—from material resource planning and procurement through pack and ship—is an invaluable learning device. Implementing companies should consider adopting this tool when process changes are fundamental and involve disparate groups.

At the completion of the second senior executive change impacts session, the group should have reached overall agreement on the importance of each major change. The group should also have agreed on the courses of action to be followed in mitigating the effects of these changes. The change management team will schedule periodic reviews with this group to discuss progress made and obstacles encountered.

19.3 Stakeholder Management

Stakeholder management represents the second element of change management. Some consider stakeholder management to simply be a marketing tool to manipulate views on the project. According to this line of thought, the project works to achieve a favorable impression—and only a favorable impression—from major stakeholders in the implementing company. Once that favorable impression is achieved, the stakeholders are considered "managed."

However, if done correctly, stakeholder management does constitute a legitimate change management activity. A more even-handed approach than that of "savvy marketing orientation" understands that company stakeholders are owners of legitimate concerns and are valuable communication links within their organizations. Negative perceptions of the project are not necessarily incorrect, and it's entirely possible that the project is not performing certain tasks well. Because stakeholders are those who will be directly or indirectly affected by the project, it is important for project management to understand the situation from their perspective.

> **Tip**
>
> Stakeholders can be your best allies. Each and every one seeks transparency and a full understanding of how the project will affect their operations. Brief them whenever the project situation changes, whether positively or negatively. They may not be happy with negative results, but they *will* understand and support your efforts.

Stakeholder management should then have the following three objectives:

1. To ensure that stakeholders throughout the project lifecycle understand project objectives and have an accurate image of its progress. Most importantly, stakeholder management ensures that every stakeholder has a complete picture of how the project impacts their functions and operations.

2. To build a two-way communications dialogue with stakeholders. This dialogue should ensure that stakeholders support the objectives of the project while being open to and soliciting critical views about project performance.

3. To seek periodic, measured feedback from stakeholders throughout the project lifecycle using surveys and interviews. This information function as a key indicator of project operating effectiveness.

To accomplish these objectives, the change management team must first identify the group of potential stakeholders. The team can form a reasonable preliminary list by working closely with project sponsors and functional process leads. This list can then be vetted by other executives for additions or changes.

Figure 19.9 through Figure 19.12 present an example for the four-step approach to stakeholder selection. It assures full representation by regions and countries. It also advocates setting up initial structured meetings, either by phone or in person, as part of the selection process. As a result of these discussions, stakeholders are mapped according to their reaction to the proposed changes and to their level of influence in the organization.

The first two steps identify individuals and groups to interview and survey as stakeholders, and then execute that information-gathering step.

19 | Change Management

Step One:
Identify individuals and groups to interview and survey

Individual stakeholders
- Executives
- Managers
- Core team
- SME

Group stakeholders: SAP/non-SAP users

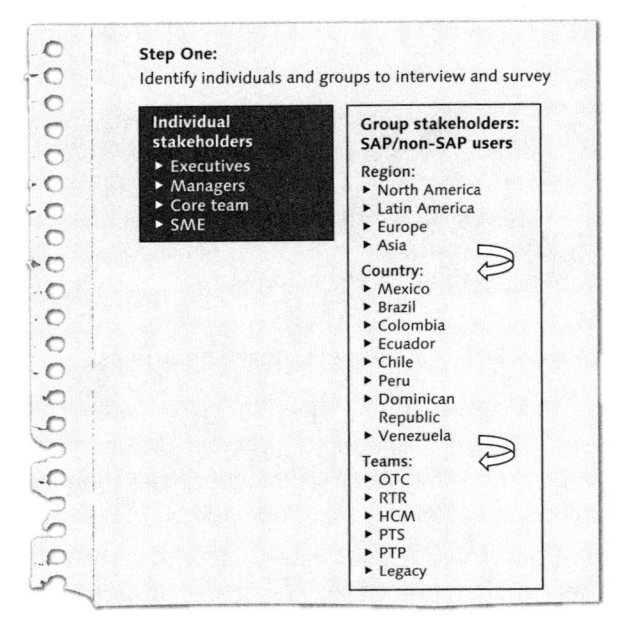

Region:
- North America
- Latin America
- Europe
- Asia

Country:
- Mexico
- Brazil
- Colombia
- Ecuador
- Chile
- Peru
- Dominican Republic
- Venezuela

Teams:
- OTC
- RTR
- HCM
- PTS
- PTP
- Legacy

Figure 19.9 Identify Survey Recipients

Step Two:
Interview individuals and survey groups

Stakeholder interview questions

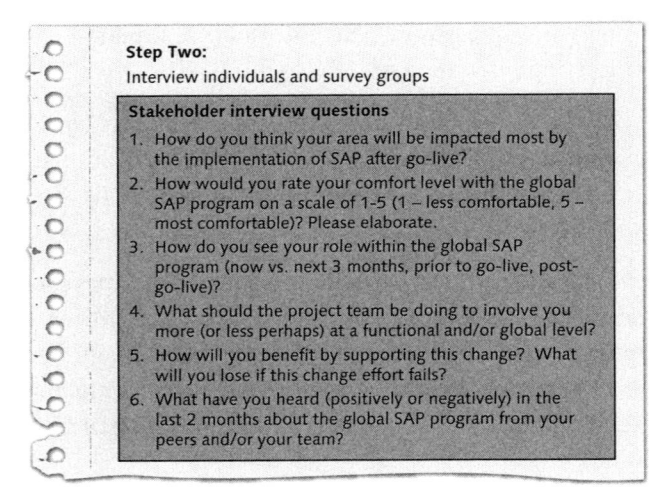

1. How do you think your area will be impacted most by the implementation of SAP after go-live?
2. How would you rate your comfort level with the global SAP program on a scale of 1-5 (1 – less comfortable, 5 – most comfortable)? Please elaborate.
3. How do you see your role within the global SAP program (now vs. next 3 months, prior to go-live, post-go-live)?
4. What should the project team be doing to involve you more (or less perhaps) at a functional and/or global level?
5. How will you benefit by supporting this change? What will you lose if this change effort fails?
6. What have you heard (positively or negatively) in the last 2 months about the global SAP program from your peers and/or your team?

Figure 19.10 Interview Questions

Step three determines group findings by region, country, and team, and then maps individuals in a matrix that measures level of influence and reaction to change.

Step Three:
Map individuals. Determine group findings by region, country, and team

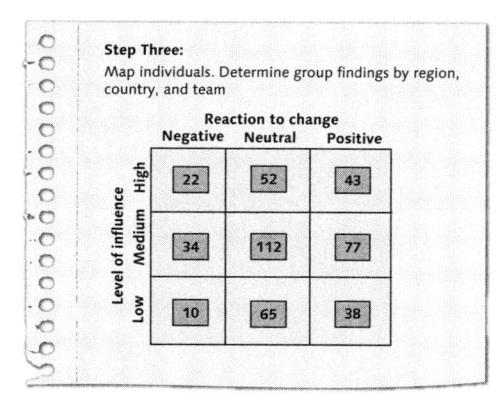

	Reaction to change		
Level of influence	Negative	Neutral	Positive
High	22	52	43
Medium	34	112	77
Low	10	65	38

Figure 19.11 Map Individuals

Finally, step four determines influence strategies and actions for individual communication and action plans.

Step Four:
Determine influence strategies and actions for individuals' communication plans and change agent network actions

Stakeholder name	Current support	What you need from stakeholder	Issues of stakeholder	Action plan	Owner	Status
Anne Jones (Manager of Airport processes, project lead)	Current support: 4 / Needed support: 4	▶ Notification or project rollout ▶ Updates on change, maintenance, and enhancements to system	▶ Concerned about legacy systems still working when project rolls out ▶ This group has "been there and done that" before. Does project management truly realize how hard it is to change a legacy function?	▶ Identify key people in group as touch points ▶ Establish open door, information communication with no secrets	Denise Baker	5/4: Carolyn Gates met with Anne. Anne or representative of her group will attend the change agent meeting in mid-May. Denise has been assigned as an extended team member for project.
Derek Collins (Airport processes and consulting)	Current support: 3 / Needed support: 4	▶ Overall buy-in of metrics	▶ Concerned that project may not truly provide a return on investment	▶ Periodic meetings with Dominic Garrison, AR to gain direction for value added "to-be analysis and direction"	Trish Kennedy	4/25: Owner switched from Debbie Crawford to Trish Kennedy
Eric Elliott (Airport processes/web development)	Current support: 2.5 / Needed support: 4	▶ Buy-in for his niche in customer services	▶ Concerned that project and his group are doing duplicate work	▶ Develop effective rapport ▶ Keep Eric in the loop on decisions made, direction, timelines, etc.	Mike Scanton	4/25: Action item: Mike to talk with Eric about the Palm notification initiative.

Figure 19.12 Determine Influence Strategies and Actions

The underlying model for this type of selection process is that stakeholders should be aware of project objectives and progress, and they should be involved in creating favorable outcomes. As Table 19.2 shows, stakeholders can fall into one of four combinations regarding awareness and involvement. Preferably they will fall into the top-left category of both aware and involved. However, this may not occur. Obviously, the worst-case scenario arises when stakeholders are neither aware nor involved, or are in the bottom-right category in the matrix. It will be up to the change management team to increase their awareness where necessary or assist with their involvement where possible.

		Awareness	
		Yes	No
Involvement	Yes	Committed to the project: Both engaged and aware of project status	Ineffective project support: Involved but unaware of project status
	No	Limited project engagement: Aware but not involved	Disengaged from the project: No awareness or involvement

Table 19.2 Stakeholder Project Involvement and Awareness Matrix

Once project sponsors are satisfied that they have achieved a solid stakeholder listing, the change management team begins the first of its periodic survey activities. These surveys should be scheduled around significant project milestones, and the team should take steps to ensure the fullest possible stakeholder participation. Survey findings should be reported to project leadership and discussed for their implications as soon as they are available. Where problem areas are revealed through the surveys, project management ensures that resolution plans are developed and their results monitored frequently.

19.4 Organizational Design

Not every project engages in organizational changes. Generally, only projects undergoing significant business transformation will include major organizational design activities. For those projects that do have organizational design in their scope, finding the right solution set for changing the company organization will be a difficult and time-consuming task.

The organizational design work begins with the definition of the desired state. But where to start? It often helps to get a clear understanding of the deficiencies in the current state. The aim is to find out what does not work now, or what will not work in the future state. These deficiencies can be outlined relative to the performance of the current organizational model used in the company. Alternatively, they can be defined relative to the model of the new system and processes that are being introduced as part of the SAP implementation project.

The scope of work in organizational redesign includes the following elements:

- Mapping the current organization and assessing its likely performance after the SAP system and new business processes are put into operation
- Planning for the organization design to fit the new system and processes
- Establishing the detail of the new organizational model to include its layers and spans of control
- Identifying any additional skills required by the new organizational model and assessing the supply of these skills in the current company organization
- Defining job roles and job descriptions for the new organizational model
- Aligning the company reward structure to provide incentives for critical roles
- Recruiting additional company staff, where necessary, to fill out the new organizational model
- Providing the training and education necessary for staff to operate in the new organizational model

Clearly, the type of organization redesign effort shown in Figure 19.13 — delivered concurrently with an SAP implementation — places a considerable strain on the project team. Activities undertaken by your company project team could include such diverse steps as designing the new organization and defining all the related components. Management must clearly understand the scheduling implications of this decision and set team priorities based on this information.

19 | Change Management

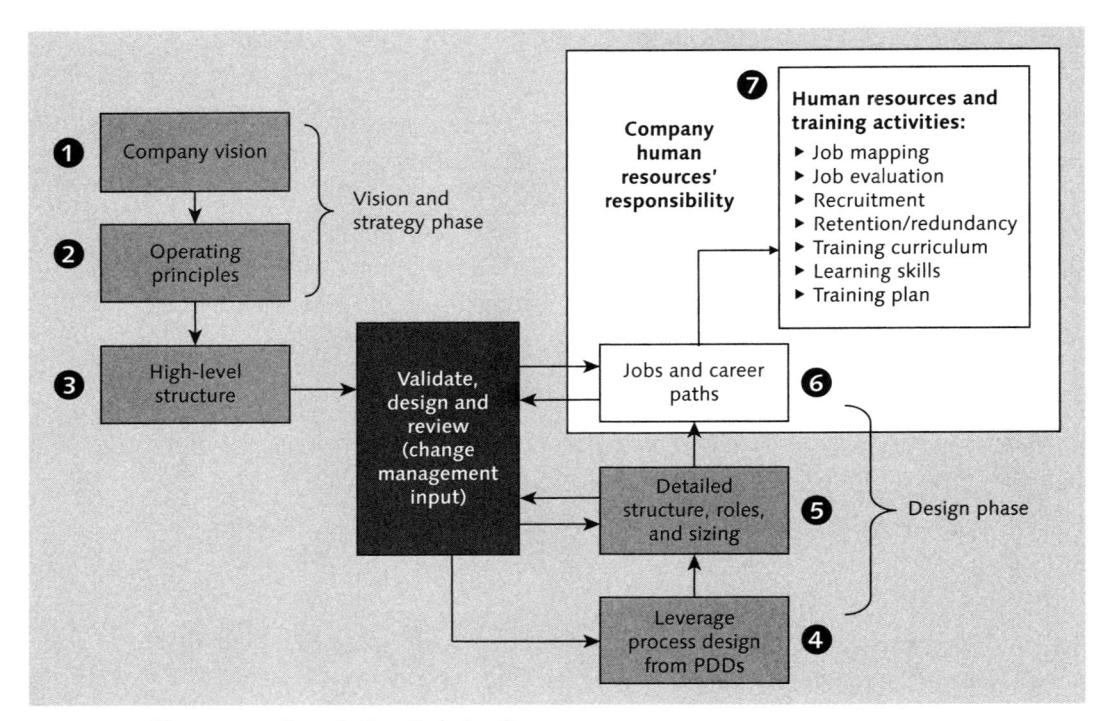

Figure 19.13 Organization Redesign Process

No doubt your project team can accomplish organizational redesign as part of the implementation project. Those steps involved and deliverables to be accomplished should be incorporated as part of your company SAP implementation project plan. For example, if the organizational redesign included shifting to a shared services procurement organization, responsibility would be assigned to the procure-to-pay team. If the organizational redesign included changes to manufacturing floor operations and the implementation of a manufacturing execution system (MES), responsibility would be assigned to the plan-to-stock team.

The underlying principle is that the SAP implementation project, due to its scope and resourcing, should take charge of all activities in its sphere of influence. In this way, the SAP implementation project has overall control of all subsidiary activities affecting its success.

19.5 Project Communication

For the project to be successful, it must communicate its messages to end users, stakeholders, and to the company at large. This communications team has responsibility for this element of the SAP implementation. The communications team prepares those messages and ensures that they are effectively delivered.

Some projects pay limited attention to their communications team. To the extent that the project team focuses exclusively on the systems deliverables facing it, the communications team may seem like an afterthought. However, for the remainder of the company—its end users and line managers—knowing about the progress of the project is essential information. If the communications team is underutilized, some important information will not be delivered.

> **Tip**
> Review the output of your communications team whenever possible. If you see that the communication does not contain enough detail, sit down with the writer and educate him or her. With the next communication, expect to see the necessary level of detail.

For the communications team to accomplish its tasks, it must become an integral part of overall project operations. To do this, every member of the communications team must become more than solely a "writer" or grammar checker for the text supplied. Team members must develop a working knowledge of project objectives and approach. They must know what content is needed and construct it where appropriate.

The communications team will develop a toolkit that provides relevant information to diverse target audiences in a wide range of locations. Some of the deliverables in Table 19.3, such as announcements and newsletters, can be scripted ahead of time. Others—such as briefings, road shows, and presentations—take place in a more ad hoc fashion, and so will be demanded and supplied in a limited time frame.

Tool	Audience	Purpose
Executive briefings	Company corporate and regional senior executives	Maintain executive engagement level and familiarity with project progress
Newsletters	Company-wide periodic distribution, including end users and non-users	Keep the project at top-of-mind among all parts of the company and ensure receipt of timely information
Announcements	Company-wide distribution primarily focused on end-users and stakeholders	Make known the accomplishment of major project milestones to include go-lives and date changes
Handouts	Targeted groups addressing specific subjects	Materials tailored to enhance understanding or awareness of important subject areas
Road shows	Site and regional audiences	In-person updates to bring the "face of the project" to sites and regions where the project will deploy
Posters	Targeted groups addressing specific important subjects	Provide interesting and thought-provoking awareness materials on an as-needed basis
Presentations	Targeted groups addressing specific important subjects	Ad hoc materials intended to address specific subjects and to targeted groups

Table 19.3 Communications Toolkit for an SAP Implementation Project

Additionally, the communications team will collect and report periodic stakeholder survey information. As shown in Figure 19.14, this information can be reported in a standardized format that supports discussions in regular project meetings. Any changes in assessment rating, description, and actions required can all be tracked and made the subject of ongoing evaluations among project leadership.

When performed well, the four components of change management outlined in this chapter can make a substantial difference in project results. An informed and prepared user base can greatly ease go-live preparation and hypercare activities.

Assessment Area	Rating	Assessment Description	Actions Required
Project awareness	Green	▸ High awareness of project ▸ Case for change articulated and cascaded effectively	▸ Reinforce the "what" and "why" of project with site location and users who approve work
Understanding of change impacts	Green	▸ Good understanding of change impacts and how users will be affected by project ▸ Ratings varied across locations but fairly high across user types	▸ Reinforce change impacts with production sites, particularly for users who approve work
Understanding of benefit opportunities	Yellow-green	▸ Good understanding of benefits, however key benefit areas may not have been thoroughly articulated or there may be a lack of understanding of how the benefits will be realized	▸ Revisit business case and benefits realization process ▸ Reinforce benefits areas, tracking, and accountability, with emphasis at manufacturing sites
Ability to adapt to policies and procedures	Yellow	▸ Solid understanding of policies and procedures, however reinforcement across locations and users may be required	▸ Revisit how users access documents ▸ Reinforce communication of policies and procedures with daily use
Effectiveness of knowledge transfer	Yellow-red	▸ Reinforced training and increased communication may be needed across locations and users	▸ Conduct refresher training and increase communication for daily and reporting users in company-specific plants
Understanding of support structure	Yellow	▸ Solid understanding of support structure, however reinforcement across locations and users may be required	▸ Reinforce communication of support mechanisms with focus on users in production sites
Effectiveness of communication mechanisms	Yellow	▸ Solid communication across locations and users, however reinforcement may be required	▸ Reinforce communication mechanisms, timing, and relevancy

Figure 19.14 Stakeholder Survey Reporting

The next chapter, on continuous user training, supplements the mission of change management. There, we'll review the instructional programs designed to improve end-user system operations.

Similar to change management, user training appears from the outside to be a very straightforward, cut-and-dried activity. However, the reality is quite different.

20 Continuous User Training

In many ways, the development and delivery of user training in an SAP implementation project qualifies it as a "project within a project." The number of interrelated items, degree of complexity, and importance to project objectives all ensure that user training ranks high as a focus for project management.

Figure 20.1 illustrates the many activities needed to carry out the development and delivery of training materials. Let's walk through it now. The process begins in blueprinting with the completion of business process procedures (BPPs). Based on the process definition documents (PDDs), the BPPs capture the steps in the process to include system entries and transactions.

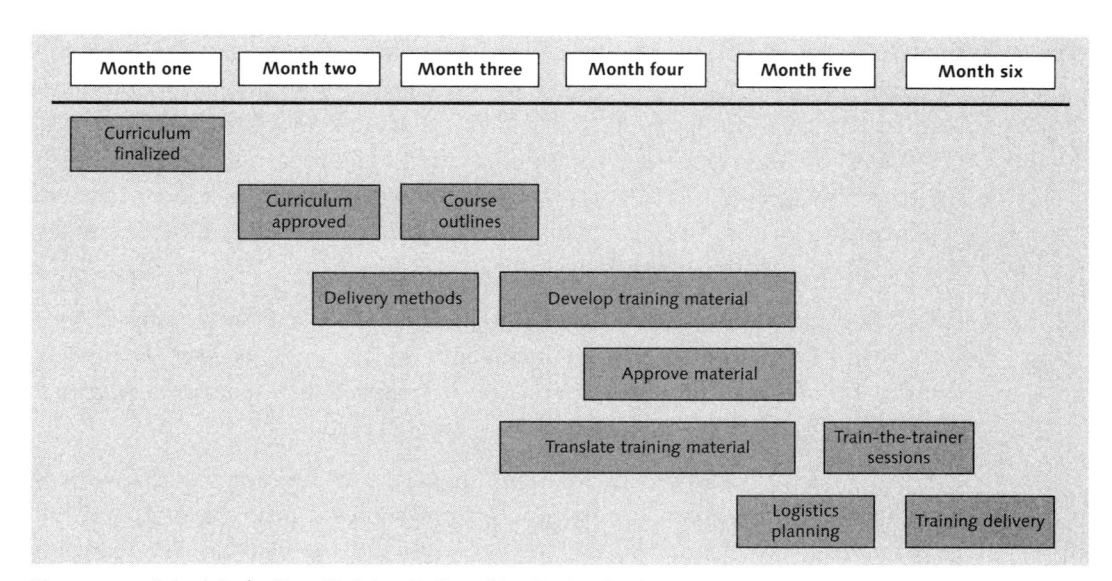

Figure 20.1 Schedule for User Training Deliverables During Realization

> **Trail Marker**
>
> Our graphic shows the training deliverables during realization. For that reason, the BPP deliverables are not included.

Using the BPP information, the training team recommends an initial curriculum. It contains an identification of courses to be developed for all functional workstreams and a short description of each course. Functional workstream leads then review the recommended curriculum and propose changes. After any suggested changes are made, the curriculum is approved and the training team begins work on content development.

The approved curriculum sets the foundation for course outlines. These are detailed summaries for each course on the approved list, and they give overviews of the content to be covered. At approximately the same time, the training team proposes delivery methods for each course in the curriculum. At first glance, it seems likely that instructor-led training (ILT) would be the primary delivery method proposed. However, other delivery methods, such as Web-based training, are available and will likely be used as part of the project training delivery.

When these preliminaries are complete, the training team begins the course development work. Course developers are assigned to the workstreams in which they have background and expertise. Functional workstream leads designate subject matter experts (SMEs) who have familiarity with your company's processes and the blueprint design for this area. Developers and SMEs work together as a team, with the developer gathering information and preparing draft versions of the course material. The SME acts as the initial review point for these drafts and offers feedback at each review point. The course design process only moves forward when the SME is satisfied with the output.

Once SMEs have agreed that the course material is ready, the process moves to its second and final approval stage. Functional workstream leads own all the decisions on training coursework prepared for their area. When the workstream lead has signed off on the course material, it is deemed ready for use.

For SAP implementations using multiple languages, the training material must be translated for those users. The training team prepares course materials and submits them for translation. Because the translations take place after review and approval, this step occurs very close to the actual presentation of materials. Thus, there is little slack in the schedule at this point. The translations must come back correct and on time.

Immediately before the instruction is to be delivered, the training team conducts train-the-trainer sessions for company instructors. Where possible, SMEs will instruct the material they helped to prepare. These train-the-trainer sessions acknowledge that many or most of the instructors will have no experience in conducting a training class. Train-the-trainer sessions build attendees' instructional delivery skills and confidence in their ability to manage a classroom.

With instructors prepared and materials ready for delivery, the training team turns its attention to the logistics planning needed for course delivery. This involves a number of components: locations, facilities, instructors, class schedules, and attendees. Because they are interrelated, all parts of the package must be handled as a whole.

When the logistics are complete, the actual end-user training begins. Generally, this takes place is a very compressed timeframe. All user training must be completed and certified before SAP UserIDs are issued at go-live. With most users enrolled in multiple courses, tracking each user's completion can become a daunting task.

The sections below will cover core aspects of the training development and delivery process: course development, trainer preparation, training delivery logistics, and post-go-live processes.

20.1 Course Development

For the project training team, course development is the most intensive part of the entire sequence of activities. The training developers are assigned to functional workstreams, and they face the challenge of integrating themselves within the workstreams' operations. Many workstream members will view training materials as a secondary activity or, at best, one that can be put off until later. One of the initial challenges for the training team will be to alter this perception. Otherwise, many training deliverables may not be ready by the time classes are scheduled.

The next challenge entails mapping instructional requirements based on the PDDs. This time-consuming activity must be done in some detail. Acting in concert with the workstream lead and assigned SMEs, the training developer will assess how to best structure the training outputs. The defined courses must cover all known end-user training needs and distribute them among recommended courses in a reasonable manner.

It is very common to have several courses developed per workstream and an even larger number of modules for each course. Preparing the coursework in a modularized fashion assists with instructional flexibility. Some classes need not cover all parts of the material, as users may already be familiar with certain topics. Limiting the session to only those areas where coverage is needed conserves valuable instructor time and keeps the classes interesting for all attendees.

20.1.1 Delivery Methods

At the time of initial development, the training team makes decisions about the presentation strategy for each class. Several options are available and some options are better suited for particular training situations. The three delivery types shown in Table 20.1 are all used in a typical SAP implementation project.

Delivery Method	Description	Best-Fit Situation
Instructor-led training (ILT)	In-classroom instruction led by an SME instructor and with approximately 20-30 attendees per session.	ILT works best where the training is locally delivered and a number of site users share the need for business process content. Its format allows for questions, answers, and in-depth explanation as needed.
Web-based training (WBT)	Pre-packaged Web-based content that is delivered remotely and that end users access on their individual work stations.	WBT works best for a course assigned to large numbers of end users and diverse sites. Users can access materials at their convenience. The material is standardized and provided in the same way to all users.
Coaching sessions	One-on-one or one-on-a-few sessions delivered either in person or via teleconference to limited attendees	Coaching works best when users require individual attention and to be shown "how-to" operate a complex process. In this format, the instructor gains real-time feedback on end-user understanding and can adjust the materials to fit the situation.

Table 20.1 Common Training Delivery Methods in SAP Projects

Not only is each delivery method suited to specific training situations, but each consumes differing amounts of training resources. ILT requires instructors for each class session and involves classroom space at the delivery site. All this must be scheduled and confirmed for each class session. ILT also requires attendee notification and the use of facilities that have work stations for the class. In terms of developmental resources, each class must be fully supplied with exercises, tests, and related content.

WBT makes minimal demands on instructor and facilities resources. WBT does not require instructors or classroom space; nor does it require attendee scheduling. The process is much simpler here. Communications are sent to each prospective attendee with guidance as to how to enroll in the course. Completion feedback built into the delivery material enables the training team to electronically monitor course attendance and completion.

So why aren't all classes prepared in a WBT format? After all, the logistics requirements are so minimal. Two reasons: First, WBT takes much longer to develop. The course designer must foresee every possible question or issue and build that information into the course content. In coaching and ILT, much of that interaction is left to the course instructor. It is assumed that the instructor will perceive where additional information is necessary and provide it on the spot. With WBT, that option is not available.

Second, WBT is not optimal for some training situations—especially those involving new business process implementation. End users will not be satisfied with one-size-fits-all instruction. They will demand an instructional mechanism that addresses their specific and detailed questions, many of which start with "What do I do if...?" Having a trained and expert instructor to provide answers to a range of potential questions is fundamental to this delivery method.

Coaching sessions provide even more tailored instruction. This delivery method encourages very close contact between instructor and end users. It works best when the subject is very complex and requires continuing interaction to explain all the permutations. Almost certainly, the instructor will be *the* company expert for a specific process. As a result, the instructor need not be fully scripted in these encounters and can adjust specific content based on the needs of attendees. Questions can be raised at any point in the session, and answers can continue until the instructor is assured that the student fully understands the lesson.

Here again, one might reasonably ask why coaching sessions are not used for most instruction. By using instructors so knowledgeable in the subject matter, the training team doesn't need to spend so much time on course development. Additionally, logistics requirements are far easier with such a small number of attendees in each session.

> **Tip**
> Coaches are even more difficult to find than classroom instructors. These are your very best performers, the ones who everyone in the company recognizes and turns to for answers. Their organizations will be reluctant to make them available.
> Sit down with the site or regional executive to explain the situation. Unless end users really understand how to perform tasks on the system, they will make errors. Cleaning up those errors takes time, and the job will often fall to process experts. It really is one of those "pay me now or pay me later" situations.

However, the coaching delivery method places extraordinary demands on instructors. Most implementing companies are likely to have only a very small number of experts in any subject area. Conducting large number of coaching sessions with end users would require instructors to forego their normal job duties and become full-time coaches for a two to three month period. Clearly, coaching fits best with small groups and with only a few sessions required. Larger groups will almost immediately shift into classroom mode due to the number of student users. Increased numbers of sessions for the same group places time demands on instructors as described above.

Most SAP projects use a combination of the three delivery methods: WBT for large-scale learning populations with similar needs, ILT for moderately sized localized groups with similar needs, and coaching for those highly specialized activities with small user populations. Each project team will identify the mix that works best for its resource base and user population.

20.1.2 Content Types

Not only will there be a mix of user training delivery methods, there will also be a mix of learning content. Table 20.2 illustrates the types of content prepared by training developers:

- *Concept slides* cover a multitude of usages. This type of content is used for process explanations and for any needed background information. Concept slides provide an overview of end-to-end processes and detailed subprocesses to help users understand the context before they begin to learn system tasks.
- *Simulations* provide the hands-on guidance needed for completing SAP system transactions. These simulations are made as realistic as possible. They not only mirror company business processes, but use online or paper-based examples of how to complete a system transaction. Often, the simulation uses company data is to make the lesson more realistic.
- *Quick reference guides* provide take-away information that the user can apply in executing required tasks. Reference guides digest much of the training content into a user-friendly format. When a user is back on the job and needs a point of reference, the quick reference guide is available to supply the information for complex or infrequently performed tasks.
- In the classroom setting, *student exercises* supplement the learning environment with company data. Here, the user can practice all aspects of the business activity or system transaction. After necessary instruction has been provided, end users are asked to perform process steps and applicable system transactions. Normally, all students in a class execute the same exercise so they can compare results and learn from one another as they complete the steps.

Knowledge Transferred	Concept slides	Simulations	Quick reference guide	Student exercise
To-be business processes	X	X	X	
Changes to job roles	X		X	
Specific business scenarios	X	X	X	X
System transactions		X	X	X

Table 20.2 Learning Content Types and Optimum Uses

Each content type can be used for any of the three delivery methods outlined in Table 20.1. Student exercises or tests are a common feature of WBT. Passing an end-of-course test demonstrates knowledge and understanding. Grades are recorded and used as proof of training for compliance purposes.

Coaching sessions often use simulations to measure learning. In coaching sessions, due to the limited number of end-user attendees, the instructor/coach can work directly with the students to assure full understanding. The coach can also assist with simulations.

20.1.3 Course Organization

Courses are divided into two types: *foundation courses* providing overview information for most end users, and *transaction courses* that provide transaction instruction for end users in specific areas.

Figure 20.2 shows how the course organization for an SAP implementation project might work. In this example, all end users would complete the project overview and the SAP overview. Content for overview courses would consist entirely of concept slides. Those responsible for accounts receivable would enroll in the accounts receivable overview.

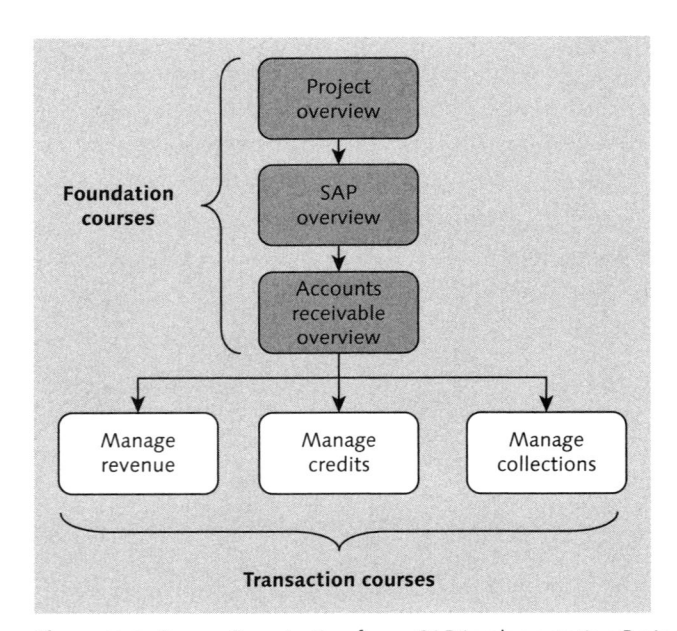

Figure 20.2 Course Organization for an SAP Implementation Project

After the third level (accounts receivable overview), users would be divided according to their roles and assigned to specific coverage areas. End users assigned to accounts receivable roles might attend three transaction classes: manage revenue, manage credits, and manage collections. These classes would present intensive information on those three processes. Each class would cover the SAP transaction set applicable for that process. Instructors would give step-by-step information on completing those transactions.

Figure 20.3 offers an example of transaction-based instruction. The instructions prepare end users to create an SAP billing document using Transaction VF01. The selection identifies the transaction code used, exceptions to the automatic process, and additional contextual information about the process. This would supply the background information needed to understand the transaction.

Instructions:

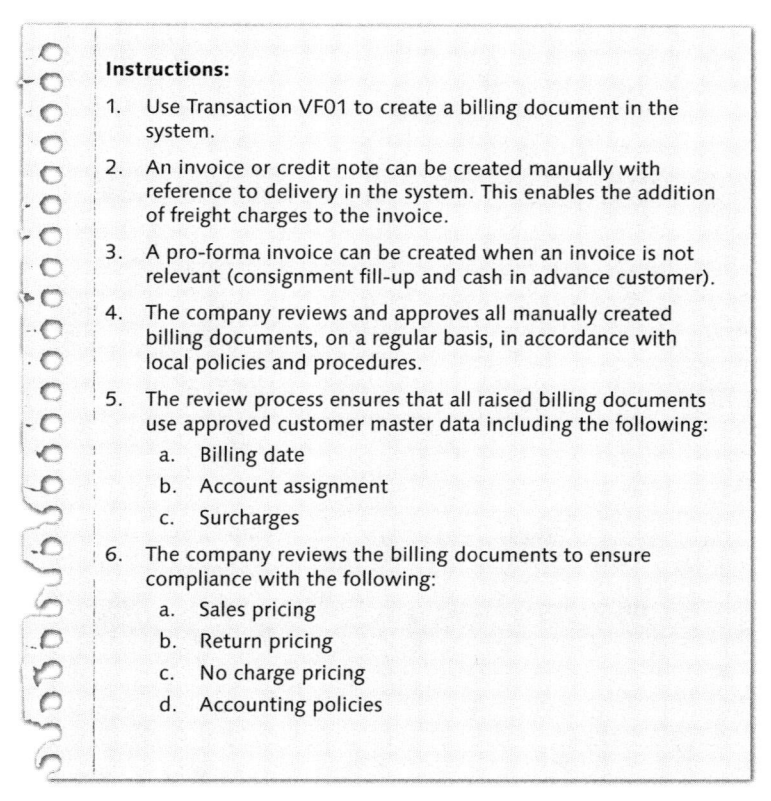

1. Use Transaction VF01 to create a billing document in the system.
2. An invoice or credit note can be created manually with reference to delivery in the system. This enables the addition of freight charges to the invoice.
3. A pro-forma invoice can be created when an invoice is not relevant (consignment fill-up and cash in advance customer).
4. The company reviews and approves all manually created billing documents, on a regular basis, in accordance with local policies and procedures.
5. The review process ensures that all raised billing documents use approved customer master data including the following:
   a. Billing date
   b. Account assignment
   c. Surcharges
6. The company reviews the billing documents to ensure compliance with the following:
   a. Sales pricing
   b. Return pricing
   c. No charge pricing
   d. Accounting policies

Figure 20.3 Transaction-Based Instructions Created by the Project Training Team

This transaction-based instruction can also be supplemented with student exercises. The training team will have prepared a special SAP environment that is restricted to training use. (Remember the training environment?) This environment

20 | Continuous User Training

contains the full range of SAP functionality needed for training, as well as subsets of company-representative data for student exercises.

Figure 20.4 shows an example of a student exercise that contains data for creating a credit memorandum. Each student user and the instructor are assigned customer numbers to complete the transaction. The data sheet provides additional required information regarding document date, amounts involved, GL account to use, and text information to be entered.

1. Create Credit Memo: FB75

Situation: Create a credit memo on a customer's account for non-material, non-invoice items.

Required data: This section provides the field data required to complete this exercise. Refer to this data sheet as necessary while performing the exercise.

Field	Value
KEYCODE	FB75
Customer	1022538/See user-specific data
Document date	06/29/20XX
Amount	100.00
Text	FI credit
G/L account	420010
Amount in doc. curr.	100.00
Item text	FI credit

User-specific data: This section provides the user-specific data required to complete this exercise.

User	Customer
Instructor	1003262
User 1	1002475
User 2	1003720
User 3	1002579
User 4	1003178
User 5	1003360

Figure 20.4 Data Sheet for Student Exercise

The instructor demonstrates credit memorandum entry using the specific customer number assigned. Members of the class would have the opportunity to view the process and ask questions. Once instructor entry is completed, each student user then creates a credit memorandum using information from the data sheet assigned. Once entry is complete, user students can compare their results with those produced by the instructor.

20.1.4 Development Tools

All training content associated with an SAP implementation project can be prepared manually. However, automated systems are available that help a great deal with the material preparation. Not only do these systems make the development process easier, but they also leave much of the content generation in the hands of the SMEs. This arrangement greatly minimizes resource demands placed on scarce training developers. Additionally, by enabling the SME as content developers, they ensure that training very closely matches company business processes.

A few of these authoring systems operate in tandem with the SAP system. This greatly adds to their value for use on an SAP implmentation project. These systems support content creation as well as automated collaboration between authors, designers, and reviewers. Many have the check-in and check-out features common to workflows in document management systems. Similar to these document management systems, authoring applications also support versioning as the training content moves through the development process.

Figure 20.5 illustrates the authoring process using an automated tool. It shows content development that begins with an author, who records information regarding a specific SAP transaction. As the document is expanded and enlarged, the authoring tool updates versions from previous edits and indicates approvals when attained. Completed course material can be stored in the company document repository for reuse as needed.

Authoring tools can be used for virtually all types of training material. Additionally, they will support completion of work instructions that may be required for life science and other validated operations. For large-scale SAP implementation projects, authoring tools greatly minimize errors in developing content and ensure that materials are "training-ready."

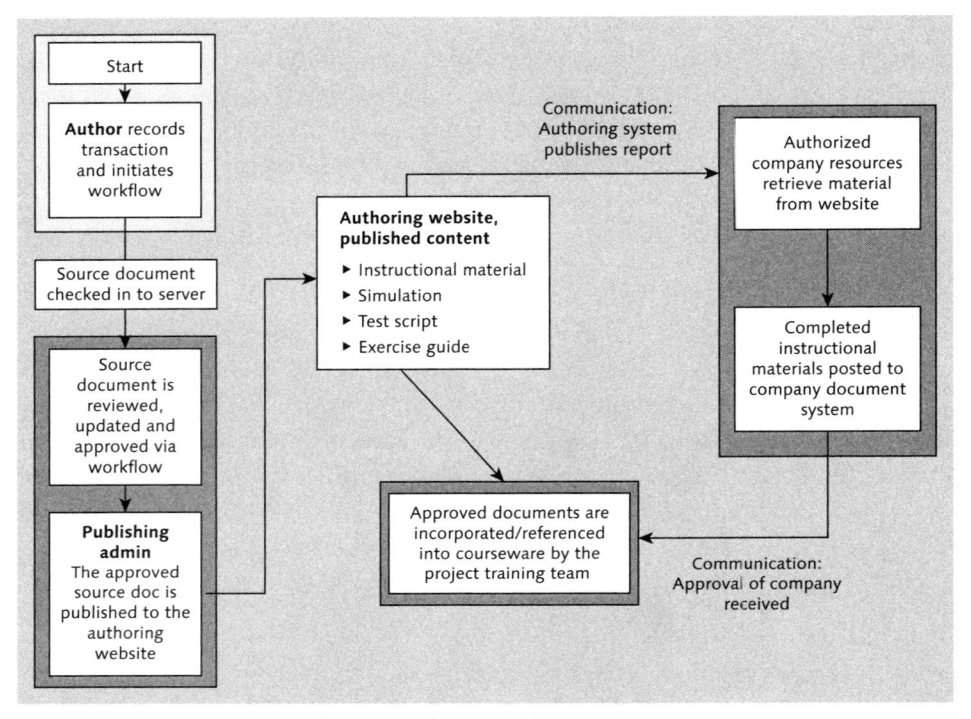

Figure 20.5 Authoring System Operations for an SAP Implementation

20.2 Trainer Preparation

An SAP implementation project team can expect anywhere from 50 percent to 75 percent of total user training to take place using ILT. This high reliance on ILT means that instructors must be identified, matched with locations and class demand, and prepared to perform as instructors well before training begins.

> **Tip**
>
> In almost all cases, your SMEs will also be your trainers. They are best prepared by their familiarity with the system. They also tend to be leaders at their sites.
>
> Take advantage of their availability, but prepare them as well. Let them know early on that they will instruct classes prior to go-live. Help them see the assignment as interesting and challenging. If you do, they will learn to see it that way too.

Virtually every trainer will be a company employee and will have participated in earlier stages of the project as SMEs. Selection criteria for instructors should emphasize just this type of preparation. It should include extensive involvement in blueprinting, documentation review, and user acceptance testing to ready prospective instructors for the subject matter demands of course instruction. However, it's likely that many of those individuals selected will be first-time instructors and require assistance in adapting to the trainer role.

Making sure that the right people are selected as instructors is the essential first step. Instructors should be content experts, and they should also have a real interest in helping others learn. Picking instructors who have little or no interest in the task will surely lead to problems. Successful projects seek to identify the best potential instructors. Effective instructors will build motivation among end-user attendees; instructors who lack the interest themselves will not build motivation and may even discourage their end-user classes.

The most effective instructors possess high levels of self-assurance and are able to think on their feet. To the extent possible, they should be organizational leaders who have the confidence of the end-user population. Where these traits are present, the instructor has already travelled at least halfway down the path of success.

The project training team can do much to augment instructional skills. The primary tool used for instructor preparation is the train-the-trainer *workshop*. These workshops are conducted just prior to the initiation of end-user training. Normally lasting for a work week, these sessions provide time for instructors to familiarize themselves with course content and to practice their classroom delivery skills.

Train-the-trainer sessions will be conducted at a site or regional location. For that reason, instructors who participate will have varying instructional assignments. Some may cover accounts payable, others may cover indirect procurement, and still others may cover plant maintenance processes. Thus, train-the-trainer sessions will focus on the overall instructional process and provide time for instructors to work with content experts on the subject matter of their specific courses.

Table 20.3 illustrates the structure of a train-the-trainer session. The topics are listed in the order that they would be addressed during the session. Most session time is devoted to applied activities, such as instructor preparation and practice sessions. These are essential to ensure familiarity with course content and to gain confidence in presentation. Equally important is the time spent in system setup and accessing data to be used in the course.

Topic	Description
Instructional skills	Covers how a classroom operates and how the instructor contributes to making the class a success.
Training course design	Outlines how the training team has constructed training courses. It explains the different types of content used and how overview and transaction courses work.
SAP transaction courses	Most instructors will provide training for transaction courses. This section provides an overview of the transactions included in each course and the use of student exercises and simulations.
Classroom setup	Presents information on collecting student attendance information, maintenance and distribution of class rosters, and timing of breaks. This section also includes how to access the training system and the data to be used in the course.
Instructor preparation	Each instructor will be given time to review classroom materials and prepare notes required for training delivery for the session.
Practice sessions	SMEs from project functional workstreams will assist instructors in presenting material and will provide feedback to instructors.
Hands-on practice	Instructors will have the opportunity to present their materials to the entire group and receive feedback.

Table 20.3 Agenda for the Train-the-Trainer Session

Once instructors have completed the train-the-trainers sessions, they are ready for the classroom teaching activities that immediately follow. Once training logistics has begun assigning trainees to classes, instructors will find their time almost entirely devoted to training for the next month or two.

20.3 Training Delivery Logistics

When all courses are developed and all instructors prepared, the training team shifts its emphasis to managing the logistics of course delivery. This is a very different role from content development and requires a different skillset. Often at this point, with development completed, the systems integrator will roll off most of its training development staff. Company project team resources now take over and handle this final step in delivering training.

20.3.1 Translation of Training Materials

For implementations that require converting training materials into different languages, translation must be completed before classroom training can begin.

Figure 20.6 outlines the process that translation will follow. The implementing company will have contracted with a professional translation service. This service provider translates course materials into the implementing company's selected languages. These often include English, Spanish, French, Mandarin Chinese, Portuguese, Japanese, and Thai.

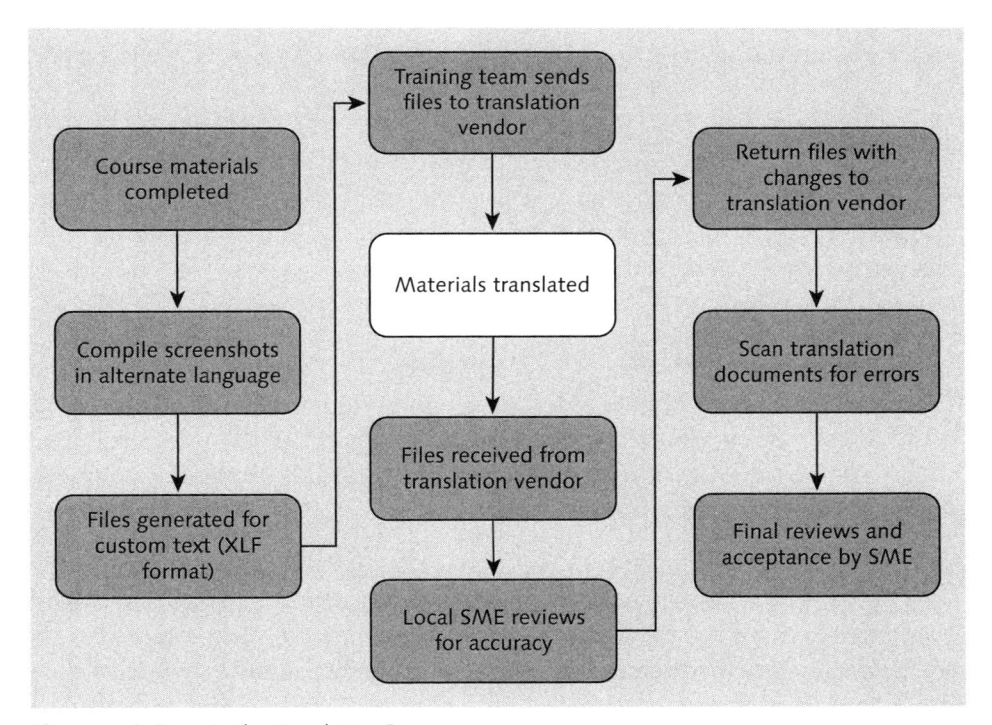

Figure 20.6 Steps in the Translation Process

From the perspective of the implementing company, materials must be prepared for translation and then reviewed for both accuracy and completeness upon receipt. The training team selects reviewers who have both subject matter experience with the content and who are native speakers in the specific language.

Many of the translations will be completed by the translation service providers' proprietary automated applications. For this reason, reviewers will especially focus on word usage. The translation must use common terms for activities or objects involved in a business process; otherwise the translation may come across as stilted or simply be unhelpful.

> **Tip**
>
> If your project is reasonably large, you will need a small team to coordinate course material translations. The job will include packaging the course material for the translation service, monitoring it through the completion stages, assigning it to native speaker SMEs for review, and returning any material errors to the translation service for repair. The training team can likely manage the team but may need assistance in finding resources.

When the completed translations are approved, the training team immediately forwards copies to the course instructors who will provide training in that language. Instructors will then have the opportunity to acclimate themselves to the translated course materials prior to beginning their classes.

20.3.2 Course Scheduling

The onset of end-user training is a very active time and requires continuous involvement from project team staff, as well as coordinators assigned from each region. Classes must be scheduled, facilities allocated, and instructors assigned — all within an approximately two-month period.

The team will face several challenges, and its capacity for adaptation will be tested fully. End users may be assigned to attend a specific class session and not attend, instructors may become sick or otherwise unavailable and their classes require rescheduling, and for whatever reason, instructional facilities may be lost — that is, assigned to other purposes.

Course scheduling entails more than assigning one end user to one class. With various users taking job assignments that cover multiple roles, many end users can expect to attend several classes.

Figure 20.7 shows how this might work in the case of a single end user. For a company financial analyst, training would mean attending nine separate classes and 21 hours of training.

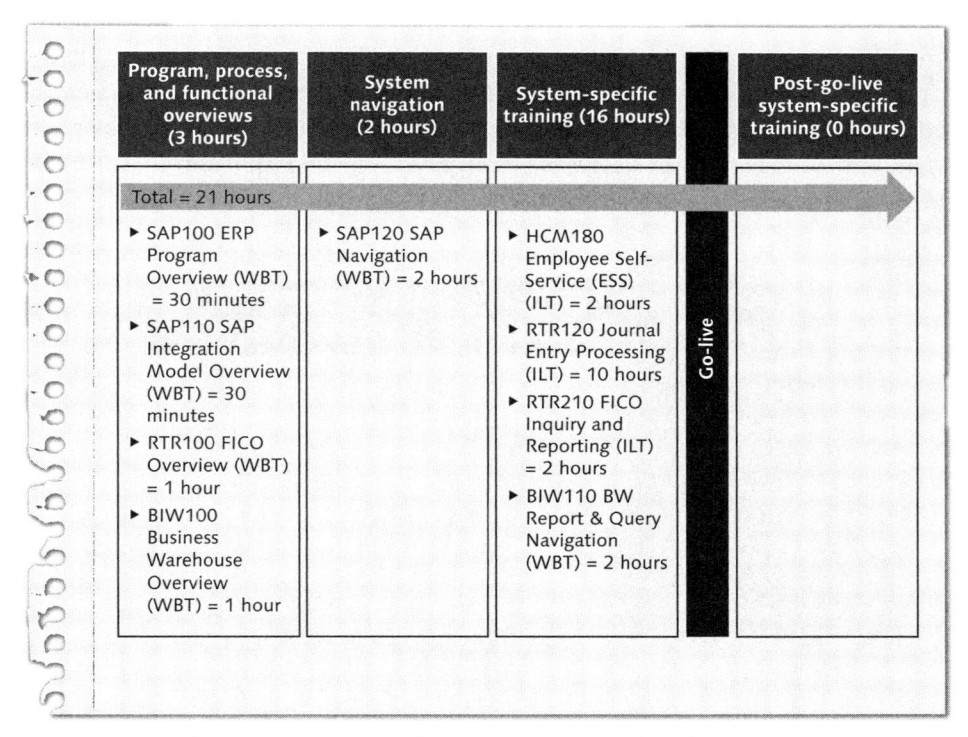

Program, process, and functional overviews (3 hours)	System navigation (2 hours)	System-specific training (16 hours)	Post-go-live system-specific training (0 hours)
Total = 21 hours			
▶ SAP100 ERP Program Overview (WBT) = 30 minutes ▶ SAP110 SAP Integration Model Overview (WBT) = 30 minutes ▶ RTR100 FICO Overview (WBT) = 1 hour ▶ BIW100 Business Warehouse Overview (WBT) = 1 hour	▶ SAP120 SAP Navigation (WBT) = 2 hours	▶ HCM180 Employee Self-Service (ESS) (ILT) = 2 hours ▶ RTR120 Journal Entry Processing (ILT) = 10 hours ▶ RTR210 FICO Inquiry and Reporting (ILT) = 2 hours ▶ BIW110 BW Report & Query Navigation (WBT) = 2 hours	

(Go-live marker between System-specific training and Post-go-live columns)

Figure 20.7 Sample Training Assignment for a Company Financial Analyst

Of the total 21 training hours, seven are assigned to WBT and 14 to ILT. The scheduling advantage of WBT is that end users can complete the course assignment at their convenience. There is no scheduling problem.

However, the remaining 14 hours of ILT must be scheduled, with completion monitored on a course-by-course basis. Training administrators must identify locations, instructors, and materials to accommodate these 14 hours of coursework. This situation will be multiplied exponentially for the total number of end users participating in training.

Figure 20.8 provides some indication of the problems that schedulers can face. In this example, three separate sites are going live with the SAP system and are now beginning end-user training. Each end user would attend the SAP overview and navigation course. This represents almost 500 individual enrollments. However, the total course enrollments for additional instructor-led courses contribute another 1,200 course attendances.

Job roles spanning multiple areas require attendance at approximately two to three additional classes per end user. These must be scheduled and resourced—all while the sites continue their normal business activities. Ensuring that all the right end users make it to classes is not an easy task and requires round-the-clock back-office operations to make it work.

Functional Area	Trainees for Site One	Trainees for Site Two	Trainees for Site Three	Course Totals
All-SAP overview and navigation	117	205	175	497
Plant operations	104	172	161	437
Manufacturing	91	102	153	346
Demand planning and forecasting	10	12	12	34
Supply chain/OTC	123	167	173	463
Finance	20	24	22	66
Direct procurement	22	24	25	71
Totals	487	706	721	1,914

Figure 20.8 Distribution of End-User Training at Three Implementation Sites

> **Tip**
>
> Especially in highly regulated companies—where class attendance is a prerequisite for obtaining an SAP UserID—course scheduling is a very demanding activity. Remember, this time is very close to go-live and there is little margin for error. Users *will* commit to attending class and then pop up on your "no show" list. Rooms will be available and then suddenly disappear. Expect the unexpected and develop plans to resolve the issues.

20.3.3 Logistics Tools

Fortunately, some systems support is available to automate these scheduling activities. Many companies have adopted learning management systems (LMS) to assist with training delivery. These applications can assist with normal company education and training operations, as well as those related to an SAP implementation. To help with the SAP implementation, they perform the following types of activities:

- **Managing training logistics**
  By connecting with the company human resources system, the LMS can access all employee master data, such as names, locations, and skill levels. This information can be used to assign users to courses, schedule classes, monitor enrollment statuses, and assign instructors. Because the system is automated, it can easily shift classes, instructors, and attendees as needed. An LMS can eliminate weeks and weeks of manual tracking activity.

- **Providing attendance and completion reports**
  The LMS can report user attendance status on all assigned classes and flag users who are not on target to complete their coursework on time. Additionally, the LMS can indicate site completion status grouped by users and functional area.

- **Generating content authoring**
  Some LMSs have content authoring functionality as well. This would allow the implementing company to prepare its own coursework and deliver that material on the same system.

- **Delivering Web-based training**
  Most LMSs support self-service delivery. This would permit an implementing company to distribute Web-based training to end users through the LMS. Moreover, the system could also automatically maintain course completion information and any test scores required.

- **Tracking skills**
  An LMS can maintain training records indicating levels of end-user proficiency and any areas where skills are in need of improvement. This automated performance tracking can be very useful in highly regulated environments where training status must be demonstrated to auditors.

Let's look briefly at where training fits into the post-go-live process.

20.4 Post-Go-Live Processes

As the implementation project winds down and the scramble to train end users comes to a conclusion, many will see the accumulated training material as artifacts of a previous experience, no longer needed.

However, even with all training delivered and the system live, the need for end-user training still remains. As new employees are hired, they must receive training. As new sites are added, users located in those sites must be trained. As new companies are acquired, the acquired staff must be trained in company systems. Training does not go away. It merely changes its emphasis.

> **Pitfall Alert**
>
> Many companies not only view the project training material in the past tense but apply the same logic to their training administrators. Many are shifted over to other assignment, sometimes out of the training field altogether. Make sure that you retain sufficient administrator expertise to handle future demand. Otherwise, you will need to find and train an entirely new set of administrators.

Company business processes will adapt and change. The existing training material must be adjusted to reflect these changes, and continuing employees must now receive amended training to remain current.

The SAP system will also adapt and change. Upgrades will be released or new functionality will be added. As the system evolves, end users now require training on the modified system. New content must be developed and integrated with the user training that was built for the implementation project. In this way, the course material is kept synchronized and suited to current conditions.

Resourcing decisions in the newly implemented company should reflect this need for ongoing training and education. Many companies come to believe that their investment in user training can be dramatically scaled back once the SAP implementation project is complete—but some level of resourcing and support for user training will still be required. Company senior management should carefully weigh the need for ongoing training with the resourcing required to provide it.

End-user training marks the demarcation point between realization and final preparation. Most of the activities to prepare for training take place in realization. The actual conduct of training takes place in final preparation. We'll continue with final preparation by next discussing the core activity of final preparation: cutover planning.

Your project is now in the express lane headed for go-live. Cutover planning focuses the team on those last activities before the system is available for all users.

21   Cutover Planning

User acceptance testing marks the final step in realization. With realization now complete, the project moves into the final preparation phase. All remaining activities necessary for go-live take place during this relatively short and very intensive period.

Most project teams find that the final preparation phase feels compressed. In fact, time really is very limited, and there are many items to complete between realization completion and system go-live. They include the following:

- Business process preparation
- Final data loads to the production system and verification of the data
- Moving of configuration and custom object builds into the production system
- User communications and training completion in support of go-live
- Go-live review and approval
- Post go-live (hypercare) planning

This chapter provides information on these items. To add clarity to the hypercare process, post-go-live planning will be covered in the next chapter (Chapter 22).

Cutover calls for very detailed planning. Each step requires careful thought and thorough monitoring. Your project leadership should designate specific individuals—generally one from the company IT organization and one from the systems integrator—to guide its cutover planning and execution. It takes staff with extensive knowledge of systems implementation and company business processes. Successful leaders also possess the ability to manage all the moving parts at an in-depth level. Potential conflicts between project needs and business requirements

21 | Cutover Planning

require constant balancing. Project leadership should give careful consideration to filling these positions.

> **Tip**
>
> Pay special attention to selecting your cutover leads. During the cutover period, these individuals directly manage the entire set of activities. They build a high-performance team for each regional wave and ensure high standards for its execution. Any errors here can have lasting business ramifications. Find the best and give them the leeway to get the job done.

Let's walk through the elements of cutover as they appear in Figure 21.1. The process uses its own special terminology, which we'll describe in cases where its meaning is not obvious. Note that some processes take place within the same time frame.

- **Quiet period**
  The project asks that business activities be limited only to those essential for production and sales. During this time, sizeable changes could cause negative impacts to SAP configuration or data load. Clearly, major activities such as product launches or product modifications should be restricted.

- **Freeze period**
  This more limited period restricts any changes to products, such as bills of material, customer information, or supplier information. Business activities now ramp down in anticipation of the imminent SAP go-live. At this time, data, custom objects, and configuration for the new SAP system are loaded. Any changes made to existing information can create discrepancies between the new system and what is required to operate the business. Thus, activities as diverse as entry of new supplier contracts or making changes to invoices are prohibited.

- **Cutover**
  Generally starting approximately a week prior to go-live, cutover marks the time when legacy applications involved in the implementation are unavailable for use. During this period, data, custom objects, and configuration are loaded into the new system, and all parts of feeder systems must be stable. For this reason, your project team minimizes any open activity that would carry over

through to go-live. This could include taking action to restrict open sales or production orders.

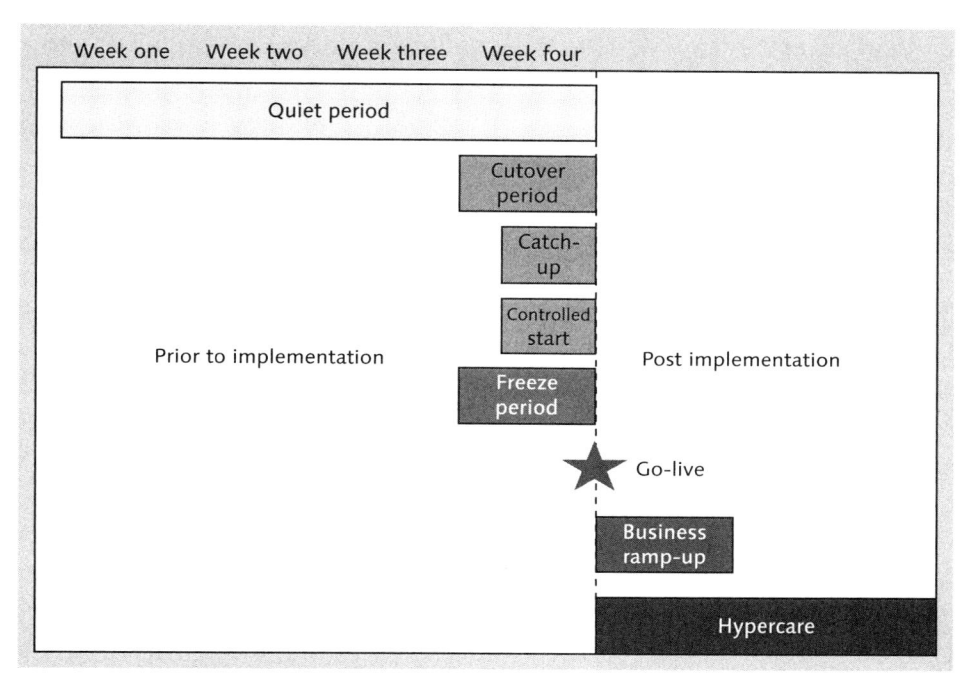

Figure 21.1 Cutover Activities

- **Catch-up**
  Occurring during the cutover period, catch-up provides time for data to be manually entered into the new SAP system. These data represent transactions from business activities taking place after the shutdown of existing company systems. Manual entry of this data into SAP assures that at go-live the system will be "caught up" with all transactions outside the data transport window. Adding emergency sales orders, purchase orders, or goods receipts also takes place at this time.

- **Controlled start**
  Taking place a few days prior to go-live but after data has been loaded, controlled start permits a small number of selected users to complete transactions prior to general use. This controlled start serves two purposes: It allows users to verify that transactions occur as planned, and it also provides time for any

needed early business activity in the system. Essential transactions, such as entering sales orders, generating invoices, and moving inventory, will take place and each receive individual verification for accuracy.

- **Go-live**
  At this point, the new SAP system is available for use. All activities expected to take place in the new system will now begin. Company employees and any business partners who integrate with the system will now use it for standard transactions.

- **Business ramp-up**
  Immediately after the system is live, functional business organizations initiate their ramp-up activities. These planned actions are orchestrated to introduce the business to the new system in a measured and structured way. Each functional organization will have identified step-by-step increases in performance, along with measures to track them. Once business ramp-up has reached its targets, your new SAP system will have proved its functionality. Only the resolution of incidents reported by end users stands in the way of full system transfer from the project team to standing business organizations.

- **Hypercare (post-go-live support)**
  This period begins immediately after go-live. Generally scheduled for 45 days, hypercare focuses the project team on immediately attending to and resolving any system-related problems.

Now that you have a good grasp of the high-level processes used in cutover, let's move on to a more detailed description.

21.1 Cutover Processes

A small team representing the project team and business operations manages cutover activities. Where the implementation involves regions and sites within the company, cutover leads are required for those regions and each major site, including countries and manufacturing plants. All those assigned to regional and site roles should have extensive knowledge of business activities performed there and should also have the confidence of regional and site management. The cutover team manages preparation and execution of cutover activities in their areas. Members will also be on point for first-line decisions regarding process and site readiness. Figure 21.2 shows the relationship of cutover teams.

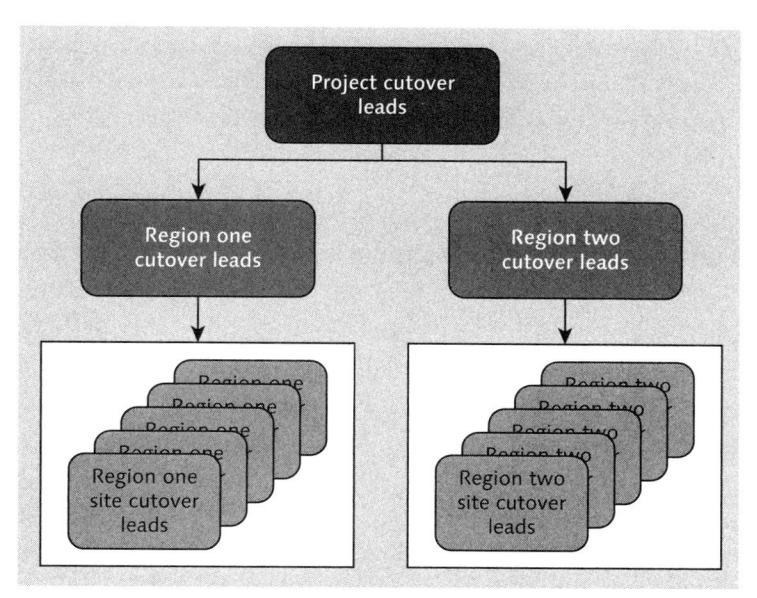

Figure 21.2 Cutover Management Team Structure

> ### Trail Marker
>
> Business ramp-up and post go-live support will be covered in Chapter 22. Our current chapter ends with the decision to go live. Ramp-up and post-go-live support take place after the project is live. They are introduced here to complete the picture regarding cutover planning.

Let's examine the four important business processes that the cutover management steam will oversee.

21.1.1 Business Preparation

A great deal of coordinated activity takes place to ready the business for go-live. This occurs in every project workstream and company location. In manufacturing plants and production-related facilities, management must decide what operations to continue during the cutover period. These decisions include potential plant shutdowns, amounts of inventory build and safety stock to have in place, and any needed business continuity planning.

> **Tip**
>
> Your company business operations will need assistance in planning the steps for go-live. Cutover leads should work with designated representatives from each involved business organization. The leads will help with the planning and then monitor the results.

Product operations management will decide on the levels of finished goods and raw material inventories they need during the cutover and ramp-up periods. These safety stock decisions are included in production plans for the periods. Cutover management acts to ensure that these stocks are in place prior to beginning cutover.

Business continuity plans should be reviewed and approved as well. For critical business processes, cutover management should verify that any needed manual operating procedures and work instructions are in place. These should be assessed in real-world practices. All key staff should receive refresh training on the work instructions and be ready to implement them if necessary.

Cutover management will plan for and track performance against business ramp-down requirements. Key areas include order management, inventory control, and monitoring of financial transactions. Any plant shutdowns agreed upon in support of the go-live are included in this tracking as well. These plans should identify actions to be taken, timing required, and who owns these actions.

Figure 21.3 provides an example of cutover key area tracking that assumes an October 25th go-live. All listed activities would again resume after go-live during the business ramp-up period.

Clearly, these activities require close cooperation between business owners and your project team. Many business owners will not have participated in the project during its earlier phases. To assure full understanding of the cutover process, your project team should arrange to brief business owners on the importance of each activity and describe reporting of progress. Regularly scheduled meetings with business owners to monitor progress will play a positive role here as well.

Any changes to existing business processes during this period can have negative impacts and must be addressed by senior executives. At this point, the SAP system build will be in its final stages. Unless they are fully understood and accounted for, changes may create effects on the system go-live. Thus, changes to business processes or market expansions must be made clearly visible. Such changes include product launches and changes, office moves, or changes to business partner relationships. Management may well decide to delay these changes in support of a smoother system go-live. Each requested change will be decided upon on an as-needed basis.

Business Area	Action	Completion Date
Order management	Eliminate generation of new indirect purchase orders	October 15
	Creation of new direct purchase orders will take place in initial MRP run after go-live	October 25
	Restriction on opening of new sales orders	October 18
	Closing of all production orders to include goods issues, goods receipts, and goods in transit	October 19
Inventory control	Establish finished goods and raw material inventories to account for cutover and business ramp-up	October 15
	Complete all inventory movements to include goods issues	October 18
	Inventory all finished goods	October 19
	Send final shipments to all order recipients	October 22
Financial transactions	Final accounts receivable cash receipt activity	October 24
	Prepare new system data for financial close	October 27
	Make necessary financial adjustments	October 27
Plant shutdowns	Two plants (China and Japan) schedule production shutdowns during cutover period	October 20 and October 19

Figure 21.3 Business Ramp-Down Control Sheet

Linking business operations closely to project cutover will greatly ease the go-live experience. Successfully ramping down business operations prior to go-live and ramping them back up again after go-live makes cutover a small bump in the road. Where business operations are not closely linked in cutover, the go-live can make for a difficult experience.

21.1.2 Data Load and Verification

During the cutover period, all necessary data to operate the business must be loaded into the production system. This includes both all master data and limited transactional data. This data includes inventory, open accounts receivable, open sales orders, and relevant financial transactions. Additionally, all data loaded into the system requires verification after load is complete but before the system (and the data) is released for use.

Figure 21.4 shows a hypothetical timeline for master and transactional data load. Data owners will review each data object for completeness and accuracy. Since this is part of the cutover period and takes place in the very limited time frame allowed, verification must be closely tracked and any data defects rapidly resolved. If the project team has utilized a test management system, it can be put to work processing verifications and managing data defect resolution.

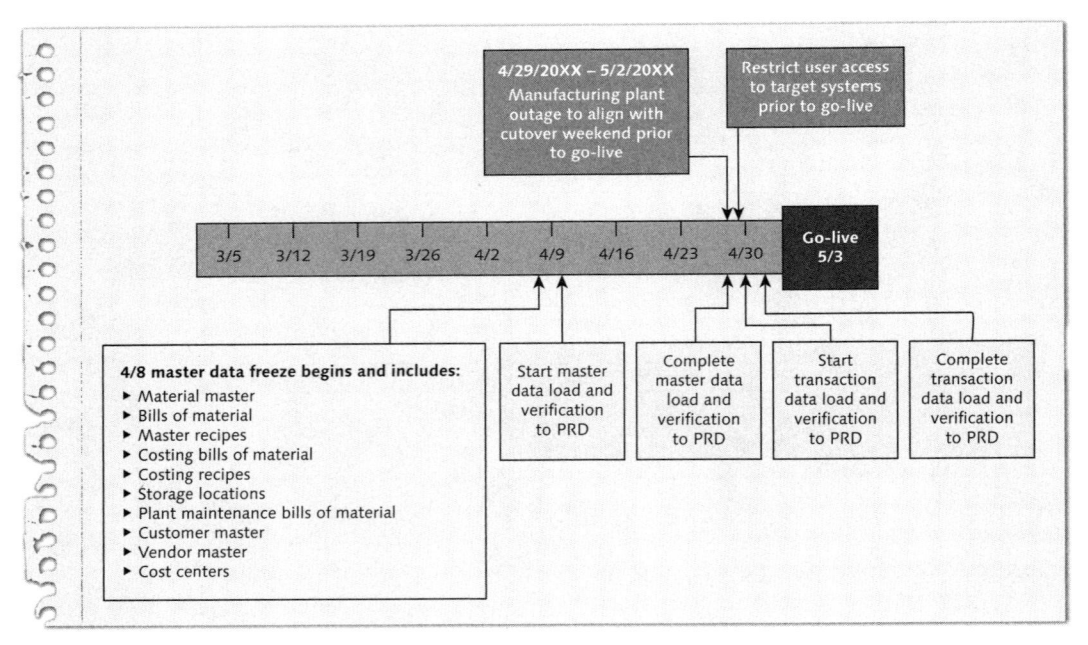

Figure 21.4 Master and Transactional Data Load Process at Cutover

The project team has little margin for error during data load. The data must be correct *and* loaded into the production system on time. Many projects use a mock data load process to practice the load sequences and timing. Taking place a few weeks prior to final data load, the mock load provides the opportunity to verify the exact process. Each step will have owners assigned and timing for completion established. Cutover leads monitor overall progress according to the timeline.

The data management team monitors mock data load as it progresses in order to identify deviations from schedule or unintended results on a real-time basis. The team can then use results from mock data loads to improve and refine the load process.

Once the final go-live data loads are ready to begin, success depends on the skills of the data team and assigned data verifiers. Master data has been locked down and restricted from change since the beginning of the quiet period, so it will be the first element to be loaded. Key objects such as customer, material, and vendor masters are large files and take some days to load. Dependent master data, such as outline agreements or bills of material, will follow those loads according to plan. Once all master data has been loaded, the focus shifts to transactional data. Items such as inventory and open accounts receivable are transferred in a shorter window during cutover.

Take care to ensure that all needed data has been accurately loaded in the system. This second review assures that the data now in the production system is correct and usable. Selected business owners review all data objects and verify correctness prior to go-live. These reviewers set the number of records in each object to be verified. Their review will include all key customers, materials, vendors, and a sample of other records. Reviewers will have participated in verification activities during previous data loads and will be familiar with the steps involved. They will be the individuals in the company most familiar with the data and the review process.

Not only do data verifiers review selected records, but they also confirm that the records are correct against any data mapping or cross reference files that have been used during load. They will check for any missing or inaccurate data. For transactional data, reviewers will use control totals to verify inventory numbers or financial balances.

Again, this is a very compressed activity. Any defects must be identified and reported to the data team. Identification, resolution, and retest will take place within the four- or five-day data load window. It is not uncommon for participants to do without sleep during this intense time.

> **Pitfall Alert**
>
> We've said it before and now we'll say it again: Production data load is an *extremely* stressful activity. Your data team will have experienced some of this stress in previous data loads. Those are difficult, yes. However, this final data load period contains no margin for error. The data must be loaded to the production system, and loaded correctly, or the project cannot go live on time. Adding to the stress is the fact that *something always goes wrong*. Be there and be ready to support your data team.

21.1.3 User Training

While the business preparation and data load activities are taking place, a similarly urgent set of actions is underway with the training team. End users who will operate the system or even to have access to it must be trained. Earlier chapters discussed creation of this training material; it will now be ready and available. The logistics steps to provide instruction to end users now begins.

In addition to the training team that is part of the core project organization, each region and site will assign local staff to coordinate training. These coordinators will work closely with the core training team. These coordinators will handle all training logistics for their sites, including the following:

- Scheduling classes at locations
- Booking facilities and classrooms
- Assigning instructors to classes and notifying them
- Assigning users to classes and notifying them
- Distributing materials to sites, ensuring classroom setup, and providing training data
- Maintaining records of attendance and class completion

For companies operating in a highly regulated environment, user training verification is taken very seriously. Users are not permitted access to the system unless they have demonstrable proof of training completion. Normally this requires attendance at all assigned classes and evidence of understanding required procedures or work instructions. Without proof of training, they will not be assigned an SAP UserID. And without the ability to log on to the system, they would be prevented from performing data verification or their normal business role after go-live.

In most cases, company subject matter experts will deliver the training classes. They have the greatest familiarity with company processes as they will take place in the SAP system. This is the same group that performed company reviews on the training materials as they were developed.

These subject matter experts will be in great demand from other parts of the project. It will be up to the training team to lock down class schedules and assure instructor availability for all sessions. Some classes may have as many as 30 attendees. Canceling a class due to instructor availability means those users may not receive their SAP UserIDs; they only receive system access when they complete all assigned training. Thus, it's vital to know which classes each user has been assigned to, and which of those have been completed

Hundreds of users will participate in training during this cutover period. Additionally, some users may have as many as five or six classes to complete. In total, this could represent 30 or more hours of classroom training. Site and regional training coordinators will prepare detailed reports on the training status of each individual. These reports outline training completion status for each individual and each site. Because of the time-sensitive nature of this information, progress reports reflecting the entire project training completion would be prepared and reviewed on a daily basis.

Users requiring early access to the system, such as data verifiers, will need to complete training prior to beginning their tasks. The schedule will reflect these and other special requirements. Site training coordinators will place users in time buckets that reflect the point at which their training must be completed.

> **Pitfall Alert**
>
> The subject of early access is a tricky one. Without completing training early, your data verifiers would not be eligible for an SAP UserID. In this case, the security team would be forced to issue SAP "firefighter" IDs. These give open-ended access to anyone who receives them. To avoid this very risky situation—your corporate audit group will be very unhappy with this course of action—you should identify those who require early access and arrange special classes for them.

Often, some sites will experience difficulty handling the complex logistics and fall behind schedule. Project management must maintain open lines of communication with site management. When problems occur, direct interventions by site management can make the difference in achieving on-time cutover completion.

Once all users have received their required training, the provisioning of SAP UserIDs can begin.

21.1.4 Cutover Communication

Regular communications regarding project progress have already been taking place during blueprint and realization. During cutover, communications intensify and messages become more targeted. These messages use several mechanisms. They will consist of broadcast emails announcing the impending go-live and the actions required to support it. These emails will address go-live timing, restrictions on some business processes during the cutover period, the need for user training attendance, any planned manufacturing plant shutdowns, and processes for distributing SAP UserIDs.

Additionally, project management provides regular project updates targeted to company management. Experience shows that having an informed, committed middle management represents one of the major keys to achieving go-live success. The project communications team prepares several messages during the cutover period that reinforce the email broadcasts. These messages would specifically target business process changes brought about by the new SAP system.

> **Tip**
>
> Get middle management on the project's side. They can either see the project as something to be tolerated, or they can give you their wholehearted support. The choice is an easy one to make. Listen to their concerns and respond to them. Once your project team adopts this approach, middle management will help you at every point possible.

These communications will focus on describing process changes in some detail, and on providing reinforcing information on the benefits to be achieved by the changes. Whenever middle management feels a strong ownership for the changes, they are more likely to be successful. Staff members who get a positive view from their manager or supervisor will see these changes as good for the company.

Conducting the "day-in-the-life" exercises described in Chapter 20 helps cement understanding of changes. During these sessions, management and staff learn to operate new business processes with the SAP system. The sessions emphasize execution of steps as they would be performed, going from upstream to downstream processes. In this way, all participants gain a firm idea of how the system will execute end-to-end business processes.

Larger gatherings of sites and functions will have a role to play as well. They provide a great opportunity for management to discuss the upcoming go-live with their staff. Managers can address any business process changes and make clear their support, and staff will of course have the opportunity to ask questions and receive detailed answers.

Using these communication tools during cutover builds enthusiasm for go-live. Additionally, this preparation produces a knowledgeable and committed staff. Viewing the implementation with anticipation can help outweigh any bumps in the road that staff will encounter during go-live.

21.2 Go-Live Authorization

With most cutover steps successfully completed, the project is ready for a go-live decision. The project team must now prove that the project is prepared to move forward to a positive implementation. Because the potential negative ramifications to company processes—and even its bottom line—are so substantial, go-live decision-making requires careful assessment. Prior to go-live, the process can be halted with data and configuration removed from the not-yet-active production system. Once implemented, the SAP system will operate major functions of the company. It will be impossible to step backwards or to run legacy systems in parallel, so the decision must be the correct one.

> **Pitfall Alert**
>
> Many believe that it's possible to dial back into the previous system after go-live, as long as you do so in the early stages. But after more than a few transactions have made their way into the system, this is an almost impossible course of action. SAP transactions are so complex and affect so many aspects of company operations that this cannot be accomplished. The only real course of action is to make sure that everything in your system is correct and reliable.

Go-live decision-making consists of several iterative reviews, each conducted at a higher level of management responsibility. The project must gain approval from each rung in the review ladder. Failure to receive approval at any step halts the cutover process. Receiving a negative go-live decision means that management feels that the project is not ready. A new date or way forward must be found that mitigates management concerns.

Figure 21.5 shows how the iterative go-live approval process would work. It contains six review steps, beginning at the base. The box shape designates approval process steps exercised by the project team, as well as steps made by affected business organizations. The ovals at the bottom identify project team decisions. The rounded rectangles above them represent business organizations' steps. The darker rectangle at the top represents the company management committee step.

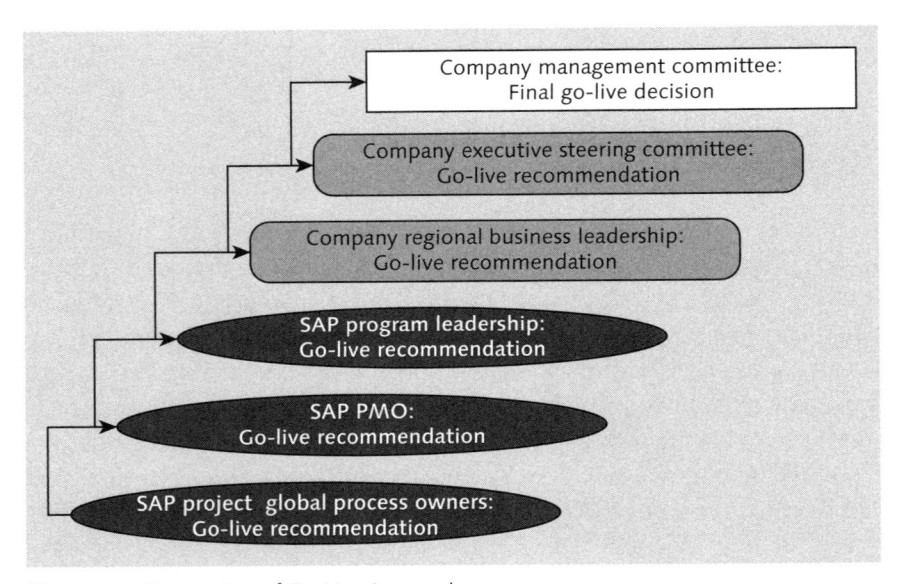

Figure 21.5 Progression of Go-Live Approval

Clearly, the first steps focus on the project view of its readiness to go live. Each global process owner or functional workstream lead makes a recommendation concerning go-live preparation. If these recommendations are all positive, the PMO takes the next review step.

In the next step, the PMO takes a broader view. It examines the performance of the entire project and makes a recommendation based on that information. If this recommendation is also positive, it passes the baton to program sponsors. These individuals, who have senior-level positions in the company, have participated in the project on a daily basis since its inception. They combine a project and systems point of view along with a business orientation. If in the third step they recommend that the project move forward to go-live, ownership for all following decisions lies with the company business organizations.

Regional business executives who will be directly affected by project go-live are next in the approval order. For the most part, they will examine how the project affects their region and the extent of regional preparedness. If their recommendation in the fourth step is a positive one, decision-making responsibility moves to the project executive steering committee in the fifth step. This group will usually contain at least one C-level company officer who is familiar with project progress. Reviewing the implications for company performance will become paramount. The steering committee looks to the project team for its readiness status and raises any questions or concerns. These will be discussed in great detail until they are better understood. The steering committee then makes its recommendation.

The final step brings together the company management committee. This group includes the CEO, COO, CFO, controller, and the senior supply chain executive, at a minimum. It will also generally comprise senior executives from the project systems integrator and from SAP. At this point, all participants are vested in project success. All participants—whether company executives, SAP, or the systems integrator—want the right decision for the client company. These are generally very intense discussions and focus on making the "right" decision.

The PMO has responsibility to prepare and present much of the information at the go-live decision meetings. This information must be impartial and aimed at assisting decision-making. It covers major aspects of project performance but is structured at a level geared to senior executives.

Figure 21.6 provides a reusable outline for go-live decision-making. It divides reporting into four readiness components: system, user, external partner, and business. These categories are intended to represent an exhaustive list of factors that could impede go-live performance. Listed under each category are the elements that comprise that particular readiness component. The structure provides top-level guidance to assessing project readiness. Project management must ensure that the pieces under each readiness component are the right ones to represent the project. Project management must also ensure that relevant and correct data are provided for each component.

21 | Cutover Planning

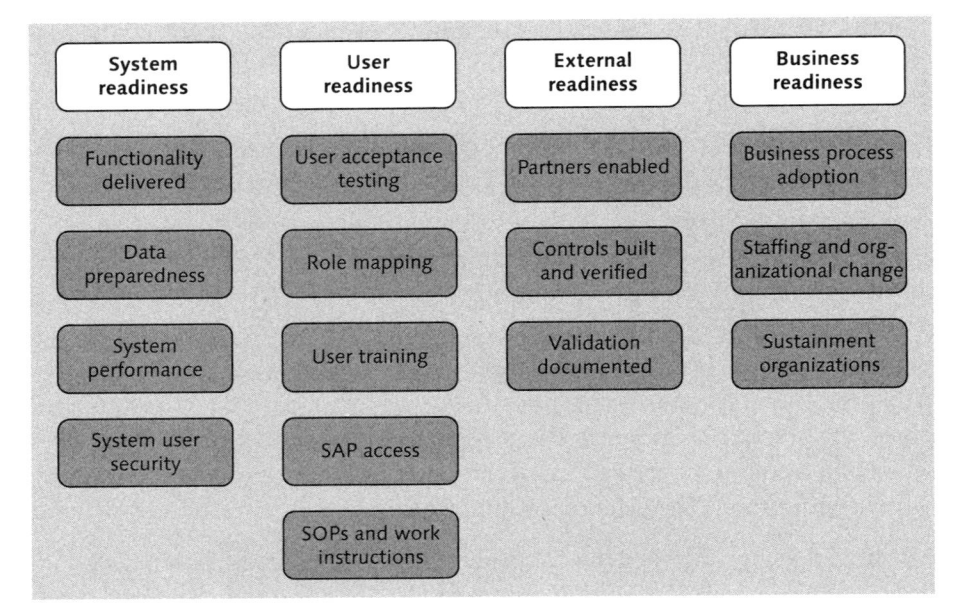

Figure 21.6 Outline for Go-Live Readiness Reporting

Figure 21.7 illustrates the concept by giving an example of the systems readiness scorecard as part of a go-live approval scenario. The systems readiness profile lists functionality delivered, data preparedness, system performance, and system user security as the evaluation criteria. The item column also contains a status indicator showing green, yellow, or red. These provide shorthand rating information for senior executives.

Remaining columns depict requirements for each category, its current status, and any significant issues affecting project performance. The requirements column shows the benchmark against which the project team is operating. These should be clearly stated and open to discussion with executives. The status column indicates whether the requirement has been met. In the example all requirements have been met. The issues column provides a field to describe any open issues. Some watch items have been identified.

The three remaining readiness scorecards provide similar information within their field of scope. Using this information, senior executives will have a view to the preparedness of the project for go-live. Discussion during the review session will follow the concerns of executives present. Their concerns likely coincide with any items listed as yellow or red on the readiness scorecards.

Item	Requirement	Status	Issues
Functionality delivered (green)	▶ All in-scope functionality in place for go-live ▶ Mitigations in place for all approved exceptions	▶ All in-scope functionality ready for go-live with three exceptions (currently in process by the project team)	▶ Customs documents ▶ Tax processing software
Data preparedness (yellow)	▶ Required legacy data is migrated via automated or manual conversion processes	▶ Data loads underway for cutover master data	▶ Verification data owners still in training
System performance (green)	▶ All in-scope functionality in place for go-live ▶ Mitigations in place for all approved exceptions	▶ Performance testing verified load handling	▶ Portal performance occasionally problematic
System user security (green)	▶ SAP user security designed to identify and remedy internal controls or validation issues	▶ Role design and role mapping complete ▶ Role testing successful during user acceptance test	▶ Role testing complete in three work-streams—PTS and RTR have small number of open items

Figure 21.7 Systems Readiness Go-Live Scorecard

Executive representatives from SAP and the systems integrator will also put forth their assessments of project go-live readiness. Company senior management will find this external viewpoint quite valuable in their decision-making. Since both sets of executives will have participated in numerous SAP implementations, their recommendations carry significant weight.

In cases where regional implementations are involved, company senior executives may decide to include readiness information from participating sites. These scorecards would follow a similar format but reflect scope specific to the sites, as shown in Figure 21.8.

The report contains status information regarding the range of activities under site auspices. As with other reports of this type, numerical updates are provided where possible and each item is coded green, yellow, or red to indicate its current level of progress. The report provides detail about project support activities as well as cutover preparation. Senior executives could request similar reports from additional sites or a single report compiled at the regional level.

Item	Status	Rating
Early access user training	35 early access users identified and trained	Green
Super users prepared	103 super users identified and trained	Green
End users trained per plan	1,536 end users trained per plan	Green
Data verifiers prepared	35 data verifiers trained and access provided	Green
Vendor and bank information submitted	Bank information submitted for 900 vendors—awaiting confirmation	Yellow
Blocked and parked invoices cleared	All 327 blocked and parked invoices cleared	Green
Inactive and aged purchase orders cleared	All 134 inactive and aged invoices cleared	Green
New customer orders and purchase orders halted	New order activity halted as of planned times	Green
Inventory in place to cover ramp-down and ramp-up	Inventory in place—amounts assume normal order volume	Yellow
Partners notified of system changeover	All partners (three PLs, banks, and vendors) notified	Green

Figure 21.8 Site Readiness Report

Assuming that the readiness data all point in a positive direction, permission for go-live is granted. Project staff then moves forward with the final cutover steps and activates the system for use.

We've now reached the closing stages of final preparation. A few more steps are needed and then we move into hypercare and incident resolution.

Go-live and hypercare focus your project team's energies on an all-out error-resolution process. Errors or incidents are a normal part of a go-live experience. Resolving them takes the concentrated effort of the project team.

22 Go-Live and Hypercare

Your project team has now received permission to go live! Over the next few days, the team will complete final activities to prepare the system for use. Once these are accomplished, user access is granted and your company will be live on its SAP system. This chapter covers those final steps to go-live and the intensive problem-resolution efforts that follow.

22.1 Final Go-Live Processes

There are several items to be completed within the last few days prior to go-live. During this very concentrated period, your team will finalize remaining deliverables to ready the system for use. Let's examine these processes now.

22.1.1 Continuing Cutover Activities

Once master and transactional data have been loaded, inventory reconciliation and cost roll-ups will be performed. Manufacturing sites will have previously conducted physical inventory counts during the earlier stages of cutover. These counts established actual on-hand inventory figures for all products as well as raw material and work-in-process inventories. Prior to releasing the system for full user access, this inventory information will be compared to inventory data posted in the new system.

Production operations will compare and reconcile the two sets of figures. The inventory counts include material held at partner locations such as third-party logistics providers and contract manufacturers. Where discrepancies are identified, the root causes of any differences must be examined. Often, tracing inventory differences and reconciling them represents a time-consuming activity—especially if inventory handling processes change as a result of introducing the SAP system.

In any case, the reconciliation must confirm that the new inventory numbers held in the SAP system are complete and correct. If analysis demonstrates that the inventory levels reported in the new SAP system are incorrect, the discrepancies must be resolved as soon as is practical.

In similar fashion, cost roll-ups should also be performed in the last stages of cutover. Cost roll-ups confirm that product costing in the new system is accurate. The project team would first execute full cost roll-up. This "explodes" (or lists) bills of material for assemblies and subassemblies. The roll-up provides the cost of assemblies at an indentured level. Beginning with the lowest level, it consolidates costs all the way to top-level assemblies. The cost roll-up confirms accuracy of the bills of material and individual component costs.

Analysis of cost roll-up data should compare data in the new SAP system with data from legacy source systems. Any discrepancies must be traced to issues with either system or to the data converted during cutover processes. The project team must resolve any inconsistencies before large-scale system usage occurs.

22.1.2 Granting System Access

Virtually the last step in cutover—just prior to releasing the system for use—is the distribution of SAP UserIDs. Once these are received by end users, they will be able to access the system and perform all transactions for which they have access.

Cutover management verifies that each end user has completed the required training before access is granted. Any end users who have not yet completed training will not receive SAP UserIDs. Both the end user and responsible manager will be notified of this situation. All other end users will receive their SAP UserIDs via email along with log-in instruction.

22.1.3 Business Ramp-Up Execution

Functional business organizations and regional operations have set transaction volume targets for this early stage of system availability. In coordination with the project team, these organizations now move forward to execute their plans. This business ramp-up provides the opportunity to make sure that the system properly performs standard business transactions at customary volumes. Figure 22.1 shows a subset of supply chain ramp-up metrics.

Supply Chain Business Ramp-Up Metrics (Raw Numbers)	Week One Planned	Week Two Planned	Week Three Planned
Sales orders processed	450	575	900
Deliveries made	210	300	450
Production orders	125	200	350
Direct purchase orders requested	400	600	800
Direct purchase orders approved	150	400	600
Intercompany stock transfer orders	125	200	350
Invoices paid	200	300	400
Indirect purchase orders requested	500	700	1,000

Figure 22.1 Supply Chain Business Ramp-Up Plans

> **Tip**
> Most of your business organizations will immediately understand the idea of ramp-down. Reducing their activities in the face of some major event, such as a product launch, is a relatively common occurrence. Ramp-up, however, may come as a more novel concept. Spend time educating business units to ensure that they understand ramp-up and have defined realistic measures to assess its performance.

These are essential business activities with numerical targets assigned over a three-week period. The first week presumes lower levels of performance as users familiarize themselves with the system. As weeks pass, the expected performance levels increase. In the final week, levels should closely conform to regular run rates. Once these are reached, business ramp-up has achieved its purpose and your project team no longer tracks these levels.

22.2 Hypercare

Once the system is live and users have access, your project team will immediately shift to problem-resolution mode. Solving problems now becomes the sole focus of the project team. This intensive support period—known as "hypercare"—remains in place until the system is validated as stable. As a general rule, hypercare takes place during the first 30 to 45 days after go-live. However, its actual duration will depend on the number of incidents (or errors) reported, their severity, and closure status. Until the system and business processes involved are deemed stable, the project team cannot move on to follow-on implementation waves or return to pre-project roles.

At go-live, many users will immediately log on to the system. Either they are able to complete all transactions as expected, or they will encounter problems that prevent transaction completion. Substantial difficulties affecting large user populations not only influence business operations, but they also create negative perceptions of system performance. When users experience significant problems, they can quickly come to believe that the system "just doesn't work." Once this perception becomes entrenched, it is very difficult to change.

For this reason, hypercare mobilizes all available project resources to find immediate solutions to major issues. Hypercare also involves new terminology, roles, and processes. This section will focus on the effective organization and management of post go-live support.

22.2.1 Hypercare Operations

The key term in hypercare is the *incident*. Essentially the same as an error or defect, an incident denotes any problem that an end user identifies in using the system. Hypercare aims to identify and resolve all incidents, which can range from users' inability to log on, to encountering errors in completing transactions.

Figure 22.2 outlines the overall flow of hypercare. It begins with an end user identifying an issue in step one and flows through contact with a super user in steps two and three. If this intervention fails to resolve the issue (step four), it is then reported to the help desk in step five. The issue now becomes an incident. It is tracked and then assigned to the applicable project team resolver group for resolution in step six. Once the incident is tested and resolved in step seven, the incident is closed in step eight.

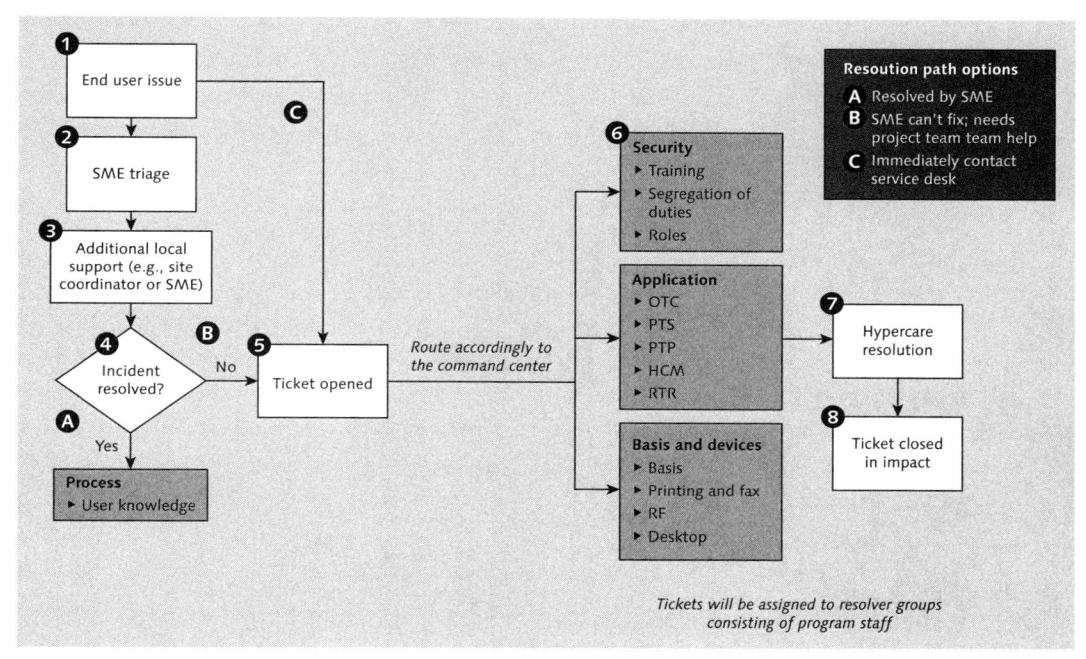

Figure 22.2 Hypercare Process Flow

The following sections describe the components of this problem-resolution process, considered the superstructure for hypercare, in greater detail.

Command Center

Each implementation requires a central control location. A central command center manages hypercare operations and houses most of the resolvers; it operates 24 hours a day and seven days a week until hypercare is closed. The implementation may create additional subsidiary command centers as needed. They will house regional or site hypercare resources.

Figure 22.3 provides an example of a single command center in North America and four designated regional command centers in Mexico City, Rio de Janeiro,

Amsterdam, and Shanghai. This arrangement supports a global implementation where simultaneous post-go-live support activities are carried on in virtually every region.

> **Tip**
>
> Your command center will become a bustling hive of activity. The project team is gathered together, doing everything possible to resolve incidents as they arrive. Organizing logistics such as phone connections, seating space for team members, and work schedules can make the command center a much more efficient hive.

While the central command center has overall control in all regions and time zones, regional command centers focus exclusively on issues within their regions. Additional, country- and site-specific activities will center primarily on business operations, making systems issues a secondary concern. The vast majority of hypercare activities are carried out at either the central or regional command centers.

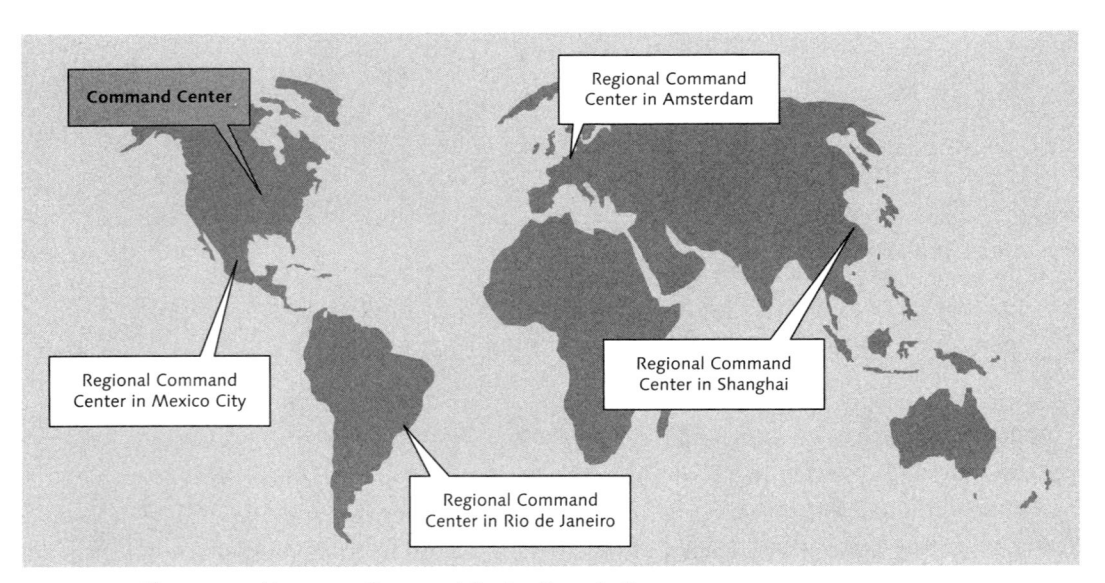

Figure 22.3 Hypercare Command Center Organization

Super Users and Subject Matter Experts

Super users and subject matter experts (SMEs) are the first line of defense in a triaged problem-resolution process. They own the performance of step one through step four in the hypercare flow outlined in Figure 22.2. These are SMEs who have participated in many project activities or expert business users who have skills to assist others. Frequently, end-user problems can be solved by trained resources who walk them through the steps of completing a transaction correctly. The user may have forgotten some aspect of training or may have encountered an issue not fully covered in training. Super users and SMEs have slightly different roles to play.

Super users will perform the following roles:

- Gather in-depth knowledge about the SAP system as it will operate at their function or site
- Serve as the initial point of contact for end-user issues
- Actively support end users in problem resolution
- Provide information about the site or functional problems to the project team
- Assist end users when reporting their issues to the help desk
- Receive and disseminate all relevant project updates to end users

SMEs will perform the following roles:

- Serve as the process or system expert for their site or function
- Deliver any needed hands-on instruction to super users or end users
- Operate as a liaison to the relevant global process owners regarding user experience
- Lead system testing for incidents identified at their site

In some cases, end users may attempt to solve their issue by directly contacting the help desk. However, the project team should strongly emphasize the preferred resolution path so end users contact a super user first. Having skilled super users available at go-live locations enables rapid response, which greatly reduces user frustration. It also the decreases demands made on project team resolvers. Effective super users working with end users can correct as many as half of issues that might otherwise be routed to the project team. Because super users can solve so many issues, project team resolvers are able to focus their attention on genuine systems issues.

The change management team takes the lead in preparing super users to handle their hypercare activities. All super users must understand the role they are to play and any specialized knowledge required. Many new procedures will be unique to hypercare, including the following:

- **End users should know their super user contact.**
  Super users must reach out to all assigned end users prior to go-live to communicate their role and let the end user know that they are there to help. Additionally, the project team should supply materials to make super users (and SMEs!) immediately identifiable. These can include specially colored shirts and buttons that super users wear throughout the hypercare period.
- **Super users should understand how to perform their role.**
  The change management team will conduct training sessions to discuss the details of hypercare and to outline special tasks assigned to super users. Super users will also receive instruction on specific problem information required to report an incident to the help desk. As a result of the training, super users should also be prepared to assist with any hands-on end-user assistance required at their site or functional area. Specific issues they would be expected to handle include the following:
  - Difficulties with log-in to the SAP system
  - Challenges with access to needed transactions
  - Issues with data displaying in transactions
  - Running or printing any required reports
- **Super users should be prepared to assist or perform required testing.**
  Testing to assure that a problem was correctly resolved is the final step prior to incident closure. Normally the user who reported the incident would perform the testing. However, some end users may be unfamiliar with testing processes or require assistance with testing. Super users for the area in question can provide assistance or even perform the testing.

> **Tip**
>
> Super users are an essential part of hypercare. Spend time finding the best candidates and educating them thoroughly. A motivated super user group will closely observe work areas for user issues and catch them right away. They can calmly assist the often-frantic end users to resolve their issues with no incident ever reported!

Figure 22.4 shows the relationship between SMEs, super users, and end users. Although some SMEs can act as super users, most often the SME acts as a coach and resource for the super user. For that reason, super users are generally collocated with the end users they support. This collocation makes for ease of access and familiarity. SMEs, however, can be located in regional offices or other centralized sites. SMEs and super users will work together to make arrangements for rapid communication using telephones or email.

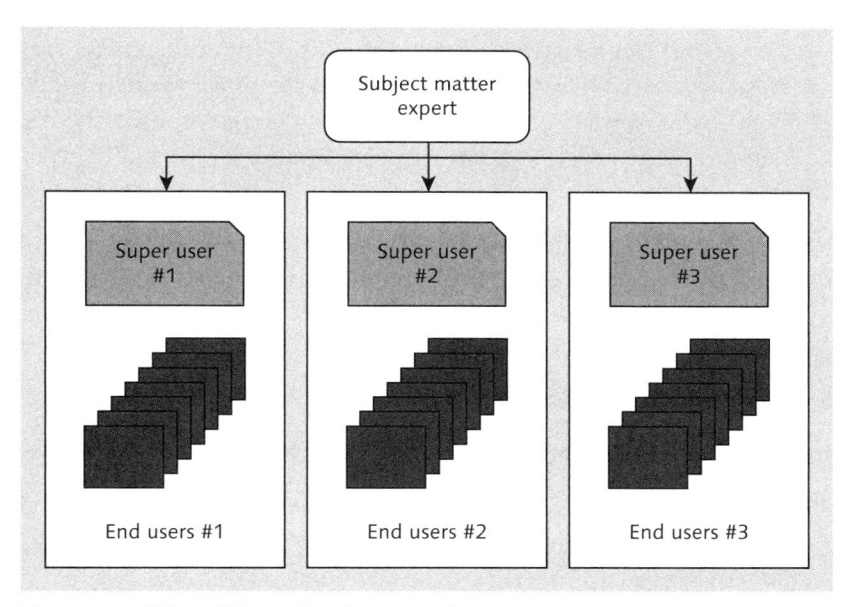

Figure 22.4 SME and Super User Assignments

Help Desk

However, not all end-user issues can be resolved through the efforts of super users. Some issues will be beyond their capability to resolve. These involve technical problems or complex business processes that do not appear to work correctly in the new SAP system. In such cases, super users will assist end users with reporting the issue to the company help desk. The most common of these issues would be the following:

- Access has been denied to the end user
- Commands in the SAP system are not operating correctly

- End-user account has been locked
- Reports are not working or are not printing
- Needed transaction codes are not available
- User has forgotten his or her password and requires a password reset

Your project team will communicate general contact numbers for reporting any systems issues. Once the call is made, the answering system filters users through the familiar set of prompts: "Press one to report a problem with XXX." In this way, the call is routed to technicians who can best assist with problems on that system. In the case of an SAP implementation, given its company-wide impact, the help desk will install special prompts for reporting project-specific issues. Additionally, help desk technicians will have received training on handling calls regarding the new system.

Thus, the prompt may indicate, "Press two to report a problem with SAP system project XXX." This step routes the call to those technicians prepared to assist with SAP go-live-related issues. With the help desk technician on the line, the end user and super user then describe the problem in as much detail as possible.

Such details will include the following:

- Contact information for both the end user and super user
- Regions or sites impacted by the issue
- SAP transaction codes or SAP menu paths associated with the issue, such as SAP error message details
- System screen shots showing the error taking place on the system

The super user participating on the help desk call ensures that all necessary information is related to the help desk technician. Even though the end user may presume that the help desk technician knows whether to request any additional information, the super user understands what additional information is needed and outlines it at the time of the call.

> **Tip**
>
> Project team resolvers without specific error information often spend unnecessary time attempting to identify the problem. Help desk tickets indicating the "SAP is not working" or "my printer is not working" give little guidance to the resolver team. Instead, stating that the user is receiving an error message when attempting to open PDF attach-

> ments from the portal inbox and that all other site users are unable to open these attachments as well would provide more specific information. Identifying any system-generated error messages received would be more helpful still.

Incident Management

Once reported, the help desk generates an incident to reflect and track the issue. The help desk utilizes special systems to input and describe reported issues. This information is reported to project team resolvers and becomes their primary tool in issue resolution. Figure 22.5 describes the major steps in the incident resolution process. Once received by the company service help desk, incidents are routed to the central command center, and are then assigned to a resolver group.

Company service desk
- Captures incidents reported by end users in incident system; creates ticket
- Handles minimum SAP-related incidents (password resets, client installation)
- Assigns initial severity level
- Routes to command center

Central command center
- Receives tickets
- Validates severity level
- Accepts ticket assignment or routes as appropriate
- Keeps tickets updated in Impact
- Assigns tickets to triage team or resolver
- Coordinates system testing and fixes
- Communicates changes

Resolver groups
- Receives tickets through incident system
- Works on resolving issues
- Requests additional information from end user if needed
- Conducts initial verification testing and root cause analysis
- Closes tickets

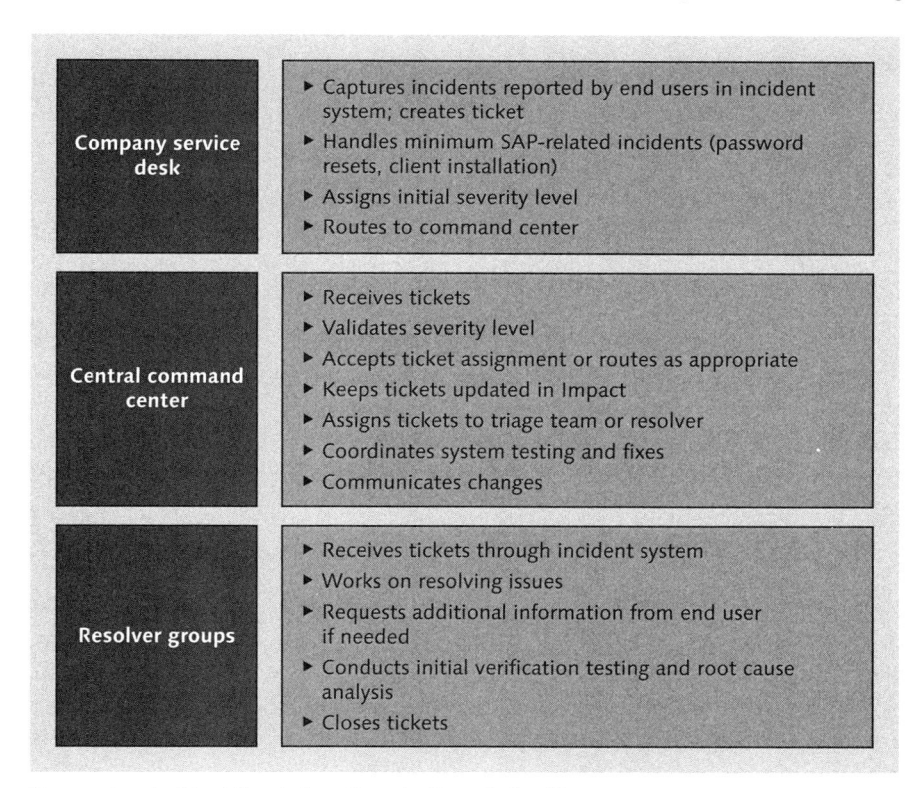

Figure 22.5 Incident Resolution Organizations during Hypercare

Let's walk through this process.

Once an end user calls the help desk to report a problem, the issue becomes an incident. Help desk technicians will have received written instructions outlining how to resolve some incidents during the initial call. In this first-line support role, help desk technicians have access to scripts describing the step-by-step procedures needed to resolve the issue. Thus, incidents such as password resets and some access issues can be handled at the help-desk level and resolved at that point without going further in the resolution process. An incident would be opened at the help desk and, assuming that the resolution generated a solution, it would be closed almost immediately.

> **Tip**
>
> Your company help desk management will prepare scripts for service agents outlining step-by-step guides for resolving certain commonly occurring issues. Conduct a walk-through with the help desk. It should include calls simulating major problem types. Note the quality of the response. If agents handle the calls in a capable manner, all is well. If not, ensure that help desk management conducts additional agent training sessions.

Any incidents that cannot be resolved by first-line support are forwarded to the project team for resolution. The central command center first reviews and categorizes incidents received. This review includes assigning a priority to each incident and deciding which project sub-team will take charge of its resolution. Recall from Figure 22.2 that assignments break down to applications, security, or Basis and device issues. Application issues focus on incidents involving the performance of the SAP application. Security issues cover access, role mapping, and user training issues. Finally, Basis and device issues address the functioning of SAP infrastructure and any devices included in the go-live, such as the previously discussed impact printers.

Either the help desk or the central command center assigns a severity to incidents as they are received. Incident severity level is very important. Severity levels dictate required response resolution times and will also dictate which resources the command center will assign to the incident. Severity levels depend on the degree of business impact and are categorized into four groups. Table 22.1 and Table 22.2 describe these severity levels in greater detail.

Category	Description	Examples
Level one—severe business impact	Critical outage! System, network, or key application outage or disruption has occurred that impacts critical business functions and multiple end users.	▸ Blocks selling, producing, or buying of product ▸ Creates critical impact at sites (plants, regions, or country headquarters) ▸ Poses environmental, health, or safety risk ▸ Prevents closing of financial books ▸ Stops completion of scheduled payroll, bonus, or sales commission runs ▸ Affects responses to regulatory authorities or to subpoenas ▸ Hinders planned product launch
Level two—major business impact	Key components are not working, leading to significant disruption of key business functions caused by system, network, or application problem.	▸ Impacts performance of one or more major user groups ▸ Affects requests from key customers or accounts ▸ Interrupts critical data flow ▸ Creates business partner outages ▸ Prevents completion of financial audit
Level three—minor business impact	Service is degraded but available, causing minor disruption to business functions or processes.	▸ Affects performance of one or more user groups due to difficulties with a minor application or process ▸ Impacts on end-user equipment or services that does not prevent delivery of service
Level four—minimal business impact	Service is fully available. There is only minimal disruption, with no business impact on business processes.	▸ Impacts application or process that is not business critical ▸ Affects small number of end users ▸ Alternative or work-around is available to perform the task

Table 22.1 Hypercare Incident Severity Levels

Incident Severity Level	Required Response Time	Required Resolution Time
Severity one (critical)	15 minutes	3 hours
Severity two (major)	1 hour	8 hours
Severity three (minor)	4 business hours	3 business days
Severity four (minimal)	1 business day	5 business days

Table 22.2 Required Response and Resolution Times by Incident Severity Level

> **Trail Marker**
>
> Level one and level two resolution times really mean solving the problem immediately. No matter what time of day those incidents are received, your team must resolve them within a three- or four-hour window. Level three and level four resolution times are stated in terms of business hours and days. The resolution clock does not start until normal business hours begin.

Each severity level has both a required response time and a required resolution time. These represent service-level expectations for the project team resolvers. Meeting these expectations will be up to them. Severity one and two incidents mandate an ability to respond according to a 24-hours-by-seven-days-a-week schedule. Severity levels three and four are handled within the parameters of normal business operating times.

Severity one incidents, as would be expected, receive emergency treatment—that is, very rapid response and constant monitoring by the central command center—due to their critical nature. Figure 22.6 shows the allocation of effort and the steps specific to the severity level. Once the central command center or help desk identify an incident as severity one, resolver teams spring into immediate action, regardless of the time of day. The central command center ensures that all resolvers have been notified. It also opens up a telephone bridge line where participants can immediately communicate questions, concerns, or potential solutions. Command center personnel remain on this line until the incident is closed.

Incidents with severity level two, three, and four are handled in a more standard fashion. The command center ensures that these incidents are assigned to the proper resolver group and tracks their resolution status according to the service levels described in Table 22.2.

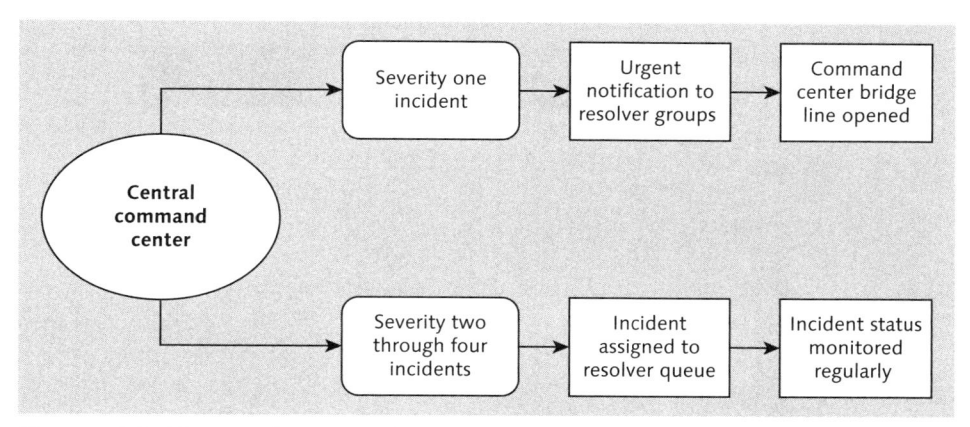

Figure 22.6 Incident Handling Process by Severity Level

As with testing and other related activities, the PMO tracks and issues reports on incident closure. Visibility to incidents opened, incidents closed, and aging enables the team to assess its performance and make changes to its resolution processes where necessary.

Figure 22.7 indicates the number of incidents opened by the project during one of the initial days of hypercare. As expected, the number of incidents received increases as their criticality decreases. This represents a positive sign for the project. Severity one and severity two incidents consume substantial amounts of available resolver resources. Receiving even a small number of the more critical severity incidents means that the project team may soon lack resources needed to address less critical incidents—and could indicate the beginning of an incident backlog.

The distribution of incidents by team will run consistent to form. In the opening days after go-live, many security incidents are reported. These often fall in the areas of access restrictions because of some mistake made during role mapping, or perhaps access is not granted due to incomplete user training. These numbers should decrease significantly as days go by. Other workstreams, such as order-to-cash, human capital management, and procure-to-pay, can be expected to receive incident activity due to the large number of users in those areas. Project team management should keep a close watch on the severity one and severity two incidents opened during this period to ensure that required service levels are met.

Resolver Group	Severity One	Severity Two	Severity Three	Severity Four	Total
Order-to-cash	1	1	3	7	12
Human capital management			4	6	10
Procure-to-pay		1	6	5	12
Plan-to-stock				3	3
Record-to-report			3	1	4
Security		2	5	20	27
Middleware	1		1	1	3
Basis					0
Reports			2	2	4
Legacy systems				4	4
Total	2	4	24	49	79

Figure 22.7 Daily Incidents Opened During Hypercare

In contrast, team effectiveness in resolving issues is shown in Figure 22.8, which charts the number of incidents closed in the previous day. Achieving an incident closure rate approximately equal to or better than the rate of incident opening demonstrates that the project team is in control of hypercare. If the rate of incidents opened greatly exceeds the rate of incidents closed, this likely means that resolver groups were insufficiently staffed or that incident rates were out of control, which might be evidence that the system implementation was flawed in some significant way.

Resolver Group	Severity One	Severity Two	Severity Three	Severity Four	Total
Order-to-cash		2	3	5	10
Human capital management			3	3	6
Procure-to-pay		1	4	5	10
Plan-to-stock			3	2	5
Record-to-report			1	1	2
Security		2	9	20	31
Middleware			1	1	2
Basis				1	1
Reports			2	3	5
Legacy systems			2	1	3
Total	0	5	28	42	75

Figure 22.8 Incidents Closed During the Previous Day

In this example, the project team comes close to the desired situation. Comparison of closure rates from the previous day with new incidents from the following day reveals approximately the same number of incidents closed in the previous day as opened in the following day. It also confirms that the closure rate for each team in one day approaches its incident-opening rate for the next day.

However, the figure does not show whether incidents are being worked and closed within the service-level resolution time. Otherwise, the project team might resolve severity four incidents within the required time frame, but complete severity one and severity two incidents outside the service-level window. Establishing resolution timeliness requires two reports: one to assess service-level performance on a daily basis and another to examine the aging of incidents since their time of reporting.

Figure 22.9 displays the project's daily service-level performance. It reflects both the number of incidents opened and closed in a single day, as well as service levels attained in doing so. Desired levels would show approximately equal amounts opened and closed in that day. It would also demonstrate that resolvers had met service levels, especially for the crucial severity one and severity two incidents.

Actual performance attained shows some disparities. Although the severity one incident was resolved within the required time frame, incidents in other categories indicate that the service levels are lagging behind resolution times. Numbers of incidents opened and closed correspond, except in the non-critical severity four category. However, the service-level figures demonstrate that many of the number that were closed represent aged incidents from previous days. Project management must closely monitor incident fix rates.

Incident Severity	Number Opened	Number Closed	Service Level Achieved
Severity one	1	1	1 attained service level
Severity two	2	1	1 attained service level
Severity three	28	25	17 attained service level
Severity four	68	54	45 attained service level
Total	99	81	64 attained service level

Figure 22.9 Incident Resolution Performance

The second resolution report, incident aging, illustrates overall time to resolve. Shown by resolver group, this report compiles incident closure time frames since system go-live. Where needed, this report could be prepared for weekly performance by severity level.

Figure 22.10 demonstrates some encouraging trends in hypercare incident resolution, but also indicates some causes for concern. On the positive side, most incidents are resolved within five days. It's likely that many of the 42 security incidents that took five or more days to resolve are minimally critical severity three and severity four levels. On the negative side, the report captures only resolved incidents. If the team had received a total of 500 incidents, this would show only about half resolved. Knowing the aging of unresolved incidents would give an important data point as well.

Resolver Group	One to Three Days	Three to Five Days	More than Five Days	Total
Order-to-cash	19	11	4	34
Human capital management	12	14	2	28
Procure-to-pay	19	6	28	55
Plan-to-stock	4	3	1	8
Record-to-report	4	3	9	16
Security	45	32	42	119
Middleware	2	1	2	5
Basis	1			1
Reports	2	3		5
Legacy systems	3			3
Total	111	73	90	274

Figure 22.10 Incident Resolution Report by Days of Aging

Project management must decide how much information to report. Too little information prevents others from seeing the entire picture, but too much information can inundate the project team and make real problem assessment difficult. Finding the right level is a decision that each project management team must make.

Incident Resolution and Change Control

In many ways, the incident resolution process during hypercare mimics defect resolution during user acceptance testing. As shown in Figure 22.11, once an incident is assigned to a resolver group and then handed over to a technical resource, the effort centers on finding a technical solution to the problem. Resolvers utilize screen shots and incident descriptions supplied by the end user as their starting point. They attempt to replicate the issue within the SAP system. If they experience difficulties in replicating the issue, they often communicate directly with the end user or his super user support.

Once the resolver has identified a fix for the incident, the resolution process then moves to test. Assuming that the test results were positive, steps would be taken to arrange for end-user testing. Only the end user who opened the incident—or his or her designee—can perform this testing. If the test produces a positive outcome, the incident is closed.

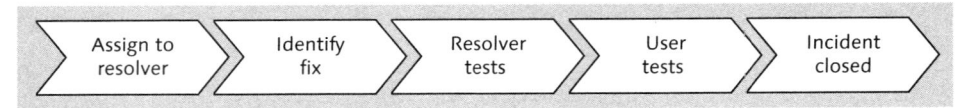

Assign to resolver → Identify fix → Resolver tests → User tests → Incident closed

Figure 22.11 Hypercare Incident Resolution Process

This resolution process is pretty standard, but there are some significant ways in which incident resolution differs from defect resolution during user acceptance testing. Since go-live has now taken place, the SAP system is now a production operation. In practice, this means the imposition of change control.

Now, it will not be sufficient to simply resolve issues, test them, and post the solutions to the system. Instead, any modifications intended for the production system must follow a rigorous change control process to ensure that only necessary and fully reviewed changes are added to the SAP production environment. The change control process operates as a line of defense against introducing error of any kind into the production system.

Once change control is initiated, several steps are added to the process outlined in Figure 22.11. Incident resolution work can begin. However, the system change control board (CCB), consisting of business users and company IT staff, must review and approve the change prior to initiating any testing. Change control personnel will ensure that CCB approval is in place to authorize the work prior to transporting the incident solution to the development system for resolver testing. This same process will be followed for solutions moved to the quality system for end-user testing.

If both sets of testing achieve target results, the configuration or code change needed for resolution will await a production release. At this point, the resolution will be grouped with other solutions and transported to the production system as part of a single release. Documentation demonstrates exactly what was added or changed in the system, and those records are permanently retained. Both the Basis team and company change control will retain these change records. This level of rigor protects system integrity and ensures that all changes are fully verified.

In many cases, companies utilize change control systems to automate these processes. These systems assure that required documentation is complete and available prior to any system changes. Accustomed to less formal change control processes, project teams often find the imposition of formal change control onerous. However, benefits to system integrity certainly outweigh these concerns. No company wants to live with the consequences of introducing unintended changes to their core system of record.

22.2.2 Hypercare Exit

Leaving the hypercare phase takes place according to one of several scenarios. The most commonly used scenario bases the decision on *incident levels* or *business performance targets*. In other cases, a project applies both methods. Often, the systems integrator will specify the scenario to be used in its statement of work.

The incident level method defines an incident quantity or ratio of newly opened incidents versus rate of closure. Once these numbers are reached, project management reaches out to project sponsors and executives in functional organizations to gain their agreement that hypercare can be closed. Formal reviews, if needed, describe current incident conditions and request approval to exit hypercare.

Using business performance metrics is an effective method as well. Its application depends on the agreement of all parties (especially the systems integrator partner) that the measures selected concretely reflect business process performance.

The items chosen, as well as the meaning of terms and methods of measurement, must be crystal clear. If not, a great deal of time can be spent discussing them.

For each measure selected, your company specifies a current baseline performance indicator. The baseline performance designates current company performance levels for the chosen indicators. These values are relatively easy to obtain and are readily accepted by all parties.

The next set of measures, *hypercare targets*, requires thorough examination. In many cases, the company will not reach currently achieved baseline numbers during hypercare simply because it takes time to adjust to new processes and systems. Thus, hypercare target numbers will often reflect this user acclimation process. The targets are set below current baseline performance. Finding the right middle ground requires some effort.

> **Tip**
>
> You can expect some degree of tension regarding hypercare exit. Your systems integrator will either want to shift resources to a subsequent wave or roll them off at project end. Specific hypercare exit measures can greatly assist here. They do not necessarily reduce the tension, but they do frame the discussion around constructive topics.

Figure 22.12 shows several stabilization metrics from an order-to-cash perspective. In all cases, the baseline values exceed or equal the hypercare target values. Project management would conduct periodic reviews for stabilization metrics applicable to each workstream. Achieving the hypercare targets for some metrics will not be difficult. For others, attaining the target values proves difficult and time-consuming. Until these targets are reached, the systems integrator must continue to focus its efforts on achieving them and will be restricted from rolling off staff on to other implementation waves or projects.

Once the requisite performance levels are acieved, hypercare comes to a close. Project staff then moves on to the next implementation wave. If this deployment represents the final wave, both company and integrator resources roll off the project. For company staff, this entails returning to their former positions. For integrator staff, it means moving on to a new project and beginning the implementation process once again.

Order-to-Cash Stabilization Metrics	Current Baseline	Hypercare Target
Shipping performance	98%	98%
Export compliance	100%	95%
Inventory availability	96%	90%
Customer invoices released	90%	85%
Invoice accuracy	95%	95%
Inventory accuracy	100%	95%
Receivables processing	90%	85%
Open accounts receivable line items	3,500	3,000

Figure 22.12 Order-to-Cash Hypercare Stabilization Metrics

As hypercare completes, the project prepares to transition to sustainment. The resources will support the system and the project team wraps up its commitments. Our next chapter describes this shift.

Once the project team has delivered the SAP implementation and hypercare has wound down, the sustainment, or steady-state, period begins.

23 Sustainment

Sustainment, or ongoing systems maintenance, can take many forms. It can be completely outsourced to a service provider based on a contractual understanding of roles and expectations; it can be handled totally with resources and management from your company; or it can be organized with a mix of company and outsourced service provider resources.

No matter what format is adopted, the responsibility for system operation ultimately lies with your company (though the temptation to assign operational responsibility to the service provider may be great). Management will now want to refocus its energies on business unit and company performance. Successful turn-key sustainment operations are nowhere to be found. Without direct guidance and oversight from your senior management, the effort will certainly encounter extreme difficulties and most likely fail.

For global projects that implement in waves, the need for sustainment support arises with the first deployment. As the project moves forward during succeeding waves, the sustainment organization simultaneously acquires an increased number of users, responsibility for any additional functionality implemented in those waves, and the potential for operating in additional languages.

The success of the sustainment organization depends on four critical success factors:

1. Strong system governance led by *engaged* senior executives who represent the major user communities
2. Excellent system guidance and technical support directed by the company's IT group
3. Clear performance expectations and visibility to sustainment execution as reported by commonly agreed-upon metrics

4. Use of financial allocations and budgets to set parameters for system workload priorities and expectations

This chapter covers the workings of the sustainment process, its relationship with the SAP implementation project, and mechanisms to make sustainment a success.

23.1 The SAP Center of Excellence

Due to its scope and complexity, the SAP system requires a sustainment center solely devoted to its operations. Services include technical activities to support the system, as well as business activities focused on the company processes that the system enables. The overall organization that houses SAP support skills for a company is known as a *center of excellence* (COE).

Typically, the COE provides all support required by the SAP system. Services are grouped in three separate areas:

- Services provided by your company's functional business organizations
- Services supplied by the your company's IT organization
- Technical services needed to operate the system, furnished either by third-party providers or your company's IT group

As you can see in Figure 23.1, these services are comprehensive in nature. Company functional organizations retain control of how business processes are performed on the system and requirements for additional functionality. The IT organization works closely with business organizations to define any additional business requirements in systems terms and to assure effective system performance. These two roles must be performed by company resources. Without their guidance and input, the system may drift away from its original design.

The third service area, technical services, may be performed by company technical staff or by an outsourced service provider. If a service provider is used, it will be up to your IT organization to provide oversight and ongoing management. It's likely that some portion of service provider operations will be housed in an offshore operation. Company IT management must understand the dynamics of offshore services and effectively supervise them.

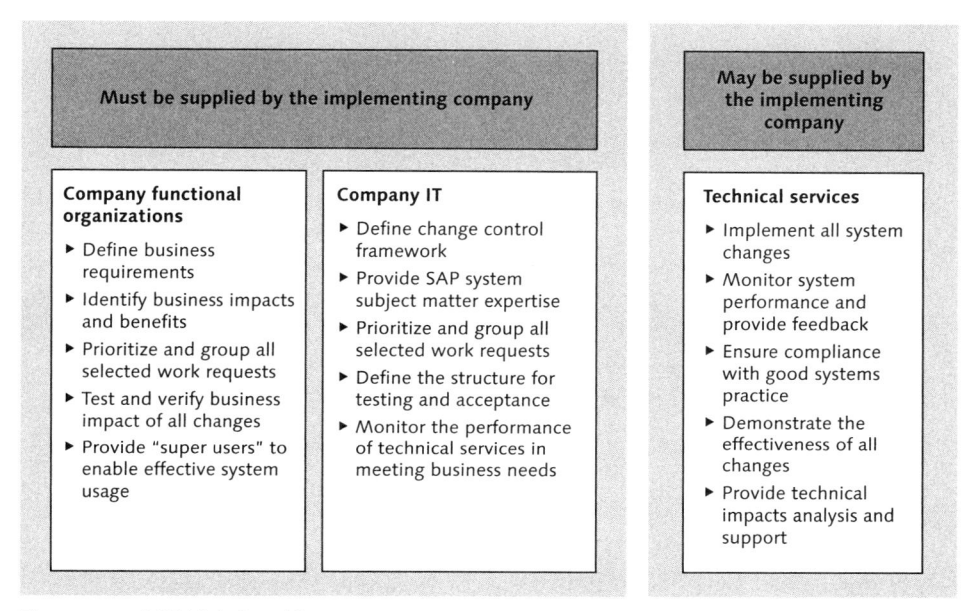

Must be supplied by the implementing company		May be supplied by the implementing company
Company functional organizations ▸ Define business requirements ▸ Identify business impacts and benefits ▸ Prioritize and group all selected work requests ▸ Test and verify business impact of all changes ▸ Provide "super users" to enable effective system usage	**Company IT** ▸ Define change control framework ▸ Provide SAP system subject matter expertise ▸ Prioritize and group all selected work requests ▸ Define the structure for testing and acceptance ▸ Monitor the performance of technical services in meeting business needs	**Technical services** ▸ Implement all system changes ▸ Monitor system performance and provide feedback ▸ Ensure compliance with good systems practice ▸ Demonstrate the effectiveness of all changes ▸ Provide technical impacts analysis and support

Figure 23.1 COE High-Level Structure

Figure 23.1 gives some idea about how your company's COE should be organized. This three-part structure is a common and successfully used approach.

23.1.1 COE Organization

Notice that Figure 23.1 divides COE duties according to their business ownership or SAP technical focus. This section outlines those duties in more detail and provides examples of how the organization as a whole might work.

Business COE

For many, the concept of a business COE may seem hard to understand. This is a quite normal reaction. When one first thinks about an SAP system, the mind indeed gravitates to very technical operations. However, as we have demonstrated in this book on several occasions, implementing and now *running* an SAP system is inherently a business operation. The system will support the business, and the business must provide direction on how to furnish that support.

23 | Sustainment

Figure 23.2 illustrates the organization of a business COE, which provides a robust set of services. Let's look at each.

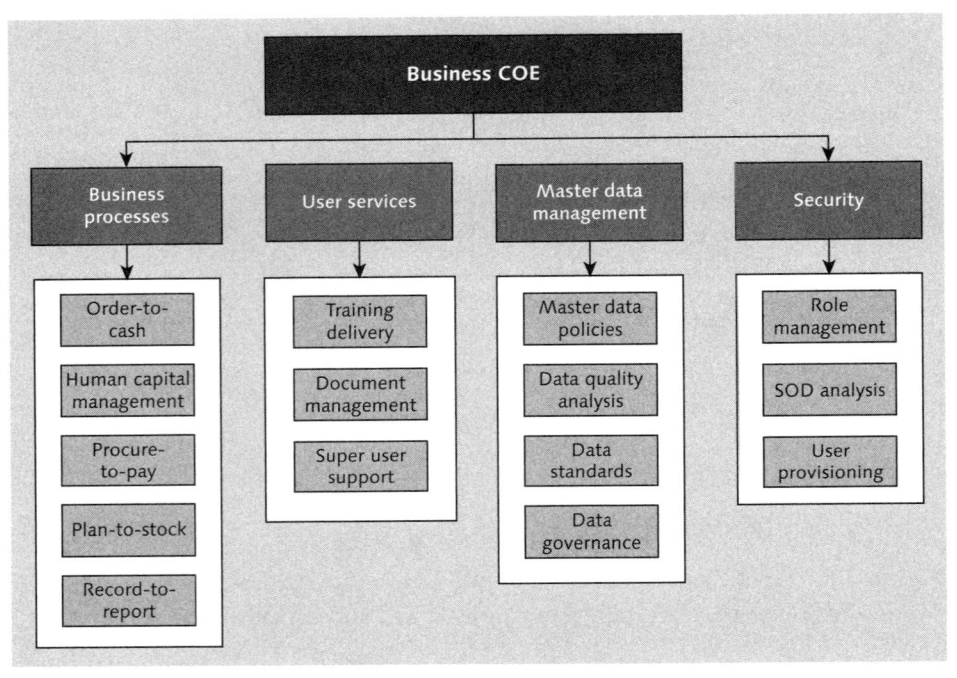

Figure 23.2 Organization of an SAP Business COE

First of all, the business COE houses the business workstreams that gave direction to your just-completed SAP implementation project. Instead of fading away, as did the project team, these functions now move over to the business COE. Global process owners still have a significant role to play. They now are charged with ensuring that the blueprint remains in place and adapts to changing company needs. This steady-state role is especially essential to maintaining system integrity in a global or multi-regional operation.

> **Tip**
>
> Your best candidates for the business COE will come from the project workstreams. Whether these individuals were functional workstream leads or members of the team, they will have knowledge of the issues involved and challenges that the business COE will face. Look here first.

Process owners represent system operations and performance in your business units. They seek out information on whether and how the system is meeting business needs. They also closely coordinate with regional leaders to give process guidance and to ensure that the blueprint continues to be followed everywhere. They own the business controls put in place for their functional area and must verify that these perform as planned. Finally, they give input to the company IT organization on changes or upgrades needed to improve the system.

Additionally, the business COE also offers user services. Many services that were formerly supplied by the project team are now made available through the business COE. These include delivery and upkeep of user training materials, managing changes to standard operating procedures and work instructions, maintaining blueprint documents such as process definition documents, and ensuring the continuing involvement of the super user team.

Chapter 17 already addressed the need for master data management. The business COE puts in place the master data governance necessary to operate a global system. Even for a moderately sized company, your new system will contain tens of thousands of customers, likely over one hundred thousand sales pricing conditions, and thousands upon thousands of vendors and materials. This is not to mention the company codes, plants, and sales organizations that were created by the project team.

These must be maintained and assessed for correct usage. The master data segment of the business COE generates policies and standards that define proper data use. Each major master data element now has a data owner who operates as the eyes and ears of the data team. The master data group also conducts periodic audits of both master and transactional data to verify that defined standards are followed.

Finally, the business COE houses a security section. It ensures that security roles and data-level security are kept up to date, and will issue security roles to new hires and conduct ongoing segregation of duties analysis.

Information Technology COE

Figure 23.3 outlines many of the responsibilities traditionally given to centers of excellence, but which we assign to a more discrete team—the information technology COE. This IT COE maintains a strong relationship with the company's IT organization and focuses its energies primarily on areas concerned with system performance.

Figure 23.3 indicates three service areas:

- Business process support works closely with global process owners in specific and with functional business organizations in general on system issues
- Release management handles nuts-and-bolts activities associated with system upkeep
- Technical monitoring attends to infrastructure and break/fix performance

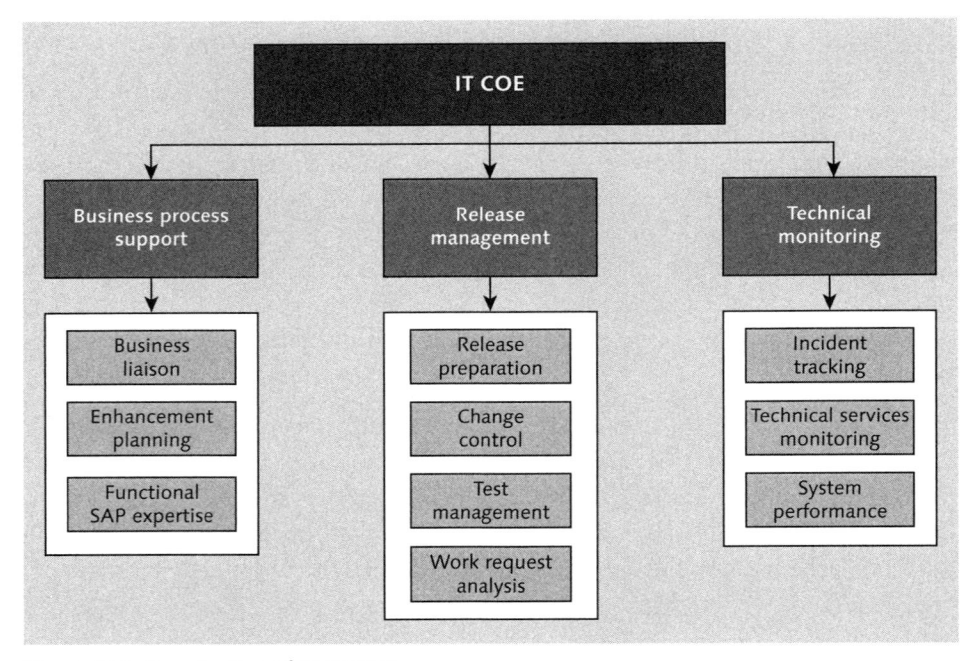

Figure 23.3 Organization of an IT COE

The business support section of the IT COE aligns closely with the global process owners. It establishes a very close working relationship between the process owner and the analysts who are giving support. Each analyst will have an extensive SAP background. As a result, analysts will have a very good idea of the problems experienced in a business function and the causes of those problems. A few business analysts from the IT COE organization provide support for each process area. For example, OTC may have separate analysts supporting accounts receivable, order management and fulfillment, and logistics operations.

> **Tip**
>
> Remember that staff in the business support section must have real SAP proficiency in the areas they would support. It is always tempting to immediately reassign project support resources to the COE. If these individuals possess expert-level SAP skills, they will likely be a good fit. If they do not, then look elsewhere. The ability to translate between business requirements and technical design is crucial here. Make sure that those selected can perform this role.

Release management in the IT COE provides more in the way of back-office service. It ensures that periodic software updates or enhancement releases work according to plan and also manages any integration or user acceptance testing required for incident resolution.

Technical monitoring assures that the overall system is performing to expectation. It examines continuing incident resolution and identifies causes for delays. It also assesses the effectiveness of solutions promoted to production and tracks infrastructure operations to include causes for scheduled and unscheduled down time.

SAP Technical Services COE

The SAP technical services COE shown in Figure 23.4 manages the operation of both the hardware that runs SAP and the SAP software applications themselves. Often the SAP technical services COE operates the data center where the SAP systems are housed. Its purview includes the actual installation of all system upgrades and releases. It is also responsible for help desk management.

The help desk played a primary role at go-live and during hypercare. It operates as the first line of defense for the SAP system. Its agents not only receive and report incidents, but they are also prepared for standard problem-solving such as password resets.

Whether the help desk is outsourced to an external services provider or internally operated by your company, help desk performance must be managed. Effective help desk management includes tracking of call queue times, abandon rates, and assessments of services provided. In a global SAP system, analysis of help desk performance involves monitoring status in regions and among language groupings as well.

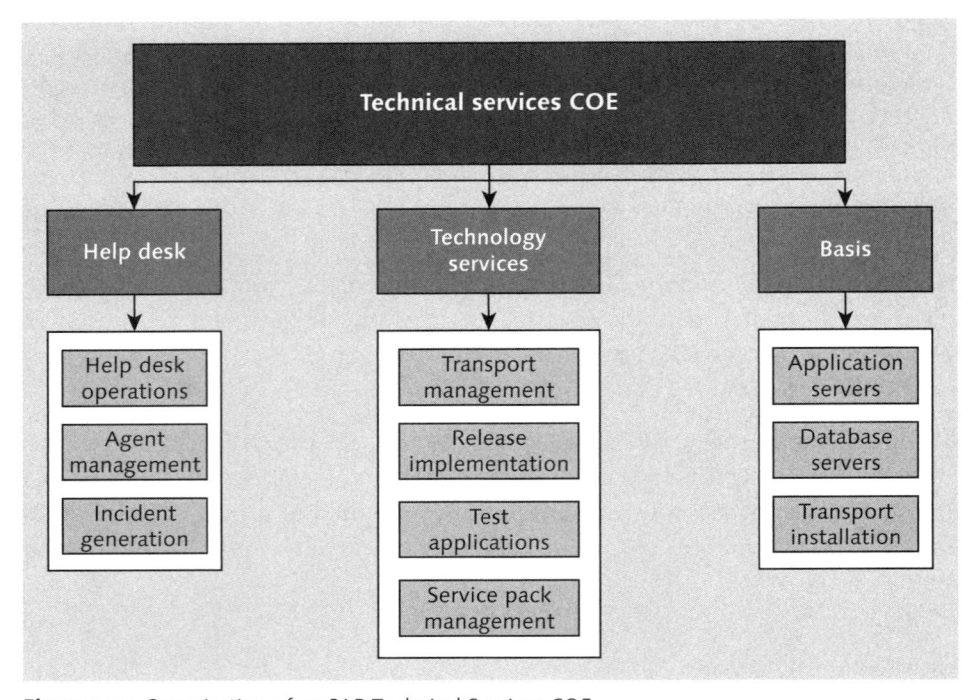

Figure 23.4 Organization of an SAP Technical Services COE

Technology services covers very traditional IT functions. Ensuring that changes to the SAP system were managed through a standard release process and that transports were handled in accordance with procedure would fall in its domain. Its purview also includes monitoring system unscheduled down time and recovery time.

Basis houses infrastructure operations for the SAP system. These data center functions involve maintaining application and database servers to include standard back-up. Even if this service is outsourced to an external service provider, your company must closely monitor infrastructure performance and service issues. Unless these run smoothly, the system will not run smoothly.

23.1.2 The COE and the Project Team

Clearly, planning for the SAP implementation project must include the COE. If one is not already in place in your company, it must be designed and delivered as part of go-live planning. Timing of COE availability will be very important. Figure 23.5 depicts a three-wave deployment process. Each wave adds successive portions of the company locations to the system. Each wave will also add increasing degrees of functionality aligned with business process requirements in those areas.

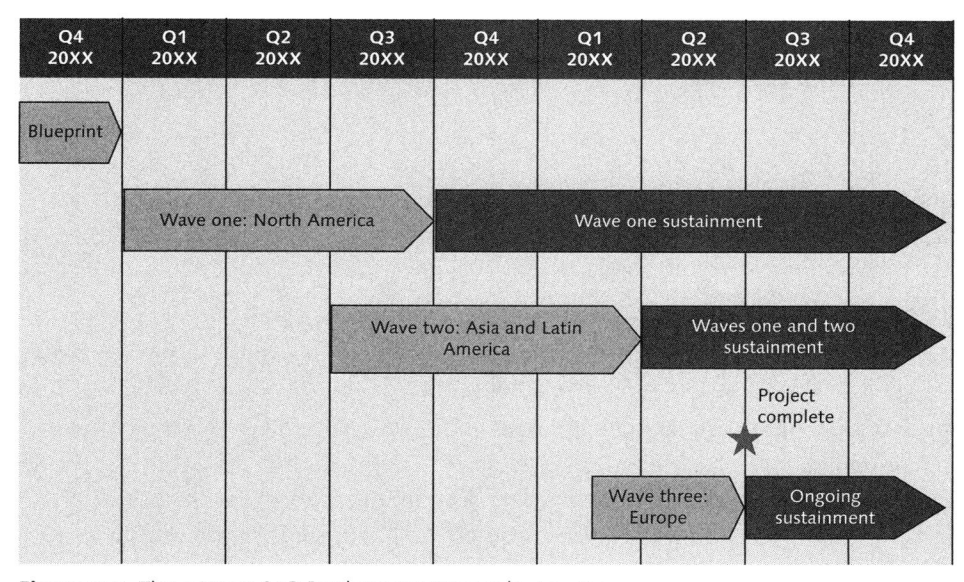

Figure 23.5 Three-Wave SAP Deployment Process by Location

The SAP implementation project team concentrates all its activities on completing hypercare and moving to the next deployment wave. So in this example, as wave one completes for North America and the system is stabilized, the project team immediately focuses its energies on wave two. Once that deployment is complete and stabilized, the team shifts its momentum to wave three.

However, the SAP system that is now live in those locations demands extensive support. End users will continue to report incidents. Functional business areas will continue to request changes and enhancements to the system. After wave three is deployed and hypercare complete, the project team will disband. With the project team gone, the COE must now stand on its own.

As Figure 23.5 illustrates, the COE ramp-up comes in stages. Staffing must be capable to deliver system support for each deployment wave that has gone live. Full support staffing must be in place after the final wave has been completed. Final preparation and go-live represent the critical periods in this transition. Not only must sustainment staff members be onboarded prior to go-live, but they must be trained on the SAP system as delivered, and they must demonstrate proficiency in resolving systems issues.

To the degree that your company has shifted from several legacy systems to a global single instance of SAP, the COE will serve as an integrating mechanism. Where regions or sites formerly experienced considerable latitude in business practices, the adoption of a single instance places unfamiliar constraints on their operations.

In a global single instance, all company regions and sites use the same system simultaneously. Major activities in the system must align. These include standardized use of master data, process steps according to guidelines, and security setup common across operating areas. The COE gives direction on the rules of the road and provides coordination for this new environment.

Let's walk through Figure 23.6, which shows how this ramp-up process would work. The sustainment team would be onboarded and trained during the final preparation phase. Each COE member is given a specific support assignment. Additionally, newly assigned COE staff would be aligned with the functional project team member who best fits that assignment. During the final preparation period, each COE staff member begins knowledge transfer by reviewing all relevant design documents and examining user acceptance test scripts.

Final preparation	Hypercare		COE cutover
★ GO-LIVE		★ CUTOVER	
Onboarding and training of COE team	Assist project team in incident resolution	Take lead in incident resolution	Responsible for incident resolution

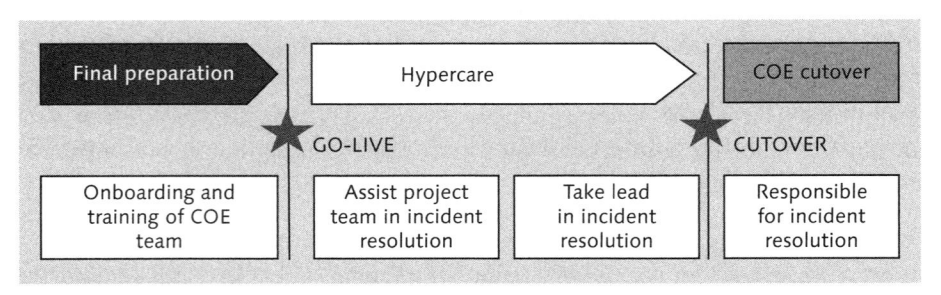

Figure 23.6 COE Onboarding Sequence

Once go-live has taken place and the project has entered hypercare, COE staff would now shift to incident resolution. Preparation begins by assisting project team staff members in their resolution activities. This hands-on, watch-and-learn process is intended to build system knowledge. COE staff would sit with their project team counterparts and handle with them whatever incidents were generated.

> **Tip**
>
> Knowledge transfer can be tricky. Each COE support resource must be trained for proficiency and then assessed to see whether he or she really has learned everything needed. COE management should recognize its vested interest in assuring that each and every resource has the necessary skill levels prior to the transition. Otherwise, management will be left with incidents unresolved and resources incapable of solving the problems.

Approximately halfway through the hypercare period, the relationship between the project team and the COE staff shifts. At this point, the COE staff takes the lead in incident resolution, with the project team members providing guidance and assistance as needed. This combined approach to incident resolution continues until hypercare is complete.

Competency assessment for members of the COE takes place on an individual basis. Project team members who formerly handled specific assignments will review knowledge transfer and sign off on the sustainment team member's competency. Full hand-over is not approved until all knowledge transfer is certified.

23.1.3 Staffing the COE

COE staffing is built around its division into business, IT, and technical services subgroups. Each group requires a mix of business expertise and technical skills, as shown in Figure 23.7. Note that the formula for success mandates that each position, regardless of organizational location, should possess some business understanding and some technical skills. This combined skill set facilitates effective communication across the diverse subjects covered by the COE.

In general terms, the COE will have three skill set types. They consist of business process experts who primarily work in the business COE, IT system analysts who are located in the IT COE, and technical resources assigned to the technical services COE. Figure 23.7 gives more information about each role and indicates the relationship between business and technical expertise needed for each role.

Business process expert	IT systems analyst	Technical resource
▸ Focuses on business use of the system ▸ Possesses deep knowledge of company business processes ▸ In-depth familiarity with system blueprint ▸ Knowledgeable of company data usage and policies ▸ Able to provide security and documentation services	▸ Understands the technical setup of the system ▸ Highly skilled on relevant modules of SAP ▸ Familiar with business uses of the SAP system ▸ Capable of translating business issues into systems operations ▸ Expert on operations and policies governing testing and release management	▸ Focuses on the technical uses of the system ▸ Expert in data center operations and the SAP applications environment ▸ Provides technical solutions to systems issues ▸ Operates under guidance from company IT systems analysts

■ Business expertise   ■ Technical expertise

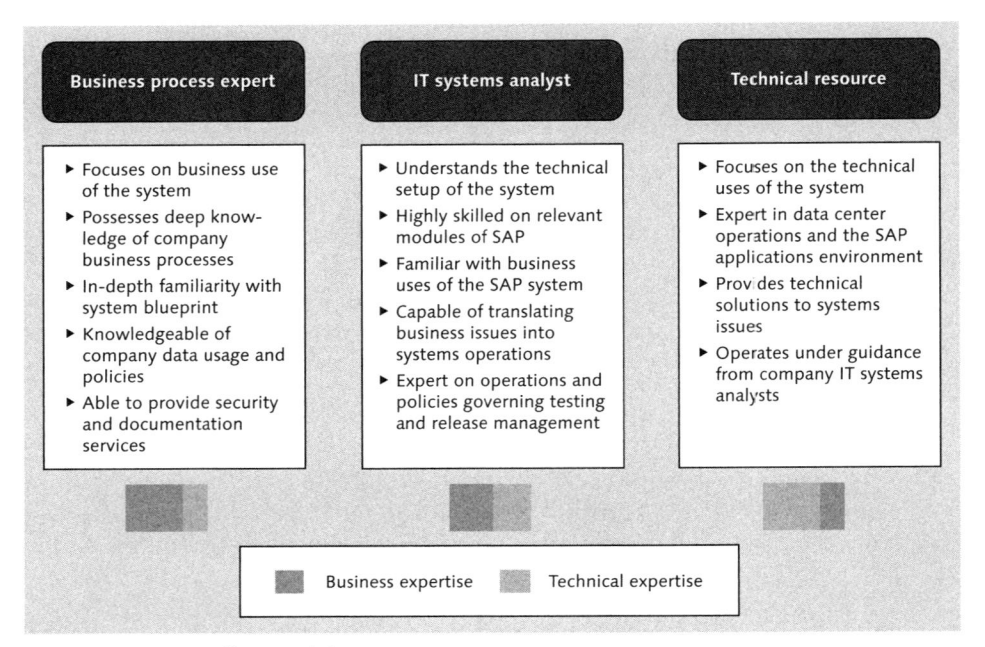

Figure 23.7 COE Staffing Model

While business process experts require deep company business skills, the role also requires a moderate level of SAP technical expertise. In a similar vein, the technical resource role centers primarily on SAP technical skills but also needs some business process knowledge. A COE functions optimally only when each segment has an understanding and appreciation of both business process and technical segments.

> **Tip**
>
> Your staffing selection process should clearly address both the business and technical requirements for each position. Remember, if business support staff cannot state a problem in SAP terminology and technical services staff have no idea of how to understand a business problem, then communication between the two groups will only lead to confusion.

Staffing levels are based on the volume and complexity of the work; in other words, it is based on COE workload. Drivers would certainly include—but not be limited to—the following:

- **Number, severity, and complexity of break/fix incidents**
  Items here fall in the defect resolution category (e.g., invoice values incorrect). They come from help desk tickets and are the most common workload producer. Generally, incidents can be quickly resolved (a two- to three-day turnaround) without major configuration or testing efforts. Incidents requiring more complex resolution processes will, of course, consume even greater resource levels.

- **System enhancements mandated by functional business organizations**
  Elective enhancements, as they are known, represent functionality improvements requested by company functional organizations (e.g., implementing a new stock transfer order process). These are significant changes to the system and require thorough testing prior to deployment. Measured in weeks or months, these can sometimes constitute small projects and require project management skills as well.

  These elective enhancements can turn out to be the most time-consuming activity facing the COE and can drive the bulk of COE staffing levels. Virtually every enhancement requires a full range of pre-implementation activity, including the following:
  - Design and configuration of the enhancement
  - Regression testing that verifies that the new enhancement will not break or alter system functionality already in place
  - Integration testing verifying that all elements of the enhancement and the current SAP system work as planned
  - User acceptance testing that verifies that the enhancement works as designed

- **Special initiatives or system upgrades adopted by the company**
  Your company may decide to implement an SAP support pack or upgrade a single application. Support packs are system improvements packaged and issued by SAP. These are complex in nature and would require careful assessment and a time-consuming deployment.

Information regarding break/fix numbers may be extrapolated from any previous deployment waves. Incident volumes by functional area will point out the need for any additional or reduced staffing. Although these numbers are higher during the hypercare period, their relative amounts can indicate which workstream faces the heaviest volumes. Paying attention to incident resolution times can also supply evidence for any needed changes in staffing levels. If resolution times are longer in one area than another, this can signal that resource levels are insufficient and need to be augmented.

23.2 Sustainment Governance

Company functional business organizations own the SAP system.

Many observers will find this a surprising statement, and their position is easy to understand. After all, SAP is a system, and for that reason it should be owned by the company's IT organization. However, the sole purpose of the SAP system is to enable business services. It has no other reason for being. For that reason, the business units own and define SAP system direction.

23.2.1 Governance Structure

As a matter of course, company business leaders may choose to assign SAP system responsibility to the company IT organization. In turn, the IT organization may be quite happy to take on the role. This arrangement can work well as long as the system operates exactly as planned and no system changes are required. Once significant problems arise or changes become necessary, this standard relationship no longer works. At that point, guidance and direction from the business is absolutely required and a mechanism must be developed to provide it. Far better to begin with a business-led governance process in place.

Figure 23.8 portrays the best-practice relationship between business functions and IT to make sustainment successful. Each organizational component has a significant role to play. Business functions, shown on top, supply guidance and feedback regarding system performance. They also provide resources as needed for testing and related purposes. IT, on the other hand, contributes system expertise and analysis and furnishes resources for system operation and management.

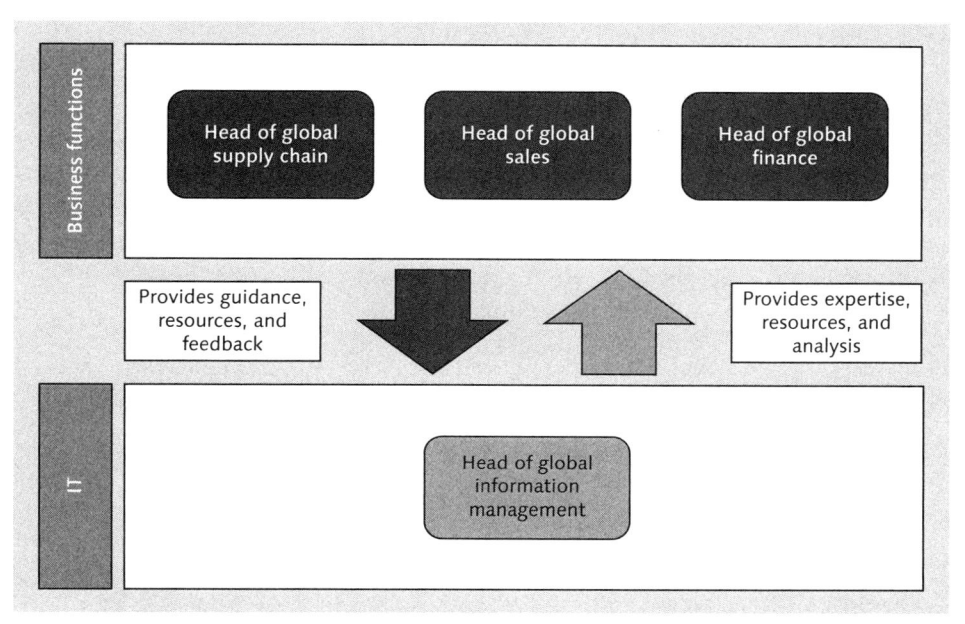

Figure 23.8 Relationship Between Business and IT to Govern Sustainment

This governance structure emphasizes business ownership of the system. Earlier discussion divided the COE workload into three categories: incident resolution, enhancement support, and handling of any special initiatives. In terms of the effort involved, elective enhancements consume by far the greatest amount of COE workload. Enhancements universally represent business requests for additional or modified system functionality.

> **Pitfall Alert**
>
> Find the senior executive who has a real interest in system performance; this person should play a lead role in sustainment governance. Some senior executive in your company has a real passion about how well SAP works. That passion, if supported, can ensure that sustainment operates as well as your implementation phase did.

Each functional business organization has its own candidates for the final approved enhancement list. Without an effective governance process in place, IT will find itself placed in a broker role that it is not equipped to handle. Moreover, unless the real principals in the decision are making the determinations, confusion and dissatisfaction will result.

Further, these decisions must be made by the most senior executives in the company. They can leave it to others to gather information and come up with recommendations, but they cannot delegate the decision-making. Placing these decisions in the hands of lower-level managers only impedes resolution. Those who disagree with the priorities of lower-level managers can simply bring their concerns to the most senior functional executives, and the reordering process begins anew. Senior executives can and should own the priorities of their organizations. They should also own the bargaining and negotiation with other functional senior executives to reconcile differing choices.

Obviously, the governance structure is key to creating ownership of the COE. The governance group establishes COE performance targets and monitors results relative to those targets. The recurring agenda for the group would include the following:

- Conducting regular reviews of COE performance against selected metrics
- Adopting annual initiatives, such as master data standardization, and evaluating the results achieved
- Setting system direction by selecting elective enhancements, extending the system to new markets, and adding or modifying current functionality
- Evaluating the accomplishments of the COE against its annual objectives

Figure 23.9 outlines a framework for the COE performance review. As the earlier discussion of key performance indicators revealed, it's essential to agree on how the measures are calculated. Participants in these discussions must have a very specific understanding of what constitutes red, yellow, and green status. These must be in place for the scorecard mechanism to operate as planned.

Number and severity of incidents reported by month	Status
Incidents resolved outside allotted closure standards	Yellow
Number of unscheduled system outages	Green
Hours of unscheduled system downtime	Green
Number and impact of severity one incidents	Red
Transaction performance time to system response	Green
Reports performance time to system response	Red
Schedule performance for elective enhancements	Yellow
Budget performance for elective enhancements	Green

Figure 23.9 COE Performance Scorecard

The measures above are divided into four groupings. These include the following:

- **Incident resolution status**
  As with hypercare, steady-state support operates according to service-level agreements. These stipulate time frames within which action and resolution are expected to take place. The COE should provide the monthly run rate of incidents in each category as a standard of comparison. Due to their significant impact on company operations, severity one incidents would be reported and discussed separately.

- **System outages and downtime**
  Any unscheduled system outage affects business operations. When the system is unavailable, users cannot process transactions or run reports. This puts much of the company at a standstill.

  Additionally, the length of time that the system is unavailable can worsen the situation. A one-hour unscheduled system downtime has far less business consequence than a two-day unscheduled downtime. During this period, all processes must be completed manually and entered into the system when it becomes available again.

  Scheduled downtimes can also be tracked, but generally do not present the same impacts. First of all, the timing is known and agreed upon by functional business owners. Additionally, these scheduled downtimes—which are often used for back-up or enhancement release activities—are scheduled for times where the system experiences minimal usage. That said, any increasing trend for scheduled downtime, or downtime that exceeds approved limits, should be closely examined by the senior executive governance group.

- **System response time for executing transactions and reports**
  System response time measurements target the time to complete a transaction or report from the time that the ENTER button is pushed. Systems that perform slowly can cause real user frustration. For those who execute multiple transactions in an hour, waiting even for two or three minutes at each transaction can negatively affect productivity.

  For reports, when a problem occurs, it is usually worse still. When a user spends time setting up a query and then waits for 30 minutes while it compiles, it creates a negative perception of the system. The senior executive governance group would review response times and assess reasons for slow system performance.

- **Budget and schedule status for elective enhancements**
  As we have discussed, elective enhancements comprise the major workload element for the COE. The COE will identify a set of enhancements in its quarterly release plan. Some larger enhancements may have their own release schedule. Nevertheless, each enhancement will have a manpower or cost figure assigned to it. Each enhancement would also have a scheduled delivery date. The senior executive governance group would monitor COE execution against those benchmarks.

COE management will distribute information on all scorecard items to governance senior executives prior to scheduled review meetings. At a minimum, these meetings review all yellow-rated indices and give special attention to those rated red. At the meeting, COE staff present any background information that is necessary to understand the issue. Staff would also present recommendations for all needed remediation activities.

With an effective structure in place, governance ensures that the system meets company needs. This governance process will identify problems and give ongoing direction to the COE. This in turn creates significant benefits for both the COE and the company.

23.2.2 Managing COE Workload

Using a budget model represents an excellent way to manage elective enhancement workload. In this way, functional organizations can ensure that their most needed enhancements are delivered, and the COE can ensure that it gets the resources necessary to produce the work. Putting a budget model in place requires some work, but the benefits far outweigh the costs.

To build the model properly, responsible process owners and COE management would review each elective enhancement and assign workload consumption estimates. This mechanism operates very similarly to the workload estimation that was part of the gap process for custom objects during blueprinting.

The senior executive governance group would establish a budget with an overall dollar amount, to be divided among the participating functional organizations. Figure 23.10 illustrates this concept with a hypothetical $10 million budget—based on COE workload capacity—to cover all approved SAP elective enhancement work. Working together, the group further subdivides the amount to global finance, global sales, and global supply chain.

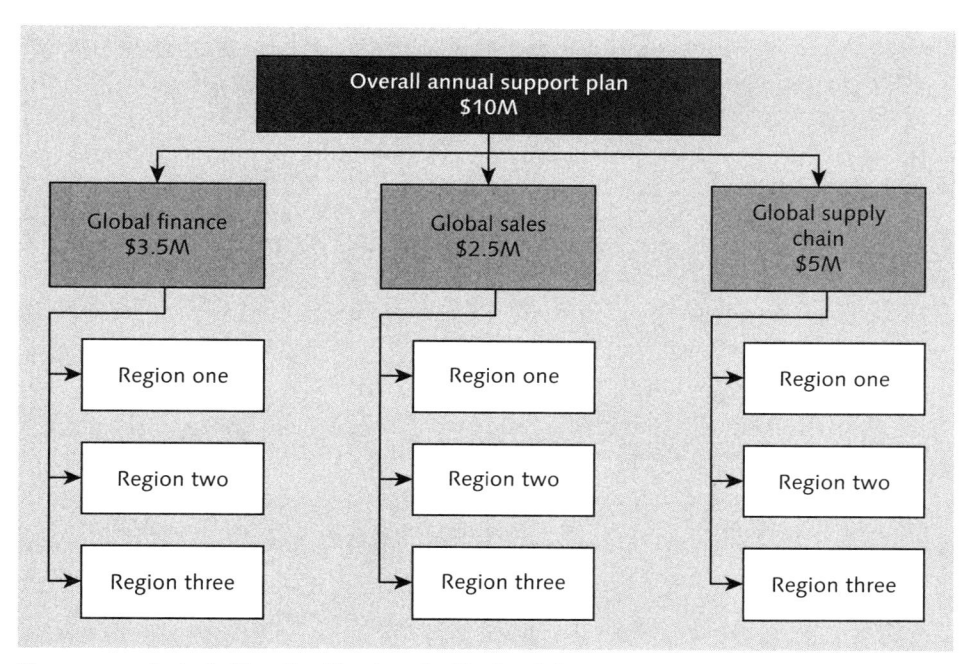

Figure 23.10 Budget Allocation Structure for Elective Enhancements

As enhancements are approved for each organization, the budget is decremented until the total is consumed. These funds would cover all COE work required, whether from the business COE, the IT COE, or technical services COE. Additionally, each approved and budgeted elective enhancement requires a separate delivery schedule. At this point, the COE annual budgets would be covered. If a functional business organization required additional elective enhancement work, that organization could separately fund it by hiring a service provider to do the work.

Covering elective enhancement approvals via this budgetary model reduces the amount of guesswork involved. By approving work that can be completed within the required time frame, it rewards accurate estimates from the COE. Additionally, it allocates some portion of the overall elective enhancement pie to each functional organization.

The scorecard shown in Figure 23.10 for COE governance reflects both the performance-to-schedule and performance-to-budget for exactly these approved elective enhancements. The senior executive governance group would review the status of major elective enhancements at its regular meetings. Issues and problems could be addressed at the meeting and immediately resolved.

23.2.3 Critical Success Factors for Sustainment Governance

It goes without saying that many companies fail to get sustainment right. And, truth to tell, it is difficult to accomplish—but *it can be done*.

There are a few critical success factors that must be achieved for sustainment to meet its goals. These success factors are divided into organizational roles:

- Business leadership requirements
    - An engaged and dedicated senior executive group that understands business needs and the importance of ongoing SAP system performance in meeting those needs
    - Key performance indicators owned by the senior executive group that demonstrate where system operations meet—or do not meet—business requirements, and which point to corrective action
    - Vigorous cross-functional dialog on requests for elective enhancements and the funding to handle workload
- IT leadership requirements
    - An active partnership with company functional organizations to understand their needs, and a commitment to translating those needs into effective system solutions
    - Full transparency with business organizations regarding workload, performance issues, and results attainment
    - Dedication to managing all technical resources to cost, schedule, and effectiveness targets

23.3 Continuing Company Projects

Likely your large-scale implementation project will be only the first of many SAP projects for the company. As upgrades are released or decisions are made to expand the application footprint—perhaps with the SAP HANA solution or SAP Global Trade Systems—projects will be required to install them. The sustainment period often leads to the start of new projects.

Previous experience with implementation projects will serve your company well. Skill sets acquired and lessons learned from prior projects serve as a foundation upon which to build, and the structure of later implementation projects remains very similar. What changes is the scope. While this does introduce complexity, much of that can be handled by the processes that proved successful in previous projects. Additionally, the guidance provided in this book still applies and can be adapted to those new challenges.

At this point, we've reached the end of our journey together. Your SAP system is now live, performing to expectations, and in good hands for its ongoing support. All this is due to your hard work and dedication. We have travelled from the idea of a project to actually bringing on a full-scale project team and now to rolling that team off to new duties and responsibilities.

Through this journey, you personally—and those around you—will have changed immeasurably. Looking back, you may be amazed at all that you've accomplished in such a short period of time. Take a moment to reflect on all the challenges you faced and overcame. Use this time to appreciate your new abilities. Don't let them grow rusty; decide how to apply them in your new role. Remember, the sky is the limit now!

The Author

Gerald Sullivan has a 25-year background in implementations. He has operated from the systems integrator side, but most of his experience has come from managing very large-scale SAP projects for implementing companies. Industries involved include life sciences, consumer-packaged goods, electronics, and financial services. His past experience as a professor in graduate schools of management and as a quality improvement executive contribute to a unique perspective and broad contextual knowledge of the challenges of implementation. He has a doctorate from the University of Wisconsin at Milwaukee.

Dr. Sullivan is the president of SAP Global Consultants, a consultancy offering project management advisory services to implementing companies. He can be reached at *jerry@sapglobalconsultants.com*.

Index

A

Abandon rates, 533
ABAP, 337
ABAP reports, 393
Accelerated SAP (ASAP), 23, 43, 77, 86, 89, 90, 142, 163, 221, 265
Accenture, 47, 117
 delivery methods, 47
Access, 58, 328, 514
Accessing unauthorized information, 346
Accountability, 179
Accounting, 83, 101, 113, 116
 document creation, 288
Accounts
 payable, 213, 272
 payable administrator, 343, 449
 receivable, 177, 180, 213, 272, 533
 receivable administrator, 448
Acquisitions, 68
Action planning, 443, 449
Active issue registry, 227
Administrator, 195
Affordable Care Act, 19, 355
Aging, 517
Aging of defects, 369
AIX, 105
Algorithms, 170
Allocated resources, 544
Alphanumerical information, 385
Americas SAP User Group (ASUG), 159
Announcements, 459
ANSI X12, 402
Answering system, 512
Application, 419, 514, 534
 development, 312
 development team, 217
 installation, 293
 lifecycle management, 49
 software installation scripts, 433
Approval, 193
Approver, 36, 351
AS2, 403
Asia, 102, 235, 253
As-is processes, 261
Assemble-to-order, 147
Assemblies, 504
Assessment checklists, 125
Asset, 391
 records, 383
Assign defects, 365
Assigning tasks, 252
Assignment of security roles, 412
Associate director, 244
Attendee, 465, 495
 list, 299
 notification, 467
Attitude, 243
Audit, 185
 auditor, 194, 373
 organization, 373
 requirements, 185
 trails, 411
Author, 350
Authoring system operations, 474
Authorization, 342
 controls, 412
Automatic three-way invoicing, 411
Automation, 34, 103
 computer-based transactions, 401
 controls, 283, 411
 efficiencies, 71
 purchase order approval, 181
 screening, 180
 testing systems, 372
Available positions, 258
Available to ship, 399
Average database execution time, 436
Average response time, 436
Average wait time, 436
Awareness training, 149

Index

B

Backfill mechanism, 228
Back-office activity, 75, 372
Back-up, 543
 data center, 434
 recovery mechanisms, 105
 system, 437
Banking, 217, 347
Barriers to communication, 251
Base SAP application, 425
Base SAP roles, 346
Basis, 514
 team, 216, 417
Believers, 449
Benefit, 223, 496
Big bang, 172
Billing and invoice processing, 288
 practices, 138
Bills of material, 167, 382, 390, 486, 493, 504
Blueprint, 242, 496, 530
 approval, 285
 completion, 230, 291
 deliverable, 185, 223
 documents, 531
 phase, 83
 workshop materials, 223
Blueprinting, 39, 51, 72, 89, 92, 108, 163, 204, 222, 261, 262, 264, 288, 291, 295, 304, 327, 424, 432, 442, 463
Book of Revelations, 379
Bottom line, 90, 497
Break-fix performance, 532, 539
Briefings, 459
Broadcast e-mails, 496
Budget, 183, 185, 220, 528
 allocation structure, 545
 and schedule status, 544
 categories, 113, 115
 model, 544
 overruns, 208
 planning, 208
Build completion, 229, 230
Build plans, 417
Building, 68
Business analysts, 75

Business as usual, 241, 257
Business blueprint, 27, 45
Business continuity, 105, 434, 489
Business controls, 185, 225, 294, 338, 531
Business Controls Identification (BCI), 282
Business impact, 514
Business interruption, 434
Business leadership requirements, 546
Business model, 77
Business partner outages, 515
Business partner relationships, 491
Business performance metrics, 59, 523
Business performance targets, 523
Business process, 67, 69, 164, 261
 changes, 70, 236, 255
 complexity, 75
 documentation, 84, 535
 experts, 537
 hierarchy (BPH), 190, 268
 leads, 175
 management, 48
 owners, 25, 225, 490
 performance, 157, 328
 preparation, 485
 procedure (BPP), 463
 support, 532
Business ramp-up, 488, 505
Business readiness, 153
Business requirements, 358, 528
Business scope, 100
Business transformation, 19, 153, 175, 199, 440
Business transformation office (BTO), 134, 205, 224
Business users, 356
Business warehouse, 396
Business-requested functionality, 82
Business-to-business (B2B) transactions, 401
Buttons, 510
Buyer, 249, 451

C

Cadre, 90, 96, 98, 99, 100, 111, 112
 members, 99
Calendar, 185, 195

Call queue times, 533
Calling card number, 254
Candidate selection, 243
Capgemini, 117
Capital versus expense reporting, 227
Carriers, 254
Carveout, 66
Cash management, 179
Catastrophic event, 434
Catch-up, 487
Categories, 443
Center of Excellence (COE)
  Annual budgets, 545
  Business, 528, 529, 537
  IT, 528, 531, 533, 537, 538
  Management, 544
  Technical Services, 528, 533, 537
  Workload, 539
Central governance, 390
Centralized sites, 511
Certified SAP partners, 141
Change control, 430, 431, 522
  procedures, 138
Change control board (CCB), 139, 522
Change impact, 225, 439, 442
  briefings, 445
  matrix, 280
Change management, 67, 133, 152, 271, 293, 310, 313, 439
  challenges, 446
  facilitator, 450
  initiatives, 224
  lead, 136
  team, 216, 280, 407, 439, 510
  training, 152
Change request, 139
Changes to invoices, 486
Changes to products, 486
Charge numbers, 228
Charts of accounts, 335
Chief executive officer (CEO), 205, 499
Chief financial officer (CFO), 126, 204, 499
Chief information officer (CIO), 203, 245, 247
Chief operating officer (COO), 204, 499
Citrix, 105

Class, 494
  completion, 494
  materials, 463
  rosters, 415
  schedules, 415, 465
Classifications, 443
Classroom, 494
  delivery skills, 475
  setup, 465, 467, 476, 494
Clean cycle, 406
C-level company officer, 499
Client, 419, 428
  arrangement, 418
  identifiers, 425
  role description, 134
Closure rates, 519
Coaching, 444
  sessions, 466
Code change, 523
Code fix, 149
Cold back-up, 437
Collaboration application, 192
Color-coding, 298, 313
Combination test, 406
Command center, 507
Commodity buyer, 449
Common area, 253
Commonality matrix, 288
Communications, 224, 459
  activities, 293
  devices, 249
  tools, 497
Company business operations, 173
Company business processes, 71, 122, 355
Company code, 346, 531
Company data, 469
Company executive committee, 227
Company executive leadership, 219
Company executive sponsors, 374
Company headcount costs, 114
Company headquarters, 113
Company initiatives, 224
Company instructors, 465
Company International trade activities, 169
Company locations, 100, 122, 166
Company management, 200, 496

Company master data, 330
Company procurement organization, 179
Company procurement staff, 121
Company revenues, 178
Company reward structure, 457
Complexity factors, 171
Compliance, 133
    problems, 344
Concept slides, 469
Conduct monthly and quarterly reviews, 208
Conference calls, 253, 254, 263
Conference room, 249, 253
Configuration, 78, 95, 104, 105, 144, 157,
    188, 211, 227, 230, 270, 305, 313, 328,
    380, 424, 432, 485, 523, 539
    analysts, 333
    decision, 185
    rationale, 185, 333
    setup, 368
    tables, 331
Configured system, 357
Consolidation, 272
Contact information, 512
Content authoring, 481
Content developers, 473
Content experts, 475
Content management, 193, 194
Content types, 468
Continuous user training, 439
Contracting, 127, 180, 228, 272
    contractors, 20, 248, 325
    contractual understanding, 249
    expirations, 180
    hires, 248
    manufacturers, 503
    new suppliers, 177
    to pay, 211
Control points, 414
Controlled document, 193, 277
    repository, 194
Controlled start, 487
Controller, 499
Controlling, 83
Conversion, 274, 388, 389
    functional specifications, 384

Conversion (Cont.)
    technical specifications, 384
    tools, 381, 387
    unit testing, 384
Coordinator, 207
Core interface (CIF), 158
Core project team, 356, 373
Corporate audit, 116, 227
Corporate level reports, 395
Corrective actions, 209
Cost accounting, 85
Cost collection mechanisms, 227
Cost control, 275
Cost estimate, 124
Cost of goods, 180
Cost parameters, 122
Cost reductions, 178
Cost risk sharing, 128
Cost roll-ups, 503
Cost savings, 163, 178
Country coordinator, 310
Course
    materials, 463
CPU usage, 157, 436
Credit check, 279
Credit master, 335
Credit memorandum, 473
Critical data flow, 515
Critical event, 436
Critical mass, 252
Critical outage, 515
Critical roles, 457
Cross reference files, 493
Cross-functional dialog, 546
Cross-functional process issues, 225
Cross-workstream coordination, 359
CTP, 211
Current office location, 252
Current state, 457
Current system modifications, 81
Custom development, 144, 319
Custom mapping requirements, 404
Custom object, 34, 64, 83, 95, 104, 107, 132,
    157, 169, 222, 274, 293, 305, 485
    development, 328, 384, 424, 432
    identifier, 281

Custom object (Cont.)
　performance, 356, 368
Customer, 217, 380, 493, 531
　address, 330
　credit limit, 358
　development, 145, 146
　exits, 145
　information, 486
　invoices, 401
　maintenance category, 79
　management scenario, 190
　master, 275, 330, 335, 358, 382, 390
　number, 33, 473
　payment, 359
　supplier purchase orders, 401
Customer relationship management (CRM), 76, 106
Customer service administrator, 448
Customer-requested add-ons, 145
Customization, 144
Customs authorities, 169
Customs documentation, 177, 275
Cutover, 381, 486, 503
　management, 49, 504
　planning, 483, 485
　team, 488
Cycle structure, 363
Cycles, 357, 406

D

Daily project operations, 207
Daily service level performance, 520
Data, 216, 379, 380
Data boundaries, 356
Data center, 81, 110, 432, 533
Data cleansing and conversion, 99, 214, 225, 246, 251, 293, 305, 313, 377, 380, 383
　conversion lead, 251
　defect resolution, 492
　definition document (DDD), 383
　entry, 373
　governance, 389
　identification, 381
　issue, 368
　level security, 346, 531
　load files, 380, 381, 386

Data cleansing and conversion (Cont.)
　maintenance, 69
　management, 49
　mapping, 381, 384
　migration, 64, 141, 167, 173
　owner, 391, 531
　preparedness, 500
　sharing process, 168
　sheet, 473
　sources, 395
　team, 389, 531
　transformation rules, 381
　transport window, 487
　verification, 251
Data warehouses, 396
Database, 105, 108, 157, 443
　performance, 157
　server, 111, 534
　volume consumption, 157
Day in the life exercise, 451
Day-in-the-life exercise, 496
Days on hand (DOH), 399
Days sales outstanding (DSO), 399
Dedicated department number, 228
Defect, 356, 506
　category, 368
　handling, 365
　identification, 363
　resolution, 110, 522
　resolution category, 539
　resolution urgency, 366
　resolver, 362
　review meetings, 368
　severity level, 366
Defining best practices, 103
Defining test data, 381
Degree of customization, 79
Deliver to schedule, 255
Deliverables, 21, 89, 90, 91, 99, 133, 185, 268, 304
　cycles, 328
　identification, 50
　scheduling and tracking, 209
　set, 46
　status, 313
　tracking, 315
Deliverables and outcome, 303

Delivery methods, 464
Delivery of service, 515
Delivery phases, 242
Deloitte, 117
Demand planner, 448
Demand planning forecasting, 435
Demonstrating leadership, 38
Demonstration, 423
Deployment, 87, 329, 535
  speed, 40
  waves, 102
Derived roles, 347
Design, 227, 539
  decisions, 262
  deliverables, 261
  document, 188
  documentation, 54, 261
  documents, 536
  meetings, 176
  objectives, 230
Designated storage location, 254
Detailed design, 264
Detective controls, 411
Development, 293, 393
Development environment, 419, 421, 426
Development system, 77
Development tools, 473
Development work, 170
Device, 514
Diplomatic skills, 289
Direct material, 181, 272
Director, 244
Display access, 414
Distribution, 83, 193, 217
  inventory, 399
Divested entity, 68
Divestiture action, 68
Document changes, 344
Document continuity, 183
Document deliverable, 183, 184
Document hierarchy, 190
Document owner, 350
Document preparation, 195
Document reviews and approvals, 33, 193, 195, 475
Document submission, 195

Document type, 184
Documentation, 293
Drilldown, 447
Due diligence, 119
Duplicate records, 384

E

Early business activity, 488
Ecuador, 177
EDIFACT, 402
Education, 457
Elective enhancements, 539
Electronic bank reconciliations, 179
Electronic communication, 169
Electronic data interchange (EDI), 217, 246, 294, 312, 363, 379, 400, 401
  810 invoice, 401
  Project deliverables, 404
  Sales order, 359
  Standards, 402, 405
Electronic documents, 36, 104, 109
Electronic funds transfer, 104
Electronic signature, 193
Electronic transactions, 217
Emergency sales orders, 487
Employee backfill, 208
Employee master data, 481
Employee roles, 439
Enabling unneeded access, 344
End user, 199, 441, 494, 535
  account, 512
  documentation, 86
  preparation, 166
  proficiency, 481
  system training, 151
  training, 171, 228, 412, 424
End-of-life support systems, 72
End-of-phase reviews, 60
End-to-end scenario, 358
End-to-end to-be overview, 267
End-user training, 53, 320
  materials, 54
Engagement lead, 135
English, 290, 477

Enhancement, 132, 145, 170, 274, 357
  Enhancement pack (EHP), 73, 76
  Enhancement Package Information Center, 77
  Enhancement Package Installer (EPHI), 78
  releases, 533
Enterprise
  Collaboration tools, 188
  Document management tools, 188
  Knowledge management, 188
Enterprise Portal, 193
Enterprise resource planning (ERP), 66
Entrance and exit criteria, 374
Environment, 418
Environmental, health, or safety risk, 515
Equipment, 391
Error, 356, 411, 506
E-signature, 193
Europe, 102, 103
Evidence of readiness, 374
Exception cycle, 406
Exception report review, 412
Executing a production order, 359
Executive risk, 233, 235, 320
Executive sponsors, 25
Exercises, 467
Existing policies, 329
Exit criteria, 376
Expected result, 358
Expense costs, 228
Expenses as a percentage of fees, 138
Experienced SAP users, 168
Exports, 371
  documentation, 33
  management, 180, 448
  operations, 101
External auditor, 116
External contractors, 199
Extract, transformation, and load (ETL), 387

F

Facilities, 298, 465, 494
  allocation, 114
  coordinator, 250
Factory shipment, 211

Failover, 104, 105
  testing, 418, 434
Fast track, 351
Feasibility check, 156
Feeder systems, 486
Fees and expenses, 137
Field length, 385
Fields, 384
Fill rates in plants, 391
Final data loads, 485
Final go-live, 257
Final go-live approval, 57
Final integrator selection, 126
Final preparation, 27, 46, 92, 95, 96, 174, 183, 204, 242, 434, 483, 485, 536
Final role mapping, 231
Final system build, 356
Finance, 279, 348
Finance and Controlling (FI-CO), 168, 212, 420
Finance organization, 98, 224
  accounts, 380
  allocations, 528
  audit, 515
  consolidation and close, 177
  controllers, 116
  forecasting, 208
  impacts, 170
  performance, 208
  planning, 209, 211
  process, 211
  projection, 90
  records, 380
  reporting, 180, 208
  services companies, 201
  transactions, 211, 492
Finished good product number (SKU), 278
Finished goods, 490
First cut integrator presentations, 125
First-line support, 514
First-time instructors, 475
Fixed assets, 213, 335
Fixed price contract, 128, 325
Folders, 194
Follow-up, 252
Forecasts, 101, 220

Formal testing, 336
Forms, 274, 357
Foundation courses, 470
Fractional share, 238
Fraud, 411
Freeze period, 486
French, 290, 477
FTP, 403
Fulfillment, 533
Full share, 238
Full transparency, 546
Full-scale implementation, 64
Full-time employee (FTE), 179
Functional access, 414
Functional approach, 203
Functional boundaries, 440
Functional business organizations, 52, 439, 441, 488, 504, 528, 539
  process area, 165
  process workstreams, 222
  processes, 101
  risk, 233, 236
Functional executives, 245
Functional senior executives, 214
Functional specification, 338, 393
Functional testing, 336
Functional workstream, 51, 52, 304, 310, 360, 444, 498
  leads, 99, 210, 243, 464
Functionality delivered, 500
Funds receipt for invoice, 211
Future state, 457
Future working capital, 179

G

General ledger accounts, 390, 472
General ledger close, 179
General ledger transactions, 383
Generating sales documents, 435
Geographic scope, 67, 133, 418
Geographical complexity, 166
German, 290
Global documents, 349
Global finance, 200, 545
Global process owner, 498, 509, 530

Global projects, 166, 527
Global requirements, 318
Global resources, 172
Global sales, 200, 545
Global SAP implementation, 163
Global single instance, 536
Global supply chain, 200
Golden rules, 20
Go-live and support, 27, 46, 172, 174, 193, 199, 206, 372, 439, 488, 503, 533
  authorization, 497
  date, 298
  decision making, 499
  planning, 535
  readiness, 231
  review and approval, 485
  system, 355
Goods receipt, 487
Governance, 55, 297
  document, 185
  model, 390
  process, 540
  structure, 181, 241, 540
Governmental agencies, 193
Governmental regulatory agencies, 373
Granting access, 504
Greenfield, 19, 66

H

Handling responsibility, 38
Handouts, 460
Hands-on instruction, 509
Hands-on practice, 476
Hard cost savings, 178
Hard dollar returns, 179
Hard-copy documents, 196
Hardware, 80, 104, 208, 418, 533
Hardware installation script, 433
Headcount charges, 227
Headcount decreases, 178
Headcount forecasting, 89
Headcount plan, 183
Headcount ramp-up process, 96
Help desk, 507
  management, 533

Help desk (Cont.)
  technicians, 512
  tickets, 512, 539
Hierarchies, 193
High-availability approach, 438
High-level project organization, 200
High-level realization plan, 296
High-level schedule, 265
High-volume transactions, 435
Hiring and training additional staff, 272
Holdback, 129
Home organization, 248
Horizontal/technical workstreams, 222, 294, 304, 312, 444
  leads, 243
  teams, 214, 375
Host country language skills, 263
Host functional organization, 202
Host nation working styles, 262
Hot back-up, 437
Hourly rate, 249
HR practitioner, 244
Human capital management (HCM), 101, 177, 211, 266, 444, 517
Human resources, 224
  function, 440
  master data, 382
  organization, 244
  process, 211
Hypercare, 58, 172, 320, 372, 485, 488, 503, 506, 533, 537
  completion, 231
  exit, 523
  operations, 506
  planning, 231
  targets, 524

I

IBM, 47, 117
Impact categories, 443
Implementation Guide (IMG), 333
Implementation guidelines, 401
Implementation model, 83
Implementation project lifecycle, 178
Implementation projects, 17

Implementation strategy, 101, 102
Implementation waves, 231, 324, 506
  framework, 173, 524
Imports, 371
Inactive status, 227
Inadequate testing, 355
Inbound messages, 401
Incentive payment, 128
Incident, 231, 430, 488, 506
  aging, 520
  closed, 517
  closure rate, 518
  closure status, 58
  levels, 231, 523
  opened, 517
  quantity, 523
  reports, 78
  resolution, 522, 533, 537
  resolution status, 543
  resolution times, 540
  severity level, 514
  volume targets, 59
  volumes, 540
Incomplete records, 384
Incomplete user training, 517
Incorrect addresses, 380
Indirect buyer, 449
Indirect procurement, 177
Individual sales companies, 179
InfoCube, 396
Informal communication, 251
Informal test scripts, 336
Information technology (IT), 202, 372
  Organization, 540
  Support, 71
InfoView, 397
Infrastructure, 157, 418, 532
  component, 232
  deliverables, 432
  delivery schedules, 235
  environment, 298, 433
  installation, 293
  operations, 534
  package, 71, 111
  power supply qualification, 433
  support, 80

Index

In-house candidates, 247
Initial curriculum, 464
Initial data loads, 424
Initial process maps, 263
Initial requirements listing, 268
Initial space planning, 90
Inputs, 302, 303
Installation, 419
Installation qualification (IQ), 433
Instance, 419
Instructor-led training (ILT), 464, 466
Instructors, 216, 465, 478, 494
  availability, 495
  certifications, 196
  preparation, 476
  skills, 476
Insufficient resources, 287
Integrated company, 31
Integrated SAP system, 189
Integration, 171, 262
  agent, 215
  management, 208
  meetings, 272
  points, 279
  solutions management, 49
Integration test, 54, 230, 336, 356, 386, 406, 421, 539
Integrator
  capabilities, 119
  contracting, 127
  development team, 276
  executive sponsors, 136
  lead, 339
  management, 368
  onboarding, 139
  project team performance, 120
  rankings and scoring, 124
  report-card, 119
  scoring, 126
  selection, 90, 91, 92, 96, 99, 108, 116, 118
  staff, 325, 356
Inter-company postings, 179
Intercompany shipments, 371
Interfaces, 68, 75, 132, 170, 274, 357
Intermediate document (IDoc), 403

Internal auditor, 449
Internal Control Standard, 283
Internal controls, 377
  analysis, 409
  requirements, 281
  team, 408
Interviews, 453
Inventory, 83, 180, 399, 492, 493
  management, 181
  reconciliation, 271, 503
  records, 380
  transaction, 358
Invoices and customs documents, 104, 275, 359, 375, 383
Issue management, 226
Issue registry, 227
Issues and risks, 194
IT staff, 522
IT system analysts, 537
Iterative go-live approval process, 498
IT-led project organization, 203

J

Japanese, 477
JD Edwards, 71
Job description, 243, 457
Job role, 343, 457, 469, 480

K

Key dependencies, 303, 304
Key design decisions, 273
Key performance indicator (KPI), 274, 397, 412, 546
Key personnel loss, 256
Key program deliverables, 224
Key vendors, 224
Kick-off, 255, 264, 298
Knowledge, 243
Knowledge management, 183
  tools, 181
Knowledge sharing, 266
Knowledge transfer, 257, 536
Knowledgeable business resource, 395

L

Labor projections, 322
Laboratory sessions, 299, 300
Languages, 527
    differences, 263
    groupings, 534
    issues, 263
    multiple, 70, 166, 464
    support, 310
Large-scale SAP implementations, 19, 63
Late delivery, 338
Latin America, 102, 236
Lay-off, 248
Leadership attributes, 243
Leadership risk, 318
Learning management systems (LMS), 188, 481
Legacy System Migration Workbench (LSMW), 389
Legacy systems, 106, 107, 166, 190, 216, 319, 380, 536
    applications, 368, 486
    ERP systems, 262
    PLM application, 167
Legal requirements, 222
Lessons learned, 172
Licensing requirements, 110
Life sciences, 193, 347
Line items, 435
Line managers, 459
Linux, 105
Load files, 381
Loading, 216, 387
Local governance, 390
Localization, 169, 222, 288
    completion, 230
    decisions, 230
Location, 465, 481
Locked, 512
Logic paths, 356
Log-in, 504, 510
Logistics, 216
    arrangements, 249
    operations, 533
    planning, 465

Long-term company asset, 40
Low-level plans, 296

M

Maintenance, 184
Maintenance technician, 448
Major milestones, 221
Manage customers, 190
Manage pricing, 190
Management reporting, 24, 393
Management review, 412
Manager, 244
Managerial level, 244
Mandarin Chinese, 290, 477
Manual clearing tasks, 179
Manual controls, 411
Manual entry, 487
Manual files, 381
Manual load-ready files, 389
Manual processes, 35, 80, 187, 274, 373, 490
Manufacturing and distribution operations, 193, 200
Manufacturing execution system (MES), 106, 458
Manufacturing floor operations, 458
Manufacturing plant shutdowns, 496
Manufacturing plants, 489
Manufacturing sites, 166, 503
Mapping tables, 388
Marketing, 200
Master data, 33, 270, 382, 421, 492, 503
    element, 531
    governance, 531
    management, 101, 531
    migration, 216
    standardization, 542
Master scheduling, 211
Master services agreement (MSA), 129
Material, 493, 494, 531
    costs decreases, 178
    handlers, 451
    master, 335, 382, 390
    number, 278

Material requirements planning (MRP), 85, 359, 452
Material spend, 180
Materials management, 168
Materials purchasing, 211
Matrix-led project organizations, 204
MaxAttention, 158
McKinsey & Company, 20
Meeting the schedule, 356
Meetings, 252
  ground rules, 289
  structure, 225
  tempo and duration, 311
Mega-scenario, 359, 371
Merger, 68
Messages, 496
Metrics, 527, 542
Middle management, 496
Middleware, 105, 403
Migrating, 69
Migrating data, 71
Milestone, 185
  recognition, 315
Minor disruption, 515
Mission-critical data, 435
Mitigation activities, 449
Mitigation strategies, 220
Mock data load, 492
Modifications, 83, 144
Modified system, 482, 542
Modules, 466
Monetary awards, 238
Monitoring time to completion, 55
Monthly reviews, 256
MS Office, 223
MS Project, 297
Multi-copy impact printers, 291
Multi-national companies, 80
Multiple ERP systems, 262
Multiple instances, 421
Multiple regions, 166
Multiple workstreams, 370
Multi-wave implementations, 172, 424
Mutually exclusive designation, 191

N

Naming conventions, 191, 193
Naming variances, 33
Native speakers, 478
Negative go-live decision, 498
Negative perceptions, 452
Network analyst, 345
Network operations, 105, 110
Network operators, 254
New employees, 259
  provisioning process, 177
  recruiting, 248
New functionality requirements, 80
New markets, 542
New organizational model, 457
New policies, 329
New processes, 261, 320
New requirement, 368
New supplier contracts, 486
New vendor, 358
Newsletters, 459
Nomenclature, 417
North America, 102, 535
Notas fiscal financial reporting, 290
Not-to-exceed fee, 137
Numeric information, 385

O

Office moves, 491
Office supplies, 114
Off-shore services, 528
Onboarding, 89, 242, 249
Ongoing maintenance, 110
On-line rebate payments, 180
Online Support System (OSS) Notes, 73, 147
On-time delivery, 170, 338, 431
Open accounts receivable, 492, 493
Open defect, 376
Open issues and concerns, 274
Open sales orders, 487, 492
Open-ended model, 138
Operate to specification, 170
Operating data, 69

Operating system, 111, 157
    installation script, 433
Operational detail, 295
Operational reporting, 394
Operator training, 110
Optimizations, 103
Order
    acknowledgement, 279
    confirmation, 278
    fulfilment process, 211
    management, 533
    processing, 211
    receipt, 279
    type, 278
Order-to-cash (OTC), 101, 177, 190, 211, 266, 444, 517
Organization changes, 48, 439
Organization hierarchy, 346
Organization redesign, 458
Organizational alignment, 441
Organizational change management team, 53
Organizational changes, 224
Organizational design, 439, 456
Organizational hierarchy, 268
Organizational impacts, 271
Organizational redesign, 441
Organizational risk, 233, 235
Organizational structure, 50
Organizational transformation, 442
Orientation mechanism, 295
Original tester, 366
Outbound messages, 401
Outcomes, 304
Outline agreements, 493
Output framework, 160
Overall sales levels, 391
Overruns, 38
Oversight and guidance, 219
Overview courses, 470
Overview sessions, 150

P

Pack and ship, 452
Package implementation plan, 85
Packing boxes, 254
Paper-based partner transactions, 401
Participant events, 299
Password reset, 512, 533
Payment for services, 211
Payment orders from customers, 401
Payments from banks, 401
PDF applications, 352
PeopleSoft, 71
Performance benchmarking database, 159
Performance expectations, 527
Performance issue, 256
Performance metrics, 220, 312
Performance targets, 542
Performance testing, 434
Performance-to-budget, 546
Performance-to-schedule, 546
Periodic audits, 411
Periodic measured feedback, 453
Periodic project reviews, 229
Periodic software updates, 533
Periodic survey activities, 456
Peripherals, 375
Permission structure, 190
Personalization, 145
Phase reviews, 229
Phasing, 133
Physical inventory, 503
Planned product launch, 515
Planning, 228, 451
Plant, 278, 531
Plant code, 346
Plant shutdowns, 489
Plant warehouse storage locations, 290
Plan-to-report, 211
Plan-to-schedule, 211
Plan-to-stock, 101, 177, 211, 266, 444
Plug and play, 432
Policies and procedures, 153, 193, 328, 412, 444, 450
Polish, 290
Poor documentation, 356
Portal, 105, 274, 357
Portal, web, and middleware, 105
Portuguese, 290, 477
Post go-live, 485
Posted sales order, 332

Index

Posters, 460
Post-execution reviewer, 362
Post-go-live operations, 40
Post-go-live processes, 465
Post-implementation support, 320
Practice sessions, 476
Pre-built package projects, 64
Predefined implementation work packages, 85
Preparatory activities, 255
Presentations, 185, 459
Presenters, 299
Preventive controls, 410
Pricing, 180, 213, 272, 278
   conditions, 382
   information, 382
   specialist, 448
PRINCE2, 47
Printing, 510, 514
Prior company usage experience, 168
Problem resolution, 506
Problem-solving, 449
Procedures, 153, 347, 494
Process, 280
Process automation, 34, 179
Process business requirements, 225
Process control definition (PCD), 409
Process deficiencies, 34
Process definition document (PDD), 225, 277, 358, 443, 465, 531
Process design, 225, 336
Process flows, 280
Process holds, 177
Process lead, 350
Process owners, 135
Process simplification, 33
Process standardization, 103, 262
Process team lead, 135
Process team member, 135
Process transformations, 30, 224
Procurement, 452
   process, 211
   shopping cart, 435
Procure-to-pay, 51, 101, 177, 210, 211, 266, 444, 517
Procure-to-pay lead, 244
Produce-to-demand, 211

Product availability check, 279
Product disposition, 181
Product expiration dates, 181
Product launches, 486, 491
Product lifecycle management (PLM), 76
Product master, 335
Product modifications, 486
Product operations management, 490
Production, 419
Production data load, 356
Production environment (PRD), 56, 57, 419, 429, 430, 431
Production forecasting and scheduling, 213
Production of product, 211
Production orders, 359, 487
Production personnel, 451
Production planning and scheduling, 211, 345, 420, 490
Production scheduler, 448
Production system, 78, 231, 275, 485, 522
Profit and cost centers, 382
Profit centers, 391
Program lifecycle, 225
Program management office (PMO), 99, 120, 164, 176, 206, 220, 276, 295, 307, 311, 315, 320, 335, 356, 407, 498
Program management review, 93
Program management workstream, 51
Program manager, 206, 243
Program performance, 224
Program progress updates, 224
Program sponsors, 498
Programmers, 337
Progress of the project, 459
Project budgeting, 90, 113, 249
Project buy-in, 202
Project chain of command, 226
Project charter, 183, 219
Project communication, 440, 459
Project complexity assessment, 164, 171
Project definition, 45
Project deliverable, 195, 204, 221
Project delivery schedules, 170
Project description, 221
Project documents, 192
   policy, 186

Project documents (Cont.)
  repository, 277
Project duration, 293
Project environment, 56, 104
Project executive steering committee, 499
Project financial control, 208, 220
Project goals, 221
Project governance, 93, 94, 97, 113, 120, 219
Project leadership, 93, 238, 456, 486
Project legitimacy, 202
Project lifecycle, 95, 99, 104, 111, 183, 209, 220, 241, 380
Project management, 22, 48, 221, 225, 310, 367, 463
Project Management Institute, 47
Project management review meetings, 286
Project management risk, 318
Project manager, 135, 248
Project meeting schedules, 89
Project objectives, 122, 459
Project operating review meeting, 93, 210
Project operational skills, 21
Project organizational structure, 122, 199, 221, 243
Project planning, 89, 93, 95, 97, 98, 111, 116, 221, 260
Project preparation, 26, 45, 183, 199, 432
  deliverables, 89
  timeline, 89
Project procurement, 90
Project results, 242
Project risk, 25, 233, 236
Project schedule, 24, 185, 207, 252
Project scope, 43, 130, 199, 265, 318
Project sponsors, 60, 142, 163, 208, 339, 379
Project staffing levels, 95
Project stakeholders, 123
Project status meetings, 296
Project support deliverables, 309
Project team, 503
  effectiveness, 153
  resolvers, 513
  skills, 30
Project timeline, 122
Project types, 163
Project watch list, 287

Promote-to-production process, 77, 429
Promotions, 259
Prompts, 512
Proposals, 99
Propriety automated applications, 478
Prototyping, 270, 423
Purchase order, 35, 278, 487
Purchase order date, 278
Purchase requisition, 382
Purchasing, 83
Purchasing information records, 335
Purchasing organization, 347
Purpose of the project, 265, 301, 303

Q

QA2, 423, 427, 429
QAS, 419, 425, 426, 427
QE1, 419
Quality assurance, 181
Quality gates, 60
Quality inspectors, 451
Quantity, 278
Query, 543
Question and answer session, 123
Quick reference guides, 153, 469
Quiet period, 486
Quotation number, 278

R

Ramp-up process, 536
Rate card, 137
Rate of incident opening, 518
Raw material, 490, 503
Readiness components, 499
Realization, 27, 46, 78, 95, 174, 204, 225, 242, 268, 293, 327, 355, 380, 408, 439, 485
  deliverables, 298
  handbook, 301
  kick-off, 295
  project plan, 295, 299
  wrap-up, 301
Real-time interaction, 251
Real-world processes, 371
Reasonable cost basis, 137

Receiving goods, 359
Receiving vendor invoices, 359
Reconciliation, 412
Record amounts, 385
Record counts, 387
Record to report, 444
Records, 384
Records of attendance, 494
Records of defect closure, 197
Records of employee attendance, 188
Records with errors, 384
Record-to-report (RTR), 101, 177, 211, 266
Recovery time, 534
Recruiter, 256, 448
Recruiting, 457
Recruit-to-retire, 211
Reduced cash flow, 179
Reducing business process variety, 83
Refreshes, 396
Regional and site management, 488
Regional operations, 504
   business executives, 499
   command centers, 507
   design differences, 261
   documents, 349
   executives, 225
   implementation waves, 237
   leaders, 306, 531
   localization sessions, 289
   market, 371
   offices, 116, 208, 511
   subject matter experts, 238
   team members, 263
   team participants, 262
   teams, 373
   variances, 32
Regions, 488, 536
Regression testing, 74, 78, 372, 539
Regular run rates, 506
Regulated companies, 193
Regulator, 194, 373
Regulatory authorities, 515
Regulatory compliance, 169
Regulatory oversight, 328
Regulatory requirement, 166, 347, 373
Reintegration, 257

Release management, 532
Release process, 534
Repatriation, 257
Replacement, 256
Reporting, 132, 274, 293, 311, 314, 357, 377, 379, 391, 421, 512
   of earnings, 211
   of systems test status, 110
   on test progress, 360
   requirements, 103
   solution, 103
   time allocations, 228
Repositories, 188, 352
Request for proposal (RFP), 90
   Reviewing responses, 121
Requests for payment, 383
Required service levels, 517
Requirement, 77, 186, 261, 395, 435
   coverage, 361
   linkage, 362
   specification, 356
   specification documents, 332
   traceability matrices, 373
Research and development, 200
Resolution timing, 231, 514
Resolve defects, 366
Resolved status, 227
Resolver group, 513
Resolvers, 58, 368
Resource requirements, 323
Resource risk, 233, 236, 319
Resourcing, 321, 448
Resourcing plan, 209
Response time, 252, 435
Restoration operations, 105
Restricted stock, 399
Retest, 366
Retest requirements, 363
Revenue-versus-plan projections, 391
Review, 195
Review board, 275
Reviewer, 36, 350
Reward funding, 237
Risk, 19, 185
   analysis, 67, 317
   classification system, 234

Risk (Cont.)
    identification, 232
    management, 209, 220, 231, 317
    mitigation skills, 232
    mitigation status, 321
    profile, 68
    recognition skills, 232
    registry, 209, 317, 320
    tracking, 193
Risk-based project schedule, 170
Road shows, 459
Role and responsibilities, 221, 281
    definitions, 271
    mapping, 53, 172, 407, 412, 514
    role-based security, 342
    specifications, 24
Role assignments, 408
Roll-off and reintegration, 242, 326
Rollouts, 133
Root cause analysis, 355, 356
RSVP date, 123
Russian, 290

S

Safeguarding, 154
Safety checks, 434
Safety stock, 490
Sales and distribution, 168
Sales and Distribution (SD), 420
Sales and inventory forecasting process, 177
Sales area, 278
Sales operations, 166, 348
Sales ordering, 420
    creation, 435
    header data, 332
    processing, 275
    volume, 435
Sales organization, 332, 347, 531
Sales pricing, 335
    conditions, 391, 531
Sales projections, 272
Sales reporting, 180
Sales transactions, 383
Sample data, 405
Sample training assignment, 479

Sanctioned party lists (SPL), 180
Sandbox (SBX), 423
    environment, 432
    system, 77
SAP ABAP programs, 338
SAP acronyms, 210
SAP Active Global Support (AGS), 154
SAP Advanced Planning and Optimization
    (APO), 125, 169, 216, 271
SAP applications, 216, 418
SAP as a company asset, 31
SAP Basis operations, 71
SAP Blue Book, 39
SAP Business One, 82
    starter package, 82
SAP Business Planning and Consolidation
    (BPC), 22, 212, 272, 392
SAP Business Suite, 76
SAP BusinessObjects BI, 168, 393, 419
SAP BusinessObjects Dashboards, 393, 398
SAP BusinessObjects Web Intelligence (WebI),
    397
SAP BW, 393
SAP certified system integrators, 146
SAP competency, 67
SAP consulting contract, 143
SAP country version, 290
SAP Crystal Reports, 83
SAP ERP, 17, 65, 75, 168, 216, 392, 419, 420
    SAP ERP 4.6, 79
    SAP ERP 6.0, 76, 79
SAP error message, 512
SAP executable transaction, 358
SAP expertise, 206
SAP Global Risk and Compliance (GRC), 422
SAP Global Trade Services (GTS), 125, 169,
    422, 547
SAP Green Book, 39
SAP HANA, 547
SAP HANA in-memory database, 79
SAP implementation methodology, 31
SAP implementation project, 90, 94, 98, 100,
    101, 107, 108, 109, 110, 113, 114
SAP installed base, 63
SAP landscape, 419
SAP licenses, 115

SAP login, 57, 190
SAP menu path, 338, 512
SAP NetWeaver, 76
SAP NetWeaver Development Studio, 422
SAP Overview and Navigation course, 480
SAP production system, 380
SAP Rapid Deployment Solutions, 18, 82
SAP security, 328
SAP service charges, 114
SAP software applications, 533
SAP Software Change Registration (SSCR), 145
SAP Solution Browser, 77
SAP Solution Manager, 187, 190, 284, 333, 422
SAP Supplier Relationship Management (SRM), 36, 189, 216, 419
　Supplier Self-Service (SUS), 429
SAP system design, 187, 417
SAP system environment changes, 80
SAP system landscape, 188
SAP system landscape profile, 81
SAP system setup, 69
SAP technical expertise, 538
SAP technical knowledge, 206
SAP Training, 149
SAP upgrade, 539
SAP UserID, 148, 342, 366, 411, 465, 494, 504
　Provisioning, 216
Sarbanes-Oxley, 348
Scenarios, 358, 361
Scheduled and unscheduled down time, 533
Scope, 221
　decisions, 267
　identification, 70
　management, 225
　of user access, 216
　parameters, 164
Scorecard, 542
Scorekeeper, 207
Screen setups, 440
Screen shots, 366
Script execution, 362
Scripts, 514
Security and internal controls, 214, 233, 377, 379, 407, 514
　design, 328, 407

Security and internal controls (Cont.)
　error, 368
　incidents, 517
　requirements, 328
　role, 216, 293, 375, 531
　setup, 190, 341, 536
　team, 407
Segregation of duty (SOD), 408, 412
　analysis, 531
　assessments, 216
　conflict, 415
　risks, 283
　violations, 409
Self-service delivery, 481
Senior advisory team, 135
Senior executive meeting, 93
Senior executives, 442, 445, 490, 527
Senior leadership roles, 97
Senior management, 244, 482, 527
Senior supply chain executive, 499
Sensitive transactions, 282, 411
Server access, 374
Server hardware, 65
Server platforms, 105
Servers, 90, 104, 110, 111
Service level resolution time, 519
Service manager, 433
Service order, 411
Service provider, 527, 545
Service-level agreements, 543
Session dress rehearsals, 299
Severe business impact, 515
Severity rating
　Four, 516
　One, 516
　rating, 367
　Three, 516
　Two, 516
Shared control, 390
Shipments, 177, 180, 383
Ship-to party, 278
Sign-offs, 196
Simulations, 469
Single building, 251
Single instance strategy, 419, 421
Single region, 166

Single source of truth, 18
Sites, 488, 536
    deliverables, 309
    operations, 373
    preparation, 171, 309
    readiness, 294
Size of user base, 70
Skills, 243, 481
    deficiency, 356
    set requirements, 439
Slow system performance, 543
Small and medium-sized businesses, 82
Small business, 85
Soft cost savings, 179
Software, 208, 418
    development lifecycles, 44
    errors, 147
    fixes, 74
    licenses, 65, 114, 115
Sold-to party, 278
Solution classes, 151
Sound station technology, 254
Sourcing, 180
Spanish, 290, 477
Spans of control, 457
Special business scenarios cycle, 406
Special configuration, 83, 270
Special matrix organization, 200
Specialized consultant resources, 142
Specialized contract recruiting companies, 248
Specialized document applications, 196
Specially colored shirts, 510
Specific business scenarios, 469
Specification, 186, 217, 293, 356
Specification documents, 190
Spend, 180
Stable operating parameters, 231
Staffing, 95, 181, 536
    levels, 319, 439
    model, 124
    needs, 209
    replacement, 326
    sources, 247
Stakeholder, 77
    approval, 123
    aware and involved, 456

Stakeholder (Cont.)
    management, 439, 452
    unaware and uninvolved, 456
Standard functionality, 270
Standard SAP ERP reports, 393
Standardize processes, 261
Standardized templates, 193
Standing operating procedures, 186
Start, 87
Start dates, 257
Starter Package scope documentation, 85
Start-up logistics, 89
Statement of work (SOW), 129, 315
Status reports, 185, 310
Statutorily required invoice, 177
Statutory financial regulations, 282
Statutory requirements, 166, 222
Statutory/legal reports, 393
Steady state, 530
Step-by-step procedures, 514
Stock option grants, 238
Stock transfer order (STO), 539
Storage and backup, 105, 110, 184
Storage location master data, 290
Storage locations, 335, 382
Storage setup, 110
String testing, 339
Strong PMO approach, 207
Structured Query Language, 157
Student exercises, 469
Subassemblies, 504
Sub-folders, 194
Subject matter expert (SME), 464, 473, 495, 509
Subpoenas, 515
Substitute resources, 136
Super user, 57, 135, 320, 506, 509
    preparedness, 231
    recruitment, 172
    team, 531
Supplier contracting, 211
Supplier information, 486
Supplier invoice payments, 177
Supplier Portal, 190, 275
Supplier relationship management (SRM), 76
Supply and inventory planning, 271

569

Supply chain, 173, 345, 545
Supply chain management (SCM), 76, 279
Supply network, 345
Supply planning, 272, 448
Support packs, 73
Supporting systems, 70
Surveys, 453
Sustainment, 186, 190, 527
    execution, 527
    governance, 540, 546
    group, 59
    organization, 40
    team, 424, 536
Swim lanes, 280
System
    administrators, 75
    architecture, 104, 111, 338
    build, 270, 327
    configuration, 64, 67, 71, 293, 411
    configurator, 136
    defects, 231
    design content, 230
    direction, 542
    downtime, 78
    enhancements, 539
    entries, 463
    go-live, 424, 485
    governance, 527
    identifier (SID), 419
    implementation, 271, 485
    integration, 70
    integrity, 341
    interface, 168
    landscape, 417
    language, 68, 289
    off-line, 78
    outages and downtime, 543
    performance, 274, 293, 319, 418, 500
    releases, 533
    replacement, 66
    response time, 543
    security, 216, 441
    support, 215
    transactions, 469
    transport, 370
    upgrades, 533

System (Cont.)
    usage patterns, 81
    user security, 500
System Administration Service, 158
System-based processes, 66
System-based transactions, 67
System-related deliverables, 90
System-related problems, 488
Systems build, 417
Systems environment, 77
Systems integrator, 20, 47, 65, 67, 117, 169, 221, 255, 332, 356, 380
    selection, 95
    senior executives, 265
    service charges, 114
    team, 45, 199
    travel and expense, 114
Systems readiness, 501
Systems test document, 197
Systems testing, 43, 64, 99, 110, 111, 173, 211, 225, 276, 312, 327, 355, 360, 381, 509

T

Table structures, 332
Table TVKO, 332
Tables, 397
Target closed date, 369
Target system, 389
Targeted communication, 318
Task assignment, 50
Tasks, 302, 303
Tax and statutory reporting, 101
Tax specialist, 449
Taxes and prices, 332
Team building, 262
Team dinners, 271
Team facilities, 250
Team folder, 195
Team leads, 195, 221
Team member performance, 256
Team members, 221
Team organization, 318
Team recruitment and selection, 242, 243
Team rewards and recognition, 220, 237
Teambuilding, 21, 242

Technical deliverables, 307
Technical design work, 217
Technical infrastructure, 222
Technical integration check, 157
Technical leads, 99, 135
Technical monitoring, 532, 533
Technical requirements, 104
Technical resources, 248, 546
Technical risk, 233, 235, 319
Technical Services, 154
Technical solution management, 49
Technical specification, 217, 338, 393
Technical support, 185, 527
Technical team, 77, 214
Technical writing companies, 348
Technicians, 512
Technology architecture, 233
Teleconferences, 248, 286
Telephone bridge line, 516
Templates, 46, 264
Temporary replacement workers, 228
Terms for payment, 399
Test
  approver, 362
  cases, 433
  completions, 110
  coordinators, 366
  data, 375
  documentation, 360
  executor, 433
  lead, 136
  management team, 341, 357, 358
  metrics, 363
  performance, 376
  planning, 359, 361
  preparation activities, 374
  record, 433
  results, 186
  scenario, 357
  sets, 363
Test scripts, 231, 358, 374, 433
  author, 362
  completions, 197
Testable, 270
Tester, 362
  error, 368

Testing, 68, 78, 133, 170, 193, 228, 293, 329, 467
  process, 360
  program, 355
  report, 395
  scope, 361
  team, 424
Thai, 290, 477
Third-party, 169
  applications, 222
  business partners, 122
  contractors, 114
  logistics providers, 141, 271, 503
  participants, 45
  systems, 359
Three-in-a-box leadership, 213
Three-letter acronym, 210
Three-wave solution, 173
Time allocation, 322
Time and material contract, 128
Time zones, 251
Timeline, 170, 493
To-be business processes, 261, 469
Tools installation script, 433
Top-level assemblies, 504
Top-level requirements, 163, 175
Top-level risks, 234
Top-ten risk list, 209
Total quality manager (TQM), 155
Traceability, 370
Tracing of requirements, 373
Tracking, 91, 106, 113
Tracking test script completions, 58
Trade promotion planning, 190
Trade promotion specialist, 448
Trading partner communications, 401
Trainer preparation, 465, 474
Training, 81, 168, 196, 357, 504
  completion, 485
  coordinators, 495
  course design, 476
  data, 494
  delivery logistics, 476
  developer, 448
  impacts, 338
  materials, 188, 196, 477, 494

Training (Cont.)
  packages, 216
  records, 481
  scope, 133
  testers, 360
Training environment (TRN), 423, 428, 471
Training team, 53, 408, 464
Training workstream, 51
Train-the-trainer, 465, 475
Transactional data, 381, 382, 492, 503, 531
Transactional data migration, 216
Transactions, 328, 330, 380, 452, 463, 487, 504
  codes, 81, 512
  courses, 470
  entries, 440
  integrity, 342
  Transaction FB04, 344
  Transaction ME21N, 342
  Transaction VF01, 471
Transformation, 216
Transformational business model, 225
Translation service provider, 464, 478
Transport, 231
Transport numbers, 370
Transportation planner, 448
Transports, 534
Travel schedules, 94
Treasury, 213
  analyst, 449
Turnover, 256
Two-way communications, 453
Type one documents, 185, 194
Type three documents, 185, 186
Type two documents, 185, 194
Types of contracts, 128
Typical full-scale project, 211

U

Unauthorized procurement, 181
Unicode, 79
Uniform data submissions, 215
Unique identifier, 191
Unit testing, 217, 338, 393, 406, 421
Universes, 397

Upgrade projects, 64
Upgrades, 146, 424, 482, 531, 546
Urgency rating, 367
US GAAP reporting, 180
User acceptance testing, 78, 171, 197, 276, 336, 356, 386, 406, 424, 475, 522, 533, 539
  Completion, 231
  Scripts, 536
User attendance status, 481
User communications, 485
User exits, 145
User familiarity, 171
User groups, 515
User interface, 440
User profile, 342
User requirements, 103
User role assignments, 216
User roles, 190
User training, 188, 271, 293, 312, 463, 494
  attendance, 496
  development, 225
  issues, 514
  materials, 531
  packages, 84
  team, 216
Utilities industries, 347

V

Vacant building space, 251
Validation organization, 347
Value management, 49, 158
Value realization, 178
Value-added networks (VANs), 403
Vanilla SAP, 152, 330, 425
Vendor, 208, 217, 335, 380, 531
  master, 275, 330, 358, 382, 390, 493
  payment, 211, 330
Verification, 485, 492
Version history, 277
Versions, 352
  upgrades, 73
Vertical leads, 212
Vertical workstream, 305

W

Warehouse, 181
Warehouse inventory, 383
Warehouse management system, 106
Warehouse stocking, 211
Warm back-up, 437
Watch list, 235
Waves, 172, 173, 527
   one, 372, 535
   three, 372, 535
   two, 372, 535
Weak PMO approach, 207
Web-based functionality, 352
Web-based training (WBT), 466, 481
Windows, 105
Work around, 515
Work breakdown structure (WBS), 47, 382
Work centers, 382
Work in process, 503
Work instructions, 153, 188, 328, 348, 452, 490
Work products, 199
Work spaces, 249
Workflow, 104, 107, 109, 132, 170, 193, 274, 357
   requirements, 411
   technology, 36
Working documents, 185
Working under pressure, 38
Workload consumption estimates, 544
Workload priorities, 528
Workstations, 111
Workstream, 47
   deliverables, 298
   leads, 207, 386
   meeting notes, 185
   scope, 211
   test coordinator and defect manager, 359, 362
WRICEFPs, 107, 132, 144, 169, 230, 316, 328, 337, 339, 391

- From in-memory basics to implementation, learn what SAP HANA is all about

- Start working in the system with step-by-step instructions for data modeling and provisioning

- Updated with new coverage of SAP HANA cloud options and native application development

Bjarne Berg, Penny Silvia

SAP HANA

An Introduction

SAP HANA is evolving rapidly—are you on top of the latest developments? The third edition of our best-selling introduction covers all ground: from the basics of in-memory technology to the most recent innovations in the HANA landscape. With new discussions of native application development, SAP HANA Cloud Platform, and more, this book is all you need to take your first HANA steps.

approx. 615 pp., 3. edition, 69,95 Euro / US$ 69.95
ISBN 978-1-4932-1164-7, Sept 2014
www.sap-press.com

Galileo Press

- Learn to easily navigate the SAP system

- Work with SAP components step by step

- Includes many examples and detailed SAP illustrations

- 2nd, revised and updated edition

Olaf Schulz

Using SAP
A Guide for Beginners and End Users

Don't get trapped in a thicket of confusing IT terms and explanations: Consult this single resource written for you, the SAP user! You'll find detailed steps and screenshots that walk you through the processes you need to do your job: logging on to the system, navigation and maintenance, creating reports, printing, and so much more. Whether you're entering data, using SAP software on a daily basis, or need a foundational knowledge of navigating the SAP system, this book will get you comfortable in no time.

approx. 392 pp., 2. edition, 29,95 Euro / US$ 29.95
ISBN 978-1-59229-981-2, July 2014
www.sap-press.com

More information: www.sap-press.com